CONTEMPORARY LINGUISTICS

AN INTRODUCTION

SEVENTH EDITION

Edited by

William O'Grady
University of Hawaii at Manoa

and

John Archibald
University of Calgary

U.S. edition prepared by

Mark Aronoff
State University of New York at Stony Brook

and

Janie Rees-Miller
Marietta College

bedford/st.martin's
Macmillan Learning

Boston | New York

For Bedford/St. Martin's
Vice President, Editorial, Macmillan Learning Humanities: Edwin Hill
Editorial Director, English: Karen S. Henry
Senior Publisher for Composition, Business and Technical Writing, Developmental Writing:
  Leasa Burton
Executive Editor: Vivian Garcia
Senior Developmental Editor: Joelle Hann
Editorial Assistants: Suzanne Chouljian, Cara Kaufman
Senior Production Editor: Harold Chester
Senior Media Producer: Allison Hart
Senior Production Supervisor: Lisa McDowell
Marketing Manager: Sophia Latorre-Zengierski
Copy Editors: Eric Raetz, Kathleen Lafferty
Senior Photo Editor: Martha Friedman
Permissions Manager: Kalina Ingham
Permissions Researcher: Jen Roach Kaveney, Lumina Datamatics
Senior Art Director: Anna Palchik
Text Design: Kyle Gell
Cover Design: William Boardman
Composition: Jouve
Printing and Binding: LSC Communications

Manufactured in the United States of America.

2   1   0   9   8   7
f   e   d   c   b   a

For information, write: Bedford/St. Martin's, 75 Arlington Street, Boston, MA 02116
  (617-399-40)

ISBN 978-1-319-03977-6

Acknowledgments
Acknowledgments and copyrights appear on the same page as the text and art selections they cover; these acknowledgments and copyrights constitute an extension of the copyright page.

To the memory of
our friend and colleague
Ewa Iwanicka
1950–1986

Convinced at once that, in order to break loose from the beaten paths of opinions and systems, it was necessary to proceed in my study of man and society by scientific methods, and in a rigorous manner, I devoted one year to philology and grammar; linguistics, or the natural history of speech, being, of all the sciences, that which best suited the researches which I was about to commence.

– PIERRE-JOSEPH PROUDHON, *What Is Property?* (1840)

CONTEMPORARY LINGUISTICS

PREFACE

Since *Contemporary Linguistics* was first published in 1989, our goal has been to provide a comprehensive introductory linguistics textbook that conveys the fascinating aspects of language study to students in an accessible and enlightening way. By including up-to-date coverage of all the important areas of linguistics—from phonology, morphology, syntax, and semantics to cross-curricular topics such as sociolinguistics and psycholinguistics—we aim to prepare students for further work in the subject. At the same time, we strive for a clear, direct presentation of the material so that students at different levels, and with different goals for taking the course, can come to appreciate how language works. To our gratification, feedback from users of previous editions indicates that *Contemporary Linguistics* has succeeded at both tasks.

While updating both presentation and content of the material in the text, we have retained those features that have proved themselves over time in a variety of classroom settings:

- *The most comprehensive and up-to-date introductory text available.* *Contemporary Linguistics* provides the most thorough coverage of core concepts of any introductory text—phonology, morphology, syntax, and semantics—while exploring key cross-curricular issues as diverse as psycholinguistics, the brain and language, and computational linguistics.

- *Presents the knowledge of working experts in the field.* Each chapter is written by an expert or a team of experts on a particular topic in linguistics, providing the most current and in-depth information available.

- *Written in a language students can understand.* We strive for a direct writing style and modular approach to make complex concepts interesting and accessible to students of all levels.

- *Offers extensive support to students and instructors.* To help students master concepts, each chapter begins with bulleted objectives and concludes with a summary, key terms, recommended reading, and exercises to reinforce material presented in the chapter. The widely praised *Study Guide for Contemporary Linguistics* gives students extra practice and support, and the helpful *Instructors' Resource Manual* provides answers to questions and ideas for teaching complex concepts.

New to This Edition

While working on *Contemporary Linguistics* through its various editions, we have enjoyed charting new developments in the field and adding material that reflects the expanding research in its various subdisciplines. As linguistics has expanded, so too has the size of the textbook, and with each expanded edition has come the risk that the book would grow into an unmanageable tome. For the fifth edition, the Canadian editors of *Contemporary Linguistic Analysis*—the book on which *Contemporary Linguistics* has always been based—moved more advanced and detailed information and exercises online, a move that we embraced in the U.S. version.

In this seventh edition, we continue to refine this balance, recognizing the growing presence of online and multimedia technology in the classroom, as well as the need to control the physical size of this textbook with LaunchPad Solo for *Contemporary Linguistics* available at **launchpadworks.com**. LaunchPad Solo offers a number of features:

- *Interactive exercises, downloadable problems, as well as advanced questions* for students who have progressed beyond the introductory level.

- *Additional review of core topics* where students need the most practice.

- *Interactive audio chart of International Phonetic Alphabet (IPA) vowels and consonants.* Audio charts of IPA vowels and consonants provide students with an excellent learning tool for chapters that deal directly with phonetics and phonology.

- *Four more chapters for further exploration* of specialized topics in linguistics: "Indigenous Languages of North America," "Sign Languages," "Animal Communication," and "Computational Linguistics."

In addition, all chapters in *Contemporary Linguistics* have been revised to reflect recent research, to include or expand material of current interest to instructors, and to streamline the presentation. In this streamlined and restructured format, fourteen core chapters remain in the book to help students and professors focus on the essential course material, and four chapters on specialized areas of linguistics mentioned above are now featured online in LaunchPad Solo for *Contemporary Linguistics*. Additionally, Chapter 8, "Historical Linguistics," has been streamlined to retain its wealth of information within a more accessible and student-friendly context.

Revised and Updated Content

- *Revised Chapter 2: Phonetics.* More in-depth detail on the sound-producing system and glottal states and a new appendix on dialectal variation in the pronunciation of American vowels help students transcribe their own speech more accurately.

- *Revised Chapter 3: Phonology.* This entirely revamped chapter clearly explains key concepts such as phonemes, allophones, and complementary distribution; reframes the treatment of syllable structure to introduce concepts of sonority and universal constraints; and provides new and revised problems so that instructions are more explicit and scaffolded.

- *Revised Chapter 4: Morphology.* The morphology chapter now features a number of new problems that increase the variety of languages and morphological phenomena.

- *Revised Chapter 5: Syntax.* Included in this chapter is new coverage on relative clauses and VP-internal subjects, as well as abbreviated tree structures without X' when there is no specifier or complement. This chapter has also replaced IP with TP.

- **Updated content:** Two additional chapters have been updated to include the most recent scholarship:

  - **Chapter 10, "Second Language Acquisition,"** includes recent work in motivation, focus on form, and education in the bilingual environment.
  - **Chapter 13, "Language in Social Contexts,"** incorporates the latest research on grammatical diversity, language change, and gender problems. Exercises at the end of the chapter have also been thoroughly revised to include a mix of fieldwork problems and linguistic problems in dialects, creoles, and code-switching.

Ancillaries

The **LaunchPad Solo for *Contemporary Linguistics*** package (ISBN: 978-1-319-11960-7) includes the following features:

- **Interactive exercises, downloadable problems, as well as advanced questions** for students who have progressed beyond the introductory level.
- **Additional review of core topics** for those subjects on which students need the most practice.
- **Interactive audio charts of IPA vowels and consonants.** Audio charts of IPA vowels and consonants provide students with an excellent learning tool for those chapters that deal directly with phonetics and phonology.
- **Four more chapters for further exploration** of specialized topics in linguistics: "Indigenous Languages of North America," "Sign Languages," "Animal Communication," and "Computational Linguistics."

The Study Guide for *Contemporary Linguistics* (ISBN: 978-1-319-04089-5), updated for the seventh edition, offers students summaries of the most important concepts from the core chapters (1–8) of *Contemporary Linguistics*, as well as a range of supplemental exercises and a helpful answer key. To order the *Study Guide* packaged with *Contemporary Linguistics* **at a discount**, use ISBN: 978-1-319-11961-4.

The Instructor's Resource Manual is downloadable from the instructor's resource tab on the *Contemporary Linguistics* catalog page at **macmillanlearning.com/linguistics7e**. This manual provides teaching advice and includes answers to the exercises at the end of each chapter, and the **PowerPoint Slides** (also downloadable from this tab) provide 103 key charts, images, and other teaching aids from the main text for use in the classroom.

For more information about these ancillaries or about ordering, go to the following page: **macmillanlearning.com/linguistics7e**.

Acknowledgments

A book such as this one, with four editors and eighteen contributors, is clearly a team effort, and the success of such an effort rests on how well the book fulfills its purpose for the instructors and students who use it. We are indeed fortunate that our colleagues have been generous in providing us with valuable feedback and suggestions based on their experiences using the text in a variety of settings, and we express our heartfelt thanks to them. For the seventh edition, we also benefited from the input of our colleagues Thomas Graf (on computational linguistics) and Daniel Feiner (on syntax).

Many individuals contributed comments and suggestions to the first six editions of the book, and their assistance continues to be reflected in this edition: Howard Aronson, Peter Avery, Barbara Bevington, Derek Bickerton, Robert Blust, Patrick Bruke, Vit Bubenik, Gary Byma, Lyle Campbell, Steven Carey, Andrew Carnie, Jack Chambers, Shuji Chiba, Vanna Condax, Eung-Do Cook, Lynda Costello, Janet Cowal, Andrea Dallas, John Davison, John DeFrancis, Nicole Domingue, Elan Dresher, Matthew Dryer, Sheila Embleton, Hana Filip, Robert Fisher, Michael Forman, Paul Franckowiak, Don Frantz, Donna Gerdts, John Haiman, Rachel Hansen, Brent Henderson, John Hewson, Joyce Hildebrand, Robert Hsu, Sarah Hulsey, James Hunter, David Ingram, Ricky Jacobs, Kyle Johnson, Kazue Kanno, Brian King, Utpal Lahiri, Yong Lang, Margaret Larock, Gary Libben, Vivian Lin, Anatole Lyovin, Monica Macaulay, Sarah Tully Marks, Joyce McDonough, Barry Meislin, Marianne Mithun, Yves-Charles Morin, Woody Mott, Robert Murray, Michael O'Grady, Douglas Parks, George Patterson, Mary Pepper, Marilyn Phillips, Tim Pulju, Thomas Purnell, R. Radhakrishnan, Laurence Reid, Lori Repetti, Keren Rice, Lorna Rowsell, Lynn Santelmann, Yataka Sato, Coral Sayce, Albert Schütz, Peter Seyffert, Patricia Shaw, Ronald Southerland, Stanley Starosta, the students in Terry Pratt's linguistics course at the University of Prince Edward Island, Allison Teasdale, Charles Ulrich, Tim Vance, Theo Venneman, Douglas Walker, Sheri Wells-Jensen, Chris Wen-Chao Li, Lydia White, Norio Yamada, Mehmet Yavas, and Nava Zaig.

For this seventh edition, we are especially grateful for the meticulous reading and detailed comments provided by our reviewers: Mary Jane Hurst (Texas Tech University), Harriet Magen (Rhode Island College), Andrew McKenzie (University of Kansas), Brad Montgomery-Anderson (Northeastern State University), Janet Randall (Northeastern University), and Carson Schutze (University of California, Los Angeles). We also owe a special debt to Joe Davis, a linguistics enthusiast at InternationalPhoneticAlphabet.org, who has granted us use of his fantastic IPA vowel and consonant charts with audio; they appear in LaunchPad Solo and add so much to students' learning of phonetics and phonology.

We are delighted to have worked once again with Bedford/St. Martin's of Macmillan Learning. Although Nancy Perry, who was instrumental in getting the first edition off the ground and gave unflagging support through many editions, is now retired, we are grateful for all the other capable people who continued to contribute their expertise: Karen Henry, publisher and editorial director for English; Vivian Garcia, executive editor; Suzanne Chouljian and Cara Kaufman, editorial assistants; and Sophia Latorre-Zengierski, marketing manager. We are grateful to Elise Kaiser, managing editor in Boston, for her patience and knowledge as the book went through production; art director Anna Palchik, who guided the art program; and Billy Boardman, who designed the book's bold new cover. We are particularly delighted to have Harold Chester working as project editor with us again. Harold distinguished himself on previous editions with his meticulous attention to detail, and his eagle eye has not dimmed.

Perhaps our greatest debt at Bedford/St. Martin's is to Joelle Hann, development editor for this seventh edition. She has once again taken the reins with professionalism and good cheer and guided us and the book from the beginning stages to the finished product. We gratefully acknowledge her efforts and thank her most sincerely.

Finally, we acknowledge our students, without whom this endeavor would be meaningless. In their questions and in their joy in discovering the elegance and beauty of language, they remind us why we have become linguists and why we are teachers.

Mark Aronoff
Janie Rees-Miller

PREFACE TO THE FIRST EDITION

Thanks to the application of rigorous analysis to familiar subject matter, linguistics provides students with an ideal introduction to the kind of thinking we call "scientific." Such thinking proceeds from an appreciation of problems arising from bodies of data, to hypotheses that attempt to account for those problems, to the careful testing and extension of the hypotheses. But science is more than a formal activity. One of the great pleasures offered introductory students of linguistics is the discovery of the impressive body of subconscious knowledge that underlies language use. This book attempts to emphasize the extent of this knowledge as well as to introduce the scientific methodology used in linguistic analysis.

Although this is the first linguistics textbook designed primarily for a Canadian readership, we have tried to do much more than simply provide coverage of linguistic phenomena peculiar to Canada. As the title suggests, we have attempted an introduction to linguistic analysis as it is practiced at this stage in the development of our discipline. While we do not ignore or reject other fruitful approaches to linguistics, we have taken the generative paradigm as basic for two reasons. First, generative linguistics provides a relatively coherent and integrated approach to basic linguistic phenomena. Phonetics, phonology, morphology, syntax, and semantics are viewed within this framework as perhaps in no other as fully integrated and interrelated. Secondly, the generative approach has been widely influential in its application to a broad range of other linguistic phenomena over the past twenty years.

The extent of our "contemporariness" has been limited by the inevitable compromise between the need to present basic concepts and the demands of sophisticated and competing recent approaches. In many cases, early versions of our chapters were judged "too contemporary" by instructors who were not specialists in the subfields in question. This led to substantial revisions and a somewhat more traditional approach to certain issues than was originally intended. Where possible, however, later sections of the chapters are used to present more contemporary material. In this way, we have attempted to provide what is promised by the title—an introductory text that provides a solid grounding in basic linguistic concepts, but one that also prepares the student to go on to current work in the discipline. For this reason, the student is introduced to multilevelled phonology (in preparation for further tiered analysis), allophonic/morphophonemic distinctions (in preparation for lexical phonology), interaction among components of the grammar (in preparation for a more extended modular approach), word-formation rules in morphology, and examples of parametric variation in syntax.

To the extent possible, we have attempted to integrate the basic mechanisms outlined in the first five chapters of the book into our discussion of phenomena in later chapters. Thus, our discussion of semantics, historical linguistics, first and second language acquisition, and neurolinguistics draws to some degree on the notions presented in our introduction to generative grammar.

No textbook can be all things to all users. We hope that this book will provide students not only with a springboard to the realm of scientific linguistic analysis, but with a greater appreciation for the wonder of human language, the variety and complexity of its structure, and the subtlety of its use.

We gratefully acknowledge the assistance of Jack Chambers and Sheila Embleton, both of whom read the manuscript in its entirety and provided invaluable comments. Thanks are also due to those who have read and commented upon individual chapters and sections, including Steven Carey, Matthew Dryer, David Ingram, Gary Byma, Gary Libben, Robert Murray, R. Radhakrishnan, Ronald Southerland, Mary Pepper, Derek Bickerton, Robert Blust, Ricky Jacobs, Don Frantz, John Haiman, John Hewson, Nicole Domingue, Lydia White, George Patterson, Donna Gerdts, Elan Dresher, Keren Rice, Robert Fisher, Marilyn Philips, Lorna Rowsell, and Joyce Hildebrand. For assistance in the planning, editing, and production of the manuscript, we are grateful to Coral Sayce, Lynda Costello, Joyce Hildebrand, Brian Henderson, Patrick Burke, Les Petriw, and our project editor at Copp Clark, Margaret Larock.

CONTENTS

t h r e e

f o u r

MORPHOLOGY: THE ANALYSIS OF WORD STRUCTURE

s e v e n

THE CLASSIFICATION OF LANGUAGES   261

e i g h t

HISTORICAL LINGUISTICS: THE STUDY OF LANGUAGE CHANGE   297

n i n e

t e n

SECOND LANGUAGE ACQUISITION

eleven

twelve

t h i r t e e n

LANGUAGE IN SOCIAL CONTEXTS

f o u r t e e n

f i f t e e n

s i x t e e n

SIGN LANGUAGES
[online only in LaunchPad Solo for *Contemporary Linguistics*
at **launchpadworks.com**]

s e v e n t e e n

ANIMAL COMMUNICATION
[online only in LaunchPad Solo for *Contemporary Linguistics*
at **launchpadworks.com**]

Eighteen

COMPUTATIONAL LINGUISTICS
[online only in LaunchPad Solo for *Contemporary Linguistics* at launchpadworks.com]

LIST OF TECHNICAL ABBREVIATIONS

*	(in syntactic rules) one or more	go	goal
*	(in historical linguistics) protoform	H	high tone
*	(in front of words or sentences) unacceptable	HAB	habitual aspect
#	word boundary	IA	inflectional affix
1	first person	IL	interlanguage
1	primary stress	INDIC	indicative
2	second person	IP	inflectional phrase
2	secondary stress	IPA	International Phonetic Alphabet
3	third person	ISL	Israeli Sign Language
A	adjective	L	low tone
AAVE	African American Vernacular English	L1	first language
ABL	ablative case	L2	second language
ABS	absolutive case	LN	last name
ACC	accusative case	Loc	location
Adv	adverb	LOC	locative case
AdvP	adverb phrase	M	mid tone
Af	affix	MEG	magnetoencephalography
ag	agent	MRD	machine readable dictionary
AP	adjective phrase	N	(first) name
ASL	American Sign Language	N	noun
Aux	auxiliary verb	N	nucleus
C	complementizer	NEG	negative
C	consonant	NOM	nominative case
caus	cause	NP	noun phrase
CG	constricted glottis	O	(direct) object
cmpl	completed action	O	onset
C_o	any number of consonants	Obl	oblique
Co	coda	OE	Old English
COM	comitative case	P	preposition, postposition
Con	conjunction	PASS	passive
CP	complementizer phrase	PET	positron emission tomography
CT	computerized axial tomography	PIE	Proto-Indo-European
DA	derivational affix	PL	plural
DAT	dative case	PP	prepositional phrase
Deg	degree word	PR	phonetic representation
Det	determiner	PRES	present tense
DR	delayed release	PROG	progressive aspect
ERG	ergative case	Pst	past tense
ERP	event-related potential	QUES	question marker
ESL	English as a second language	R	rhyme
fMRI	functional magnetic resonance imaging	R	rounded
Fut	future tense	rc	relative clause
GEN	genitive case	REA	right ear advantage
		recip	recipient

S	subject		TOP	topic
σ	syllable		UG	Universal Grammar
SG	singular		UR	underlying representation
SG	spread glottis		UR	unrounded
SLA	second language acquisition		V	verb
T	title alone		V	vowel
t	topicalization		VP	verb phrase
th	theme		Wd	word
TLN	title + last name			

LANGUAGE MATTERS BOXES

CONTEMPORARY LINGUISTICS

one

Language: A Preview

William O'Grady

> *The gift of language is the single human trait that marks us all genetically, setting us apart from the rest of life.*
> —LEWIS THOMAS, *The Lives of a Cell*

OBJECTIVES

In this chapter, you will learn:
- that human beings are specialized for language
- that all human languages are creative, have a grammar, and change over time
- that all grammars are alike in basic ways
- that grammatical knowledge is subconscious in all native speakers of a language

 **LaunchPad Solo**
macmillan learning | For more helpful content and quizzes, go to the LaunchPad Solo for *Contemporary Linguistics* at **launchpadworks.com**.

Language is at the heart of all things human. We use it when we're talking, listening, reading, writing—and thinking. It underpins social relationships and communities; it forges the emotional bond between parent and child; it's the vehicle for literature and poetry. Language is not just a part of us; language *defines* us. All normal human beings have at least one language, and it is difficult to imagine much significant social, intellectual, or artistic activity taking place without the opportunities for communication offered by language.

Linguistics is the study of how language works—how it is used, how it is acquired, how it changes over time, how it is represented in the brain, and so on. It is concerned not only with the properties of the world's more than 7,000 living languages but also with the abilities and adaptations that have made it possible for our species to create and use language in the first place.

1 Specialization for Language

Modern *Homo sapiens* (our species) made its appearance 100,000 to 200,000 years ago, by many estimates. Early humans were anatomically like us—they had large brains and vocal tracts capable of producing speech. Archaeological evidence (such as tools, carvings, and cave paintings) suggests that they also had the type of intellect that could accompany language.

LANGUAGE MATTERS   How Many Languages Are There in the World Today?

That's not an easy question, since little is known about the linguistic situation in many parts of the world. The most complete compilation to date can be found at **www.ethnologue.com**, which lists 7,102 living languages as of 2015.

But this is not the whole story. Many languages have only two or three hundred speakers (or fewer), and many others are in grave danger of demise as indigenous peoples throughout the world lose their traditional cultures and homelands. You can find out more by reading *Language Death* by David Crystal (Cambridge, UK: Cambridge University Press, 2002) or *Vanishing Voices: The Extinction of the World's Languages* by Daniel Nettle and Suzanne Romaine (New York: Oxford University Press, 2000). Up-to-date information is also available at the websites of the Endangered Languages Project and Terralingua, among others.

Hundreds of thousands of years of evolution created a special capacity for language in humans that is not found in any other species. The evidence is literally inside us. Our speech organs (the lungs, larynx, tongue, teeth, lips, soft palate, and nasal passages) were—and still are—primarily concerned with breathing and eating. However, they have also all become highly specialized for use in language. Their structure and shape is unique to our species, as is the highly developed network of neural pathways that controls them during speech production (see Table 1.1). Indeed, the bundle of nerves controlling the vocal cords is among the densest in the entire body.

Human beings are also specially equipped for the perception of speech. Newborns respond differently to human voices than to other types of sounds, and six-month-old infants are able to perceive subtle differences among sounds in languages that they have never heard before.

Of course, language is much more than just speech sounds and does not even have to be oral. In sign languages, meaning is conveyed via gestures, body posture, and facial expressions rather than through sounds. Moreover, much of what makes language special can be neither heard nor seen because it involves the way in which the human mind goes about forming words, building sentences, and interpreting meaning.

Table 1.1 The dual functions of the speech organs

Organ	Survival function	Speech function
Lungs	to exchange carbon dioxide and oxygen	to supply air for speech
Vocal cords	to create seal over passage to lungs	to produce vibrations for speech sounds
Tongue	to move food to teeth and back into throat	to articulate vowels and consonants
Teeth	to break up food	to provide place of articulation for consonants
Lips	to seal oral cavity	to articulate vowels and consonants
Nose	to assist in breathing and smelling	to provide nasal resonance during speech

LANGUAGE MATTERS   Sign Language

There are many misconceptions about sign languages, the most prevalent being that they are just a way to spell out an oral language. Although finger spelling of words from an oral language is sometimes used (to indicate names or technical terms, for instance), sign languages are independent systems of communication, with their own vocabulary and grammatical rules. That's why British Sign Language and American Sign Language (ASL) are mutually unintelligible. And it's why Quebec Sign Language (Langue des signes québécoise) is similar in many respects to American Sign Language, despite major differences between French and English. You can find out more about ASL by going to the U.S. National Institutes of Health website.

2 A Creative System

What, precisely, is language? What does it mean to know a language? To answer these questions, it is first necessary to understand the resources that a language makes available to its **native speakers**, those who have acquired it as children in a natural setting (say, a home rather than a classroom).

The breadth and diversity of human thought and experience place great demands on language. Because there are always new things to say, new experiences to report, and new challenges to confront, language has to be creative, giving us the freedom to produce and understand new words and sentences as the need arises.

The **creativity** of language goes hand in hand with a second defining characteristic—the presence of systematic constraints that establish the boundaries within which innovation can occur. We can be innovative in our use of language, but there are rules to the game—and those rules are an integral part of our knowledge of language. As a preliminary illustration of this, consider the process that we use to create verbs from nouns in English, as shown in Table 1.2. (For now, you can think of verbs as words that name actions and nouns as words that name things.)

Table 1.2 Nouns used as verbs

Noun use	Verb use
pull the boat onto the *beach*	*beach* the boat
keep the airplane on the *ground*	*ground* the airplane
tie a *knot* in the string	*knot* the string
put the wine in *bottles*	*bottle* the wine
catch the fish with a *spear*	*spear* the fish
clean the floor with a *mop*	*mop* the floor

As the sentences in *1* show, we have a great deal of freedom to innovate in the formation of such verbs.

1) a. I *wristed* the ball over the net.
   b. He would try to *stiff-upper-lip* it through.
   c. She *Houdini'd* her way out of the locked closet.

However, this freedom also has limits. For instance, a new verb is rarely coined if a word with the intended meaning already exists. Although we say *jail the robber* to mean 'put the robber in jail', we do not say *prison the robber* to mean 'put the robber in prison'. This is because the well-established verb *imprison* already has the meaning that the new form would have.

There are also special constraints on the meaning and use of particular subclasses of these verbs. One such constraint involves verbs that are created from time expressions such as *summer, vacation,* and so on.

2) a. Julia *summered* in Paris.
   b. Harry *wintered* in Mexico.
   c. Bob *vacationed* in France.
   d. Harry and Julia *honeymooned* in Hawaii.

Although the sentences in *2* all sound natural, not all time expressions can be used in this way. (Throughout this book, an asterisk is used to indicate that an utterance is unacceptable.)

3) a. *Jerome *midnighted* in the streets.
   b. *Andrea *nooned* at the restaurant.
   c. *Philip *one o'clocked* at the airport.

These examples show that when a verb is created from a time expression, it must be given a very specific interpretation—roughly paraphrasable as 'to be somewhere for the period of time X'. Thus, *to summer in London* is 'to be in London for the

---

LANGUAGE MATTERS   Disagreeing about Language Use

People sometimes object to innovation in language. The following letter to the editor is a case in point:

"I was shocked and appalled to read in yesterday's newspaper the following phrase: *Nash's knee injury impacted his ability to score.* As anyone with a modicum of education or who owns a dictionary will tell you, *impact* is a noun. You have used it as a verb. This is clearly nonsensical and provides further evidence of the crumbling of our public education system and the decline of language in general. If your editorial offices are not in the possession of a suitable dictionary, I would be happy to provide one for you."

Languages change, and so do dictionaries. While the fifth edition of the *American Heritage Dictionary* (2011) lists *impact* as a verb, it notes that a majority of its usage panel still rejects this usage. The *New York Times* publishes a long-running column titled "On Language" (available online through its website). Often witty and insightful, it helps document (sometimes disapprovingly) changes to contemporary English.

---

summer', *to vacation in France* is 'to be in France for the vacation', and so on. Since *noon* and *midnight* express *points* in time rather than extended *periods* of time, they cannot be used to create new verbs of this type.

Moreover, there are constraints on what verbs that are derived from nouns can mean. For instance, *winter in Hawaii* can only mean 'spend the winter in Hawaii', not 'make it snow in Hawaii' or 'stay in Hawaii until winter begins'. Without such constraints, creativity would run amok, undermining rather than enhancing communication.

Systematic rule-governed creativity is the hallmark of all aspects of language. For instance, consider how sounds are combined to form words. Certain patterns of sounds, like the novel forms in *4*, have the look of English words—all they lack is a meaning.

4) a. prasp
   b. flib
   c. traf

In contrast, the forms in *5* contain combinations of sounds that English does not permit; they simply do not have the shape of English words.

5) a. *psapr
   b. *bfli
   c. *ftra

Still other constraints determine how special endings can be used to create words from other words. Imagine, for example, that the word *soleme* entered the English language (used perhaps for a newly discovered atomic particle). As a speaker of

English, you would then automatically know that something with the properties of a soleme could be called *solemic*. You would also know that to make something solemic is to *solemicize* it, and you would call this process *solemicization*. Further, you would know that the *c* is pronounced as *s* in *solemicize* but as *k* in *solemic*, and that both words are pronounced with the stress on the second syllable. (You would say *soLEmic*, not *SOlemic* or *soleMIC*.)

Nowhere is the ability to deal with novel utterances more obvious than in the production and comprehension of sentences. Apart from a few fixed expressions and greetings (*What's up?*, *How're things?*, *No way!*), much of what you say, hear, and read in the course of a day consists of sentences that are new to you. In conversations, lectures, newscasts, and textbooks, you are regularly exposed to novel combinations of words, unfamiliar ideas, and new information. Consider, for instance, the paragraph that you are currently reading. While each sentence is no doubt perfectly comprehensible to you, it is extremely unlikely that you have ever seen any of them before.

Not all new sentences are acceptable, however. The words in *6* are all familiar, but they are simply not arranged in the right way to make a sentence in English.

6) *Frightened dog this the cat that chased mouse a.
   (cf. This dog frightened the cat that chased a mouse.)

As with other aspects of language, the ability to form and interpret sentences is subject to systematic limitations.

3   Grammar and Linguistic Competence

As we have just seen, speakers of a language are able to produce and understand an unlimited number of utterances, including many that are novel and unfamiliar. At the same time, they are able to recognize that certain utterances are not acceptable and do not belong in their language. Knowledge of this type, which is often called **linguistic competence**, constitutes the central subject matter of linguistics and of this book.

In investigating linguistic competence, linguists focus on the mental system that allows human beings to form and interpret the sounds, words, and sentences of their language. Linguists often call this system a **grammar** and break it down into the components in Table 1.3.

Table 1.3   The components of a grammar

Component	Domain
Phonetics	the articulation and perception of speech sounds
Phonology	the patterning of speech sounds
Morphology	word formation
Syntax	sentence formation
Semantics	the interpretation of words and sentences

As you can see, the term *grammar* is used in a special way within linguistics. To a linguist, a grammar is not a book, nor is it concerned with just the form of words and sentences. Rather, it is the intricate network of knowledge that underlies our ability to use language.

The study of grammar lies at the core of our attempts to understand what language is and what it means to know a language. Five simple points should help clarify why the investigation of grammatical systems is so important to contemporary linguistic analysis.

3.1   Generality: All Languages Have a Grammar

One of the most fundamental claims of modern linguistic analysis is that all languages have a grammar. It could not be any other way. If a language is spoken, it must have a phonetic and phonological system; since it has words and sentences, it must also have a morphology and a syntax; and since these words and sentences have systematic meanings, there must be semantic principles as well.

It is not unusual to hear the remark that some language—say, Puerto-Rican Spanish, American Sign Language, or Swahili—has no grammar. (This is especially common in the case of languages that are not written or are not taught in schools and universities.) Unfamiliar languages sometimes appear to an untrained observer to have no grammar, perhaps because their grammatical systems are different from those of more frequently studied languages. In Walpiri (an indigenous language of Australia), for example, the relative ordering of words is so free that the English sentence *The two dogs see several kangaroos* could be translated by the equivalent of any of the following sentences. (The word 'now' is used informally to help express present tense.)

7) a. Dogs two now see kangaroos several.
   b. See now dogs two kangaroos several.
   c. See now kangaroos several dogs two.
   d. Kangaroos several now dogs two see.
   e. Kangaroos several now see dogs two.

Although Walpiri does not restrict the order of words in the way English does, its grammar imposes other types of requirements. For example, in the sentence above, Walpiri speakers must place the ending *lu* on the word for 'dogs' to indicate that it names the animals that do the seeing rather than the animals that are seen. In English, by contrast, this information is conveyed by placing *two dogs* in front of the verb and *several kangaroos* after it.

Rather than showing that Walpiri has no grammar, such differences simply demonstrate that it has a grammar that is unlike the grammar of English in certain respects. This point holds across the board: although no two languages have exactly the same grammar, every language has a grammar.

A similar point can be made about different varieties of the same language. Appalachian English, Jamaican English, and Hawaiian English each have pronunciations, vocabulary items, and sentence patterns that may appear unusual to outsiders. But this does not mean that they have no grammar; it just means that their grammars differ in particular ways from those of more familiar varieties of English.

LANGUAGE MATTERS   Regularization

Why and how does the English spoken in one area end up being different from the English spoken in other places? One powerful force is **regularization**—the tendency to drive out exceptions by replacing them with a form that fits with a more general pattern.

With one exception, English verbs all have a single past tense form no matter what the subject is—*I just arrived, you just arrived, s/he just arrived*, and so on. The exception is the verb *be*, which has two forms—*was* and *were*: *I was there, you were there, s/he was there*.

Regularization has taken care of this anomaly in at least two varieties of English. In Yorkshire English (northern England), only *were* is used: *I were there, you were there, s/he were there*. In Appalachian English (West Virginia and parts of nearby states), things have gone the other way—only *was* has been retained: *I was there, you was there, s/he was there, we was there*.

3.2   Parity: All Grammars Are Equal

Contrary to popular belief, there is no such thing as a primitive language, even in places untouched by modern science and technology. Indeed, some of the most complex linguistic phenomena we know about are found in societies that have neither writing nor electricity.

Moreover, there is no such thing as a good grammar or a bad grammar. In fact, all grammars do essentially the same thing: they tell speakers how to form and interpret the words and sentences of their language. The form and meaning of those words and sentences vary from language to language and even from community to community, of course, but each language works for its speakers.

Linguists sometimes clash over this point with people who are upset about the use of nonstandard varieties of English that permit sentences such as *I seen that, They was there, He didn't do nothing, She ain't here*, and so forth. Depending on where you live and who you talk to, speaking in this way can have negative consequences: it may be harder to win a scholarship, to get a job, or to be accepted in certain social circles. This is an undeniable fact about the social side of language. From a purely linguistic point of view, however, there is absolutely nothing wrong with grammars that permit such structures. They work for their speakers, and they deserve to be studied in the same objective fashion as the varieties of English spoken by the rich and educated.

The bottom line for linguists is that the analysis of language must reflect the way it is actually used, not someone's idealized vision of how it should be used. The psychologist Steven Pinker offers the following illustration to make the same point.

> Imagine that you are watching a nature documentary. The video shows the usual gorgeous footage of animals in their natural habitats. But the voiceover reports some troubling facts. Dolphins do not execute their swimming strokes properly. White-crowned

sparrows carelessly debase their calls. Chickadees' nests are incorrectly constructed, pandas hold bamboo in the wrong paw, the song of the humpback whale contains several well-known errors, and the monkey's cries have been in a state of chaos and degeneration for hundreds of years. Your reaction would probably be, What on earth could it mean for the song of the humpback whale to contain an "error"? Isn't the song of the humpback whale whatever the humpback whale decides to sing?

As Pinker goes on to observe, language is like the song of the humpback whale. The way to determine whether a particular sentence is permissible is to find people who speak the language and observe how they use it.

In sum, linguists don't even think of trying to rate languages as good or bad, simple or complex. Rather, they investigate language in much the same way that other scientists study snails or stars—with the goal of figuring out how it works. This same point is sometimes made by noting that linguistics is **descriptive**, not **prescriptive**. Its goal is to describe and explain the facts of languages, not to change them.

3.3   Universality: All Grammars Are Alike in Basic Ways

In considering how grammars can differ from each other, it is easy to lose sight of something even more intriguing and important—the existence of principles and properties shared by all human languages.

For example, all languages use a small set of contrastive sounds that help distinguish words from each other (like the *t* and *d* sounds that allow us to recognize *to* and *do* as different words). There are differences in precisely which sounds particular languages use, but there are also fundamental similarities. For instance, all languages have more consonant sounds (*p*, *t*, *d*, etc.) than vowel sounds (*a*, *e*, *i*); any language that has a *d* sound almost certainly has a *t* sound as well; and all languages have a vowel that sounds like the "ah" in *far*.

There are also universal constraints on how words can be put together to form sentences. For example, in describing a situation in which Ned lost his own wallet, many languages can use the equivalent of the first sentence below, with *his* coming after *Ned*, but no language can use the second sentence, with *he* coming before *Ned*.

8) a. Ned lost his wallet.
   b. He lost Ned's wallet.

Moreover, even when languages do differ from each other, the amount of variation is restricted in certain ways. For example, some languages (like English) place question words at the beginning of the sentence. In *9*, for example, the word *what* originates after *donate* and is moved to the beginning of the sentence to create the question.

9) What did Mary donate to the library?

Other languages, like Mandarin, make no such changes.

10) Mali juan shenme gei tushuguan?
     Mary donate what to library

LANGUAGE MATTERS   Don't End That Sentence with a Preposition

One of the better-known prescriptive rules of English is "Don't end a sentence with a preposition." (In other words, say "To whom were you talking?," not "Who were you talking to?") The problem with this rule is that people don't speak that way. Prepositions often occur at the end of a sentence in English, and trying to prevent this from happening leads to all sorts of unnatural-sounding constructions, as Winston Churchill illustrated (in a famous but possibly apocryphal story) when he said, tongue in cheek, "This is the kind of tedious nonsense up with which I will not put."

Here's an extreme case of prepositions ending a sentence. A young girl, unhappy with the book that her father had brought upstairs for her bedtime story, was heard to say: "What did you bring the book I didn't want to be read to out of up for?" This sentence ends with five prepositions—an extreme case, admittedly, but it's still English!

But no language uniformly places question words at the *end* of the sentence.

In other cases, variation is constrained by strong tendencies rather than absolute prohibitions. Take three-word sentences such as *Canadians like hockey*, for instance. Such sentences have six logically possible orders.

11) a. Canadians like hockey.
    b. Canadians hockey like.
    c. Like Canadians hockey.
    d. Like hockey Canadians.
    e. Hockey like Canadians.
    f. Hockey Canadians like.

All other things being equal, we would expect to find each order employed in about one-sixth of the world's languages. In fact, more than 95 percent of the world's languages adopt one of the first three orders for basic statements (and the vast majority of those use one or the other of the first two orders). Only a handful of languages use any of the last three orders as basic.

These are not isolated examples. As you'll see as you continue your study of linguistics, languages are fundamentally alike in important ways.

3.4   Mutability: All Grammars Change Over Time

The features of language that are not universal and fixed are subject to change over time. Indeed, the grammars of all languages are constantly changing. Some of these changes are relatively minor and occur very quickly (for example, the addition of new words such as *bitcoin*, *twerk*, *selfie*, *defriend*, and *geekery* to the vocabulary of English). Other changes have a more dramatic effect on the overall form of the language and typically take place over a long period of time. One such change involves the manner in which we negate sentences in English. Prior to 1200, English formed negative constructions by placing *ne* before the verb and a variant of *not* after it.

12) a. Ic *ne* seye *not*. ('I don't say.')
　　b. He *ne* speketh *nawt*. ('He does not speak.')

By 1400 or thereabouts, the use of *ne* had decreased dramatically, and *not* (or *nawt*) typically occurred by itself after the verb.

13) a. I seye *not* the wordes. ('I don't say the words.')
　　b. We saw *nawt* the knyghtes. ('We didn't see the knights.')

It was not until several centuries later that English adopted its current practice of allowing *not* to occur after only certain types of verbs (*do, have, will,* and so on).

14) a. I will *not* say the words. (versus *I will say not the words.)
　　b. He did *not* see the knights. (versus *He saw not the knights.)

　　These changes illustrate the extent to which grammars can be modified over time. The structures exemplified in *13* are archaic by today's standards, and those in *12* sound completely foreign to speakers of modern English.

　　Through the centuries, those who believed that certain varieties of language are better than others frequently expressed concern over what they perceived to be the deterioration of English. In 1710, for example, the writer Jonathan Swift (author of *Gulliver's Travels*) lamented "the continual Corruption of our English Tongue." Among the corruptions to which he objected were contractions such as *he's* for *he is*, although he had no objection to *'tis* for *it is*!

　　Similar concerns have been expressed about the state of American English. In the nineteenth century, Edward S. Gould, a columnist for the New York *Evening Post*, published a book entitled *Good English; or, Popular Errors in Language*, in which he accused newspaper writers and authors of "sensation novels" of ruining the language

---

LANGUAGE MATTERS　Verbs Again

A thousand years ago, more than three hundred English verbs formed their past tense by making an internal change (*drive/drove, eat/ate,* etc.) rather than by adding a suffix (*walk/walked, dance/danced*). Today, about half as many verbs do this. The past tense of *heave* used to be *hove*; now it is *heaved*. The past tense of *thrive* used to be *throve*; now it is *thrived*. The past tense of *chide* ('scold') used to be *chid*; now it is *chided*. And so on. These past tense forms have all changed to the more regular *-ed* pattern.

　　Then why aren't all verbs regular? One factor involves frequency: more frequent forms tend to resist regularization. That's why the most enduring irregular past tense forms in English (*was* and *were* for *be, had* for *have, went* for *go, came* for *come,* and so on) involve high-frequency verbs. To find out more, read *Words and Rules* by Steven Pinker (New York: Basic Books, 1999).

by introducing "spurious words" like *jeopardize, leniency,* and *underhanded.* The tradition of prescriptive concern about the use of certain words continues to this day in the work of such popular writers as Edwin Newman and John Simon, who form a kind of self-appointed language police.

Linguists reject the view that languages attain a state of perfection at some point in their history and that subsequent changes lead to deterioration and corruption. As noted above, there are simply no grounds for claiming that one language or variety of language is somehow superior to another.

3.5   Inaccessibility: Grammatical Knowledge Is Subconscious

Knowledge of a grammar differs in important ways from knowledge of arithmetic, traffic rules, and other subjects that are taught at home or in school: it is largely subconscious and not accessible to introspection—you can't figure out how it works just by thinking about it. As an example of this, consider your pronunciation of the past tense suffix, written as *ed*, in the following words.

15) a. hunted
    b. slipped
    c. buzzed

You probably didn't notice it before, but the *ed* ending has three different pronunciations in these words. Whereas you say *id* in *hunted,* you say *t* in *slipped* and *d* in *buzzed.* Moreover, if you heard the new verb *flib,* you would form the past tense as *flibbed* and pronounce the ending as *d.* If you are a native speaker of English, you acquired the grammatical subsystem regulating this aspect of speech when you were a child, and it now exists subconsciously in your mind, allowing you to automatically make the relevant contrasts.

The same is true for virtually everything else about language. Once we go beyond the most obvious things (such as whether words like *the* and *a* come before or after a noun), the average person can't say much about how language works. For example, try explaining to someone who is not a native speaker of English why we can say *I went to school* but not **I went to supermarket.* Or try to figure out for yourself how the word *or* works. Matters are seemingly straightforward in a sentence such as the following, which means something like 'Either Mary drank tea, or she drank coffee—I don't know which.'

16) Mary drank tea or coffee.

But *or* has a different interpretation in the next sentence.

17) Mary didn't drink tea or coffee.

Now it seems to mean 'and'—'Mary didn't drink tea and she didn't drink coffee', not 'Mary didn't drink tea or she didn't drink coffee—I don't know which'.

As you can see, being able to interpret these sentences is not the same thing as knowing *why* they have the particular meanings that they do. Speakers of a language know what sounds right and what doesn't sound right, but they are not sure how they know.

Because most of what we know about our language is subconscious, the analysis of human linguistic systems requires considerable effort and ingenuity. As is the case in all scientific endeavors, observable facts (about the pronunciation of words, the interpretation of sentences, and so on) must be used to draw inferences about the sometimes invisible mechanisms (atoms, cells, or grammars, as the case may be) that are ultimately responsible for these phenomena.

Summing Up

Human language is characterized by creativity. Speakers of a language have access to a grammar, a mental system that allows them to form and interpret both familiar and novel utterances. The grammar governs the articulation, perception, and patterning of speech sounds; the formation of words and sentences; and the interpretation of utterances. All languages have grammars that are equal in their expressive capacity, and all speakers of a language have (subconscious) knowledge of its grammar. The existence of such linguistic systems in humans is the product of unique anatomical and cognitive specialization not found in other species.

Key Terms

creativity   linguistics
descriptive (grammar)   native speakers
grammar   prescriptive (grammar)
linguistic competence   regularization

Recommended Reading

Bickerton, Derek. 1990. *Language and Species*. Chicago: University of Chicago Press.
Crystal, David. 2003. *The Cambridge Encyclopedia of the English Language*. 2nd ed. New York: Cambridge University Press.
Crystal, David. 2010. *The Cambridge Encyclopedia of Language*. 3rd ed. New York: Cambridge University Press.
Pinker, Steven. 1994. *The Language Instinct: How the Human Mind Creates Language*. New York: Morrow.

Exercises

1. The following sentences contain verbs created from nouns in accordance with the process described in Section 2 of this chapter. Describe the meaning of each of these new verbs.
   a) We techno'd the night away.
   b) She dog-teamed her way across the Arctic.

    c) We Harleyed to Oregon.

    d) You should Band-Aid that cut.

    e) He LeBron'd his way to the basket.

    f) We Greyhounded to Columbus.

    g) We'll have to Ajax the sink.

    h) He Windexed the windows.

    i) You should Clairol your hair.

    j) Let's carton the eggs.

2. Using the examples in the preceding exercise as a model, create five new verbs from nouns. Build a sentence around each of these new verbs to show its meaning.

3. Which of the following forms are possible words of English? Show the words to an acquaintance and see if you agree on your judgments.

    a) mbood   e) sproke

    b) frall   f) flube

    c) coofp   g) wordms

    d) ktleem   h) bsarn

4. Imagine that you are an advertising executive and that your job involves inventing new names for products. Create four new forms that are possible words of English and four that are not.

5. Part of linguistic competence involves the ability to recognize whether novel utterances are acceptable. Consider the following sentences and determine which are possible sentences in English. For each unacceptable sentence, change the sentence (as little as possible) to make it acceptable, and compare the two.

    a) Jason's mother left himself with nothing to eat.

    b) Miriam is eager to talk to.

    c) This is the man who I took a picture of.

    d) Colin made Jane a sandwich.

    e) Is the dog sleeping the bone again?

    f) Wayne prepared Zena a cake.

    g) Max cleaned the garden up.

    h) Max cleaned up the garden.

    i) Max cleaned up it.

    j) I hope you to leave.

    k) That you likes liver surprises me.

6. Consider the following sentences, each of which is acceptable to some speakers of English. Try to identify the prescriptive rules that are violated in each case.

    a) He don't know about the race.

    b) You was out when I called.

    c) There is twenty horses registered in the show.

    d) That window's broke, so be careful.

    e) Jim and me are gonna go campin' this weekend.

    f) Who did you come with?

g) I seen the parade last week.
h) He been lost in the woods for ten days.
i) My car needs cleaned 'cause of all the rain.
j) Julie ain't got none.
k) Somebody left their book on the train.
l) Murray hurt hisself in the game.

What is the reaction of linguists to the claim that sentences of this sort are wrong?

7. An interesting feature of the variety of English spoken in Hawaii involves the form of the possessive pronoun that shows up in the following context.

   That belongs to me. It's *mines*.

Make a list of other possessive pronoun forms in standard English by filling in the spaces below.

   That belongs to you. It's _____.
   That belongs to him. It's _____.
   That belongs to her. It's _____.
   That belongs to us. It's _____.
   That belongs to them. It's _____.

What process in language change appears to be responsible for the form *mines*?

 **LaunchPad Solo** | For more helpful content and quizzes, go to the LaunchPad Solo
macmillan learning | for *Contemporary Linguistics* at **launchpadworks.com**.

t w o

Phonetics: The Sounds of Language

Michael Dobrovolsky

I shall whisper
Heavenly labials in a world of gutturals.
—Wallace Stevens, *"The Plot against the Giant"* (1917)

OBJECTIVES

In this chapter, you will learn:

- how we use special symbols to represent all the different sounds in human languages, beginning with English
- how to write down your own speech using these symbols
- how we use articulators in the vocal tract to produce specific sounds
- how we can group language sounds into classes
- how human languages use tone, intonation, and sound length to create meaning
- how language sounds in context can be modified by neighboring sounds

 **LaunchPad Solo** | For more helpful content and quizzes, go to the LaunchPad Solo
macmillan learning | for *Contemporary Linguistics* at **launchpadworks.com**.

We do not need to speak in order to use language. Language can be written, manually signed, mechanically reproduced, and even synthesized by computers with considerable success. Nevertheless, speech remains the primary way in which humans express themselves through language. Our species spoke long before we began to write, and this long history of spoken language is reflected in our anatomical specialization for speech. Humans also appear to have specialized neural mechanisms for the perception of speech sounds. Because language and speech are so closely linked, we begin our study of language by examining the inventory and structure of the sounds of speech. This branch of linguistics is called **phonetics**.

Human languages display a wide variety of sounds, called **phones** (from Greek *phōnē* 'sound, voice') or **speech sounds**. The class of possible speech sounds is finite, and a portion of the total set will be found in the inventory of any human language. Humans can also make sounds with the vocal tract that do not occur in speech, such as the sound made by inhaling through one corner of the mouth or the "raspberry" produced by sticking out the tongue and blowing hard across it. Nonetheless, a very wide range of sounds is found in human language (600 consonants and 200 vowels, according to one estimate), including the click made by drawing the tongue hard away from the upper molars on one side of the mouth (imagine making a sound to get a horse to move) or the sound made by constricting the upper part of the throat while breathing out. Any human, child or adult, can learn to produce any human speech sound.

Linguists undertake the study of phonetics in two ways. One approach involves analyzing the physiological mechanisms of speech production. This is known as **articulatory phonetics**. The other approach, **acoustic phonetics**, is concerned with measuring and analyzing the physical properties of the sound waves we produce when we speak. Both approaches are indispensable to an understanding of speech. This chapter focuses on articulatory phonetics but also makes some reference to the acoustic properties of sounds and to acoustic analysis.

1   Phonetic Transcription

Since the sixteenth century, efforts have been made to devise a universal system for transcribing the sounds of speech. The best-known system, the **International Phonetic Alphabet (IPA)**, has been evolving since 1888. This system of transcription attempts to represent each sound of human speech with a single symbol. These symbols are enclosed in brackets [ ] to indicate that the transcription is phonetic and does not represent the spelling system of a particular language. For example, the sound spelled *th* in English *this* is transcribed as [ð] (the symbol is called *eth*, as in *weather*). The IPA uses this symbol to represent that sound in whichever language it is heard, whether it is English, Spanish, or Arabic, as shown in Table 2.1.

Table 2.1   Use of [ð] in transcribing speech phonetically

Language	Spelling	IPA	Meaning
English	<u>th</u>is	[ðis]	'this'
Spanish	bo<u>d</u>a	[boða]	'wedding'
Arabic	ذِباب	[ðuba:b]	'flies'

The use of a standardized phonetic alphabet with a one-to-one correspondence between sound and symbol enables linguists to transcribe languages consistently and accurately. Although we use the IPA in this book, it is not the only system of phonetic transcription; there is also a North American system, in which some symbols are different. You can see a comparison of the North American system and IPA at **launchpadworks.com**.

LANGUAGE MATTERS   Sounds and Spelling

Although the relationship between sound and symbol in IPA is one to one, things are very different in the writing system of English—as a quick look at the words *rough, through, bough, though,* and *cough* illustrates. All these words contain *ough,* but the letters represent different sounds in each word—and sometimes even a different number of sounds. In the word *rough,* they represent two sounds, while in *through,* they represent only one. The absence of a one-to-one correspondence between a symbol and a sound in English spelling is also evident when we look at the letter *o,* which is pronounced differently in *go, hot, women, more,* and *mutton.*

George Bernard Shaw, the famous playwright who described a character in his play *Pygmalion* as an "energetic phonetic enthusiast" (a description that we think could just as easily be applied to Shaw himself), illustrated the problem in the following anecdote. Imagine a new word coming into the English language that is spelled *ghoti.* How would this word be pronounced? In an attempt to demonstrate what he felt were the inadequacies of the English spelling system, Shaw argued that the word could be pronounced as "fish". How so? Note the pronunciations of the underlined segments in the following words:

enou*gh* → f

w*o*men → i

na*ti*on → sh

Shaw felt that any writing system that could possibly represent "fish" with the string of letters *ghoti* was in desperate need of reform.

If you wish to start practicing the phonetic transcription of English, turn to Tables 2.16 and 2.17 for examples.

1.1   Units of Representation

Anyone who hears a language spoken for the first time finds it hard to break up the flow of speech into individual units. Even when hearing our own language spoken, we do not focus attention on individual sounds as much as we do on the meanings of words, phrases, and sentences.

The IPA represents speech in the form of **segments**—individual phones like [p], [s], or [m]. Segments are produced by coordinating a number of individual articulatory gestures including jaw movement, lip shape, and tongue placement.

1.2   Segments

We have defined the segment as an individual speech sound (phone). The analysis of speech in terms of sound segments, or phones, is supported by several kinds of evidence.

LANGUAGE MATTERS   The Muscles of Speech

The bundle of nerves controlling the vocal folds is among the densest in the entire body. There are about forty different muscles in the vocal tract. Although they aren't all used for all sounds, coordinating those that are used at any particular moment requires exquisite timing. In fact, it's been estimated that 225 muscle activations are needed to produce just one second of speech.

Information from: Peter F. MacNielage, *The Origin of Speech* (New York: Oxford University Press, 2008), p. 4.

Errors in speech production provide one kind of evidence for the existence of segments. Slips of the tongue such as *renumeration* for *remuneration* and *melcome wat* for *welcome mat* show segments shifting and reversing position within and across words. This suggests that segments are individual units of linguistic structure that should be represented individually in a system of transcription.

The relative invariance of speech sounds in human language also suggests that segmental phonetic transcription is a well-motivated way of transcribing speech. The sounds of speech remain invariant enough from language to language for us to transcribe them consistently. A *p* sound is much the same in English, Russian, or Uzbek. The fact that when producing a *p* sound, English speakers press their lips together while Russian speakers draw theirs slightly inward does not make the sounds different enough to warrant separate symbols. But the sounds *p* and *t* are distinct enough from each other in languages the world over to be consistently transcribed with separate symbols.

When we use the same symbol to represent two sounds that are not exactly the same phonetically, we are making a **broad transcription**. A broad transcription uses a relatively simple set of symbols to represent contrasting segments but does not show all phonetic detail. If we wish to show more phonetic detail, we can use a more elaborate set of symbols and **diacritics**. In this case, we are making a **narrow transcription**. The terms *broad* and *narrow* are relative, not absolute: the less phonetic detail we show, the broader the transcription; the more phonetic detail, the narrower the transcription.

2   The Sound-Producing System

Sound is produced when air is set in motion. Think of the speech production mechanism as consisting of an air supply, a sound source that sets the air in motion in ways specifically relevant to speech production, and a set of filters that modify the sound in various ways (see Figure 2.1). The air supply is provided by the lungs. The sound source is in the **larynx**, where a set of muscles called the **vocal folds** (or **vocal cords**—not *chords*) is located. The filters are the passages above the larynx, collectively known as the **vocal tract**: the tube of the throat between the larynx and the oral cavity, which is called the **pharynx**; the oral cavity; and the nasal cavity.

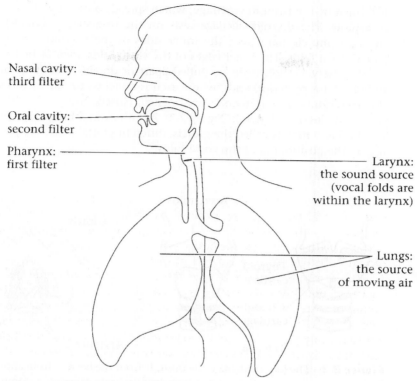

Figure 2.1 The sound-producing system

2.1 The Lungs

In order to produce the majority of sounds in the world's languages, we take air into the lungs and expel it during speech. (A small number of phones are made with air as it flows *into* the vocal tract.)

A certain level of air pressure is needed to keep the speech mechanism functioning steadily. The pressure is maintained by the action of various sets of muscles coming into play during the course of an utterance. The primary muscles are the **intercostals** (the muscles between the ribs) and the **diaphragm** (the large sheet of muscle separating the chest cavity from the abdomen). The intercostals raise the ribcage to allow air to flow into the lungs during inhalation, while the diaphragm helps control the release of air during exhalation for speech so that we can speak for a reasonable period of time between breaths.

2.2 The Larynx

As air flows out of the lungs up the **trachea** (windpipe), it passes through a boxlike structure made of cartilage and muscle; this is the larynx (commonly known as the voice box or Adam's apple), as shown in Figure 2.2. The main portion of the larynx is formed by the **thyroid cartilage**, which spreads outward at its front like the head of a plow. The thyroid cartilage rests on the ring-shaped **cricoid cartilage**. Fine sheets of muscle flare from the inner sides of the thyroid cartilage, forming the paired vocal folds. The inner edges of the vocal folds are attached to the vocal ligaments. The vocal folds can be pulled apart or drawn closer together, especially at their back (or posterior) ends, where each is attached to one of two small cartilages, the **arytenoids**. The arytenoids are opened, closed, and rotated by several pairs of small muscles (not shown in Figure 2.2). As air passes through the space between the vocal folds, which is called the **glottis**, different glottal states are produced, depending on the positioning of the vocal folds.

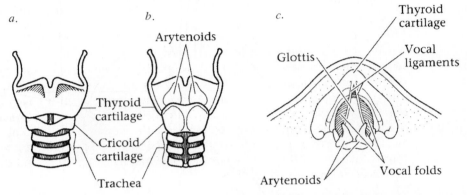

Figure 2.2   The larynx: *a.* from the front; *b.* from the back; *c.* from above, with the vocal folds in open position. The striated lines in *c.* indicate muscles, a number of which have been eliminated from the drawings in order to show the cartilages more clearly.

2.3   Glottal States

The vocal folds may be positioned in a number of ways to produce different glottal states. The first two glottal states presented in Figure 2.3 are commonly encountered in most of the world's languages. The third diagram describes the glottal state that underlies a common speech phenomenon, and the fourth illustrates one of a number of glottal states not encountered in English.

Voiceless

When the vocal folds are pulled apart as illustrated in the first drawing in Figure 2.3, air passes directly through the glottis without much interference. Any sound made with the vocal folds in this position is said to be **voiceless**. The initial sounds of *fish*, *sing*, and *house* are all voiceless. You can confirm a sound's voicelessness by touching your fingers to your larynx as you produce it. You will not feel any vibration from the vocal folds being transmitted to your fingertips. Voicelessness is a true speech state distinct from breathing; the vocal folds are not as far apart during speech voicelessness as they are in silent breathing.

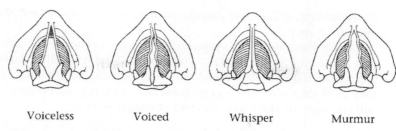

Voiceless   Voiced   Whisper   Murmur

Figure 2.3   Four glottal states: the drawings represent the vocal folds and glottis from above; the anterior (front) portion of the larynx is at the top. The small triangles represent the arytenoid cartilages, which help spread or close the vocal folds.

Voiced

When the vocal folds are brought close together but not tightly closed, air passing between them causes them to vibrate, producing sounds that are said to be **voiced**. (See the second illustration in Figure 2.3.) You can determine whether a sound is voiced in the same way you determined voicelessness. By lightly touching your fingers to your larynx as you produce an extended version of the initial sounds of the words _zip_ or _vow_, or any vowel, you can sense the vibration of the vocal folds within the larynx. It can be helpful to contrast voiced versus voiceless sounds while resting your hand on your throat. Produce the following pairs of sounds and decide which are voiced and which are voiceless.

[fffffffffffffffffffffffffvvvvvvvvvvvvvvvvvvvvvvv]
[ssssssssssssssssssssssssszzzzzzzzzzzzzzzzzzzzzzz]

On which sounds did you feel vibration? Some people find it easier to hear this distinction in another way. Perform the same exercise as given above but this time with your fingers in your ears. You will feel much greater resonance with the sounds that are voiced. These techniques can be helpful as you try to hear which phones are voiced and which are voiceless.

Whisper

Another glottal state produces a **whisper**. Whispering is voiceless, but, as shown in Figure 2.3, the vocal folds are adjusted so that the anterior (front) portions are pulled close together, while the posterior (back) portions are apart.

Murmur

Yet another glottal state produces a **murmur**, also known as **breathy voice**. Sounds produced with this glottal configuration are voiced, but the vocal folds are relaxed to allow enough air to escape to produce a simultaneous breathy effect. There are languages in the world that use breathy voice as an integral part of the sound system. Although it is difficult to generalize, sometimes when you see words or place names that have been borrowed into English with spellings such as <bh> as in

Bhagavad-Gita, <dh> as in *dharma* or *dhal*, or <gh> as in *ghee*, they can represent murmured sounds.

These four glottal states represent only some of the possibilities of sound production at the glottis. The total number of glottal states is still undecided, but there are more than a dozen. Combined with various articulations made above the larynx, they produce a wide range of phones. Before examining phones in more detail, we will consider the three major classes of speech sound.

3   Sound Classes

The sounds of language can be grouped into **sound classes** based on the phonetic properties that they share. You have already seen what some of these properties can be. All voiced sounds, for example, form a class, as do all voiceless sounds. The most basic division among sounds is into two major classes, **vowels** and **consonants**. Another class of sounds, the **glides**, shares properties of both vowels and consonants. Each class of sounds has a number of distinguishing features.

3.1   Vowels and Consonants

Vowels and consonants can be distinguished on the basis of differences in articulation or by their acoustic properties. We can also distinguish among these elements with respect to whether they function as **syllabic** or **nonsyllabic** elements.

The Articulatory Difference

Consonantal sounds, which may be voiced (e.g., [v]) or voiceless (e.g., [f]), are made with either a complete closure (e.g., [p]) or a narrowing (e.g., [f]) of the vocal tract. The airflow is either blocked momentarily or restricted so much that noise is produced as air flows past the constriction. In contrast, vowels, which are usually voiced, are produced with little obstruction in the vocal tract (you will note that for all vowels the tip of your tongue stays down by your lower front teeth).

The Acoustic Difference

As a result of the difference in articulation, consonants and vowels differ in the way they sound. Vowels are more **sonorous** (acoustically powerful) than consonants, and so we perceive them as louder and longer lasting.

Syllabic and Nonsyllabic Sounds

The greater sonority of vowels allows them to form the basis of **syllables**. A syllable can be defined as a peak of sonority surrounded by less sonorous segments. For example, the words *a* and *go* each contain one syllable, the word *laughing* two syllables, and the word *telephone* three syllables. In counting the syllables in these words, we are in effect counting the vowels. A vowel is thus said to form the **nucleus** of a syllable. In Section 5.7, we will see that certain types of consonants can form syllabic nuclei as well. It is a good idea, therefore, to think of vowels and consonants not simply as types of articulations but as elements that may or may not be syllabic.

In *1*, the initial sounds of the words in the left column are all consonants; those on the right are all vowels.

1) take   above
   cart   at
   feel   eel
   jump   it
   think   ugly
   bell   open

Table 2.2 sums up the differences between consonants and vowels.

Table 2.2   Major differences between syllabic and nonsyllabic elements

Vowels (and other syllabic elements)	Consonants (nonsyllabic elements)
• are produced with relatively little obstruction in the vocal tract	• are produced with a complete closure or narrowing of the vocal tract
• are more sonorous	• are less sonorous

3.2   Glides

A type of sound that shows properties of both consonants and vowels is called a glide. Glides may be thought of as rapidly articulated vowels—this is the auditory impression they produce. Glides are produced with an articulation like that of a vowel. However, they move quickly to another articulation, as do the initial glides in *yet* or *wet*, or quickly terminate, as do the word-final glides in *boy* and *now*. You can feel how little movement is necessary to move from a vowel articulation to a glide articulation when you pronounce the following phrases:

see *y*ou later
wh*o* *w*ould do that

Make the vowel sound in the word *see* ([i]) and then make the glide in the word *you* ([j]). Now go back and forth from [i] to [j] and note that the small articulatory movement can cause us to perceive one sound as a vowel and the other as a glide. The same pattern emerges when you produce the vowel in *who* ([u]) and the glide in *would* ([w]).

Even though they are vowel-like in articulation, glides pattern as consonants. For example, glides do not form the nucleus of a syllable. Since glides show properties of both consonants and vowels, the terms *semivowel* and *semiconsonant* may be used interchangeably with the term *glide*.

4   Consonant Articulation

Airflow is modified in the vocal tract by the placement of the tongue and the positioning of the lips. These modifications occur at specific **places of articulation**. The major places of articulation used in speech production are outlined in this section. Figure 2.4 provides a midsagittal section, or cutaway view, of the vocal tract on which each place of articulation has been indicated.

4.1   The Tongue

The primary articulating organ is the tongue. It can be raised, lowered, thrust forward or retracted, and even rolled back. The sides of the tongue can also be raised or lowered.

Phonetic description refers to five areas of the tongue. The **tip** is the narrow area at the front. Just behind the tip lies the **blade**. The main mass of the tongue is called the **body**, and the hindmost part of the tongue that lies in the mouth (versus the throat) is called the **back**. The body and back of the tongue can also be referred to jointly as the **dorsum**. The **root** of the tongue is contained in the upper part of the throat (pharynx).

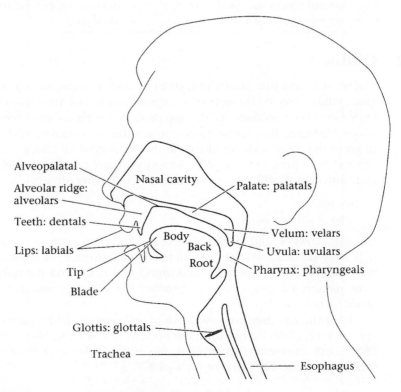

Figure 2.4   The vocal tract and places of articulation

4.2   Places of Articulation

Each point at which the airstream can be modified to produce a different sound is called a place of articulation. Places of articulation are found at the lips, within the oral cavity, in the pharynx, and at the glottis (see Figure 2.5 *a–f*).

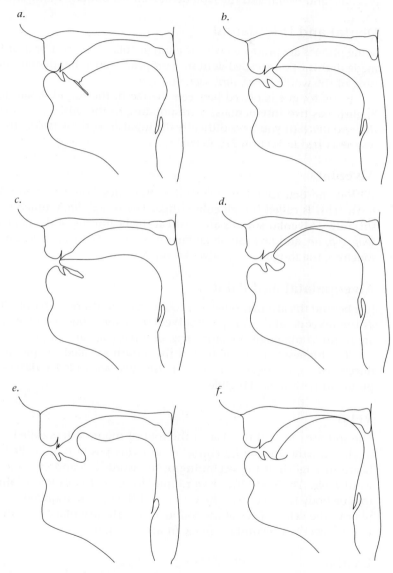

Figure 2.5   Places of articulation: *a.* the labial sound at the beginning of *peer*; *b.* the alveolar sound at the beginning of *top*; *c.* the interdental sound at the beginning of *this*; *d.* the alveopalatal sound at the beginning of *show*; *e.* the retroflex sound at the beginning of *red*; *f.* the velar sound at the beginning of *call*.

Labial

Any sound made with closure or near-closure of the lips is said to be **labial**. Sounds involving both lips are termed **bilabials**; sounds involving the lower lip and upper teeth are called **labiodentals**. English includes the bilabials heard word-initially in *peer, bin,* and *month* and the labiodentals heard initially in *fire* and *vow*.

Dental and Interdental

Some phones are produced with the tongue placed against or near the teeth. Sounds made in this way are called **dentals**. European French has dental sounds at the beginning of the words *temps, dire, sept,* and *zizi*.

If the tongue is placed between the teeth, the sound is said to be **interdental**. English has two interdentals, corresponding to the initial consonants of the words *this* and *thing*. (If you have difficulty distinguishing these two sounds, try the voicing test described in Section 2.3 above.)

Alveolar

Within the oral cavity, a small ridge protrudes from just behind the upper front teeth. This is called the **alveolar ridge**. The tongue may touch or be brought near this ridge. **Alveolar sounds** are heard at the beginning of the English words *top, deer, soap, zip, lip,* and *neck*. Some languages, such as Spanish, have an *r* that is made by touching the tongue to the alveolar ridge.

Alveopalatal and Palatal

Just behind the alveolar ridge, the roof of the mouth rises sharply. This area is known as the **alveopalatal** area (**palatoalveolar** in some books). Alveopalatal consonants are heard in the English words *show, measure, chip,* and *judge*.

The highest part of the roof of the mouth is called the **palate**, and sounds produced with the tongue on or near this area are called **palatals**. The word-initial phone in *yes* is a palatal glide.

Velar

The soft area toward the rear of the roof of the mouth is called the **velum**. Sounds made with the tongue touching or near this position are called **velars**. Velars are heard in English at the beginning of the words *call* and *guy*, and at the end of the word *hang*. The glide heard word-initially in *wet* is called a **labiovelar**, since the tongue body is raised near the velum and the lips are rounded at the same time. We refer to the velar aspect of the sound as its **primary place of articulation** while the labial aspect is a **secondary place of articulation**.

Uvular

The small fleshy flap of tissue known as the **uvula** hangs down from the velum. Sounds made with the tongue near or touching this area are called **uvulars**. English has no uvulars, but the *r* sound of standard European French is uvular.

Pharyngeal

The area of the throat between the uvula and the larynx is known as the pharynx. Sounds made through the modification of airflow in this region by retracting the tongue or constricting the pharynx are called **pharyngeals**. Pharyngeals can be found in many dialects of Arabic, but not in English.

Glottal

Sounds produced using the vocal folds as primary articulators are called **glottals**. The sound at the beginning of the English words _heave_ and _hog_ is made at the glottis. You can also hear a glottal sound in the Cockney English pronunciation of the _tt_ in words like _better_ or _bottle_.

5 Manners of Articulation

The lips, tongue, velum, and glottis can be positioned in different ways to produce different sound types. These various configurations are called **manners of articulation**.

5.1 Oral versus Nasal Phones

A basic distinction in manner of articulation is between **oral** and **nasal phones**. When the velum is raised, cutting off the airflow through the nasal cavity, oral sounds are produced. The velum can also be lowered to allow air to pass through the nasal cavity, producing a sound that is nasal. Both consonants and vowels can be nasal, in which case they are generally voiced. (All nasals represented in this chapter are voiced.) The consonants at the end of the English words _sun_, _sum_, and _sung_ are nasal. For many speakers of English, the vowels of words such as _bank_ and _wink_ are also slightly nasal because of their proximity to nasal consonants.

5.2 Stops

Stops are made with a complete closure either in the oral cavity or at the glottis. In the world's languages, stops are found at bilabial, dental, alveolar, alveopalatal, palatal, velar, uvular, and glottal places of articulation.

In English, bilabial, alveolar, and velar oral and nasal stops occur in the words shown in Table 2.3. Note that [ŋ] does not occur word-initially in English, though it can in other languages.

The glottal stop is commonly heard in English in the expression _unh-unh_ [ʔʌ̃ʔʌ̃], meaning 'no'. The two vowels in this utterance are each preceded by a momentary closing of the airstream at the glottis. In some British dialects, the glottal stop is commonly heard in place of the [t] in a word like _bottle_. You may see this glottal stop spelled with an apostrophe (_bo'l_).

Table 2.3   English stops and their transcription

Place of articulation			Transcription
Bilabial			
Oral	Voiceless	span	[p]
	Voiced	ban	[b]
Nasal	(Voiced)	man	[m]
Alveolar			
Oral	Voiceless	stun	[t]
	Voiced	done	[d]
Nasal	(Voiced)	none	[n]
Velar			
Oral	Voiceless	scold	[k]
	Voiced	gold	[g]
Nasal	(Voiced)	long	[ŋ]
Glottal			
	Voiceless	uh-oh	[ʔ]

A Grid for Stops

Table 2.4 presents a grid on which the stop consonants of English are arranged horizontally according to place of articulation. As you can see, each oral stop, with one exception, has voiced and voiceless counterparts. The nasal stops are always voiced in English. The glottal stop is always voiceless. It is produced with the vocal folds drawn firmly together and the arytenoids drawn forward; since no air can pass through the glottis, the vocal folds cannot be set in motion.

Table 2.4   English stop consonants

		Bilabial	Alveolar	Velar	Glottal
Nonnasal	Voiceless	[p]	[t]	[k]	[ʔ]
	Voiced	[b]	[d]	[g]	
Nasal	(Voiced)	[m]	[n]	[ŋ]	

5.3   Fricatives

Fricatives are consonants produced with a continuous airflow through the mouth. They belong to a large class of sounds called **continuants** (a class that also includes vowels and glides), all of which share this property. The fricatives form a special class of continuants; during their production, they are accompanied by a continuous

The words in the first column have the stops ([pʰ], [tʰ], and [kʰ]) released into the following vowel. However, in the second column, it is quite common not to release word-final stops at all. When you pronounce the word *cap* you may well end with your lips closed, and in *pot* and *back* your tongue can stay on the roof of your mouth. The phonetic symbol for this is a raised [˺] as in [p˺]. In some languages, a word-final stop is always unreleased. This is the case in Korean, where *pap* 'rice' is always pronounced [pap˺]. (Since transcribing all phonetic details can become cumbersome, the symbols indicating aspiration or an unreleased stop are sometimes omitted in the remainder of this chapter when they are not relevant to the point being discussed.)

5.6   Liquids

Among the sounds commonly found in the world's languages are *l* and *r* and their numerous variants. They form a special class of consonants known as **liquids**. Although there is a great deal of variation in the production of *l*s and *r*s in the languages of the world, they are nonetheless similar enough to be grouped together in a single category: they are all oral sonorous consonants.

English Laterals

Varieties of *l* are called **laterals**. The most commonly used lateral liquid in English, transcribed as [l], is articulated with the tip of the tongue touching the alveolar ridge while air escapes through the mouth along the lowered sides of the tongue.

Because laterals are generally voiced, the term *lateral* is usually used to mean 'voiced lateral'. Still, there are instances of voiceless laterals in speech. The voiceless dental or alveolar lateral is written with an additional phonetic symbol, called a diacritic. In this case, the diacritic is a circle beneath the symbol: [l̥]. Voiceless laterals can be heard in the pronunciation of the English words *please* and *clear*.

LANGUAGE MATTERS   Another Kind of *l*

Pronounce the words in the following two lists:

leaf	fall
lie	milk
lawn	steal

In most dialects of English, the *l* sounds are not pronounced in the same way. For some speakers, the *l* in the first column is made with the tongue tip touching the alveolar ridge (as described in Table 2.10). This *l* sound is known as a **clear l**. In the second column, however, the *l* sound is made with additional constriction further back in the mouth (at the velum). This type of *l* is known technically as a **velarized l** and more casually as a **dark l**. It is represented by the phonetic symbol [ɫ].

English *r*s

Numerous varieties of *r* are also heard in the world's languages. This section describes the types found in English. The *r* of English as it is spoken in the United States and Canada is made by curling the tongue tip back and bunching the tongue upward and back in the mouth, as shown in panel *e* in Figure 2.5 on page 27. This *r*, which is known as a **retroflex** *r*, is heard in *ri*de and *car*. In a broad transcription, the symbol [r] can be used for the English *r* as well as *r*s in other languages. However, in narrower IPA transcription, [r] is reserved for a trilled *r*, as in Spanish *perro* 'dog'. The IPA transcription for the retroflex *r* is [ɹ], and that is the symbol we will use in this book for the English *r*.

Another sound commonly identified with *r* is the **flap**. The flap is produced when the tongue tip strikes the alveolar ridge as it passes across it. It is heard in the North American English pronunciation of *bitter* and *butter*, and in some British pronunciations of *very*. It is commonly transcribed as [ɾ] and is generally voiced. Table 2.10 presents the liquids *r*, *l*, and the flap of American English.

Table 2.10 English liquids

		Alveolar	
Laterals		voiced	[l]
		voiceless	[l̥]
*r*s	retroflex	voiced	[ɹ]
		voiceless	[ɹ̥]
	flap		[ɾ]

5.7 Syllabic Liquids and Nasals

Liquids and nasals are more sonorous than other consonants and in this respect are more like vowels than are the other consonants. In fact, they are so sonorous that they may function as syllabic nuclei. When they do so, they are called **syllabic liquids** and **syllabic nasals** (see Table 2.11). Syllabic liquids and nasals are found in many of the world's languages, including English. In transcription, they are usually marked with a short diacritic line underneath.

Table 2.11 Syllabic liquids and nasals in English

	Syllabic		*Nonsyllabic*
bottle	[bɑɾl̩]	lift	[lɪft]
funnel	[fʌnl̩]	pill	[pʰɪl]
bird	[be˞d]	rat	[ɹæt]
her	[he˞]	car	[kʰɑɹ]
teacher	[titʃɹ̩]	now	[naw]
hidden	[hɪdn̩]	mat	[mæt]
'm-m'	[ʔm̩ʔm̩] (meaning 'no')		

To be clear, then, the [n] in a word like *no* is not syllabic because it does not form the nucleus of the syllable. *No* is a one-syllable word and has one vowel. However, the [n] in some two-syllable words is syllabic. The second syllable in *hidden*, for example, has [n] as its nucleus. Therefore, whether a segment is syllabic or not is directly related to how it functions in the syllable.

Unfortunately for beginning linguistics students, linguists are not always consistent in the transcription of syllabic liquids and nasals, and there is some dialectal variation as well. A broad transcription simply uses schwa plus the liquid or nasal. In this book, we will transcribe a nasal as syllabic in English when it occurs in an unstressed syllable at the end of a word after a stop, affricate, or fricative. We will transcribe a liquid as syllabic in English when it occurs in an unstressed syllable at the end of a word after any consonant. We will use the symbol [ɚ] for *r* in words like *bird*, *earth*, and *girl* and [ɻ̩] for syllabic *r* in unstressed syllables.

5.8 Glides

Recall that a glide is a very rapidly articulated nonsyllabic segment. The two glides of American English are [j] of *yes* and *boy* and [w] of *wet* and *now*.

The [j] is a palatal glide (sometimes described as alveopalatal as well) whose articulation is virtually identical to that of the vowel [i] of *see*. You can verify this by pronouncing a [j] in an extended manner; it will sound very close to an [i].

The glide [w] is made with the tongue raised and pulled back near the velum and with the lips protruding, or rounded. For this reason, it is sometimes called a labio-velar. The [w] corresponds closely in articulation to the vowel [u] of *who*. This can be verified by extending the pronunciation of [w]. We will consider [w] a rounded velar glide for purposes of description. Some speakers of English also have a voiceless (labio)velar glide, transcribed [ʍ], in the words *when*, *where*, and *which* (but not in *witch*).

LANGUAGE MATTERS   Which Witch Is Which?

Do you make a distinction in your pronunciation of the following pairs of words?

weather	whether
witch	which
wither	whither

Ask some of your friends (of different ages and geographical origins) to pronounce these words. Do they make a distinction?

You can see a dialect map showing where the /w/ versus /ʍ/ distinction is maintained at the Telsur Project site hosted by the University of Pennsylvania (online).

Table 2.12 provides a summary of the places and manners of articulation of English consonants.

Table 2.12 English consonants: places and manners of articulation

Manner of articulation		Place of articulation							
		Bilabial	Labiodental	Interdental	Alveolar	Alveopalatal	Palatal	Velar	Glottal
Stop	voiceless	p			t			k	ʔ
	voiced	b			d			g	
Fricative	voiceless		f	θ	s	ʃ			h
	voiced		v	ð	z	ʒ			
Affricate	voiceless					tʃ			
	voiced					dʒ			
Nasal	voiced	m			n			ŋ	
Liquid	voiced lateral				l				
	voiced retroflex				ɹ				
Glide	voiced	w					j	w	
	voiceless	ʍ						ʍ	

LANGUAGE MATTERS   What's the World's Most Unusual Speech Sound?

Pirahã, a language with only a couple of hundred speakers in Brazil, has a sound that is produced as follows: the tongue tip first touches the alveolar ridge and then comes out of the mouth, almost touching the upper chin as the underblade of the tongue touches the lower lip. Technically speaking, this is known as a "voiced, lateralized apical-alveolar/sublaminal-labial double flap with egressive lung air." (Fortunately, for all concerned, the sound is only used in "certain special types of speech performance.")

Information from: Peter Ladefoged and Ian Maddieson, *The Sounds of the World's Languages* (Malden, MA: Blackwell, 1996); Daniel Everett, "Phonetic Rarities in Pirahã," *Journal of the International Phonetic Association* 12, 2 (1982): 94–96.

---

6 Vowels

Vowels are sonorous, syllabic sounds made with the vocal tract more open than it is for consonant and glide articulations. Different vowel sounds (also called **vowel qualities**) are produced by varying the placement of the body of the tongue (remember that for vowels your tongue tip is behind your lower front teeth) and shaping the lips. The shape of the vocal tract can be further altered by protruding the lips to produce **rounded vowels** or by lowering the velum to produce a nasal vowel. Finally, vowels may be tense or lax, depending on the degree of vocal tract constriction during their articulation. This section on vowels introduces most of the basic vowels of English.

Note that vowels are particularly subject to dialectal variation. The appendix at the end of this chapter lists a number of examples.

6.1   Simple Vowels and Diphthongs

English vowels are divided into two major types, **simple vowels** and **diphthongs**. Simple vowels do not show a noticeable change in quality during their articulation. The vowels of *pit*, *set*, *cat*, *dog*, *but*, *put*, and the first vowel of *suppose* are all simple vowels.

Diphthongs are vowels that exhibit a change in quality within a single syllable. English diphthongs show changes in quality that are due to tongue movement away from the initial vowel articulation toward a glide position. In the vowels classified as **major diphthongs**, the change in articulation is quite extreme and hence easy to hear. Listen to the change in articulation in the following words: *buy* ([aj]), *boy* ([ɔj]), and *now* ([aw]). Each of these diphthongs starts in one position (e.g., [a]) and ends up in another position (e.g., [w]). In **minor diphthongs**, the change in position of the articulators is less dramatic. If you listen carefully and note the change in your tongue position as you say *play* ([ej]) and your lip position as you say *go* ([ow]), you will realize that in each of these diphthongs, too, the starting position is different from the ending position. In the vowels of words like *heed* and *lose*, the change is more difficult to hear and in fact is not made by all English speakers, so we will not

---

LANGUAGE MATTERS   **Cross-Dialectal Variation**

One of the best ways to learn to appreciate some of these fine differences in vowel articulation is to think of some cross-dialectal variation in English. Let us first consider the question of the minor diphthongs in [ej] and [ow]. In American English, these sounds are diphthongs (as reflected in our transcription), but this is not the case in *all* dialects of English. In Jamaican English, words like *go* and *say* have simple vowels and would be transcribed as [go] and [se].

Comparison across dialects can also help us understand why we have used the [a] symbol in the major diphthongs. In articulatory terms, the [a] sound is made at the front of the mouth with the tongue a bit lower than [æ]. You can hear this sound in many Romance languages (like French or Spanish) in words like *la* or *gato*. This [a] vowel is, in fact, where we start articulating our diphthongs. If you try to say words like *ride* and *round* with an [ɑ] sound rather than an [a], you will find yourself speaking with one variety of a British accent.

transcribe these as diphthongs. Some instructors, however, may ask that you transcribe them in the diphthongized form.

Table 2.13 presents the simple vowels and diphthongs of American English. The diphthongs are transcribed as vowel-glide sequences. Although diphthongs are complex in an articulatory sense (in that they are transcribed as a vowel plus a glide), they still act as a single vowel in some respects. For example, our judgments tell us that both *pin* (simple vowel) and *pint* (diphthong) are single-syllable words. Having a diphthong doesn't add a syllable to a word.

Table 2.13   Some simple vowels and diphthongs of American English

Simple vowels		Minor diphthongs		Major diphthongs	
pit	[ɪ]	say	[ej]	my	[aj]
set	[ɛ]	grow	[ow]	now	[aw]
put	[ʊ]			boy	[ɔj]
cut	[ʌ]				
bought	[ɔ]				
mat	[æ]				
pot	[ɑ]				
heat	[i]				
lose	[u]				

6.2   Basic Parameters for Describing Vowels

Vowel articulations are not as easy to feel at first as consonant articulations because the vocal tract is not narrowed as much. To become acquainted with vowel articulation, alternately pronounce the vowels of *he* and *ah*. You will feel the tongue move from a **high** front to a **low** back position. Once you feel this tongue movement, alternate between the vowels of *ah* and *at*. You will feel the tongue moving from the low **back** to low **front** position. Finally, alternate between the vowels of *he* and *who*. You will notice that in addition to a tongue movement between the high front and high back positions, you are also rounding your lips for the [u]. Figure 2.9 shows a midsagittal view of the tongue position for the vowels [i], [ɑ], and [u] based on X-ray studies of speech.

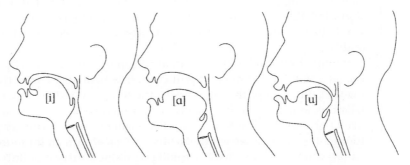

Figure 2.9   Tongue position and transcription for three English vowels

Vowels for which the tongue is neither raised nor lowered are called **mid vowels**. The front vowel of English *ma̲de* or *fa̲me* is mid, front, and unrounded. The vowel of *co̲de* and *so̲ak* is mid, back, and rounded. In the case of diphthongs, the articulatory descriptions refer to the tongue position of the vowel nucleus, not the following glide. The vowels presented so far in this section are summed up in Table 2.14. Note that in describing the vowels, the articulatory parameters are presented in the order *height, backness, rounding.*

Table 2.14 Basic phonetic parameters for describing American English vowels

h̲e̲at	[i]	high front unrounded
fa̲te	[ej]	mid front unrounded
ma̲sh	[æ]	low front unrounded
S̲u̲e	[u]	high back rounded
bo̲at	[ow]	mid back rounded
ca̲ught	[ɔ]	mid back rounded (in some dialects)
su̲n	[ʌ]	mid central unrounded
co̲t	[ɑ]	low back unrounded

As Table 2.14 shows, the vowel of *caught* (and certain other words such as *law*) is the mid back rounded lax vowel [ɔ] in many dialects of English, both in the United States and worldwide. However, in some dialects of North American English, the vowel [ɔ] has merged with the vowel [ɑ], and there is, therefore, no difference between *cot* and *caught;* the vowel in both words is [ɑ].

Tongue positions for some English vowels are illustrated in Figure 2.10. The trapezoid corresponds roughly to the space within which the tongue moves, which is wider at the top of the oral cavity and more restricted at the bottom. Nonfront vowels are traditionally divided into central and back vowels (see Figures 2.10 and 2.11); often the term *back* alone is used for all nonfront vowels.

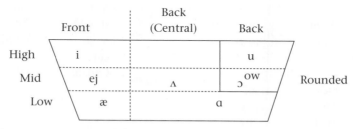

Figure 2.10 Basic tongue positions for English vowels

6.3 Tense and Lax Vowels

All the vowels illustrated in Figure 2.10 except [æ] and [ʌ] are tense. **Tense vowels** are produced with greater vocal tract constriction than nontense vowels and are longer in duration than nontense vowels. Some vowels of English are made with roughly the same tongue position as the tense vowels but with a less constricted articulation; they are called **lax vowels**. The representation of vowels and their artic-ulatory positions (Figure 2.10) is expanded in Figure 2.11 to include both tense and lax vowels, as well as the major diphthongs.

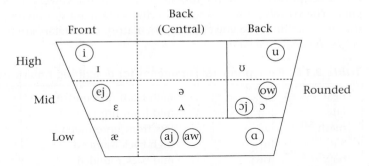

Figure 2.11 American English vowels (tense vowels are circled)

Table 2.15 provides examples from English comparing tense and lax vowels. Note that not all the vowels come in tense/lax pairs. The difference between two of the vowels illustrated in Table 2.15 is often not easy to hear at first. Both the vowel [ʌ] in c*u*t, d*u*d, pl*u*ck, and H*u*n, and the vowel [ə] of Can*a*da, *a*bout, tom*a*hawk, and sof*a* are mid, central, unrounded, and lax. The vowel of the second set of examples, called **schwa**, is referred to as a **reduced vowel**. In addition to being lax, its duration is briefer than that of any of the other vowels.

Table 2.15 Tense and lax vowels in American English

Tense		*Lax*	
h*ea*t	[i]	h*i*t	[ɪ]
m*a*te	[ej]	m*e*t	[ɛ]
—	—	m*a*t	[æ]
sh*oo*t	[u]	sh*ou*ld	[ʊ]
c*oa*t	[ow]	*ou*ght	[ɔ] (in some dialects)
—	—	c*u*t	[ʌ]
—	—	Can*a*da	[ə]
l*o*ck	[ɑ]	—	—
l*ie*s	[aj]		
l*ou*d	[aw]		
b*oy*	[ɔj]		

A simple test can help determine whether vowels are tense or lax. In English, monosyllabic words spoken in isolation do not end in lax vowels (except for [ɔ]). We find *see* [si], *say* [sej], *Sue* [su], *so* [sow], and *spa* [spɑ] in English, but not *[sɪ], *[sɛ], *[sæ], *[sʊ], or *[sʌ]. Schwa, however, frequently appears in unstressed syl-lables (syllables perceived as less prominent) in polysyllabic words like *sof*[ə] and *Can*[ə]*d*[ə]. (See Section 8.3 for a discussion of stress.) It should be pointed out—especially for those who think their ears are deceiving them—that many speakers produce the final vowel in the last two examples as [ʌ], not as [ə].

This rather formidable crowd of vowels should not intimidate you. If you are a native speaker of English, you have been using these vowels most of your life. Learning to hear them consciously and transcribe them is not a difficult task.

7 Phonetic Transcription of American English Consonants and Vowels

Tables 2.16 and 2.17 present the phonetic symbols for consonants and vowels commonly used to transcribe American English. To illustrate how each symbol is used, one word is transcribed completely, and then some other words in which the same sound is found are given. You will notice that in the example words, the spelling of the sound may vary. Be careful of this when you transcribe words phonetically—the sound of a word, not its spelling, is what is transcribed!

Table 2.16   Transcribing English consonants

	Symbol	Word	Transcription	More examples
Stops	[p]	spit	[spɪt]	spar, crispy, upper, culprit, bumper
	[b]	bib	[bɪb]	boat, liberate, rob, blast
	[t]	stuck	[stʌk]	stem, hunter, nasty, mostly
	[d]	dip	[dɪp]	dust, sled, draft
	[k]	skip	[skɪp]	scatter, uncle, blacklist, likely
	[g]	get	[gɛt]	gape, mugger, twig, gleam
Aspirated Stops	[pʰ]	pit	[pʰɪt]	pain, upon, apart
	[tʰ]	tick	[tʰɪk]	tell, attire, terror, tutu
	[kʰ]	keep	[kʰip]	cow, kernel, recur
Affricates	[tʃ]	chip	[tʃɪp]	lunch, lecher, ditch, belch
	[dʒ]	judge	[dʒʌdʒ]	germ, journal, budge, wedge
Fricatives	[f]	fit	[fɪt]	flash, coughing, proof, phlegmatic, gopher
	[v]	vat	[væt]	vote, oven, prove
	[θ]	thick	[θɪk]	thought, ether, teeth, three, bathroom
	[ð]	though	[ðow]	then, bother, teethe, bathe
	[s]	sip	[sɪp]	psychology, fasten, lunacy, bass, curse, science
	[z]	zap	[zæp]	Xerox, scissors, desire, zipper, fuzzy
	[ʃ]	ship	[ʃɪp]	shock, nation, mission, glacier, wish
	[ʒ]	rouge	[ɹuʒ]	measure, azure, visual, garage (for some speakers)
	[h]	hat	[hæt]	who, ahoy, forehead, behind

Table 2.16 Continued

	Symbol	Word	Transcription	More examples
Nasals	[m]	moat	[mowt]	mind, humor, shimmer, sum, thumb
	[n]	note	[nowt]	now, winner, angel, sign, wind
	[ŋ]	sang	[sæŋ]	singer, longer, bank, twinkle, speaking
Syllabic Nasals	[m̩]	m-m	[ʔm̩ʔm̩]	bottom, prism
	[n̩]	button	[bʌtn̩]	Jordan, fatten
Liquids	[l]	leaf	[lif]	loose, lock, alive, hail
	[ɹ]	reef	[ɹif]	rod, arrive, tear
Flap	[ɾ]	hitting	[hɪɾɪŋ]	butter, madder, writer, rider, pretty, amity
Syllabic Liquids	[l̩]	huddle	[hʌdl̩]	bottle, needle (for many speakers)
	[ɚ]	bird	[bɚd]	early, hurt, stir, purr
	[ɹ̩]	doctor	[dɑktɹ̩]	summer, eraser, eager
Glides	[j]	yet	[jɛt]	_use, c_ute, yes
	[w]	witch	[wɪtʃ]	wait, weird, queen, now
	[ʍ]	which	[ʍɪtʃ]	what, where, when (only for some speakers)

Table 2.17 Transcribing English vowels

Symbol	Word	Transcription	More examples
[i]	fee	[fi]	she, cream, believe, receive, serene, amoeba, highly
[ɪ]	fit	[fɪt]	hit, income, definition, been (for some speakers)
[ej]	fate	[fejt]	they, clay, grain, gauge, engage, great, sleigh
[ɛ]	let	[lɛt]	led, head, says, said, sever, guest
[æ]	bat	[bæt]	lab, racket, laugh, pal
[u]	boot	[but]	do, two, loose, brew, Louise, Lucy, through
[ʊ]	book	[bʊk]	should, put, hood
[ow]	note	[nowt]	no, throat, though, slow, toe, oaf, O'Conner
[ɔ]	fought	[fɔt]	caught, normal, all
[ɔj]	boy	[bɔj]	voice, boil, toy
[ɑ]	rob	[ɹɑb]	cot, father, body
[ʌ]	shut	[ʃʌt]	other, udder, tough, lucky, what, flood
[ə]	suppose	[səpʰowz]	collide, telegraph, about, hinted (in some dialects)
[aw]	crowd	[kɹawd]	(to) house, plow, bough
[aj]	lies	[lajz]	my, tide, thigh, buy

8 Suprasegmentals

All phones have certain inherent **suprasegmental** or **prosodic properties** that form part of their makeup no matter what their place or manner of articulation. These properties are **pitch**, **loudness**, and **length**.

All sounds give us a subjective impression of being relatively higher or lower in pitch. Pitch is the auditory property of a sound that enables us to place it on a scale that ranges from low to high. Pitch is especially noticeable in sonorous sounds: vowels, glides, liquids, and nasals. Even stop and fricative consonants convey different pitches. This is particularly noticeable among the fricatives, as you can hear by extending the pronunciation of [s] and then of [ʃ]; the [s] is clearly higher pitched. All sounds have some degree of intrinsic loudness as well, or they could not be heard. Moreover, all sounds occupy a certain stretch of time—they give the subjective impression of length.

8.1 Pitch: Tone and Intonation

Speakers of any language have the ability to control the level of pitch in their speech. This is accomplished by controlling the tension of the vocal folds and the amount of air that passes through the glottis. The combination of tensed vocal folds and greater air pressure results in higher pitch on vowels and sonorant consonants, whereas less tense vocal folds and lower air pressure result in lower pitch. Two kinds of controlled pitch movement found in human language are called **tone** and **intonation**.

Tone

A language is said to have tone or to be a **tone language** when differences in word meaning are signaled by differences in pitch. Pitch on forms in tone languages functions very differently from the movement of pitch in a nontone language. When a speaker of English says *a car?* with a rising pitch, the word *car* refers to the same type of object as when it is pronounced on a different pitch level or with a different pitch contour. In contrast, when a speaker of the tone language Mandarin pronounces the form *ma* [mà] with a falling pitch, it means 'scold', but when the same form (*ma*) is pronounced with a rising pitch, as [má], the meaning is 'hemp' (see Figure 2.14). There is no parallel to anything like this in nontone languages such as English and French.

Unlike Mandarin, which has falling and rising tones, some languages show only what are known as level tones. Tsúut'ína (or Sarcee), an Athabaskan language spoken in Alberta, Canada, has high-, mid-, and low-pitch level tones. In Figure 2.12, the uppercase letters H, M, and L stand for high, mid, and low tones, respectively. An **association line** drawn from the letters to the vowels links the segments with their respective tones.

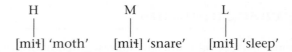

Figure 2.12 Tsúut'ína level tones ([ɬ] is a voiceless lateral fricative) Data from: E. D. Cook, "Vowels and Tones in Sarcee" in *Language* 47: 164–79.

Level tones that signal meaning differences are called **register tones**: two or three register tones are the norm in most of the world's register tone languages, though four have been reported for Mazatec, a language spoken in Mexico.

A single tone may be associated with more than one syllabic element. In Mende, spoken in West Africa, certain polysyllabic forms show the same tone on each syllable. (In Table 2.18, the diacritic [´] indicates a high tone and the diacritic [`] indicates a low tone.)

Table 2.18 High-tone and low-tone words in Mende

pélé	'banana'
háwámá	'waistline'
kpàkàlì	'tripod chair'

The notation in Figure 2.13 allows us to represent the tone as characteristic of an entire form. The single underlying tone unit is associated with all vowels.

Figure 2.13 Tone as a word feature in Mende

In some languages, tones can change pitch within a single syllabic element. Moving pitches that signal meaning differences are called **contour tones**. In Mandarin, both register and contour tones are heard. Contour tones are shown by pitch level notation lines that converge above the vowel. Figure 2.14 shows one (high) register tone and three different contour tones.

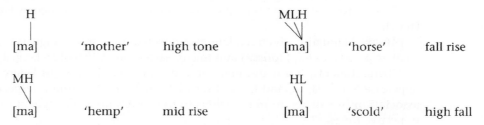

Figure 2.14 Register and contour tones in Mandarin

Tone can sometimes have a grammatical function. In Bini, a language spoken in Nigeria, tone can signal differences in the tense of a verb (such as past versus present), as Figure 2.15 shows.

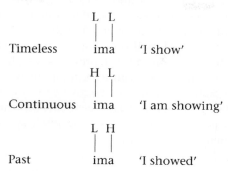

Figure 2.15 Tense and tone in Bini

Although tones may seem exotic to native speakers of Western European languages, they are very widespread. Tone languages are found throughout North and South America, sub-Saharan Africa, and the Far East.

Intonation

Pitch movement in spoken utterances that is not related to differences in word meaning is called intonation. It makes no difference to the meaning of the word *seven*, for example, whether it is pronounced with a rising pitch or a falling pitch.

Intonation often does serve to convey information of a broadly meaningful nature, however. For example, the falling pitch we hear at the end of a statement in English such as *Fred parked the car* signals that the utterance is complete. For this reason, falling intonation at the end of an utterance is called a **terminal (intonation) contour**. Conversely, a rising or level intonation, called a **nonterminal (intonation)**

LANGUAGE MATTERS   Intonation and Punctuation

Punctuation marks in English often serve to indicate intonation patterns. If you just read an unpunctuated sequence such as

   John said William is brilliant

you might not recognize the ambiguity of the utterance, as shown below:

   John said, "William is brilliant."

   "John," said William, "is brilliant."

Repeat each of the above sentences and note how your intonation helps to convey the right meaning.

contour, often signals incompleteness. Nonterminal contours are often heard in the nonfinal forms found in lists and telephone numbers.

In questions, final rising intonations also signal a kind of incompleteness in that they indicate that a conversational exchange is not finished: *Are you hungry?* However, English interrogatives that contain question words like *who, what, when,* and *how* (for example, *What did you buy?*) ordinarily do not have rising intonation. It is as if the question word itself is enough to indicate that an answer is expected.

Although intonation can be represented graphically as in Figures 2.16 and 2.17, a more formal way of representing intonation is shown in Figure 2.18. Here, as in tonal representation, L and H are relative terms for differences in pitch. The letters H and L are placed above the syllabic elements on which the pitch change occurs. The dotted lines indicate that the lowering pitch spreads across the remaining pitch-bearing elements.

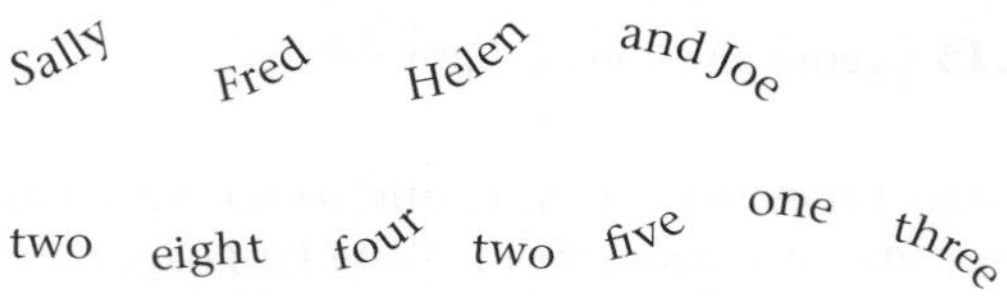

Sally   Fred   Helen   and Joe

two   eight   four   two   five   one   three

Figure 2.16   Rising nonterminal intonations in a list and a telephone number

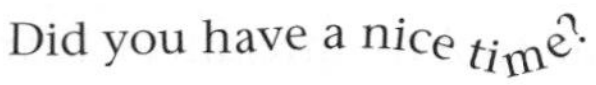

Did you have a nice time?

Figure 2.17   Nonterminal intonation in a question

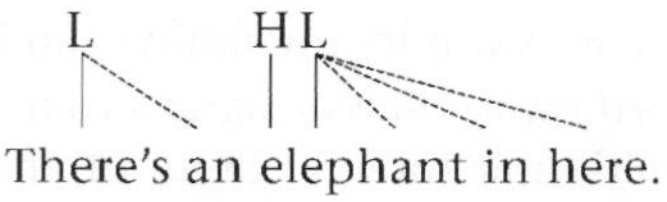

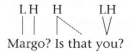

There's an elephant in here.

Figure 2.18   A terminal contour

Rising intonation on names or requests is commonly heard in addressing people. Its use indicates that the speaker is opening a conversation or that some further action is expected from the addressee, as shown in Figure 2.19.

Margo? Is that you?

Figure 2.19   Two nonterminal contours

The complex use of intonation has just been touched on here. For example, rising intonation is often used to express politeness, as in *Please sit down*. Some linguists think that this is an extension of the open-ended mode of intonation and that since a rising intonation indicates that a further response is expected (but not demanded) of the addressee, a sentence uttered with a rising intonation sounds less like an order and so is more polite.

Intonation and Tone

Tone and intonation are not mutually exclusive. Tone languages show intonation of all types. This is possible since tones are not absolute but relative pitches. For example, a tone is perceived as high if it is high relative to the pitches around it. As long as this relative difference is maintained, the pitch distinctions will also be maintained. This is shown graphically in Figure 2.20, which represents the overall pitch of a declarative sentence in Igbo, a West African language with register tones. Note how an Igbo speaker clearly maintains the distinction among the pitch registers even as the overall pitch of the utterance falls. Each high tone is always lower than the preceding high tone but higher than the low tone that immediately precedes it. This phenomenon is known as **downdrift**.

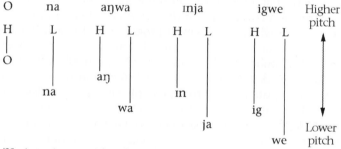

'He is trying to ride a bicycle.'

Figure 2.20 Tone and intonation: downdrift in Igbo

8.2 Length

Many languages have vowels and consonants whose articulation takes longer relative to that of other vowels and consonants. This phenomenon, known as length, is widespread in the world's languages. Length is indicated in phonetic transcription by the use of an IPA-style colon [ː] placed after the segment in question.

Hungarian, German, Cree, and Finnish are a few of the many languages that have long and short vowels. Yapese, a language spoken on the island of Yap in the Western Pacific, shows **short vowels** and **long vowels** in pairs of words such as those in Table 2.19.

Table 2.19 Short and long vowels in Yapese

[θis]	'to topple'	[θiːs]	'(a) post'
[pul]	'to gather'	[puːl]	'moon'
[ʔer]	'near you'	[ʔeːr]	'part of a lagoon'

Italian has short consonants and long consonants (called **germinates**) in pairs of words such as those shown in Table 2.20. Long and short consonants are also found in many other languages, including Finnish, Turkish, and Hungarian.

Table 2.20 Short and long consonants in Italian

fato	[fatɔ]	'fate'	fatto	[fatːɔ]	'fact'
fano	[fanɔ]	'grove'	fanno	[fanːɔ]	'they do'
tufo	[tufɔ]	'volcanic rock'	tuffo	[tufːɔ]	'dive'

8.3 Stress

In any utterance, some vowels are perceived as more prominent than others. In a word such as *banana,* the second syllable is more prominent than the other two. In a word such as *telegraphic* [ˌtɛləˈgɹæfɪk], the two vowel nuclei that are more prominent than the others are [ɛ] and [æ]. A syllabic nucleus that is perceived to be more prominent than other nuclei in the word is said to be stressed.

Stress is a cover term for the combined effects of pitch, loudness, and length—the result of which is perceived prominence. In each language, the effect of these prosodic features varies. In general, English stressed vowels are higher in pitch, longer, and louder than unstressed ones. In some languages, the impression of vowel prominence results from a different interaction of the prosodic parameters than is found in English. In Modern Greek, for example, syllables tend to be of equal length. Stress, therefore, is manifested by a change only in pitch and loudness and not in syllable length. Tone languages do not change the pitch level or contour of tones to mark stress. In many of these languages, relative prominence is marked by exaggerating the vowel length or pitch contour.

There are various ways to mark stress in phonetic transcription. IPA uses a superscript prime ['] before the syllable that receives the most prominent or **primary stress** and a subscript prime [ˌ] to mark the second most prominent or **secondary stress** (or stresses). Stress can also be marked by placing numbers above the stressed vowels, usually ^{1} for a primary stress and ^{2} for a secondary stress. The word *telegraphic* can therefore be transcribed in either of the following ways:

2)

$$[\text{ˌtɛləˈgɹæfɪk}] \quad \text{or} \quad [\text{tɛlə}\overset{2}{\text{g}}\overset{1}{\text{ɹæfɪk}}]$$

The examples in Table 2.21 illustrate some differences in English stress placement.

Table 2.21 Differing stress placement in English

(an) áddress	[ˈædɹɛs]	(to) addréss	[əˈdɹɛs]
(a) présent	[ˈpɹɛznt̩]	(to) presént	[pɹəˈzɛnt]
télegràph	[ˈtɛləˌgɹæf]		
telégraphỳ	[təˈlɛgɹəfi]		
tèlegráphic	[ˌtɛləˈgɹæfɪk]		

In these examples, you can also see that the quality of certain vowels varies depending on whether they are stressed or unstressed. This phenomenon is common in English, Russian, Palauan, and many other languages, but is not universal.

9 Speech Production

Up to this point we have, for the most part, been describing phonetic segments as if they existed in isolation and did not affect one another. However, speech production is not a series of isolated events. The phenomenon is a complex one, as the articulatory organs interact with each other (as we saw in Section 5.5) and many fine adjustments are carried out very rapidly as we speak. As a consequence, speech production often results in the articulation of one sound affecting that of another sound.

9.1 Coarticulation

In order to articulate a sequence of phonetic segments, we have to plan a complex series of muscular movements. Due to the rapidity of speech (we can produce many segments in a second) and the design of the vocal tract, if our goal is to produce a [pl] sequence, we cannot produce the two sounds independently of each other. Indeed, early speech synthesizers that produced speech in this way were practically unintelligible. Rather, as the sequence [pl] is produced, the tongue tip will start to move toward the alveolar ridge *before* the lips separate. The term **coarticulation** is used for situations such as this in which more than one articulator (here the lips and the tongue tip) is active.

9.2 Processes

Articulatory adjustments that occur during the production of connected speech are called **articulatory processes**. Processes change the nature of the individual segment. Their cumulative effect often results in making words easier to articulate, and in this sense, they are said to make speech more efficient. For example, when speakers of English say the word *bank*, they do not delay lowering the velum until the exact moment the nasal consonant articulation is reached. Instead, most English speakers begin lowering the velum for a nasal consonant almost as soon as they begin to articulate the vowel that precedes it.

In a parallel manner, when speakers use a palatal [ḵ] in a word such as *key* (the [ˌ] indicates a palatal articulation), they are speaking more efficiently since they are making a less drastic adjustment in moving from the articulation of a more palatal [ḵ] to that of a high front vowel than they would make in moving from a velar [k] to a high front vowel. Even more drastically, a speaker of English who says [pɹejd] for *parade* is making a major adjustment that results in a more efficient articulation: the two syllables of a careful pronunciation of *parade* are reduced to one by dropping the unstressed vowel of the first syllable; the tongue position for [ɹ] is anticipated during pronunciation of the [p]; and the voicelessness of the initial stop is carried on through the [ɹ̥] (the [̥] signals voicelessness).

Some processes appear to make articulation less, not more, efficient. For example, English speakers often lengthen consonants and vowels when they are asked to repeat a word that someone has not heard clearly. The following kind of exchange is typical.

3) "It's Fred."
"Did you say, 'It's red'?"
"No, I said, 'Fffreeed!'"

Lengthening segments results in a greater articulatory effort, but the process results in a more distinct form that is easier to perceive.

Another process that results in more easily perceivable speech adds a segment under certain conditions. When speaking slowly and carefully in a noisy environment, for example, English speakers often insert a vowel inside a group of consonants. This breaks up the sequence of consonants into separate syllables. To judge from the use people often make of this process when they wish to be clearly understood, it may well make words easier to perceive.

4) "Stop screaming!"
"What? Stop dreaming?"
"I said, 'Stop sc[ə]reaming!'"

These examples show that there are two basic reasons for the existence of articulatory processes. Some processes result in a *more efficient articulation* of a series of sounds in that the precise timing and coordination of speech is relaxed to various degrees. Other processes result in a *more distinct output*, which is easier to perceive than fluent or rapid everyday speech. Although these two types of processes might at first appear to be contradictory, each serves a particular end in speech production.

9.3   Some Common Articulatory Processes

Only a finite number of processes operate in language, though their end result is a great deal of linguistic variability. In this section, we survey some of the most common of these processes.

Assimilation

A number of different processes, collectively known as **assimilation**, result from the influence of one segment on another. Assimilation always results in a sound becoming more like another nearby sound in terms of one or more of its phonetic characteristics.

Nasalization of a vowel before a nasal consonant (nasal assimilation) is caused by speakers anticipating the lowering of the velum in advance of a nasal segment. The result is that the preceding segment takes on the nasality of the following consonant as in [kæ̃nt] 'can't'. (Nasality is marked with a tilde [˜].) This type of assimilation is known as **regressive assimilation**, since the nasalization is, in effect, moving *back-wards* to a preceding segment.

The nasalization of vowels following nasal consonants in Scots Gaelic is an example of **progressive assimilation**, since the nasality moves *forward* from the nasal consonant onto the vowel (see Table 2.22). It results from not immediately raising the velum after the production of a nasal stop.

Table 2.22   Progressive nasalization of vowels in Scots Gaelic

[mõːr]	'big'
[nĭ]	'cattle'
[mũ]	'about'
[nẽːl]	'cloud'

Voicing assimilation is also widespread. For many speakers of English, voiceless liquids and glides occur after voiceless stops in words such as *please* [pl̥iz], *try* [tɹ̥aj], and *cure* [kju̥ɹ]. These sounds are said to be devoiced in this environment. **Devoicing** is a kind of assimilation since the vocal folds are not set in motion immediately after the release of the voiceless consonant closure. The opposite of devoicing is **voicing**. In Dutch, voiceless fricatives assimilate to the voicing of the stops that follow them, in anticipation of the voiced consonant. For example, the word *af* [ɑf] 'off, over' is pronounced with a [v] in the words *afbellen* 'to cancel' and *afdekken* 'to cover'.

Assimilation for place of articulation is also widespread in the world's languages. Nasal consonants are very likely to undergo this type of **place assimilation**, as shown in Table 2.23.

Table 2.23   Assimilation for place of articulation in English

possible	impossible
potent	impotent
tolerable	intolerable
tangible	intangible

The negative form of each of these words is made with either *im-* or *in-*. In both cases, the form shows a nasal consonant that has the same place of articulation as the stop consonant that follows it: labial in the case of *possible* and *potent*, and alveolar in the case of *tolerable* and *tangible*. In informal speech, many English speakers pronounce words like *inconsequential* and *inconsiderate* with an [ŋ], assimilating the nasal to the place of articulation of the [k] that follows it, even though the spelling remains *n*. Assimilation can also be heard in pronunciations such as *A*[ŋ]*chorage*. Assimilation may even cross the boundary between words. In rapid speech, it is not uncommon to hear people pronounce phrases such as *in code* as [ɪŋkʰowd].

The preceding English examples show regressive assimilation for place of articulation. The following example, taken from German, shows progressive assimilation that again affects nasal consonants (see Table 2.24). In careful speech, certain

German verb forms are pronounced with a final [ən], as in *laden* 'to invite', *loben* 'to praise', and *backen* 'to bake'. In informal speech, the final [ən] is reduced to a syllabic nasal, which takes on the place of articulation of the preceding consonant. (Recall that the diacritic line under the phonetically transcribed nasals indicates that they are syllabic.)

Table 2.24   Progressive place assimilation in German

	Careful speech	Informal speech	
laden	[laːdən]	[laːdn̩]	'to invite'
loben	[loːbən]	[loːbm̩]	'to praise'
backen	[bakən]	[bakŋ̩]	'to bake'

Flapping is a process in which a dental or alveolar stop articulation changes to a flap [ɾ] articulation. In English, this process applies to [t] and [d] when they occur between vowels, the first of which is generally stressed. Flaps are heard in the casual speech pronunciation of words such as *butter, writer, fodder,* and *wading,* and even in phrases such as *I bought it* [ajˈbɔɾɪt]. The alveolar flap is always voiced. Flapping is considered a type of assimilation because it involves a stop consonant being weakened and becoming less stop-like when it occurs between vowels, which involve no closure at all in the vocal tract.

Dissimilation

Dissimilation, the opposite of assimilation, results in two sounds becoming less alike in articulatory or acoustic terms. The resulting sequence of sounds is easier to articulate and distinguish. It is a much rarer process than assimilation. One commonly heard example of dissimilation in English occurs in words ending with three consecutive fricatives, such as *fifths*. Many speakers dissimilate the final [fθs] sequence to [fts], apparently to break up the sequence of three fricatives with a stop.

Deletion

Deletion is a process that removes a segment from certain phonetic contexts. Deletion occurs in everyday rapid speech in many languages. In English, a schwa [ə] is often deleted when the next vowel in the word is stressed, as shown in Table 2.25. (Notice that in the first two words in Table 2.25, the deletion of the schwa creates the environment for the [ɹ] to become devoiced.)

Table 2.25   Deletion of [ə] in English

Slow speech	Rapid speech	
[pəˈɹejd]	[ˈpɹ̥ejd]	parade
[kəˈrowd]	[ˈkɹ̥owd]	corrode
[səˈpowz]	[ˈspowz]	suppose

Deletion also occurs as an alternative to dissimilation in words such as *fifths*. Many speakers delete the [θ] of the final consonant cluster and say [fɪfs]. In very rapid speech, both the second [f] and the [θ] are sometimes deleted, resulting in [fɪs].

Epenthesis

Epenthesis is a process that inserts a syllabic or a nonsyllabic segment within an existing string of segments. For example, in careful speech, the words *warmth* and *something* are pronounced [wɔɹmθ] and [sʌ̃mθɪ̃ŋ] (see Table 2.26). It is common in casual speech for speakers to insert a [p] between the [m] and the [θ] and pronounce the words [wɔɹmpθ] and [sʌ̃mpθɪ̃ŋ]. Consonant epenthesis of this type is another example of a coarticulation phenomenon. In English, the articulatory transition from a sonorant consonant to a nonsonorant appears to be eased by the insertion of a consonant that shares properties of both segments. Notice that the epenthesized consonants are all nonsonorant, have the same place of articulation as the sonorant consonant before them, and have the same voicing as the nonsonorant consonant after them.

Table 2.26 Some examples of English consonant epenthesis

Word	Nonepenthesized pronunciation	Epenthesized pronunciation
something	[sʌ̃mθɪ̃ŋ]	[sʌ̃mpθɪ̃ŋ]
warmth	[wɔɹmθ]	[wɔɹmpθ]
length	[lɛ̃ŋθ]	[lɛ̃ŋkθ]
prince	[prɪ̃ns]	[prɪ̃nts]
tenth	[tɛ̃nθ]	[tɛ̃ntθ]

Vowels may also be inserted epenthetically. In Turkish, a word never begins with two consonants. When words are borrowed into Turkish, an epenthetic vowel is inserted between certain sequences of two initial consonants, creating a new and permissible sequence (see Table 2.27). (While the reason for the differences among the inserted vowels need not concern us here, note that they are always high; see Section 10 for more of these and other unfamiliar symbols.)

Table 2.27 Vowel epenthesis in Turkish

Source word	Turkish form
train	[tiɾen]
club	[kylʏp]
sport	[sɯpoɾ]

Metathesis

Metathesis is a process that reorders a sequence of segments. This often results in a sequence of phones that is easier to articulate. It is common to hear metathesis in the speech of children, who often cannot pronounce all the consonant sequences that adults can. For example, some English-speaking children pronounce *spaghetti* as *pesghetti* [pəskɛɾi]. In this form, the initial sequence [spə], which is often difficult for children to pronounce, is metathesized to [pəs].

The pronunciation of *ask* as a[ks] is an example of metathesis that is common in adult speech. It is interesting that historically in English the word was a[ks] and underwent metathesis in the past to become a[sk].

Vowel Reduction

In many languages, the articulation of vowels may move to a more central position when the vowels are unstressed. This process is known as **(vowel) reduction**. Typically, the outcome of vowel reduction is a schwa [ə]; this can be observed in pairs of related words that show different stress placement such as *Canada* [ˈkʰænədə] versus *Canadian* [kʰəˈnejdiən]. If you listen carefully to these words, you'll notice that the first vowel is [æ] when stressed (in *Canada*) but schwa when unstressed (in *Canadian*). And the second vowel is [ej] when stressed (in *Canadian*) but schwa when unstressed (in *Canada*). Since we cannot predict what vowel a schwa may turn into when it is stressed, we assume that [æ] and [ej] are basic to the words in question and are reduced in unstressed position.

10   Other Vowels and Consonants

So far, this chapter has described only the vowels and consonants of English. Many but not all of these sounds are found in other languages. Moreover, many of the sounds found in other languages do not occur in English. Tables 2.28 and 2.29 introduce a number of novel vowels and consonants that are relevant to the discussion and problems throughout this book. Once the basic articulatory parameters have been understood, it's not a big jump to describe and to pronounce new and unfamiliar sounds.

Table 2.28   Modified IPA chart for vowels, including the vowels of American English (shaded) and many of those found in other languages. Where symbols appear in pairs, the phone on the left is unrounded, and the one on the right is rounded.

	Front		(Central)		Back		
High	i y		ɨ ʉ			ɯ	u
	ɪ ʏ						ʊ
Mid	e ø		ə			ɤ	o
	ɛ œ		ʌ				ɔ
Low	æ		a		ɑ ɒ		

Table 2.29   Modified IPA chart for consonants, including the sounds of English (shaded) and many of those found in other languages. Where symbols appear in pairs, the phone on the left is voiceless, and the one on the right is voiced. The term *approximant* is used by the IPA to include glides and some liquids in which there is a relatively free flow of air with no friction.

	Bilabial	Labiodental	Interdental	Alveolar	Alveopalatal	Retroflex	Palatal	Velar	Uvular	Pharyngeal	Glottal
Stop	p b			t d		ʈ ɖ	c ɟ	k g	q ɢ		ʔ
Fricative	ɸ β	f v	θ ð	s z	ʃ ʒ	ʂ ʐ	ç ʝ	x ɣ	χ ʁ	ħ ʕ	h ɦ
Nasal	m	ɱ		n		ɳ	ɲ	ŋ	N		
Trill				r					R		
Flap				ɾ							
Approximant	ʍ w ɥ			ɹ		ɻ	j ɥ	ʍ w			
Lateral Approximant				l̥ l			ɭ ʎ				
Lateral Fricative			ɬ ɮ								

Data from: International Phonetic Alphabet Data from the International Phonetic Association, Aristotle University, School of English, Department of Theoretical and Applied Linguistics, Thessaloniki, 54124, Greece, www.langsci.ucl.ac.uk/ipa/.

Remember that phonetic descriptions are universal—they apply to the sounds of any human language. If you encounter the description "voiced velar fricative," you know that the sound is a voiced continuant consonant made at the velum (i.e., the same place as the stop [g]). If you want to make this sound, the articulatory description can guide you: make a near closure at the velum and allow airflow to pass through. If you come across the description "high front rounded vowel", and want to produce this sound, make the high front unrounded vowel [i] and then round the lips to produce the high front rounded vowel [y].

Summing Up

The study of the sounds of human language is called **phonetics**. These sounds are widely transcribed by means of the **International Phonetic Alphabet**.

The sounds of language are commonly described in **articulatory** and **acoustic** terms and fall into two major types: syllabic sounds (**vowels, syllabic liquids**, and **syllabic nasals**) and nonsyllabic sounds (**consonants and glides**). Sounds may be **voiced** or **voiceless**, and **oral** or **nasal**. Consonants and glides are produced at various **places of articulation**: **labial, dental, alveolar, alveopalatal, palatal, velar, uvular, glottal**, and **pharyngeal**. At the places of articulation, the airstream is modified by different **manners of articulation** and the resulting sounds are **stops, fricatives, affricates, liquids**, or **glides**. Vowels are produced with less drastic closure and are described with reference to tongue position (**high, mid, low, back**, and **front**), tension (**tense** or **lax**), and lip rounding (**rounded** or **unrounded**). Language also exhibits **suprasegmental** phenomena such as **tone, intonation**, and **stress**.

Key Terms

General terms

acoustic phonetics	narrow transcription
articulatory phonetics	phones
broad transcription	phonetics
diacritics	segments
International Phonetic Alphabet (IPA)	speech sounds

Parts of the vocal tract below the mouth

arytenoids	pharynx
cricoid cartilage	thyroid cartilage
diaphragm	trachea
glottis	vocal folds (vocal cords)
intercostals	vocal tract
larynx	

Terms concerning glottal states

breathy voice	voiceless (sounds)
murmur	whisper
voiced (sounds)	

Terms concerning sound classes

consonants	sound classes
glides	syllabic
nonsyllabic	syllables
nucleus	vowels
sonorous (sounds)	

Terms concerning the mouth and articulators

alveolar ridge	tongue body
dorsum	tongue root
palate	tongue tip
tongue back	uvula
tongue blade	velum

Types of sounds based on places (points) of articulation

alveolar sounds	labiovelar (sounds)
alveopalatal (palatoalveolar)	palatals
bilabial (sounds)	pharyngeals
dentals	places (points) of articulation
glottals	primary place of articulation
interdental (sounds)	secondary place of articulation
labial (sounds)	uvulars
labiodentals	velars

General terms concerning manners of articulation

manners of articulation
nasal phones

oral phones

Terms for consonant sounds based on manner of articulation

affricates
aspiration
clear *l*
continuants
dark *l*
flap
fricatives
laterals
liquids

nonstrident
retroflex
sibilants
stops
stridents
syllabic liquids
syllabic nasals
unreleased stop
velarized *l*

Terms used for vowel sounds

back
diphthongs
front
high
lax vowels
low
major diphthongs
mid vowels

minor diphthongs
reduced vowel
rounded vowels
schwa
simple vowels
tense vowels
vowel qualities

Terms concerning suprasegmental properties

association line
contour tones
downdrift
geminates
intonation
length
long vowels
loudness
nonterminal (intonation) contour
pitch

primary stress
prosodic properties
register tones
secondary stress
short vowels
stress
suprasegmental properties
terminal (intonation) contour
tone
tone language

Terms concerning sounds in context

articulatory processes
assimilation
coarticulation
deletion
devoicing
dissimilation
epenthesis
flapping

metathesis
nasalization
place assimilation
progressive assimilation
regressive assimilation
voicing
voicing assimilation
(vowel) reduction

Recommended Reading

Catford, J. C. 2001. *A Practical Introduction to Phonetics*. 2nd ed. New York, NY: Oxford University Press.

Kent, Ray D., and Charles Read. 1993. *The Acoustic Analysis of Speech*. San Diego, CA: Singular Publishing Group.

Ladefoged, Peter, and Keith Johnson. 2014. *A Course in Phonetics*. 7th ed. Stamford, CT: Cengage Learning.

Ladefoged, Peter, and Ian Maddieson. 1995. *The Sounds of the World's Languages*. Cambridge, MA: Blackwell.

Pullum, Geoffrey K., and William A. Ladusaw. 1996. *Phonetic Symbol Guide*. 2nd ed. Chicago: University of Chicago Press.

Rogers, Henry. 1991. *Theoretical and Practical Phonetics*. Toronto: Copp Clark Pitman.

Shearer, William M. 1968. *Illustrated Speech Anatomy*. Springfield, IL: Charles C. Thomas.

Appendix:
Dialectal Variation in Pronunciation of Vowels

Vowels in American English show considerable dialectal variation, and we describe a few of those variations in Chapter 13. The linguistics student learning to do phonetic transcription would find a full catalog of variations overwhelming if even such a catalog could be compiled. What follows is a listing of some dialectal variation in vowel pronunciation (with implications for transcription), and students are encouraged to discuss possible dialectal variations with their professors.

High Vowels

- As suggested in Section 6.1 of this chapter, some speakers pronounce the high tense vowels [i] and [u] with an off-glide. In that case, the sounds could be transcribed as [ij] and [uw].

- Some dialects also tense the high front vowel [ɪ] before the velar nasal [ŋ] in words such as *thinking* or *sink*. Instead of pronouncing *think* as [θɪŋk], a speaker of one of these dialects would say [θiŋk]. In southern Appalachia, this vowel is lowered and pronounced as [æ] in a stressed syllable, so *think* would be pronounced as [θæŋk].

- Most speakers of American English pronounce the first vowel in words such as *eagle* and *league* with the high front tense vowel [i], so *eagle* would be transcribed as [igl̩]. However, in Philadelphia and extending along to the Ohio River valley and environs, the high front tense vowel [i] may be laxed when it occurs before [g]. Thus, the word *eagle* rhymes with *wiggle* and would be transcribed [ɪgl̩]. For some speakers, this laxing extends to front mid vowels as well, so the word *pagan* [pejgn̩] is pronounced as [pɛgn̩].

Vowels before Liquids and Nasals and Syllabic Liquids and Nasals

When a vowel occurs before *r* or *l*, the liquid affects the vowel, and the effect is different in different dialects.

- In words such as *beer* and *cheer*, speakers may produce the vowel as a full tense vowel with a schwa before the *r*, as a full tense vowel without schwa, or as a lax vowel. Thus, the word *beer* could be pronounced as [biəɹ], as [biɹ], or as [bɪɹ].

- Similarly, there is a widespread tendency for tense vowels to be laxed before *l*. The result is that a word such as *sale* [sejl] may sound the same as *sell* [sɛl]. In some areas, this also extends to [u] and [ʊ] in words such as *pool* [pul] and *pull* [pʊl]. It may also extend to [i] and [ɪ] in words such as *field* [fild] and *filled* [fɪld].

- There is also dialectal variation in the pronunciation of syllabic liquids and nasals. For example, in words such as *Jordan*, *garden*, or *student*, some younger speakers in southern California pronounce a full vowel instead of a syllabic consonant in the final syllable. For example, *student* [studn̩t] would be pronounced as [studɛnt] by these speakers. A student who does not hear the syllabic consonant as he or she pronounces a word should check with the professor.

- For speakers in the southern Midland and in the South of the U.S., the sound [ɛ] becomes [ɪ] before the nasal in words such as *pen*, *hem*, and *length*. In this dialect, the word *length* [lɛŋθ] is pronounced [lɪŋθ].

Schwa

In this book, we have transcribed the underlined unstressed vowels in the following words as a schwa: *roses*, *wanted*, *sofa*. Not all speakers, however, pronounce a schwa in these words.

- Speakers in the southern Midland distinguish between schwa in *Rosa's* [ɹowzəz] and a mid high unrounded vowel [ɨ], called "barred i", in *roses* [ɹowzɨz].

- Some speakers pronounce the past tense ending –*ed* in words such as *wanted*, *visited*, and *boarded* as [əd], while other speakers pronounce the –*ed* with a high front lax vowel: [ɪd].

- As mentioned in the text, for many speakers, the unstressed vowel at the end of *sofa* and *Canada* is a schwa, but other speakers pronounce it as [ʌ].

Back Vowels [ɔ], [ɑ], and [o]

Vowel Contrasts: [ɔ] and [ɑ]: For many speakers of American English, the vowels in the word pairs *tot* and *taut*, *hock* and *hawk*, and *Don* and *dawn* are pronounced differently; these speakers pronounce *tot*, *hock*, and *Don* with the low back unrounded vowel [ɑ] and pronounce *taut*, *hawk*, and *dawn* with the mid back lax rounded vowel [ɔ]. However, for a growing number of younger speakers, this is not the case. For these speakers, there is only one vowel for the words in the pairs, and that vowel is [ɑ]. This seems to be a change in progress.

Vowels [ɔ] and [o]: The vowel [ɔ] is also used in this book for the vowel in words such as *or*, *for*, and *more*. Some speakers, however, produce this vowel as the tense vowel [o] (without the off-glide [w]). Similarly, some speakers may produce the tense vowel [o] instead of [ɔ] as the first element in the diphthong [ɔj] in words such as *toy* and *boil*. For these speakers, the word *toy* [tɔj] would be pronounced [toj].

"Short a": [æ]

Variation in the pronunciation of the vowel [æ] has been noted since at least the 1920s, with speakers raising [æ] in a complex set of circumstances. Now, however, while the so-called "short *a* split" is still documented, the conditioning factors seem to have simplified. For younger speakers in multiple locations such as New York City, Philadelphia, the West, and cities in the Midwest, [æ] is raised before nasals. For these speakers, *pan* has a higher vowel than *pal*, and a words like *thanks* [θæŋks] may end up sounding closer to *thinks* [θɪŋks].

Diphthongs [aj] and [aw]

- Speakers in the southern states are well known for their pronunciation of the vowel in words such as *time*, *ride*, and *I*. Instead of pronouncing a diphthong [aj], these speakers produce a monophthong [a]; thus *time* [tajm] becomes [tam], and *ride* [ɹajd] becomes [ɹad].
- Speakers in Canada and in some northern states in the U.S. may pronounce words such as *right* and *ride* with different vowels. For these speakers, the diphthong in *ride* is [aj], while the diphthong in *right* is [ʌj]. Similarly, they pronounce the diphthong in *loud* as [aw], while the diphthong in *lout* is [ʌw]. This is known as Canadian raising and will be described more fully in Chapter 3.

Northern Cities Shift and California Shift

- One particularly noticeable characteristic of speakers from cities around the Great Lakes is the fronting of the vowel [ɑ] in words such as *hot* with the result that it has almost approached the low mid vowel [a] for some speakers. Another tendency is for [æ] to become raised and made into a diphthong [ɪə] in some or all environments, so that the name *Ann* sounds almost like *Ian*. These two variations are part of what is known as the Northern Cities Shift, which is described in Chapter 13.
- Conversely, in the West, especially in southern California, the lax front vowels [ɪ] and [ɛ] are lowered, and the vowel [æ] in a word like *black* is backed, approaching the low mid vowel [a]. In the West, the vowels [ɑ] and [ɔ] are merged to a backed [ɑ]. This variation in pronunciation of the system of vowels is called the California Shift and is also described more fully in Chapter 13.

Exercises

1. In order to become more aware of the differences between English spelling and pronunciation, do the following (see Sections 1 and 7):
   a) Give as many examples as you can of different ways to pronounce the letter <u>.
   b) Give two examples of words where the <gh> in the spelling is pronounced (e.g., *cough*) and two examples of words where the <gh> in the spelling is not pronounced (e.g., *taught*).
   c) Give examples of different letter combinations that can represent the [ej] sound in English spelling.

2. How many segments are there in the following words? (See Section 1.2.)
   a) up   c) pure   e) pterodactyl   g) attack
   b) think   d) walked   f) chiropractic   h) offending

3. Is the first sound in each of the following words voiced or voiceless? (See Section 2.3.)
   a) thus   e) Virginia   i) sure   m) wing
   b) moth   f) Honolulu   j) lumpy   n) ghoul
   c) xylophone   g) post   k) doll   o) knee
   d) chasm   h) thumb   l) unite   p) juice

4. Using the words in question 3, state whether the last sound of each word is voiced or voiceless.

5. For each of the following pairs of sounds, state whether they have the same or different places of articulation. Then identify the place of articulation for each sound. (See Section 4.2.)
   a) [g] : [ŋ]   e) [m] : [n]   i) [t] : [tʃ]
   b) [p] : [k]   f) [ð] : [s]   j) [f] : [v]
   c) [t] : [d]   g) [θ] : [ð]   k) [l] : [ɹ]
   d) [w] : [j]   h) [s] : [t]   l) [h] : [ʃ]

6. For each of the following pairs of sounds, state whether they have the same or different manners of articulation. Then identify the manner of articulation for each sound. (See Section 5.)
   a) [b] : [t]   e) [v] : [θ]   i) [tʃ] : [ʃ]
   b) [d] : [z]   f) [l] : [ɹ]   j) [l] : [j]
   c) [v] : [h]   g) [w] : [j]   k) [b] : [g]
   d) [tʃ] : [dʒ]   h) [m] : [ŋ]   l) [p] : [f]

7. For each of the following articulatory descriptions, write the symbol for the sound described. (See Sections 4, 5, 6.)
   a) voiced velar stop   e) voiceless alveolar fricative
   b) voiced palatal glide   f) high back rounded tense vowel
   c) voiceless labiodental fricative   g) voiced interdental fricative
   d) voiced bilabial nasal   h) low front unrounded vowel

8. Which of the following pairs of words have the same vowel in your dialect? Mark each pair as *same* or *different*. Then transcribe the vowel in each word. (See Sections 6 and 7.)

   a) ban   hand   h) nail   whale
   b) push   food   i) line   take
   c) cot   bought   j) cloud   run
   d) ghost   lock   k) plan   hat
   e) mush   what   l) lunch   whoosh
   f) seem   sit   m) bid   key
   g) catch   watch   n) get   frame

9. For each of the following groups of sounds, name one phonetic characteristic shared by all the members of the group. *Example:* [b d g u m j] are all *voiced*. (See Sections 4, 5, 6.)

   a) [p t k g]   e) [f v θ z h]
   b) [u ʊ o]   f) [t d n l ɹ]
   c) [ɪ ɛ æ ʊ]   g) [p t k s f θ tʃ]
   d) [aj aw ɔj]   h) [v ð ʒ æ]

10. Transcribe the following words. (See Section 7.)

   a) rich   g) ridge   m) guess   s) yes
   b) his   h) hiss   n) vex   t) should
   c) things   i) myth   o) wring   u) cup
   d) debt   j) shock   p) Butch   v) lathe
   e) could   k) top   q) zinc   w) buff
   f) jug   l) gem   r) Scotch   x) sham

11. Transcribe the following words. These words will allow you to pay particular attention to whether the voiceless stops are aspirated. (See Sections 5.5 and 7.)

   a) tog   g) juice   m) sigh   s) accord
   b) kid   h) thimble   n) hulk   t) astound
   c) attain   i) peas   o) explode   u) pure
   d) despise   j) stun   p) tube   v) wheeze
   e) elbow   k) Oscar   q) spell   w) remove
   f) haul   l) cooler   r) cord   x) clinical

12. Using H, L, and association lines, transcribe the intonation of the following English phrases. Compare your results with the transcriptions of some classmates. Are they the same? If they aren't, what factors (e.g., emotion or context) might account for the differences? (See Section 8.1.)

   a) Are you leaving?
   b) What are you doing over there?
   c) Take a seat, please.

13. Mark primary and (where necessary) secondary stresses on the following words. It is not necessary to transcribe them. (See Section 8.3.)

a) Florida
b) bookcase
c) return
d) greenhouse
e) anecdote

f) (the) record
g) (to) record
h) cinema
i) attain
j) aroma

k) Floridian
l) government
m) governmental
n) control
o) New York Mets

14. Find a fluent speaker of a language other than English and transcribe phonetically ten words of that language. If you encounter any sounds for which symbols are not found in this chapter, attempt to describe them in phonetic terms and then invent diacritics to help you transcribe them. (See Tables 2.28 and 2.29.)

15. Name the articulatory process responsible for the change from standard Spanish to the dialectal variant in each item below. (See Section 9.3.)

a) [poβɾe]   →   [pɾoβe] (U.S. southwestern Spanish) 'poor'
b) [grasjas]   →   [grasja] (Caribbean Spanish) 'thank you'
c) [gatito]   →   [gatiko] (Costa Rican Spanish) 'kitty'
d) [kaɾne]   →   [kanne] (Cuban Spanish) 'meat'
e) [pesos]   →   [pesos̞] (Mexican Spanish) 'pesos'
f) [estomaɣo] →   [estoɣamo] (U.S. southwestern Spanish) 'stomach'
g) [alβɾisjas] →   [aβɾisjas] (U.S. southwestern Spanish) 'gift, reward'

16. Compare the careful speech and rapid speech pronunciations of the following English words and phrases. Then name the process or processes that make the rapid speech pronunciation different from the careful speech. (Stress is omitted here.) (See Section 9.)

		Careful speech	Rapid speech
a)	in my room	[ɪn maj rum]	[ɪm maj rum]
b)	I see them	[aj si ðɛm]	[aj siəm]
c)	I see him	[aj si hɪm]	[aj siəm]
d)	within	[wɪθɪn]	[wɪðɪn]
e)	balloons	[bəlunz]	[blunz]
f)	careful	[kʰɛɹfʊl]	[kʰɛɹfl̩]
g)	sit down	[sɪt dawn]	[sɪɾawn]
h)	sandwich	[sændwɪtʃ]	[sæmwɪtʃ]
i)	protection	[pɹ̥owtʰɛkʃn̩]	[pɹ̥tʰɛkʃn̩]
j)	hand me that	[hænd mi ðæt]	[hæmiðæt]
k)	Pam will seat you	[pæm wɪl sit ju]	[pæml̩sitʃju]

 **LaunchPad Solo**
macmillan learning

For more helpful content and quizzes, go to the LaunchPad Solo for *Contemporary Linguistics* at **launchpadworks.com.**

For the Student Linguist

DON'T WORRY ABOUT SPELLING

What if you had to choose: either nobody would read and write ever again, or nobody would speak or hear language? This is a total nonchoice for me—I'd pitch out liner notes and lyric sheets in a second, but would be really upset about losing all my Ella Fitzgerald CDs. Not that it would be easy to function without reading and writing. Road signs, for example, are pretty important, and even linguistics textbooks have their uses. But the point is, I think spoken language is more fundamental than reading or writing. Let's assume it is, but let's also assume that writing is pretty important to modern society. The question, then, is how closely writing should resemble speaking.

Current spelling is much closer to the way English *used* to be spoken than the way it's spoken today, and for years various folks have been proposing spelling reforms. Would learning to read be easier if you didn't have to deal with spelling nightmares like *night, though, tough, cough, two, due, who, threw, shoe, through,* or *answer*? Some of these words are already being changed informally in advertising, pop music, and casual writing. For example, when my best friend sends me e-mails, she always writes *nite, tho, tuff, cough, 2, due, who, threw, shoe, thru,* and *anser*. Are these spellings any better? For someone who's learning to read English, it could be hard to figure out that *tho* and *who* aren't supposed to rhyme but *2, due, who, threw, shoe,* and *thru* are supposed to rhyme, although there's now a difference in spelling for the nonrhyming *tho* and *tuff*.

Phonetic transcription—using the IPA—is unambiguous about what rhymes with what. For every sound there's exactly one symbol (except for a couple of substitutions for different keyboards), and for every symbol there's exactly one sound. Thus the word list becomes: najt, ðow, tʰʌf, kʰɔf, tʰu, du, hu, θɹu, ʃu, θɹu, and ænsɹ̩. Making the changeover from standard spelling to IPA would be a nightmare, though. We'd have to reconfigure our keyboards, for starters. Instead of five vowel symbols (and many combinations of them) and twenty-one consonants, we'd have about eighteen vowels and twenty-five consonants.

Imagine all the changeover details could be taken care of (including instantly teaching everyone the IPA). Think about how much richer writing could be if it included all the information you get from hearing someone speak. You'd have information about the writer's regional background and class, plus information about the level of formality of the piece you were reading. Depending on how detailed the writing system was, you would be able to read all sorts of nuances of stress and intonation.

I've transcribed the same piece of dialogue in several different systems below. The first system is probably the hardest to read, and the following systems get progressively easier. Try to figure out the dialogue from the first system, checking the later ones for clarification if you get stuck. Also try to figure out the stylistic differences among the different versions of the dialogue.

1. ʃiləˀejtʰejlaɹdʒpʰʌmpkʰɪnpʰaj ˀəwɛɹðæt ˀələnwəzwatʃɪŋ o̥ːw̥ ˀæ̃lə̃n̥
   ʃisɛdbɹɛθili pʰæ̥smi̥ ð̥i̥ w̥ɪptʰ kʰɹ̥i̥m ʃilə hiwajnd ˀajmtʃɹajɪŋ
   tʰufɪnɪʃgɹajndɪŋðikʰɔfi

2. ʃiləˀejɾəlaːdʒpʰʌmpkʰɪnpʰaj ˀəwɛɹðæˀæln̩wəzwatʃno̥ːw ˀæln ʃisɛˀbɹɛθli
   pʰæsmiðəwɪpkʰɹim ʃilə hiwajnd ˀajmtʃɹajntʰəfɪnɪʃgɹajndn̩ðəkʰɔfi

3. ˈʃiləˀejɾəlaːdʒpʰʌmpkʰɪnˈpʰaj ˀəwɛɹðæˀæln̩wəzˈwatʃn̩ oːw ˀˀæln ʃisɛˀbɹɛθli
   pʰæsmiðəwɪpˈkʰɹim ˈʃilə hiˈwajnd ˀajmˈtʃɹajntʰəfɪnɪʃˈgɹajndn̩ðəˈkʰɔfi

4. ʃilə ejt ej laɹdʒpʰ ʌmpkʰɪn pʰaj ˀəwɛɹ ðæt ˀælən wəz watʃɪŋ oːw ˀæln
   ʃi sɛd bɹɛθili pʰæs mi ði wɪptʰ kʰɹim ʃilə hi wajnd ˀajm tʃɹajɪŋ tʰu
   fɪnɪʃ gɹajndɪŋ ði kʰɔfi

5. ʃilə ejt ej laɹdʒ pʰʌmpkʰɪn pʰaj, ˀəwɛɹ ɹæt ˀælən wəz watʃɪŋ. "oːw
   ˀæln," ʃi sɛd bɹɛθili, "pʰæs mi ði wɪptʰ kʰɹim." "ʃilə," hi wajnd, "ˀajm
   tʃɹajɪŋ tʰu fɪnɪʃ grajndɪŋ ði kʰɔfi."

The downside of this type of writing is that there'd be so much variability. For instance, you might care about the accent or tone of a character in a novel, but do you really need to know where the journalist who wrote this morning's article on the economy was raised? And what if his or her editor were from someplace else? Whose accent would get printed? Not to mention the difficulties of something like a GRE exam or SAT test written in someone else's dialect.

Of course, the degree of variability depends on how extreme the system is. There's a wide gap between standard spelling and the fairly narrow (detailed) transcription system used in examples *1* through *3*. Writing could be more phonetic than it is now, but we don't have to force people to include every minor variation in pronunciation. We could forget about stress marks and anything to show intonation—except for a few simple things like question marks and exclamation points. We could also leave off fairly predictable things like aspiration (you'll discover how predictable aspiration is in the next chapter). Examples *4* and *5* are probably a lot easier to understand than *1* through *3*, since *4* and *5* are not as detailed (broad transcription) and, most importantly, because they have spaces between the words. Putting in spaces makes the writing less like the actual pronunciation, but it also takes away the ambiguity of figuring out whether something like [ʃilə] is supposed to be *she lo* . . . (as in *she locked the door* . . .) or *Sheila*.

In fact, the new writing system could keep punctuation, keep word spaces, and have nothing but the bare minimum to distinguish the way one word sounds from the way other words sound. The trick, then, is to figure out what the bare minimum is. It's a pretty difficult question, and before you can answer it, you'll need to read about phonology and morphology. You'll also need to figure out what exactly a word *is*, anyway. So, read the next two chapters and then come back to this section and read it again. Then devise the perfect writing system, use it for your senior thesis, patent it, market it, make a fortune off of it, and retire to a lovely little tropical island (with good food) where they don't speak English.

three

Phonology: Contrasts and Patterns

William O'Grady
Carrie Dyck
Yvan Rose
Ewa Czaykowska-Higgins
Michael Dobrovolsky

> *A person's tongue is a twisty thing, there are plenty of words there of every kind, and the range of words is wide, and their variation.*
>
> —HOMER, *The Iliad*

OBJECTIVES

In this chapter, you will learn:

- how we know which language sounds are distinctive in a particular language
- how distinctive sounds in a particular language can vary systematically according to the context in which they occur
- how we use transcription to represent distinctive sounds and systematic variations of these sounds
- how syllables are constructed and the influence of language-specific syllable structure
- how individual sounds can be broken down further, according to specific features
- how we can construct rules to explain systematic variations in the production of sounds

 | For more helpful content and quizzes, go to the LaunchPad Solo
for *Contemporary Linguistics* at **launchpadworks.com**.

As the study of phonetics shows, human beings can produce and perceive a very large number of speech sounds. Of course, no human language exploits *all* of these possibilities. Instead, every language makes its own particular selection from the range of possible speech sounds and organizes them into a system of contrasts and patterns. This system makes up a language's **phonology**.

Phonological analysis takes place at three levels. First, and most obviously, it is concerned with the relationships among individual speech sounds, or **segments**. But there is also a need for analysis at both a higher level and a lower level.

At a higher level, it is necessary to think about how sounds are organized into **syllables**, units of phonological organization that are crucial to the patterning of sounds, as we will soon see. And at a lower level, we consider **features**, the articulatory and acoustic building blocks of sounds that are also crucial to understanding why sounds systems have the particular contrasts and patterns that they do. Let's begin by looking at segments and how they are used to make the contrasts that allow us to distinguish words from each other.

1   Segments

Speakers make dozens, perhaps hundreds, of phonetic distinctions as they use their language. One such distinction, which is easy to notice for speakers of English, is the difference between [n] and [ŋ] in words like *win* [wɪn] and *wing* [wɪŋ].

Another distinction, which is much less obvious, involves the difference between the [n] in *one time*, which is alveolar (tip of the tongue making contact with the alveolar ridge), and the [n̪] in *one thing*, which is dental (tip of the tongue on the back of the upper front teeth).

> [wʌn] *one time*   [wʌn̪] *one thing*

This is a real difference, but you'll notice it only if you pay deliberate attention to exactly where the tip of your tongue touches as you say the last sound in *one* in each of these phrases.

What is happening here is that /n/ has a dental pronunciation in front of another dental consonant (the [θ] of *thing*) but retains its usual alveolar place of articulation elsewhere. This is an automatic adjustment, of which speakers are typically not even conscious since it doesn't affect the meaning of the word *one*. But the choice of the final consonant in *sun* and *sung* is deliberate and creates a contrast between two different words. Herein lies a key insight of phonological analysis.

1.1   Phonemes and Allophones

Linguists organize a language's sounds into contrastive units called **phonemes** based on the phonetic properties of the sounds and whether those properties can be used to distinguish between words. The sounds that are assigned to the same phoneme (its **allophones**) don't contrast with each other, but phonemes contrast with other phonemes.

So [n] and [n̪] are analyzed as allophones of the same phoneme, since the difference between them (alveolar versus dental point of articulation) is not used to distinguish between words in English and indeed, *o*[n]*e* and *o*[n̪]*e* are perceived as the same word. In contrast, [n] and [ŋ] must be assigned to separate phonemes, since the difference between them (alveolar versus velar point of articulation) can in fact be used to distinguish one word from another. Thus, *sun* and *sung* are perceived as different words.

When representing a phoneme and its allophones, we coopt the symbol for the most widely used allophone (if there is more than one) to represent the phoneme, which we write between slashes. The phonological status of the sounds [n], [n̪], and [ŋ] can be represented as shown in Figure 3.1:

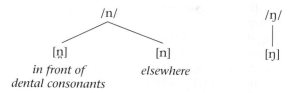

Figure 3.1 The phonemes /n/ and /ŋ/ and their allophones

As depicted here, the sounds [n] and [n̪] are allophones of the same phoneme because they don't contrast with each other. On the other hand, thanks to contrasts such as *sun-sung* and *run-rung*, we can conclude that /n/ and /ŋ/ are separate phonemes.

The same sort of analysis applies to vowels. If you're a native speaker of English, it's easy to hear the difference between [i] and [ɪ] in words like *beat* [bit] and *bit* [bɪt]. So we know that there's a phoneme /i/ and a phoneme /ɪ/. But more than that is going on here. Notice that the /i/ in *bead* takes longer to say than the /i/ in *beat*.

[biːd] *bead*   [bit] *beat*

What is happening, roughly speaking, is that English vowels of all types are automatically lengthened in front of voiced **obstruents** (stops, fricatives, and affricates) like [d] but not in other positions. Although this difference is a natural part of speech in English, it is not used to distinguish between words—even if you deliberately lengthen the vowel in *beat*, it's still the same word. This tells us that [iː] and [i] should be assigned to the same phoneme, as illustrated in Figure 3.2.

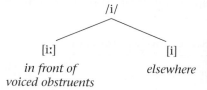

Figure 3.2 The phoneme /i/ and its allophones

It might help to think about phonemes and allophones as follows. Phonemes are mental categories—they exist in your mind for the purpose of creating contrasts among words. Allophones are physical sounds that occur in particular positions when words are spoken—they are produced in your vocal tract as you speak.

Organizing a language's sounds into phonemes requires special attention to two factors—minimal pairs and complementary distribution.

1.2 Minimal Pairs

A **minimal pair** consists of two words that differ by only one segment in the same position as shown in *1*. Thus, *sun* and *sung* make up a minimal pair since they differ only in terms of their final consonant. And *beat* and *bit* constitute a minimal pair since they too differ by just one segment (the vowel in the middle of the word).

1) Some other minimal pairs:
   a. contrast in initial position:
      [θaj] *thigh* — [ðaj] *thy*
   b. contrast in medial position:
      [lejsi] *lacy* — [lejzi] *lazy*
   c. contrast in final position:
      [sʌm] *sum* — [sʌn] *sun*

When two sounds can create a minimal pair, we know that they belong to separate phonemes. So /θ/ and /ð/ are separate phonemes, as are /s/ and /z/, and /m/ and /n/.

Table 3.1 presents some minimal pairs that illustrate various consonant contrasts in English. It is important to remember that minimal pairs are established on the basis of sound and not spelling, so *cheap* and *jeep* make up a minimal pair despite the multiple differences in the way they are spelled.

Table 3.1 Some consonant contrasts in English

feel	/f/	*ether*	/θ/	*sip*	/s/	*cheap*	/tʃ/
veal	/v/	*either*	/ð/	*zip*	/z/	*jeep*	/dʒ/
sum	/m/	*leaf*	/l/	*yet*	/j/		
sun	/n/	*reef*	/ɹ/	*wet*	/w/		
sung	/ŋ/						

As the examples in Table 3.2 show, vowel contrasts in English can also be established with the help of minimal pairs. (For now, we will treat diphthongs as single segments.)

Table 3.2 Some vowel contrasts in English

beet	/i/	*bait*	/ej/
bit	/ɪ/	*bet*	/ɛ/
bat	/æ/		
		coat	/ow/
cooed	/u/	*cot*	/ɑ/
could	/ʊ/	*caught*	/ɔ/
		cut	/ʌ/
loud	/aw/		
lied	/aj/		
Lloyd	/ɔj/		

1.3 Complementary Distribution

What about allophones of the same phoneme—such as [n] and [n̪] or [i] and [i:] in English? Noncontrastive differences like these typically arise when a segment's articulation is affected by its neighbors: that is, it has one pronunciation in one position or **environment** and another pronunciation in other environments. When two sounds occur in nonoverlapping, mutually exclusive environments, they are said to be in **complementary distribution.**

As we have seen, English [n̪] and [n] work this way: we find dental [n̪] in front of other dental sounds, and we find [n] elsewhere. Some familiar and new examples are presented in 2.

2) Complementary distribution: dental and alveolar /n/:
   a. [n̪] occurs in front of dental consonants such as [θ] and [ð]:
       e.g., *one thing, on them, in there*
   b. [n] occurs elsewhere:
       e.g., *one ship, one egg, one cent, one dollar*

And of course English [i:] and [i] are in complementary distribution too: [i:] occurs in front of voiced obstruents, and [i] occurs elsewhere—in front of voiceless obstruents like [t] in *heat* and [s] in *cease*, in front of the nasal consonant in *lean*, and so on. This is shown in 3.

3) Complementary distribution: long and short /i/:
   a. [i:] occurs in front of voiced obstruents:
       e.g., *heed, seize, leave*
   b. [i] occurs elsewhere:
       e.g., *heat, cease, leaf, lean, sea*

In sum, phonetic distinctions may or may not create contrasts that distinguish between words. When they do, the sounds in questions belong to separate phonemes; when they don't, the sounds in question are allophones of the same phoneme. An appendix at the end of the chapter lays out a detailed procedure for identifying a language's phonemes and allophones.

Canadian Raising

An example of complementary distribution that is strongly associated with Canadian English but also occurs in some dialects of American English involves the diphthongs /aj/ and /aw/. In this dialect, the [a] portion of these diphthongs raises to [ʌ] in certain predictable positions. This phenomenon has been dubbed **Canadian raising.**

Table 3.3 Some examples of Canadian raising

Raising		No raising	
[ʌjs]	ice	[ajz]	eyes
[lʌjs]	lice	[lajz]	lies
[tɹʌjt]	trite	[tɹajd]	tried
[tɹʌjp]	tripe	[tɹajb]	tribe
[flʌjt]	flight	[flaj]	fly
[hʌws]	house (noun)	[hawz]	(to) house (verb)
[lʌwt]	lout	[lawd]	loud
[skʌwt]	scout	[kaw]	cow

As you can see, the diphthongs [ʌj] and [aj] are in complementary distribution: [ʌj] occurs before the class of voiceless consonants ([s, t, p], etc.) and [aj] occurs elsewhere. A parallel relationship holds between the vowels [aw] and [ʌw] (see Figure 3.3).

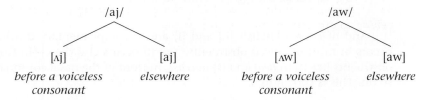

Figure 3.3 Allophones of /aj/ and /aw/ in Canadian raising

We can predict that the word *shout*, for example, would be pronounced [ʃʌwt], and that the work *Skype* would be pronounced [skʌjp] because in each case the diphthong comes before a voiceless consonant. Similarly, we can predict the pronunciation of words such as *bough* [baw], *proud* [pɹawd], *cry* [kɹaj], and *hive* [hajv] because the diphthong is *not* followed by a voiceless consonant. In Canadian raising, therefore, we know that [aj] and [ʌj] are allophones of one phoneme, and that [aw] and [ʌw] are allophones of another phoneme because in each pair the allophones are phonetically similar, they occur in different and mutually exclusive environments (i.e., are in complementary distribution), and are predictable based on the environment.

1.4 Language-Specific Contrasts

Sounds that contrast with each other in one language might not do so in another. For example, the difference between the vowels [ɛ] and [æ] is crucial to English, as we can see from minimal pairs like *Ben* [bɛn] and *ban* [bæn]. But in Turkish, this difference is not contrastive. A Turkish speaker may pronounce the word for 'I' as [bɛn] or [bæn], with no difference in meaning.

Table 3.4   Language-specific vowel contrasts: English versus Turkish

English		Turkish	
[bɛn]	'Ben'	[bɛn]	'I'
[bæn]	'ban'	[bæn]	'I'

Conversely, sounds that do not contrast in English, such as long and short vowels, may contrast in another language. There are no minimal pairs of the type [si]/[si:] in English. But in Japanese and many other languages, short and long vowels contrast, as the examples in Table 3.5 show.

Table 3.5   Short/long vowel contrasts in Japanese

[toɾi]	'bird'	[mesi]	'meal'
[toɾi:]	'shrine gate'	[me:si]	'business card'

So whereas the sounds [i:] and [i] belong to the same phoneme in English, they belong to different phonemes in Japanese.

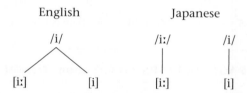

Figure 3.4   A phonological difference between English and Japanese

An analysis of voiceless stops in English and Khmer (Cambodian) illustrates the same point.

Table 3.6   Voiceless stops in English and Khmer

English		Khmer	
[p]	[pʰ]	[p]	[pʰ]
[t]	[tʰ]	[t]	[tʰ]
[k]	[kʰ]	[k]	[kʰ]

As can be seen in Table 3.6, both languages have aspirated and unaspirated voiceless stops. In English, the difference between the two types of stop is not contrastive: there are no minimal pairs like [pɪk] and [pʰɪk]. In Khmer, though, unaspirated and aspirated voiceless stops contrast with each other, as the minimal pairs in Table 3.7 show.

Table 3.7 Some Khmer minimal pairs

| [pɔːŋ] | 'to wish' | [tɔp] | 'to support' | [kat] | 'to cut' |
| [pʰɔːŋ] | 'also' | [tʰɔp] | 'be suffocated' | [kʰat] | 'to polish' |

So although English and Khmer have phonetically similar sounds, they are very different phonologically, as Figure 3.5 shows.

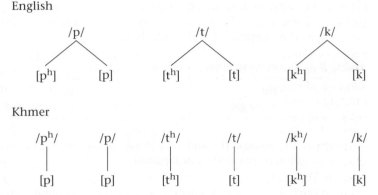

Figure 3.5 A phonological difference between English and Khmer

---

LANGUAGE MATTERS   What about Dental and Alveolar *n*?

The distinction between dental [n̪] and alveolar [n] is not contrastive in English. That seems natural to us, since the difference seems so hard to hear. But in some languages, that very difference is used to distinguish between words, and there are minimal pairs to prove it. One such language is Malayalam (a Dravidian language of south India); another is Arrernte (a language of Australia), from which the following minimal pair is taken.

　　[n̪əmə] 'fall (rain)'　　　[nəmə] 'sit'

The existence of minimal pairs means that /n̪/ and /n/ are separate phonemes in those languages.

Information from: V. Anderson, *The Perception of Coronals in Western Arrernte*, Proceedings of the Fifth European Conference on Speech Communication and Technology 1 (1997): 389–392.

1.5   In the Absence of Minimal Pairs

As we've already seen, the simplest and best way to show that two sounds contrast with each other (that is, that they belong to separate phonemes) is to find a minimal pair. Occasionally, though, gaps in a language's vocabulary make it difficult to find minimal pairs for contrasting sounds, or your data set may not include them even if they exist. Under these circumstances, it is sometimes possible to rely on **near-minimal pairs** that contain differences other than the one involving the key contrast, as long as the extra differences don't involve sounds right next to the contrast. One such example in English is [mɪʃn̩] and [vɪʒn̩], *mission* and *vision*. Although not a perfect minimal pair, these words can help establish that [ʃ] and [ʒ] contrast with each other if actual minimal pairs are not available. (In fact, there are even a few minimal pairs for the [ʃ]/[ʒ] distinction, such as *mesher* and *measure*, but they are few and far between, and could easily be missed.)

Sometimes, even near-minimal pairs are not available to establish that two sounds contrast with each other. A notorious example of this involves [h] and [ŋ] in English. Because [h] occurs only at the beginning of syllables and [ŋ] occurs only at the end of syllables, we don't find the usual minimal or near-minimal pairs. There are lots of words like *hope* and *ham*, with [h] in initial position, but no words like *ngope* and *ngam* to contrast with them. And there are lots of words like *long* and *king*, with [ŋ] in final position, but no words like *loh* and *kih*. This does not mean that [h] and [ŋ] are allophones of the same phoneme, though. As our earlier definition makes clear, the allophones of a phoneme must be phonetically similar to each other. Because [h] and [ŋ] are so different phonetically, we can be confident in assigning them to separate phonemes even in the absence of minimal and near-minimal pairs.

1.6 Differences in the Distribution of Allophones across Languages

Just as the phonemic contrasts found in each language are specific to that language, so the distribution of individual allophones can vary from language to language. The phenomenon of vowel nasalization illustrates this.

It is common to have nasal allophones for vowels when there is a nasal consonant nearby. In Malay, a language spoken in Malaysia and Singapore, both vowels and glides are nasalized when they come after a nasal sound, but not before, as shown in Table 3.8.

Table 3.8 Nasalization in Malay

Unnasalized vowel before a nasal consonant	Nasalized vowel after a nasal consonant	Gloss
[məlaraŋ]	[mə̃laraŋ]	'forbid'
[mākan]	[mākan]	'eat'
[rumāh]	[rumāh]	'house'
	[nãɛ̃ʔ]	'ascend'

We can summarize this pattern as in *4*:

4) In Malay, nasal allophones of vowels and glides are found right after a nasal consonant.

In Scots Gaelic, however, vowels are nasalized on both sides of a nasal consonant.

Table 3.9 Nasalization in Scots Gaelic

Before a nasal consonant		After a nasal consonant	
[rũːn]	'secret'	[mõːr]	'big'
		[nĩ]	'cattle'
		[nẽːl]	'cloud'

The generalization governing the distribution of nasal vowels in Scots Gaelic can be stated as follows.

5) Nasal allophones of vowels in Scots Gaelic are found right before or right after a nasal consonant.

1.7 Phonetic and Phonemic Representations

So far, we have seen that each language has a set of contrastive phonemes (which can be established largely by means of the minimal pair test) and that phonemes can have predictable phonetic variants or allophones (which are in complementary distribution with each other). We can transcribe a word phonemically or phonetically, depending on how much and what kind of information we want to represent.

As the examples in Table 3.10 show, a word's **phonemic representation** consists just of its component phonemes, but its **phonetic representation** carries additional information about phonetic details—including aspiration, devoicing of liquids, vowel lengthening, nasalization, and so on. All this phonetic information is predictable in English: simplifying just a bit, a voiceless stop at the beginning of a stressed syllable is aspirated in front of a vowel, a liquid that occurs after a voiceless stop is voiceless, a vowel that occurs right before a nasal consonant is nasalized, and so on. These phonetic characteristics have nothing to do with contrasts and therefore need not be stated in the phonemic representation; because they involve noncontrastive details of speech, they belong only in the phonetic representation. (Because narrow phonetic representations become very complex if every fine point of speech is included, it is common to use broader transcription and omit phonetic details that are not directly relevant to the point at hand. We follow that practice here.)

Table 3.10 Sample phonemic and phonetic representations in English

Word	Phonemic representation	Phonetic representation	Extra information in the phonetic representation
tied	/tajd/	[tʰajd]	aspiration
creep	/kɹip/	[kɹ̥ip]	voicelessness of the liquid
bead	/bid/	[biːd]	vowel lengthening
on	/ɔn/	[ɔ̃n]	nasalization of the vowel

Remember that the phonemic representation corresponds to what is in your head, while the phonetic representation corresponds to what comes out of your mouth. Because phonetic details are added as we speak, the phonetic representation ends up being much more specific than the phonemic representation, which includes only contrastive sounds.

Mid Vowels and Glides in English

Sometimes it is possible to predict not only the choice of allophones in the phonetic representation, but also the appearance of entirely new segments. One example of this concerns the mid tense vowels [e] and [o], which are diphthongized in most dialects of English: [e] occurs with [j], as in [dej] *day*, and [o] occurs with [w], as in [dow] *dough*. The choice of glide is not arbitrary: [w] is back and rounded, just like [o], and [j] is nonback and unrounded, like [e]:

[dej] *day*	[dow] *dough*
[e] + [j]	[o] + [w]
(both nonback and unrounded)	(both back and rounded)

The following generalization states the distribution of the two glides.

6) A mid tense vowel in English is predictably followed by a glide that has the same backness and roundness.

Thus, although the phonetic representations of English mid tense vowels include the glides, the corresponding phonemic representations do not (see Table 3.11).

Table 3.11   Phonemic and phonetic representations for English mid tense vowels

Word	Phonemic representation	Phonetic representation	Extra segment in the phonetic representation
day	/de/	[dej]	the glide [j]
dough	/do/	[dow]	the glide [w]

Once again, we see that the phonemic representation contains only information that is not predictable. Phonetic details—whether they are about vowel nasalization or which glide follows a mid vowel—are added later. We'll return to this point in Section 4, where we discuss the operations that add these details.

2   Syllables

The syllable is a highly perceptible phonological unit. Speakers of a language are generally aware of syllables, and they typically have no trouble counting them. (A dot is used to mark the boundary between two syllables.)

Table 3.12 Some examples of English syllables

/ə.plɔd/	applaud
/di.klajn/	decline
/ɪg.zɪst/	exist
/ɪm.pɹə.vajz/	improvise

What most speakers don't consciously know, however, is just how important syllables are to the phonology of their language.

LANGUAGE MATTERS   That's Not the Right Word

Syllables also matter for how words are organized in our mental dictionary. We can see this in *malapropisms*—mischosen words such as *equivocal* for *equivalent*, *emanate* for *emulate*, or *participate* for *precipitate*. Malapropisms tend to be phonologically similar to the intended word, and in the vast majority of cases, they have the same number of syllables, too.

Information from: D. Faye and A. Cutler, "Malapropisms and the Structure of the Mental Lexicon," *Linguistic Inquiry* 8 (1977): 505–520.

2.1   Types of Syllable Patterns

Languages differ from each other in terms of the complexity of the syllables that they allow. In some languages, a (C)V template is strictly followed—all syllables consist of either a vowel by itself or a consonant followed by a vowel. Hawaiian works this way. The Hawaiian greeting *aloha* illustrates both types of syllables within a single word:

/a.lo.ha/
V.CV.CV

When a word with a different type of syllable structure is borrowed into Hawaiian from another language, adjustments have to be made. That's why the borrowed English word *cloak* /klok/ is pronounced /ko.lo.ka/ in Hawaiian, with each syllable consisting of a consonant and a vowel.

Korean has the somewhat more complex syllable template (C)V(C)—it allows the syllable types exemplified in Table 3.13.

Table 3.13 Syllable types in Korean

V only	/i/	'teeth'
CV	/pʰa/	'onion'
VC	/il/	'work'
CVC	/son/	'hand'

French is one step more complex in that it allows up to two consonants at the beginning and end of a syllable.

Table 3.14 Some syllable types in French

V only	/o/	*eau* 'water'
CV	/fu/	*fou* 'fool'
CVC	/mas/	*masse* 'mass'
CCV	/pʁi/	*prix* 'prize'
VCC	/ɛst/	*est* 'east'

Still more complex is the syllable template for English, which allows up to three consonants at the beginning of a syllable, as in *stream* /stɹim/, and up to four at the end, as in *sixths* /sɪksθs/. Very few words have this sort of complexity in their syllable structure, however, and special constraints are in play in such cases. For instance, three-consonant sequences are possible at the beginning of a syllable only if the first consonant is /s/, the second a voiceless stop, and the third a liquid or glide, as happens in *stream, spring, squeak,* and so forth. The term **phonotactics** is used for the branch of phonology that is concerned with permissible combinations of phonemes.

Although English allows many different types of syllables, not all phonotactic possibilities are permitted, of course. That is why English-speaking students learning Russian often react to the consonant cluster at the beginning of a word like *vprog* (/fprɔk/ 'value, good') by either adding a vowel (/fəprɔk/) or deleting the initial consonant (/prɔk/).

Some phonotactic constraints are quite language-specific (like the prohibition against having more than one consonant at the beginning of a syllable). Others are much more general: very few languages allow a syllable to begin with a liquid followed by a stop (compare /lbu/ to /blu/ *blue,* with the reverse order). In Section 2.3, we will consider two factors that help determine why some phonotactic sequences are more likely than others in the world's languages.

2.2 Syllable Structure

Syllables comply with the following basic design.

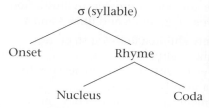

Figure 3.6 The basic syllable and its constituents

LANGUAGE MATTERS   Speaking Pig Latin

One version of the English language game known as Pig Latin is played by displacing the onset of the first syllable of a word to the end of the word and then tacking on the vowel *ay* [ej]: thus *long* becomes *ong-l-ay*, and *sweet* becomes *eet-sw-ay*.

ong [l] + ay   eet [sw] + ay

In the vast majority of languages, the **nucleus** of a syllable has to be a vowel or diphthong. However, some languages are more permissive. For example, English allows sonorant consonants to function as syllabic nuclei in words such as *rhythm* /ɹɪ.ðm̩/ or *pickle* /pɪ.kl̩/. (A consonant that functions as a syllabic nucleus is marked by the diacritic [̩] and is often called a syllabic consonant.)

All languages appear to allow an **onset** consisting of at least one consonant before the nucleus, and some (e.g., Senufo, Klamath) even require that every syllable have an onset. As we have already seen, there are differences among languages in terms of how many consonants appear in onsets—Korean allows just one, French permits two, English allows up to three, and so on.

Many languages permit a **coda** consisting of one or more consonants after the nucleus, but many ban codas altogether (e.g., Hua, Cayuvava, Sesotho, in addition to Hawaiian), and no language requires that every syllable have a coda. The nucleus plus the coda (if there is one) is called the **rhyme**. In addition, we often find a larger number of consonant types in onsets than in codas. For example, German allows both voiced and voiceless obstruents in onsets, but voiced obstruents are prohibited in codas leading to **devoicing** of word-final voiced obstruents. That's why the German word for 'dog', *Hund*, is pronounced [hʊnt].

LANGUAGE MATTERS   Why Rhymes Are Called Rhymes

It's no coincidence that the word *rhyme* is used for the portion of the syllable consisting of the nucleus and the coda, since that is the part of the syllable that creates rhyming in poetry. The first five lines of "Paul Revere's Ride" by Henry Wadsworth Longfellow provide an illustration. Pay special attention to the last words in lines 1, 2, and 5 and lines 3 and 4.

Listen, my children and you shall hear
Of the midnight ride of Paul Revere,
On the eighteenth of April in Seventy-five;
Hardly a man is now alive
Who remembers that famous day and year.

Building Syllable Structure

A simple three-step procedure governs the construction of syllables.

Step a *Nucleus formation:* Since the syllable nucleus is the only obligatory constituent of a syllable, it is constructed first. Each vowel segment in a word makes up a syllabic nucleus. To represent this, link a vowel to an N symbol above it by drawing an **association line**. Above each nucleus symbol, place an R symbol (for rhyme), and above that, place a σ symbol (for syllable).

Figure 3.7 The first step of syllable building: nucleus formation

Step b *Onset formation:* The longest permissible sequence of consonants before each nucleus is the onset of the syllable. Link these consonants to an O(nset) symbol and join it to the σ symbol above the vowel to the right (see Figure 3.8). In the word *entry*, the first syllable has no onset. The second nucleus is preceded by three consonants, but the longest permissible sequence is just /tɹ/—recall that English allows three consonants in a row at the beginning of a syllable only if the first one is /s/.

Figure 3.8 The second step of syllable building: onset formation

Step c *Coda formation:* Any remaining unassociated consonants to the right of each nucleus form the coda and are linked to a Co(da) symbol above them. This coda is then associated with the syllable nucleus, making up the rhyme. A syllable with a coda is called a **closed syllable**, while a syllable without a coda is called an **open syllable**. As can be seen in Figure 3.9, the first syllable in *entry* is closed and the second one is open.

Figure 3.9   The third step of syllable building: coda formation

2.3   Basic Syllables

In languages that allow more than one consonant to appear in onsets and codas, two general principles apply. The first principle, stated in *7*, makes reference to **sonority** (roughly, a sound's degree of resonance).

7) **The Sonority Requirement**
In basic syllables, sonority rises before the nucleus and declines after the nucleus.

A **sonority scale** is provided in Figure 3.10, with the numbers from 0 to 4 indicating relative sonority levels. (Remember that an obstruent is an oral stop, a fricative, or an affricate.)

0	1	2	3	4
Obstruent	Nasal	Liquid	Glide	Vowel

Figure 3.10   The sonority scale

The sonority profile of basic syllables can be seen in a monosyllabic word like *grant* /gɹænt/. There is rising sonority within the onset and falling sonority within the coda, as shown in Figure 3.11.

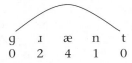

Figure 3.11   The sonority profile of *grant*

In contrast, there are no words such as */ɹgænt/, with falling sonority in the onset.

ɹ   g   æ   n   t
2   0   4
↑   ↑

falling sonority in the onset

And there are no words such as */gɹætn/, with rising sonority in the coda.

$$
\begin{array}{ccccc}
g & \text{ɹ} & \text{æ} & t & n \\
0 & 2 & 4 & 0 & 1 \\
& & & \uparrow & \uparrow
\end{array}
$$

rising sonority in the coda

Don't be fooled by words such as *button* /bʌtn/. It consists of two syllables: /bʌ.tn̩/, with /t/ in the onset of the second syllable and /n̩/ functioning as the nucleus. Table 3.15 illustrates the Sonority Requirement in onset combinations in English.

Table 3.15 Some onsets in English that comply with the Sonority Requirement

Labial + sonorant		Alveolar + sonorant		Velar + sonorant	
/pl/	please	/tɹ/	trade	/kl/	clean
/pɹ/	proud	/tw/	twin	/kɹ/	cream
/pj/	pure	/sɹ/	Sri Lanka	/kw/	queen
/bɹ/	bring	/sl/	slow	/kj/	cute
/bl/	blight	/dɹ/	dry	/gɹ/	grow
/fɹ/	free			/gl/	glow

The second major principle with which basic syllables must comply can be stated as follows in *8*.

8) The Binarity Requirement

Within basic syllables, each constituent can be at most binary (i.e., branching into two).

This means that an onset or coda can't contain more than two consonants. Thus, a word such as *grant*, with two consonants in its onset and two in its coda, represents the most complex basic syllable permitted in English, as shown in Figure 3.12. We know, however, that English has words such as *scrimps* [skɹɪmps], which seem to violate this constraint. The next section will explain how we deal with this apparent contradiction.

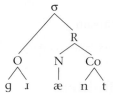

Figure 3.12 The syllable structure of *grant*

2.4   Syllables with a More Complex Structure

In fact, of course, English permits syllables whose structure is more complex than that of *grant*—for example, *stream* has three consonants in its onset, and *ranks* has three in its coda. Not only do these syllables have too many consonants in their onsets and codas (remember the Binarity Requirement), but they also violate the Sonority Requirement. In *stream*, the initial /st/ has a flat rather than rising sonority profile—both segments are voiceless obstruents. And in *ranks*, the final /ks/ is also flat, rather than falling.

```
s    t    ɹ    i    m              ɹ    æ    ŋ    k    s
0    0         2                        1    0    0
↑    ↑                                       ↑    ↑
```
flat sonority in the onset   *flat sonority in the coda*

Interestingly, such complex syllables are rare in the world's languages and are subject to special restrictions in languages in which they occur.

- Extra consonants tend to occur at word edges—either at the beginning or the end, as in the case of the /s/ in *stream* and *ranks*.

- In English, only /s/ can serve as an extra consonant in onsets, which is why all CCC onsets begin with /s/ (*stream*, *split*, *scream*, etc.). In coda position, the extra consonant is always voiceless and made with the tip of the tongue, such as the /s/ in *ranks* /ɹæŋk̲s̲/, the /t/ in *clamped* /klæmp̲t̲/, and the /θ/ in *twelfth* /twɛlf̲θ̲/. It's also worth noting that the extra coda consonant in these and many other cases is not an inherent part of the word—it's added as a grammatical ending (suffix) to mark past tense, plurality, or some other contrast.

When drawing the structure of these more complex syllables, some linguists place consonants that violate the Sonority and/or Binarity Requirements in an appendix position, outside the onset or coda of the syllable with which they are associated, as shown in Figure 3.13.

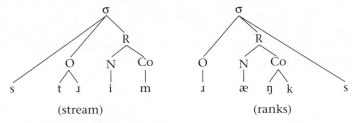

Figure 3.13   Appendix consonants

2.5   Stress and Syllables

A basic feature of English pronunciation is the use of stress to increase the acoustic prominence of particular syllables: the stress falls on the first syllable in *Canada*, the second syllable in *agenda*, and so on. Because English vocabulary is so varied, with mixed Germanic and Latinate origins, the location of stress is sometimes unpredictable. Nonetheless, we know that syllable structure affects stress placement in a large number of cases.

Stress placement in English is sensitive to **syllable weight**, which is determined by the composition of its rhyme. Whereas the rhyme in a **heavy syllable** consists of a vowel plus at least one other element (a glide or a consonant), the rhyme in a **light syllable** consists of just a vowel or a syllabic consonant such as [ŋ] or [ḷ]. Thus the syllables *bad* (vowel plus consonant) and *by* (vowel plus glide) are heavy, while the syllable *bee* is light.

The basic stress rule for English verbs (ignoring suffixes, which have effects of their own) can be stated as follows in *9*.

9) Basic stress rule for English verbs with more than one syllable:

Stress falls on the final syllable if it is heavy;
otherwise, it falls on the second-to-last (penultimate) syllable.

Table 3.16 presents some examples illustrating the effect of this rule. (Stress in transcriptions is marked by the symbol ['] at the beginning of the syllable.)

Table 3.16 Stress in English verbs

Final syllable is heavy (stress falls on that syllable)	Final syllable is light (stress falls on the penultimate syllable)
arrive /ə.'ɹajv/	hurry /'hʌ.ɹi/
destroy /də.'stɹɔj/	button /'bʌ.tn̩/
advise /əd.'vajz/	cancel /'kæn.sḷ/
insist /ɪn.'sɪst/	study /'stʌ.di/
consult /kən.'sʌlt/	carry /'kæ.ɹi/ or /'kɛ.ɹi/
allow /ə.'law/	belittle /bi.'lɪ.tḷ/
interrupt /ɪn.tə.'ɹʌpt/	recover /ɹi.'kʌ.vɹ̩/

Exceptions include *edit*, *promise*, *astonish*, and *embarrass*, all with stress on the second-to-last syllable despite the presence of an apparently strong final syllable.

The basic rule for nouns (once again ignoring suffixes) can be stated as follows in *10*.

10) Basic stress rule for English nouns with more than one syllable:
Stress falls on the second-to-last (penultimate) syllable.

The effect of this rule can be seen in the pronunciation of words such as *English*, *city*, *kidney*, *elbow*, and *effort*, all of which have stress on the penultimate syllable. Its effects can also be seen in the contrasts between noun-verb pairs in Table 3.17, with stress on the second-to-last syllable in the case of nouns and on the final syllable in the case of verbs.

Table 3.17   Stress in English noun and verb pairs

Nouns	Verbs
a <u>con</u>vert	to con<u>vert</u> someone
a <u>con</u>vict	to con<u>vict</u> someone
a <u>dis</u>count	to dis<u>count</u> something
an <u>in</u>crease	to in<u>crease</u> something
a <u>re</u>fill	to re<u>fill</u> something
a <u>per</u>mit	to per<u>mit</u> something
a <u>sus</u>pect	to sus<u>pect</u> someone

A further effect of syllable structure can be seen in nouns that are longer than two syllables. In such cases, we generally find stress on the second-to-last syllable if that syllable is heavy; otherwise, the stress falls on the third-to-last (antepenultimate) syllable. (See Table 3.18.)

Table 3.18   Stress in English nouns longer than two syllables

Penultimate syllable is heavy (stress on penultimate syllable)	Penultimate syllable is light (stress on antepenultimate syllable)
ho<u>ri</u>zon /hə.'ɹaj.zn̩/	<u>Ca</u>nada /'kæ.nə.də/
va<u>ca</u>tion /və.'kej.ʃn̩/	<u>ci</u>tizen /'sɪ.tə.zn̩/
a<u>ro</u>ma /ə.'ɹow.mə/	<u>ci</u>nema /'sɪ.nə.mə/
po<u>ta</u>to /pə.'tej.to/	A<u>me</u>rica /ə.'mɛ.ɹə.kə/
ve<u>ran</u>da /və.'ɹæn.də/	a<u>na</u>lysis /ə.'næ.lə.səs/
a<u>gen</u>da /ə.'dʒɛn.də/	a<u>rith</u>metic /ə.'ɹɪθ.mə.tɪk/

Exceptions to these generalizations include *result*, *giraffe*, *sardine*, *ballet*, and *Tennessee*, all of which have stress on the final syllable, as well as *banana*, *Alabama*, and *committee*, with stress on a light second-to-last syllable.

LANGUAGE MATTERS   Syllabification in Writing

It is important not to confuse phonological syllable structure with the breaks that are used when a word won't fit at the end of a line in writing. These breaks, marked by hyphens, often align with phonological syllable boundaries—as in *re-write*, *un-der*, and *da-ta*. But one case in particular creates serious divergences: in writing, a consonant that occurs between vowels goes with the first vowel if that vowel is lax. Check the words *digit* and *method* in your dictionary, and you'll see that they're syllabified as *dig-it* and *meth-od*, compared to /dɪ.dʒɪt/ and /mɛ.θəd/ in phonology. Which better corresponds to the pronunciation?

2.6   Syllable-Based Phonology

Syllables play a major role in the operation of phonological processes, including some that are vital to English.

Aspiration in English

We have already seen that the English voiceless stops /p, t, k/ can be aspirated, as in *pan* [pʰæn], *tan* [tʰæn], and *kin* [kʰɪn]. But what are the precise conditions under which the aspirated allophone is used? Table 3.19 provides some relevant data.

Table 3.19   English aspiration

A (aspiration)		B (no aspiration)		C (no aspiration)	
[pʰæn]	pan	[spæn]	span	[slæp]	slap
[tʰæn]	tan	[stæn]	Stan	[slɑt]	slot
[kʰɪn]	kin	[skɪn]	skin	[sɪk]	sick
[pʰl̥æn]	plan	[splɪt]	split		
[tʰɹ̥aj]	try	[stɹɔŋ]	strong		
[kʰl̥in]	clean	[skɹim]	scream		

A preliminary generalization can be stated very simply in *11* with reference to syllable structure.

11)   English voiceless stops are aspirated syllable-initially.

This statement accounts for all the data in column A of Table 3.19, where voiceless stops appear syllable-initially. No aspiration is found in the words in columns B and C since the voiceless stops appear either as the second segment in a syllable onset (in *span*, *skin*, etc.), or in a coda, as in *slap* and *slot*.

So far, so good. But when we look *inside* words, aspiration is more puzzling—the syllable-initial voiceless stops in column A of Table 3.20 are aspirated but those in column B are not.

Table 3.20   Syllables and English aspiration

A (aspiration)		B (little or no aspiration)	
upon	[ə.ˈpʰɔn]	upper	[ˈʌ.pɹ̩]
atomic	[ə.ˈtʰɑ.mɪk]	atom	[ˈæ.təm] or [ˈæ.ɾəm]
attack	[ə.ˈtʰæk]	attic	[ˈæ.tɪk] or [ˈæ.ɾɪk]
akin	[ə.ˈkʰɪn]	aching	[ˈej.kɪŋ]

We can make sense of this if we take into account the fact that syllables can be stressed or unstressed. (Recall that a stressed syllable is perceived to be more prominent than its neighbors—compare *phoneme*, with stress on the first syllable, with *phonemic*, which has stress on the second syllable.)

Notice that the aspirated stops in Table 3.20 all occur at the beginning of a stressed syllable, marked here by the diacritic [']. Stress seems not to matter when the voiceless stop is at the beginning of a word—the /p/ of *police* [pʰə.'lis] and *parade* [pʰə.'ɹejd] is aspirated even though the initial syllable is unstressed. But it does matter when the syllable occurs inside the word. The right generalization seems to be something like *12.*

12) English voiceless stops are aspirated when they occur at the beginning of a syllable that is word-initial or that is stressed.

Vowel Length in English

Vowel length in English offers yet another example of the phonological relevance of syllables. We have already seen that, as a first approximation, vowels are lengthened in front of a voiced obstruent in English, but not elsewhere. This is shown in Table 3.21.

Table 3.21   Phonetic vowel length in English

A (vowel lengthening)		B (no vowel lengthening)	
bad	[bæːd]	bat	[bæt]
Abe	[eːjb]	ape	[ejp]
phase	[feːjz]	face	[fejs]
leave	[liːv]	leaf	[lif]
tag	[tʰæːg]	tack	[tʰæk]
brogue	[bɹoːwg]	broke	[bɹowk]
		say	[sej]
		meal	[mil]
		soar	[sɔɹ]
		show	[ʃow]

It turns out, though, that this is not quite right: lengthening takes place only if the voiced obstruent is in the coda position of *the same syllable* as the vowel. As the next examples show in Table 3.22, if the consonant is in the onset of the next syllable, the vowel is not lengthened.

Table 3.22   Short vowels before a voiced onset obstruent in the next syllable

obey	[ow.bej]	(compare to *lobe* [loːwb])
redo	[ɹi.du]	(compare to *read* [ɹiːd])
regard	[ɹi.gɑɹd]	(compare to *league* [liːg])
ogre	[ow.gɻ]	(compare to *brogue* [bɹoːwg])
Odin	[ow.dɪn]	(compare to *ode* [oːwd])

Once again, syllable structure is crucial, as stated in *13*.

13) English vowels are lengthened when followed by a voiced obstruent in the coda position of the same syllable.

Uvular Consonants in Quechua

Yet another syllable-based phenomenon occurs in Quechua (spoken in Peru), where the voiceless uvular stop /q/ has two allophones. The fricative allophone [χ] is found in coda positions—that is, at the end of syllables.

[tʃeχ.niŋ] 'he hates'   [soχ.ta] 'six'   [al.qoχ] 'dog'
    ↑   ↑   ↑

The stop allophone [q] is found elsewhere (i.e., at the beginning of syllables).

[qaŋ] 'you'   [no.qa] 'I'   [al.qoχ] 'dog'
↑   ↑   ↑

The generalization can be stated as follows in *14*:

14) The [χ] allophone of /q/ is used in the coda position in Quechua.

As these and other examples show, the use of syllabic representations in phonology permits us to make more accurate statements about allophonic patterns in language than would otherwise be possible.

3   Features

As noted at the beginning of the chapter, linguists consider features to be the most basic units of phonology. Features are like atoms; they are the basic building blocks of speech sounds.

3.1   Features as Phonetically Grounded Elements

The study of phonetics shows that speech is produced by a number of independent but coordinated articulatory activities such as voicing, tongue position, lip rounding, and so on. For example, when we produce the voiceless bilabial stop [p], the vocal cords in the larynx are open and not vibrating; hence, the sound is voiceless. At the same time, the lips are pressed together to block the flow of air through the vocal tract, thereby creating a labial stop. Features such as [± voice], [LABIAL], and the like allow us to identify the building blocks of phonemes. This has advantages for various aspects of phonological analysis.

Features and Natural Classes

A first advantage of features is that they give us an economical way of characterizing natural classes. **Natural classes** are groups of sounds with similar properties. Consider, for example, the set of English sounds in Figure 3.14.

[− sonorant]

[− voice]			[+ voice]		
p				b	
t	tʃ		dʒ	d	[− continuant]
k				g	
f				v	
θ				ð	[+ continuant]
s				z	
ʃ				ʒ	

Figure 3.14 Natural classes: obstruents in English

In fact, by using just three features, we can group these sounds into nine different natural classes:

- To capture the fact that all these sounds are obstruents, we can say that they are all [–sonorant], meaning they are not sonorants.

- We can distinguish the subset of sounds that are voiced from those that are voiceless with the feature [±voice].

- The feature [±continuant] refers to whether or not a sound is produced with a continuous flow of air through the oral cavity. Stops and affricates, which are [–continuant], can thus be distinguished from fricatives, which are [+continuant].

Table 3.23 shows the nine natural classes captured by the three features [sonorant], [voice], and [continuant].

Table 3.23 Nine natural classes: obstruents in English

Obstruents	Stops/ Affricates	Fricatives	Voiceless obstruents	Voiced obstruents	Voiceless stops/affricates	Voiced stops/ affricates	Voiceless fricatives	Voiced fricatives
[−sonorant]	[−sonorant −continuant]	[−sonorant +continuant]	[−sonorant −voice]	[−sonorant +voice]	[−sonorant −continuant −voice]	[−sonorant −continuant +voice]	[−sonorant −continuant −voice]	[−sonorant +continuant +voice]
p t k	p t k	f θ s ʃ	p t k	b d g	p t k	b d g	f θ s ʃ	v ð z ʒ
b d g	b d g	v ð z ʒ	f θ s ʃ	v ð z ʒ	tʃ	dʒ		
f θ s ʃ	tʃ		tʃ	dʒ				
v ð z ʒ	dʒ							
tʃ								
dʒ								

The importance of natural classes in phonology stems from the fact that the members of a natural class tend to behave alike with respect to patterns and processes. In English, for instance, the class of voiceless stops /p, t, k/, defined by the features [–sonorant, –continuant, –voice, –delayed release], are the only segments that can be aspirated. The consonants before which vowels can lengthen also make up a natural class—they are all voiced obstruents ([–sonorant, +voice]). Thus, having the right system of features is essential for grouping sounds together in an insightful way.

Features and Contrasts

A second advantage of features is that they provide insights into a language's system of phonemic contrasts. We are missing something important about English if we simply say that that /p/ contrasts with /b/, /t/ with /d/, /f/ with /v/, /θ/ with /ð/, /s/ with /z/, and so on. The key point is that voiced obstruents contrast with voiceless obstruents. Put another way, [voice] is a **distinctive feature** in English—which is why voiced phonemes contrast with their voiceless counterparts.

In contrast, aspiration, which is characterized by the feature [+spread glottis], is not distinctive in English. That's why we don't find contrasts between [p] and [pʰ], [t] and [tʰ], or [k] and [kʰ] in English. Of course, just the opposite is true in Khmer, where aspiration is distinctive (see Section 1.4).

Other features provide for other contrasts. For example, we can capture the contrast between /t/ and /s/ in English with the feature [continuant]. Both /t/ and /s/ are voiceless and have an alveolar point of articulation. By viewing the relevant distinctive feature as [continuant], we can use the same feature to distinguish between /p/ and /f/, /b/ and /v/, and /d/ and /z/ (see Table 3.24).

Table 3.24 Stop-fricative contrasts captured by a distinctive feature

[–continuant]	[+continuant]
p	f
b	v
t	s
d	z

By systematically examining the phonemic contrasts of a language, we can extract the distinctive features and use these irreducible linguistic elements to describe the phonemic inventory.

Features, Processes, and Allophonic Variation

A third reason for using features in phonology is that they enable us to describe allophonic variation more precisely. Viewed from the perspective of features, allophonic variation is not simply the substitution of one allophone for another but rather the environmentally conditioned change or specification of a feature or features. For instance, English vowels have nasalized allophones when in front of [m], [n], or [ŋ]: e.g., [θʌ̃m] *thumb*, [tʌ̃n] *ton*, and [bʌ̃ŋk] *bunk*. Features allow an elegant statement of this generalization: vowels become [+nasal] in front of a [+nasal] consonant in the same syllable.

3.2   Feature Representations

In this section, we present and define features that are needed to analyze the sound system of English, as well as of many other languages.

Defining the Features of English

Most features have labels that reflect traditional articulatory terms such as [voice], [consonantal], and [nasal]. These features require little further description. A few features have less familiar labels, such as [CORONAL] and [anterior]. Most of the features given below are written in lower case and are **binary features**; in other words, they can have one of two values, "+" or "−". For example, voiced sounds are [+voice], while voiceless sounds are [−voice]. In contrast with the binary features, the three place features [LABIAL], [CORONAL], and [DORSAL] are written in upper case and have only one value. These features refer to the articulators that are used to produce sounds. Thus, [LABIAL] represents sounds made using the lips, [CORONAL] represents sounds made with the tongue tip or tongue blade, and [DORSAL] represents sounds made with the tongue body/back.

Table 3.25 summarizes each feature category and its features, with defining characteristics and examples of each feature.

- **Major class features** *features that represent the classes consonant, obstruent, and sonorant (nasal, liquid, glide, vowel)*

  [±consonantal] Sounds that are [+consonantal] are produced with a major obstruction in the vocal tract. All consonants are [+consonantal], except for the glottals [h] and [ʔ], which are produced at the glottis rather than in the vocal tract. Like glides and vowels, they are [−consonantal].

  [±sonorant] All and only those sounds that are singable are [+sonorant]; they include vowels, glides, liquids, and nasals (even if the sounds are devoiced). All nonsingable sounds (namely, obstruents) are [−sonorant].

  [±syllabic] Sounds that can act as syllabic nuclei are [+syllabic]; this includes vowels, syllabic liquids, and syllabic nasals. All other sounds are [−syllabic].

Table 3.26 illustrates how the major class features are used to divide sounds into classes. Note that nasals and liquids have the same values for the three major class features; to distinguish these two classes from each other, additional (manner) features are therefore needed.

Table 3.25 Features and their characteristics

Category	Features	Characteristics	Examples
Major class	+consonantal	major obstruction in vocal tract	consonants (except glides)
	+sonorant	singable, acoustically powerful	nasals, liquids, glides, vowels
	+syllabic	can be nucleus of syllable	vowels, syllabic liquids/nasals
Manner	+nasal	air allowed through nasal cavity	nasal consonants
	+continuant	continuous airflow through oral cavity	fricatives, liquids, glides
	+lateral	air escapes over side of tongue	varieties of *l*
	+DR (delayed release)	slow release of initial stop	affricates
Laryngeal	+voice	vocal cords vibrate	voiced obstruents, all sonorants
	+CG (constricted glottis)	vocal folds closed	glottal stop
	+SG (spread glottis)	vocal folds open	aspirated voiceless stops
Place	✓LABIAL	produced with lips	bilabials, labiodentals
	+round	lips protrude	rounded vowels and consonants
	✓CORONAL	produced with tongue tip or blade	interdentals, alveolars, alveopalatals
	+anterior	in front of alveopalatal region	alveolars, interdentals
	+strident	noisy fricatives and affricates	alveolar fricatives; affricates
	✓DORSAL	produced with body of tongue	palatals, velars, vowels
	+high	tongue body is raised	high vowels; palatal, velar consonants
	+low	tongue body is lowered	low vowels
	+back	tongue body behind palate	back vowels, velar consonants
	+tense	tense tongue body	tense vowels
	+reduced	exceptionally brief (vowel)	schwa

Table 3.26 Use of major class features

	Obstruents	Nasals	Liquids	Glides	Vowels
[±consonantal]	+	+	+	−	−
[±sonorant]	−	+	+	+	+
[±syllabic]	−	−/+	−/+	−	+
Examples:	p d v tʃ	m n ŋ	l ɹ	j w	i ɑ

The manner features given next represent manners of articulation. Their use is particularly important in distinguishing the following classes: stops/affricates from fricatives ([±continuant]), affricates from stops ([±delayed release]), nasals from nonnasals ([±nasal]), and laterals from nonlaterals ([±lateral]).

- **Manner features** *features that represent manner of articulation*

  [±nasal] Sounds produced with a lowered velum—nasal stops and all nasalized sounds—are [+nasal]. Sounds that are oral, and thus produced with a raised velum, are [−nasal].

  [±continuant] Sounds produced with free or nearly free airflow through the oral cavity—vowels, glides, liquids, and fricatives—are [+continuant]. All other sounds are [−continuant]; noncontinuants include nasal and oral stops as well as affricates.

  [±lateral] All and only varieties of *l* are [+lateral], with air escaping along the lowered sides of the tongue. All other sounds are [−lateral].

  [±delayed release] **([±DR])** When an affricate sound such as [tʃ] is produced, the tongue is slower in leaving the roof of the mouth than when a stop like [t] is produced on its own. Hence, affricates are said to be produced with delayed release of air. All and only affricates such as [tʃ] and [dʒ] are [+DR]. All other sounds are [−DR].

Voicing, aspiration, and glottal constriction are all the result of laryngeal activity. To represent different laryngeal states, we use the features [±voice], [±constricted glottis], and [±spread glottis].

- **Laryngeal features** *features that represent laryngeal activity*

  [±voice] All voiced sounds are [+voice]; all voiceless sounds are [−voice].

  [±constricted glottis] **([±CG])** All sounds made with a closed glottis are [+CG]; all others are [−CG]. In English only the glottal stop [ʔ] is [+CG].

  [±spread glottis] **([±SG])** All aspirated consonants and [h] are [+SG]; all others are [−SG]. The use of this feature reflects the fact that aspiration occurs when the vocal folds remain open (spread) after the release of a consonant's closure.

The last category of features represents the supralaryngeal place of articulation (i.e., above the larynx): [LABIAL], [CORONAL], and [DORSAL]. These three nonbinary place features refer to the involvement of the lips [LABIAL], the tongue tip or blade [CORONAL], or the tongue back [DORSAL] in articulating a sound. If an articulator is not used for a particular sound, then that place feature simply does not appear in the feature matrix. Each of these three nonbinary place features can be further refined by the use of binary features specific to that place of articulation.

- **Place of articulation features** *features that represent supralaryngeal activity*

[LABIAL] Any sound that is produced with involvement of one or both of the lips is [LABIAL]. This includes bilabial and labiodental sounds.

> **[±round]** A labial sound may be produced by protruding the lips—such sounds are [+round] (rounded vowels and the rounded labiovelar glide [w]); labial sounds made with no lip protrusion are [−round] (e.g., [p, b, f, v]).

[CORONAL] Any sound that is produced with involvement of the tongue tip or blade raised is [CORONAL]. Interdental, alveolar, and alveopalatal sounds are all [CORONAL].

> **[±anterior]** All coronal sounds articulated in front of the alveopalatal region (interdentals and alveolars) are [+anterior]; coronal sounds articulated at or behind the alveopalatal region (alveopalatals) are [−anterior].

> **[±strident]** All "noisy" coronal fricatives and affricates ([s, z, ʃ, ʒ, tʃ, dʒ]) are [+strident]; all other coronal fricatives and affricates ([θ, ð]) are [−strident].

[DORSAL] All sounds that are produced with involvement of the body of the tongue are [DORSAL]. This includes vowels as well as palatal and velar consonants.

> **[±high]** Dorsal consonants (velars and palatals) and vowels produced with the tongue body raised from a central position in the oral cavity are [+high]. Sounds produced with a neutral or lowered tongue body are [−high].

> **[±low]** Vowels produced with the tongue body lowered from a central position in the oral cavity are [+low]. All other vowels are [−low]. Consonants in English do not need the feature [low], although it may be used in languages that have uvular or pharyngeal consonants.

> **[±back]** Dorsal consonants and vowels produced with the tongue body behind the palatal region (hard palate) in the oral cavity are [+back]. Velars and uvulars are [+back], while palatals are [−back].

> **[±tense]** Vowels that are tense are [+tense]; vowels that are lax are [−tense]. In some analyses, the feature [tense] is replaced by the feature [advanced tongue root] ([ATR]), in recognition of the fact that the tongue root adopts a somewhat higher position in the vocal tract for tense vowels than for their lax counterparts.

> **[±reduced]** The schwa ([ə]) is a lax and exceptionally brief vowel and is therefore [+reduced]; all other vowels are [−reduced].

Generally speaking, the binary place features are specific to individual articulators and will not appear in the feature matrix if that articulator is not active.

Using Place of Articulation Features

To see exactly how the articulator features are used to represent the various places of articulation of the consonants found in English, let us look at Table 3.27. In the feature representations, a checkmark indicates that the relevant articulator is active in the production of a sound. Where no checkmark is present, the articulator is inactive. Using [p] as an example, the feature representations in Table 3.27 can be understood as follows:

- [p] is produced with the lips in an unrounded state. It is therefore a [LABIAL], [–round] sound. The tongue blade and the tongue body are not used in the production of [p], and therefore [p] has no feature specifications for the coronal and dorsal articulators.

Table 3.27 Use of place of articulation features to represent some English consonants

	Labials		Interdentals	Alveolars	Alveopalatals	Palatals	Velars
	p	w	θ	s	ʃ	j	k
LABIAL	✓	✓					
[±round]	–	+					
CORONAL			✓	✓	✓		
[±anterior]			+	+	–		
[±strident]			–	+	+		
DORSAL		✓				✓	✓
[±high]		+				+	+
[±back]		+				–	+

- [θ s ʃ] are all [CORONAL] sounds because they are produced with the tongue blade. [θ s] are produced with the tongue blade in front of the alveopalatal region and are therefore [+anterior], while [ʃ] is produced with the tongue blade at the alveopalatal region and is therefore [–anterior]. [θ] is produced with a quiet airflow and thus is [–strident], while [s ʃ] are produced with noisy airflow and thus are [+strident]. Since neither the lips nor the tongue body are used to produce these sounds, they have no specifications for the [LABIAL] or [DORSAL] features.

- [j k] are both produced with the tongue body and are therefore [DORSAL] sounds. Both have a raised tongue body, so are [+high], but [j] is pronounced with the tongue body at the hard palate, so it is [–back]. In contrast, [k] is pronounced with the tongue body behind the hard palate, so it is [+back]. Finally, since neither the lips nor the tongue blade are used to produce these sounds, they have no specifications for the features [LABIAL] or [CORONAL].

- [w] is a labiovelar sound and is thus coarticulated: it is produced with both a tongue body that is raised and behind the hard palate *and* with lip rounding. This means that both the dorsum and the lips are used to produce [w], so it is executed with two articulators acting simultaneously. It is therefore both [LABIAL] and [DORSAL]; as a [LABIAL] sound, it is [+round], and as a [DORSAL] sound, it is [+high, +back]. Since the tongue blade is not used to produce this sound, it has no specifications for the [CORONAL] feature.

Table 3.28 exemplifies how the place of articulation features are used to represent vowels in English. All vowels are produced with an active tongue body and therefore are [DORSAL]. Vowels that involve lip rounding are also produced with the [LABIAL] articulator. [CORONAL] is never used in the feature representations of vowels. All vowels except schwa are unreduced and therefore specified as [–reduced].

Table 3.28 Use of place of articulation features to represent some English vowels

	ɛ	ə	u	ɑ
LABIAL			✓	
[±round]			+	
DORSAL	✓	✓	✓	✓
[±high]	–	–	+	–
[±low]	–	–	–	+
[±back]	–	+	+	+
[±tense]	–	–	+	+
[±reduced]	–	+	–	–

- [ɛ] is a mid front lax unrounded vowel. Since it is unrounded, it does not use the labial articulator. As a mid vowel, it has neither a raised nor a lowered tongue body, so it is [DORSAL] and specified as both [–high] and [–low]. As a front vowel, it is [–back], and as a lax vowel, it is [–tense].

- [ə] is a mid central unrounded lax reduced vowel. As a mid vowel, it is [DORSAL, –high and –low]. As a central and therefore nonfront vowel, it is [+back]. (All central vowels are [+back] in feature representations.) Being unrounded, it does not involve the labial articulator. Because it is a lax reduced vowel, it is [–tense] and [+reduced].

- [u] is a high back tense vowel and is therefore specified as [+high], [+back], and [+tense]. Since it is round, it is [LABIAL, +round] in addition to being [DORSAL]. Since it is [+high], it is also [–low]. (Because the tongue body cannot be both raised and lowered at the same time, all [+high] vowels are also [–low].)

- [ɑ] is a low back unrounded tense vowel. Since it is produced with a lowered tongue body it is [DORSAL, +low]; because a lowered tongue body cannot be simultaneously raised, it is also [–high]. Since it is back, it is [+back]. Being tense, it is [+tense], and being unrounded, it has no labial specifications.

Feature notation does not provide a convenient way to distinguish diphthongs such as [aj], [aw], and [ɔj] from the other vowels. These diphthongs may be treated as vowel-glide sequences when using features.

Tables 3.29 and 3.30 provide the feature representations for all the consonants and vowels of English. As you go through these tables, notice that features are listed in the following order for every sound: major class features, manner features, laryngeal features, and place of articulation features.

Table 3.29 Feature matrix for English consonants

		Stops						Fricatives								Affricates		Nasals			Liquids		Glides			Glottals	
		p	b	t	d	k	g	f	v	θ	ð	s	z	ʃ	ʒ	tʃ	dʒ	m	n	ŋ	l	ɹ	j	w	ʍ	h	ʔ
Major class features	[consonantal]	+	+	+	+	+	+	+	+	+	+	+	+	+	+	+	+	+	+	+	+	+	-	-	-	-	-
	[sonorant]	-	-	-	-	-	-	-	-	-	-	-	-	-	-	-	-	+	+	+	+	+	+	+	+	-	-
	[syllabic]	-	-	-	-	-	-	-	-	-	-	-	-	-	-	-	-	-	-	-	-	-	-	-	-	-	-
Manner features	[nasal]	-	-	-	-	-	-	-	-	-	-	-	-	-	-	-	-	+	+	+	-	-	-	-	-	-	-
	[continuant]	-	-	-	-	-	-	+	+	+	+	+	+	+	+	-	-	-	-	-	+	+	+	+	+	+	-
	[lateral]	-	-	-	-	-	-	-	-	-	-	-	-	-	-	-	-	-	-	-	+	-	-	-	-	-	-
	[delayed release]	-	-	-	-	-	-	-	-	-	-	-	-	-	-	+	+	-	-	-	-	-	-	-	-	-	-
Laryngeal features	[voice]	-	+	-	+	-	+	-	+	-	+	-	+	-	+	-	+	+	+	+	+	+	+	+	-	-	-
	[CG]	-	-	-	-	-	-	-	-	-	-	-	-	-	-	-	-	-	-	-	-	-	-	-	-	-	+
	[SG]	-	-	-	-	-	-	-	-	-	-	-	-	-	-	-	-	-	-	-	-	-	-	-	-	+	-
Place of articulation features	LABIAL	✓	✓					✓	✓									✓						✓	✓		
	[round]	-	-					-	-									-						+	+		
	CORONAL			✓	✓					✓	✓	✓	✓	✓	✓	✓	✓		✓		✓	✓					
	[anterior]			+	+					+	+	+	+	-	-	-	-		+		+	+					
	[strident]			-	-					-	-	+	+	+	+	+	+		-		-	-					
	DORSAL					✓	✓													✓			✓	✓	✓		
	[high]					+	+													+			+	+	+		
	[back]					+	+													+			-	+	+		

Note: [low], [tense], and [reduced] are not used for English consonants.
Aspirated stops [pʰ, tʰ, kʰ] will have the feature [+SG].
Syllabic liquids and nasals will have the feature [+syllabic].

Table 3.30 Feature matrix for English vowels

		i	ɪ	e	ɛ	æ	ə	ʌ	u	ʊ	o	ɔ	ɑ/a*
Major class features	[consonantal]	–	–	–	–	–	–	–	–	–	–	–	–
	[sonorant]	+	+	+	+	+	+	+	+	+	+	+	+
	[syllabic]	+	+	+	+	+	+	+	+	+	+	+	+
Manner feature	[continuant]	+	+	+	+	+	+	+	+	+	+	+	+
Laryngeal feature	[voice]	+	+	+	+	+	+	+	+	+	+	+	+
Place of articulation features	LABIAL								✓	✓	✓	✓	
	[round]								+	+	+	+	
	DORSAL	✓	✓	✓	✓	✓	✓	✓	✓	✓	✓	✓	✓
	[high]	+	+	–	–	–	–	–	+	+	–	–	–
	[low]	–	–	–	–	+	–	–	–	–	–	–	+
	[back]	–	–	–	–	–	+	+	+	+	+	+	+
	[tense]	+	–	+	–	–	–	–	+	–	+	–	+
	[reduced]	–	–	–	–	–	+	–	–	–	–	–	–

*Note: While [a] and [ɑ] are phonetically different, in English they have the same phonological features because they are not contrastive—and remember, central vowels (like [ə]) are [+back]. For languages in which they contrast phonemically, the two sounds would have distinct feature specifications.

Table 3.31 illustrates how an individual sound can be described and distinguished through a full **feature matrix**. However, as Table 3.31 also shows, we will often abbreviate the matrix to include only the salient features for a particular problem or language. In English, since all vowels are [–consonantal, +syllabic, +sonorant, +continuant, +voice], we may use V to stand for these features shared by all English vowels. Furthermore, in the specific example in Table 3.31, the abbreviated matrix leaves out [–low] since a [+high] vowel is by definition [–low]. Similarly, we do not include [–reduced] since the features [+high, –back, +tense] together preclude the possibility that the vowel is a schwa.

Table 3.31 Feature matrix for [i]

Full feature matrix [i]	Abbreviated matrix [i]
–consonantal	V
+syllabic	DORSAL
+sonorant	+high
+continuant	–back
+voice	+tense
DORSAL	
+high	
–low	
–back	
+tense	
–reduced	

4   Derivations and Rules

As explained in Section 1, the segments making up words can be associated with two different types of representations. On the one hand, there are phonological representations, consisting of phonemes, which contain just information about contrasts. On the other hand, there are phonetic representations, made up of allophones, which contain a great deal of additional information about the details of pronunciation.

> *tab*
> /tæb/   ← Phonological representation (shows contrasts only)
> [tʰæ:b] ← Phonetic representation (shows details of pronunciation)

As already noted, one way to understand the difference between the two representations is to say that the **phonological representation** (also called the **underlying representation**) corresponds to what is in the mind while the phonetic representation corresponds to what comes out of the mouth. As we'll see next, general processes, often called **phonological rules**, apply to phonological representations to derive the phonetic representation by filling in the various predictable phonetic details that contribute to a word's actual pronunciation.

4.1   Derivations

When we apply phonological rules to the underlying representation, we can derive the phonetic representation. This is illustrated in Figure 3.15 (UR = underlying representation; PR = phonetic representation).

UR →	/tæp/ 'tap'	/pæd/ 'pad'	/slæp/ 'slap'
Aspiration	tʰæp	pʰæd	—
V-lengthening	—	pʰæ:d	—
PR →	[tʰæp]	[pʰæ:d]	[slæp]

Figure 3.15   The derivations of three English words

Two rules are at work in these examples of **derivations**. Aspiration applies to the syllable-initial voiceless stops in *tap* and *pad*, and vowel lengthening applies to the vowel in *pad*, which precedes a voiced obstruent in the same syllable. The end result—the phonetic representation—reflects the addition of predictable phonetic details to a less specific mental representation of the word.

Rule Application

The environments in which aspiration and vowel lengthening apply (onset and pre-coda position, respectively) are entirely different. The two rules therefore do not interact or affect each other in any way; the order in which they apply makes no difference to the outcome of the derivation. As Figure 3.16 shows, there is no difference in the outcome if the rules are applied in reverse order.

UR →	/tæp/ 'tap'	/pæd/ 'pad'
V-lengthening	—	pæːd
Aspiration	tʰæp	pʰæːd
PR →	[tʰæp]	[pʰæːd]

Figure 3.16 Aspiration and vowel lengthening applied in reverse order

We therefore say that the rules of aspiration and vowel lengthening are **unordered** with respect to each other.

In some cases, though, order matters because the application of one rule creates an environment that makes possible the application of another rule. One such case of **ordered rule application** involves the rule that devoices the liquids /l/ and /ɹ/ when they occur in a syllable onset right after a syllable-initial voiceless stop. (If you pronounce the words in *15* slowly while holding a finger on your larynx, you'll notice few if any vocal cord vibrations during the production of the liquid; vibrations don't begin in earnest until the start of the vowel. We ignore aspiration here.)

15) *pry* [pɹ̥aj] (compare to *rye*: [ɹaj])
  true [tɹ̥u] (compare to *rue*: [ɹu])
  claw [kl̥ɔ] (compare to *law*: [lɔ])
  etc.

In careful speech, the word *police* in English is pronounced [pəˈlis], but in colloquial speech the schwa in the first syllable is often deleted because it is unstressed and in an open syllable. This leaves the liquid /l/ directly after a voiceless stop, making it subject to the rule of liquid devoicing, as illustrated in Figure 3.17.

UR →	/pəlis/
Stress assignment	pəˈlis
Schwa deletion	ˈplis
Liquid devoicing	ˈpl̥is

Figure 3.17 Rule order in a derivation

The key steps here are boxed: the rule for assigning stress must apply before the rule for schwa **deletion**, since the deletion of schwa is sensitive to a word's stress pattern. And the rule of schwa deletion must apply before liquid devoicing, since the liquid occurs in a devoicing position only after the schwa has been deleted.

4.2   The Form of Rules

So far, we have been stating rules informally (e.g., a vowel is lengthened before a voiced obstruent in the same syllable). This is fine as a first step, but phonologists typically try to make rules more precise by stating them in a formal way, following the template in *16*.

16) A → B / X _____ Y

In this notation, *A* stands for the input to the rule (i.e., what we start with), *B* for the output of the rule (i.e., what we end with), and *X* and *Y* for the environment in which the rule applies. The slash separates the statement of the change from the statement of the conditioning environment, and can be thought of as meaning 'in the environment of'. The rule in *16* is therefore read as *A becomes B in the environment between X and Y*. (Some rules make reference only to the preceding environment and some only to the following environment, depending on which is relevant to the change.)

As an illustration of how all this works, we can translate our informal generalization about vowel lengthening as follows in *17*, with σ signifying a syllable boundary.

17) V → long / _____ voiced obstruent σ

The rule in *17* means: A vowel becomes long when it comes before a voiced obstruent at the end of a syllable.

At an even greater level of precision, rules are written using a combination of symbols and features to make explicit the natural classes of sounds to which the rule is sensitive as shown in *18*.

18) V → [+long] / ___ $\begin{bmatrix} +\text{cons} \\ -\text{syllabic} \\ -\text{sonorant} \\ +\text{voice} \end{bmatrix}$ σ

Another example of a formal rule involves the phenomenon of vowel nasalization, whose effects are heard in words such as [ɔ̃n] 'on' and [ɹũm] 'room', where a vowel comes right before a nasal consonant.

19) V → [nasal] / ___ $\begin{bmatrix} +\text{cons} \\ +\text{nasal} \end{bmatrix}$

This rule is particularly revealing: the [+nasal] feature is added to the vowel under the influence of the [+nasal] feature in the adjacent consonant.

Yet another example involves liquid devoicing, which we have been stating informally as follows.

20) Liquids become voiceless after syllable-initial voiceless stops.

We can now state this more formally as follows.

21) $\begin{bmatrix} +\text{cons} \\ +\text{sonorant} \\ -\text{syllabic} \\ -\text{nasal} \end{bmatrix}$ → [−voice] / σ $\begin{bmatrix} +\text{cons} \\ -\text{sonorant} \\ -\text{continuant} \\ -\text{DR} \\ -\text{voice} \end{bmatrix}$ ___

Using feature notation, this rule groups together the class of liquids (sounds that are [+consonantal, +sonorant, –syllabic, and –nasal], as outlined in Table 3.29), and states that they take on the [–voice] feature of a preceding syllable-initial stop. (As you can see by consulting Table 3.29, voiceless stops have in common the features [+consonantal, –sonorant, –continuant, –DR, and –voice].)

Deletion and Epenthesis as Rules

We have already seen that English speakers (optionally) drop a schwa [ə] in an open syllable when it is followed by a stressed syllable, as in *police* [pl̥is] and *parade* [pɹe:jd]. The rule can be formalized as in *22*.

22) Schwa deletion in English:

$$[ə] → Ø / C \underline{\quad} σ \quad C...V$$
$$[+stress]$$

Now consider the reverse process of **epenthesis**, which adds a vowel where previously there was none. This can happen when an impermissible syllable structure is encountered in a borrowed word, as in the English pronunciation of the name *Dmitri* [dəmitɹi] in which [ə] is used to break up the first two consonants. In addition, there are dialects of English that do not permit a coda consisting of [l] and another consonant. In these dialects, *milk* is pronounced [mɪlək] and *film* [fɪləm], in accordance with the following insertion rule.

23) Schwa insertion in English:

$$Ø → [ə] / [+lateral] \underline{\quad} \begin{bmatrix} +cons \\ -syllabic \end{bmatrix} σ$$

Summing Up

Phonology is the study of the contrasts and patterns that underlie the use of sounds to communicate meaning. The single most important unit in phonology is the **phoneme**, which consists of a group of phonetically similar sounds (its **allophones**) that do not contrast with each other but do contrast with other sounds. Phonemes are identified with the help of **minimal pairs**, while **complementary distribution** offers a key test for identifying allophones of the same phoneme.

Phonemes are grouped together into **syllables**, each consisting of a **nucleus** and (optionally, depending on the language) an **onset** and a **coda**. Many phonological phenomena, including a great deal of allophonic variation, are sensitive to syllable structure, as is rhyming in poetry.

Phonemes can be broken down into **features**, which help define **natural classes** of sounds that behave alike with respect to phonological processes such as aspiration, nasalization, vowel lengthening, and so on.

The relationship between a word's **phonological representation** and its **phonetic representation** can be captured by formal rules, stated in terms of features, which capture significant generalizations about a language's sound pattern.

Key Terms

General terms

feature   segment
phonology   syllable

Distinctive sounds and their variations

allophones   minimal pair
Canadian raising   near-minimal pairs
complementary distribution   phonemes
contrast   phonemic representation
environment   phonetic representation

Terms concerning syllable structure

association line   onset
Binarity Requirement   open syllable
closed syllable   phonotactics
coda   rhyme
devoicing   sonority
heavy syllable   sonority scale
light syllable   Sonority Requirement
nucleus   syllable weight

General terms concerning classes of sounds and features

binary features   feature matrix   sonorant
consonantal   natural classes   syllabic
distinctive feature   obstruents

Manner features

continuant   lateral
delayed release (DR)   nasal

Laryngeal features

constricted glottis (CG)   spread glottis (SG)   voice

Place features

anterior   high   round
back   LABIAL   strident
CORONAL   low   tense
DORSAL   reduced

Terms concerning rules, representations, and processes

deletion   phonological representation
derivations   phonological rules
epenthesis   underlying representation
ordered (rule application)   unordered (rule application)

Recommended Reading

Anderson, Stephen R. 1985. *Phonology in the Twentieth Century: Theories of Rules and Theories of Representations*. Chicago: University of Chicago Press.

Avery, Peter, B. Elan Dresher, and Keren Rice, eds. 2008. *Contrast in Phonology: Theory, Perception, Acquisition*. Berlin: Mouton de Gruyter.

Blevins, Juliette. 2004. *Evolutionary Phonology: The Emergence of Sound Patterns*. Cambridge: Cambridge University Press.

Carr, Philip. 1993. *Phonology*. London: Macmillan.

Goldsmith, John A., ed. 1999. *Phonological Theory: The Essential Readings*. Malden, MA: Blackwell.

Goldsmith, John, Jason Riggle, and Alan C. L. Yu, eds. 2011. *The Handbook of Phonological Theory*. 2nd ed. Hoboken, NJ: Wiley-Blackwell.

Odden, David. 2005. *Introducing Phonology*. Cambridge: Cambridge University Press.

Pellegrino, François, Egidio Marsico, Ioana Chitoran, and Christophe Coupé, eds. 2009. *Approaches to Phonological Complexity*. Berlin: Mouton de Gruyter.

Appendix: Hints for Solving Phonology Problems

The task of solving a phonology problem is made easier if certain facts presented in this chapter and summarized here are kept in mind.

1. In the following data from Tagalog (Filipino), a language spoken in the Philippines, consider the sounds [h] and [ʔ] and determine whether they contrast or are allophones of one phoneme.

a) kahon	'box'		d) ʔariʔ	'property'
b) hariʔ	'king'		e) daʔiŋ	'to complain'
c) ʔumagos	'to flow'		f) humangos	'to pant'

    In order to determine whether the sounds contrast, we begin by looking for minimal pairs. These establish which segments are contrastive. A minimal pair occurs in items b–d, and there is even a near-minimal pair in c–f. We therefore have very good evidence that [h] and [ʔ] contrast with each other and belong to separate phonemes.

2. Now consider the following data from Swampy Cree, a Native American language of the Algonquian family that is spoken in Canada. Determine whether the sounds [k] and [g] contrast or are allophones of one phoneme. (Note the symbol [ː] indicates that the preceding vowel is long.)

a) niska	'goose'		f) niːgi	'my house'
b) kodak	'another'		g) koːgoːs	'pig'
c) waskoːw	'cloud'		h) tahki	'often'
d) paskwaːw	'prairie'		i) ospwaːgan	'pipe'
e) oːgik	'these'		j) tʃiːgahigan	'axe'

    Since the data contain no minimal pairs that contrast [k] and [g] and because the two sounds are phonetically similar (both are velar stops), we suspect that they are allophones of the same phoneme and we must look to see whether they are in complementary distribution.

In checking to see whether two (or more) sounds are in complementary distribution, the best thing to do is to list the environments in which the sounds occur:

[g] occurs:	[k] occurs:
between two vowels (data in e, f, g, i, j)	word-initially (data in b, g)
	word-finally (data in b, e)
	after a consonant (data in a, c, d, h)

We quickly notice that the sounds occur in mutually exclusive environments; in other words the environments do not overlap. The sound [g] occurs between vowels, but [k] does not. In contrast, [k] appears elsewhere—word-initially, word-finally, and after a consonant, whereas [g] does not appear in these environments. We thus have complementary distribution, and we can conclude that the two sounds are allophones of the same phoneme.

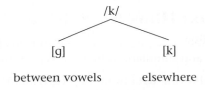

The key to this step in the analysis is to make the most general statements allowed by the data about the distribution of the individual allophones. So when you notice that [g] occurs between two [i]s in (f), between two [o]s in (g), between two [a]s in (i), and between [i] and a back vowel in (e) and (j), look for what all these environments have in common: in all cases, the [g] is between two vowels. Since [k] never occurs in this context and it only occurs elsewhere, then you have complementary distribution.

3. In a more advanced analysis, it is common to write a rule that will derive the appropriate allophone(s) from the underlying phoneme(s). Such a rule in this case would look like this:

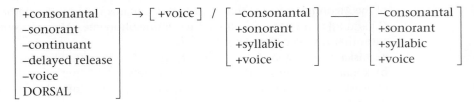

Because /k/ belongs to the natural class of voiceless stops, we might wonder whether the rule that applies to /k/ could also extend to other voiceless stops between vowels. For this, we need more data:

k) asaba:p 'thread' q) pimi: 'lard'
l) namwa:tʃ 'not at all' r) mide 'heart'
m) midʒihtʃij 'hand' s) tʃi:ma:n 'canoe'
n) nisto 'three' t) wa:bos 'rabbit'
o) adim 'dog' u) na:be:w 'man'
p) mi:bit 'tooth' v) mi:dʒiwin 'food'

In fact, we discover that not only does the voiceless velar stop become voiced between vowels, but so do the voiceless stops /p/ and /t/, as well as the voiceless affricate /tʃ/. We can then generalize our rule:

Voiceless stops and affricates become voiced between vowels.

Written with features, the rule would look like this:

$$
\begin{bmatrix} +\text{consonantal} \\ -\text{sonorant} \\ -\text{continuant} \\ -\text{voice} \end{bmatrix} \rightarrow \begin{bmatrix} +\text{voice} \end{bmatrix} \; / \; \begin{bmatrix} -\text{consonantal} \\ +\text{sonorant} \\ +\text{syllabic} \\ +\text{voice} \end{bmatrix} \underline{} \begin{bmatrix} -\text{consonantal} \\ +\text{sonorant} \\ +\text{syllabic} \\ +\text{voice} \end{bmatrix}
$$

Here's a flow chart that summarizes the analytic steps described above.

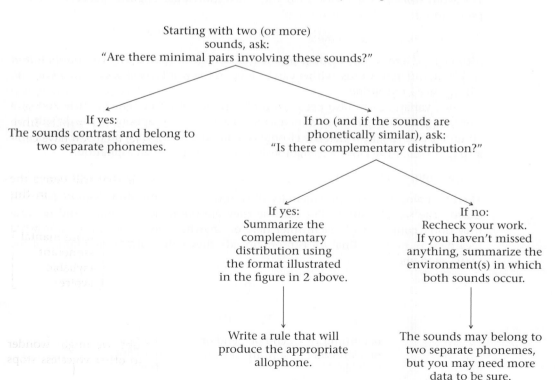

Starting with two (or more) sounds, ask:
"Are there minimal pairs involving these sounds?"

If yes:
The sounds contrast and belong to two separate phonemes.

If no (and if the sounds are phonetically similar), ask:
"Is there complementary distribution?"

If yes:
Summarize the complementary distribution using the format illustrated in the figure in 2 above.

If no:
Recheck your work. If you haven't missed anything, summarize the environment(s) in which both sounds occur.

Write a rule that will produce the appropriate allophone.

The sounds may belong to two separate phonemes, but you may need more data to be sure.

Hints for Solving Advanced Phonology Problems

In more advanced work (but not in the practice exercises that follow), you may have to deal with two additional factors—neutralization and free variation.

Neutralization involves the loss of a contrast between two phonemes in certain circumstances because of a shared allophone. For example, /t/ and /d/ are clearly distinct phonemes in English, as shown by minimal pairs such as *tie–die* and *mate–made*. Between vowels, however, both phonemes may be pronounced as the flap [ɾ]. This leads to the loss of the /t/–/d/ contrast in words such as *rating* and *raiding*, each of which is pronounced [rejɾɪŋ]. The resulting phonological system looks like this:

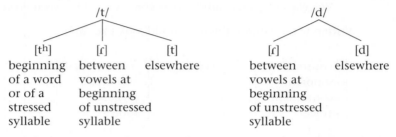

Free variation occurs when a single word has more than one pronunciation. The word *economics* is a case in point, since individual English speakers regularly pronounce it in either of two ways:

[ikənamɪks]   [ɛkənamɪks]

Although /i/ and /ɛ/ are distinct phonemes in English (that's why we interpret *beat* and *bet* as different words), either can be used in the word *economics* without creating a difference in meaning.

Free variation can also occur with allophones of a phoneme. At the end of a word, English stop consonants such as /p/ have several allophones—the default [p], an unreleased [p̚], in which the closure is maintained past the end of the word, and a [pʼ], in which the closure is vigorously released, with added aspiration.

stop: [stap], [stap̚], [stapʼ]

There's obviously no complementary distribution here—the three sounds occur in exactly the same position. But because they are phonetically similar and because they don't contrast with each other here or anywhere else (*stop* is the same word regardless of how the final /p/ is pronounced), they still count as allophones of the same phoneme.

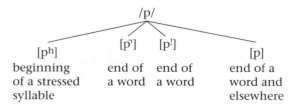

PHONOLOGY: CONTRASTS AND PATTERNS 111

Exercises

All data are presented using IPA.

1. *Korean* (Korean is the national language of Korea.)
   Consider the following data from Korean.

   a) pʰul   'glue'   f) pap   'food'
   b) pam   'night'   g) pʰal   'arm'
   c) sɨlpʰə 'sad'   h) apʰə   'hurt'
   d) pi   'rain'   i) pul   'fire'
   e) pʰjo   'ticket'   j) pan   'half'

   Do [p] and [pʰ] belong to separate phonemes in Korean or are they allophones of the same phoneme? Be sure to support your answers with reference to the presence or absence of minimal pairs. (See Section 1, especially 1.2.)

2. *Inuktitut* (Inuktitut is an indigenous language of Canada.)
   Consider the following data from Inuktitut. Note: [ː] after a consonant indicates that it is doubled.

   a) iglumut   'to a house'   f) pinːa   'that one up there'
   b) aniguvit   'if you leave'   g) ani   'female's brother'
   c) aglu   'seal's breathing hole'   h) iglu   '(snow)house'
   d) iglumit   'from a house'   i) panːa   'that place up there'
   e) anigavit   'because you leave'   j) ini   'place, spot'

   i)   Do [i] and [u] belong to separate phonemes in Inuktitut? What about [a] and [u]? What about [i] and [a]? Be sure to support your answers with reference to minimal pairs and/or complementary distribution (see Sections 1.2 and 1.3).

   Now consider the data again; here it is transcribed in narrower transcription. In it, there are phonetically similar segments that are in complementary distribution. Look for them and then answer the questions that follow the data.

   aa) iglumut   'to a house'   ff) pinːa   'that one up there'
   bb) aniguvit   'if you leave'   gg) anɪ   'female's brother'
   cc) aglʊ   'seal's breathing hole'   hh) iglʊ   '(snow)house'
   dd) iglumit   'from a house'   ii) panːa   'that place up there'
   ee) anigavit   'because you leave'   jj) inɪ   'place, spot'

   Review Sections 1.1 and 1.3. The sounds [ɪ] and [ʊ] are allophones of existing vowel phonemes.

   ii) Fill in the blanks in these sentences: [ɪ] is an allophone of the phoneme /___/. [ʊ] is an allophone of the phoneme /___/.

   iii) Using Figure 3.2 as a model, fill in the following diagrams with the respective phonemes and their elsewhere allophones. Fill in the information about the occurrence of [ɪ] and [ʊ]:

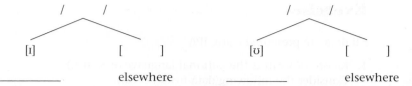

/   /   /   /

[ɪ]   [   ]   [ʊ]   [   ]

_____   elsewhere   _____   elsewhere

iv)   What features are shared by both the underlying phoneme of [ɪ] and the underlying phoneme of [ʊ]? What single feature distinguishes both [ɪ] from its underlying phoneme and [ʊ] from its underlying phoneme?

3. *Mokilese* (Mokilese is an Austronesian language of the South Pacific.)
   Examine the following data from Mokilese.

   a) pi̥san   'full of leaves'   g) uduk   'flesh'
   b) tu̥pu̥kta   'bought'   h) kaskas   'to throw'
   c) pu̥ko   'basket'   i) poki   'to strike something'
   d) ki̥sa   'we two'   j) pil   'water'
   e) su̥pwo   'firewood'   k) apid   'outrigger support'
   f) kamwɔki̥ti   'to move'   l) ludʒuk   'to tackle'

   Do [i] and [i̥] belong to separate phonemes, or are they allophones of the same phoneme? What about [u] and [u̥]?

   • If you decide that a pair of sounds represents separate phonemes, cite evidence from the data set to show that there are minimal pairs (see Section 1.2) or that the items in the pair occur in the same environment (see Section 1.5).
   • If you decide that the two sounds are allophones of one phoneme in complementary distribution, then describe the phonetic similarities of the two sounds and the mutually exclusive environments in which each sound occurs (see Sections 1.1 and 1.3). Use natural classes (Section 3.1) or features (Section 3.2) in your description.

4. *Hindi* (Hindi is an Indo-European language spoken in India.)
   Consider the segments [b] and [b̤] in the data below and answer the questions that follow. The segment transcribed [b̤] is a murmured voiced stop. (See Section 1, especially 1.5.)

   a) bara   'large'   f) b̤ɛd   'disagreement'
   b) b̤ari   'heavy'   g) bais   'twenty-two'
   c) bina   'without'   h) b̤əs   'buffalo'
   d) b̤ir   'crowd'   i) bap   'father'
   e) bori   'sackcloth'   j) b̤ag   'part'

   Are [b] and [b̤] allophones of the same phoneme, or do they belong to separate phonemes?

   • If you decide that a pair of sounds represents separate phonemes, cite evidence from the data set to show that there are minimal pairs (see Section 1.2) or that the items in the pair occur in the same environment (see Section 1.5).
   • If you decide that the two sounds are allophones of one phoneme in complementary distribution, then describe the phonetic similarities of the two sounds

and the mutually exclusive environments in which each sound occurs (see Sections 1.1 and 1.3). Use natural classes (Section 3.1) or features (Section 3.2) in your description.

5. *Gascon* (Gascon is spoken in southwestern France.)
Consider the following data from Gascon. Note: [β] is a voiced bilabial fricative; [ɣ] is a voiced velar fricative; [y] is a high front tense rounded vowel. A tilde over a segment means it is nasalized.

a)	brẽn	'endanger'	n)	gat	'cat'
b)	bako	'cow'	o)	lũŋg	'long'
c)	ũmbro	'shadow'	p)	saliβo	'saliva'
d)	krãmbo	'room'	q)	noβi	'husband'
e)	dilys	'Monday'	r)	aβe	'to have'
f)	dũŋko	'until'	s)	ʃiβaw	'horse'
g)	duso	'sweet'	t)	byðɛt	'gut'
h)	taldepãn	'leftover bread'	u)	eʃaðo	'hoe'
i)	pũnde	'to lay eggs'	v)	biɣar	'mosquito'
j)	dudze	'twelve'	w)	riɣut	'he laughed'
k)	guteʒa	'flow'	x)	agro	'sour'
l)	ẽŋgwãn	'this year'	y)	ʒuɣɛt	'he played'
m)	puðe	'to be able'			

Do [b] and [β] belong to different phonemes or are they allophones of the same phoneme? What about [d] and [ð]? And [g] and [ɣ]?

- If you decide that a pair of sounds represents separate phonemes, cite evidence from the data set to show that there are minimal pairs (see Section 1.2) or that the items in the pair occur in the same environment (see Section 1.5).
- If you decide that the two sounds are allophones of one phoneme in complementary distribution, then describe the phonetic similarities of the two sounds and the mutually exclusive environments in which each sound occurs (see Sections 1.1 and 1.3). Use natural classes (Section 3.1) or features (Section 3.2) in your description.

6. *Passamaquoddy* (Passamaquoddy is a Native American language of the Algonquian family spoken in Maine and New Brunswick.)
The following data from Passamaquoddy show a number of different voiced and voiceless consonants. Note: [kʷ] and [gʷ] are labiovelar stops.

a)	mɛtka	'he stops dancing'
b)	keguw	'all day'
c)	pak	'fib'
d)	altɛstagən	'wooden dish used in dice game'
e)	tʃibilkʷe	'he has epilepsy'
f)	padazikhal	'he makes him choke on smoke'
g)	kʷədagən	'his throat'
h)	kadʒiptun	'he takes it by hiding it'
i)	satkʷ	'300'
j)	ptəgʷap	'bag'

k)	wabɛjidʒik	'white men'
l)	hustiwin	'host'
m)	mitsut	'fork'
n)	hezis	'older brother'
o)	tabagən	'sled'
p)	əbəs	'tree'
q)	alkʷɛbu	'he sits around'
r)	əptan	'woman's coat'
s)	litpəzuwin	'tribal countil member'
t)	tʃiksədəmən	'he listens to it'

i)   Do [p] and [b] belong to separate phonemes or are they allophones of one phoneme?

- If they are separate phonemes, cite evidence from the data set to show that there are minimal pairs (see Section 1.2) or that the two sounds occur in the same environments (see Section 1.5).

- If they are allophones of the same phoneme in complementary distribution (Sections 1.1, 1.3), explain the ways in which they are phonetically similar. Then describe the environment in which each allophone occurs.

ii)   Do you expect your conclusions from i) to apply to the following pairs: [t] and [d]; [k] and [g]; [kʷ] and [gʷ]; [tʃ] and [dʒ]; and [s] and [z]? If your answer is *no*, explain why. If your answer is *yes*, explain why and write a rule using features to account for all the pairs of sounds (see Sections 3–4).

7. First, transcribe each of the following words; then using the syllabification procedure outlined in Section 2.2, draw the syllable structure for each word.

a) Hindi	c) praying	e) depth
b) resent	d) dinosaurs	f) explanation

8. *English*

Many speakers of English use two variants of [l]. One, called *clear l*, is transcribed as [l] in the following data. The other, called *dark l*, is transcribed as [ł]. Examine the data, and answer the questions that follow.

a)	lajf	'life'	e)	dilajt	'delight'	i)	hɛłp	'help'
b)	lip	'leap'	f)	slip	'sleep'	j)	bʌłk	'bulk'
c)	luːz	'lose'	g)	pʰɪł	'pill'	k)	sowłd	'sold'
d)	ilowp	'elope'	h)	fił	'feel'	l)	fʊł	'full'

Do [l] and [ł] belong to separate phonemes or are they allophones of the same phoneme? (See Section 1.) If you think they belong to separate phonemes, answer question i). If you think they are allophones of the same phoneme, answer questions ii) and iii).

i)   State the evidence that makes your case for treating [l] and [ł] as separate phonemes.

ii)   State the distribution of [l] and [ł] in words. (Hint: look at syllable structure and review Section 2.) Which variant makes the best underlying form? Why?

iii) If you have covered formal rule notation (Section 4), write the rule governing the distribution of *clear l* and *dark l*.

9. *Korean* (Korean is the national language of Korea.)
Consider the following data from Korean. Note: [ɨ] is a high mid unrounded vowel.

a) pi   'rain'
b) saŋdʒa   'box'
c) ta   'all'
d) ɨmak   'music'
e) page   'in the gourd'
f) tʃunbi   'preparation'
g) melda   'far'
h) madʒa   'correct'
i) tʃalba   'short'
j) puldʒirɨda   'set fire'
k) ipku   'entrance'
l) kɨktoro   'extremely'

m) kæ   'dog'
n) ip   'mouth'
o) tʃa   'ruler'
p) mat   'taste'
q) tʃogæ   'clam'
r) podo   'grape'
s) ibul   'comforter'
t) ilgə   'read'
u) kanda   'go'
v) paŋgɨm   'just now'
w) hakpu   'undergraduate school'

Do [p] and [b] belong to different phonemes or are they allophones of the same phoneme? What about [t] and [d]? [k] and [g]? [tʃ] and [dʒ]?

- If you decide that a pair of sounds represents separate phonemes, cite evidence from the data set to show that there are minimal pairs (see Section 1.2) or that the items in the pair occur in the same environment (see Section 1.5).
- If you decide that the two sounds are allophones of one phoneme in complementary distribution, then describe the phonetic similarities of the two sounds and the mutually exclusive environments in which each sound occurs (see Sections 1.1 and 1.3). Use natural classes (Section 3.1) or features (Section 3.2) in your description.

10. There are a number of natural classes in the vowel and consonant data below. Circle three natural classes in each set of data. Indicate which feature or features define the class, as in the example. The phone [x] is a voiceless velar fricative. (See Section 3.)

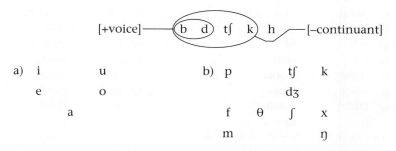

11. Name the single feature that distinguishes the sounds in each of the following pairs. (See Section 3.2 and Tables 3.29 and 3.30.)

a) θ : ð   e) b : m   i) ʌ : ə
b) p : f   f) s : ʃ   j) s : θ
c) u : ʊ   g) i : ɪ   k) e : ɛ
d) i : e   h) k : g   l) u : o

12. Complete the feature matrix for each of the sounds indicated. The V abbreviates the features [+syllabic, –consonantal], and the C abbreviates the features [–syllabic, +consonantal]. (See Section 3.2.)

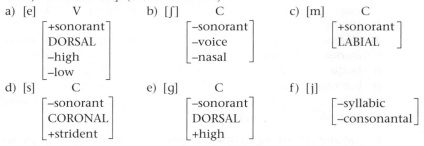

a) [e]   V
  ⎡ +sonorant ⎤
  ⎢ DORSAL   ⎥
  ⎢ –high   ⎥
  ⎣ –low   ⎦

b) [ʃ]   C
  ⎡ –sonorant ⎤
  ⎢ –voice   ⎥
  ⎣ –nasal   ⎦

c) [m]   C
  ⎡ +sonorant ⎤
  ⎣ LABIAL   ⎦

d) [s]   C
  ⎡ –sonorant ⎤
  ⎢ CORONAL   ⎥
  ⎣ +strident ⎦

e) [g]   C
  ⎡ –sonorant ⎤
  ⎢ DORSAL   ⎥
  ⎣ +high   ⎦

f) [j]
  ⎡ –syllabic   ⎤
  ⎣ –consonantal ⎦

13. *Canadian French*

In the following data from Canadian French, the sounds in each pair are in complementary distribution.

[i] and [ɪ] are allophones of one phoneme
[y] and [ʏ] are allophones of a second phoneme
[u] and [ʊ] are allophones of a third phoneme

The symbol [y] represents a high front rounded tense vowel while [ʏ] represents a high front rounded lax vowel.

Examine the data and answer the questions that follow.

a) pilʏl   'pill'   o) fini   'finished'
b) griʃe   'to crunch'   p) fɪj   'girl'
c) grɪʃ   'it crunches'   q) dzʏr   'hard'
d) pətsi   'little (masc.)'   r) tryke   'to fake'
e) pətsɪt   'little (fem.)'   s) fʊl   '(a) crowd'
f) vitamɪn   'vitamin'   t) plʏs   'more'
g) saly   'hi'   u) ru   'wheel'
h) ʒʏp   'skirt'   v) rʊt   'road'
i) fyme   'smoke'   w) suvã   'often'
j) lynɛt   'glasses'   x) trupo   'herd'
k) tɔrdzy   'twisted'   y) sʊp   'flexible'
l) lʏn   'moon'   z) tʊʃ   'touch'
m) pɪp   'pipe'   aa) fu   'crazy (masc.)'
n) grimas   'grimace'   bb) trʏk   '(a) trick'

i)   With the help of reference to syllable structure (Section 2), make a general statement about the distribution of [i] and [ɪ], [y] and [ʏ], [u] and [ʊ] in words.

ii) If you have completed the section on rule formalization (Section 4), write a single rule that derives the allophones of each phoneme from the underlying form. Use features! (Section 3.) Be sure to give your rule a name; use this name as you complete the derivations in iii.

iii) Provide derivations for the following underlying forms (see Section 4.1).

UR	/	/	'vitamin'	/	/	'glasses'
PR	[vitamɪn]			[lynɛt]		

14. *English*

The following data contains both careful speech and fast speech forms. Note the differences and answer the questions that follow. Some phonetic detail irrelevant to the question has been omitted from the transcription. Remember that an asterisk before a form indicates that it is not acceptable to (most) native speakers.

	Careful speech	*Fast speech*	*Spelled form*
a)	æspəɹən	æspɹ̩n	aspirin
b)	pɔɹsələn	pɔɹsl̩n	porcelain
c)	næʃənəlajz	næʃnəlajz	nationalize
d)	ɹizənəbl̩	ɹiznəbl̩	reasonable
e)	ɪmædʒənətɪv	ɪmædʒnətɪv	imaginative
f)	sɛpəɹəbɪlɪɾi	sɛpɹəbɪlɪɾi	separability
g)	mɛməɹajz	mɛməɹajz *mɛmɹajz	memorize
h)	kənsɪdəɹejʃn̩	kənsɪdəɹejʃn̩ *kənsɪdɹejʃn̩	consideration

i) The deletion of schwa in rapid speech is constrained by a number of factors, one of which is illustrated in the examples given. State the simple generalization that distinguishes the acceptable instances of deletion in a) to f) from the unacceptable ones in g) and h).

ii) If you have completed the section on rule formalization, state your generalization using formal notation. (See Section 4.)

15. Change the following statements into rule notation. Be sure to name the process in question for each case. (See Chapter 2, Section 9.3, for a discussion of phonetic processes and Chapter 3, Section 4, for rule notation.)
a) Voiceless stops become corresponding fricatives between vowels.
b) A schwa is inserted between a voiced stop and a word-final voiced fricative.
c) Low unrounded vowels become rounded before [m].

16. Change each of the following rules to a statement, making reference to natural classes and common linguistic processes (# marks a word boundary). (See Sections 3.2 and 4.2.)

Example: $\begin{bmatrix} +consonantal \\ -sonorant \\ -syllabic \end{bmatrix}$ → ø / _____ # (*An obstruent is deleted word-finally.*)

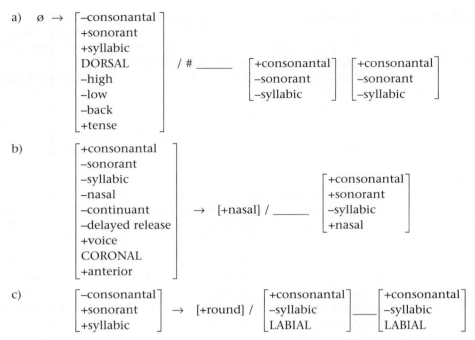

a) ø → [−consonantal, +sonorant, +syllabic, DORSAL, −high, −low, −back, +tense] / # _____ [+consonantal, −sonorant, −syllabic] [+consonantal, −sonorant, −syllabic]

b) [+consonantal, −sonorant, −syllabic, −nasal, −continuant, −delayed release, +voice, CORONAL, +anterior] → [+nasal] / _____ [+consonantal, +sonorant, −syllabic, +nasal]

c) [−consonantal, +sonorant, +syllabic] → [+round] / [+consonantal, −syllabic, LABIAL] _____ [+consonantal, −syllabic, LABIAL]

17. *Tamil* (Tamil is a Dravidian language spoken in southern India and Sri Lanka.) In the following Tamil data, some words begin with glides while others do not. The symbol [ɖ] represents a voiced retroflex stop and the diacritic [̪] indicates dentals.

Initial j-glide		*Initial w-glide*		*No initial glide*	
a) jeli	'rat'	f) woɖi	'break'	k) arivu	'knowledge'
b) jiː	'fly'	g) woːlaj	'palm leaf'	l) ai̪ntu	'five'
c) jilaj	'leaf'	h) wuːsi	'needle'	m) aːsaj	'desire'
d) jeŋgeː	'where'	i) wujir	'life'	n) aːru	'river'
e) jiɖuppu	'waist'	j) woːram	'edge'	o) aːdi	'origin'

i)   The occurrence of these glides is predictable. Using your knowledge of natural classes, make a general statement about the distribution of the glides. (See Section 3.)

ii) Assuming the glides are not present in the underlying representations, name the process that accounts for their presence in the phonetic forms. (See Section 4.2.)

For the Student Linguist

THE FEATURE PRESENTATION

You've already read that features are the fundamental building blocks of phonemes. By writing rules with features, you can describe simply a change that happens to an entire class of sounds. You also make a stronger statement when you use features in a rule. For example, rule *1* says something about all the stops in a language, but rule *2* only says something about a list of sounds.

1) [–continuant] → [–voice] / ___ #
   (stops become voiceless at the end of a word)
2) {p,t,k,b,d,g} → {p,t,k,p,t,k} / ___ #
   (p "becomes" p at the end of a word;
   b becomes p at the end of a word; etc.)

If you're just listing sounds, nothing requires them to have anything in common with each other. The sounds in the list could be a totally random selection of sounds turning into another totally random selection of sounds, as in rule *3*, and you'd have no way of predicting that *3* should be less common than *2*.

3) {e,t,w,b,n,h} → {ʃ,p,tʃ,g,a,m} / ___ #
   (e becomes ʃ at the end of a word; etc.)

If you use features, you can predict that the set of changes described by rule *2* should be common (because once the rule is translated to features, it's merely rule *1*, a delightfully simple rule), but the set of changes described by rule *3* should be weird and unlikely. To describe rule *3* with features, you'd have to write six different rules, and each rule would be ugly and complicated. (I'm assuming that the more features you have to include in a rule, the more complicated it is.) For example, the first rule, changing [e] to [ʃ], would be:

4) $\begin{bmatrix} -consonantal \\ +voice \\ -high \\ -low \\ -back \\ +tense \end{bmatrix} \rightarrow \begin{bmatrix} +consonantal \\ -voice \\ CORONAL \\ +continuant \\ +strident \\ -anterior \\ -delayed\ release \end{bmatrix}$ / ___ #

However, you can accept the brilliance of features without buying the idea of using a matrix of binary features (like you've done so far) or a hierarchy of binary features. Features could have only one value (these are called "monovalent" or "privative" features). So instead of, say, [–nasal] and [+nasal], there'd only be [nasal]. Sounds that had [nasal] in the matrix/representation would be nasal; everything else would be oral. How is that any different from using a binary feature? The difference is that with a binary feature, you can write rules about things that are [–nasal]. You could write a rule like this:

5) $\begin{bmatrix} \text{–continuant} \\ \text{–nasal} \end{bmatrix} \rightarrow \begin{bmatrix} \text{–voice} \end{bmatrix} / \underline{\quad} \#$
   (oral stops become voiceless at the end of a word)

But if [–nasal] didn't exist, the only rule you could write would be:

6) $\begin{bmatrix} \text{–continuant} \end{bmatrix} \rightarrow \begin{bmatrix} \text{–voice} \end{bmatrix} / \underline{\quad} \#$
   (all stops, including nasal stops, become voiceless at the end of a word)

If [–nasal] did exist, you could write rule *5 or* rule *6.* Monovalent features, then, give you fewer possible rules. That's great if you can still write all the rules you need for every language, but awful if you can't write every rule you need.

Having fewer possible rules isn't important just because it would make this unit of linguistics easier. It's also important because, theoretically, if there are fewer possible rules in a language, it's easier for a child trying to learn the language to figure out how the sound system in that language works. He or she has fewer options to consider.

What if features could have three values? Or four? Or an infinite number of values? For example, there could be four features for the different laryngeal states: [A laryngeal], for glottal stops; [B laryngeal], for voiced sounds; [C laryngeal], for voiceless unaspirated sounds; and [D laryngeal], for voiceless aspirated sounds. Just like nothing can be both [+voice] and [–voice] at the same time, nothing could be [A laryngeal] and [B laryngeal] at the same time (or [A laryngeal] and [C laryngeal], etc.). Place of articulation could be handled the same way: [A place] for labials, [B place] for dentals, [C place] for alveolars, etc.

With this type of multivalued system, none of the subgroups (like dentals and alveolars) could be lumped together in a rule. Thus, for the place system I described, you couldn't talk about all of the coronals at once—you could only talk abouf the dentals or the alveolars or the alveopalatals and so forth. Once again, whether this is good or bad depends on how well it describes actual languages. (You might want to try out a multivalued feature system for place on some of the phonology problems you've already solved for homework or in class discussions, and see if they're harder or easier to do this way than with a binary feature system.)

These are just a couple of the possible variations on feature systems. I haven't even begun to question the merit of these *features*—that is, do we *really* need [voice]? Or [strident]? Or [delayed release]? Think about this as you work on a few phonology problems, and see if you can come up with a better feature system. There's a lot of room for change here.

four

Morphology: The Analysis of Word Structure

William O'Grady
Videa de Guzman

Carve every word before you let it fall.
—OLIVER WENDELL HOLMES, SR., *Urania: A Rhymed Lesson (1846)*

OBJECTIVES

In this chapter, you will learn:

- how we analyze the structure of words
- how we form words by adding prefixes, suffixes, and infixes
- how we form words by putting two or more existing words together
- how we mark words to show grammatical concepts such as number, case, agreement, and tense
- how we form words by other processes
- how the processes of word formation interact with phonology

 **LaunchPad Solo** | For more helpful content and quizzes, go to the LaunchPad Solo
macmillan learning | for *Contemporary Linguistics* at **launchpadworks.com**.

Nothing is more important to language than words. Unlike phonemes and syllables, which are simply elements of sound, words carry meaning. And unlike sentences, which are created as needed and then discarded, words are permanently stored in a speaker's mental dictionary, or lexicon. They are arguably the fundamental building blocks of communication.

The average high school student knows about sixty thousand basic words—items such as *read*, *language*, *on*, *cold*, and *if*, whose meaning cannot be predicted from their component parts. Countless other words can be constructed and comprehended by

---

LANGUAGE MATTERS   How Many Words Does English Have?

The *Oxford English Dictionary* (20 volumes), whose stated goal is to present all of English vocabulary "from the time of the earliest records to the present day," contains a total of 616,500 word forms. But no dictionary can ever be up to date, because new words and new uses of old words are being added to the language all the time. The *Oxford English Dictionary* offers quarterly updates (http://public.oed.com/the-oed-today/recent-updates-to-the-oed/), and the online *Urban Dictionary* (www.urbandictionary.com) adds hundreds of new definitions EVERY DAY!

Information from: The *Oxford English Dictionary*, 2nd ed. (1989).

---

the application of general rules to these and other elements. For example, any speaker of English who knows the verb *phish* ('fraudulently obtain sensitive information via e-mail') recognizes *phished* as its past tense form and can construct and interpret words such as *phisher, phishing,* and *unphishable.*

Linguists use the term **morphology** to refer to the part of the grammar that is concerned with words and word formation. As we will see, the study of morphology offers important insights into how language works, revealing the need for different categories of words, the presence of word-internal structure, and the existence of operations that create and modify words in various ways.

1   Words and Word Structure

As speakers of English, we rarely have difficulty segmenting a stream of speech sounds into words or deciding where to leave spaces when writing a sentence. What, though, is a word?

Linguists define the **word** as the smallest **free form** found in language. A free form is simply an element that does not have to occur in a fixed position with respect to neighboring elements; in many cases, it can even appear in isolation. Consider, for instance, the following sentence.

1) Dinosaurs are extinct.

We all share the intuition that *dinosaurs* is a word here and that the plural marker *-s* is not. But why? The key observation is that *-s* is not a free form: it never occurs in isolation and cannot be separated from the noun to which it belongs. (Elements that must be attached to something else are written here with a hyphen; an asterisk indicates unacceptability.)

2) *Dinosaur are -s extinct.

In contrast, *dinosaurs* is a word because it can occur both in isolation, as in example *3*, and in different positions within sentences, as in example *4*:

3) Speaker A: What creatures do children find most fascinating?
   Speaker B: Dinosaurs.

4) a. Paleontologists study *dinosaurs.*
   b. *Dinosaurs* are studied by paleontologists.
   c. It's *dinosaurs* that paleontologists study.

Some words—like *are*—normally do not occur in isolation. However, they are still free forms because their positioning with respect to neighboring words is not entirely fixed, as shown in *5*.

5) a. Dinosaurs *are* extinct.
   b. *Are* dinosaurs extinct?

1.1   Morphemes

Words have an internal structure consisting of smaller units organized with respect to each other in a particular way. The most important component of word structure is the **morpheme**, the smallest unit of language that carries information about meaning or function. The word *builder*, for example, consists of two morphemes: *build* (with the meaning 'construct') and *-er* (which indicates that the entire word functions as a noun with the meaning 'one who builds'). Similarly, the word *houses* is made up of the morphemes *house* (with the meaning 'dwelling') and *-s* (with the meaning 'more than one').

Some words consist of a single morpheme. For example, the word *tremble* cannot be divided into smaller parts (say, *tr* and *emble* or *t* and *remble*) that carry information about the word's meaning or function. Such words are said to be **simple words** and are distinguished from **complex words**, which contain two or more morphemes (see Table 4.1).

Table 4.1   Words consisting of one or more morphemes

One	Two	Three	More than three
and			
couple	couple-s		
hunt	hunt-er	hunt-er-s	
act	act-ive	act-iv-ate	re-act-iv-ate

Free and Bound Morphemes

A morpheme that can be a word by itself is called a **free morpheme**, whereas a morpheme that must be attached to another element is a **bound morpheme**. The morpheme *boy*, for example, is free because it can be used as a word on its own; plural *-s*, however, is bound.

Concepts that are expressed by free morphemes in English do not necessarily have the same status in other languages. For example, in Hare (an Athabaskan language spoken in Canada's Northwest Territories), morphemes that indicate body parts must always be attached to a morpheme designating a possessor, as shown in Table 4.2. (The diacritic [´] marks a high tone.)

Table 4.2   Some body part names in Hare

Without a possessor		With a possessor	
*fí	'head'	sefí	'my head'
*bé	'belly'	nebé	'your belly'
*dzé	'heart'	ʔedzé	'someone's heart/a heart'

In English, of course, body part names are free morphemes and do not have to be attached to another element.

Conversely, there are also some bound forms in English whose counterparts in other languages are free. The notion 'past' or 'completed' is expressed by the bound morpheme *-ed* in English (as in *I wash<u>ed</u> the car*, or *a wash<u>ed</u> car*), but by the free morpheme *lɛɛw* in Thai. As the following sentence shows, *lɛɛw* can even be separated from the verb by an intervening word. (Tone is not marked here.)

6) Boon   thaan   khaaw   lɛɛw.
   Boon   eat   rice   PAST
   'Boon ate rice.'

Allomorphs

The variant pronunciations of a morpheme are called its **allomorphs**. The morpheme used to express indefiniteness in English has two allomorphs—*an* before a word that begins with a vowel sound and *a* before a word that begins with a consonant sound.

7) an orange   a building
   an accent   a car
   an eel   a girl

Note that the choice of *an* or *a* is determined on the basis of pronunciation, not spelling, which is why we say <u>an</u> *M.A. degree* and <u>a</u> *U.S. dollar*.

Another example of allomorphic variation is found in the pronunciation of the plural morpheme *-s* in the following words.

8) cats
   dogs
   judges

Whereas the plural is /s/ in *cats*, it is /z/ in *dogs*, and /əz/ in *judges*. Here again, selection of the proper allomorph is dependent on phonological facts. (For more on this, see Section 6.)

Yet another case of allomorphic variation is found in the pronunciation of the prefix *in-*, with the meaning 'not'. The final consonant is pronounced as /n/ in most cases—*indirect*, *inactive*, and so on. But it is pronounced as /m/ in front of another labial consonant (*impossible*, *immodest*), as /l/ in front of another /l/ (*illegal*), and as /ɹ/ in front of another /ɹ/ (*irregular*). These changes are easy to spot because of the spelling, but remember that allomorphic variation involves pronunciation. In some cases, this is reflected in the spelling, but in other cases (such as plural *-s*), it is not.

1.2 Analyzing Word Structure

In order to represent the internal structure of words, it is necessary not only to identify each of the component morphemes but also to classify them in terms of their contribution to the meaning and function of the larger word.

Roots and Affixes

Complex words typically consist of a **root** morpheme and one or more **affixes**. The root constitutes the core of the word and carries the major component of its meaning. Roots typically belong to a **lexical category**, such as noun (N), verb (V), adjective (A), or preposition (P).

Unlike roots, affixes do not belong to a lexical category and are always bound morphemes. For example, the affix *-er* is a bound morpheme that combines with a verb such as *teach*, giving a noun with the meaning 'one who teaches'. The internal structure of this word can be represented in Figure 4.1. (*Af* stands for affix.)

Figure 4.1   The internal structure of the word *teacher*

LANGUAGE MATTERS   Having Trouble Figuring Out a Word's Category?

Here are some traditional rules of thumb that you may have learned in school:

- Nouns typically refer to people and things (*citizen*, *tree*, *intelligence*, etc.).
- Verbs tend to denote actions, sensations, and states (*depart*, *teach*, *melt*, *remain*, etc.).
- Adjectives usually name properties (*nice*, *red*, *tall*, etc.).
- Prepositions generally encode spatial relations (*in*, *near*, *under*, etc.).

These traditional rules of thumb can suffice for now, but in Chapter 5 we will look at how to categorize words in a more sophisticated way.

Figure 4.2 provides some additional examples of word structure.

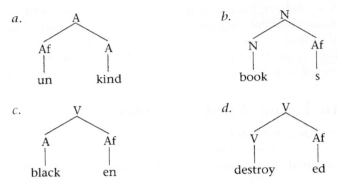

Figure 4.2 Some other words with an internal structure consisting of a root and an affix

The structural diagrams in Figures 4.1 and 4.2 are often called **trees**. The information they depict can also be represented by using labeled bracketing—[$_A$ [$_{Af}$ un] [$_A$ kind]] for *unkind* and [$_N$ [$_N$ book] [$_{Af}$ s]] for *books*. (This is somewhat harder to read, though, and we will generally use tree structures in this chapter.) Where the details of a word's structure are irrelevant to the point being considered, it is traditional to use a much simpler system of representation that indicates only the location of the morpheme boundaries: *un-kind*, *book-s*, and so on.

Bases

A **base** is the form to which an affix is added. In many cases, the base is also the root. In *books*, for example, the element to which the affix *-s* is added corresponds to the word's root. In other cases, however, the base can be larger than a root, which is always just a single morpheme. This happens in words such as *blackened*, in which the past tense affix *-ed* is added to the verbal base *blacken*—a unit consisting of the root morpheme *black* and the suffix *-en*.

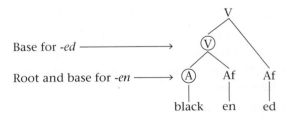

Figure 4.3 A tree diagram illustrating the difference between a root and a base

In this case, *black* is not only the root for the entire word but also the base for *-en*. The unit *blacken*, however, is simply the base for *-ed*.

Types of Affixes

An affix that is attached to the front of its base is called a **prefix**, whereas an affix that is attached to the end of its base is termed a **suffix**. Both types of affix occur in English, as shown in Table 4.3.

Table 4.3   Some English prefixes and suffixes

Prefixes	Suffixes
de-activate	faith-*ful*
re-play	govern-*ment*
il-legal	hunt-*er*
in-accurate	kind-*ness*

We will consider the nature and properties of English affixes in more detail in Sections 2.1 and 4.1.

Far less common than prefixes and suffixes are **infixes**, a type of affix that occurs within another morpheme. The data in Table 4.4 from the Philippine language Tagalog contains examples of the infix *-in-*, which is inserted after the first consonant of the root to mark a completed event.

Table 4.4   Examples of the Tagalog infix *-in-*

Base		Infixed form	
bili	'buy'	b-*in*-ili	'bought'
basa	'read'	b-*in*-asa	'read' (PAST)
sulat	'write'	s-*in*-ulat	'wrote'

Beginning students sometimes think that a morpheme such as *-en* in *black-en-ed* is an infix since it occurs between two other morphemes (*black* and *-ed*), but this is not right: *-en* is a suffix that combines with the adjective *black* to give the verb *blacken*, to which the suffix *-ed* is then added (see Figure 4.3). To be an infix, an affix must occur *inside* another morpheme (as when Tagalog *-in-* appears inside *sulat* 'write'). Nothing of this sort happens in the case of *-en*.

A very special type of infixing system is found in Arabic and other Semitic languages, in which a typical root consists simply of three consonants. Various combinations of vowels are then inserted among the consonants to express a range of grammatical contrasts. (In the examples that follow, the segments of the root are written in boldface.)

9) **kataba**   **kutib**   **aktub**
   'wrote'   'has been written'   'am writing'

One way to represent the structure of such words is as follows, with the root and affixal vowels assigned to different **tiers**, or levels of structure, that combine with each other to give the word's pronunciation (see Figure 4.4).

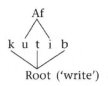

Figure 4.4 Two tiers used to represent the structure of the infixed word meaning 'has been written' in Arabic

Tagalog and Arabic offer examples of **nonconcatenative morphology**, in that words are not always built in the linear, additive fashion illustrated by English words such as *travel-er-s* and *creat-iv-ity*.

Problematic Cases

The majority of complex words in English are built from roots that are free morphemes. In the words *re-do* and *treat-ment*, for example, the root (*do* and *treat*, respectively) can itself be used as a word. Because most complex words work this way in English, English morphology is said to be **word-based morphology**.

There is no such requirement in morpheme-based systems. In Japanese and Spanish, for instance, verbal roots are always bound and can therefore not stand alone: *camin* is not a word in Spanish, *arui* is not a word in Japanese, and so on.

10) a. Spanish

camin-ó	**escuch**-ó	**limpi**-ó
walk-PAST	listen-PAST	wipe-PAST

b. Japanese

arui-ta	**kii**-ta	**hui**-ta
walk-PAST	listen-PAST	wipe-PAST

English too has a sizeable number of bound roots. For example, the word *unkempt* seems to consist of the prefix *un-* (with the meaning 'not') and the root *kempt* (meaning 'groomed' or 'combed'), even though *kempt* cannot be used by itself. *Kempt* was once a word in English (with the meaning 'combed'), and it was to this base that the affix *un-* was originally attached. However, *kempt* later disappeared from the

---

LANGUAGE MATTERS   Word Play

The following excerpt from the humorous essay "How I Met My Wife" by Jack Winter plays on the fact that certain English roots are bound and cannot be used as words:

> I was **furling** my **wieldy** umbrella for the coat check when I saw her standing alone in the corner. She was a **descript** person, a woman in a state of total **array**. Her hair was **kempt**, her clothing **shevelled**, and she moved in a **gainly** way. (From *The New Yorker*, July 25, 1994).

language, leaving behind the word *unkempt*, in which an affix appears with a bound root.

Still other words with bound roots were borrowed into English as whole words. *Inept*, for instance, comes from Latin *ineptus*, 'unsuited'. Its relationship to the word *apt* may have been evident at one time, but it now seems to consist of a prefix meaning 'not' and a bound root.

Another class of words that are problematic for morphological analysis includes items such as *receive, deceive, conceive*, and *perceive*, or *permit, submit*, and *commit*. These items were borrowed into English from Latin (usually via French) as whole words, and their component syllables have no identifiable meaning of their own. Unlike the *in-* of *inept*, which retains the meaning of negation, the *re-* of *receive* does not have the sense of 'again' that it does in *redo*, and no specific meaning can be assigned to *-ceive* or *-mit*. For this reason, we will not treat these word parts as morphemes.

2 Derivation

Derivation uses an affix to build a word with a meaning and/or category distinct from that of its base. One of the most common derivational affixes in English is the suffix *-er*, which combines with a verb to form a noun with the meaning 'one who Vs' as shown in Table 4.5. (Do not confuse this suffix with the *-er* that applies to a noun in cases such as *New Yorker* and *islander* or the *-er* that combines with an adjective in cases such as *taller* and *smarter*.)

Table 4.5 The derivational affix *-er*

Verb base	Derived noun
sell	sell-er (one who sells)
write	writ-er (one who writes)
teach	teach-er (one who teaches)
sing	sing-er (one who sings)
think	think-er (one who thinks)

Other examples of derivation include *treatment*, in which the suffix *-ment* combines with the verb *treat* to give the noun *treatment*; *unkind*, in which the prefix *un-* combines with the adjective *kind* to give a new adjective with a different meaning; and the other derived words illustrated in Figure 4.5.

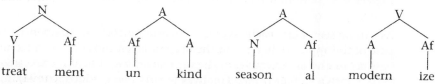

Figure 4.5 Some words formed by derivation

Once formed, derived words become independent lexical items that receive their own entry in a speaker's mental dictionary. As time goes by, they often take on special senses that are not predictable from the component morphemes. The word *writer*, for example, is often used not just for someone who can write but rather for someone who writes for a living (e.g., *She's a writer*); *comparable* (with stress on the first syllable) means 'similar' rather than 'able to be compared'; *profession* usually denotes a career rather than the act of professing; and so on.

2.1   Some English Derivational Affixes

Table 4.6 provides a partial list of English derivational affixes, along with information about the category of their usual base (ignoring bound roots) and of the resulting derived word. The entry for *-able*, for example, states that it applies to a verb base and converts it into an adjective. Thus, if we add the affix *-able* to the verb *fix*, we get an adjective (with the meaning 'able to be fixed').

The category of the base to which an affix attaches is sometimes not obvious. In the case of *worker*, for instance, the base (*work*) is sometimes used as a verb (as in *They work hard*) and sometimes as a noun (as in *The work is time-consuming*). How then can we know the category of the base for *-er*? The key is to find words such as *teacher* and *writer*, in which the category of the base can be unequivocally determined. Because *teach* and *write* can only be verbs, we can infer that the base with which *-er* combines in the word *worker* is also a verb.

Complex Derivations

Since derivation can apply to a word more than once, it is possible to create words with multiple layers of internal structure, as in the following example.

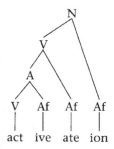

Figure 4.6   A word with a multilayered internal structure

As can be seen here, each layer of structure reflects the attachment of an affix to a base of the appropriate type. In the deepest layer, the affix *-ive* attaches to the verbal base *act* to give an adjective. In the next layer, *-ate* attaches to the adjective and converts it into a verb (*activate*). Finally, the affix *-ion* is added, converting the verb into the noun *activation*.

Table 4.6 Some English derivational affixes

Affix	Change	Examples
Suffixes:		
-able	V → A	fix-able, do-able, understand-able
-ing₁	V → A	the sleep-ing giant, a blaz-ing fire
-ive	V → A	assert-ive, impress-ive, restrict-ive
-al	V → N	refus-al, dispos-al, recit-al
-ant	V → N	claim-ant, defend-ant
-(at)ion	V → N	realiz-ation, assert-ion, protect-ion
-er	V → N	teach-er, work-er
-ing₂	V → N	the shoot-ing, the danc-ing
-ment	V → N	adjourn-ment, treat-ment, amaze-ment
-dom	N → N	king-dom, fief-dom
-ful	N → A	faith-ful, hope-ful, dread-ful
-(i)al	N → A	president-ial, nation-al
-(i)an	N → A	Arab-ian, Einstein-ian, Minnesot-an
-ic	N → A	cub-ic, optimist-ic, moron-ic
-less	N → A	penni-less, brain-less
-ous	N → A	poison-ous, lecher-ous
-ize₁	N → V	hospital-ize, vapor-ize
-ish	A → A	green-ish, tall-ish
-ate	A → V	activ-ate, captiv-ate
-en	A → V	dead-en, black-en, hard-en
-ize₂	A → V	modern-ize, national-ize
-ly	A → Adv	quiet-ly, slow-ly, careful-ly
-ity	A → N	stupid-ity, prior-ity
-ness	A → N	happi-ness, sad-ness
Prefixes:		
anti-	N → N	anti-hero, anti-depressant
ex-	N → N	ex-president, ex-wife, ex-friend
de-	V → V	de-activate, de-mystify
dis-	V → V	dis-continue, dis-obey
mis-	V → V	mis-identify, mis-place
re-	V → V	re-think, re-do, re-state
un-₁	V → V	un-tie, un-lock, un-do
in-	A → A	in-competent, in-complete
un-₂	A → A	un-happy, un-fair, un-intelligent

In some cases, the internal structure of a complex word may not be so transparent. The word *unhappiness*, for instance, could apparently be analyzed in either of the ways indicated in Figure 4.7. However, by considering the properties of the affixes *un-* and *-ness*, it is possible to determine that the structure in Figure 4.7a is the right one. The key observation is that the prefix *un-* combines quite freely with adjectives but not with nouns, as shown in Table 4.7.

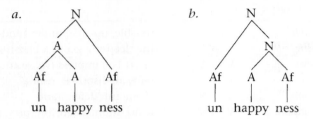

Figure 4.7 Two possible structures for the word *unhappiness*

Table 4.7 The prefix *un-*

un + A	un + N
unable	*unknowledge
unkind	*unhealth
unhurt	*uninjury

This suggests that *un-* must combine with the adjective *happy* before it is converted into a noun by the suffix *-ness*, exactly as depicted in Figure 4.7a.

By contrast, in a word such as *unhealthy*, the prefix *un-* can be attached only AFTER the suffix has been added to the root. That is because *-y* turns nouns into adjectives (as in *wealthy* and *cloudy*), creating the category of word with which *un-* can combine (see Figure 4.8).

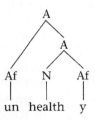

Figure 4.8 The internal structure of the word *unhealthy*

Constraints on Derivation

Derivation is often subject to special constraints and restrictions. For instance, the suffix *-ant* (see Table 4.6) can combine with bases of Latin origin, such as *assist* and *combat*, but not with those of native English origin, such as *help* and *fight*. Thus, we find words such as *assistant* and *combatant* but not **helpant* and **fightant*.

In other cases, derivation may be blocked by the existence of an alternative word. For instance, the word *cooker* in American English (to mean 'one who cooks') is blocked by the existence of the word *cook*, which already has that meaning; *famosity* (from *famous*) is blocked by *fame*; and so on.

Sometimes, a derivational affix is able to attach only to bases with particular phonological properties. A good example of this involves the suffix -en, which can combine with some adjectives to create verbs with a causative meaning as shown in Table 4.8 (*whiten* means roughly 'cause to become white').

Table 4.8 Restrictions on the use of *-en*

Acceptable	Unacceptable
whiten	*abstracten
soften	*bluen
madden	*angryen
quicken	*slowen
liven	*greenen

The contrasts illustrated here reflect the fact that *-en* can be attached only to a monosyllabic base that ends in a consonant other than /l/, /ɪ/, /m/, or /n/. Thus, it can be added to *white*, *quick*, *mad*, and *live*, which are monosyllabic and end in a consonant of the right type. But it cannot be added to *abstract*, which has more than one syllable; to *slow* or *blue*, which end in a vowel; or to *green*, which ends in the wrong type of consonant.

2.2   Two Classes of Derivational Affixes

It is common to distinguish between two types of derivational affixes in English. **Class 1 affixes** often trigger changes in the pronunciation of the base's consonants and vowels, and may affect stress placement as well. In addition, they often combine with bound roots, as in the last of the examples in Table 4.9.

Table 4.9 Typical effects of Class 1 affixes

Affix	Sample word	Change triggered by affix
-ity	san-ity; public-ity	vowel in the base changes from /e/ to /æ/ (cf. *sane*), final consonant of the base changes from /k/ to /s/, stress shifts to second syllable (cf. 'public vs. pub'licity)
-y	democrac-y	final consonant of the base changes from /t/ to /s/, stress shifts to second syllable (cf. 'democrat vs. de'mocracy)
-ive	product-ive	stress shifts to second syllable (cf. 'product vs. pro'ductive)
-(i)al	part-ial	final consonant of the base changes from /t/ to /ʃ/ (cf. *part* vs. *partial*)
-ize	critic-ize	final consonant of the base changes from /k/ to /s/ (cf. *critic* vs. *criticize*)
-ion	nat-ion	final consonant of the base changes from /t/ to /ʃ/ (cf. *native* vs. *nation*)

In contrast, **Class 2 affixes** tend to be phonologically neutral, having no effect on the segmental makeup of the base or on stress placement (see Table 4.10).

Table 4.10 Some typical Class 2 affixes

Affix	Sample word	Change triggered by affix
-ness	prompt-ness	None
-less	hair-less	None
-ful	hope-ful	None
-ly	quiet-ly	None
-er	defend-er	None
-ish	self-ish	None

As the following examples illustrate, a Class 2 affix cannot intervene between the root and a Class 1 affix.

11) relat-ion-al   divis-ive-ness   *fear-less-ity   fear-less-ness
    ROOT 1 1   ROOT 1 2   ROOT 2 1   ROOT 2 2

Notice that all combinations of Class 1 and Class 2 affixes are found in English words, except one—a Class 2 suffix followed by a Class 1 suffix.

3 Compounding

Another common technique for word building in English involves **compounding**, the combination of two already existing words (see Figure 4.9). With very few exceptions, the resulting **compound word** is a noun, a verb, or an adjective. (Possible examples of compound prepositions include the words *into* and *onto*.)

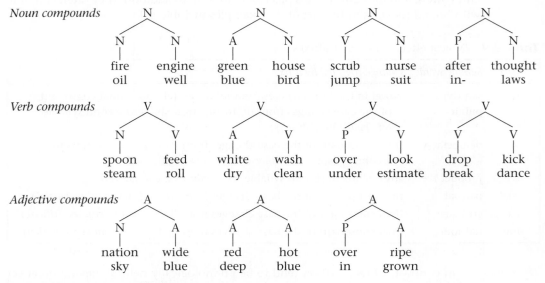

Figure 4.9 Some English compounds

In the most common type of English compound, the rightmost morpheme determines the category of the entire word. Thus, *bluebird* is a noun because its rightmost component is a noun, *spoonfeed* is a verb because *feed* also belongs to this category, and *nationwide* is an adjective just as *wide* is. The morpheme that determines the category of the entire word is called the **head**.

Once formed, compounds can be combined with other words to create still larger compounds, as the examples in Figure 4.10 show.

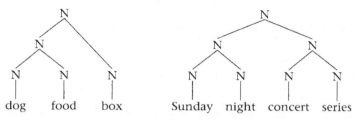

Figure 4.10   Compounds formed from smaller compounds

In addition, compounding can interact with derivation, yielding forms such as *abortion debate*, in which the first word in the compound is the result of derivation, as shown in Figure 4.11.

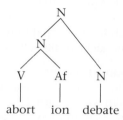

Figure 4.11   The interaction of derivation with compounding

Compounding is an inexhaustible source of new words in English, as can easily be seen by perusing the new-word updates offered by Oxford Dictionaries Online. Additions for 2013 included the following items, among many others.

Table 4.11   Some new compounds recognized by Oxford Dictionaries Online in 2013

New compound	Meaning
bitcoin	a digital currency
buzzworthy	likely to arouse public interest and attention
cake pop	a piece of cake on a stick
digital detox	refraining from using electronic devices
hackerspace	a community-operated workspace where people with common interests can socialize and collaborate
space tourism	travel to space for recreational purposes

3.1   Properties of Compounds

English orthography is not consistent in representing compounds, which are sometimes written as single words, sometimes with a hyphen, and sometimes as separate words. In terms of pronunciation, however, an important generalization can be made (see Table 4.12): adjective–noun compounds are characterized by more prominent stress on their first component. In noncompounds consisting of an adjective and a noun, in contrast, the second element is generally stressed.

Table 4.12   Compounds versus noncompounds

Compound word		Noncompound expressions	
'greenhouse	'a glass-enclosed garden'	green 'house	'a house painted green'
'blackboard	'a chalkboard'	black 'board	'a board that is black'
'wet suit	'a diver's costume'	wet 'suit	'a suit that is wet'

A second distinguishing feature of compounds in English is that tense and plural markers can typically not be attached to the first element, although they can be added to the compound as a whole. (There are some exceptions, however, such as *craftsman* and *parks supervisor*.)

12) a. Compound verb with internal tense:
       *The player [dropped kick] the ball through the goal post.
     b. Compound verb with external tense:
       The player [drop kick]ed the ball through the goal post.

13) a. Compound noun with internal plural:
       *The [ducks hunter] didn't have a license.
     b. Compound noun with external plural (different meaning):
       The [duck hunter]s didn't have a license.

LANGUAGE MATTERS   Do You Say Brothers-in-Law or Brother-in-Laws?

Is it *attorneys-general* or *attorney-generals*? *Maids-of-honor* or *maid-of-honors*? *Runners-up* or *runner-ups*? There is now variation on this point. For some people, at least some expressions of this type have become compounds, which is why the plural marker cannot occur inside, as it once had to.

3.2   Endocentric and Exocentric Compounds

In most cases, a compound denotes a subtype of the concept denoted by its head (the rightmost component). Thus, *dog food* is a type of food, a *caveman* is a type of man, *sky blue* is a type of blue, and so on. Such compounds are said to be (semantically) **endocentric compounds**. In a smaller number of cases, however, the meaning of the compound does not follow from the meaning of its parts in this way. Thus, although *redneck* is a noun (like *neck*), it denotes a type of person, not a type of neck. Similarly, a *hot dog* is a type of meat rather than a type of dog. Such compounds are **exocentric compounds**.

A very striking difference between English endocentric and exocentric compounds sometimes shows up in cases where the head is a word like *tooth* or *foot*, which has an irregular plural form. Consider in this regard the examples in Table 4.13.

Table 4.13 Pluralization in English compounds

In endocentric compounds	*In exocentric compounds*
wisdom t<u>ee</u>th	saber-t<u>oo</u>ths (an extinct species of carnivore)
club f<u>ee</u>t	bigf<u>oo</u>ts (a mythical creature, Sasquatch)
police<u>me</u>n	Watch<u>ma</u>ns (a type of portable TV)
oak lea<u>ve</u>s	Maple Leaf<u>s</u> (Toronto's NHL hockey team)

Notice that whereas the endocentric compounds employ the usual irregular plural (*teeth*, *feet*, etc.), the exocentric compounds permit the regular plural suffix *-s*.

3.3 Compounds in Other Languages

The practice of combining words (especially nouns) to build a more complex word is very widespread in the languages of the world. With the exception of Tagalog, in which compounds are left-headed, the languages exemplified in Table 4.14 all have compounds in which the rightmost element is the head. In right-headed Korean, for example, the head of *kot elum* 'icicle' is *elum* 'ice' since icicles are a type of ice, and the head of the *nwun mwul* 'tears' is *mwul* 'water' since tears are a type of water. In left-headed Tagalog, in contrast, the head of *tubig-alat* 'sea water' is *tubig* 'water' since sea water is a type of water, and in *bayad-utang* 'debt payment', the head is *bayad* 'payment' since a debt payment is a type of payment.

Table 4.14 Noun compounds in various languages

Korean		
kot elum	isul pi	nwun mwul
straight ice	dew rain	eye water
'icicle'	'drizzle'	'tears'
Tagalog		
tubig-alat	isip-lamok	bayad-utang
water salt	mind mosquito	payment debt
'sea water'	'weak mind'	'debt payment'
German		
Gast-haus	Wort-bedeutungs-lehre	Fern-seher
guest-house	word-meaning-theory	far-seer
'inn'	'semantics'	'television'

Table 4.14 Continued

Finnish		
lammas-nahka-turkki	elin-keino-tulo-vero-laki	
sheep-skin-coat	life's-means-income-tax-law	
'sheepskin coat'	'income tax law'	

Cree		
mishtikw naapeu	piyesuu upiiwiih	ishkuteu utaapan
wood man	duck feather	fire vehicle
'carpenter'	'duck feather'	'train'

Data from: East Cree Compound Nouns: http://www.eastcree.org/cree/en/grammar/southern-dialect/word-formation/noun-structure/compound-nouns-a1/.

4 Inflection

Virtually all languages have contrasts such as singular versus plural and present versus past. Such contrasts are often marked with the help of **inflection**, the modification of a word's form to indicate grammatical information of various sorts. (The base to which an inflectional affix is added is sometimes called a **stem**.)

4.1 Inflection in English

Inflection is most often expressed via **affixation**, and many languages (e.g., Japanese, Swahili, Inuktitut, and Finnish) have dozens of inflectional affixes. With only eight inflectional affixes (all suffixes), English is not a highly inflected language. Table 4.15 lists the inflectional affixes of English.

Table 4.15 The English inflectional affixes

Nouns	
Plural -*s*	the book<u>s</u>
Possessive (genitive) -*'s*	John<u>'s</u> book

Verbs	
3rd person singular nonpast -*s*	He read<u>s</u> well.
Progressive -*ing*	He is work<u>ing</u>.
Past tense -*ed*	He work<u>ed</u>.
Past participle -*en/-ed*	He has eat<u>en</u>/studi<u>ed</u>.

Adjectives	
Comparative -*er*	the small<u>er</u> one
Superlative -*est*	the small<u>est</u> one

Although most inflection in English involves affixation, some words mark inflectional contrasts in other ways. This is most obvious in the case of verbs, a number of which indicate past tense by substituting one form with another (as in *am-was* or *go-went*) or by internal changes of various sorts (*come-came*, *see-saw*, *fall-fell*, *eat-ate*). We will consider these processes in more detail in Section 5.

4.2   Inflection versus Derivation

Because inflection and derivation are both commonly marked by affixation, the distinction between the two can be subtle. Four criteria are commonly used to help distinguish between inflectional and derivational affixes.

Category Change

Inflection does not change either the syntactic category or the type of meaning found in the word to which it applies, as shown in Figure 4.12.

Figure 4.12   The output of inflection: there is no change in either the category of the base or the type of meaning it denotes

The form produced by adding the plural suffix *-s* in Figure 4.12a is still a noun and has the same type of meaning as the base. Even though *hearts* differs from *heart* in referring to several things rather than just one, the type of thing(s) to which it refers remains the same. Similarly, a past tense suffix such as the one in Figure 4.12b indicates that the action took place in the past, but the word remains a verb and it continues to denote the same type of action.

In contrast, derivational suffixes usually change the category and/or the type of meaning of the form to which they apply. Consider the examples of derivation given in Figure 4.13.

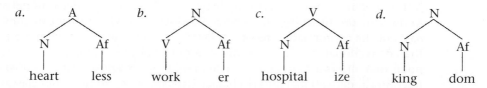

Figure 4.13   The output of derivation: there is a change in the category of the base and/or the type of meaning it denotes

As Figure 4.13a shows, *-less* makes an adjective out of a noun, changing the type of meaning it expresses from a thing (*heart*) to a property (*heartless*). Parallel changes in category and type of meaning are brought about by *-er* (V to N) and *-ize* (N to V). Matters are a little different in the case of *-dom*, which does not bring about a category change in the word *kingdom* since both the base and the resulting word are nouns. However, *-dom* does modify the type of meaning from a person (*king*) to a place (*kingdom*).

It should be noted here that the suffixes *-ing* and *-en/-ed*, which were introduced in Table 4.15 as inflectional affixes, can also function as derivational suffixes. The suffix *-ing* can change a verb to a noun, as in *the singing of the choir*. Both *-ing* and *-en/-ed* can change a verb to an adjective, as in *the sleeping giant, a broken record*, or *the escaped convict*.

Order

A second property of inflectional affixes has to do with the order in which they are combined with a base relative to derivational affixes. As Figure 4.14 illustrates, a derivational affix must combine with the base before an inflectional affix does (IA = inflectional affix; DA = derivational affix).

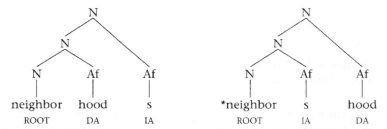

Figure 4.14   The relative positioning of derivational and inflectional affixes: the derivational affix must be closer to the root

The positioning of inflectional affixes outside derivational affixes in these examples reflects the fact that inflection applies to the output of derivation.

Productivity

A third criterion for distinguishing between inflectional and derivational affixes has to do with **productivity**, the relative freedom with which they can combine with bases of the appropriate category. Inflectional affixes are typically more productive than derivational affixes. The suffix *-s*, for example, can combine with virtually any noun that allows a plural form (aside from a few exceptions such as *oxen* and *feet*). In contrast, derivational affixes characteristically apply to restricted classes of bases. Thus, *-ize* can combine with only certain adjectives to form a verb.

14) modern-ize   *new-ize
        legal-ize   *lawful-ize
        final-ize   *last-ize

In the case of verbs, matters are somewhat more complicated, since many English verbs have irregular past tense forms (*saw, left, went,* and so on). Nonetheless, the inflectional affix *-ed* is much more generally applicable than a derivational affix such as *-ment*. All the verbs in Table 4.16 can take the regular past tense ending, but only those in the top three rows are able to take the *-ment* suffix.

Table 4.16 Compatibility of verb bases with inflectional *-ed* and derivational *-ment*

Verb	With *-ed*	With *-ment*
confine	confined	confinement
align	aligned	alignment
treat	treated	treatment
arrest	arrested	*arrestment
straighten	straightened	*straightenment
cure	cured	*curement

Semantic Transparency

Finally, the contribution of an inflectional affix to the word's meaning is usually completely transparent and consistent. Adding a plural suffix gives the meaning 'more than one' (*cat-cats, tree-trees*), adding a past tense suffix gives the meaning 'prior to the present' (*walk-walked, play-played*), and so forth.

Things are not always so straightforward in the case of derivation, where it is often not possible to predict the word's meaning from its parts. An *actor* is someone who acts, but a *professor* is not someone who professes. The word *teacher* often refers to someone who holds a teaching job, but no such implication is associated with *walker*. *Government* can be used to refer either to an institution (as in *the government's agenda*) or the act of governing (as in *government by the people*), but *abandonment* lacks the first type of meaning.

4.3   Other Inflectional Phenomena

Inflection is a very widely used morphological process, and its effects can be seen in far more cases than can be discussed here. Nonetheless, two additional phenomena are worth mentioning, however briefly, because of their importance and frequency in languages of the world.

Case inflection indicates a word's grammatical role in the sentence (subject, direct object, and so on). A very simple example of this can be seen in English, where the pronoun form *he* is used for subjects and the form *him* is employed for direct objects. There is a comparable contrast between *I* and *me, she* and *her, we* and *us,* and *they* and *them*.

15) *He* met the new professor.   The new professor met *him*.
    ↑   ↑
  subject   direct object

Agreement takes place when one word is inflected to match certain grammatical properties of another word. Especially common is agreement for number (singular vs. plural) and for person (first person—speaker; second person—addressee; third person—anyone else). Here again, English offers a simple example: the suffix *-s* appears on a present tense verb when the subject is third person singular.

16) That woman speak<u>s</u> French.

(Compare: *I speak French* or *They speak French*, with no *-s* suffix.)

5   Other Morphological Phenomena

No introductory textbook can hope to offer a full survey of the processes that contribute to word formation in human language. The preceding sections have touched upon many of the most common and central processes, but a number of others merit consideration as well. We will divide these into two groups—those that pertain primarily to inflection and those that involve other sorts of phenomena.

5.1   Processes Primarily Related to Inflection

Internal Change

Internal change is a process that substitutes one nonmorphemic segment for another to mark a grammatical contrast, as illustrated in the following pairs of words in Table 4.17.

Table 4.17   Internal change in English

s<u>i</u>ng (present)	s<u>a</u>ng (past)
s<u>i</u>nk (present)	s<u>a</u>nk (past)
dr<u>i</u>ve (present)	dr<u>o</u>ve (past)
f<u>oo</u>t (singular)	f<u>ee</u>t (plural)
g<u>oo</u>se (singular)	g<u>ee</u>se (plural)

Verbs such as *sing*, *sink*, and *drive* form their past tense by changing the vowel (e.g., from *i* to *a* in the first two examples). The term **ablaut** is often used for vowel alternations that mark grammatical contrasts in this way.

Some internal changes reflect phonologically conditioned alternations from an earlier stage in the language's history. The irregular plurals *geese* and *feet* came about in this way: the original back vowel /o/ in the words *goose* and *foot* was fronted under the influence of the front vowel in the old plural suffix /i/, which was subsequently dropped. This type of change in English and other Germanic languages is known as **umlaut**.

17) Old singular form of *goose*: /gos/
      Old plural form: /gos-i/
      Umlaut: /gœs-i/(/œ/ is a mid front rounded vowel)
      Loss of the plural suffix: /gœs/
      Other changes: /ges/ and then /gis/ 'geese'

Internal change differs from infixing in important ways. As shown by the Tagalog examples in Table 4.4, the base into which an infix is inserted typically exists as a separate form elsewhere in the language (compare *sulat* 'write' with *s-in-ulat* 'wrote'). Matters are quite different in the case of alternations such as *foot/feet* or *sing/ sang* in English, since we have no form *ft* meaning 'lower extremity of the leg' or *sng* meaning 'produce words in a musical tone'. Moreover, in contrast to the situation in Tagalog, the segments that alternate when there is internal change are not systematically associated with a particular meaning and therefore do not count as morphemes: the *a* of *ran* and the *o* of *drove* do not in general carry the meaning 'past' in English any more than the *ee* of *geese* normally carries the meaning 'plural'.

Suppletion

Suppletion replaces a morpheme with an entirely different morpheme in order to indicate a grammatical contrast. Examples of this phenomenon in English include the use of *went* as the past tense form of the verb *go*, and *was* and *were* as the past tense forms of *be*. (See Table 4.18 for examples of suppletion in some other European languages.)

Table 4.18 Suppletion in some European languages

Language	Basic form	Suppletive form
French	*aller* 'to go'	*ira* '(s/he) will go'
Spanish	*ir* 'to go'	*fue* '(s/he) went'
German	*ist* 'is'	*sind* 'are'
Russian	*xorošij* 'good'	*lučše* 'better'

In some cases, it is hard to distinguish between suppletion and internal change. For example, are the past tense forms of *think* (*thought*) and *seek* (*sought*) instances of suppletion or internal change? This type of alternation is sometimes treated as an extreme form of internal change, but the term **partial suppletion** is also used by some linguists.

Reduplication

A common morphological process in some languages involves **reduplication**, which marks a grammatical or semantic contrast by repeating all or part of the base to which it applies. Repetition of the entire base yields **full reduplication**, as in the data from Turkish and Indonesian given in Table 4.19.

Table 4.19   Examples of full reduplication

Base		Reduplicated form	
Turkish (in Turkish orthography)			
çabuk	'quickly'	çabuk çabuk	'very quickly'
yavaş	'slowly'	yavaş yavaş	'very slowly'
iyi	'well'	iyi iyi	'very well'
güzel	'beautifully'	güzel güzel	'very beautifully'
Indonesian (in Indonesian orthography)			
orang	'man'	orang orang	'men'
anak	'child'	anak anak	'children'
mangga	'mango'	mangga mangga	'mangoes'

In contrast, **partial reduplication** copies only part of the base. In the data from Tagalog in Table 4.20, for instance, reduplication affects the first consonant-vowel sequence rather than the entire word.

Table 4.20   Examples of partial reduplication in Tagalog

Base		Reduplicated form	
takbo	'run'	tatakbo	'will run'
lakad	'walk'	lalakad	'will walk'
pili	'choose'	pipili	'will choose'

English makes limited use of partial reduplication in various semi-idiomatic expressions such as *hocus pocus*, *razzle dazzle*, and *nitty gritty*, but this process does not mark grammatical information and is not productive.

Tone Placement

In Mono-Bili (spoken in the Congo), **tone placement** is used to make the distinction between past and future tense. (A high tone is marked by [´] and a low tone by [`] in Table 4.21.)

Table 4.21   Past and future tense in Mono-Bili

Past		Future	
dá	'spanked'	dà	'will spank'
zí	'ate'	zì	'will eat'
wó	'killed'	wò	'will kill'

5.2 Other Processes

Cliticization

Some morphemes behave like words in terms of their meaning and function but are unable to stand alone as independent forms for phonological reasons. Called **clitics**, these elements must always be pronounced with another word (known as a **host**). A good example of this can be found in English, where certain verb forms have reduced variants (*'m* for *am*, *'s* for *is*, and *'re* for *are*) that cannot stand alone. Cliticization occurs, attaching these elements to the preceding word.

18) a. I*'m* leaving now.
  b. Mary*'s* going to succeed.
  c. They*'re* here now.

Cliticization is also common in French, which has a set of unstressed clitic object pronouns that must be attached to the verb. The two are then pronounced as if they formed a single word.

19) Jean *t*'aime.   Suzanne *les* voit.
   John you-likes   Suzanne them-sees
   'John likes you.'   'Suzanne sees them.'

Clitics that attach to the end of their host (as in the English examples) are called **enclitics**; those that attach to the beginning of their host (as in the French examples) are known as **proclitics**.

The effects of cliticization can bear a superficial resemblance to affixation: in both cases, a morpheme that cannot stand alone is attached to a word belonging to a syntactic category, such as a noun or a verb.

Conversion

Conversion is a process that assigns an already existing word to a new syntactic category. Even though it does not add an affix, conversion is often considered to be a type of derivation because of the change in category and meaning that it brings about. For this reason, it is sometimes called **zero derivation**. Table 4.22 contains examples of the three most common types of conversion in English.

Table 4.22 Examples of conversion

V derived from N	N derived from V	V derived from A
ink (a contract)	(a long) run	dirty (a shirt)
butter (the bread)	(a hot) drink	empty (the box)
ship (the package)	(a pleasant) drive	better (the old score)
nail (the top down)	(a brief) report	right (a wrong)
button (the shirt)	(an important) call	total (a car)

Information from: Laurie Bauer, *English Word Formation* (New York: Cambridge University Press, 1983), pp. 229–31, and John Jensen, *Morphology: Word Structure in Generative Grammar* (Amsterdam: John Benjamins Publishing, 1990), pp. 92–93.

Less common types of conversion can yield a noun from an adjective (*the poor, gays*) and even a verb from a preposition (*down a beer, up the price*).

A notorious recent example of conversion involves the use of the noun *friend* as a verb to mean 'add someone as a friend on a social networking website', making it distinct from the already existent word *befriend*, which refers to a more conventional social relationship. The transition to verbhood in this case is confirmed by the appearance of derived words such as *unfriend* and *defriend*, created with the help of prefixes used for other verbs in the language (*untie, deactivate*).

Conversion is usually restricted to words containing a single morpheme, although there are some exceptions, such as *refer-ee* (noun to verb) and *dirt-y* (adjective to verb). In addition, it is common in English to form nouns from verb + preposition combinations—a *toss-up*, a *slowdown*, a *dropout*, and so on. The result is a **headless compound**—the category of the entire word (noun) cannot be traced to either of its component parts.

Conversion in two-syllable words is often accompanied by stress shift in English. As the examples in Table 4.23 show, the verb has stress on the final syllable while the corresponding noun is stressed on the first syllable. (Stress is represented here by ['].)

Table 4.23   Stress shift and conversion of two-syllable words

Verb	Noun
im'plant	'implant
im'port	'import
pre'sent	'present
sub'ject	'subject
con'test	'contest
slow 'down	'slowdown

Clipping

Clipping is a process that shortens a polysyllabic word by deleting one or more syllables. Some of the most common products of clipping are names—*Liz, Ron, Rob, Sue*, and so on. Clipping is especially popular in casual speech, where it has yielded forms

LANGUAGE MATTERS   Some Cases of Clipping That Might Surprise You

zoo < zoological garden

fax < facsimile

fan (as in sports) < fanatic

flu < influenza

van < caravan

mob < mobile vulgus (Latin, for 'fickle crowd')

like *prof* for *professor*, *psych* for *psychology*, *doc* for *doctor*, and *burger* for *hamburger*. However, many clipped forms have also been accepted in general usage: *app*, *ad*, *auto*, *lab*, *sub*, *deli*, *porn*, *demo*, and *condo*.

An interesting recent clip is *blog*, from *Web log*—a personal website-based log of events, comments, and links. Once formed, *blog* quickly appeared in compounds (*blog archive*, *blogosphere*) and has undergone conversion to a verb (as in 'things to blog about'). The verb, in turn, has undergone derivation, resulting in the noun *blogger*. No wonder *blog* was voted the new word most likely to succeed at the 2003 meeting of the American Dialect Society!

Blending

Blending creates words from nonmorphemic parts of two already existing items, usually the first part of one and the final part of the other. Recent innovations of this type include *froyo* (from *frozen yogurt*), *wi-fi* (from *wireless* and *hi-fi*), and *bromance* (from *brother* and *romance*). Older and perhaps more familiar examples include *brunch* from *breakfast* and *lunch*, *smog* from *smoke* and *fog*, *motel* from *motor* and *hotel*, *telethon* from *telephone* and *marathon*, *Chunnel* (for the tunnel under the Channel between Britain and France) from *channel* and *tunnel*, and *infomercial* from *information* and *commercial*.

Blending is commonly used to create names for crossbred animals:

20) a. lion + tiger > liger, tigon
     b. zebra + donkey > zedonk, zonkey
     c. camel + llama > cama
     d. grizzly + polar bear > grolar, pizzly

Another type of blend, common in languages of Asia, is strongly syllable-oriented: two or more words each contribute a syllable to the blend.

21) a. Tagalog
       tap-si-log < tapa sinangag itlog
       breakfast combination (from 'dried meat – fried rice – egg')
     b. Malay
       pulada < pusat latihan darat
       army training camp (from 'center – training – army')

Sometimes, a word is formed by a process that is on the borderline between compounding and blending in that it combines all of one word with part of another. Examples of this in English include *e-mail*, *perma-press*, *workaholic*, *medicare*, *guesstimate*, and *Amerindian*. Even *blog* has managed to participate in this process—*blogma* is a blend of *blog* and *dogma*.

Backformation

Backformation is a process that creates a new word by removing a real or supposed affix from another word in the language. *Resurrect* was originally formed in this way from *resurrection*. Other backformations in English include *enthuse* from *enthusiasm*, *donate* from *donation*, and *self-destruct* from *self-destruction*.

LANGUAGE MATTERS   Some Words That Originated as Blends

Some words become part of the language without its users having any idea of their origin. For example, all of the following words began as blends.

bit (unit of information in computer science) < binary + digit

modem < modulator + demodulator

pixel < picture + element

quasar < quasi + stellar

chortle < chuckle + snort

spam (the sandwich meat) < spiced + ham

Sometimes, backformation involves an incorrect assumption about a word's form: for example, the word *pea* was derived from the singular noun *pease*, whose final /z/ was incorrectly interpreted as the plural suffix.

Words that end in *-or* or *-er* have proven very susceptible to backformation in English. Because hundreds of such words are the result of affixation (*runner, walker, collector,* etc.), any word with this shape is likely to be perceived as a verb + *-er* combination. The words *editor, peddler,* and *swindler* were reanalyzed in just this way, resulting in the creation of the verbs *edit, peddle,* and *swindle,* as shown in Table 4.24.

Table 4.24   Some examples of backformation

Original word	Reanalysis	Verb formed by backformation
editor	edit + or	edit
peddler	peddle + er	peddle
swindler	swindle + er	swindle

Two relatively recent backformations are *lase* and *tase*, from *laser* and *taser*, respectively, each of which have their own unusual origin (see "Acronyms and Initialisms" on the next page).

LANGUAGE MATTERS   Word of the Year for 2013

Every year, Oxford Dictionaries picks a "word of the year." The winner for 2013 was *selfie*—a root-plus-suffix combination that refers to a photo that one has taken of oneself, usually with a smart phone. Runner-ups included *showrooming* (a suffixed compound that describes the practice of examining a product in a store before buying it at a lower price online) and *twerk* (dance to popular music in a sexually provocative manner)—a word that Oxford lexicographers think may be a blend of *twist* or *twitch* and *work*.

Backformation continues to produce new words in modern English—*aggress* (from *aggression*), *allegate* (from *allegation*), *liaise* (from *liaison*), *administrate* (from *administration*), *claustrophobe* (from *claustrophobia*), and *liposuct* (from *liposuction*) have all been derived in this way.

Acronyms and Initialisms

Acronyms are formed by taking the initial letters of (some or all) the words in a phrase or title and pronouncing them as a word. This type of word formation is especially common in names of organizations and in military and scientific terminology. Common examples include *UNICEF* for United Nations International Children's Emergency Fund, *NATO* for North Atlantic Treaty Organization, and *AIDS* for acquired immune deficiency syndrome. More recent innovations include *MOOC* (massive open online course), *YOLO* (you only live once), *FOMO* (fear of missing out), and *BOGO* (buy one, get one [free]).

Acronyms are to be distinguished from **initialisms** such as *DC* for District of Columbia or *USA* for United States of America, not to mention *BYOB* for bring your own booze, all of which are pronounced as a series of letters rather than as a word. An intermediate case is *CD-ROM*, a compound consisting of the initialism *CD* (compact disk) and the acronym *ROM* (read-only memory).

Some words enter the language as acronyms without speakers' knowledge of their origins, perhaps because they sound similar to other words in the language or because they have been in the language for more than one generation. Four commonly used words of this type are *radar* (from radio detecting and ranging), *scuba* (self-contained underwater breathing apparatus), *laser* (light amplification by stimulated emission of radiation), and *taser* (named by its inventor after his hero, Tom Swift: Thomas A. Swift's electrical rifle)!

Onomatopoeia

All languages have some words that have been created to sound like the thing that they name. Examples of such **onomatopoeic words** in English include *buzz*, *hiss*, *sizzle*, and *cuckoo*. Since onomatopoeic words are not exact phonetic copies of noises, their form can differ from language to language, as shown in Table 4.25.

Table 4.25 Onomatopoeia across languages

English	Japanese	Tagalog
cock-a-doodle-doo	kokekokko	tik-tilaok
meow	njaa	ŋijaw
chirp	pii-pii	tiɾiɾit
bow-wow	wan-wan	aw-aw

English does not always have an equivalent for the onomatopoeic words found in other languages. The Athabaskan language Slavey, for instance, has the onomatopoeic word [sah sah sah] for 'the sound of a bear walking unseen not far from camp', [ðik] for 'the sound of a knife hitting a tree', and [tɬóòtʃ] for 'the sound of an egg splattering'.

Other Sources of New Words

Sometimes, a word may be created from scratch. Called **word manufacture** or **coinage**, this phenomenon is especially common in the case of product names, including *Kodak*, *Dacron*, *Orlon*, and *Teflon*. (Notice how the *on* of the final three words makes them sound more scientific, perhaps because an affix with this form occurs in science-related words of Greek origin such as *phenomenon* and *automaton*.)

New words can also sometimes be created from names, including those listed in Table 4.26. Words created in this way are called **eponyms**.

Table 4.26 Some English words created from names

Word	Name of the person
watt	James Watt (late 18th-century scientist)
curie	Marie and Pierre Curie (early 20th-century scientists)
Fahrenheit	Gabriel Fahrenheit (18th-century scientist)
boycott	Charles Boycott (19th-century land agent in Ireland who was ostracized for refusing to lower rents)

In still other cases, brand names can become so widely known that they are accepted as generic terms for the product with which they are associated. The words *kleenex* for 'facial tissue' and *xerox* for 'photocopy' are two obvious examples of this, as is the verb *google* in the sense of 'conduct an Internet search'.

Finally, languages frequently look to other languages for new words. English has always been open to **borrowing** of this sort, and the language continues to absorb new words from many different sources—*latte* from Italian, *feng shui* from Chinese, *jihad* from Arabic, and so forth.

LANGUAGE MATTERS   What's the Longest Word in English?

Is it

ANTIDISESTABLISHMENTARIANISM (28 letters)
('the belief that opposes removing the tie between church and state')?

Or is it

SUPERCALIFRAGILISTICEXPIALIDOCIOUS (34 letters)
('extremely wonderful' from the Disney movie *Mary Poppins*)?

Neither! The longest English word in any dictionary is

PNEUMONOULTRAMICROSCOPICSILICOVOLCANOCONIOSIS
(45 letters; also spelled <. . . koniosis>)
('a lung disease caused by breathing in particles of siliceous volcanic dust').

6 Morphophonemics

A word's pronunciation can be affected by morphological factors, including its internal structure. The study of these effects is known as **morphophonemics** (or **morphophonology**).

 A well-known example of a morphophonemic phenomenon in English involves the plural suffix -*s*, which can be /s/, /z/, or /əz/, depending on the context, as mentioned in Section 1.1.

22) lip/s/
 pill/z/
 judg/əz/

This alternation is, in part, the result of phonetic factors: voiceless /-s/ occurs after voiceless sounds (such as /p/), voiced /-z/ occurs after voiced sounds (such as /l/), and the /-əz/ form shows up only when a vowel is needed to break up a non-English consonant cluster (no English syllable ends with the coda /dʒz/). What makes the alternation morphophonemic is its interaction with two additional factors.

 First, the alternation involves separate phonemes—/s/ and /z/. In this, it differs from a purely phonetic alternation, such as aspiration of the /t/ in *top* but not *stop*, a variation that involves allophones of the same phoneme.

 Second, morphological structure matters. It is perfectly possible to have /s/ after /l/ in English when they are both in the same morpheme, as in the word *pulse*. But when the <s> represents the plural as it does in *pills*, and is therefore a separate morpheme, only /z/ is permitted. Alternations like this that occur specifically at morpheme boundaries are sometimes referred to as **sandhi**, a Sanskrit word used to describe similar phenomena in the languages of India, where morphophonological analysis was being done in the 4th century B.C.

 Another example of morphophonemic alternation, also mentioned in Section 1.1, involves the variant forms of the prefix *in-*, whose final consonant is /n/ in *inactive*, /m/ in *impossible*, /l/ in *illegal*, and /ɪ/ in *irregular*. Here again, the alternation involves distinct phonemes and is associated with a particular morpheme in a particular context. (The final consonant of the semantically similar prefix *un-* does not change to /l/ in *unlawful* or to /ɪ/ in *unreadable*.)

Summing Up

This chapter has focused on the structure and formation of **words** in human language. **Morphemes** are the basic building blocks for words. These elements can be classified in a variety of ways (**free** versus **bound**, **root** versus **affix**, **prefix** versus **suffix**) and can be combined and modified under various conditions to build words.

 The two basic types of word formation in English are **derivation** and **compounding**. **Inflection**, a change in the form of a word to convey grammatical information such as plurality or tense, can be expressed via **affixation**, **internal change**,

reduplication, and **tone placement**. Other important morphological phenomena include **cliticization, conversion, clipping, blending,** and **backformation**.

Key Terms

General terms

allomorphs	morpheme
bound morpheme	morphology
complex words	simple words
free form	word
free morpheme	

General terms concerning word structure

affixes	root
base	suffix
infixes	tiers
lexical category	trees
nonconcatenative morphology	word-based morphology
prefix	

Terms concerning derivation and compounding

Class 1 affixes	derivation
Class 2 affixes	endocentric compounds
compounding	exocentric compounds
compound word	head

Terms concerning inflection

ablaut	partial suppletion
affixation	productivity
agreement	reduplication
case	stem
full reduplication	suppletion
inflection	tone placement
internal change	umlaut
partial reduplication	

Other kinds of morphological phenomena

acronyms	enclitics
backformation	eponyms
blending	headless compound
borrowing	host
clipping	initialisms
cliticization	onomatopoeic words
clitics	proclitics
coinage	word manufacture
conversion	zero derivation

Terms concerning the interaction of morphology and phonology

morphophonemics   sandhi
morphophonology

Recommended Reading

Anderson, Stephen. 1988. "Morphological Theory." In *Linguistics: The Cambridge Survey*. Vol. 1. Edited by F. Newmeyer, 146–191. New York: Cambridge University Press.

Aronoff, Mark, and Kirsten Fudeman. 2010. *What Is Morphology?* 2nd ed. Boston: Wiley-Blackwell.

Bauer, Laurie. 2003. *Introducing Linguistic Morphology*. Washington, DC: Georgetown University Press.

Bauer, Laurie, Rochelle Lieber, and Ingo Plag. 2013. *The Oxford Reference Guide to English Morphology*. Oxford, UK: Oxford University Press.

Booij, Geert. 2005. *The Grammar of Words*. Oxford, UK: Oxford University Press.

Gleason, Henry Allan. 1955/1961. *An Introduction to Descriptive Linguistics*. New York: Holt, Rinehart and Winston.

Katamba, Francis. 1993. *Morphology*. London: Macmillan.

Pinker, Steven. 1999. *Words and Rules*. New York: Basic Books.

Appendix: How to Identify Morphemes in Unfamiliar Languages

An important part of morphological analysis involves identifying morphemes in unfamiliar languages and determining the nature of the information that they carry. (A number of the problems in the set of exercises at the end of this chapter will give you an opportunity to practice this type of analysis.) The key procedure for working on this sort of problem can be stated simply as follows:

- Identify recurring strings of sounds and match them with recurring meanings.

Consider in this regard the following small sample of data in Table 4.27 from Turkish, consisting of four words along with their English translations. (A more realistic data sample would not only be much larger but would also include sentences in which it might well be unclear where the word boundaries should be placed.)

Table 4.27   Some Turkish words

/mumlaɾ/	'candles'
/toplaɾ/	'guns'
/adamlaɾ/	'men'
/kitaplaɾ/	'books'

As you can probably see, the syllable /laɾ/ occurs in all four items in our sample. From the translations of these items, you can see that a particular feature of meaning—namely, plurality—is present in all four cases as well. Using the procedure just stated, we therefore hypothesize that /-laɾ/ is the morpheme marking plurality in Turkish. Once this has been determined, we can then infer that /mum/ in /mumlaɾ/ is also a morpheme (with the meaning 'candle'), that /top/ in /toplaɾ/ is a morpheme (with the meaning 'gun'), and so on. A larger sampling of Turkish data would confirm the correctness of these inferences.

In doing morphological analysis in unfamiliar languages, a number of pitfalls must be avoided. For the type of data normally investigated at the introductory level, the following guidelines are especially important.

- Do not assume that the morpheme order in the language you are analyzing is the same as in English. In Korean, for example, morphemes indicating location (the rough equivalent of 'at', 'in', and so forth) follow rather than precede the noun (*hakkyo-eyse* 'at school' is literally 'school at').

- Do not assume that every semantic contrast expressed in English will also be manifested in the language you are analyzing. Turkish, for instance, has no equivalent for English *the* and *a*. Mandarin has no *he-she* distinction: the same pronoun form can be used to refer to a male or a female.

- Conversely, do not assume that every contrast expressed in the language you are analyzing is manifested in English. For example, some languages distinguish more than two number categories (Inuktitut distinguishes singular, dual, and plural), and some languages make multiple tense contrasts (ChiBemba has an eight-way distinction).

- Remember that a morpheme can have more than one form, or allomorph. For example, further study of Turkish would reveal that the plural suffix in this language can also be realized as /-leɾ/, depending on the vowel in the base to which the suffix is attached.

Exercises

Note: Data from languages other than English is sometimes presented in transcribed form (in which case it appears between slashes) and sometimes in the native orthography or romanization.

1. Consider the following words and answer the questions below. (See Section 1.)

    a) fly   f) reuse   k) spiteful   p) preplan
    b) desks   g) triumphed   l) suite   q) optionality
    c) untie   h) delight   m) fastest   r) prettier
    d) tree   i) justly   n) deform   s) mistreat
    e) dislike   j) payment   o) disobey   t) premature

    i)   For each word, determine whether it is simple or complex.
    ii) Circle all the bound morphemes. Underline all the roots.

2. The following problem, from the Lukunosh dialect of Mortlockese (a language of Micronesia), was authored by Emerson Lopez Odango. Data are in orthography.

    Note: INCL = inclusive (the speaker and the addressee)
    EXCL = exclusive (the speaker and someone other than the addressee)
    PL = plural
    SG = singular

    a) ngiij   'my tooth'   e) ngiimam   'our (EXCL) tooth'
    b) ngiimw   'your (SG) tooth'   f) ngiimi   'your (PL) tooth'
    c) ngiin   'his/her/its tooth'   g) ngiir   'their tooth'
    d) ngiish   'our (INCL) tooth'

    i)   Identify the morpheme corresponding to each of the following:
         tooth _____   our (INCL) _____
         my _____   our (EXCL) _____
         your (SG) _____   your (PL) _____
         his/her/its _____   their _____

    ii) Given that the word for 'leg/foot' in Mortlockese is *peshe*, how would you say each of the following?
         your (SG) leg/foot _____
         his/her/its leg/foot _____
         our (EXCL) leg/foot _____

3. The following problem, from Irarutu (an Austronesian language spoken in West Papua, Indonesia) was authored by Jason Jackson. Data are in orthography.

    a) adena   'my mother'   i) ifra   'his/her hand'
    b) odena   'your mother'   j) atgrag   'my ear'
    c) idena   'his/her mother'   k) otgram   'your ear'
    d) ambamba   'my elder brother'   l) itgra   'his/her ear'
    e) ombamba   'your elder brother'   m) aftag   'my stomach'
    f) imbamba   'his/her elder brother' n) oftam   'your stomach'
    g) afrag   'my hand'   o) ifta   'his/her stomach'
    h) ofram   'your hand'

    i)   Irarutu has different strategies for expressing possession in the case of kinship and possession in the case of body parts. Based on the data above, identify the morphemes used to express each type of possession.

    ii) Given that *mce* means 'eye' and that *nfut* means 'younger sibling', how would you say each of the following in Irarutu?
         his/her younger sibling _____
         my eye _____
         his/her eye _____

4. Consider the following data from Kwakum, a Bantu language spoken in Cameroon.
    a) /sɛbɔmmɛ/   'We bought (a long time ago).'
    b) /sɛbɔmko/   'We bought (recently).'
    c) /sɛbɔmkowɛɛ/   'We did not buy (recently).'

d) /njebɔmmɛ/   'I bought (a long time ago).'
e) /ɔbɔmmɛ/   'You (SG) bought (a long time ago).'
f) /jebɔmko/   'They bought (recently).'
g) /nɛbɔmko/   'You (PL) bought (recently).'
h) /abɔmmɛwɛɛ/   'S/he did not buy (a long time ago).'

i) What are the Kwakum morphemes for each of the following concepts?

I ____   we ____
you (SG) ____   you (PL) ____
s/he ____   they ____
buy ____
negation (not) ____
recent past (recently) ____
remote past (a long time ago) ____

ii) How would you say the following in Kwakum?
I bought (recently). _____
I didn't buy (recently). _____
They bought (a long time ago). _____

(Data from: Malcolm Guthrie, *The Bantu Languages of Western Equatorial Africa* [Oxford: Oxford University Press, 1953].)

5. All the following Persian words (presented in Roman orthography) consist of two or more morphemes. (Note: *xar* means 'buy' and *-id* designates the past tense.)

a) xaridam   'I bought'
b) xaridi   'you (SG) bought'
c) xarid   '(he) bought'
d) naxaridam   'I did not buy'
e) namixaridand   'they were not buying'
f) naxaridim   'we did not buy'
g) mixarid   '(he) was buying'
h) mixaridid   'you (PL) were buying'

i) Match each of the following notions with a morpheme in the Persian data.

I   ____   they   ____
you (SG) ____   not   ____
we   ____   was/were + -ing (CONTINUOUS) ____
you (PL) ____

ii) How would you say the following in Persian?
They were buying. _____
You (SG) did not buy. _____
You (SG) were buying. _____

6. Consider the following data from Zapotec, an indigenous language of Mexico. Data are in the orthography of the source.

a) racañeea   'I help'   racañeetonoo 'we help'
b) racañeelo   'you (SG) help'   racañeetoo   'you (PL) help'
c) racañeeni   's/he helps'   racañeeni   'they help'

d) cocañeea	'I helped'		cocañeetonoo	'we helped'
e) cocañeelo	'you (SG) helped'		cocañeetoo	'you (PL) helped'
f) cocañeeni	's/he helped'		cocañeeni	'they helped'
g) cacañeea	'I will help'		cacañeetonoo	'we will help'
h) cacañeelo	'you (SG) will help'		cacañeetoo	'you (PL) will help'
i) cacañeeni	's/he will help'		cacañeeni	'they will help'

Match each of the following notions with a Zapotec morpheme.

help	____	I	____	we	____
PRESENT	____	you (SG)	____	you (PL)	____
PAST	____	he/she/they	____		
FUTURE	____				

(Data from *Gramática de la lengua zapoteca*, by an anonymous author. Mexico: Oficina Tip. de la Secretaría de Formento, 1897, p. 8.)

7. Consider the following data from Turkish, presented in phonemic transcription.

a) /lokanta/	'a restaurant'		/lokantada/	'in/at a restaurant'
b) /kapɨ/	'a door'		/kapɨda/	'in/at a door'
c) /ɾandevu/	'an appointment'		/ɾandevuda/	'in/at an appointment'
d) /baʃ/	'a head'		/baʃta/	'in/at a head'
e) /kitap/	'a book'		/kitapta/	'in/at a book'
f) /koltuk/	'an armchair'		/koltukta/	'in/at an armchair'
g) /taɾaf/	'a side'		/taɾafta/	'in/at a side'

   i)   What are the allomorphs for the Turkish morpheme meaning 'in/at'?
   ii)   Describe the distribution of the allomorphs as generally as possible.

8. The following problem, from Serbian (a Slavic language), was authored by Diana Stojanovic. Note: [ç] is a voiceless palatal fricative.

a) /hrabra/	'brave (FEM SG)'		/hrabrija/	'braver (FEM SG)'
b) /hrabro/	'brave (NEUT SG)'		/hrabrije/	'braver (NEUT SG)'
c) /pametna/	'smart (FEM SG)'		/pametnija/	'smarter (FEM SG)'
d) /pametno/	'smart (NEUT SG)'		/pametnije/	'smarter (NEUT SG)'
e) /sretçna/	'happy (FEM SG)'		/sretçnija/	'happier (FEM SG)'
f) /sretçno/	'happy (NEUT SG)'		/sretçnije/	'happier (NEUT SG)'
g) /lepo/	'beautiful (NEUT SG)'		/lepʃe/	'more beautiful (NEUT SG)'
h) /lako/	'light (NEUT SG)'		/lakʃe/	'lighter (NEUT SG)'

   i)   Make a list of the morphemes in the above data and indicate the meaning of each.
   ii)   If your analysis of the above data is correct, you will have noticed instances of allomorphic variation. Under what conditions does each allomorph occur?

9. Consider the following words.

a) desks	e) triumphed	i) prearrange	m) optionality
b) untie	f) ageless	j) smartest	n) prettier
c) insincere	g) loser	k) redistribute	o) mistreat
d) disprove	h) payment	l) disobey	p) resell

    i)   Draw a tree structure for each word. (See Section 2.)

    ii)   For the word *optionality*, what is the base for the affix *-ion*? What is the base for the suffix *-ity*? Are either of these bases also the root for the entire word? If so, which one?

10. The following problem, from Puyuma (a Formosan language, spoken in Taiwan), was authored by Yen-hsin Chen. Data are in orthography of the source.

a) sanay	'a song'	semanay	'to sing'
b) treli	'a decrease in weight'	tremeli	'to lighten'
c) traetra	'a lock'	tremaetra	'to lock'
d) sapuk	'a seedling'	semapuk	'to sow'
e) seber	'a bud'	semeber	'to bud'
f) garutr	'a comb'	gemarutr	'to comb'
g) sungal	'a bow'	semungal	'to bow (to someone)'

    i)   What is the affix that converts nouns into verbs in Puyuma? (See Section 1.2.)

    ii)   What type of affix is it?

11. In this chapter, an argument was presented in favor of the following structure for the word *unhappiness*. (See Section 2.1.)

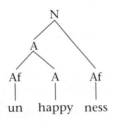

Using the same type of argument, draw and justify tree structures for the words *unresourceful*, *redisposal*, and *disinvestment*. (*Hint*: This will involve determining the type of syntactic category with which the affixes in these words can combine; see Table 4.6.)

12. In English, the suffix *-er* can be added to a place name. Examine the words in the two columns below. (See Section 2.)

Column 1	*Column 2*
Long Islander	*Denverer
Vermonter	*Philadelphiaer
New Yorker	*Delawarer
Marylander	*Atlantaer
Londoner	*Miamier

    i)   In general terms, what does the suffix *-er* mean in these words?

    ii)   How is this *-er* different in meaning from the *-er* found in the words *skater* and *walker*?

    iii) State the constraint on the distribution of *-er* illustrated in this data set.

    iv) Does this constraint also apply to the type of *-er* used in the word *skater*? (*Hint*: What would you call 'one who discovers' or 'one who rows'?)

13. The following words have all been formed by compounding. Draw a tree structure for each word. If you are in doubt as to the lexical category of the compound, remember that the category of the head determines the category of the word. (See Section 3.)

a) football
b) billboard
c) sunspot
d) in-crowd
e) fast food
f) softball
g) freeze-dry
h) oversee
i) tree trunk
j) lead-free
k) home plate
l) girlfriend
m) city center
n) failsafe
o) potato peel
p) bittersweet
q) hockey match
r) coffee table
s) flower pot
t) blueprint
u) red alert
v) space ship

14. Examine the following compounds and answer the questions below. (See Section 3.)

a) loudmouth
b) skinhead
c) killjoy
d) bath towel
e) death blow
f) airhead
g) snowman
h) cutthroat
i) pickpocket
j) spoilsport
k) crybaby
l) brain-dead
m) blow-dry
n) armchair

i) For each of the compounds determine whether it is endocentric or exocentric.
ii) How do you form the plural of *snowman* and *loudmouth*? (*Hint*: See Table 4.13. Also, pay special attention to the pronunciation of *mouth*. Is it any different here than when it is an independent word?)

15. English contains many verbal expressions that consist of a verb plus a preposition:
hold up (a bank)
carry on (a conversation)
drop out (of school)
back down (from a challenge)
take over (a company)

Should these sorts of expressions be considered compounds? In answering this question, be sure to refer to the properties of compounds discussed in Section 3.
   Now consider the nouns that are derived from these verbal expressions via conversion: *a holdup, a dropout, a takeover*. According to the criteria you used to answer the preceding question, should they be considered compounds?

16. State whether the words in each of the following groups are related to one another by process of inflection or derivation. (See Section 4.2.)

a) go, goes, going, gone
b) discover, discovery, discoverer, discoverable, discoverability
c) lovely, lovelier, loveliest
d) inventor, inventor's, inventors, inventors'
e) democracy, democrat, democratic, democratize

17. The following sentences contain both derivational and inflectional affixes. Underline all of the derivational affixes and circle the inflectional affixes. (See Sections 2 and 4.)
    a) The farmer's cows escaped.
    b) It was raining.
    c) Those socks are inexpensive.
    d) Jim needs the newer copy.
    e) The strongest rower continued.
    f) The pitbull has bitten the cyclist.
    g) She quickly closed the book.
    h) The alphabetization went well.

    (Data from: A. Koutsoudas, *Writing Transformational Grammars* [New York: McGraw-Hill, 1966].)

18. Each of the following columns illustrates a different way of marking inflection. (See Section 5.)

Column 1	*Column 2*	*Column 3*
a) mouse/mice	f) go/went	k) record/recorded
b) dive/dove	g) is/was	l) arrive/arrived
c) take/took	h) good/better	m) start/started
d) man/men	i) she/her	n) discuss/discussed
e) eat/ate	j) am/are	o) try/tried

    i) How is inflection expressed in column 1? column 2? column 3?
    ii) Think of at least one more English example to add to each column.

19. Consider the following data from Samoan, presented in the native orthography. (The [ʻ] symbol represents a glottal stop.) (See Section 5.1.)

a) mate	'he dies'	mamate	'they die'
b) nofo	'he stays'	nonofo	'they stay'
c) galue	'he works'	galulue	'they work'
d) tanu	'he buries'	tatanu	'they bury'
e) alofa	'he loves'	alolofa	'they love'
f) taʻoto	'he lies'	taʻoʻoto	'they lie'
g) atamaʻi	'he is intelligent'	atamamaʻi	'they are intelligent'

    i) What morphological process is used to express the inflectional contrast between singular and plural here?
    ii) Describe how it works in your own words.
    iii) If 'he is strong' is *malosi* in Samoan, how would you say 'they are strong'?

20. The following words from Chamorro, spoken in Guam and the Mariana Islands, all involve derivation. (Data are presented in Chamorro orthography.) (See Sections 2 and 5.)

I. Root		*Derived word*	
a) adda	'mimic'	aadda	'mimicker'
b) kanno	'eat'	kakanno	'eater'
c) tuge	'write'	tutuge	'writer'

II. Root   *Derived word*
d) atan   'look at'   atanon   'nice to look at'
e) sangan   'tell'   sanganon   'tellable'
f) guaiya   'love'   guaiyayon   'lovable'
g) tulaika   'exchange'   tulaikayon   'exchangeable'
h) chalek   'laugh'   chalekon   'laughable'
i) ngangas   'chew'   ngangason   'chewable'

III. Root   *Derived word*
j) nalang   'hungry'   nalalang   'very hungry'
k) dankolo   'big'   dankololo   'very big'
l) metgot   'strong'   metgogot   'very strong'
m) bunita   'pretty'   bunitata   'very pretty'

Like inflection, derivation can be expressed in a variety of ways—including by affixation of various types (prefixation, suffixation, infixation) and by reduplication.

i)   What morphological process is manifested in I? in II? in III?
ii) Formulate a general statement that describes how the derived words in I are formed. Do the same for II and III.
iii) One of these derivational processes consists of affixation involving allomorphs. What are the allomorphs, and what is the distribution of the allomorphs?

21. The following words can be either nouns or verbs.
    a) record   f) outline   k) report
    b) journey   g) convict   l) assault
    c) exchange   h) imprint   m) answer
    d) remark   i) reply   n) import
    e) surprise   j) retreat   o) cripple

    i) For each word, determine whether stress placement can be used to make the distinction between noun and verb. (See Section 5.2.)
    ii) Think of two more English examples illustrating the process of stress shift to mark a category distinction.

22. Indicate the morphological phenomenon illustrated by the items in column 2. (See Section 5.2.)

    Column 1   *Column 2*
    a) automation   → automate
    b) humid   → humidifier
    c) information, entertainment   → infotainment
    d) love, seat   → loveseat
    e) 'progress   → pro'gress
    f) typographical error   → typo
    g) aerobics, marathon   → aerobathon

h) act   → deactivate
i) curve, ball   → curve ball
j) methamphetamine   → meth
k) (the) comb   → comb (your hair)
l) beef, buffalo   → beefalo
m) random access memory   → RAM
n) megabyte   → meg
o) Federal Express   → FedEx
p) applications (for a computer)   → apps
q) They have finished   → They've finished
r) Global Positioning System   → GPS

23. Here are ten instances where a new word is needed. Create a word for each of these definitions in the manner indicated. (See Section 5.2.)

a) Use an acronym . . . for your uncle's second oldest brother.
   "We visited my _____ at Christmas."

b) Use onomatopoeia . . . for the sound of a dishwasher at work.
   "I can't concentrate because my dishwasher is _____ ing."

c) Use conversion . . . for wrapping something breakable in bubble wrap.
   "You'd better _____ that ornament or else it might break."

d) Use a compound . . . for the annoying string of cheese stretching from a slice of hot pizza to one's mouth.
   "As the _____ hung precariously from my lips, our eyes met!"

e) Use backformation . . . for the action of backformation.
   "We had to _____ words in linguistics class today."

f) Use a product name . . . for the act of cleaning a mirror with Windex.
   "I _____ed the mirror to get rid of the fingerprints."

g) Use a proper name . . . for the act of breaking dishes, which Jonathan does regularly.
   "He's going to _____ all of my best dishes."

h) Use clipping . . . for a course in ovinology (the study of sheep).
   "Have you done your _____ assignment yet?"

i) Use derivation . . . for being able to be contacted.
   "The counselor is not very _____."

j) Use a blend . . . for a hot drink made with chocolate and ginseng.
   "I'll have a _____ and two peanut butter cookies, please."

24. In Korean, /p/ and /m/ are distinct phonemes, as shown by contrasts such as the following:
/pap/ 'food'   /pam/ 'night'

However, under the circumstances illustrated below, /p/ is converted to /m/.

/pap/ 'food' + /məkə/ 'eat' becomes /pammməkə/ 'eat food'
/sip/ 'ten' + /njən/ 'year' becomes /simnjən/ 'ten years'
/ip/ 'mouth' + /man/ 'only' becomes /imman/ 'mouth only'

i) What type of phenomenon is this? (See Section 6.)
ii) Describe the process that is involved in terms of the change that takes place and the context in which it occurs.
iii) Now consider the following additional data.

/hak/ 'school' + /njən/ 'year' becomes /haŋnjən/ 'school year'
/ot/ 'clothes' + /mana/ 'be many' becomes /onmana/ 'there are many clothes'

Based on this data, how would you modify the statement that you made in response to question (ii)?

 For more helpful content and quizzes, go to the LaunchPad Solo for *Contemporary Linguistics* at **launchpadworks.com**.

For the Student Linguist

BAMBIFICATION

Well, of course, language is productive. You can't possibly read this chapter without being completely convinced of how very easy it is to make up new words. Morphological productivity is mildly interesting when you're creating transparent new words, such as when you have a verb like *fax* and create a new verb like *refax* (fax again) or *speed-fax* (fax fast) or an adjective like *faxable* (can be faxed), but it's not exactly earth-shattering.

What amazes me, though, is running across a new word, knowing it's a perfectly good word in English, knowing exactly how to pronounce it, and not having a clue about what it means. I'm not talking about knowing *frete* could be a word because it doesn't break any phonological rules of English. I'm talking about a word whose meaning remains mysterious even though that word can be broken down into recognizable, meaningful parts. Take the word *Brazilification*, which appears in Douglas Coupland's novel *Generation X*. *Brazilification* might appear in a sentence like "The recent Brazilification seen in the United States will have a large impact on tax reform plans." *Brazilification* could mean 'the replacement of forests with cattle ranches' or 'the improved quality of coffee' or many other things; it actually means 'the widening gulf between the rich and the poor and the accompanying disappearance of the middle classes' (p. 11). From this, the meaning of *Brazilify* is transparent: make the gulf between the rich and the poor wider, thereby causing the disappearance of the middle classes.

Now consider *Bambification*, another morphologically complex word from Coupland's book. It means 'make like X', where X is a variable that can be replaced by *Brazil*, or *Bambi*, or some other noun. *Bambification* doesn't mean 'make like Bambi's economic system', although theoretically it could. It means 'the mental conversion of flesh and blood living creatures into cartoon characters possessing bourgeois Judeo-Christian attitudes and morals' (p. 48).

Morphology is even more interesting when you look at compounds. The four words below, also gleaned from *Generation X*, could each be interpreted in a few ways. For each word, I've given the real definition and my own, made-up definition (Coupland's are made up too, but his were first, so I count them as the real definitions). I've also given the morphological structure that matches one of the definitions. Your task is to figure out if and how the structure would be different for the other definition.

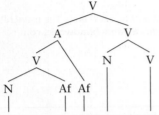

VACCIN ATE D TIME TRAVEL
To fantasize about traveling backward in time, but only with the proper vaccinations. (p. 11)

VACCINATED TIME TRAVEL
To travel freely in time, but only to times and places worth going to.

GREEN DIVISION
Sorting waste into chic recycling bins, showing how environmentally aware you are to all your friends.

GREEN DIVIS ION
Knowing the difference between envy and jealousy. (p. 150)

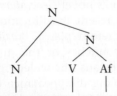

DUMPSTER CLOCK ING
The tendency when looking at objects to guesstimate the amount of time they will take to eventually decompose: *"Ski boots are the worst. Solid plastic. They'll be around till the sun goes supernova."* (p. 162)

DUMPSTER CLOCKING
Reckoning time by the amount and nature of the contents of the dumpster: *"An old couch, three textbooks, and twenty pounds of notebooks beneath a case of empties. Must be late May."*

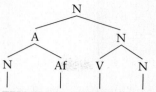

TERMINAL WANDERLUST
The inescapable urge, when seated at a computer, to do *anything* else as long as it involves getting away from the machine. Often involves coffee and cigarettes.

TERMIN AL WANDER LUST
A condition common to people of transient middle-class upbringings. Unable to feel rooted in any one environment, they move continually in the hopes of finding an idealized sense of community in the next location. (p. 171)

five

Syntax: The Analysis of Sentence Structure

William O'Grady

> *. . . the game is to say something new with old words.*
> –Ralph Waldo Emerson, *Journals,* 1849

OBJECTIVES

In this chapter, you will learn:
- how we categorize words
- how words can be combined into phrases and sentences according to a systematic schema
- that words "choose" what they can combine with in the same phrase
- how to diagram the structure of sentences
- how questions are derived from statements
- how all languages are alike in the way sentences are constructed
- how languages can differ systematically in the way sentences are constructed

 **LaunchPad Solo** macmillan learning | For more helpful content and quizzes, go to the LaunchPad Solo for *Contemporary Linguistics* at **launchpadworks.com**.

Not much can be said in English with a single word. If we are to use language to express complex thoughts and ideas, we must be able to combine and organize words into sentences. Not just any combination of words will do, however: the pattern in *1* is not permissible, even though the same words can be combined in a different way to form the acceptable sentence in *2*.

1) *House painted student a the.
2) A student painted the house.

We say that an utterance is **grammatical** if native speakers judge it to be a possible sentence of their language. Hence, *2* is grammatical, but *1* is not.

This chapter will focus on **syntax**, the component of grammar that is concerned with the form of grammatical sentences. The starting point for work on syntax is the universally accepted idea that words belong to categories of different types (nouns, verbs, and so on) and that these categories can be combined in particular ways to form phrases—and ultimately, sentences. One widely accepted way to represent the internal structure of sentences makes use of tree diagrams, like the simplified one in Figure 5.1.

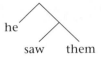

Figure 5.1   A simplified syntactic structure (tree diagram)

As we will see a little later in this chapter, structures like this are built by two interacting operations. A **Merge** operation combines words to create larger phrases and sentences, and a **Move** operation can carry an element to a new position within the structure. Before examining these operations, however, it is necessary to have a look at words and the categories to which they belong.

LANGUAGE MATTERS   What's the Longest Sentence in English?

George Bernard Shaw wrote one that was 110 words long. William Faulkner's novel *Absalom, Absalom!* includes a 1,300-word sentence. James Joyce managed to produce a 4,391-word sentence (that goes on for forty pages) in *Ulysses*. But even that's not the longest known sentence—*The Rotter's Club* by Jonathon Coe contains a sentence that is 13,955 words long!

The bottom line is that there's no such thing as the world's longest sentence—any sentence can be made longer. That's because the operations that combine words can be used over and over again, without limit.

It's the right answer
I think it's the right answer
You know I think it's the right answer
Harry said you know I think it's the right answer.

. . . .

a book
a book on the table
a book on the table near the bookcase
a book on the table near the bookcase in the office

Repeated application of the same rule to create an ever more complex structure is called **recursion**, and it's an essential part of our ability to build sentences.

1   Categories and Structure

A fundamental fact about words in all human languages is that they can be grouped together into a relatively small number of classes called **syntactic categories** or **parts of speech**. This classification reflects a variety of factors, including the types of meaning that words express, the types of affixes that they take, and the types of structures in which they can occur.

1.1   Categories of Words

Table 5.1 provides examples of the word-level categories that are most central to the study of syntax. The four most studied syntactic categories are **noun (N)**, **verb (V)**, **adjective (A)**, and **preposition (P)**. These elements, which are often called **lexical categories**, play a very important role in sentence formation, as we will soon see. A fifth and less studied lexical category consists of **adverbs (Adv)**, most of which are derived from adjectives.

Table 5.1   Syntactic categories

Lexical categories (content words)	Examples
Noun (N)	Harry, boy, wheat, policy, moisture, bravery
Verb (V)	arrive, discuss, melt, hear, remain, dislike
Adjective (A)	good, tall, old, intelligent, beautiful, fond
Preposition (P)	to, in, on, near, at, by
Adverb (Adv)	slowly, quietly, now, always, perhaps
Nonlexical categories (functional categories)	*Examples*
Determiner (Det)	the, a, this, these, no (as in *no books*)
Degree word (Deg)	too, so, very, more, quite
Auxiliary (Aux)	
Modal	will, would, can, could, may, must, should
Nonmodal	be, have, do
Conjunction (Con)	and, or, but

Languages may also contain **nonlexical** or **functional categories**, including **determiner (Det)**, **auxiliary verb (Aux)**, **conjunction (Con)**, and **degree word (Deg)**. Such elements generally have meanings that are harder to define and paraphrase than those of lexical categories. For example, the meaning of a determiner such as *the* or an auxiliary such as *would* is more difficult to describe than the meaning of a noun such as *hill* or *vehicle*.

A potential source of confusion in the area of word classification stems from the fact that some items can belong to more than one category.

3) *comb* used as a noun:
The woman found a comb.

comb used as a verb:
The boy should comb his hair.

4) *near* used as a preposition:
The child stood near the fence.

near used as a verb:
The runners neared the finish line.

near used as an adjective:
The end is nearer than you might think.

How then can we determine a word's category?

Meaning

One criterion involves meaning. For instance, nouns typically name entities (people and things), including individuals (*Harry, Sue*) and objects (*book, desk*). Verbs characteristically designate actions (*run, jump*), sensations (*feel, hurt*), and states (*be, remain*). Consistent with these tendencies, *comb* in *3* refers to an object when used as a noun but to an action when used as a verb.

The typical function of an adjective is to designate a property or attribute of the entities denoted by nouns. Thus, when we say *that tall building*, we are attributing the property *tall* to the building designated by the noun.

In a parallel way, adverbs typically denote properties and attributes of the actions, sensations, and states designated by verbs. In the following sentences, for example, the adverb *quickly* indicates the manner of Janet's leaving, while the adverb *early* specifies its time.

5) Janet left quickly.
Janet left early.

A word's category membership does not always bear such a straightforward relationship to its meaning, however. For example, nouns such as *difficulty, truth,* and *likelihood* do not name entities in the strict sense. Moreover, even though words for actions tend to be verbs, some nouns also express this type of meaning (e.g., *push* in *give someone a push* and *run* in *have a run*).

Matters are further complicated by the fact that in some cases, words with very similar meanings belong to different categories. For instance, the words *like* and *fond* are very similar in meaning (as in *Mice like/are fond of cheese*), yet *like* is a verb and *fond* is an adjective.

Inflection

Most linguists believe that meaning is only one of several criteria that enter into determining a word's category. As shown in Table 5.2, inflection can also be very useful for distinguishing among different categories of words.

Table 5.2   Lexical categories and their inflectional suffixes in English

Category	Inflectional suffix	Examples
Noun	plural -*s* possessive -*'s*	books, chairs, doctors John's, (the) man's
Verb	past tense -*ed* progressive -*ing* third person singular -*s*	arrived, melted, hopped arriving, melting, hopping arrives, melts, hops
Adjective	comparative -*er* superlative -*est*	taller, faster, smarter tallest, fastest, smartest

However, even inflection does not always provide the information needed to determine a word's category. In English, for example, not all adjectives can take the comparative and superlative suffixes (**intelligenter*, **beautifulest*) and some nouns cannot be pluralized (*moisture, bravery, knowledge*).

Distribution

A third and often more reliable criterion for determining a word's category involves the type of elements (especially functional categories) with which it can co-occur (its **distribution**). For example, nouns can typically appear with a determiner, verbs with an auxiliary, and adjectives with a degree word in the patterns illustrated in Table 5.3.

Table 5.3   Distributional properties of nouns, verbs, and adjectives

Category	Distributional property	Examples
Noun	occurrence with a determiner	a car, the wheat
Verb	occurrence with an auxiliary	has gone, will stay
Adjective	occurrence with a degree word	very rich, too big

In contrast, a noun cannot occur with an auxiliary, and a verb cannot occur with a determiner or degree word.

6) a noun with an auxiliary:
  *will destruction

  a verb with a determiner:
  *the destroy

  a verb with a degree word:
  *very appreciate

Distributional tests for category membership are simple and highly reliable. They can be used with confidence when it is necessary to categorize unfamiliar words.

LANGUAGE MATTERS   A Poem That Syntacticians Love

Thanks to distributional and inflectional clues, it's often possible to identify a word's category without knowing its meaning. The poem "Jabberwocky" by Lewis Carroll illustrates this point in a particularly brilliant way—it's interpretable precisely because readers are able to figure out that *gyre* is a verb (note the auxiliary verb to its left), that *borogoves* is a noun (it's preceded by a determiner and takes the plural ending), and so on.

> 'Twas brillig, and the slithy toves
> Did gyre and gimble in the wabe;
> All mimsy were the borogoves,
> And the mome raths outgrabe.
>
> "Beware the Jabberwock, my son!
> The jaws that bite, the claws that catch!
> Beware the Jubjub bird, and shun
> The frumious Bandersnatch!"

1.2   Phrase Structure

Sentences are not formed by simply stringing words together like beads on a necklace. Rather, they have a hierarchical design in which words are grouped together into ever larger structural units called **phrases**—*the door, to the door, go to the door,* and so on.

The Blueprint

As a first approximation, it is often suggested that the internal structure of phrases follows the design shown in Figure 5.2, which is called the **X′ Schema** (X′ is pronounced 'X-bar').

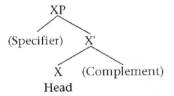

Figure 5.2   The X′ Schema—a template for phrase structure

Heads

The **head** is the obligatory nucleus around which a phrase is built. For now we will focus on four categories that can function as the head of a phrase—nouns (N), verbs (V), adjectives (A), and prepositions (P).

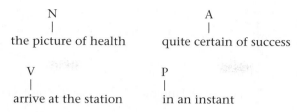

Figure 5.3   Some examples of heads

Specifiers

Specifiers have no single semantic function. Structurally, though, they are alike in that they occur at the edge of a phrase. As illustrated in Table 5.4, the specifier position in English is at the beginning of a phrase.

Table 5.4   Some specifiers

Head	Specifier	Examples
N	Determiner (Det) *the, a, some, this, those* . . .	*a picture,* ***the*** *map,* ***those*** *people,* ***some*** *guests*
V	Preverbal adverb (Adv) *never, perhaps, often,* *always, almost* . . .	***never*** *quit,* ***perhaps*** *go,* ***often*** *failed,* ***almost*** *forgot*
A or P	Degree word (Deg) *very, quite, more, almost* . . .	***very*** *smart,* ***quite*** *rich,* ***almost*** *in*

Note: *Almost* can be either an adverb or a degree word, depending on whether it is followed by a V or by an A or a P.

Complements

Complements, which are always phrases, provide information about entities and locations implied by the meaning of the head. For example, the meaning of *protect* implies something that is protected (*protect the environment*); the meaning of *in* implies a location (*in the house*); the meaning of *map* implies an area that is depicted, as in *a map of Oklahoma*; and so on.

As illustrated in Figure 5.4, the X' Schema ensures that when a phrase includes both a specifier and a complement in addition to the head, the specifier will occur higher than the complement. To simplify here, we don't show the internal structure of the complement phrases.

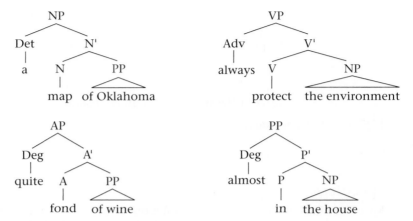

Figure 5.4   Phrases containing a head, a specifier, and a complement

However, it is common (and practical!) to represent tree structures in an abbreviated way, without the intermediate X', when there is no specifier and/or complement, as shown in Figures 5.5 and 5.6.

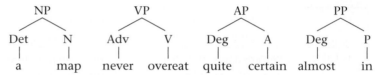

Figure 5.5   Phrases consisting of just a specifier and a head

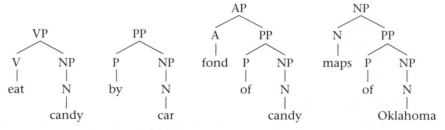

Figure 5.6   Phrases consisting of just a head and a complement

Only when the phrase contains both a specifier and a complement in addition to the head is it necessary to make use of the intermediate X' level.

In the interests of being able to consider the largest number of patterns possible, we will adopt two common additional assumptions. First, we will treat both names (*Mary, Bob,* etc.) and *pronouns* (*she, he, him, her,* etc.) as instances of the N category that do not normally take either specifiers or complements as shown in Figure 5.7.

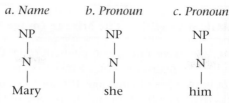

Figure 5.7   Names and pronouns

Second, we will assume that possessives (e.g., *the child's, Mary's, his*, etc.) are NPs that occur in the specifier position of a larger NP as shown in Figure 5.8.

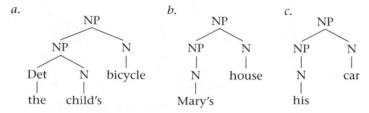

Figure 5.8   Possessives: NPs inside NPs

An appendix at the end of the chapter offers detailed instructions on how to draw tree structures; exercises 3 and 4 provide an opportunity to practice.

The Merge Operation

We can now formulate the following operation for sentence building.

7) *Merge*

   Combine words in a manner compatible with the X' Schema.

As illustrated in Figure 5.9, the Merge operation is able to take a determiner such as *the* and combine it with the N *house* to form the NP *the house*. It is then able to take a preposition such as *in* and combine it with the NP *the house* to form the PP *in the house*.

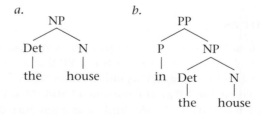

Figure 5.9   The Merge operation in action

LANGUAGE MATTERS   The Mirror Image

Many languages have a head-complement order that is the mirror image of the one found in English—the complement occurs before the head rather than after it. (In both types of language, the specifier appears before the head.) Japanese works that way: the V occurs at the end of the VP, the P at the end of the PP, and so on.

[sono gakkō]-ni   [sono hon] yonda
that school at   that book read (+Pst)
'at that school'   'read that book'

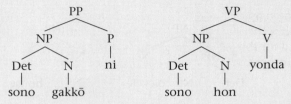

The version of the X' Schema needed for these languages looks like this—with the head after its complement:

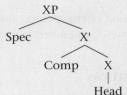

About half of the world's languages use this version of the X' Schema.

Further application of the Merge operation to additional words can lead to the formation of phrases and sentences of unlimited complexity.

1.3   Sentences

The largest unit of syntactic analysis is the sentence. Sentences typically consist of an NP (often called "the subject") and a VP that are linked together by an abstract category dubbed T (for tense). As illustrated in Figure 5.10, T serves as the head of the sentence, taking the VP as its complement and the subject NP as its specifier (+Pst = past, –Pst = nonpast). What we think of as a sentence or a sentential phrase, then, is really a TP.

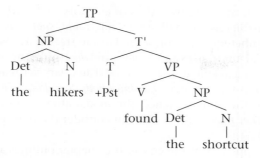

Figure 5.10   The structure of a typical sentence

The tense feature in T must be compatible with the form of the verb. So a sentence like the one above, whose head contains the feature +Pst, must contain a verb marked for the past tense (hence, *found* rather than *find*).

Although somewhat abstract, this analysis has the advantage of giving sentences the same internal structure as other phrases (with a specifier, a head, and a complement), making them consistent with the X' Schema. Moreover, because T, like all heads, is obligatory, we also account for the fact that all sentences have tense (i.e., they are all past or nonpast).

The TP structure also provides us with a natural place to locate **modal auxiliaries** such as *can*, *may*, *will*, and *must*, most of which are inherently nonpast, as shown by their incompatibility with time adverbs such as *yesterday*: **He can/will/must work yesterday.* (The modals *could* and *would* can be either past or nonpast: *He could swim when he was three/He could swim tomorrow.*) Although traditionally called auxiliary verbs, modals are treated as instances of the T category in contemporary syntactic analysis, as depicted in Figure 5.11. (Because modals have inherent tense, we will assume that it is not necessary to have the feature ±Pst in the T position when they are used.)

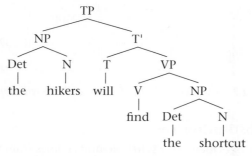

Figure 5.11   A sentence with an auxiliary verb in the T position

This structure neatly accounts not only for the fact that modals express an inherent tense but also for their positioning between the subject (the specifier) and the VP (the complement)—in the position reserved for the head of the sentence.

In fact, there are two types of auxiliary verbs, which differ in crucial ways. The modal auxiliaries are: *will, would, can, could, shall, should, may, must, might*. Because of their inherent tense, only modals are treated as instances of the T category. The **nonmodal auxiliaries** are *be, have,* and *do*. Unlike the modals, which are not inflected for tense or agreement, the nonmodal auxiliary verbs are marked for tense and agreement: *am-is-was; are-were; has-have-had; does-do-did*. When both types of auxiliaries appear in the same sentence, the modal always comes first, as in *They <u>should</u> have gone* or *They <u>may</u> be going*. We will consider the nonmodal auxiliaries further in Section 4.1.

The appendix at the end of the chapter outlines a procedure that will help you assign the right structure to sentences. Exercise 5 provides an opportunity to practice this procedure.

1.4   Tests for Phrase Structure

How can linguists be sure that they have grouped words together into phrases in the right way? The existence of the syntactic units, or **constituents**, found in tree structures can be independently verified with the help of special tests, although it must be noted that not every test works for every constituent. Consider, for instance, the tree structure that the X' Schema requires for the sentence *The children will stop at the corner* as shown in Figure 5.12.

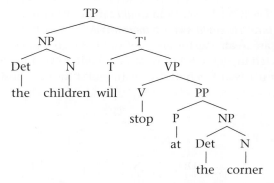

Figure 5.12   The tree structure for *The children will stop at the corner*

The Substitution Test

One piece of evidence for syntactic units comes from the fact that they can often be replaced by an element such as *they, she, he, it, do so,* and so on. (This is called a **substitution test**.)

As illustrated in 8, *the children* can be replaced by *they*, and *stop at the corner* can be replaced by *do so*—confirming that each is a syntactic unit, just as the tree structure shows by grouping the component parts together under a phrasal label such as NP, VP, and so on.

8) [$_{NP}$ The children] will [$_{VP}$ stop at the corner]. *They* always *do so.*
     (*they = the children; do so = stop at the corner*)

A substitution test also confirms that *at the corner* is a unit, as it can be replaced by a single word in a sentence such as *9*.

9) The children stopped [$_{PP}$ at the corner] and we stopped *there* too.
     (*there = at the corner*)

Elements that do not form a constituent cannot be replaced in this way. Thus, there is no word in English that we can use to replace *children stopped*, for example, or *at the*.

The Movement Test

A second indication that *at the corner* forms a constituent in Figure 5.12 is that it can be moved as a single unit to a different position within the sentence. (This is called a **movement test**.) In *10*, for instance, *at the corner* can be moved from a position after the verb to the beginning of the sentence.

10) They stopped [$_{PP}$ at the corner]. → [$_{PP}$ At the corner], they stopped.

Of course, *at the*, which is not a syntactic unit, cannot be fronted in this manner (**At the, they stopped corner*). Note that the movement test often works better for PP than for other phrases.

The Coordination Test

Finally, we can conclude that a group of words forms a constituent if it can be joined to another group of words by a conjunction such as *and*, *or*, or *but*. (This is known as the **coordination test** since patterns built around a conjunction are called **coordinate structures**.) The sentence in *11* illustrates how coordination can be used to help establish that *stop at the corner* is a constituent.

11) The children will [$_{VP}$ stop at the corner] *and* [$_{VP}$ look both ways].

2   Complement Options

How can we be sure that individual words will occur with a complement of the right type in the syntactic structures that we have been building? Information about the complements permitted by a particular head is included in that head's entry in a speaker's lexicon. For instance, the lexicon for English includes an entry for *devour* that indicates that it requires an NP complement.

12) a. *devour* with an NP complement:
        The child devoured [$_{NP}$ the sandwich].
     b. *devour* without an NP complement:
        *The child devoured.

The term **subcategorization** is used to refer to information about a word's complement options, such as the fact the verb *devour* belongs to a verb subcategory that requires an NP complement.

2.1   Complement Options for Verbs

Table 5.5 illustrates some of the more common complement options for verbs in English. The subscripted prepositions indicate subtypes of PP complements, where this is relevant. *Loc* stands for any preposition expressing a location (such as *near*, *on*, and *under*).

Table 5.5   Some examples of verb complements

Complement option	Sample heads	Example
Ø	vanish, arrive, die	The rabbit vanished.
NP	devour, cut, prove	The professor proved [$_{NP}$ *the theorem*].
AP	be, become	The man became [$_{AP}$ *very angry*].
PP$_{to}$	dash, talk, refer	The dog dashed [$_{PP}$ *to the door*].
NP NP	tell, hand, give	We handed [$_{NP}$ *the man*] [$_{NP}$ *a map*].
NP PP$_{to}$	hand, give, send	She gave [$_{NP}$ *a diploma*] [$_{PP}$ *to the student*].
NP PP$_{for}$	buy, cook, reserve	We bought [$_{NP}$ *a hat*] [$_{PP}$ *for Andy*].
NP PP$_{loc}$	put, place, stand	Chris put [$_{NP}$ *the muffler*] [$_{PP}$ *on the car*].
PP$_{to}$ PP$_{about}$	talk, speak	I talked [$_{PP}$ *to a doctor*] [$_{PP}$ *about Sue*].
NP PP$_{for}$ PP$_{with}$	open, fix	We opened [$_{NP}$ *the door*] [$_{PP}$ *for Andy*] [$_{PP}$ *with a crowbar*].

The verbs in the first line of Table 5.5 (*vanish*, *arrive*, and *die*) don't take a complement, those in the second line take an NP complement, and so on.

When a verb's complement options include an NP, as in the case of *devour*, *give*, *buy*, and so on, it is said to be **transitive**, and its NP complement is often referred to as its **direct object**. Verbs like *vanish*, *arrive*, and *dash* that don't have an NP complement are called **intransitive**.

A word can belong to more than one subcategory. The verb *eat*, for example, can occur either with or without an NP complement and therefore belongs to both of the first two subcategories in Table 5.5.

13) After getting home, they ate (a snack).

Of course, not all verbs exhibit this flexibility. As we have already seen, *devour*—although similar in meaning to *eat*—requires an NP complement and therefore belongs only to the second subcategory in our table.

As the examples in Table 5.5 also show, some heads can take more than one complement. The verb *put* is a case in point, since it requires both an NP complement and a PP complement (or a locative adverb such as *there*).

14) a. *put* with an NP complement and a PP complement:
   The librarian put [$_{NP}$ the book] [$_{PP}$ on the shelf].

   b. *put* without an NP complement:
   *The librarian put [$_{PP}$ on the shelf].

   c. *put* without a PP complement:
   *The librarian put [$_{NP}$ the book].

The VP *put the book on the shelf* has the structure in Figure 5.13, in which the VP consists of the head *put* and two complements—the NP *the book* and the PP *on the shelf*.

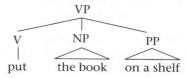

Figure 5.13   A verb with two complements

2.2   Complement Options for Other Categories

Various complement options are also available for Ns, As, and Ps. Tables 5.6, 5.7, and 5.8 provide examples of just some of the possibilities.

Table 5.6   Some examples of noun complements

Complement option	Sample heads	Example
Ø	car, boy, electricity	the car
PP$_{of}$	memory, failure, death	the memory [$_{PP}$ *of a friend*]
PP$_{of}$ PP$_{to}$	presentation, description, donation	the presentation [$_{PP}$ *of a medal*] [$_{PP}$ *to the winner*]
PP$_{with}$ PP$_{about}$	argument, discussion, conversation	an argument [$_{PP}$ *with Stella*] [$_{PP}$ *about politics*]

Table 5.7   Some examples of adjective complements

Complement option	Sample heads	Example
Ø	tall, green, smart	very tall
PP$_{about}$	curious, glad, angry	curious [$_{PP}$ *about China*]
PP$_{to}$	apparent, obvious	obvious [$_{PP}$ *to the student*]
PP$_{of}$	fond, full, sick	fond [$_{PP}$ *of chocolate*]

Table 5.8 Some examples of preposition complements

Complement option	Sample heads	Example
Ø	near, away, down	(he got) down
NP	in, on, by, near	in [$_{NP}$ *the house*]
PP	down, up, out	down [$_{PP}$ *into the cellar*]

Here again, subcategorization ensures that particular heads can appear in tree structures only if there is an appropriate type of complement. Thus, the adjective *sick* takes an *of*-PP as its complement, while the adjective *satisfied* takes a *with*-PP.

15) a. sick [$_{PP}$ of cafeteria food] (compare: *sick with cafeteria food)
    b. satisfied [$_{PP}$ with cafeteria food] (compare: *satisfied of cafeteria food)

A good deal of what we know about our language consists of information about words and the type of complements with which they can appear. Much of this information must be stored in the lexicon, since it cannot be predicted from a word's meaning.

2.3 Complement Clauses

All human languages allow sentential phrases (or **clauses**, as they are often called) to function as complements. A simple example of this from English is given in *16*.

16)   complement clause
                                     ↓
[The fans hope [**that the team won**]].
          ↑
    matrix clause

The boldface bracketed phrase in *16* is called a **complement clause**; the larger underlined phrase in which it occurs is called the **matrix clause**. Words such as *that*, *whether*, and *if* are known as **complementizers** (Cs). Together with their TP complement, they form the CP (complementizer phrase) depicted in Figure 5.14.

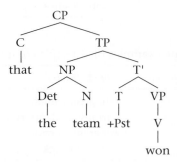

Figure 5.14 The internal structure of a CP

As we will see in Section 3.2, there is even a type of element that can occur in the specifier position under CP.

When a CP occurs in a sentence such as *16*, in which it serves as complement of the verb *hope*, the entire sentence has the structure shown in Figure 5.15.

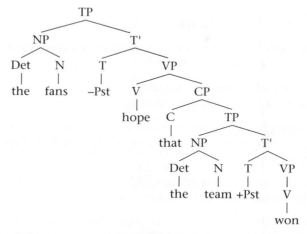

Figure 5.15 The structure of a sentence with an embedded CP

There is no limit on the number of embedded clauses that can occur in a sentence, as *17* shows.

17) Harry said [CP that you know [CP that I think [CP that . . .

Table 5.9 provides examples of some verbs that are often found with a CP complement.

Table 5.9 Some verbs permitting CP complements

Complement(s)	Sample heads	Example
CP	believe, know, think, remember	They believe [CP *that Eric left*].
NP CP	persuade, tell, convince, promise	They told [NP *Mary*] [CP *that Eric had left*].
PP to CP	concede, admit	They admitted [PP *to Mary*] [CP *that Eric had left*].

3 Move

As we have seen, it is possible to build a very large number of different sentences by allowing the Merge operation to combine words and phrases in accordance with the

X' Schema and the subcategorization properties of individual words. Nonetheless, there are still many kinds of sentences that we cannot build. This section considers two such patterns and discusses the sentence-building operation needed to accommodate them.

3.1   *Yes-No* **Questions**

The sentences in *18* are examples of ***yes-no* questions** (so called because the expected response is usually "yes" or "no").

18) a. **Should** those guys leave?
    b. **Can** we meet at the library?

A defining feature of *yes-no* questions is that the auxiliary verb occurs at the beginning of the sentence rather than in its more usual position after the subject, as illustrated in *19*.

19) a. Those guys **should** leave.
    b. We **can** meet at the library.

How does the word order in *18* come about? The formation of question structures requires the use of an operation that we can call Move. Traditionally known as a **transformation** because it transforms an existing structure, Move transports the item in the T position to a new position in front of the subject.

20) Should those guys __ leave?

This analysis has at least two advantages. First, it allows us to avoid positing two types of modal auxiliary verbs in English: one that occurs between the subject and the VP and one that occurs in front of the subject. Thanks to Move, all modal auxiliaries belong in the same place—in the T position, from which they can then be moved in front of the subject in order to signal a question.

Second, the use of Move automatically captures the fact that the sentence *Should those guys leave?* is the question structure corresponding to *Those guys should leave*. According to the analysis presented here, both sentences initially have the same basic composition. They differ only in that the Move operation has applied to the T category in the question structure.

A Landing Site for T

In what position does the modal auxiliary land when it is moved in front of the subject? One promising idea assumes that TPs occur within a larger CP shell, in which the C position carries information about whether the sentence is a statement or a question. For the sake of illustration, we use the symbol +Q to indicate a question; sentences with the feature –Q in their C position will be interpreted as statements.

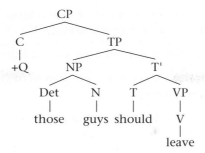

Figure 5.16   A TP inside a CP shell, with the C carrying the +Q feature

In some languages, the **Q feature** is spelled out as a separate morpheme (see the example from Yoruba in the box on page 187). In languages like English, where there is no such morpheme, the feature must attract another element to its position. The modal auxiliary in the T position is that element. As illustrated in Figure 5.17, T is drawn to the C position, where it attaches right next to the +Q feature.

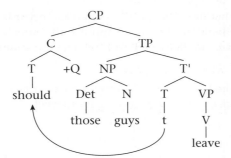

Figure 5.17   The T moves to the C position

A Move operation can do no more than change an element's position. It does not change the categories of any words and it cannot eliminate any part of the structure created by the Merge operation. Thus, *should* retains its T label even though it is moved into the C position (it changes its address, not its name). Moreover, the position that T formerly occupied remains in the tree structure. Called a **trace** and marked by the symbol *t*, it records the fact that the moved element comes from the head position within TP.

The Move operation used for *yes-no* questions is often informally called **Inversion**; it can be formulated as follows.

21) *Inversion*
    Move T to the C position.

Interesting evidence that T does in fact end up in the C position comes from patterns such as *22*, which contain an embedded CP.

22) I wonder [$_{CP}$ whether those guys should leave].

Here, as Figure 5.18 shows, the C position in the embedded clause is occupied by the complementizer *whether*.

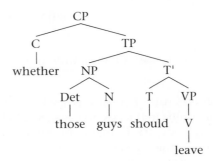

Figure 5.18   The C position in the embedded CP is filled by *whether*

Assuming that no more than one word can occur in a head position, we predict that Inversion should not be able to apply in the embedded clause since there is nowhere for the moved auxiliary verb to land. The ungrammaticality of *23* shows that this is correct.

23) Attempted inversion when there is a complementizer—the landing site is full:
   *I wonder [$_{CP}$ **whether** those guys t leave].
   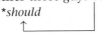
   should

Crucially, the acceptability of Inversion improves quite dramatically when there is no complementizer in the C position. (In fact, such sentences are perfectly acceptable in Appalachian English. For other English speakers, they may sound most natural when the embedded clause is interpreted as an indirect question.)

24) Inversion in an embedded CP that does not have a complementizer:
   I wonder [$_{CP}$ should those guys *t* leave].

To summarize before continuing, we have introduced two changes into our system of syntactic analysis. First, we assume that TPs occur inside CP shells even when there is no visible complementizer. Second, we assume that the Inversion transformation moves T (and its contents) to the C position in order to indicate a question. In addition to giving the correct word order for the question structure, this analysis helps explain why the result of applying Inversion sounds so unnatural when the C position is already filled by another element, as in *23*.

LANGUAGE MATTERS   Another Way to Ask a *Yes-No* Question

Although Inversion is a widely used question-marking strategy around the world, many languages go about things in an entirely different way. Instead of moving something to the C position, they place a special question morpheme there to begin with. Yoruba (a Benue-Congo language spoken in Nigeria) works that way.

Yoruba
Ṣé   Olú wá?
+Q   Olu come
'Did Olu come?'

```
        CP
       /  \
      C    TP
      |    /\
     Ṣé  Olú wá
```

Information from: Oluseye Adesola, *Yoruba: A Grammar Sketch*, Version 1.0, http://www.africananaphora.rutgers.edu/images/stories/downloads/casefiles/YorubaGS.pdf.

3.2   *Wh* Questions

Consider now the question construction exemplified in *25*. These sentences are called **wh questions** because of the presence of a question word beginning with *wh*.

25) a. [~NP~ Which languages] can Jerry speak?
    b. [~NP~ What] will they talk about?

Depending on the *wh* word and its place in the sentence, *wh* words can belong to various syntactic categories, as Table 5.10 shows.

Table 5.10   The syntactic category of *wh* words

Wh *word*	*Syntactic category*	*Examples*
who	N	*Who did you contact?*
what	N, when it occurs by itself	*What did you see?*
	Det, when it occurs with a noun	*What movie do you want to see?*
which	N, when in occurs by itself	*Which do you prefer?*
	Det, when it occurs with a noun	*Which car do you prefer?*
where	Adv	*Where are you going?*
when	Adv	*When did you move to Texas?*
why	Adv	*Why did you leave the room?*
how	Adv, when it asks about a verb	*How did they escape?*
	Deg, when it occurs with an adjective	*How rich are they?*

There is reason to believe that the *wh* elements at the beginning of sentences such as those in *25* have been moved there from the positions indicated in *26*.

26) a. Jerry can speak [NP which languages]
    b. They will talk about [NP what]

As illustrated here, *which languages* corresponds to the complement of *speak* (compare: *Jerry can speak two languages*) and *what* corresponds to the complement of *about* (compare: *They will talk about politics*).

How, then, do the *wh* phrases end up at the beginning of the sentence? The answer is that they are attracted there by the +Q feature, which triggers the application of a Move operation known as **Wh Movement**.

27) a. [**Which languages**] can Jerry speak *t*?
        ↑   *Wh* Movement

    b. [**What**] will they talk about *t*?
       ↑   *Wh* Movement

A Landing Site for *Wh* Words

Because *wh* phrases end up in front of the C position (filled in *27* by a moved modal), we can infer that they end up in the specifier of CP—the only available position in that region of the sentence. We can make this idea precise by formulating the **Wh Movement** operation as follows.

28) Wh *Movement*
    Move a *wh* phrase to the specifier position under CP.

The sentence *Which languages can Jerry speak?* can now be analyzed in steps, the first of which involves formation of the structure in Figure 5.19a, which includes an open specifier position under CP. *Wh* Movement and Inversion then apply, as depicted in Figures 5.19b and 5.19c.

LANGUAGE MATTERS   Pied Piping

In more formal varieties of English, there is a second possibility—the entire PP containing the *wh* word can undergo *Wh* Movement.

Movement of the PP *about what*:
[PP About what] will they   *t*   talk *t*?
    ↑   ↑*Inversion*
        Wh Movement

This phenomenon is known as *pied-piping*, a whimsical reference to the folk tale *The Pied Piper of Hamelin*, in which (in the words of Robert Browning) "the Piper advanced and the children followed."

---

a. The structure produced by the Merge operation, with *which languages* functioning as complement of *speak*

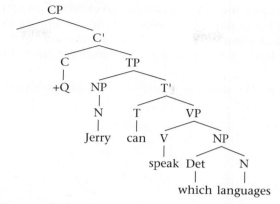

b. Inversion: T moves to the C position

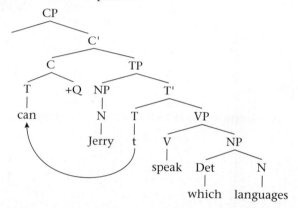

c. *Wh* Movement: the *wh* phrase moves to the specifier position in CP

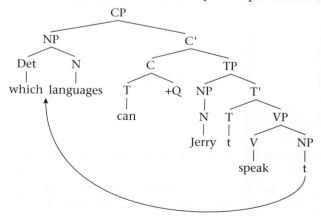

Figure 5.19 Steps for forming the sentence *Which languages can Jerry speak?*

Like Inversion, *Wh* Movement cannot eliminate any part of the previously formed structure. The position initially occupied by the *wh* phrase is therefore not lost. That is because the Move operation leaves behind an empty category (known as a trace) that marks the earlier position of the moved element. In the case at hand, the trace indicates that the NP *which languages* originates as the complement of the verb *speak*.

Figure 5.20 provides a second example, involving sentence *27b*.

a. The structure produced by the Merge operation

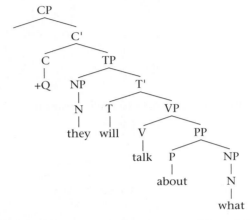

b. Inversion and *Wh* Movement (compressed here into a single step to save space)

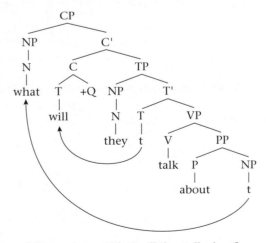

Figure 5.20   Formation of the sentence *What will they talk about?*

In the examples considered so far, the *wh* word originates as the complement of a verb or preposition. In sentences such as the following, however, the *wh* word asks about the subject (the person who will walk the dog).

29) Who will walk the dog?

The *wh* word in these patterns originates in the subject position. For the sake of generality, we assume that it subsequently moves to the specifier position in CP, even though the actual order of the words in the sentence does not change as a result of this movement (see Figure 5.21). (We will assume that there is no Inversion in this type of question structure.)

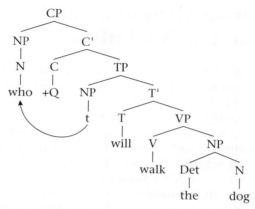

Figure 5.21   Movement of a subject *wh* phrase

3.3   Deep Structure and Surface Structure

The preceding examples show that two distinct types of mechanisms are involved in structure building. The first is the Merge operation, which creates tree structures by combining categories in a manner consistent with their subcategorization properties and the X' Schema. The second is the Move operation, which can modify these tree structures by moving an element from one position to another.

In the system sketched here, all instances of the Merge operation take place before any instances of the Move operation. This yields two distinct levels of syntactic structure, as shown in Figure 5.22. The first, called **deep structure** (or **D-structure**), is formed by the Merge operation.

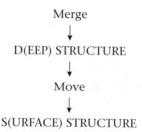

Figure 5.22   Structure-building operations

The second level of syntactic structure corresponds to the final syntactic form of the sentence. Called **surface structure** (or **S-structure**), it results from applying whatever Move operations are appropriate for the sentence in question.

A system that explicitly builds syntactic structure in this way is often called a **(transformational) generative grammar**.

4 Universal Grammar and Parametric Variation

An intriguing aspect of work on syntax is the emphasis on **Universal Grammar (UG)**, the system of categories, operations, and principles shared by all languages. The key idea is that despite the many superficial differences among languages, there are certain commonalities with respect to how syntax works, including categories such as noun and verb, structure-building operations such as Merge and Move, and general constraints such as those imposed by the X' Schema.

This does not mean that languages must be alike in every way, though. Universal Grammar leaves room for variation, allowing individual languages to differ with respect to certain **parameters**. (You can think of a parameter as the set of options that UG permits for a particular phenomenon.) We have already seen one example of this sort of variation with regard to the X' Schema, which allows the head to precede its complement (as in English) or to follow it (as in Japanese). This illustrates the **head-complement parameter** stated in *30*:

30) *The Head-Complement Parameter*
   Option a: The head precedes its complement.
   Option b: The head follows its complement.

Another parameter involves the placement of *wh* words. As we have seen, *wh* words move to the specifier position under CP in simple *wh* questions in English. In Chinese, though, they stay in their original position.

31) Ni mai le **shenme**?
   you buy PAST **what**
   'What did you buy?'

This suggests the existence of a ***Wh* Movement parameter** with the two options summarized in *32*.

32) *The* Wh *Movement Parameter*
   Option a: *Wh* words move to the specifier position in CP.
   Option b: *Wh* words don't move.

The next section presents yet another example of parametric variation, this one involving verb movement.

LANGUAGE MATTERS   When *Wh* Words Don't Move in English

English requires *Wh* Movement when the question is a simple request for information but not in certain other types of questions.

1. *Incredulity questions, expressing disbelief or surprise.* Such questions usually have a high-rising intonation and heavy stress on the *wh* word.

   Speaker A: The President appointed his brother to the cabinet.
   Speaker B: The President appointed WHO to the cabinet?!!

2. *Pure echo questions, which request a repetition due to partial unintelligibility.* They also manifest a rising intonation and stress on the *wh* word, although perhaps less extreme than in the case of incredulity questions.

   Speaker A: The President appointed [mumble, mumble] to the cabinet.
   Speaker B: The President appointed WHO to the cabinet?

3. *Quizmaster questions, sometimes used by courtroom attorneys and quiz program announcers.* They have a flat or falling intonation.

   Now, Mr. Smith, you said you were where the night the Stanley Cup was stolen?
   For $15,000, the Lewis and Clark expedition began in what year?

Information from: J.-Marc Authier, "Nonquantificational *Wh* and Weakest Crossover," *Linguistic Inquiry* 24, 1 (1993): 161–168.

4.1 Verb Raising

Consider the contrast between the following two English sentences.

33) a. Paul always works.
    b. *Paul works always.

The ungrammaticality of the second sentence is expected since the preverbal adverb *always* functions as specifier of the verb and therefore should occur before it, as in *33a*. Surprisingly, however, the equivalent adverb must follow the verb in French, even though specifiers in French normally precede the head, just as they do in English.

34) a. If the adverb precedes the verb, the sentence is ungrammatical:
       *Paul **toujours** travaille. (= English *33a*)
       Paul **always** work
       'Paul always works.'

    b. If the adverb follows the verb, the sentence is grammatical:
       Paul travaille **toujours**. (= English *33b*)
       Paul work **always**
       'Paul always works.'

Why should this be? One possibility is that the tense feature in the T category attracts the verb to the T position in French, just as the Q feature can attract T to the C position in some languages. As a result, French has the **Verb Raising** rule outlined in *35*.

35) *Verb Raising*
  Move V to the T position.

This Move operation brings about the change depicted in Figure 5.23, adjoining the verb to the tense feature with which it is associated.

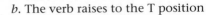

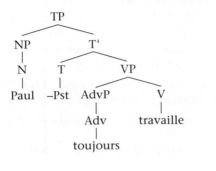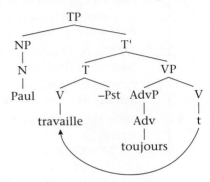

Figure 5.23   Verb Raising in French

An important piece of independent evidence for the existence of Verb Raising in French comes from Inversion. As we have already seen (Section 3.1), this operation moves the T category to the C position. In English, only auxiliary verbs occur in the T position, which explains why only they can undergo Inversion.

36) a. Inversion of an auxiliary verb in English:
      Will you *t* stay for supper?

  b. Inversion of a nonauxiliary verb in English:
      *Stay you *t* for supper?

In French, however, ordinary verbs can occur in the T position, thanks to Verb Raising. This predicts that Inversion in French should be able to apply to these verbs as well as to auxiliaries. This is correct. Like English, French can form a question by moving an auxiliary leftward (when the subject is a pronoun) as illustrated in *37*.

37) Inversion of an auxiliary:
  As-tu *t* essayé?

  'Have you tried?'

However, unlike English, French also allows inversion of nonauxiliary Vs.

38) Inversion of a nonauxiliary verb:
    Vois-tu *t* le livre?

    see you the book
    'Do you see the book?'

Figure 5.24 depicts the interaction between Verb Raising and Inversion: the V first raises to the T position; the T complex then moves to the C position.

a. Verb Raising: the V raises to T   *b.* Inversion: the T complex moves to C

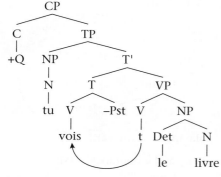
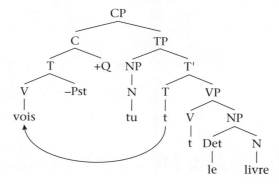

Figure 5.24 A *yes-no* question in French

Verb Raising in English

At this point, it might seem that there is a simple Verb Raising parameter with two options—raising (as in French) and no raising (as in English). This neatly accounts for the facts that we have considered so far, but matters are not so simple. As we'll see next, Verb Raising can apply in English, but only to *have* and *be*.

To begin, consider the sentences in *39*, which contain two auxiliaries—one modal and one nonmodal.

39) a. The students should have finished the project.
               ↑   ↑
            modal nonmodal

    b. The children could be playing in the yard.
            ↑ ↑
         modal nonmodal

As we have already seen, modal auxiliaries occur under T, but what about nonmodal auxiliaries? As depicted in Figure 5.25, they are considered to be a special type of V that takes a VP complement.

a.

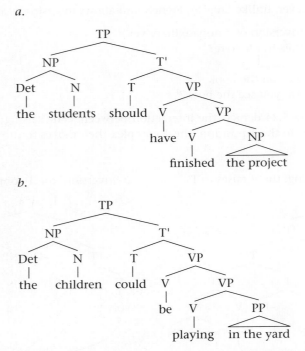

b.

Figure 5.25   Patterns containing a modal auxiliary and a nonmodal auxiliary

As expected, only the modal auxiliary can undergo Inversion in these structures.

40) a. The modal auxiliary verb moves to the C position (grammatical):
[_CP Should [_TP the students *t* have finished the project]]?

b. The nonmodal auxiliary moves to the C position (ungrammatical):
*[_CP Have [_TP the students should *t* finished the project]]?

Crucially, however, a nonmodal auxiliary can undergo Inversion when there is no modal.

41) [_CP Have [_TP the students *t* finished the project]]?

(from: The students have finished the project.)

Since Inversion involves movement from T to C, the auxiliary in *41* must have moved to the T position, and from there to the C position, as depicted in Figure 5.26.

a. Before Verb Raising

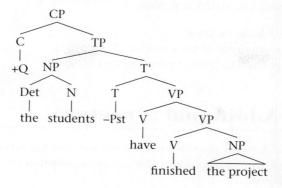

b. Verb Raising

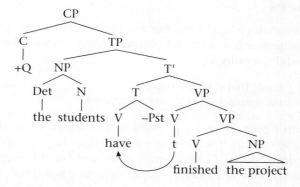

c. Inversion (raising of the T complex to C)

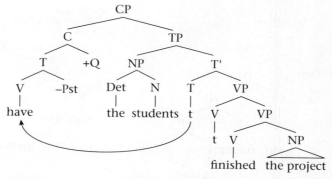

Figure 5.26   The V moves to the T position (Verb Raising); the T complex then raises to C (Inversion)

In sum, then, it appears that the two options permitted by the Verb Raising parameter should be stated as follows.

42) *The Verb Raising Parameter*
     Option a: Any type of verb raises to T (French).
     Option b: Only auxiliary verbs raise to T (English).

5   Some Additional Structures

Now that we have in place a basic system for forming sentences, it is possible to extend it to encompass various other syntactic phenomena, four of which will be considered here.

5.1   Modifiers

The term **modifier** is used for words and phrases that denote properties of heads. For example, adjective phrases (APs) commonly serve as modifiers of Ns, while adverb phrases (AdvPs) modify Vs.

43) a. a [$_{AP}$ good] friend of the family
     b. read the instructions [$_{AdvP}$ very carefully]

The adjective *good* denotes a property of the friend, while the AdvP *very carefully* describes the manner in which the reading occurred.

How do modifiers fit into phrase structure? For the purposes of this introduction to syntax, we will assume (as most syntacticians do) that they occur in an intermediate position, lower than specifiers but higher than complements, as illustrated in Figure 5.27.

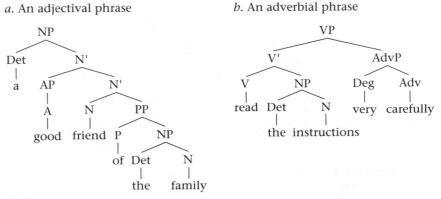

Figure 5.27   The place of modifiers in phrase structure

In Figure 5.27a, the modifier (on the left side of the head) occurs lower than the specifier (the determiner *a*), but higher than the complement (the PP *of the family*), creating two intermediate levels in the phrase. In Figure 5.27b, the modifier (the adverbial phrase) occurs on the right side of the head, once again above the complement.

5.2   Relative Clauses

Sometimes even CPs can serve as modifiers. In the following sentence, for instance, a special type of CP called a **relative clause** provides information about the N before it.

44) a. The friend [$_{CP}$ who Leslie visited _] lives in Colorado.
      b. the choice [$_{CP}$ which most people prefer _]

Relative clause structures resemble *wh* questions in two respects. First, they can begin with a *wh* word such as *who* or *which* (a so-called **relative pronoun**). Second, there is an empty position within the sentence from which the *wh* phrase has apparently been moved. (In *44a* and *b*, that position occurs right after the transitive verb.)

The first step in the formation of the relative clause in *44a* involves the D-structure in Figure 5.28; the **+Rel feature** in the C position indicates that the CP is a relative clause. (The CP here includes an open specifier position for subsequent use as a landing site for *Wh* Movement.)

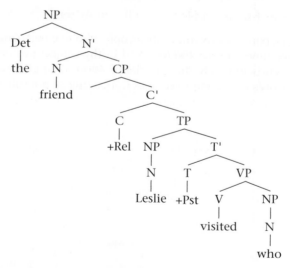

Figure 5.28   The D-structure for a relative clause

Here, the *wh* word *who* occurs as complement of the verb *visit* since it corresponds to the direct object (the person who was visited). The next step involves the application of *Wh* Movement (triggered by the +Rel feature in the C position) to give the structure in Figure 5.29, with the *wh* word ending up in the specifier position within CP.

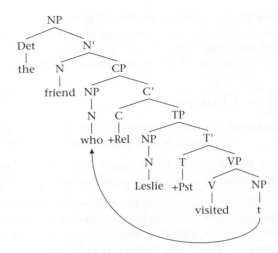

Figure 5.29   The S-structure for a relative clause: the *wh* word moves to the specifier position in CP

In the preceding example, the *wh* word originates in the direct object position. In *45*, in contrast, it originates in the subject position.

45) Sue met some people [ₒₚ who live in Arizona].

Here *who* corresponds to certain people who live in Arizona. The D-structure for this sentence therefore has the *wh* word in the subject position. Like other *wh* words, it subsequently moves to the specifier position within CP even though the actual order of the words in the sentence does not change as a result of this movement.

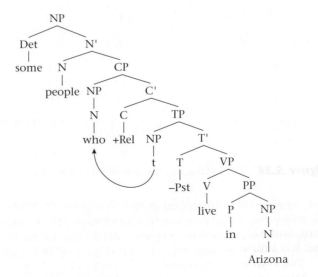

Figure 5.30   A subject relative clause

5.3   Passives

Another important syntactic phenomenon involves the relationship between the two sentence types exemplified in *46*. (The first type is called **active** because the subject denotes the **agent** or instigator of the action denoted by the verb, while the second is called **passive**.)

46) a. Active sentence type:
      A thief stole the painting.

   b. Passive sentence type:
      The painting was stolen (by a thief).

We will focus here on two key properties of passive constructions. First, passive constructions involve a major reduction in the importance of the agent. Whereas the agent serves as subject of an active clause, it is not expressed at all in the vast majority of passive sentences in English.

47) The painting was stolen.

Second, some other NP—usually the direct object of the corresponding active sentence—functions as subject in the passive sentence. This too can be seen in example *47*, where the NP *the painting* serves as direct object in the active sentence and as subject in the passive sentence.

The D-structure for a passive sentence such as *The painting was stolen* is depicted in Figure 5.31. Note that the auxiliary *be* is treated as a V that takes a VP complement. We include an empty subject position under TP. (When the agent is expressed as part of a PP [e.g., *by the thief*], the PP is attached to the lower VP, to the right of the verb's NP complement.)

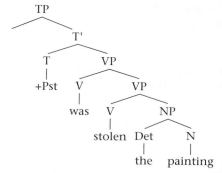

Figure 5.31   The D-structure for the passive sentence *The painting was stolen*

This D-structure is admittedly abstract—it does not sound like any sentence that we actually utter. However, it neatly captures the two key properties of passive constructions. First, the agent is not expressed, leaving the subject position open. Second, the verb has a direct object that can take over as subject.

The D-structure in Figure 5.31 is converted into an S-structure with the help of the Move operation in *48*, known as **NP Movement**.

48) *NP Movement*
    Move NP into the specifier position in TP.

Movement of the NP *the painting* to the subject position gives the S-structure depicted in Figure 5.32.

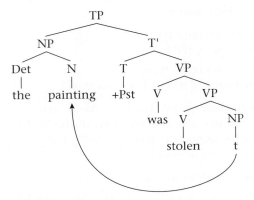

Figure 5.32   S-structure resulting from NP Movement

5.4   VP-Internal Subjects

As we have just seen, the subject in a passive sentence originates in the complement position within the VP. Interestingly, there is reason to think that (contrary to what we have been assuming) subjects of active sentences also originate inside the VP—in the specifier position. (If this is right, then preverbal adverbs such as *perhaps* and *always* would have to be treated as modifiers rather than as specifiers of VP—a relatively minor adjustment.)
    Sentence *49* provides a preliminary illustration of how this works.

49) Children are playing in the yard.

As illustrated in Figure 5.33, the sentence's subject (*children*) occurs in the specifier position in VP in D-structure.

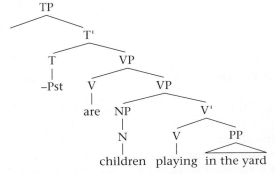

Figure 5.33   D-structure for the sentence *Children are playing in the yard*

It subsequently moves (via NP Movement) to the specifier position in TP.

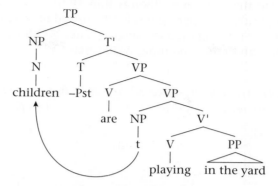

Figure 5.34 Movement to the specifier position in TP, via NP Movement

Various facts make this analysis attractive; we will mention just two here.

First, there are patterns in which the would-be subject is trapped inside the VP, in the specifier position. One such pattern is illustrated in *50*, where the subject position is occupied by *there*—a special place-filling NP with no meaning of its own.

50) [$_{TP}$ There are [$_{VP}$ children playing in the yard]].

As illustrated in Figure 5.35, the presence of *there* in the specifier position in TP forces the NP that would otherwise be the subject (*children*) to remain in its point of origin—the specifier position inside VP.

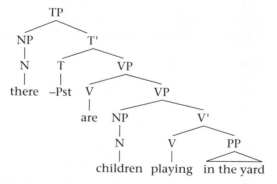

Figure 5.35 An NP trapped inside a VP

Second, we now have a tantalizing explanation for patterns in which the verb comes before the subject—the preferred word order in about 10 percent of the world's languages. The following example is from Welsh.

51) Gwelodd Siôn ddraig.
    saw   John dragon
    'John saw a dragon.'

It is hard to see how this order can be accommodated in tree structures that place subjects in the specifier position within TP. However, a straightforward analysis is possible if subjects originate inside VP: instead of raising the subject to the specifier position in TP as English does, languages like Welsh leave the subject where it is but raise the verb to the T position. As illustrated in Figure 5.36, this gives verb–subject order.

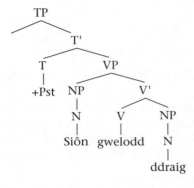
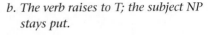
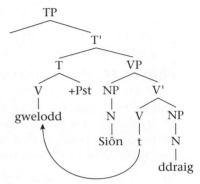

a. The verb and the subject NP in their original positions

b. The verb raises to T; the subject NP stays put.

Figure 5.36   Verb Raising in Welsh (Welsh data in this section from: Richard Sproat, "Welsh Syntax and VSO Structure" in *Natural Language and Linguistic Theory* 3 (1985): 173–216.

This idea makes a crucial prediction: the verb should have to stay inside the VP in cases where the T position is already filled. This seems to be exactly right: when the T position is occupied by the special auxiliary verb *gwnaeth* 'did', the main verb *weld* 'see' (without tense) remains inside the VP after the subject *Siôn*.

52) Gwnaeth Siôn weld draig.
    did   John see   dragon
    'John saw a dragon.'

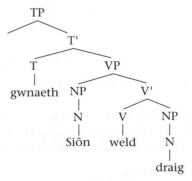

Figure 5.37   Sentence in which the T position is filled

LANGUAGE MATTERS   The World's Most Controversial Language

In 2005, a startling report was published on Pirahã, a language spoken by a few hundred mostly monolingual tribespeople in the rainforest of northwestern Brazil. Pirahã, it was reported, lacks complex syntactic structure in general, including complement clauses and coordination: unlike every other known language, it supposedly permits only short, simple sentences. (It is also said to lack color terms, numerals, and quantity-denoting expressions such as *every* and *some*.) Although the report has received widespread attention in the media, its conclusions are being hotly debated within linguistics. A great deal of additional research and scrutiny will be required before a consensus is reached on the status of this fascinating language.

Information from: John Colapinto, "The Interpreter," *The New Yorker*, April 16, 2007, 118–137.
Daniel Everett, "Pirahã Culture and Grammar: A Response to Some Criticisms," *Language* 85, 2 (2009): 405–442.
Andrew Nevins, David Pesetsky, and Cilene Rodrigues, "Pirahã Exceptionality: A Reassessment," *Language* 85, 2 (2009): 355–404.

The possibility of VP-internal subjects obviously has wide-ranging consequences. If it is right, then we need to rethink how we define subjects (they are no longer just specifiers of TP) and what D-structure looks like. Your instructor will decide whether you should revise the way you draw tree structures or whether the VP-internal subject analysis should be set aside for now.

Summing Up

Syntactic structure is built by two basic operations. A **Merge** operation combines words in accordance with their **syntactic category** and their **subcategorization** properties, creating a representation called **D(eep) Structure**. D-structure must comply with the **X' Schema**, which stipulates the place of **heads**, **specifiers**, and **complements** in phrase structure. **Move** operations can modify D-structure by moving words and phrases in particular ways to produce a **S(urface) structure**.

   Although the form of sentences can vary considerably from language to language, **Universal Grammar** appears to provide all languages with the same general type of syntactic mechanisms. Differences among languages can, for the most part, be attributed to a small set of **parameters**, each of which makes available a variety of alternatives from which individual languages may choose.

Key Terms

General terms

grammatical	recursion	syntax

Terms concerning syntactic categories

adjective (A)	modal auxiliaries
adverbs (Adv)	nonlexical (functional) categories
auxiliary verb (Aux)	nonmodal auxiliaries
conjunction (Con)	noun (N)
degree word (Deg)	parts of speech
determiner (Det)	preposition (P)
distribution	syntactic categories
lexical categories	verb (V)

Terms concerning combining words into phrases

complements	intransitive	specifiers
direct object	Merge	transitive
head	phrases	X' Schema

Terms concerning tests for phrase structure

constituents	movement test
coordinate structures	substitution test
coordination test	

Terms concerning complement options

clauses	matrix clause
complement clause	subcategorization
complementizers (C)	

Terms concerning the Move operation and parametric variation

deep structure (D-structure)	transformation
Head-Complement Parameter	(transformational) generative grammar
Inversion	Universal Grammar (UG)
Move	Verb Raising
parameters	*Wh* Movement
Q feature	*Wh* Movement Parameter
surface structure (S-structure)	*wh* questions
trace	*yes-no* questions

Terms concerning additional structures

active	passive
agent	+Rel feature
modifier	relative clause
NP Movement	relative pronoun

Recommended Reading

Adger, David. 2003. *Core Syntax.* Oxford: Oxford University Press.
Beockx, Cedric. 2011. *The Oxford Handbook of Linguistic Minimalism.* Oxford: Oxford University Press.

Appendix: How to Build Tree Structures

In building a tree structure from scratch for a phrase or sentence that you are analyzing, you will probably find it easiest to proceed in steps, working from the bottom up and from right to left. As an illustration, let us first consider the phrase *a picture of Mary.*

Using Merge to Build Simple Phrases

The first step involves assigning each word to the appropriate category, as depicted in Figure 5.38.

```
Det      N        P       N
 |       |        |       |
 a     picture   of     Mary
```

Figure 5.38   The first step: determining the word-level categories

Then, working from right to left, the appropriate phrasal structure is built above each head. Thus, since the preposition to the left of *Mary* cannot function as a specifier of an NP, we build an NP above the N *Mary*.

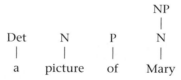

Figure 5.39   Construction of the NP

Next, we carry out the same procedure for the P *of*, combining it with the NP *Mary* (its complement), as depicted in Figure 5.40.

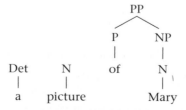

Figure 5.40   Combination of the P *of* with its complement NP, resulting in a PP

Next, the N *picture* combines with the PP, to give an N'.

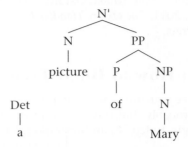

Figure 5.41   Combination of the N *picture* with its complement PP

Finally, the determiner is added as specifier of the N, giving the full NP depicted in Figure 5.42.

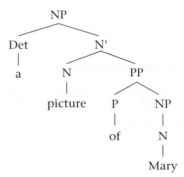

Figure 5.42   Addition of the Det *a*

Using Merge to Build Sentence Structure

Consider now how we proceed in the case of a complete sentence such as *The dog might bite that man*. Assignment of each word to the appropriate category gives the structure depicted in Figure 5.43.

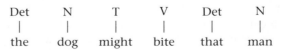

Figure 5.43   Category assignment

Then, working from right to left, it is easy to see that *bite that man* forms a VP.

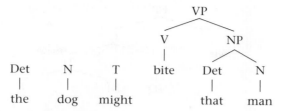

Figure 5.44   The VP *bite that man*

Next, the T *might* combines with the VP, creating a T', which is then merged with the subject NP *the dog*. The resulting TP is then embedded in a CP, whose head carries the feature –Q, indicating a statement rather than a question.

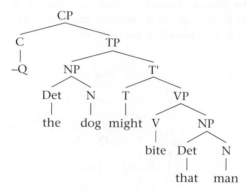

Figure 5.45   The complete sentence

Using Move

Recognizing that a Move operation such as Inversion or *Wh* Movement has applied is relatively simple: if a sentence contains an auxiliary verb in front of the subject, then Inversion has applied; if it begins with a *wh* word, then *Wh* Movement has applied. In the sentence *What should the farmers plant?*, then, both operations have applied.

In order to represent the deep structure, we must place the auxiliary verb in its normal position under T and we must determine the position from which the *wh* word has been moved. Since the *wh* word in the sentence *What should the farmers plant?* asks about the complement of the verb (the thing that is planted), we place *what* in the complement position within VP in deep structure. This gives the deep structure depicted in Figure 5.46.

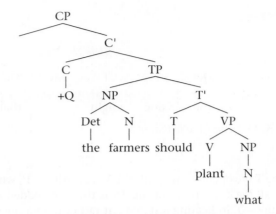

Figure 5.46 The D-structure for *What should the farmers plant?*

Attracted by the +Q feature, *should* then moves to the C position (Inversion) and *what* moves to the specifier position under CP (*Wh* Movement), yielding the complete S-structure depicted in Figure 5.47.

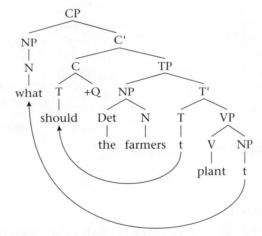

Figure 5.47 Application of Inversion and *Wh* Movement gives the S-structure

---

Some things to remember

- A sentence is a TP, with a T as its head.
- The T position contains either a modal auxiliary (if there is one) or the ±Pst tense feature.
- Every T takes a VP as its complement.
- Every T has an NP specifer (the subject).
- Every TP occurs inside a CP shell (although this is sometimes not represented for reasons of space).

Exercises

1. Place an asterisk next to any of the sentences that are ungrammatical for you. Can you figure out what makes these sentences ungrammatical?
   a) The instructor told the students to study.
   b) The instructor suggested the students to study.
   c) The customer asked for a cold beer.
   d) The customer requested for a cold beer.
   e) He gave the Red Cross some money.
   f) He donated the Red Cross some money.
   g) The pilot landed the jet.
   h) The jet landed.
   i) A journalist wrote the article.
   j) The article wrote.
   k) Jerome is satisfied of his job.
   l) Jerome is tired of his job.

2. Indicate the category of each word in the following sentences. (It may help to refer back to Section 1.1.)
   a) That glass broke.
   b) A jogger ran toward the end of the lane.
   c) These tall trees are blocking the road.
   d) The detective looked through the records.
   e) The peaches never appear quite ripe.
   f) Jeremy will play the trumpet and the drums in the orchestra.

3. Each of the following phrases consists of a specifier and a head. For each example, draw a tree structure that complies with the X' Schema. (See Section 1.2.)
   a) the zoo   f) this house
   b) always try   g) very competent
   c) so witty   h) quite cheap
   d) perhaps pass   i) never surrender
   e) less bleak   j) those books

4. The following phrases include a head, a complement, and (in some cases) a specifier. For each example, draw a tree structure that complies with the X' Schema, following the same abbreviatory conventions adopted in the chapter. (See Section 1.2.)
   a) into the house
   b) fixed the printer
   c) full of mistakes
   d) more toward the window
   e) a film about pollution
   f) always study this material
   g) perhaps earn the money
   h) that argument with Owen
   i) the success of the program

5. Drawing on the X' Schema, draw trees for each of the following sentences. (See Section 1.3.)
   a) Those guests should leave.
   b) Maria never ate a brownie.
   c) That shelf will fall.
   d) The glass broke.
   e) The student lost the debate.
   f) The manager may offer a raise.
   g) The judge never jails shoplifters.
   h) The teacher often organized a discussion.
   i) A psychic will speak to this group.
   j) Marianne could become quite fond of Larry.

6. Apply the substitution test to determine which of the bracketed sequences in the following sentences form constituents. (See Section 1.4.)
   a) [The news] upset the entire family.
   b) They hid [in the cave].
   c) The [computer was very] expensive.
   d) [The houses] will be rebuilt.
   e) Jane will [leave town].
   f) The goslings [swam across] the lake.

7. Apply the movement test to determine which of the bracketed sequences in the following sentences form constituents. (See Section 1.4.)
   a) We ate our lunch [near the river bank].
   b) Steve looked [up the number] in the book.
   c) The [island has been] flooded.
   d) I love [peanut butter and bacon sandwiches].
   e) The environmental [movement is gaining momentum].

8. Lexical categories are divided into subcategories on the basis of their complements. For each of the following words, two potential complement options are given. (See Sections 2.1 and 2.2.)

   i)   For each word, determine which one of the two options better matches its subcategorization requirements.
   ii) Justify your choice by creating a sentence using that complement option.

Verb	Options		Verb	Options
a) expire	Ø *or* NP NP		e) clean	NP PP$_{for}$ *or* NP NP
b) destroy	NP *or* Ø		f) mumble	NP *or* NP NP
c) observe	NP *or* PP$_{to}$ PP$_{about}$		g) throw	Ø *or* NP PP$_{loc}$
d) discuss	NP *or* Ø		h) paint	NP PP$_{to}$ *or* NP PP$_{for}$

Noun	Options
i) debate	PP$_{of}$ PP$_{to}$ *or* PP$_{with}$ PP$_{about}$
j) hammer	Ø *or* PP$_{with}$ PP$_{about}$
k) success	PP$_{of}$ PP$_{to}$ *or* PP$_{of}$
l) transfer	PP$_{with}$ PP$_{about}$ *or* PP$_{of}$ PP$_{to}$
m) sickness	Ø *or* PP$_{with}$ PP$_{about}$

Adjective	Options
n) strong	Ø *or* PP$_{about}$
o) sick	NP *or* PP$_{of}$
p) happy	PP$_{with}$ *or* PP$_{of}$
q) knowledgeable	PP$_{to}$ *or* PP$_{about}$
r) small	PP$_{of}$ *or* Ø

9. The following sentences all contain embedded clauses that function as complements of a verb. Draw a tree structure for each sentence. (See Section 2.3.)
   a) The reporter said that an accident injured a woman.
   b) The fishermen think that the company polluted the bay.
   c) Bill reported that a student asked whether the eclipse would occur.

10. The derivations of the following sentences involve the Inversion transformation. Draw tree structures for the deep structure and the surface structure for each sentence. (See Sections 3.1 and 3.3.)
    a) Will the boss hire Hillary?
    b) Can the dog fetch the frisbee?
    c) Should the student report the incident?
    d) Must the musicians play that sonata?
    e) Might that player leave the team?

11. The following sentences involve the rules of *Wh* Movement and Inversion. Draw the trees to show the deep structure and the surface structure for each of these sentences. (See Sections 3.2 and 3.3.)
    a) Who should the director call?
    b) What can Joanne eat?
    c) Who will the visitors stay with?
    d) What might Terry sing?
    e) What could Anne bring to the gathering? (Hint: See Figure 5.13.)
    f) Who should call the director? (Hint: See Figure 5.21.)

12. The following data illustrate the formation of *yes-no* questions in German.
    a) Das Kind wird die Schwester lehren.
       the child will the sister teach
       'The child will teach the sister.'
    b) Wird das Kind die Schwester lehren?
       will the child the sister teach
       'Will the child teach the sister?'
    c) Der Mann liebt die Frau.
       the man loves the woman
       'The man loves the woman.'
    d) Liebt der Mann die Frau?
       loves the man the woman
       'Does the man love the woman?'

Assuming that German makes use of the same Inversion operation as English (i.e., "Move T to the C position"), what do the above data tell us about whether German employs the Verb Raising operation? (See Section 4.1.)

13. Draw the tree structure for the following sentences, each of which contains one or more modifiers. (Because no movement is involved in any of these sentences, the deep structure and surface structure will be alike.) (See Section 5.1.)
    a) The efficient workers finished very quickly.
    b) A very clever engineer designed this new car.
    c) The large tiger suddenly leapt into the tree.

14. Each of the following phrases contains a relative clause. Draw the deep structure and the surface structure for each. (See Section 5.2.)
    a) the girl who Jane befriended
    b) the girl who Millie talked to
    c) the cyclist who the hiker met
    d) the cyclist who met the hiker
    e) the tree which the President stood under

 **LaunchPad Solo** | For more helpful content and quizzes, go to the LaunchPad Solo
macmillan learning | for *Contemporary Linguistics* at **launchpadworks.com**.

For the Student Linguist

BACKWARDS

Sometimes poetry frustrates me because of all the seemingly nonsensical sentence bits I get after my brain automatically inserts a dramatic pause at the end of each line. Because I'm stuck, waiting for my eyes to get to the next line as I try to figure out what's so incredibly significant about a line consisting of "Eskimo" or "his amber eyes" or "detritus" and nothing else. But I really like Lesléa Newman's work because the line divisions actually seem meaningful and because she seems to be having so much fun arranging these sentence bits.

Tiff and I*

Tiff and I sit
in Tompkins Square Park
reading poetry
under a sky
full of clapping pigeons.
He calls them flying rats
but I think
the pink and green circles
around their necks
like greasy oil puddles are
beautiful.

> Tiff says
> all my poems sound better
> backwards.
>
> Backwards
> all my poems sound better
> Tiff says.
> Beautiful
> like greasy oil puddles
> around their necks are
> the pink and green circles
> but I think
> he calls them flying rats.
> Full of clapping pigeons
> under a sky
> reading poetry
> in Tompkins Square Park
> Tiff and I sit.

If you read the poem as if it were prose, I think the first half sounds pretty bland and the second half is just plain loopy:

> Tiff and I sit in Tompkins Square Park reading poetry under a sky full of clapping pigeons. He calls them flying rats but I think the pink and green circles around their necks like greasy oil puddles are beautiful. Tiff says all my poems sound better backwards.

> Backwards all my poems sound better Tiff says. Beautiful like greasy oil puddles around their necks are the pink and green circles but I think he calls them flying rats. Full of clapping pigeons under a sky reading poetry in Tompkins Square Park Tiff and I sit.

In fact, I can't read the second half in prose format without imagining flying poems that have greasy pink and green circles around their necks, a sky that is reading poetry, and two people who've spent the afternoon eating live pigeons.

What is it about the change from prose to poetry that makes this string of words interesting and meaningful? (We've got to drudge through some syntax here, but trust me, it's relatively painless and worth it.) Assume that the first half of the poem has three untransformed sentences, and the second half has sentences that have undergone transformations. Also notice that one word—*are*—gets switched into a different line in the second stanza. It shouldn't be too hard to draw tree structures for the sentences in the first stanza *if* you do it line by line (i.e., first draw the tree for "Tiff and I sit," then for "in Tompkins Square Park," etc., and then hook them together).

The sentences in the second stanza will be harder to draw trees for, but if you do the first stanza line by line, those parts will be the same, except for where the word *are* is switched. So all you really need to do is figure out which parts of the trees got moved, and in which order. Actually, that's not even too hard to do, since only constituents can be moved.

You've probably figured out by now why this poem is in the syntax chapter: it does a good job of showing off what constituents are and of showing how the same words, even the same phrases, can have a different meaning when they're moved. However, this poem does more than show off constituents. I also like the rhythm of the poem—the way some of the lines seem to invite me to pause after them, and other lines lead me quickly on to the next line. Take a look at the subcategorizations of the last word of each line. Some of them lead you to expect a complement and others don't. Try reading the poem again and see if the subcategorization frames make a difference in how much emphasis you put on each line.

Finally, look at some other poetry that you love or hate and see what sort of match there is between grouping in lines or stanzas and grouping into constituents. Look at some different types of writing and their phrase structures; since punctuation is sadly limited in how well it can show pauses or emphasis or any sort of complex tone, the actual structure of the sentence can be crucial if the sentence is to be read with the right emphasis. And look in particular at some of your own writing and at how transformations of sentences could make a difference in their clarity. All of this theory might actually improve your writing.

*Newman, Lesléa, "Tiff and I," in *Sweet Dark Places* (Santa Cruz, CA: HerBooks, 1991).

Semantics: The Analysis of Meaning

William O'Grady

In every object there is inexhaustible meaning.
—THOMAS CARLYLE, *The French Revolution* (1848)

OBJECTIVES

In this chapter, you will learn:

• how we derive meaning from words and sentences
• how different languages encode concepts in words and sentences
• how we use sentence structure to produce and understand meaning
• how speaker beliefs and attitudes, setting, and context contribute to meaning

 **LaunchPad Solo** | For more helpful content and quizzes, go to the LaunchPad Solo
macmillan learning | for *Contemporary Linguistics* at **launchpadworks.com**.

In order for language to fulfill its communicative function, utterances must convey a message; they must have content. Speaking very generally, we can refer to an utterance's content as its **meaning**.

This chapter is concerned with **semantics**, the study of meaning in human language. Because some work in this complicated area of linguistic analysis presupposes considerable knowledge of other disciplines (particularly logic, mathematics, and philosophy), not all aspects of contemporary semantics are suitable for presentation in an introductory linguistics textbook. We will restrict our attention here to four major topics in semantics: (1) the nature of meaning, (2) some of the properties of the conceptual system underlying meaning, (3) the contribution of syntactic structure to the interpretation of sentences, and (4) the role of nongrammatical factors in the understanding of utterances.

1   The Nature of Meaning

Long before linguistics existed as a discipline, thinkers were speculating about the nature of meaning. For thousands of years, this question has been considered central to philosophy; more recently, it has come to be important in other disciplines as well—including of course linguistics and psychology. Contributions to semantics have come from a diverse group of scholars, ranging from Plato and Aristotle in ancient Greece to Bertrand Russell in the twentieth century. Our goal in this section will be to explore, in a very general way, what this research has revealed about meaning in human language. We will begin by considering some of the basic analytic notions used in evaluating the meanings of words and sentences.

1.1   Semantic Relations among Words

Words and phrases can enter into a variety of semantic relations with each other. Because these relations help identify those aspects of meaning relevant to linguistic analysis, they constitute a good starting point for this chapter.

Synonymy

Synonyms are words or expressions that have the same meaning in some or all contexts. The pairs of words in Table 6.1 provide plausible examples of synonymy in English.

Table 6.1   Some synonyms in English

filbert	hazelnut
youth	adolescent
automobile	car
remember	recall
purchase	buy
big	large

Because it would be inefficient for a language to have two words or phrases with absolutely identical meanings, perfect synonymy is rare, if not impossible. For example, although *youth* and *adolescent* both refer to people of about the same age, only the latter word can be used to imply immaturity—as in "He's acting like such an adolescent!"

Antonymy

Antonyms are words or phrases that are opposites with respect to some component of their meaning. The pairs of words in Table 6.2 provide examples of antonymy.

Table 6.2 Some antonyms in English

dark	light
boy	girl
hot	cold
up	down
in	out
come	go

In each of these pairs, the two words contrast with respect to at least one aspect of their meaning. For instance, the meanings of *boy* and *girl* are opposites with respect to gender, although they are alike in other respects (both are human). Similarly, *come* and *go* are opposites with respect to direction, although both involve the concept of movement.

LANGUAGE MATTERS Hypernyms and Related Relations

There are also various less-known relations among words—such as the relationship between the word *dog* and the words for various types of dogs (*spaniel, collie, beagle*, etc.). The word for the general class (here, *dog*) is called the *hypernym*, whereas the words for the members of that class are its *hyponyms*. Of course, *dog* has a hypernym too—*animal*.

Meronyms designate the parts of a whole, and a *holonym* is the whole to which parts belong. Meronyms for *dog* include *head, nose, paws, tail*, and so forth. Conversely, *dog* is the holonym for those parts.

You can find a large online database of these relations at Princeton University's *WordNet: A Lexical Database for English* (http://wordnet.princeton.edu).

Polysemy and Homophony

Polysemy occurs where a word has two or more related meanings. Table 6.3 contains some examples of polysemous words in English.

Table 6.3 Some polysemy in English

Word	Meaning a	Meaning b
bright	'shining'	'intelligent'
to glare	'to shine intensely'	'to stare angrily'
a deposit	'minerals in the earth'	'money in the bank'

If you consult a reasonably comprehensive dictionary for any language, you will find numerous examples of polysemy. For example, my dictionary lists several related meanings for the word *mark*.

1) Polysemy in the meaning of *mark*:
   - a visible trace or impression on something (*The tires left a mark on the road.*)
   - a written or printed symbol (*You need a punctuation mark here.*)
   - an exam score, as in school (*He got a good mark on the math test.*)
   - a target (*She hit the mark every time.*)
   - an indication of some quality or property (*The mark of a good diplomat is the ability to negotiate.*)

Homophony exists where a single phonetic form has two or more entirely distinct meanings (see Table 6.4). In such cases, it is assumed that these are separate words with the same pronunciation rather than a single word with different meanings.

Table 6.4   Some homophones in English

Word	Meaning a	Meaning b
light	'not heavy'	'illumination'
bank	'a financial institution'	'the land at the edge of a river'
club	'a social organization'	'a blunt weapon'
pen	'a writing instrument'	'an enclosure'

Homophones need not have identical spellings—*write* and *right* are homophones, as are *piece* and *peace*.

Polysemy and homophony create **lexical ambiguity**, in that a single form has two or more meanings. Thus, a sentence such as *2* could mean either that Liz purchased an instrument to write with or that she bought an enclosure.

2) Liz bought a pen.

Of course, in actual speech the surrounding words and sentences usually make the intended meaning clear. The potential lexical ambiguity in sentences such as the following therefore normally goes unnoticed.

3) He got a loan from the *bank*.

4) She sat on the *bank* of the river and watched the boats go by.

LANGUAGE MATTERS   Similar in Other Ways

Different words with the same spelling are called **homographs**. The examples in Table 6.4 are therefore homographs as well as homophones, whereas *write* and *right* are just homophones. In contrast, the *bow* that means 'weapon for shooting arrows' and the *bow* that means 'bend at the waist' are homographs but not homophones since they have different pronunciations—[bow] and [baw], respectively. Words that are both homophones and homographs are commonly called **homonyms**.

LANGUAGE MATTERS   The Pinnacle of Polysemy

The most ambiguous word in English may well be the word *set*. In an entry that extends over nineteen pages, the *Oxford English Dictionary* lists more than 150 meanings and uses. Here are some examples:

Set the box on the floor.

Set the wood on fire.

Set the table.

Let's play a *set* of tennis.

a *set* of golf clubs

a *set* time

1.2   Semantic Relations Involving Sentences

Like words, sentences have meanings that can be analyzed in terms of their relation to other meanings. Three such relations—paraphrase, entailment, and contradiction—are particularly important.

Paraphrase

Two sentences that have essentially the same meaning are said to be **paraphrases** of each other. The following pairs of sentences provide examples of paraphrase.

5) a. The police chased the burglar.
   b. The burglar was chased by the police.

6) a. I gave the summons to Erin.
   b. I gave Erin the summons.

7) a. It is unfortunate that the team lost.
   b. Unfortunately, the team lost.

8) a. Paul bought a car from Sue.
   b. Sue sold a car to Paul.

9) a. The game will begin at 3:00 p.m.
   b. At 3:00 p.m., the game will begin.

The *a* and *b* sentences in each of the above pairs are obviously very similar in meaning. Indeed, it would be impossible for one sentence to be true without the other also being true. Thus, if it is true that the police chased the burglar, it must also be true that the burglar was chased by the police. (Sentences whose meanings are related to each other in this way are said to have the same **truth conditions**—that is, they are true under the same circumstances.)

For some linguists, this is enough to justify saying that the two sentences have the same meaning. However, you may notice that there are subtle differences in emphasis between the *a* and *b* sentences in *5* to *9*. For instance, it is natural to interpret *5a* as a statement about what the police did and *5b* as a statement about what happened to the burglar. Similarly, *9b* seems to place more emphasis on the starting time of the game than *9a* does. As is the case with synonymy, many linguists feel that languages do not permit two or more structures to have absolutely identical meanings and that paraphrases are therefore never perfect.

Entailment

When the truth of one sentence guarantees the truth of another sentence, we say that there is a relation of **entailment**. This relation is mutual in the case of examples *5* to *9* since the truth of either sentence in the pair guarantees the truth of the other. In examples such as the following, however, entailment is asymmetrical.

10) a. The park wardens killed the bear.
    b. The bear is dead.

11) a. Prince is a dog.
    b. Prince is an animal.

If it is true that the park wardens killed the bear, then it must also be true that the bear is dead. However, the reverse does not follow since the bear could be dead without the park wardens having killed it. Similarly, if it is true that Prince is a dog, then it is also true that Prince is an animal. Once again, though, the reverse does not hold: even if we know that Prince is an animal, we cannot conclude that he is a dog rather than, say, a horse or a cat.

Contradiction

Sometimes it turns out that if one sentence is true, then another sentence must be false. This is the case with the examples in *12*.

12) a. Charles is a bachelor.
   b. Charles is married.

If it is true that Charles is a bachelor, then it cannot be true that he is married. When two sentences cannot both be true, we say that there is a **contradiction**.

1.3   What Is Meaning?

Although it is relatively easy to determine whether two words or sentences have identical or different meanings, it is much more difficult to determine precisely what meaning is in the first place. In fact, despite many centuries of study, we still know very little about the nature of meaning or how it is represented in the human mind. Nonetheless, it is worthwhile to review briefly some of the better-known proposals and the problems that they encounter.

LANGUAGE MATTERS   Meaning and the Body

The meanings of many words are tightly integrated with physical experience. Indeed, studies have shown that exposure to verbs denoting various physical actions trigger involuntary activation of the part of the brain responsible for controlling those actions. Seeing the word *chew* leads to activation of the part of the brain that controls movement of the mouth, seeing *kick* stimulates the part of the brain associated with leg movements, and so on.

Information from: F. Pulvermüller, M. Härle, and F. Hummel, "Walking or Talking? Behavioral and Neurophysiological Correlates of Action Verb Processing," *Brain and Language* 78 (2001): 143–168; O. Hauk, I. Johnsrude, and F. Pulvermüller, "Somatotopic Representation of Action Words in Human Motor and Premotor Cortex," *Neuron* 41, 2 (2004): 301–307.

Connotation

One notion that is closely linked with the concept of meaning is **connotation**, the set of associations that a word's use can evoke. For most Minnesotans, for example, the word *winter* evokes thoughts of snow, bitter cold, short days, frozen fingertips, and the like. These associations make up the word's connotation, but they cannot be its meaning (or at least not its entire meaning). The word *winter* does not become meaningless just because it is a mild year or because one moves to Florida in November. We must therefore look beyond connotation for our understanding of what meaning is.

Denotation

One well-known approach to semantics attempts to equate the meaning of a word or phrase with the entities to which it refers—its **denotation** or **referents**. The denotation of the word *winter*, for example, corresponds to the season between the winter solstice and the spring equinox, regardless of whether it is cold and unpleasant. Similarly, the denotation of the word *dog* corresponds to the set of canines, and so on.

Although a word's denotation is clearly connected to its meaning in some way, they cannot be one and the same thing. This is because there are words such as *unicorn* and phrases such as *the present king of France*, which have no referents in the real world even though they are far from meaningless.

A problem of a different sort arises with expressions such as *the Speaker of the House* and *the leader of the House Republicans*, both of which refer (in 2015, at least) to Paul Ryan. Although these two expressions may have the same referent, it seems wrong to say that they mean the same thing. Thus, we would not say that the phrase *the Speaker of the House* is defined as 'the leader of the House Republicans' or that the definition of the phrase *leader of the House Republicans* is 'the Speaker of the House'.

Extension and Intension

The impossibility of equating an element's meaning with its referents has led to a distinction between **extension** and **intension**. Whereas an expression's extension corresponds to the set of entities that it picks out in the world (its referents), its intension corresponds to its inherent sense, the concepts that it evokes. Thus, the extension of *woman* is a set of real world entities (women) while its intension involves notions like 'female' and 'human'. Similarly, the phrase *the Chief Justice of the Supreme Court* has as its extension an individual (John Roberts), but its intension involves the concept 'presiding judge of the Supreme Court' (see Table 6.5).

Table 6.5 Extension versus intension

Phrase	Extension	Intension
Chief Justice of the Supreme Court	John Roberts	presiding judge of the Supreme Court
Super Bowl champions	Denver Broncos (2016)	winners of the NFL championship
Capital of Missouri	Jefferson City	city containing the state legislature

The distinction between intension and extension does not allow us to resolve the question of what meaning is. It simply permits us to pose it in a new way: What are intensions?

One suggestion is that intensions correspond to mental images. This is an obvious improvement over the referential theory since it is possible to have a mental image of a unicorn or even of the king of France even though no such entities exist in the real world. However, problems arise with the meanings of words such as *dog*, which can be used to refer to animals of many different sizes, shapes, and colors. If the meaning of this word corresponds to a mental image, that image would have to be general enough to include chihuahuas and St. Bernards, yet still exclude foxes and wolves. If you try to draw a picture that satisfies these requirements, you will see just how hard it is to construct an image for meanings of this sort.

Componential Analysis

Still another approach to meaning tries to represent a word's intension by breaking it down into smaller semantic components. Sometimes known as **componential analysis** or **semantic decomposition**, this approach has often been used to analyze the meaning of certain types of nouns in terms of **semantic features**. The analysis in Figure 6.1 for the words *man*, *woman*, *boy*, and *girl* illustrates how this works.

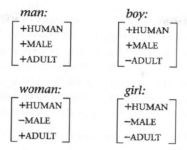

Figure 6.1   Semantic feature composition for *man, woman, boy, girl*

An obvious advantage of this approach is that it allows us to group entities into natural classes. Hence, *man* and *boy* could be grouped together as [+human, +male] while *man* and *woman* could be put in a class defined by the features [+human, +adult].

LANGUAGE MATTERS   Images Are Real

Images may not work for everything, but we do construct images of various sorts as we interpret sentences. In an elegant experiment, people were shown (for example) a picture of a nail and asked whether the corresponding word had appeared in the previously presented sentence *The man hammered the nail into the wall.*

It took less time to answer the experimenter's question when the picture provided a horizontal depiction of the nail (as above) than when it provided a vertical depiction. The reverse was true for the sentence *The man hammered the nail into the floor.* This suggests that the participants in the experiment had constructed a mental image of a horizontally oriented nail as they heard "into the wall", making it easier to recognize the object in the picture as something that had been named in the sentence.

Information from: Robert A. Stanfield and Rolf A. Zwan, "The Effect of Implied Orientation Derived from Verbal Context on Picture Recognition," *Psychological Science* 12, 2 (2001): 153–156.

This in turn can be useful for stating generalizations of various sorts. For instance, there are certain verbs—such as *marry*, *argue*, and the like—that we expect to find only with subjects that are [+human]. Moreover, within the English pronoun system, *he* is used to refer to [+human] entities that are [+male] while *she* is used for [+human] entities that are [−male].

There are limits on the insights into word meaning offered by componential analysis. What value, for example, is there in characterizing the meaning of *dog* as [+animal, +canine] as long as there is no further analysis of these features? Similarly, do we say that the meaning of *blue* consists of the feature [+color] and something else? If so, what is that other thing? Isn't it blueness? If so, then we have not really broken the meaning of *blue* into smaller components, and we are back where we started.

To date, componential analysis has given its most impressive results in the study of verb meaning. A typical component of verb meaning is the concept GO, which is associated with change of various sorts. (The components of verb meaning tend not to be binary features. We use uppercase letters to represent a semantic concept.)

13) Manifestations of the concept GO:

    a. positional change:
       Harvey went from Denver to Sacramento.

    b. possessional change:
       The inheritance went to Marla.

    c. identificational change:
       J. K. Rowling went from being an unemployed single parent to being a best-selling author.

Despite their somewhat different senses, all three uses of the verb *go* have something in common that can be traced to the GO component of their meaning—they typically occur with a phrase that denotes the entity undergoing change (e.g., the subject in these examples) and with a phrase expressing the endpoint of that change (the *to* phrases).

The GO concept is manifested in the meaning of verbs other than just *go*. For instance, positional GO is present in the meaning of *fly* ('go through the air'), *walk* ('go on foot'), *crawl* ('go on hands and knees'), and so forth. Possessional GO is manifested in the meaning of *give*, *buy*, and *inherit*, all of which involve a change of possession, while identificational GO shows up in *become* and *turn into*. Because these verbs all share the abstract GO meaning, they are all typically used with a phrase denoting the entity undergoing the change (marked below by a single underline) and a phrase denoting the endpoint of that change (marked by a double underline).

14) a. positional GO:
      The bird flew to its nest.

    b. possessional GO:
      The coach gave a new ball to the children.

    c. identificational GO:
      The caterpillar turned into a butterfly.

Verb Meaning and Subcategorization

Sometimes, quite surprising features of verb meaning can be relevant to the choice of accompanying phrases. Consider, for instance, the contrast between the verbs in list *a*, which can occur with two NP complements, and the verbs in list *b*, which cannot.

15) a. throw [$_{NP}$ the boy] [$_{NP}$ a ball]   b. *push [$_{NP}$ the boy] [$_{NP}$ the package]
    toss   *pull
    kick   *lift
    fling   *haul

Can you see the semantic difference? The verbs in list *a* all denote ballistic motion that results from the instantaneous application of force to an object at its point of origin. (When we throw something, for example, we thrust it forward and then release it.) In contrast, the verbs in list *b* all denote motion that is accompanied by the continuous application of force to the object as it moves from one point to another. (For instance, pulling typically involves the extended use of force as the object moves, rather than a single quick motion.)

Now think about the contrast between the following two sets of verbs.

16) a. fax [$_{NP}$ Helen] [$_{NP}$ the news]   b. *murmur [$_{NP}$ Helen] [$_{NP}$ the news]
    e-mail   *mumble
    text   *mutter
    phone   *shriek

Once again, componential analysis reveals a subtle semantic contrast. The first group of verbs (*phone, e-mail*, etc.) have meanings that include the means by which a message was communicated (by phone, by e-mail, and so on). In contrast, the verbs in the second group all have meanings that describe the type of voice that was used to communicate the message (murmuring, mumbling, shrieking, etc.). For reasons that are not yet fully understood, meaning differences like these help determine the type of complements that these and other verbs (belonging to still other classes) can select.

2 The Conceptual System

Underlying the use of words and sentences to express meaning in human language is a conceptual system capable of organizing and classifying every imaginable aspect of our experience, from inner feelings and perceptions, to cultural and social phenomena, to the physical world that surrounds us. This section focuses on what the study of this conceptual system reveals about how meaning is expressed through language. We will begin by considering some examples that illustrate the way in which these concepts are structured, extended, and interrelated.

2.1   Fuzzy Concepts

We tend to think that the concepts expressed by the words and phrases of our language have precise definitions with clear-cut boundaries. Some concepts may indeed be like this. For example, the concept expressed by the word *Senator* seems to have a clear-cut definition: one is a Senator if and only if one is duly elected to a particular legislative body; no other person can be truthfully called a Senator.

But are all concepts so straightforward? Consider the concept associated with the word *rich*. How much does a person have to be worth to be called rich? Five hundred thousand dollars? Eight hundred thousand? A million? Is there any figure that we can give that would be so precise that a person who is short by just five cents would not be called rich? It seems not. While one could miss out on being a Senator by five votes, it does not seem possible to miss out on being rich by just five cents. Moreover, whereas some people clearly qualify as rich and others uncontroversially do not, an indefinitely large number of people fall into the unclear area at the borderline of the concept, and it is just not possible to say definitively whether they count as rich. This is because the notion of "richness" does not have clear-cut boundaries; it is what we call a **fuzzy concept**.

This type of fuzziness pervades the human conceptual system. With only a little effort, you should be able to think of many everyday concepts whose boundaries are fuzzy—TALL, OLD, HEAVY SMOKER, STRONG, GRAY-HAIRED, GENIUS, CLEAN, and BARGAIN are just a few examples.

A second important fact about concepts is that their members can be graded in terms of their typicality. Consider first a fuzzy concept such as TENNIS STAR. Of the people who we can agree are tennis stars, some provide better examples of this concept than others. At the time of writing, for instance, Serena Williams is a better example of a tennis star than are most other professional tennis players. Although tennis fans agree that many players are stars, Serena Williams has won more matches and awards, received more media attention, and so on. This makes her a better example of a star than, say, Venus Williams.

Even concepts whose boundaries can be scientifically defined exhibit this type of **graded membership**. A good example of this involves the concept BIRD as shown in Figure 6.2. Even assuming that all English speakers think of birds as 'warm-blooded, egg-laying, feathered vertebrates with forelimbs modified to form wings' (the dictionary definition), they still feel that some of these creatures are more bird-like than others. For instance, robins and sparrows are intuitively better examples of birds than are hummingbirds, ostriches, or penguins. Examples like these suggest that concepts have an internal structure, with the best or **prototypical** exemplars (Serena Williams in the case of TENNIS STAR, robins in the case of BIRD) close to the core and less typical members arranged in successively more peripheral regions.

The existence of fuzzy concepts and of graded membership provides important insights into the nature of the human conceptual system. In particular, it seems that many (perhaps even most) concepts expressed in language are not rigid all-or-nothing notions with precise and clear-cut boundaries. Rather, they exhibit degrees of typicality and fuzzy boundaries that sometimes overlap with those of other concepts.

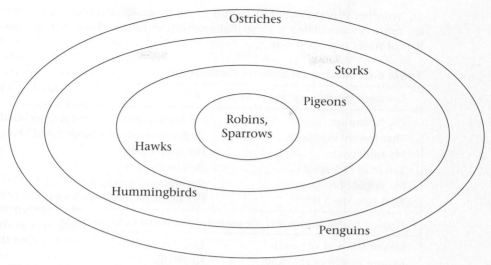

Figure 6.2 Internal structure of the concept BIRD

2.2 Metaphor

The concepts expressed by language make up a giant network, with many inter-connections and associations. A good example of these interconnections involves **metaphor**, the understanding of one concept in terms of another.

Many people think of metaphor as a literary device reserved for the use of authors and poets. In fact, however, it has a prominent place in the conceptual system shared by all human beings. This can be seen in the way that we use language to talk about even commonplace notions such as time.

The dominant metaphor for talking about time involves treating it as if it were a concrete commodity that can be saved, wasted, and invested just like other valuable things.

17) a. You're *wasting* my time.
    b. This gadget will *save* you hours.
    c. How do you *spend* your time these days?
    d. I have *invested* a lot of time in that project.
    e. You need to *budget* your time.
    f. Is that *worth* your while?
    g. He's living on *borrowed* time.
    h. You don't use your time *profitably*.

What is the basis for this metaphor? There is no objective, inherent similarity between time and commodities such as gold or money. What brings these concepts together is the *perception* that time is a valuable commodity that can be gained and lost.

Another very prevalent metaphor in our language involves the use of words that are primarily associated with spatial orientation to talk about physical and psychological states (see Table 6.6).

Table 6.6 Metaphorical use of spatial terms

Emotions: happy *is up*; sad *is down*	
I'm feeling *up*.	I'm feeling *down*.
That *boosted* my spirits.	He *fell* into a depression.
My spirits *rose*.	Her spirits *sank*.
You're in *high* spirits.	He's feeling *low*.
the *height* of ecstasy	the *depths* of depression
That gave me a *lift*.	Her mood *dropped* even lower.
Physical health: health *and* life *are up;* sickness *and* death *are down*	
He's at the *peak* of health.	He's *sinking* fast.
Lazarus *rose* from the dead.	He *fell* ill.
He's in *top* shape.	He came *down* with the flu.
	Her health is *declining*.
	She's feeling *under* the weather.

The basis for these metaphors appears to lie in our physical experience. Unhappiness and ill health tend to be associated with lethargy and inactivity, which often involve being on one's back (physically down). In contrast, happiness and good health are often correlated with energy and movement, which involve being on one's feet (physically up).

These few examples illustrate the point that the concepts expressed through language are interrelated in special and intriguing ways. By investigating phenomena such as the use of metaphor to represent abstract concepts in terms of more basic physical and cultural experience, we can gain valuable insights into how language is used to communicate meaning.

2.3 The Lexicalization of Concepts

Do all human beings share the same conceptual system? Do all languages express concepts in the same way? These are questions that have fascinated and puzzled researchers for many decades. At the present time, there is no reason to believe that human beings in different linguistic communities have different conceptual systems. But there is ample evidence that languages can differ from each other in terms of how they organize and express particular concepts.

Lexicalization across Languages

A notorious example of how languages can supposedly differ from each other in the expression of concepts involves the number of words for 'snow' in Inuktitut. Sometimes estimated to be in the hundreds, the number is actually much, much smaller.

In fact, one dictionary gives only the four items in Table 6.7 (although other dictionaries give a few more, at least for some varieties of Inuktitut).

Table 6.7 Words for 'snow' in Inuktitut

aput	'snow on the ground'
qana	'falling snow'
piqsirpoq	'drifting snow'
qimuqsuq	'snow drift'

As you can see, there is nothing particularly startling about this list of words. In fact, even English has several words for describing snow in its various forms—*snow*, *slush*, *blizzard*, and *sleet* come to mind.

These examples illustrate the phenomenon of **lexicalization**, the process whereby concepts are encoded in the words of a language. Inuktitut lexicalizes the concepts FALLING and SNOW in a single word (*qana*) while English uses two separate words. While some lexicalization differences may correlate with cultural factors (the relative importance of types of snow in traditional Inuit culture), this is not always so. For example, English has an unusually rich set of vocabulary items pertaining to the perception of light (see Table 6.8).

Table 6.8 Some verbs pertaining to light in English

glimmer	glisten
gleam	glow
glitter	flicker
shimmer	shine
flare	glare
flash	sparkle

Although English speakers know and use the words in this list, it is hard to see how the richness in this particular area of vocabulary can be traced to the culture(s) of English-speaking communities.

As we have tried to emphasize throughout this book, linguistic analysis focuses on the *system* of knowledge that makes it possible to speak and understand a language. The fact that a particular language has more words pertaining to snow or light does not in and of itself provide any insight into the nature of the human linguistic system, and therefore does not merit special attention. However, as we will see in the next subsection, certain lexicalization differences do shed light on how language expresses meaning.

Motion Verbs

All languages have words that describe motion through space (English has *come*, *go*, and *move*, among many others). However, there are systematic differences in terms of how languages express motion and the concepts related to it. In English, for example, there are many verbs that simultaneously express both the concept of motion and the manner in which the motion occurs (see Table 6.9).

Table 6.9   Some verbs expressing motion and manner in English

> The rock *rolled* down the hill.
> The puck *slid* across the ice.
> She *limped* through the house.
> The smoke *swirled* through the opening.

Notice how each of these verbs expresses both the fact that something moved and the manner in which it moved (by rolling, sliding, limping, and so on). We describe this fact by saying that English lexicalization includes a **conflation pattern** that combines manner and motion into a single verb meaning.

Interestingly, Romance languages (descendants of Latin) generally don't express motion events in this way. Thus, while French has a verb *rouler* with the meaning 'to roll', it does not use this verb to simultaneously express both manner and motion as English does.

18) *La bouteille a roulé dans la caverne.
    'The bottle rolled into the cave.'

Instead, the motion and its manner have to be expressed separately.

19) La bouteille est entrée dans la caverne en roulant.
    'The bottle entered the cave, rolling.'

Although French does not have the motion + manner conflation pattern, it does have verbs whose meaning brings together the concepts of motion and path (see Table 6.10). As the English translations show, French verbs of motion express both the concept of movement and the direction of its path—down, up, back, across, out, and so forth. (English too has verbs that can express both motion and path—*mount*, *descend*, *return*, and so on—but these words are not part of its native vocabulary; rather, they were borrowed into English from Latinate sources, usually through French.)

Table 6.10   Some verbs expressing motion and path in French

L'enfant	*monte*	l'escalier.
'The child	goes up	the stairs.'
L'enfant	*descend*	l'escalier.
'The child	goes down	the stairs.'
Les passagers	*retournent*	à l'aéroport.
'The passengers	go back	to the airport.'
Le bateau	*traverse*	l'océan.
'The ship	goes across	the ocean.'
L'ours	*sort*	de la caverne.
'The bear	comes out	of the cave.'

Yet another conflation pattern is found in the now-extinct Native American language Atsugewi, in which verbs express both motion and the type of thing that moves (see Table 6.11).

Table 6.11 Some verb roots expressing motion and the thing moving in Atsugewi

lup	for movement of a small, shiny, spherical object (a hailstone)
t	for movement of a smallish, flat object that can be attached to another (a stamp, a clothing patch, a shingle)
caq	for movement of a slimy, lumpish object (a toad, a cow dropping)
swal	for movement of a limp linear object, suspended by one end (a shirt on a clothesline, a hanging dead rabbit)
qput	for movement of loose, dry dirt
staq	for movement of runny, unpleasant material (manure, guts, chewed gum, rotten tomatoes)

We learn two things from these facts. First, the concept of motion is associated with a number of other concepts, including PATH, MANNER OF MOVEMENT, and MOVING THING. Second, the way in which these concepts are combined for the purposes of lexicalization can differ systematically from language to language. Languages such as English have a class of verbs that conflate motion and manner while other languages have verbs that conflate motion and path (French) or motion and the type of thing that moves (Atsugewi).

The general picture that is emerging from this type of work is consistent with the key idea underlying componential analysis (Section 1.3). In particular, it seems that at least within certain semantic domains, there may be a small universal set of concepts (motion, manner, path, thing that moves, and so on) and a small set of options for how these concepts can be combined for purposes of lexicalization (see Figure 6.3).

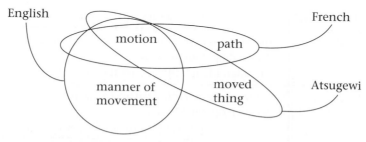

Figure 6.3 Systematic differences in conflation patterns

Unlike the lexicalization differences involving snow and light discussed earlier, these differences appear to be highly systematic and to reveal some general tendencies about the organization of the human conceptual system and the way in which meaning is expressed in language.

2.4   Grammatical Concepts

Of the indefinitely large set of concepts expressible in human language, a relatively small subset is **grammaticalized**—that is, they are encoded as affixes and nonlexical (functional) categories that express grammatical contrasts of various sorts. Some of the concepts that are treated this way in English are listed in Table 6.12.

Table 6.12   Some concepts associated with affixes and nonlexical categories in English

Concept	*Affix*
PAST	-ed
MORE THAN ONE	-s
AGAIN	re-
NEGATION	in-, un-

Concept	*Nonlexical category*
OBLIGATION	must
POSSIBILITY	may
DEFINITE, SPECIFIC	the
INDEFINITE, NONSPECIFIC	a
DISJUNCTION	or
NEGATION	not
CONJUNCTION	and

Some concepts—such as NEGATION, TENSE, and NUMBER—are grammaticalized in a very large number of languages. Others, such as contrasts involving **evidentiality** (the source of a speaker's evidence for a statement), are less commonly treated in this way. As illustrated in Table 6.13, a refined set of grammaticalized evidentiality contrasts is found in Hidatsa (a Siouan language spoken in North Dakota).

Table 6.13   Evidentiality morphemes in Hidatsa

ski	THE SPEAKER IS CERTAIN OF THE STATEMENT'S TRUTH Waceo iikipi kure heo -<u>ski</u>. 'The man (definitely) carried the pipe.'
c	THE SPEAKER BELIEVES THE STATEMENT TO BE TRUE Waceo iikipi kure heo -<u>c</u>. 'The man (supposedly) carried the pipe.'
wareac	THE SPEAKER REGARDS THE STATEMENT TO BE COMMON KNOWLEDGE Waceo iikipi kure heo -<u>wareac</u>. 'The man carried the pipe (they say).'
rahe	THE STATEMENT IS BASED ON AN UNVERIFIED REPORT FROM SOMEONE ELSE Waceo wiira rakci heo -<u>rahe</u>. 'The man roasted the goose (it is rumored).'

Table 6.13 Continued

toak	THE TRUTH OF THE STATEMENT IS UNKNOWN TO BOTH SPEAKER AND LISTENER
	Waceo cihpa rakci heo -<u>toak</u>.
	'The man roasted the prairie dog (perhaps).'

Choice of the appropriate sentence-ender is extremely important in Hidatsa. Speakers who utter a false sentence marked by the morpheme *-ski* are considered to be liars. Had they used the morpheme *-c*, however, it would be assumed that they simply made a mistake. While English has ways of indicating these contrasts (by using expressions such as *perhaps*, *I heard that*, and *I guess*), it does not have a grammatical system of affixes to encode this information.

LANGUAGE MATTERS   Where Do Grammaticalized Forms Originate?

In many cases, the forms expressing grammatical concepts were originally ordinary nouns and verbs. Over time and through frequent use, their form was reduced and their meaning was modified to express a related grammatical notion.

A good example of this can be found in English, where the verb *going*, whose literal meaning involves directional motion, has come to be used (with the pronunciation "gonna") as a future marker. (This is a relatively recent innovation; *go* was not used to express the future tense in Shakespeare's time.)

I'm going to school now. (directional motion)
The snow is going to (gonna) melt. (future time)

The two principal sources of future tense markers in languages of the world are verbs of motion and verbs of wanting. English provides a good illustration of the second case as well: the auxiliary *will* evolved from the verb *willan*, which meant 'to want'.

Information from: Joan Bybee, "Cognitive Processes in Grammaticalization," in *The New Psychology of Language*, vol. 2, ed. M. Tomasello, 145–167 (Mahwah, NJ: Lawrence Erlbaum, 2003).

---

3 Syntax and Sentence Interpretation

The two preceding sections have focused on the meaning conveyed by the individual words and phrases that make up a sentence. In this section, we turn to the problem of sentence interpretation, with an emphasis on how the positioning of words and phrases in syntactic structure helps determine the meaning of the entire sentence, consistent with the **Principle of Compositionality**.

20) *The Principle of Compositionality*
   The meaning of a sentence is determined by the meaning of its component parts and the manner in which they are arranged in syntactic structure.

Syntactic structure is relevant to meaning in a variety of ways. For purposes of illustration, we will consider four aspects of its contribution to the interpretation of sentences—constructional meaning, the representation of structural ambiguity, the assignment of thematic roles, and the interpretation of pronouns.

3.1   Constructional Meaning

There is reason to believe that structural patterns can have a meaning of their own, independent of the meaning of their component parts. One example of this **constructional meaning** can be seen in the caused-motion construction. (PP$_{dir}$ represents a PP in which the preposition denotes a direction.)

21) The caused-motion construction:
   Form: NP   V   NP   PP$_{dir}$
   Meaning: 'X   causes   Y   to go somewhere'

Simple examples of the caused-motion construction include sentences such as the following.

22) a. Seymour pushed the toy off the table.
   b. Mabel moved the car into the garage.
   c. Perry pulled the dog into the swimming pool.

The first sentence describes a situation in which Seymour causes the toy to go off the table by pushing it; the second sentence is used for situations in which Mabel causes the car to go into the garage; and so on.
   The evidence that the caused-motion construction has a meaning above and beyond the meaning of its component parts comes from sentences such as the following.

23) a. Boris sneezed the handkerchief right across the room.
   b. The audience laughed the poor guy off the stage.
   c. Morley squeezed the shirt into the suitcase.

There is nothing in the meaning of verbs such as *sneeze*, *laugh*, and *squeeze* that implies caused motion. Yet when they occur in the NP V NP PP$_{dir}$ pattern, the resulting sentence has a meaning in which X causes Y to go somewhere. Sentence *23a* means that Boris caused the handkerchief to fly across the room by sneezing; *23b* means that the audience forced someone off the stage by laughing at him; and so on. The motion part of the meaning comes from the construction itself.
   Another example of constructional meaning can be found in patterns such as the following.

24) a. Jerry sent Lou a present.
   b. The company gave its employees a bonus.
   c. The secretary handed Mary a message.
   d. Marvin threw Harry the ball.

These sentences are instances of the so-called ditransitive construction, which consists of a verb and two NP complements and is typically associated with the meaning 'X causes Y to have Z'. Thus *24a* describes a situation in which Jerry causes Lou to have a present by sending it to him, for example.

25) The ditransitive construction:
   Form: NP   V   NP   NP
   Meaning: 'X   causes Y   to have Z'

   An indication that the structure itself contributes part of the meaning associated with ditransitive constructions comes from sentences such as *Jerry baked Lou a cake*. This sentence describes a situation in which Lou ends up with a cake, even though there is clearly nothing in the meaning of *bake* that implies that one person causes another person to have something. This part of the sentence's meaning comes from the structure itself—another example of constructional meaning.

LANGUAGE MATTERS   What's This Fly Doing in My Soup?

A defining feature of constructions is that at least some aspect of their meaning cannot be determined from the meaning of their parts. A good example of this involves sentences of the type 'What's X doing . . . ?'

   What's this scratch doing on my new car?
   What's this hotel room doing without a decent bed?
   What's my wallet doing in your pocket?

Even though the verb *do* normally denotes an activity (as in, "What are you doing?"), these sentences are used to demand an explanation for an unexpected and inappropriate situation that doesn't even involve an activity—the construction has taken on a special meaning of its own. An old and famous joke plays on this fact.

   Diner: Waiter, what's this fly doing in my soup? [special construction-based meaning intended]
   Waiter: Madam, I believe that's the backstroke. [pretending to get only the literal meaning]

Source: "What's this Fly Doing in My Soup?" by Paul Kay. Reprinted by permission of the author.

3.2   Structural Ambiguity

Some sentences are **structurally ambiguous** in that their component words can be combined in more than one way. A simple example of this is found in the phrase *wealthy men and women*, where *wealthy* can be seen as a property of just the men alone or of both the men and the women. These two interpretations (or **readings**) can be depicted as follows (ignoring details), with *wealthy* grouped with *men* in the first case, but with the phrase *men and women* in the second case.

26) a. [wealthy men] and women   b. wealthy [men and women]
     (only the men are wealthy)   (both the men and the women are wealthy)

Another case of structural ambiguity is found in sentences such as the following.

27) Nicole saw the people with binoculars.

In one interpretation, *with binoculars* describes an attribute of the people (they had binoculars when Nicole noticed them). This is represented (details aside) by placing the PP inside the NP headed by the noun *people*, as in *28*.

28) Nicole [$_{VP}$ saw [$_{NP}$ the people *with binoculars*]]

In a second interpretation, *with binoculars* describes the seeing action denoted by the verb (Nicole saw people by using binoculars). This is represented by placing the PP inside the VP headed by the verb *see* but outside the NP headed by *people*, as in *29*.

29) Nicole [$_{VP}$ saw [$_{NP}$ the people] *with binoculars*]

In sum, the manner in which words are grouped together in syntactic structure reflects the way in which their meanings are combined. Sometimes, as in the examples we have just considered, identical strings of words can be combined in more than one way, creating structural ambiguity that can be neatly captured with the help of tree structures.

3.3   Thematic Roles

Another aspect of semantic interpretation involves determining the role that the referents of NPs play in the situations described by sentences. Consider in this regard the sentence in *30*.

30) The courier carried the document from Boston to Los Angeles.

It would be impossible to understand this sentence if we could not identify the courier as the person who is responsible for carrying something, the document as the thing that is carried, Boston as the point of origin, and Los Angeles as the destination. Linguists often use **thematic roles** to categorize the relation between a sentence's parts and the event that it describes. In most linguistic analyses, at least the thematic roles in Table 6.14 are recognized.

Table 6.14   Thematic roles

Agent	the entity that performs an action
Theme*	the entity undergoing an action or a movement
Source	the starting point for a movement
Goal	the end point for a movement
Location	the place where an action occurs

*also sometimes called "undergoer" or "patient"

Examples of these thematic roles can be seen in sentences such as the following.

31) a. The courier carried the document from Boston to Los Angeles.
           agent   *theme*   *source*   *goal*
      b. The athletes practiced in the stadium.
           agent   *location*

The notion of movement used in the definition of **theme**, **source**, and **goal** is intended to involve not only actual physical motion, as in *Sam went to school*, but also changes in possession, as in *32*, and identity, as in *33*.

32) Terry gave the skis to Mary.
     agent   *theme*   *goal*

33) The magician changed the ball into a rabbit.
         agent   *theme*   *goal*

As you may recall, we observed something similar in the case of the GO concept discussed in Section 1.3. This is no coincidence. Thematic roles can be traced to particular aspects of word meaning, and the presence of GO in a verb's meaning is specifically linked to the presence of a theme role and a goal role.

Thematic Role Assignment

How does the grammar ensure that the appropriate thematic role is associated with each NP in a sentence? As we have just seen, thematic roles originate in word meaning. Thus, if the sentence *Marvin purchased a pen at the bookstore* contains an **agent** and a theme, it is because the verb *purchase* has the type of meaning that implies an entity that does the purchasing (an agent) and an entity that gets purchased (a theme). Similarly, *the bookstore* is taken to denote the **location** of the action because of the meaning of the preposition *at*. Information about the thematic roles assigned by a particular lexical item is recorded in a **thematic grid**, as depicted in Table 6.15.

Table 6.15   Some words and the thematic roles implied by their meanings

purchase	<ag, th>	*from*	<so>
walk	<ag>	*at*	<loc>
to	<go>		

ag = agent, th = theme, go = goal, so = source, loc = location

The thematic roles implied by the meanings of lexical items are assigned to NPs based on their position in syntactic structure, with each NP receiving a single role. As a first example of this, let us consider the complement of a preposition. In such cases, the process of thematic role assignment can be summarized as follows:

34) A P assigns a thematic role to its complement NP.

This is illustrated in Figure 6.4.

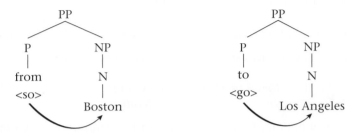

Figure 6.4 Thematic role assignment by prepositions

Matters are slightly more complicated in the case of Vs. Here, we must distinguish between the theme role, which is assigned to the verb's complement, and the agent role, which is assigned to its subject.

35) A V assigns a theme role (if it has one) to its complement NP.
    A V assigns an agent role (if it has one) to its subject NP.

This is exemplified in the structures in Figure 6.5, in which the theme role is assigned to the V's NP complement while the agent role is assigned to the subject.

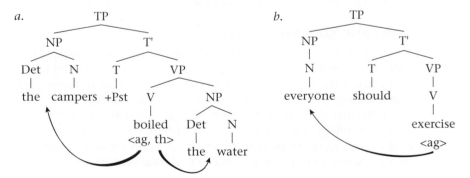

Figure 6.5 Thematic role assignment by verbs

The structure in Figure 6.6 illustrates the assignment of thematic roles in a sentence that contains a P in addition to a V. Here, the P *to* assigns its goal role to its complement NP (*the door*) while the verb *dash* assigns its agent role to the subject *the children*.

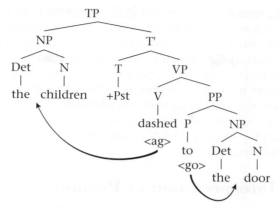

Figure 6.6 Thematic role assignment by a verb and a preposition

Deep Structure and Thematic Roles

In the examples considered to this point, it is unclear whether an NP receives its thematic role on the basis of its position in deep structure or surface structure (sometimes referred to as D-structure and S-structure). This is because our example sentences are all formed without the help of the Move operation, so that each NP occupies the same position in both deep structure and surface structure. But now consider a sentence such as *36*, which is formed with the help of *Wh* Movement.

36) Which book should the students read?

This sentence has the deep structure depicted in Figure 6.7.

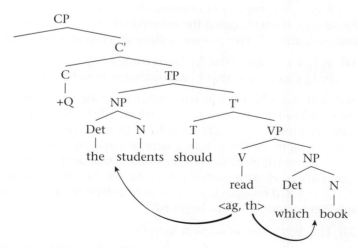

Figure 6.7 Thematic role assignment in a *wh* question

Since the theme role is assigned to the complement of V, it follows that the NP *which book* in the above example receives this role by virtue of its position in deep structure, not surface structure (where it occurs in the specifier of CP position).

In sum, an NP's initial position in syntactic structure (the result of the Merge operation) determines its thematic role. The Move operation may subsequently transport the NP to another position (as is the case with *wh* words), but the original thematic role remains unchanged. The relationship between syntactic structure and the part of a sentence's meaning represented by thematic roles is thus very intricate, reflecting the structural relations manifested in deep structure rather than position in surface structure.

3.4   The Interpretation of Pronouns

Syntactic structure also has an important role to play in the interpretation of **pronouns**, including **pronominals** such as *he, him, she,* and *her* and **reflexive pronouns** such as *himself* and *herself* (see Table 6.16).

Table 6.16   Pronouns in English

	Pronominals		Reflexives	
	SG	PL	SG	PL
1st person	I, me	we, us	myself	ourselves
2nd person	you	you	yourself	yourselves
3rd person	he, him		himself	
	she, her	they, them	herself	themselves
	it		itself	

A defining property of pronouns is that their interpretation can be determined by another element, called the **antecedent**. As the sentences in *37* help show, pronominals and reflexive pronouns differ in terms of where their antecedents occur.

37) a. [_{TP} Claire knew that [_{TP} Alexis trusted *her*]].
       b. [_{TP} Claire knew that [_{TP} Alexis trusted *herself*]].

Notice that *her* in *37a* can refer either to Claire or to someone not mentioned in the sentence but that *herself* in *37b* refers only to Alexis. This reflects the fact that a reflexive pronoun typically must have an antecedent in the same clause (or tense phrase [TP], to use the technical term preferred by many linguists).

A somewhat more abstract feature of syntactic structure enters into the interpretation of the reflexive pronoun in a sentence such as *38*, which has the tree structure in Figure 6.8. (Pronouns are treated as an N-type category. Possessor NPs occur in the specifier position within a larger NP.)

38) That boy's teacher admires himself.

Although there are two NPs in the same TP as *himself* (namely, *that boy's* and *that boy's teacher*), only one (*that boy's teacher*) can serve as antecedent for the reflexive pronoun. Thus, the person who is admired in *38* must be the boy's teacher, not the boy.

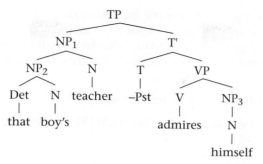

Figure 6.8   Structure containing a reflexive pronoun

Principles A and B

The principle needed to ensure the right interpretation for reflexive pronouns makes use of the notion **c-command**, which is defined as follows.

39) NP_a c-commands NP_b if the first category above NP_a contains NP_b.

We can now formulate the constraint on the interpretation of reflexives, called **Principle A**, as follows.

40) *Principle A*

A reflexive pronoun must have an antecedent that c-commands it in the same clause.

When using Principle A, the key step involves determining whether a potential antecedent c-commands the reflexive pronoun. Compare in this regard the status of the NPs *that boy's* and *that boy's teacher* in Figure 6.9.

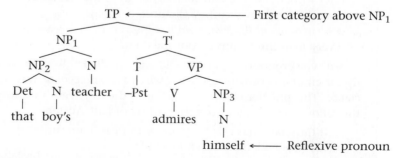

Figure 6.9   Structure illustrating c-command relations. NP_1 c-commands NP_3 but NP_2 does not.

Since the first category above NP_1 *that boy's teacher* (namely, TP) contains the reflexive, this NP c-commands *himself*, according to our definition of c-command, and can therefore serve as its antecedent. In contrast, NP_2 *that boy's* cannot be the antecedent for *himself* because the first category above NP_2 is NP_1, and it does not contain the reflexive. Therefore, the NP *that boy's* does not c-command the reflexive pronoun and is hence not an eligible antecedent.

Now let us examine the interpretation of pronominals. As the example in *41* shows, the interpretation of the pronominal *him* contrasts sharply with that of the reflexive *himself* in the structure that we have been considering. Thus, *him* can refer to the boy, but not to the boy's teacher—the opposite of what we observed for *himself*.

41) That boy's teacher admires him.

How are we to account for these facts? The relevant constraint, called **Principle B**, is stated in *42*.

42) *Principle B*
A pronominal must not have an antecedent that c-commands it in the same clause.

To see how this principle works, consider the structure in Figure 6.10. In this structure, NP_1 (*that boy's teacher*) c-commands *him* since the first category above it (namely, TP) also contains *him*. Principle B therefore prevents NP_1 from serving as

---

LANGUAGE MATTERS   It Wasn't Always That Way

In earlier varieties of English, simple pronouns could be used in positions where today we must use a reflexive.

.hweðer *he hine* gefreclsian wolde (from the Old English *Blickling Homilies*, c. 971).
. . . *whether he him set-free would*
'. . . whether he would set himself free'

Every wight out at the dore *him* dighte (from the Middle English poem *Troilus and Criseyde* by Geoffrey Chaucer, c. 1385).
every man out at the door him threw
'Every man threw himself out the door.'

Self-type pronouns existed in Old and Middle English but were used primarily for emphasis or contrast, even when the antecedent was not in the same clause. This practice continued well into the nineteenth century, as shown in the following examples from the writing of Jane Austen:

If *Cassandra* has filled my bed with fleas, I am sure they must bite *herself* (from a letter written in 1814).
But *Marianne* . . . could easily trace it to whatever cause best pleased *herself* (*Sense and Sensibility*, 1811).

Information from: C. L. Baker, "Contrast, Discourse Prominence, and Intensification, with Special Reference to Locally Free Reflexives in British English," *Language* 71, 1 (1995): 63–101; Edward L. Keenan, "Explaining the Creation of Reflexive Pronouns in English," in *Studies in the History of English: A Millennial Perspective*, ed. D. Minkova and R. Stockwell, 325–355 (New York: Mouton de Gruyter, 2002).

antecedent for *him*. In contrast, NP$_2$ (*that boy's*) does not c-command *him* since the first category above it (namely, NP$_1$) does not contain the pronoun. Thus, nothing prevents the interpretation in which *him* and *that boy's* refer to the same person.

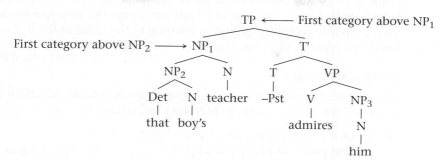

Figure 6.10   Structure containing a pronominal

There is much more that can and should be said about the interpretation of pronouns. However, the examples above suffice to illustrate the crucial point in all of this, which is that syntactic structure plays an important role in the interpretation of both pronominals and reflexive pronouns.

4   Other Factors in Sentence Interpretation

Syntactic structure provides only some of the information needed to interpret a sentence. Other necessary information comes from **pragmatics**, the strategies (above and beyond the grammar) that guide the way speakers use and interpret language. Pragmatic strategies are sensitive to the background attitudes and beliefs of the speaker and **addressee**, their understanding of the context in which a sentence is uttered, and their knowledge of how language can be used to inform, to persuade, to mislead, and so forth. This section focuses on the role of pragmatics in sentence interpretation.

4.1   The Role of Beliefs and Attitudes

As we saw in the preceding section, the grammar includes a structural principle (Principle B) that regulates the interpretation of pronominals such as *he* and *they*. However, as the following sentences show, nonlinguistic knowledge and beliefs can also play an important role in selecting the antecedent for a pronominal.

43) a. The judge denied the prisoner's request because he was cautious.
  b. The judge denied the prisoner's request because he was dangerous.

These two sentences have identical syntactic structures, differing only in the choice of the adjective in the second clause (*cautious* in the first sentence versus *dangerous* in the second). Yet most people feel that *he* refers to the judge in *43a* but to the prisoner in *43b*. Why should this be?

The crucial factor involves our beliefs about people in our society and their likely characteristics and behavior. All other things being equal, we are more likely to believe that a judge is cautious and a prisoner dangerous than vice versa. This in turn leads us to interpret the pronoun as referring to the judge in the first sentence in *43* but to the prisoner in the second.

Presupposition

There are many other ways in which a speaker's beliefs can be reflected in language use. Compare in this regard the following two sentences.

44) a. Have you stopped exercising regularly?
    b. Have you tried exercising regularly?

Use of the verb *stop* implies a belief on the part of the speaker that the listener has been exercising regularly. No such assumption is associated with the verb *try*.

The assumption or belief implied by the use of a particular word or structure is called a **presupposition**. The following two sentences provide another example of this.

45) a. Nick admitted that the team had lost.
    b. Nick said that the team had lost.

Choice of the verb *admit* in *45a* indicates that the speaker is presupposing the truth of the claim that the team lost. No such presupposition is associated with choice of the verb *say* in *45b*, where the speaker is simply reporting Nick's statement without taking a position on its accuracy.

Still another type of presupposition is illustrated in *46*.

46) a. Abraham Lincoln was assassinated in 1865.
    b. Abraham Lincoln was murdered in 1865.

Notice that use of the verb *assassinate* in *46a* involves the assumption that Abraham Lincoln was a prominent person, but no such presupposition is associated with the verb *murder*.

4.2 Setting

As noted at the beginning of this section, the pragmatic factors relevant to sentence interpretation can include knowledge of the context in which a sentence is uttered, including its physical environment or **setting**.

All languages have forms whose use and interpretation depend on the location of the speaker and/or hearer within a particular setting. Called spatial **deictics**, these forms are exemplified in English by words such as *this* and *here* (proximity to the speaker) versus *that* and *there* (proximity to the hearer and/or distance from the speaker). Thus, if Steve and Brian are sitting across from each other at a table, each would refer to a plate directly in front of him as *this plate* and to a plate in front of the other or a plate distant from both as *that plate*. Without an understanding of how the setting in which a sentence is uttered can influence the choice of words such as *this* and *that*, it would be impossible for speakers of English to use or interpret these forms correctly.

As the preceding examples show, English makes a two-way distinction in its expression of deictic contrasts. However, many languages have a three-way system that may be sensitive to distance from the speaker, the addressee, or both (depending on the language; see Table 6.17).

Table 6.17   Languages with a three-way deictic distinction

Language	'this'	'that'	'that over there'
Spanish	este	ese	aquel
Japanese	kono	sono	ano
Korean	i	ku	ce
Palauan*	tia	tilẹcha	se
Turkish	bu	şu	o

*Palauan is spoken in the Pacific islands of Palau and Guam.

An even more complex system is found in the Native American language Tlingit (spoken in Alaska and British Columbia), which makes a four-way distinction: *yáa* 'this one right here', *héi* 'this one nearby', *wée* 'that one over there', and *yóo* 'that one far off'.

Determiners are not the only type of element whose use and interpretation require reference to features of the setting. Deictic contrasts are also crucial to the understanding of such commonly used verbs as *come* and *go*. Notice in this regard the striking difference in perspective found in the following two sentences.

47) a. The bear is coming into the tent!
    b. The bear is going into the tent!

Whereas *come* with a third-person subject implies movement toward the speaker (hence we can infer that the person who utters *47a* is in the tent), *go* with the same type of subject suggests movement away from the speaker.

4.3 Discourse

An additional source of contextual information relevant to sentence interpretation can be found in **discourse**, the connected series of utterances produced during a conversation, a lecture, a story, or other speech act. The importance of discourse stems from the fact that individual sentences commonly include elements whose interpretation can only be determined with the help of information in preceding utterances. For instance, each of the italicized words in the following passage relies for its interpretation on information encoded in a preceding sentence.

48) A little girl went for a walk in the park. While *there*, *she* saw a rabbit. Since *it* was injured, *she* took *it* home.

We interpret *there* with reference to *in the park,* *she* with reference to *a little girl,* and *it* with reference to *a rabbit.*

One of the most important contrasts in the study of discourse involves the distinction between new and old information. **Old (or given) information** consists of the knowledge that the speaker assumes is available to the addressee at the time of the utterance, either because it is obvious or because it has been previously mentioned in the discourse. In contrast, **new information** involves knowledge that is introduced into the discourse for the first time. Consider the contrast between the following two sentences.

49) a. The man is at the front door.
    b. A man is at the front door.

The choice of *the* as the determiner for *man* in *49a* suggests that the referent of the phrase is someone who has already been mentioned in the discourse and is therefore known to the addressee (old information). In contrast, the choice of the determiner *a* in *49b* implies that the referent is being introduced into the discourse for the first time (new information).

Notice that both sentences in *49* use *the* as the determiner for *front door* and that the indefinite determiner *a* would not be natural in this context. This is because the setting for the conversation is likely to include only one front door. Since this information is presumably known to both the speaker and the addressee (i.e., it is old information), *the* is the right determiner to use in this context.

Topics

Another important notion for the study of discourse is that of **topic**, which corresponds to what a sentence or a portion of the discourse is about. Consider the following passage:

50) Once upon a time there was a merchant with two sons. The older son wanted to be a scholar. He spent his time reading and studying. As for the younger son, he preferred to travel and see the world.

The first sentence in this passage introduces a merchant and his two sons as new information. A topic (the older son) is selected in the second sentence and maintained in the third, in which *he* refers back to the older son. The final sentence then switches to a new topic (the younger son), providing some information about him. This switch is facilitated by the expression *as for,* which can be used in English to mark new topics.

There is a strong tendency in language to encode the topic as subject of a sentence. This is why (as mentioned in Section 1.2) it is natural to interpret the active sentence in *51a* as being about the police and the passive sentence in *b* as being about the burglar.

51) a. The police chased the burglar.
    b. The burglar was chased by the police.

In some languages, a special affix is used to identify the topic. The following sentences from Japanese illustrate this phenomenon (NOM = nominative, the subject marker; TOP = topic marker; QUES = question marker).

52) *Speaker A:*   Dare-ga kimasita-ka?
        Who-NOM came-QUES?
        'Who came?'

   Speaker B: John-ga kimasita.
        John-NOM came.
        'John came.'

   Speaker A: John-wa dare-to kimasita-ka?
        John-TOP who-with came-QUES?
        'Who did John come with?'

The topic marker in Japanese (the suffix *-wa*) is distinguished from the subject marker (*-ga*) by its use to mark old or background information. This is why speaker B responds to A's first question by using the subject marker on the NP *John*, which provides new information (in answer to A's question). And it is why the second use of the NP *John*, which is now associated with previously established information, is accompanied by the topic suffix *-wa*.

4.4   Grice's Conversational Maxims

In addition to background beliefs, the setting, and the discourse, there is at least one other major type of information that enters into the interpretation of utterances. This information has to do with the "rules for conversation"—our understanding of how language is used in particular situations to convey a message. For example, if I ask you, "Would you like to go to a movie tonight?" and you respond by saying, "I have to study for an exam," I know that you are declining my invitation even though there is nothing in the literal meaning of the sentence that says so. Moreover, I recognize that this is a perfectly appropriate way to respond. (Notice that the same could not be said of the response "It's a bit warm in here.")

As speakers of a language, we are able to draw inferences about what is meant but not actually said. Information that is conveyed in this way is called a **conversational implicature**. The ease with which we recognize and interpret implicatures stems from our knowledge of how people in our linguistic community use language to communicate with each other.

H. Paul Grice called the general overarching guideline for conversational interactions the **Cooperative Principle**.

53) *The Cooperative Principle*
   Make your contribution appropriate to the conversation.

More specific **conversational maxims** or guidelines ensure that conversational interactions actually satisfy the Cooperative Principle, as shown in Table 6.18. These maxims are responsible for regulating normal conversation, but as we will see, each can be suspended under certain circumstances to create particular effects.

Table 6.18   Grice's conversational maxims

The Maxim of Relevance Be relevant.
The Maxim of Quality Try to make your contribution one that is true. (Do not say things that are false or for which you lack adequate evidence.)
The Maxim of Quantity Do not make your contribution more or less informative than required.
The Maxim of Manner Avoid ambiguity and obscurity; be brief and orderly.

Relevance

The **Maxim of Relevance** gives listeners a bottom line for inferring the intent of other speakers. It is because of this maxim that we are able to interpret the utterance "I have to study for an exam" (in response to the question "Would you like to go to a movie?") as a 'no'.

Failure to respect the Maxim of Relevance creates a peculiar effect. For example, if someone asks you, "Have you finished that term paper yet?" and you respond, "It's been raining a lot lately, hasn't it?," you violate the Maxim of Relevance by not responding in a relevant way. But by giving this response, you signal that you want to change the topic of conversation.

Quality

The **Maxim of Quality** requires that the statements used in conversations have some factual basis. If, for example, I ask, "What's the weather like?" and someone responds, "It's snowing," I will normally assume that this statement provides reliable information about the current weather.

Considerations of kindness and politeness can justify suspension of the Maxim of Quality. For instance, in order to avoid hurt feelings, you might congratulate a fellow student on a presentation, even though you were not impressed by it.

Quantity

The **Maxim of Quantity** introduces some very subtle guidelines into a conversation. Imagine, for example, that someone asks me where a famous author lives. The nature of my response will depend in large part on how much information I believe to be appropriate for that point in the conversation. If I know that the other person is simply curious about which part of the country the author lives in, it might suffice to respond "in Maine." However, if I know that the person wants to visit the author, then much more specific information (perhaps even an address) is appropriate.

Manner

The **Maxim of Manner** imposes several constraints on language use. For example, imagine that I refer to a particular person as "the man who Mary lives with." A listener would be justified in concluding that the man in question is not Mary's husband. This is because, by the Maxim of Manner, a briefer and less obscure description, *Mary's husband*, would have been used if it could have correctly described Mary's companion.

Summing Up

The study of **semantics** is concerned with a broad range of phenomena, including the nature of **meaning**, the role of syntactic structure in the interpretation of sentences, and the effect of **pragmatics** on the understanding of utterances. Although much remains to be done in each of these areas, work in recent years has at least begun to identify the type of relations, mechanisms, and principles involved in the understanding of language. These include the notions of **extension** and **intension** in the case of word meaning, **thematic roles** in the case of NPs, and **c-command** in the case of pronouns. Other factors known to be involved in an utterance's interpretation include **constructional meaning**, the speaker's and hearer's background beliefs (as manifested, for example, in **presuppositions**), the context provided by the setting and the **discourse**, and the **maxims** associated with the **Cooperative Principle**.

Key Terms

General terms

meaning	semantics

Terms concerning semantic relations among words

antonyms	lexical ambiguity
homographs	polysemy
homonyms	synonyms
homophony	

Terms concerning semantic relations in sentences

contradiction	paraphrases
entailment	truth conditions

Terms concerning meaning

componential analysis	intension
connotation	referents
denotation	semantic decomposition
extension	semantic features

Terms concerning how concepts are encoded

conflation pattern   grammaticalized (concepts)
evidentiality   lexicalization
fuzzy concept   metaphor
graded membership   prototypical

General terms concerning the interpretation of sentences

constructional meaning   readings
Principle of Compositionality   structurally ambiguous

Terms concerning thematic roles in sentences

agent   thematic grid
goal   thematic roles
location   theme
source

Terms concerning the interpretation of pronouns

antecedent   pronominals
c-command   pronouns
Principle A   reflexive pronouns
Principle B

Terms concerning pragmatics

addressee   Maxim of Quantity
conversational implicature Maxim of Relevance
conversational maxims   new information
Cooperative Principle   old (given) information
deictics   pragmatics
discourse   presupposition
Maxim of Manner   setting
Maxim of Quality   topic

Recommended Reading

Chierchia, Gennaro, and Sally McConnell-Ginet. 2000. *Meaning and Grammar.* 2nd ed. Cambridge, MA: MIT Press.

Cruse, Alan. 2011. *Meaning in Language: An Introduction to Semantics and Pragmatics.* 3rd ed. Oxford, UK: Oxford University Press.

Kearns, Kate. 2011. *Semantics.* 2nd ed. London: Palgrave Macmillan.

Kövecses, Zoltán. 2010. *Metaphor: A Practical Introduction.* 2nd ed. Oxford, UK: Oxford University Press.

Exercises

1. Two relations involving word meanings are antonymy and synonymy. Which relation is illustrated in each of the pairs of words below? (See Section 1.1.)
   - a) flourish-thrive
   - b) intelligent-stupid
   - c) casual-informal
   - d) young-old
   - e) uncle-aunt
   - f) intelligent-smart
   - g) flog-whip
   - h) drunk-sober

2. It was noted in this chapter that a single form can have two or more meanings. Depending on whether these meanings are related to each other, this phenomenon involves polysemy or homophony. Which of these two relations is exemplified by the forms below? (See Section 1.1.)
   - a) *weed:* unwanted plant; marijuana
   - b) *leech:* a bloodsucking worm; a hanger-on who seeks advantage
   - c) *range:* a cooking stove; a series of mountains
   - d) *key:* an instrument used to apply to a lock; an answer sheet for a test or assignment
   - e) *steal/steel:* rob; a type of metal
   - f) *race:* a competition, often involving speed; people belonging to the same genetic grouping
   - g) *flower/flour:* a type of plant; finely ground wheat

3. Three semantic relations among sentences were covered in this chapter: paraphrase, entailment, and contradiction. Which of these relations is exemplified in each of the following pairs of sentences? (See Section 1.2.)
   - a) I saw Timothy at the anniversary party.
     It was Timothy that I saw at the anniversary party.
   - b) Jules is Mary's husband.
     Mary is married.
   - c) My pet cobra likes the taste of chocolate fudge.
     My pet cobra finds chocolate fudge tasty.
   - d) Vera is an only child.
     Olga is Vera's sister.
   - e) It is fifty miles to the nearest service station.
     The nearest service station is fifty miles away.
   - f) My cousin Bryan teaches at the community college for a living.
     My cousin Bryan is a teacher.

4. In discussing the nature of meaning, we noted that it is necessary to distinguish between intension and extension. Describe the intensions and the extensions of each of these phrases. (See Section 1.3.)
   - a) the president of the United States
   - b) the Queen of England
   - c) the capital of the United States
   - d) women who have walked on the moon
   - e) my linguistics professor

5. In our discussion of semantic decomposition, we noted that at least some words have meanings that can be represented in terms of smaller semantic features. Four such words are *dog, puppy, cat,* and *kitten.* (See Section 1.3.)

   i)   Attempt to provide semantic features associated with each of these words.
   ii) How are the pairs *dog-puppy* and *cat-kitten* different from *man-boy* and *woman-girl*?
   iii) Try to provide semantic features for the words *circle, triangle,* and *quadrangle.* What problems do you encounter?

6. Each of the following words is associated with a concept. (See Section 2.1.)

   a) island   e) food
   b) soft   f) husband
   c) white   g) baseball bat
   d) wristwatch   h) mountain

   i)   Determine which of these examples involve fuzzy concepts.
   ii) Choose one of the fuzzy concepts above. Name one prototypical member of that concept and one member that is closer to the concept boundary.

7. Draw a diagram for the concept DWELLING similar to that of Figure 6.2 in this chapter. Do the same for the concept VEHICLE.

8. Examine the following sets of sentences. (See Section 2.2.)

   a) She gave him an icy stare.
      He gave her the cold shoulder.
      He exudes a lot of warmth toward people.
      They got into a heated argument.
   b) He drops a lot of hints.
      The committee picked up on the issue.
      She dumps all her problems on her friends.
      Although he disagreed, he let it go.
   c) the eye of a needle
      the foot of the bed
      the hands of the clock
      the arm of a chair
      the table legs
   d) This lecture is easy to digest.
      He just eats up the lecturer's words.
      Chew on this thought for a while.
      Listen to this juicy piece of gossip.

   For each set of sentences:

   i)   Identify the words or phrases that are used metaphorically in each sentence.
   ii) Determine the basis for each of these metaphor sets.

   Use the pattern: "The metaphors in (x) describe _____ in terms of _____."

   Example: The metaphors in (a) describe human relationships in terms of temperature.

9. The section on lexicalization of concepts (Section 2.3) discussed how some languages simultaneously express motion and path, motion and manner, and/or motion and thing moving in motion verbs. Change the sentence *He moved the goods by truck to the warehouse* so that both the movement and the vehicle used for the move are lexicalized in one verb. Give another verb that expresses a similar combination of concepts.

10. Consider the following Fijian pronouns. (Refer to Section 2.4.)

au	1st person singular 'me'
iko	2nd person singular 'you'
koya	3rd person singular 'him/her/it'
kedaru	1st person dual 'you and me'
keirau	1st person dual 'one other (not you) and me'
kemudrau	2nd person dual 'you two'
rau	3rd person dual 'those two'
kedatou	1st person trial 'two others (including you) and me'
keitou	1st person trial 'two others (excluding you) and me'
kemudou	2nd person trial 'you three'
iratou	3rd person trial 'those three'
keda	1st person plural 'us' (more than three, including you)
keimami	1st person plural 'us' (more than three, excluding you)
kemuni:	2nd person plural 'you' (more than three)
ira	3rd person plural 'them' (more than three)

   i) What concepts are grammaticalized in the Fijian pronoun system that are not grammaticalized in the English pronoun system?
   ii) Which concept is grammaticalized in the English pronoun system but not in the Fijian system?

11. With the help of bracketing, describe the ambiguity in each of the following examples. (See Section 3.2.)
   a) yellow cars and motorcycles
   b) I followed the man on a bicycle.
   c) He said he left yesterday.

12. Each NP in the following sentences has a thematic role that represents the part that its referent plays in the situation described by the sentence. (See Section 3.3.)
   a) The man chased the intruder.
   b) The cat jumped from the chair onto the table.
   c) Aaron wrote a letter to Marilyn.
   d) The President entertained the guests in the Blue Room.
   e) Henry mailed the manuscript from Boise.

Using the terms described in this chapter, label the thematic role of each NP in these sentences and identify the assigner for each thematic role.

Example: <u>Beth</u> wrote <u>a novel</u> in <u>the park</u>
            <ag, th>   <loc>

13. Each of the following sentences has undergone a movement transformation. (See Section 3.3.)
    a) What should Larry give to the bride?
    b) Who will Liane kiss?
    c) Which house will the group leave from?
    d) What might Marvin forget on the bus?

    Write out the deep structure string for each of these sentences and mark all thematic roles and thematic role assigners.

    Example: a) Larry should give what to the bride

    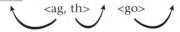

14. It is often suggested that *each other* (a so-called reciprocal pronoun) behaves like reflexive pronouns in obeying Principle A. How does this idea explain the acceptable and unacceptable uses of *each other* illustrated in the following sentences? (See Section 3.4.)

    i)   The men admire *each other*.
    ii) *The men's boss admires *each other*.
    iii) *The men think that [_TP the boss admires *each other*].

15. In the following sentence, the pronoun *she* could, according to Principle B, refer to either *the architect* or *the secretary*. (See Section 4.1.)

    The architect gave the secretary a raise after she typed the report.

    i)   Which interpretation for *she* comes to mind first?
    ii) Why?
    iii) What happens to the pronoun's interpretation if you change the word *secretary* to *janitor*?

16. In each of the following pairs of sentences, one of the sentences contains a presupposition relating to the truth of the complement clause. (See Section 4.1.)
    a) John regrets that Maria went to the graduation ceremony.
       John believes that Maria went to the graduation ceremony.
    b) The captain thought that the ship was in danger.
       The captain realized that the ship was in danger.
    c) It is significant that the criminal was sentenced.
       It is likely that the criminal was sentenced.

    For each pair:

    i)   Identify the sentence that contains the presupposition.
    ii) Locate the word that is responsible for the presupposition.

17. The syntactic construction *It was _____ that _____* is called a "cleft construction" and is used in certain discourse contexts. Consider the following conversations involving cleft constructions. (See Section 4.3.)
    a) *A:* Did Sally claim that she saw a flying saucer last night?
       B: No, it was a meteorite that Sally claimed she saw last night.

b) *A:* Did Sally claim that she saw a flying saucer last night?

   B: No, it was <u>Sally</u> that <u>claimed she saw a meteorite last night</u>.

c) *A:* Did Sally claim that she saw a flying saucer last night?

   B: No, it was <u>last week</u> that <u>Sally claimed she saw a flying saucer</u>.

i)   In which example is B's response inappropriate?

ii) Focus first on contexts in which B's response is appropriate. How do the underlined parts correspond to new and old information?

iii) Explain why the cleft construction is unacceptable in one of the examples.

18. Each of the following examples contains a conversational implicature. (See Section 4.4.)

a) *A:* Have you washed the floor and done the dishes?

   B: I've washed the floor.

b) *A:* Did you get hold of Carl yet?

   B: I tried to call him yesterday.

c) *A:* What did you think of the movie?

   B: Well, the supporting actor was great.

d) *A:* Do you have any pets?

   B: I have a goat.

What is the implicature for each example?

 **LaunchPad Solo** | For more helpful content and quizzes, go to the LaunchPad Solo
macmillan learning | for *Contemporary Linguistics* at **launchpadworks.com**.

For the Student Linguist

ELVIS'S BIGGEST FAN CLEANS OUT BANK— ACCOMPLICE LAUNDERS THE DOUGH

PEORIA—Blanche VanBuren, an old Elvis fan from Oneida, Illinois, cleaned out the Peoria Institution for Savings yesterday with nothing but a sawed-off broom and old shotgun.

Darrel Apley, the owner of Union Electric and a shocked witness who preferred to remain anonymous said, "Blanche should be at home at this time of the day. Her favorite soap is on the TV."

A teller said, "Someone came in a truck. I heard some screams coming from inside. People were rolling on the floor. Then it was over and I smoked a pack of cigarettes on the way home."

By the time the Bureau had been hauled in, the local pigs had decided someone else had done it. But the tipoff, by Oneida Otters star center Billie Jones, was about her partner. "Everyone thought two people were involved from the beginning," Jones claimed. "But it was when I saw the suds in the record store behind the pizzeria that it all came together."

The King could not be reached for comment by press time.

It's surprisingly easy to write an article in which every sentence is ambiguous. It's much harder—maybe even impossible—to write one that isn't ambiguous, or to write anything that isn't ambiguous. Maybe this explains why legal language is so tedious in its attempt to be unambiguous and why our court system is so clogged (obstructed, that is, not filled with Dutch wooden shoes), and why multiple-choice exams are so awful.

To show that the sentences in this article really are ambiguous, I'll attempt to disambiguate the first couple of paragraphs of Blanche's story in painstaking detail. By the time I'm done, you'll probably be able to see ambiguity everywhere you go.

Blanche VanBuren is an elderly Elvis aficionado who resides in Oneida, Illinois. And she's just plain old, all would agree (see tree *1B*). Or, when considering Elvis fans from Oneida, she's getting up in years (see tree *1A*), but in some other context she'd be considered pretty young (because most of the Elvis fans in Oneida are teeny-boppers, whereas Blanche is pushing thirty). Maybe Blanche has been an Elvis fan for a long time (*1B*). Or maybe, just maybe, most Oneidan Elvis fans are new to their admiration of him (it began with the postage stamp), but Blanche has loved Elvis since 1984, when she encountered him on a spaceship, and is therefore, comparatively speaking, an old Elvis-fan-from-Oneida (tree *1A*). Of course, she could also be a fan of only the *old* Elvis—that is, she liked his Vegas days but hated the early stuff. You can figure out the tree for this reading.

Let's assume Blanche is elderly. And a neat freak, because she washed the Peoria Institution for Savings from top to bottom (taking the shotgun to teach a lesson to litterbugs). Then again, she might be an incredibly compulsive cleaner in her own house and spend so much money on lemon-scented antiseptics that she robbed the P.I.S. and took along that sawed-off broom because she was delirious from inhaling ammonia all day. Let's consider her implements. The shotgun was old. The broom was sawed-off. Was the broom old? We don't know; the story doesn't provide information on its age. Was the shotgun sawed-off? This is a classic case of structural ambiguity, made famous by the example "the old men and women," and the answer should be obvious by now (but see trees *2A* and *2B* for confirmation).

The article does make clear that the event of interest took place yesterday, but I'm wondering whether Blanche habitually cleans out banks, and it just happened to be the P.I.S. yesterday, or if this was an out-of-the-blue cleaning or what. Could be that she cleans the P.I.S. every day, but usually she has more equipment than a broom and a gun.

Then there's the possibility that Blanche is an early model electric cooling device (or an antique paper and balsa wood construction), once owned (and affectionately named) by Elvis, which either: (a) blew all the dirt out of the bank or (b) was brought to life and performed the robbery. You never know.

What about Darrel Apley? If the writer of this article had any ethics, he (Darrel) is not the person who owns Union Electric, nor is he (Darrel) a shocked witness who preferred to remain anonymous. If the writer had ethics there would have to have been three different people who all said "Blanche should be at home . . ." and one of them is Darrel, one's the owner of U.E., and the third is shocked and prefers anonymity (tree *3A*). However, sloppy writing and broken promises are everywhere, and it's quite possible that *the owner of Union Electric and a shocked witness who preferred to remain anonymous* are actually intended to describe Darrel (tree *3B*).

"Blanche should be at home at this time of the day." Should? As in, given her normal patterns, the most likely case is that Blanche is at home? Or *should* as in if that lowdown, bank-thieving woman knew what was good for her she'd be at home watching *General Hospital*?

"Her favorite soap is on the TV." This one's easy; it's nothing but lexical ambiguity. Her favorite soap could be Ivory Family Size or the aforementioned *General Hospital*. If this were spoken instead of written, we'd have to explore the option that her favorite soap is called "On the TV," and actually, considering the doubts you might have about the writer's integrity, that could have been what Darrel (and maybe two others) meant. Of course, "on" is ambiguous between "being broadcast" or "on top of" but enough is enough.

The rest of the article you can disambiguate on your own. It's useful to draw trees for the structurally ambiguous parts and make sure the different interpretations match the trees. Every *written* sentence—every portion of material from one period to another—is ambiguous, but not every *TP* in the technical, linguistic sense is ambiguous. Be sure to look for lexical ambiguity, structural ambiguity, and pronouns that could refer to a few different people. Also look carefully at Jones's quote—this one is hard but interesting. Finally, check out your local newspaper. I predict that many of the sentences in it are as ambiguous as the ones in this article. You could even examine the instructions for your next linguistics homework assignment and (politely) tease your instructor if they're not crystal clear. Be careful, though—he or she might hold you to the same standard in your writing.

TREES:

(1A)

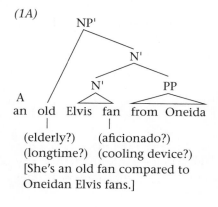

A an old Elvis fan from Oneida

(elderly?)   (aficionado?)
(longtime?)   (cooling device?)
[She's an old fan compared to Oneidan Elvis fans.]

(1B)

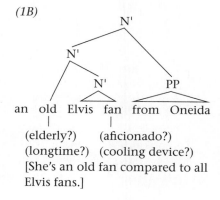

an old Elvis fan from Oneida

(elderly?)   (aficionado?)
(longtime?)   (cooling device?)
[She's an old fan compared to all Elvis fans.]

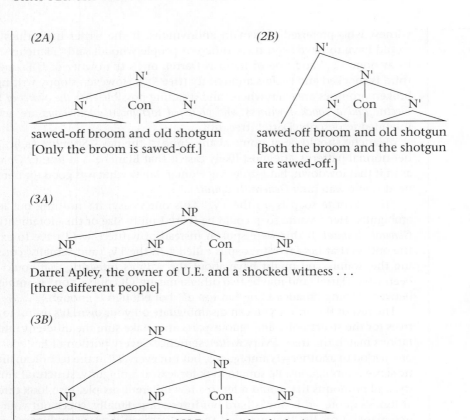

(2A)

sawed-off broom and old shotgun
[Only the broom is sawed-off.]

(2B)

sawed-off broom and old shotgun
[Both the broom and the shotgun
are sawed-off.]

(3A)

Darrel Apley, the owner of U.E. and a shocked witness . . .
[three different people]

(3B)

Darrel Apley, the owner of U.E. and a shocked witness . . .
[One person: "Darrel Apley, (who is) the owner . . . ," after "who is" has been
deleted. Don't worry about the details of this structure.]

seven

The Classification of Languages

Aleksandra Steinbergs
William O'Grady

*Everything it is possible for us to analyze depends on a clear method
which distinguishes the similar from the not similar.*
—LINNEUS, *Genera Plantarum* (1754)

OBJECTIVES

In this chapter, you will learn:

- how we define a language and the extent of linguistic diversity
- how different languages can be classified according to similarities in their phonology, morphology, and syntax
- how languages are related to one another genetically
- how languages in the Indo-European family are related

 **LaunchPad Solo**
macmillan learning | For more helpful content and quizzes, go to the LaunchPad Solo
for *Contemporary Linguistics* at **launchpadworks.com**.

There are more than 7,000 languages in the world today, each with its own sound patterns, syntax, and vocabulary. But underlying these differences are similarities that allow languages to be classified and grouped in various ways. This chapter focuses on the methods of classification used by linguists and on some of the similarities and differences that have been uncovered in comparative research on the world's languages. First, though, some preliminary discussion is in order.

1   Basic Issues and Concerns

In an attempt to bring some order to the linguistic diversity found in the world's speech communities, linguists attempt to distinguish **dialect** from language and to classify languages in various ways. In this section, we explore some of the results of their work, as well as the alarming threat to the survival of a large number of the world's languages.

1.1   Dialect and Language

It is sometimes difficult to determine whether two linguistic communities speak different languages or merely different dialects of the same language. One test that linguists use to decide this involves the criterion of **mutual intelligibility**. Mutually intelligible varieties of the same language can be understood by speakers of each variety. According to this criterion, the English of Milwaukee, the English of Toronto, and the English of London qualify as dialects of the same language. In contrast, if two speakers cannot understand one another, then linguists normally conclude that they are speaking different languages. The Italian of Florence and the French of Paris are examples of varieties of speech that are not mutually intelligible.

Political, cultural, social, historical, and religious factors frequently interfere when determining linguistic boundaries. (In fact, it is sometimes said that a language is just a dialect with an army and a navy!) For example, Serbs and Croats—with their different histories, cultures, and religions—often claim that they speak different languages. However, even though Serbian and Croatian are written with different alphabets, they are actually mutually intelligible dialects of the same language, which used to be called Serbo-Croatian when Serbs, Croats, and Bosnians lived in the united country of Yugoslavia. In contrast, we often speak of Chinese as if it were a single language, even though it is actually a number of individual, mutually unintelligible languages (Mandarin, Cantonese, Taiwanese, Wu, and so on), each with a multitude of dialects of its own.

In addition to the problems presented by these nonlinguistic considerations, complications arise when we try to divide a continuum of mutually intelligible dialects whose two endpoints are not intelligible. Dutch and German, for example, are mutually intelligible around the border area between Germany and the Netherlands; however, the Dutch of Amsterdam and the German of Munich are not. Similarly, Palestinian Arabic and Syrian Arabic are mutually intelligible, but Moroccan Arabic and Saudi Arabian Arabic are not.

1.2   The Threat to Human Linguistic Diversity

Taking these considerations into account, how many languages are spoken in the world today? The best available estimate, from the website of the Ethnologue organization, places the figure at 7,106, with the geographic distribution shown in Table 7.1.

Table 7.1 The geographical distribution of the world's living languages

Region	Number of languages	% of the total
The Americas	1,060	14.9
Africa	2,146	30.2
Europe	285	4.0
Asia	2,303	32.4
The Pacific	1,312	18.5
Total	**7,106**	100%

© SIL, The geographical distribution of the world's living languages. Used by permission, © SIL International, *Ethnologue: Languages of the World*,17th Edition, further redistribution prohibited without permission.

Table 7.2 presents the estimated speaker populations for the world's twenty most-spoken languages. (Except where otherwise indicated, estimates include only native speakers; L2 = second language.) These are large numbers, but they are not typical. Five thousand languages have fewer than 100,000 speakers, and over 3,000 have fewer than 10,000 speakers; at least 500 languages had fewer than 100 speakers at the turn of the millennium. According to a UNESCO report, 96 percent of the world's languages are spoken by just 3 percent of the world's population, leaving much of the world's linguistic diversity in the hands of a very small number of speakers.

Table 7.2 The world's twenty most-spoken languages and estimated number of speakers as of 2014

Mandarin	847,755,970 [+178,000,000 L2 speakers]
Spanish	405,638,110 [+60,000,000 L2 speakers]
English	334,800,758 [+430,000,000 L2 speakers]
Hindi	260,302,820 [+120,000,000 L2 speakers]
Portuguese	202,468,100 [+15,000,000 L2 speakers]
Bengali (Bangladesh, India)	193,263,700
Russian	161,727,650 [+110,000,000 L2 speakers]
Japanese	122,072,000 [+1,000,000 L2 speakers]
Javanese (Indonesia)	84,308,740
German	83,812,810 [+28,000,000 L2 speakers]
Wu (China)	77,202,480
Telugu (India)	74,049,000 [+5,000,000 L2 speakers]
Vietnamese	73,600,000
Marathi (India)	71,780,000 [+3,000,000 L2 speakers]
Tamil (India, Sri Lanka)	68,763,360 [+8,000,000 L2 speakers]
French	68,458,600 [+50,000,000 L2 speakers]
Korean	68,418,320
Urdu (India, Pakistan)	63,431,800 [+104,000,000 L2 speakers]
Yue (China)	62,239,960
Turkish	50,733,420

© SIL, The world's twenty most-spoken languages and estimated number of speakers as of 2014.

Ask the average person to name a dead language, and he or she is likely to mention Latin. In fact, Latin did not really die; rather, it evolved over a period of centuries into French, Spanish, Italian, Portuguese, Romanian, and the other modern-day Romance languages (see Section 3.1).

Contrast this with the situation of Manx, a Celtic language indigenous to the Isle of Man, a small island midway between Ireland and Great Britain. Its last speaker, Ned Maddrell, died in 1974. Just one hundred years earlier, 12,000 people had spoken Manx. Now no one does. Manx didn't just change over time; it eventually ceased to be spoken. A similar fate befell the Eyak language of Alaska in 2008 and the language Bo (once spoken in India's Andaman Islands) in 2010. The last native speaker of the Salish language Klallam (spoken in Washington State) died in early 2014, at the age of 103. These are all examples of **language death**, a term used when a language no longer has native speakers.

On average, a language is lost every three months, accelerating a process that has been underway for several centuries. According to the most recent estimates, 45 percent of the world's languages are at risk, with few, if any, children learning them. The situation is grim in many different areas of the world. Of the 300 languages spoken in the area corresponding to the United States at the time of Columbus, only 175 are still spoken, and many of these are on the verge of disappearing. Just four of the sixty indigenous languages once spoken in Canada—Cree, Ojibwe, Inuktitut, and Dene Sųłiné—have large enough speaker populations to have a good chance of surviving over the long term. Ninety percent of Australia's 250 Aboriginal languages are near extinction. A language whose death seems likely is said to be an **endangered language**. You can find up-to-date information on the plight of hundreds of endangered languages at the website of the Endangered Languages Project.

The death of languages is lamentable for a variety of reasons. From a purely linguistic perspective, the loss of linguistic diversity means that we have much less information about how language works and about the different forms that it can take. For example, when the last speaker of Ubykh (a North Caucasian language spoken in Turkey) died in 1992, linguists lost the opportunity to study a very unusual phonological system—Ubykh had eighty-one consonants and just three vowels. (In contrast, a typical variety of American English has twenty-four consonants and around fifteen vowels and diphthongs.)

Just as serious is the loss of cultural knowledge that accompanies language death. A language's vocabulary encodes much of a community's cultural and scientific knowledge, including the distinctions that it makes among the plants and animals in its environment. This knowledge, accumulated over centuries, is not insignificant: many indigenous languages distinguish among thousands of species of plants, fish, and animals based on their appearance, behavior, edibility, and even medicinal properties.

How and why do languages die? In some cases, they die because the people who speak them perish as the result of war or disease. Indeed, according to some estimates, up to 95 percent of the Native population of North America died from diseases brought to their continent by European colonists.

More commonly these days, however, languages die because their speakers gradually use them less and less in favor of a language that appears to offer greater economic or educational opportunities. English, Spanish, and French are obvious examples of international languages that acquire new speakers in this way, but many other languages are dominant on a more local scale: Mandarin Chinese, Thai, Bahasa Indonesia, the East African language Swahili, and Filipino (Tagalog) are all threats to smaller languages in their respective territories. The classic pattern of language loss involves **language shift** that takes place over three generations: the parents are monolingual, their children become bilingual by adopting a new language, and their children's children grow up monolingual in the new language—unable to speak to their own grandparents.

With about 7,000 languages in the world today and only about 200 countries, the vast majority of the world's languages do not have the protection of a national government. Smaller linguistic communities are therefore often left without the economic or educational resources needed to compete with the larger languages that surround them.

The ongoing pervasive threat to the world's linguistic diversity is of great concern to linguists, many of whom are actively involved in studying and documenting languages on the verge of extinction. Where feasible, linguists are also seeking ways to improve the prospects for endangered languages by participating in linguistic, social, and educational programs designed to promote and protect the use of indigenous languages.

1.3 Types of Classification

Within the field of linguistics, three different approaches to language classification are used.

A first approach, **linguistic typology**, classifies languages according to their structural characteristics. For example, typologists might group together languages with similar sound patterns or those with similar grammatical structures. Typological studies also endeavor to identify **linguistic universals**: that is, structural characteristics that occur in all or most languages. We discuss linguistic typology further in Section 2.

A second approach, **genetic classification**, categorizes languages according to their descent. Languages that developed historically from the same ancestor language are grouped together and are said to be **genetically related**. This ancestor may be attested (that is, texts written in this language have been discovered or preserved, as in the case of Latin), or it may be a reconstructed **protolanguage** for which no original texts exist (as is the case for Indo-European). Section 3 of this chapter presents an overview of some languages and the families to which they belong.

Genetically related languages need not look alike. For example, both Latvian and English belong to the European branch of the Indo-European family, but their morphological structure is quite different. Indeed, the English sentence *It has to be figured*

LANGUAGE MATTERS   Language Immersion to the Rescue?

In the 1960s, a group of Canadian parents and educators, taking advantage of children's natural abilities as language learners, launched "French immersion"—a wildly successful program that made French the language of instruction for English-speaking schoolchildren. This same idea underlies a series of exciting immersion initiatives whose goal is the survival of indigenous languages. Following the pioneering effort of the Maori in New Zealand in the early 1980s, immersion programs have been implemented with varying degrees of success for many endangered languages, including Hawaiian, Blackfoot, Navajo, and Mohawk.

Information from: Leanne Hinton and Ken Hale, eds., *The Green Book of Language Revitalization in Practice* (San Diego: Academic Press, 2001); Pūnana Leo, www.ahapunanaleo .org (website for Hawaiian preschool immersion program); "Mohawk Immersion Pilot Programs," http://www.mohawkcommunity.com/languageimmersion.html; "French Immersion in Canada," University of Michigan, http://sitemaker.umich.edu/356.hess /research_on_french-immersion_programs.

---

out can be expressed in Latvian by the single word *ja-izgudro*. Of course, Latvian and English are very distantly related, and languages that are more closely related typically manifest greater similarity. At the same time, even languages that are totally unrelated may be similar in some respects. For instance, English, Thai, and Swahili, which are unrelated to each other, all employ subject-verb-object word order in simple declarative sentences.

1) *Swahili*
   Maria anapenda   Anna.
   Maria likes   Anna
   'Maria likes Anna.'

2) *Thai*
   Roudbuntuk ding roud.
   truck   push car
   'Trucks push cars.'

Finally, **areal classification** identifies characteristics shared by languages that are in geographical contact. Under these circumstances, languages often borrow words, sounds, morphemes, and even syntactic patterns from one another. As a result, neighboring languages can come to resemble each other, even though they may not be genetically related. Areal classification is a challenging endeavor that requires detailed knowledge of a region's speech communities and their languages. For reason of space, we will not be able to discuss this type of research further in this chapter.

2 Typological Classification

Linguists who study language typology group languages together on the basis of similarities in their syntactic patterns, morphological structure, and/or phonological systems. An important area of research within the study of linguistic typology is the search for linguistic universals. Structural patterns and traits that occur in all languages are called **absolute universals** (one such universal is that all languages have syntactic structure), while those that occur in most languages are known as **universal tendencies**.

Many typological generalizations involve **implicational universals**, which specify that the presence of one trait implies the presence of another (but not vice versa). For instance, the presence of nasal vowel phonemes implies the presence of oral vowel phonemes, but not vice versa. In such situations, we say that oral vowels are **unmarked** (or more common in world languages), and nasal vowels are **marked** (less common in world languages).

Implicational universals such as the one exemplified in Table 7.3 allow us to make predictions about what types of languages are possible and impossible. The following sections present some of the typological generalizations and universals that have been proposed in the areas of phonology, morphology, and syntax.

Table 7.3 Oral and nasal vowel phonemes: nasal vowels imply oral vowels

Nasal vowels	Oral vowels	
no	yes	possible (English, Japanese)
yes	yes	possible (French, Portuguese)
yes	no	**impossible**

2.1 Phonology

In this section, we represent vowel and consonant systems phonemically. However, the exact phonetic realization of these systems may vary in the individual languages.

Vowel Systems

Languages are often classified according to the size and pattern of their vowel systems. The most common vowel system has five phonemes—two high vowels, two mid vowels, and one low vowel (see Figure 7.1). The front vowels are unrounded, as is the low vowel, and the back vowels are rounded. About half the world's languages—including Basque (spoken in Spain), Hawaiian, Hebrew, Spanish, and Swahili—have such a system.

i   u

e   o

a

Figure 7.1 The most common vowel system

The majority of the world's other languages have vowel systems with three to nine different vowels (disregarding contrasts based on length or nasalization, which can double or triple the number of vowel phonemes). Languages with fewer than three or more than nine distinctive vowels are rare. Some typical vowel systems are presented in Figure 7.2.

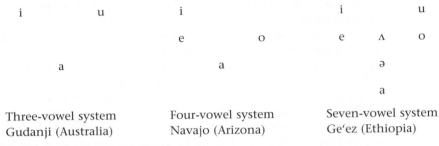

| Three-vowel system | Four-vowel system | Seven-vowel system |
| Gudanji (Australia) | Navajo (Arizona) | Ge'ez (Ethiopia) |

Figure 7.2   Common vowel systems

Analysis of many languages has led to the discovery of a number of universal tendencies pertaining to vowel systems. Some of these tendencies are listed here, along with a description of the most commonly occurring vowels.

- The most commonly occurring vowel phoneme is /a/, which is found in almost all the languages of the world. The vowels /i/ and /u/ are almost as common as /a/.
- Front vowel phonemes (e.g., /i, e, ɛ, æ/) are generally unrounded, while nonlow back vowel phonemes (e.g., /ɔ, o, u/) are generally rounded.
- Low vowels (e.g., /æ, a, ɑ/) are generally unrounded.

Although American English has an above-average number of vowels, they all conform to the above tendencies. Thus, American English has only front unrounded vowels, all the low vowel phonemes are unrounded, and all of the back, nonlow vowels are rounded. The vowel system of American English is represented in Figure 7.3.

i   u

ɪ   ʊ

e   o

ɛ   ʌ   ɔ

æ   ɑ

Figure 7.3   The vowel system of American English

As already noted with respect to nasal and oral vowels, the relationship between certain contrasting vowel types can be expressed in terms of implicational universals, since the presence of one vowel phoneme type implies the presence of another (but not vice versa).

- As already noted, if a language has nasal vowel phonemes, then it will also have oral vowel phonemes. For example, French contrasts different nasal vowels—as in *long* /lɔ̃/ 'long' versus *lent* /lã/ 'slow'. And it contrasts oral vowels with nasal vowels, as in *las* /la/ 'weary' versus *lent* /lã/ 'slow'. Predictably, French also contrasts different oral vowels, as in *clos* /klo/ 'shut' versus *clou* /klu/ 'nail'. English shows contrasts among oral vowels but does not contrast nasal vowels with oral vowels. There are no contrasts in English like /bɔt/ 'bought' and */bɔ̃t/.

- If a language has long vowel phonemes, then it will also have short vowel phonemes. For example, Finnish has contrasting long vowels, and, predictably, contrasting short vowels (see Table 7.4).

Table 7.4   Finnish vowel contrasts

Long versus long	/viːli/ 'junket'	/vaːli/ 'election'
Short versus short	/suka/ 'bristle'	/suku/ 'family'
Short versus long	/tuli/ 'fire'	/tuːli/ 'wind'

The reverse is not necessarily the case—in fact, a language need not have long vowel phonemes at all. English works that way, since it has no phonemic contrast between long and short vowels.

Table 7.5   Long and short vowel phonemes: long vowels imply short vowels

Contrasting long vowels	*Contrasting short vowels*	
no	yes	possible (English)
yes	yes	possible (Finnish)
yes	no	**impossible**

Consonant Systems

It is not particularly useful to classify languages according to the number of consonants that they contain, since there is a great deal of variation in the size of consonant inventories (see the Language Matters box, "Record-Breaking Languages," on page 271). Nevertheless, typological analysis of consonant systems has produced a number of well-substantiated universals:

- All languages have stops.

- The most common stop phonemes are /p, t, k/. Very few languages lack any one of these, and there are no languages that lack all three. If any one of these three stops is missing, it will probably be /p/; for example, Arabic, Nubian, and Wichita have no /p/ phoneme. The most commonly occurring phoneme of the three is /t/.

- The most commonly occurring fricative phoneme is /s/. If a language has only one fricative, it is most likely to be /s/. It is the only fricative found in Nandi (a language of Kenya) and Weri (a language of New Guinea). The next most common fricative is /f/.

- The vast majority of languages have at least one nasal phoneme. In cases where a language has only one nasal phoneme, that phoneme is usually /n/ (as in Arapaho, spoken in Wyoming). If there are two contrasting nasals, they are normally /m/ and /n/.

- Most languages have at least one phonemic liquid. However, a relatively small number of languages have none at all: for example, Blackfoot and Dakota (Native American languages), Efik (spoken in Nigeria), and Siona (found in Ecuador). English, of course, has two: /l/ and /ɹ/.

Consonant phonemes are also subject to various implicational universals:

- If a language has voiced obstruent phonemes (stops, fricatives, or affricates), then it will almost always have corresponding voiceless obstruent phonemes (see Table 7.6). The reverse is not necessarily true; for example, Ainu (a language of northern Japan) has only voiceless obstruent phonemes: /p, t, k, tʃ, s/.

Table 7.6 Obstruent phonemes: voiced obstruents imply voiceless obstruents

Voiced obstruents	Voiceless obstruents	
no	yes	possible (Ainu)
yes	yes	possible (English)
yes	no	**very rare** (Canela-Krahô [Brazil])

- Sonorant consonants are generally voiced. Very few languages have voiceless sonorant phonemes; those that do always have voiced sonorant phonemes as well (see Table 7.7). For example, Burmese contrasts voiced and voiceless nasals and laterals.

Table 7.7 Sonorant phonemes: voiceless sonorants imply voiced sonorants

Voiceless sonorants	Voiced sonorants	
no	yes	possible (English)
yes	yes	possible (Burmese)
yes	no	**impossible**

- If a language has fricative phonemes, then it will also have stop phonemes (see Table 7.8). There are no languages that lack stops; however, there are some languages that lack fricatives. For example, Kiribati (Gilbert Islands), Kitabal (eastern Australia), and Nuer (southeastern Sudan) have no fricatives.

Table 7.8 Stop and fricative phonemes: fricatives imply stops

Fricatives	Stops	
no	yes	possible (Nuer)
yes	yes	possible (English)
yes	no	**impossible**

- Languages that have affricates will also have fricatives and stops (see Table 7.9). This is not surprising, since an affricate is, in essence, a sequence of a stop followed by a fricative. However, many languages lack affricate phonemes altogether. For example, French has fricative and stop phonemes, but no affricate phonemes. In contrast, English has all three consonant types.

Table 7.9 Types of obstruent phonemes: affricates imply fricatives; fricatives imply stops

Affricates	Fricatives	Stops	
yes	yes	yes	possible (English)
no	yes	yes	possible (French)
no	no	yes	possible (Kitabal)
yes	yes	no	**impossible**
no	yes	no	**impossible**
yes	no	no	**impossible**

LANGUAGE MATTERS   Record-Breaking Languages

There are no official "world records" within linguistics, but it's natural to wonder about languages that are "extreme" in some way. Here are some languages that are frequently mentioned for the unusual size (large or small) of their phonological inventory.

- *Fewest consonants*: Rotokas has just 6 consonant phonemes. (A Papuan language, Rotokas has about 4,300 speakers in Papua New Guinea.)

- *Most consonants*: !Kung, a language with a speaker population of about 4,000 in Namibia and Angola, has 96 consonant phonemes.

- *Fewest vowels*: Some dialects of Abkhaz have just 2 vowel phonemes. (This North Caucasian language has approximately 106,000 speakers, mostly in the Republic of Georgia.)

- *Fewest overall number of phonemes*: Rotokas again (11).

- *Greatest overall number of phonemes*: By some counts, !Xóõ has 77 consonant phonemes, including dozens of clicks, and 31 vowel phonemes. (You can hear samples of !Xóõ, a language of Botswana, at the website of the UCLA Phonetics Lab and on YouTube.)

Suprasegmental Systems

Languages can also be classified according to their suprasegmental (or prosodic) type. Languages that use pitch to make meaning distinctions between words are called **tone languages.** As illustrated in Table 7.10, Mandarin has four contrastive tones.

Table 7.10   Tone contrasts in Mandarin

High tone	dā	'build'
Low rising tone	dá	'achieve'
Falling rising tone	dǎ	'hit'
High falling tone	dà	'big'

The other Chinese languages, as well as many languages of Southeast Asia, Africa, and the Americas, are also tone languages. A few tone languages are also found in Europe; for example, one of the dialects of Latvian makes a three-way tonal distinction (see Table 7.11).

Table 7.11   Tone contrasts in Latvian

Falling tone	loks	[lùoks]	'arch, bow'
Level (high) tone	loks	[lūoks]	'green onion'
Rising falling (broken) tone	loks	[lûoks]	'window'

There are two types of tones: level tones and contour tones. Tone languages most often contrast only two tone levels (usually high and low). However, contrasts involving three tone levels (such as high, low, and mid) are also relatively common. Five or more levels of tonal contrast are practically unknown.

Tone systems, too, exhibit various universal tendencies:

- If a language has contour tones (such as rising or falling tones), then it will also have level tones (such as high, mid, or low tones), as outlined in Table 7.12. Burmese, Crow (spoken in Montana), Latvian, and Mandarin are examples of languages that fit this pattern. The reverse pattern (languages with contour tones but no level tones) is extremely rare; Dafla, spoken in northern India, has such a system.

Table 7.12   Tone contrasts: contour tones imply level tones

Contour tones	Level tones	
no	yes	possible (Sarcee)
yes	yes	possible (Mandarin)
yes	no	**very rare** (Dafla)

Differences in stress are also useful in classifying languages. **Fixed stress languages** are those in which the position of stress on a word is predictable. For example, in Modern Hebrew and K'iché (a Mayan language), stress always falls on the last syllable of a word; in Polish, Swahili, and Samoan, stress falls on the penultimate (second-to-last) syllable of words, while in Czech, Finnish, and Hungarian, the stressed syllable is always the first syllable of a word. In **free stress languages**, the position of stress varies. Free stress is also called phonemic stress because of its role in distinguishing between words. Russian is an example of a language with free stress, as shown in Table 7.13.

Table 7.13 Stress contrasts in Russian

'muka	'torture'	mu'ka	'flour'
'zamok	'castle'	za'mok	'lock'
'ruki	'hands'	ru'ki	'hand's' (POSSESSIVE SINGULAR)

Syllable Structure

The CV and V syllable types are unmarked. They are found in all languages (with the possible exception of the Australian language Arrernte, which seems to have only the VC and V types) and are learned first by children.

In any given language, onsets may be structured differently from codas. For example, in English, a nasal + stop sequence is permitted in the coda (in a word like *hand*) but not in the onset (no English words begin with the sequence *nd*). However, Swahili has precisely the opposite restrictions: the *nd* sequence is permitted in onset position (in words like *ndizi* 'banana') but not in coda position. In fact, Swahili syllables are codaless—they can only end in vowels.

Two examples of implicational universals for syllable structure are presented below.

- If a language permits sequences of consonants in the onset, then it will also permit syllables with single consonant onsets (see Table 7.14).

Table 7.14 Onsets: multiple consonant onsets imply single consonant onsets

Multiple C onsets	Single C onsets	
no	yes	possible (Hawaiian)
yes	yes	possible (English)
yes	no	**impossible**

- If a language permits sequences of consonants in the coda, then it will also permit syllables with single consonant codas and syllables with no coda at all (see Table 7.15).

Table 7.15 Codas: multiple consonant codas imply single consonant codas/ no codas

Multiple C codas	Single C codas/no codas	
no	yes	possible (Cantonese)
yes	yes	possible (English)
yes	no	**impossible**

2.2 Morphology

Both words and morphemes are found in all languages. However, there are clear differences in whether and how individual languages combine morphemes to form words. Four types of systems can be distinguished.

The Isolating Type

An **isolating** (or **analytic**) **language** avoids affixes, using free forms to express notions such as tense and number. Mandarin shows strong isolating tendencies, as exemplified by the fact that the morpheme used to indicate completed actions can appear in more than one position in the sentence.

3) a. Ta chi fan   *le*.
      he eat meal PAST
      'He ate the meal.'

   b. Ta chi *le*   fan.
      he eat PAST   meal
      'He ate the meal.'

Other languages that are primarily isolating include Cantonese, Vietnamese, Laotian, and Khmer (Cambodian).

The Agglutinating Type

An **agglutinating language** makes widespread use of affixes, each of which typically expresses a single piece of grammatical information. The following examples are from Turkish.

4) a. [kœj]
      'village'

   b. [kœj-leɾ]
      village-PL
      'villages'

   c. [kœj-leɾ-in]
      village-PL-GEN
      'of the villages'

As can be seen here, Turkish words can have a complex morphological structure, but each morpheme typically has a single, clearly identifiable function. In *4c*, for instance, *-leɾ* marks plurality and *-in* marks possession, giving the meaning 'of the villages'.

The Fusional Type

Words in a **fusional** or (**inflectional**) **language** can also consist of root + affix combinations. However, in contrast to agglutinating systems, the affixes in fusional languages often express several bits of grammatical information simultaneously. In Russian, for example, a single inflectional suffix marks the noun's gender class (masculine, feminine, or neuter), its number (singular or plural), and its grammatical role (subject, direct object, and so on). This is illustrated in 5 for the suffix *–u*, which designates feminine gender, singular number, and accusative case (used for the direct object).

5) My   vidim   ruk-u.
   we   see   hand-FEM.SG.ACC
   'We   see a/the hand.'

The Polysynthetic Type

In a **polysynthetic language**, single words can consist of long strings of roots and affixes that often express meanings associated with entire sentences in other languages. The following word from Inuktitut illustrates this.

6) Qasuiirsarvigssarsingitluinarnarpuq.
   Qasu -iir -sar   -vig   -ssar   -si -ngit-luinar   -nar   -puq
   tired not cause-to-be place-for suitable find not completely someone 3.SG
   'Someone did not find a completely suitable resting place.'

Polysynthesis is common in many Native American languages, including Inuktitut, Cree, and Sarcee.

Mixed Types

Many (perhaps most) languages do not belong exclusively to any of the four categories just outlined. For example, English employs isolating patterns in many verbal constructions, where each notion is expressed by a separate word. The future, for instance, is indicated by the independent word *will* (rather than by an affix) in structures such as *I will leave*. However, English exhibits considerable agglutination in derived words, such as *re-en-act-ment*, which consist of a series of clearly identifiable morphemes, each with its own unique meaning and function. Furthermore, the English pronoun system is largely fusional, since a single form can be used to indicate person, number, gender, and case. The word *he*, for instance, is used to express a third-person, singular, masculine subject.

Since many, if not most, of the world's languages exhibit mixed patterns, it has been suggested that terms like *isolating*, *agglutinating*, and *fusional* should be used to refer not to a language as a whole but to particular structures within a language. It is also important to recognize that these classifications do not take into consideration morphological processes such as compounding (e.g., English *greenhouse*), reduplication (e.g., Tagalog *sulat* 'write' versus *susulat* 'will write'), grammatical use of stress or tone (e.g., the noun *'present* versus the verb *pre'sent* in English), and internal word change (e.g., vowel alternation contrasting present and past, as in English *run* versus *ran*).

Implicational Universals: Morphology

A variety of generalizations can be made about word structure in human language.

- If a language has inflectional affixes, it will also have derivational affixes. For example, English has not only inflectional suffixes such as the past tense *-ed* and plural *-s* but also derivational suffixes like *-ment* (*treatment, discernment*) and *-able* (*doable, readable*).

- If a word has both a derivational and an inflectional affix, the derivational affix is closer to the root (see Table 7.16).

Table 7.16   The ordering of derivational and inflectional affixes

English					
king	-dom	-s	*king	-s	-dom
Root	DA	IA	Root	IA	DA
Turkish					
iʃ	-tʃi	-ler	*iʃ	-ler	-tʃi
work	-er	-PL	work	-PL	-er
Root	DA	IA	Root	IA	DA

DA = *derivational affix;* IA = *inflectional affix*

- If a language has only suffixes, it will also have only postpositions. (In languages that place the head at the end of the phrase, postpositions are the equivalent of prepositions.) Turkish, for example, has only suffixes; as expected, it also has postpositions rather than prepositions. This is illustrated in the following sentence.

7) Hasan   Ebru   itʃin   kitap   al-dɨ.
    Hasan   Ebru   for   book   buy-PST
    'Hasan bought a book for Ebru.'

2.3   Syntax

Work on syntactic universals often takes as its starting point the relative order of the subject (S), the direct object (O), and the verb (V) in simple declarative sentences such as *The men built the house*. The three most common word orders (in descending order of frequency) are SOV, SVO, and VSO. Of languages with an identifiable basic word order, about 47 percent employ SOV, 41 percent use SVO, and 8 percent prefer VSO.

8) SOV (Turkish):
    Hasan   œkyz-y   al-dɨ.
    Hasan   ox-ACC   buy-PST
    'Hasan bought the ox.'

9) SVO (English):
   The athlete broke the record.

10) VSO (Welsh):

Lladdodd	y	ddraig	y	dyn.
killed	the	dragon	the	man

    'The dragon killed the man.'

The prevalence of the S-before-O pattern (more than 95 percent of the languages studied) may be due to the fact that the subject usually coincides with the topic of the sentence (i.e., what the sentence is about) and therefore is more useful at an early point in the utterance.

While an overwhelming majority of the world's languages place the subject before the direct object in their basic word order, this pattern is not universal. There are a small number of VOS languages, of which the best-known example is Malagasy.

11) VOS (Malagasy):

Nahita	ny	mpianatra	ny	vehivavy.
Saw	the	student	the	woman

    'The woman saw the student.'

In addition, there are a very few OVS and OSV languages, all of which seem to be found in South America:

12) OVS (Hixkaryana):

Kana	janimno	birjekomo.
Fish	caught	boy

    'The boy caught a fish.'

13) OSV (Apuriña):

Anana	nota	apa.
Pineapple	I	fetch

    'I fetch a pineapple.'

Word Order Universals

Sometimes, the order of elements within one kind of structure has implications for the order of elements in other structures. Many of these implications concern the relationship between the verb and its (direct) object.

- If a language has VO word order, then it will almost always have prepositions rather than postpositions. Languages of this type include Berber (spoken in Morocco), Hebrew, Maori (spoken in New Zealand), Maasai (spoken in Kenya), Welsh, and Irish Gaelic.

14) *Irish Gaelic*

   a. VSO pattern:

Chonaic	mé	mo	mháthair.
Saw	I	my	mother

      'I saw my mother.'

b. Preposition pattern:
sa teach
in house
'in the house'

- If a language has OV word order, then it will probably have postpositions rather than prepositions. Languages with this structural pattern include Basque, Burmese, Hindi, Japanese, Korean, Quechua (spoken in the Andean regions of South America), Turkish, and Guugu Yimidhirr, an Aboriginal language of Australia (ERG = ergative, an affix used for the subject of a transitive verb).

15) *Guugu Yimidhirr*

a. SOV pattern:
Gudaa-ngun   yarrga   dyindaj.
dog-ERG   boy   bit
'The dog bit the boy.'

b. Postposition pattern:
yuwaal   nganh
beach   from
'from the beach'

- PPs almost always precede the verb in OV languages and usually follow the verb in VO languages.

16) *Japanese*

a. SOV pattern:
Gakusei-ga   hon-o   yonda.
student-NOM   book-ACC   read
'The student read a book.'

b. PP precedes verb:
Taroo-ga   [$_{PP}$ nitiyoobi   ni]   tsuita.
Taroo-NOM   Sunday   on   arrived
'Taroo arrived on Sunday.'

17) *English*

a. SVO pattern:
I like candy.

b. PP follows verb:
George left [$_{PP}$ on Sunday].

- Manner adverbs overwhelmingly precede the verb in OV languages and generally follow the verb in VO languages.

18) *Japanese* (SOV pattern, as seen in *16a*)
Manner adverb precedes verb:
Joozu   hasiru.
Well   run
'(He) runs well.'

19) *English* (SVO pattern, as seen in *17a*)
Manner adverb follows verb:
John runs well.

- There is an overwhelming preference for Possessor + N order in OV languages, and a (somewhat weaker) preference for N + Possessor order in VO languages (GEN = genitive, an affix used to mark a possessor).

20) *Japanese* (SOV pattern, as seen in *16a*)
Possessor precedes head N:
Taroo-no   hon
Taroo-GEN   book
'Taroo's book'

21) *French*

   a. SVO pattern:
     Pierre   aime   Marie.
     'Pierre   likes   Marie.'

   b. Possessor structure follows head N:
     la   maison   de   Marie
     the   house   of (GEN)   Marie
     'Marie's house'

English, although an SVO language, exhibits both Possessor + N and N + Possessor patterns:

22) a. Possessor + N pattern:
    the country's laws

   b. N + Possessor pattern:
    the laws of the country

Grammatical Hierarchies

Implicational universals are often stated in terms of **grammatical hierarchies** of categories or relations. One of the most important hierarchies of this type refers to the grammatical relations of subject and direct object.

23) The grammatical relation hierarchy:
    subject > direct object > other

According to this hierarchy, a process that applies only to subjects is less marked than a process that applies to direct objects. In other words, if a particular phenomenon applies to direct objects, it should also apply to subjects. In contrast, it would not be surprising to find a process that applies to subjects but not direct objects.

Among the many typological phenomena that conform to this hierarchy is verb agreement. As the following examples show, in some languages, the verb agrees only with the subject, and in others, it agrees with both the subject and the direct object (3 = 3rd person; SG = singular; PL = plural).

24) Agreement with subject only (Spanish):

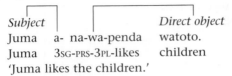

Subject
Juan   ley-ó   dos libros.
Juan   read-SG.PST   two books
'Juan read two books.'

25) Agreement with subject and direct object (Swahili):

Subject   *Direct object*
Juma   a- na-wa-penda   watoto.
Juma   3SG-PRS-3PL-likes   children
'Juma likes the children.'

However, as predicted by the hierarchy, there are no languages in which the verb agrees only with the direct object.

LANGUAGE MATTERS   The Ergative Way

In some languages, the verb agrees with the subject of an intransitive verb and the direct object of a transitive verb, but not with the subject of a transitive verb. The following example (provided by Farooq Babrakzai) is from Pashto, one of the major languages of Afghanistan.

a. *Agreement with the 3rd person subject of an intransitive verb:*
   xəza   də-daftar -na   raɣ-a.
   woman   POSS-office-from   came-3FS*
   'The woman came from the office.'

b. *Agreement with the 3rd person direct object of a transitive verb:*
   ma xəza   wəlid-a.
   I   woman saw-3FS
   'I saw the woman.'

A grammatical rule that treats the subject of an intransitive verb and the direct object of a transitive verb alike is said to be **ergative**. The existence of such phenomena suggests that the grammatical hierarchy in *23* may represent just one option—although a very common one—for creating syntax.

*3FS = third person feminine singular

2.4   Explaining Universals

Linguists are still uncertain about how to explain the existence of many linguistic universals. Nonetheless, a number of interesting proposals have been made, and it is worthwhile to consider some of them here.

Phonology

Perceptual factors play a role in shaping phonological universals. For example, the fact that /s/ is the most commonly occurring fricative may have to do with its acoustic prominence: varieties of /s/ are inherently louder and more strident than other kinds of fricatives.

Vowel systems (discussed in Section 2.1) develop so as to keep vowel phonemes as different from each other as possible. A three-vowel system such as the one in Figure 7.4 allows for plenty of "space" around each vowel, which probably makes each vowel easier to distinguish from the others.

i   u

a

Figure 7.4   A three-vowel system

The distribution of stop phonemes is also sensitive to perceptibility. The reason that /p/, /t/, and /k/ are the three most common stops in languages is probably that they occur at three maximally distant places of articulation within the supralaryngeal vocal tract. These three stops are much easier to distinguish perceptually than a sequence of dental, alveolar, and palatal stops, for example, all of which are produced in the central region of the oral cavity.

It has been suggested that consonant systems in general respond to the articulatory pressures that give rise to unmarked sounds and systems. Articulatorily basic obstruents such as /p/, /t/, and /k/ are found much more commonly than more complex articulations such as /tɬ/ and /qw/. Table 7.17 presents the set of obstruents that is most widely used across human languages.

Table 7.17   Obstruents most often found cross-linguistically

p	t	k	ʔ
b	d	g	
f	s		h
	tʃ		

Languages tend to have consonant systems that consist of about 70 percent obstruents and 30 percent sonorants, no matter what the total size of their consonant inventories may be. These figures reflect the articulatory possibilities available for contrast: more distinctions can be made among obstruents than among sonorants. There are, for example, no nasal fricatives, because the air pressure needed to force air through a narrow opening (which is necessary for the production of fricatives) cannot be built up when so much air is flowing through the nasal passage at the same time.

Morphology

Other types of explanations are appropriate for morphological universals. For example, the fact that languages with suffixes but no prefixes always have postpositions

(Section 2.2) may have a historical explanation. Because suffixes often evolve from postpositions, the coexistence of the two types of morphemes is expected.

An example of this very phenomenon can be seen in the closely related languages Finnish and Estonian. Their ancestor language (Proto-Balto-Finnic) contained a postposition *kanssa* 'with', which is still evident in Standard Finnish but has evolved into the suffix -*ga* in Estonian (see Table 7.18).

Table 7.18   Proto-Balto-Finnic postposition *kanssa* becomes suffix -*ga*

GEN = genitive case, often used to express possession; COM = comitative, a case expressing accompaniment				
Standard Finnish: postposition *kanssa* 'with'				
poja	'boy'	poja-n	kanssa	'with the boy'
		boy-GEN	with	
Estonian: case suffix -*ga*				
poja	'boy'	poja-ga		'with the boy'
		boy-COM		

The requirement that derivational affixes occur closer to the root than inflectional affixes has another type of explanation. Derivation typically forms new words, while inflection marks the subclass (for example, plural for Ns, past tense for Vs) to which a word belongs. Given that a word must be formed before its subclass can be determined, it follows that derivational processes will precede inflection. This is reflected in word structure, where derivational affixes appear closer to the root than inflectional markers. In Figure 7.5, for instance, the verbal root *treat* is converted into a noun by the affix -*ment* before the plural inflectional marker is added.

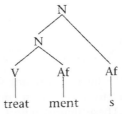

Figure 7.5   The structure of a word containing a derivational affix and an inflectional affix

Syntax

At least some syntactic universals may be explained in terms of the way that the human brain processes sentence structure. Consider the summary of word order patterns in Table 7.19, which is based on the implicational universals discussed in Section 2.3.

Table 7.19 Word order patterns

Constituents	Order in VO language	Order in OV language
P & NP	preposition-NP	NP-postposition
V & PP	verb-PP	PP-verb
V & manner Adv	verb-manner Adv	manner Adv-verb
Poss & N	noun-possessor	possessor-noun

One explanation as to why word order properties cluster together involves the contrast between right-branching and left-branching languages. In right-branching languages, the more elaborate part of a phrase's structure occurs on its right branch; in left-branching languages, it occurs on the left. Thus, a verb-object pattern is right-branching since a phrasal constituent (an XP) appears on its right branch, but an object-verb pattern is left-branching, as shown in Figure 7.6.

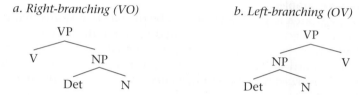

Figure 7.6 Right-branching and left-branching patterns

As you can easily determine for yourself, the P-NP, V-PP, V-Adv, and N-POSS patterns commonly associated with VO languages are also all right-branching. (Possessors are a type of NP, and manner adverbs are a type of AdvP.) In contrast, the NP-P, PP-V, Adv-V, and POSS-N patterns typically found in OV languages are all left-branching.

LANGUAGE MATTERS   Typology and Geography

Thanks to the collaboration of dozens of linguists, there is now a major online source of information on the distribution of various linguistic features (vowel inventories, morphological structure, word order, and so on) throughout the world. *The World Atlas of Language Structures*, with more than 140 maps and data from more than 2,500 languages, can be accessed at the website of the World Atlas of Linguistic Structures (WALS).

---

3 Genetic Classification

The goal of genetic classification is to group languages into families based on evidence of a common origin established through use of the comparative method. This work is difficult and challenging for a variety of reasons.

Perhaps the biggest problem is simply the amount of data that must be collected before linguists can be confident about the status of a group of languages. For example, it is only in the last few decades that enough information has been accumulated to propose a detailed classification of the languages of Africa. Moreover, many of the languages of South America, New Guinea, and Australia are still relatively unknown.

Matters are further complicated by the fact that entirely unrelated languages may be similar in various ways. This is particularly likely if the languages have been in contact long enough to have borrowed a large number of words, sounds, morphemes, or syntactic structures from one another.

Even languages that are related may not look that similar. The more distant the genetic relationship between languages, the less likely that a large number of obvious similarities will be found, especially since sound changes can obscure relationships between words that descended from a common source—as happened with English *water* and Russian *voda* 'water' and with French *eau* and Spanish *agua*, among many other examples.

Research is also made difficult by the fact that words that may be excellent indicators of a genetic relationship can drop out of the lexicon. For example, Old English had a word *leax* 'salmon' (which was cognate with German *Lachs* and Yiddish *lox*), but this lexical item has since been lost from the native English lexicon. (*Lox* has been borrowed back into some varieties of English as the name for a popular delicatessen food.)

Since word loss is a common historical event, linguists prefer to use the oldest available form of a language for their research. Thus, our knowledge of Proto-Indo-European is drawn largely from the study of Old English, Sanskrit, Latin, and so on, rather than their modern descendants such as English, Hindi-Urdu, and French.

Some language families contain many hundreds of languages. In other cases, only one language may remain to represent a family. In still other cases, families have become extinct. The following section summarizes some of what we know about the Indo-European family of languages. Although it might appear to be overly Eurocentric to focus on this particular family, you will see that the homelands of the various Indo-European languages extend well beyond Europe into the Middle East and India. It is also worth noting that a number of languages spoken in Europe (Finnish, Hungarian, and Basque, to name three) do not belong to the Indo-European family.

3.1   The Indo-European Family

If we consider only living languages, the **Indo-European family** currently has nine branches, which are listed in Table 7.20.

Table 7.20   Main branches of the Indo-European family

Germanic	Hellenic	Baltic
Celtic	Albanian	Slavic
Italic (Romance)	Armenian	Indo-Iranian

Germanic

The Germanic branch of Indo-European can be divided into three sub-branches: East, North, and West. The East Germanic branch included Gothic, the oldest Germanic language for which written texts exist (dating from the fourth century AD). Gothic and any other languages belonging to this branch of Germanic have long been extinct.

The North Germanic (or Scandinavian) branch originally included Old Norse (also known as Old Icelandic), which was the language of the Vikings and the ancestor of modern Icelandic, Norwegian, and Faroese (spoken on the Faroe Islands, north of Scotland). Swedish and Danish are two other familiar North Germanic languages.

The West Germanic branch includes English, German, Yiddish, Dutch, Afrikaans, and Frisian. Afrikaans is descended from the Dutch spoken by seventeenth-century settlers (known as Boers) in South Africa. Frisian, generally thought to be the language most closely related to English, is spoken on the north coast of Holland and on the Frisian Islands just off the coast, as well as on the northwestern coast of Germany. English descended from the speech of the Angles, Saxons, and Jutes— Germanic tribes who lived in northern Germany and southern Denmark (in an area just east of the Frisians) before invading England in 449 AD and settling there.

The organization of the Germanic branch of languages is illustrated in Table 7.21. (In this and other tables, parentheses are used to indicate languages that no longer have any native speakers. The tables are intended to illustrate the membership and organization of the families; they do not necessarily provide a complete list of the languages in each family.)

Table 7.21 The Germanic branch

(East Germanic)	North Germanic	West Germanic
(Gothic)	Icelandic	English
	Faroese	German
	Norwegian	Dutch
	Danish	Frisian
	Swedish	Afrikaans
		Yiddish

Although we use tables to represent family groupings in this book, trees of the sort illustrated in Figure 7.7 are widely used as well.

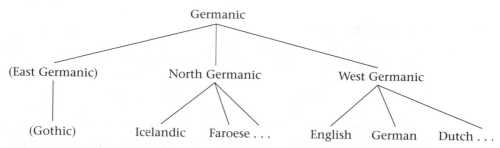

Figure 7.7 Tree depicting the organization of the Germanic branch

---

LANGUAGE MATTERS   A Sister for English?

Although Frisian is generally considered to be the closest living relative of English, there is another contender for that title. Scots (also call Lallands), the language of the famed eighteenth-century Scottish poet Robert Burns, has been spoken for centuries in the Lowlands and Northern Isles of Scotland. Not to be confused with Scottish English or with Gaelic, it is sometimes claimed to be a language in its own right. Is Scots distinct enough from English in terms of mutual intelligibility to merit status as a distinct language rather than a dialect? You can find out more about Scots and listen to some samples at the website of the Scots Language Centre.

Celtic

The Celtic branch of Indo-European (see Table 7.22) has two main sub-branches: Insular and Continental (now extinct). Gaulish, a member of the Continental branch, was once spoken in France (the Gauls were the tribe Julius Caesar defeated), but it has long been extinct.

The Insular sub-branch can be subdivided into two groups of languages: Brythonic or British (also called P-Celtic) and Goidelic or Gaelic (also called Q-Celtic). Brythonic languages include Welsh and Breton (which is spoken in northwestern France) as well as Cornish, which was once spoken in southwest Britain but no longer has any native speakers. The Goidelic branch contains Irish (or Irish Gaelic), which is still spoken natively in the western parts of Ireland; the now extinct Manx; and Scots Gaelic, which is spoken in parts of northwestern Scotland (especially the Hebrides Islands) and, to a lesser extent, on Cape Breton Island in Nova Scotia.

Table 7.22   The Celtic branch

Insular		(Continental)
Brythonic	*Goidelic*	
Welsh	Irish [= Irish Gaelic]	(Gaulish)
Breton	Scots Gaelic	
(Cornish)	(Manx)	

Italic (Romance)

The Italic branch originally had a number of sub-branches, which included several now-extinct languages spoken in the area corresponding roughly to modern-day Italy. The only Italic languages that are presently spoken all descended from Latin, the language of the Roman Empire (hence the term *Romance languages*).

These languages are commonly divided into four groups. Ibero-Romance includes Portuguese and Spanish, while Gallo-Romance contains French, Catalan (spoken in northeastern Spain, around Barcelona), and Romansch (one of the four official languages of Switzerland). The Italo-Romance branch includes Italian and Sardinian; Romanian is the best-known language in the Balkano-Romance group (see Table 7.23).

Table 7.23 The Romance branch

Ibero-Romance	Gallo-Romance	Italo-Romance	Balkano-Romance
Spanish Portuguese	French Catalan Romansch	Italian Sardinian	Romanian

Hellenic

The Hellenic branch of Indo-European has only one living member, Greek. All modern Greek dialects are descended from the classical dialect known as Attic Greek, which was the speech of Athens during the Golden Age of Greek culture (approximately 500 to 300 BC).

Hellenic Greek, which was used in subsequent centuries, was the language of commerce throughout the Middle East. (Hellenic Greek was also Cleopatra's native language; she was descended from one of Alexander the Great's generals.)

Albanian

The Albanian branch of Indo-European has only one member, Albanian, which is spoken not only in Albania but also in parts of the former Yugoslavia, Greece, and Italy.

Armenian

The Armenian branch also has only one member, Armenian. This language is centered in the Republic of Armenia but is also spoken in Turkey, Iran, Syria, Lebanon, and Egypt.

Baltic

The Baltic branch contains only two surviving languages, Latvian (or Lettish) and Lithuanian. They are spoken in Latvia and Lithuania (located just west of Russia and northeast of Poland). Lithuanian has an elaborate case system, which resembles the one proposed for Proto-Indo-European.

Slavic

The Slavic branch of Indo-European can be divided into three sub-branches: East, West, and South. The East Slavic branch is made up of Russian (also called Great Russian), Ukrainian, and Belarusian (or White Russian). The latter is spoken in Belarus, which is just east of northern Poland. The West Slavic branch includes Czech, Slovak, and Polish. The South Slavic branch includes Bulgarian, Macedonian, Serbian and Croatian (which used to be grouped together as Serbo-Croatian), and Slovene (or Slovenian).

The organization of the Slavic group of languages is represented in Table 7.24.

Table 7.24   The Slavic branch

East Slavic	South Slavic	West Slavic
Russian	Bosnian	Polish
Ukrainian	Croatian	Czech
Belarusian	Bulgarian	Slovak
	Macedonian	
	Serbian	
	Slovene	

Indo-Iranian

The Indo-Iranian branch of Indo-European is divided into the Iranian and Indic sub-branches. The Iranian sub-branch contains about two dozen different languages, including Modern Persian (also called Parsi or Farsi, spoken in Iran), Pashto (the principal language of Afghanistan), and Kurdish (found in Iran, Iraq, Turkey, and Syria). Other Iranian languages are spoken in Pakistan, Afghanistan, Tajikistan, and parts of Turkey, Russia, and China.

There are about thirty-five Indic languages. Most of the languages spoken in northern India, Pakistan, and Bangladesh belong to this branch of Indo-European. Some of the most widespread (in terms of number of speakers) are Hindi-Urdu, Bengali, Marathi, and Gujarati. Although there is a high degree of mutual comprehensibility between colloquial Hindi and Urdu (sometimes jointly referred to as Hindustani), they have totally different writing systems and are associated with different cultures. Urdu is spoken principally in Pakistan by Muslims while Hindi is spoken primarily in India by Hindus. For this reason, we listed them as separate languages in Table 7.2.

A less-known Indic language is Romany, or Gypsy. It is now believed that the Gypsies (or Roma) fled to Turkey from northwestern India during the Middle Ages, after being defeated by Islamic invaders. Subsequently they spread throughout Europe: Gypsies are found as far west as Ireland and as far east as Russia. Many now also live in North America. Romany contains many borrowed words—particularly from Greek, which was widely spoken in Turkey during the Middle Ages.

Table 7.25 depicts the organization of Indo-Iranian.

Table 7.25   The Indo-Iranian branch

Iranian	Indic
Persian	Hindi-Urdu
Pashto	Bengali
Kurdish	Marathi
	Gujarati
	Romany [= Gypsy]

The map in Figure 7.8 illustrates the geographic location of the Indo-European branches identified in this chapter.

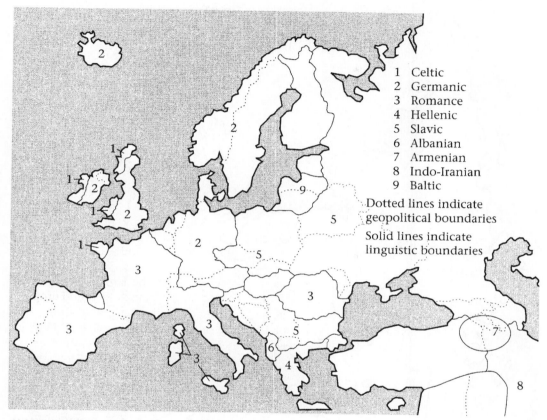

1 Celtic
2 Germanic
3 Romance
4 Hellenic
5 Slavic
6 Albanian
7 Armenian
8 Indo-Iranian
9 Baltic

Dotted lines indicate geopolitical boundaries

Solid lines indicate linguistic boundaries

Figure 7.8 Location of Indo-European languages.

3.2   Some Other Families

Although no introductory text could hope to present a complete survey of all of the world's language families, you can find maps and descriptions of other language families on the LaunchPad Solo for *Contemporary Linguistics* at **launchpadworks.com**. Language families found in Asia, Africa, and the Pacific are among those discussed. The maps in Figures 7.9 and 7.10 show the location of some of these language families.

Not all of the world's languages have been placed in families at this point in time. Languages with no known relatives are called **isolates**. Basque (spoken in northern Spain and southwestern France), Ainu (northern Japan), Burushaski (Pakistan), Kutenai (British Columbia), Gilyak (Siberia), Zuni (Arizona), and Yukagir (Siberia) are among the languages that are widely considered to be isolates.

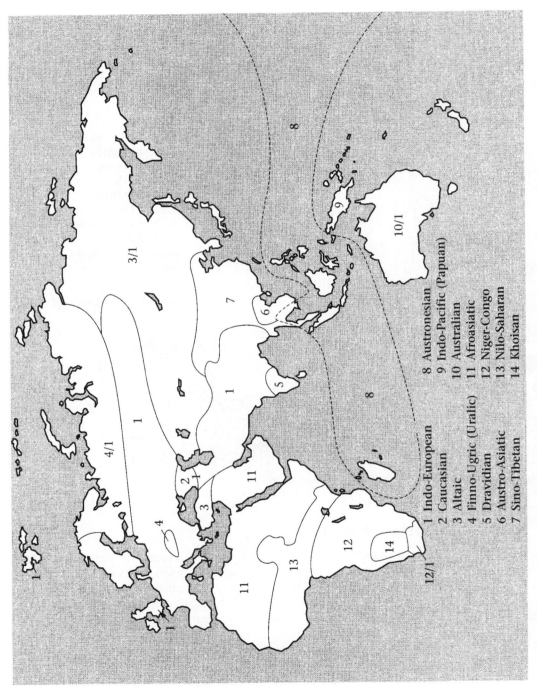

Figure 7.9 Location of some major language families

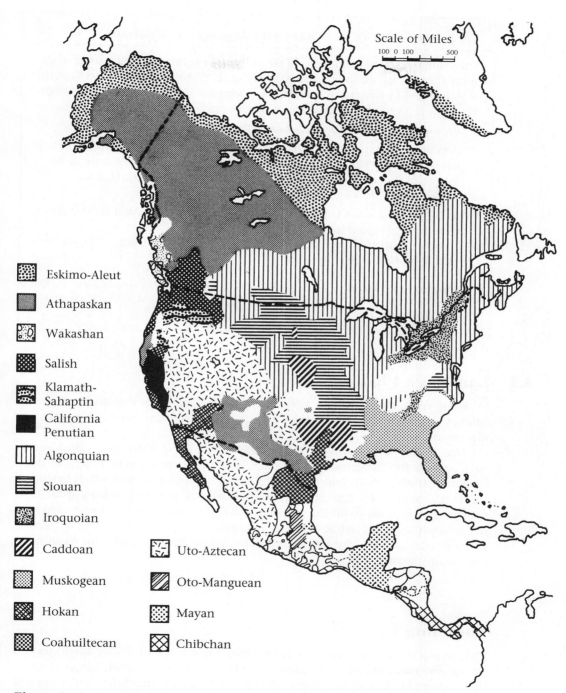

Figure 7.10 North and Central American language groups

Legend:
- Eskimo-Aleut
- Athapaskan
- Wakashan
- Salish
- Klamath-Sahaptin
- California Penutian
- Algonquian
- Siouan
- Iroquoian
- Caddoan
- Muskogean
- Hokan
- Coahuiltecan
- Uto-Aztecan
- Oto-Manguean
- Mayan
- Chibchan

Scale of Miles
100 0 100   500

LANGUAGE MATTERS   Could All Languages Be Related?

Some linguists have even gone so far as to begin reconstructing a single common ancestor for all human languages. Called Proto-World, or Proto-Sapiens, it is assumed to have been spoken approximately 60,000 to 70,000 years ago. Here is a proposed reconstruction of one word:

Proto-World *_mena_ 'to think (about)'

Possible cognates: Latin *men(s)* 'mind', Basque *munak* (pl) 'brains', Hungarian *mon(-d)* 'say', Telugu *manavi* 'prayer, humble request', Shawnee *menw* 'prefer, like', Bambara *mɛ* 'know', Tumale *aiman* 'think', Songhai *ma* 'understand', Masa *min* 'wish'.

Work along these lines is both intriguing and entertaining, but its validity is not currently accepted by most professional linguists.

For more on this topic, read "Quest for the Mother Tongue," by Robert Wright (*Atlantic Monthly*, April 1991).

Information from: Bengtson, J. D., and Ruhlen, M. (1994). "Global etymologies." *On the Origin of Languages: Studies in Linguistic Taxonomy*, ed. by Ruhlen, M., 277–336. Stanford: Stanford University Press.

3.3 Language Phyla

In recent years, attempts have been made to place many of the world's language families in even larger groupings called **phyla** (singular phylum), **stocks**, or **macrofamilies**.

One of the best known of the proposed phyla is Nostratic (also called Eurasiatic). Supposedly dating back 20,000 years, this hypothetical phylum includes Indo-European, Uralic, Altaic, and (depending on the proposal) various other languages and language families. This proposal is controversial, however, and most linguists remain very skeptical about the evidence and conclusions associated with comparative research involving a time depth greater than eight or ten thousand years because phonetic changes over longer periods obscure the similarities needed for meaningful comparative work.

Summing Up

The focus of this chapter is on the criteria that linguists use to classify languages and on the enormous variety of languages found throughout the world. Linguists sometimes attempt to classify languages solely in terms of their structural similarities and differences (that is, in terms of their **linguistic typology**). Analysis of cross-linguistic data has identified a number of **linguistic universals** indicating the most common characteristics of human language. The other major type of classificatory work in linguistics is concerned with **genetic relationships**—establishing language families such as **Indo-European** whose members are descended from a common ancestor. While research in this area is hampered by both the large number of languages involved and the scarcity of data, a sizable portion of the world's several thousand languages have been placed in families.

Key Terms

General terms and terms concerning types of classification

areal classification	language death
dialect	language shift
endangered language	linguistic typology
genetic classification	linguistic universals
genetically related (languages)	mutual intelligibility

Terms concerning typological classification

absolute universals	implicational universals
agglutinating language	isolating (analytic) language
ergative	marked (traits)
fixed stress languages	polysynthetic language
free stress languages	tone languages
fusional (inflectional) language	universal tendencies
grammatical hierarchies	unmarked (traits)

Terms concerning genetic classification and language phyla

Indo-European family	phyla
isolates	protolanguage
macrofamilies	stocks

Recommended Reading

Comrie, Bernard. 1989. *Language Universals and Linguistic Typology*. 2nd ed. Oxford: Blackwell.

Croft, William. 2003. *Typology and Universals*. 2nd ed. New York: Cambridge University Press.

Dryer, Matthew S., and Martin Haspelmath, eds. 2013. *The World Atlas of Language Structures Online*. Leipzig, Germany: Max Planck Institute for Evolutionary Anthropology.

Lewis, M. Paul, Gary F. Simons, and Charles D. Fennig, eds. 2015. *Ethnologue: Languages of the World*. 18th ed. Dallas, TX: SIL International. Also accessible online.

Lyovin, Anatole V. 1997. *An Introduction to the Languages of the World*. New York: Oxford University Press.

Newmeyer, Frederick. "Universals in Syntax." *Linguistic Review* 25 (2008): 35–82.

Palosaari, Naomi, and Lyle Campbell. 2011. "Structural Aspects of Language Endangerment." In *The Cambridge Handbook of Endangered Languages*. Edited by Peter K. Austin and Julia Sallabank, 100–119. Cambridge: Cambridge University Press.

Ruhlen, Merritt. 1994. *On the Origin of Languages*. Stanford, CA: Stanford University Press.

"The Case for Linguistic Diversity." 2011. *Terralingua Langscape* 2, 8.

Exercises

The data for exercises 1 to 3 are from Merritt Ruhlen, *A Guide to the Languages of the World* (Stanford, CA: Stanford University, Language Universals Project, 1976).

1. Which tendencies and universals are manifested in the following vowel systems? (See Section 2.1.)

   a) *Afrikaans* (South Africa) ([y] and [ø] are front rounded vowels)

i	y		u
	ø	ə	o
ɛ			ɔ
		a	

   b) *Squamish* (British Columbia)

i	u
	ə
	a

2. As noted in Section 2.1, the presence of long and nasal vowel phonemes is governed by implicational universals. In what ways do the vowel systems below comply or not comply with the implicational universals that make reference to length and nasality?

   a) *Maltese Arabic*

i	u	iː	uː
e	o	eː	oː
	a		aː

   b) *Awji* (North New Guinea)

i		u	ĩ		ũ
e	ə	o	ẽ	ɔ̃	õ
	a			ã	

3. Consider the following consonant systems. In what ways do these consonant systems comply or not comply with the implicational universals mentioned in Section 2.1?

   a) *Tahitian* (Tahiti)

p	t	ʔ
f		h
v	ɾ	
m	n	

b) *Palauan* (Palau Islands)

```
        t     k     ʔ
  b
        ð
        s
  m           ŋ
      1, r
```

c) *Nengone* (Loyalty Islands, South Pacific)—Stop and nasal system only

```
  pʰ    tʰ    ʈʰ          kʰ    ʔ
  b     d     ɖ           g
  m     n           ɲ     ŋ
  m̥     n̥                 ŋ̥
```

(*Note*: [ʈ] and [ɖ] are retroflex consonants; [̥] marks a voiceless nasal; [ɲ] represents a palatal nasal.)

d) *Mixe* (South Mexico)

```
  p     t           k     ʔ
        d           g
        ts    tʃ
        s           x     h
  v                 ɣ
  m     n
```

(*Note*: /x/ is a voiceless velar fricative, and /ɣ/ is a voiced velar fricative.)

4. Describe the morphological characteristics of each of the following languages in
   terms of the four-way system of classification outlined in Section 2.2.
   a) *Siberian Yupik*
      Angya-ghlla-ng -yug -tuq.
      Boat -big -get -want-3SG
      'He wants to get a big boat.'

   b) *Latvian*

las-u	las-ām	rakst-u	rakst-ām
read-1SG.PRES	read-1PL.PRES	write-1SG.PRES	write-1PL.PRES
'I read'	'we read'	'I write'	'we write'

   c) *Japanese*
      Gakusei-wa   home-rare-na-i.
      student-TOPIC   praise-PASSIVE-NEG-PRES
      'The student is not praised.'

5. Do a morphological analysis of the following data from Latvian. First, list each
   morpheme and its meaning. Then, describe how the data reflect the implicational
   universals in Section 2.2.
   a) lidotājs   'aviator' (NOMINATIVE)
   b) lidotāju   'aviator' (ACCUSATIVE)
   c) lidotājam   'to the aviator' (DATIVE)

d) lidot   'to fly'
e) rakstītājs   'writer' (NOMINATIVE)
f) rakstītāja   'writer's' (GENITIVE)
g) rakstīt   'to write'

6. Note the following data from Malagasy, an Austronesian language spoken on the island of Madagascar. The data are from Catherine J. Garvey, *Malagasy: Introductory Course* (Washington: Center for Applied Linguistics, 1964). In what ways does Malagasy comply or not comply with all the word order tendencies mentioned in Section 2.3?

   a) amin'   ny   restauranta
      to   the   restaurant
      'to   the   restaurant'

   b) Enti'n   ny   labiera   ny   mpiasa.
      brings   the   beer   the   waiter
      'The waiter brings the beer.'

   c) Avy   any   Amerika   izy.
      come   from   America   he
      'He comes from America.'

7. Using Figure 7.7 of the Germanic branch as a model, draw a similar tree to depict the organization of the Romance branch of the Indo-European family. (See Table 7.23.)

LaunchPad Solo
macmillan learning | For more helpful content and quizzes, go to the LaunchPad Solo for *Contemporary Linguistics* at **launchpadworks.com**.

eight

Historical Linguistics: The Study of Language Change

Robert W. Murray

> *Many men sayn that in sweveninges*
> *Ther nys but fables and lesynges;*
> *But men may some swevenes sene*
> *Whiche hardely that false ne bene,*
> *But afterwarde ben apparaunt.*
>
> —Chaucer, *The Romance of the Rose* (c. 1370)

OBJECTIVES

In this chapter, you will learn:

- how and why languages change over time
- how and why sound changes occur
- what kinds of changes occur in morphology and syntax
- ways in which words change
- how linguists can reconstruct languages spoken in earlier times, based on the existing languages that are descended from them

 **LaunchPad Solo** | For more helpful content and quizzes, go to the LaunchPad Solo
macmillan learning | for *Contemporary Linguistics* at **launchpadworks.com**.

Language change is both obvious and rather mysterious. The English of the late fourteenth century, for example, is so different from Modern English that without special training it is difficult to understand the opening lines to *The Romance of the Rose* cited above. Not only would these sentences have a foreign sound, but words and structures such as *sweveninges, lesynges,* and *false ne bene* are unfamiliar.* The existence of such differences between early and later variants of the same language raises questions as to how and why languages change over time.

Historical linguistics is concerned with both the description and explanation of language change. In this chapter we examine the nature and causes of language change and survey phonological, morphological, syntactic, lexical, and semantic change. We also explore techniques used to reconstruct linguistic prehistory and briefly discuss related research into language acquisition and linguistic universals.

1   The Nature of Language Change

All languages change over time. English has undergone continuous and dramatic change throughout its three major periods: Old English (roughly from 450 to 1100 AD), Middle English (from 1100 to 1500), and Modern English (from 1500 to the present). Although Chaucer's Middle English is at least partially comprehensible today, Old English looks like a completely foreign language. The following is an extract from an eighth-century Old English document, a translation of Bede's Latin history of England. (The letter þ, called "thorn", represented the phoneme /θ/ in Old English; here and elsewhere in this chapter ¯ marks a long vowel in the orthography.)

1) and Seaxan þā sige geslōgan.
   and Saxons the victory won
   'And the Saxons won the victory.'

   þā sendan hī hām ǣrenddracan.
   then sent they home messenger
   'Then they sent home a messenger.'

These Old English sentences differ from their Modern English counterparts in many respects. In terms of pronunciation, for instance, the Old English word *hām* [haːm] 'home' in the second sentence became [hɔːm] in Middle English, and then [howm] in Modern English. In its morphology, Old English differed significantly from Modern English. The suffix *-an* on the Old English word for 'sent' indicates both past tense and plurality of the subject (*hī* 'they'). Differences in word order are also readily apparent, with the verb following both the subject and the direct object in the first sentence and preceding both the subject and the direct object in the second. Neither of these word orders would be acceptable in the Modern English forms of these sentences.

*The translation for the passage is as follows:
Many men say that in dreams
There is nothing but talk and lies
But men may see some dreams
Which are scarcely false
But afterward come true.

LANGUAGE MATTERS   What Did Old English and Middle English Sound Like?

Thanks to the efforts of linguists and literary scholars, a great deal has been learned about what Old English and Middle English sounded like, and trained readers often recite literary works from those periods. For a sample of Old English, go to the website of the English Companions organization (Tha Engliscan Gesithas). For Middle English, go to the website of the Luminarium Encyclopedia Project. Want to learn to write and communicate in Old English? Go to the Englisc Listserv web page hosted by the University of Rochester.

In addition, some Old English words have disappeared from use, as the unfamiliar *ǣrenddracan* 'messenger' and *sige* 'victory' indicate. Still other words have been maintained, but with a change in meaning. For example, the Old English word *geslōgan* (which we translated as 'won') is the past tense of the verb *slēan*, the Old English predecessor of our word *slay*. Although the Modern English meaning of this word in normal usage is restricted to the act of killing, the Old English verb could also mean 'to strike, beat, coin (money), and forge (weapons)'. As these examples imply, all components of the grammar from meaning (semantics) to individual sounds (phonology) are subject to change.

1.1   Systematicity of Language Change

A striking fact about language change in general is its regularity and systematicity. For example, the development of a fixed subject-verb-direct object (SVO) word order in English did not affect just a few verbs; all verbs in Modern English appear before rather than after the direct object. Similarly, the changes affecting the vowel in the word *hām* did not occur in that word only; they represent the regular development of the Old English vowel *ā* ([aː]). (See Table 8.1.)

Table 8.1   Changes affecting Old English [aː]

Old English	Middle English	Modern English	
[baːt]	[bɔːt]	[bowt]	'boat'
[aːθ]	[ɔːθ]	[owθ]	'oath'
[staːn]	[stɔːn]	[stown]	'stone'

1.2   Causes of Language Change

The inevitability of language change is guaranteed by the way in which language is passed on from one generation to the next. Children do not begin with an intact grammar of the language being acquired but rather must construct a grammar on the basis of the available data. In such a situation, it is hardly surprising that differences arise, even if only subtle ones, from one generation to the next. Moreover, since all children draw on the same physiological and cognitive endowment in learning language, it is to be expected that the same patterns of change will be consistently and repeatedly manifested in all languages. Following is a brief overview of the principal causes of language change.

Articulatory Simplification

As might be expected, most sound changes have a physiological basis. Since such sound changes typically result in **articulatory simplification**, they have traditionally been related to the idea of ease of articulation. Although this notion is difficult to define precisely, we can readily identify cases of articulatory simplification in our everyday speech. For example, the three consonants in the coda of *fifths* [fθs] might be simplified to two [fɪfs], while the two consonants in the niddle of *athlete* [θl] might be simplified by inserting a vowel between them to yield [æθəlit].

Spelling Pronunciation

Not all changes in pronunciation have a physiological motivation. A minor, but nevertheless important, source of change in English and other languages is **spelling pronunciation**. Since the written form of a word can differ significantly from the way it is pronounced, a new pronunciation can arise that seems to reflect more closely the spelling of the word. A case in point is the word *often*. Although this word was pronounced with a [t] in earlier English, the voiceless stop was subsequently lost, resulting in the pronunciation [ɔfən] (compare *soften*). However, since the letter *t* was retained in the spelling, [t] has been reintroduced into many speakers' pronunciation of this word.

Analogy and Reanalysis

Cognitive factors also play a role in change in all components of the grammar. Two sources of change having a cognitive basis are **analogy** and **reanalysis**. Analogy reflects the preference of speakers for regular patterns over irregular ones. It typically involves the extension or generalization of a regularity on the basis of the inference that if elements are alike in some respects, they should be alike in others as well. Both phonological and semantic characteristics can serve as a basis for analogy. For example, on the basis of its phonological similarity with verbs such as *sting/stung* and *swing/swung*, in some dialects *bring* has developed a form *brung*, as in *I brung it into the house*. The effects of analogy can also be observed in the speech of children, who often generalize the regular *-ed* past tense form to produce forms such as *goed* and *knowed*. As we will see shortly, analogy plays a very important role in morphological change as well.

Reanalysis is particularly common in morphological change. Morphological reanalysis typically involves an attempt to attribute a compound or root + affix structure to a word that formerly was not broken down into component morphemes. A classic example in English is the word *hamburger*, which originally referred to a type of meat patty deriving its name from the city of Hamburg in Germany. This word has been reanalyzed as consisting of two components, *ham + burger*. The latter morpheme has since appeared in many new forms including *fishburger*, *chickenburger*, and even as the free morpheme *burger*. (Note that the reanalysis need not be correct. There is usually no ham in a burger—especially a *veggie burger*!)

Language Contact

Another cause of language change is **language contact**. Language contact refers to the situation where speakers of a language frequently interact with the speakers of another language or dialect. As a consequence, extensive **borrowing** can occur, particularly where there are significant numbers of bilinguals or multilinguals. Although borrowing can affect all components of the grammar, the lexicon is typically most affected. English, for example, has borrowed many words from Native American languages including *skunk, moccasin, totem, tomahawk, chinook, moose,* and *Canada.*

Among the effects that borrowing can have on the sound system are the introduction of new phonemes or allophones and changes in their distribution. If there are a significant number of borrowings from another language, the borrowed foreign segment can eventually become a new phoneme. In the early Middle English period, the London dialect had [f] but not [v] in word-initial position. The [v] was introduced later as a result of contact with other English dialects and with French, in which it did occur word-initially. This contact was a likely factor in the development of a contrast between /f/ and /v/ word-initially, as found in Modern English pairs such as *file* and *vile.*

Language (as well as dialect) contact also results in another minor but nevertheless important source of language change, **hypercorrection**. Hypercorrection occurs when a speaker who is attempting to speak another dialect or language overgeneralizes particular rules. An example of hypercorrection is the use of *I* in constructions such as *He saw John and I.* This usage is an overgeneralization of the rule that only *I* should be used in subject position, never *me*. According to this rule, *John and I are going* is correct but *John and me/Me and John are going* is incorrect. For some speakers, hypercorrection has resulted in the inference that all coordinate phrases containing *me* (such as *John and me*) are incorrect even when they serve as direct object (complement) of the verb. Note that even a person who says *He saw John and I* would not say **He saw I.*

2   Sound Change

Although all components of the grammar are susceptible to change over time, some types of change yield more obvious results than others. Variation and change are particularly noticeable in the phonology of a language. Several common types of sound change can be distinguished.

Most sound changes begin as subtle alterations in the sound pattern of a language in particular phonetic environments. The linguistic processes underlying such **phonetically conditioned change** are identical to the ones found in the phonology of currently spoken languages. The application of such processes usually brings about an articulatory simplification, and over time significant changes in the phonology of a language can result.

Although all aspects of a language's phonology (e.g., tone, stress, and syllable structure) are subject to change over time, we will restrict our attention here to change involving segments. Since most sound changes involve sequences of segments, the main focus will be on **sequential change**. However, we will also discuss one common type of **segmental change**, involving the simplification of an affricate. In addition, in order to demonstrate that more than just articulatory factors play a role in sound change, we will discuss a case of sound change based on auditory factors. All important sound changes discussed in this section and referred to in this chapter are found in the catalog of sound changes in Table 8.2.

Table 8.2 Catalog of sound changes

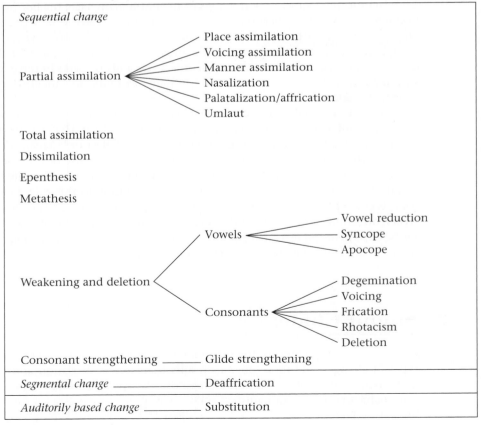

2.1 Sequential Change

Assimilation

The most common type of sequential change is **assimilation**, which has the effect of increasing the efficiency of articulation through a simplification of articulatory movements. We will focus here on the main types indicated in the catalog in Table 8.2.

Partial assimilation means that a segment becomes more like a neighboring segment in place of articulation, voicing, or manner. In Table 8.3, the Spanish example of **place assimilation** shows the nasal consonant assimilating to the CORONAL place of the following [d]. In the Old English example of **voicing assimilation**, the voiced [d] became voiceless next to the voiceless [p]. In a form of **manner assimilation**, the [f] in Old English *stefn* became a nasal [m] next to another nasal consonant. And the Portuguese and French examples of **nasalization** show the influence of an earlier nasal consonant on the preceding vowel.

Table 8.3 Forms of partial assimilation

(Note that in these and other examples, actual spelling is used where these clearly reflect the sound changes in question. Phonetic transcriptions are provided when this is not the case.)					
Place assimilation					
Old Spanish	semda	>	Modern Spanish	senda	'path'
Voicing assimilation					
Early Old English	slæpde	>	Later Old English	slæpte	'slept'
Manner assimilation					
Early Old English	stefn	>	Later Old English	stemn	'stem'
Nasalization (of a vowel)					
Latin	bon-	>	Portuguese	[bõ]	'good'
Latin	un-	>	French	[œ̃]	'one'

Note: It is traditional in historical linguistics to use the sign > to mean 'changed into'.

Total assimilation is illustrated in Table 8.4. A stop in Latin assimilated totally to a following stop, resulting in a **geminate**, or extra long, consonant in Italian.

Table 8.4 Total assimilation in Italian

Latin	*Italian*	
octo (*c* = [k])	otto	'eight'
septem	sette	'seven'
damnum	danno	'damage'

Another type of assimilation is **palatalization**—the effect that front vowels and the palatal glide [j] typically have on velar, alveolar, and dental stops, making their place of articulation more palatal. If you compare your pronunciation of *keep* and *cot*, you will notice that the pronunciation of [k] in *keep* is much more palatal than in *cot* due to the influence of [i]. Palatalization is often the first step in **affrication**, a change in which palatalized stops become affricates: [ts] or [tʃ] if the original stop was voiceless, and [dz] or [dʒ] if the original stop was voiced (see Table 8.5).

Table 8.5 Palatalization/affrication induced by front vowels and [j]

Examples from the Romance languages					
Latin	centum [k]	Italian	cento	[tʃ]	'one hundred'
Latin	medius [d]	Italian	mezzo	[dz]	'half'
Latin	gentem [g]	Old French	gent	[dʒ]	'people', 'tribe'

Although assimilation is probably most common in the case of adjacent segments, it can also apply at a distance. A case in point is **umlaut**, the effect a vowel or sometimes a glide in one syllable can have on the vowel of another syllable, usually a preceding one. Umlaut is the source of irregular plurals such as *goose/geese* and *mouse/mice* in English. (See Table 8.6.) The plural of the pre-Old English words *gōs* 'goose' and *mūs* 'mouse' was formed by adding the suffix [-i]. Because the [i] is a front vowel, the vowel in the preceding syllable of each word was also fronted. Thus, [ō] became [ø̄] (the mid front, rounded vowel), and [ū] became [ȳ] (the high front rounded vowel). By early Old English, the suffix [-i] had been lost in a separate change, leaving the umlauted vowel as the marker of the plural form. (Subsequent changes account for the modern pronunciation.)

Table 8.6 Umlaut in English plurals

Pre-Old English 1		*Pre-OE 2*		*Early OE*		*Modern English, after subsequent changes*	
[gōs]	>	[gōs]	>	[gōs]	>	[gus]	'goose'
[gōsi]	>	[gø̄si]	>	[gø̄s]	>	[gis]	'geese'
[mūs]	>	[mūs]	>	[mūs]	>	[maws]	'mouse'
[mūsi]	>	[mȳsi]	>	[mȳs]	>	[majs]	'mice'

Dissimilation

Dissimilation, the process whereby one segment is made less like another segment in its environment, is much less frequent than assimilation. This type of change typically occurs when it would be difficult to articulate or perceive two similar sounds in close proximity. The word *anma* 'soul' in Late Latin, for example, was modified to *alma* in Spanish, thereby avoiding two consecutive nasal consonants. Like assimilation, dissimilation can also operate at a distance to affect nonadjacent segments. For instance, the Latin word *arbor* 'tree' became *árbol* in Spanish and *albero* in Italian, thereby avoiding two instances of *r* in adjacent syllables. (By contrast, dissimilation did not occur in French, where *arbre* has retained both instances of *r*.)

Epenthesis

Another common sound change, **epenthesis**, involves the insertion of a consonant or vowel into a particular environment (see Table 8.7).

Table 8.7   Epenthesis

	Earlier form	*Later form*	
Old English	ganra	gan<u>d</u>ra	'gander'
	æmtig	æm<u>p</u>tig	'empty'
Latin > Spanish	<u>sc</u>hola [sk]	<u>esc</u>uela [esk]	'school'
	<u>sc</u>ribere [sk]	<u>esc</u>ribir [esk]	'write'

In the Old English examples, the epenthetic [d] and [p] have the place of articulation of the preceding nasal but agree with the following segment in terms of voice and nasality. The epenthetic segment therefore serves as a bridge for the transition between the segments on either side. In the Spanish examples, vowel epenthesis serves to break up the sequence of sounds [sk] that would otherwise be difficult to pronounce and inconsistent with the phonotactic patterns of the language.

Metathesis

Metathesis involves a change in the relative positioning of segments. This change, like assimilation and dissimilation, can affect adjacent segments. For example, early Old English *wæps* ('wasp') later became *wæsp*, and *þridda* ('third') became *þirdda*.

   Metathesis at a distance is found in the change from Latin *mīrāculum* 'miracle' to Spanish *milagro*, in which [r] and [l] have changed places although they were not adjacent (see Figure 8.1).

Figure 8.1   Metathesis of nonadjacent segments in Spanish

LANGUAGE MATTERS   Metathesis in Sign Language

Although users of signed languages do not use their oral articulators to produce speech sounds, they do nonetheless *articulate*. The difference is that they use the shape, position, and orientation of the hands to create meaning. These gestures are subject to processes very much like the ones found in speech. For example, the sign for *deaf* in American Sign Language was originally made by touching the jaw beside the ear with the index finger, and then touching the cheek beside the mouth. Over time, the movement changed from upper jaw to lower cheek, to lower cheek to upper jaw, especially when following a sign that ended near the jaw. Today, both versions are acceptable.

Weakening and Deletion

Both vowels and consonants are also susceptible to outright **deletion** as well as to various **weakening** processes. We will first treat the effects of these processes on vowels and then turn to their effects on consonants.

LANGUAGE MATTERS   Frequency Contributes to Shortening

More frequent words are, in general, more likely to have a shortened pronunciation than are less common words. That's why the middle vowel in *every* is far more likely to be dropped than the middle vowel in *summery* (in the sense of 'summerlike'). Words such as *memory* and *family*, which are intermediate in frequency, permit more variation in terms of whether the middle vowel is lost or retained.

Vowel deletion is commonly preceded in time by **vowel reduction**, in which a full vowel is reduced to a schwa-like vowel (i.e., short lax central [ə]). Vowel reduction typically affects short vowels in unstressed syllables and may affect all or only a subset of the full vowels (see Figure 8.2).

Figure 8.2   Vowel reduction

Vowel reduction can be followed by deletion of a word-final vowel (**apocope**) or a word-internal vowel (**syncope**). Table 8.8 shows vowel reduction in Middle English with subsequent vowel deletion in Early Modern English.

Table 8.8   Vowel reduction and deletion in English

	Old English		Middle English (vowel reduction)		Early Modern English (vowel deletion)	
Deletion of word-internal	stānas	[a]	ston<u>e</u>s	[ə]	ston<u>e</u>s	Ø
vowel (syncope)	stān<u>e</u>s	[e]	ston<u>e</u>s	[ə]	stone's	Ø
Deletion of word-final	nam<u>a</u>	[a]	nam<u>e</u>	[ə]	nam<u>e</u>	Ø
vowel (apocope)	tal<u>u</u>	[u]	tal<u>e</u>	[ə]	tal<u>e</u>	Ø

Consonant deletion is also a very common sound change. For example, the word-initial cluster [kn] was found in Old and Middle English, as the spelling of such words as *knight, knit, knot,* and *knee* implies, but the [k] was subsequently lost, giving us our modern pronunciation. The loss of word-final consonants has played a major role in the evolution of Modern French. The final letters in the written forms of the words in Table 8.9 reflect consonants that were actually pronounced at an earlier stage of the language.

Table 8.9 Consonant loss in French

French spelling (masculine form)	Current pronunciation	
gros	[gʁo]	'large'
chaud	[ʃo]	'warm'
vert	[vɛʁ]	'green'

Just as vowel reduction can be identified as a weakening process since it represents an intermediate step on the pathway from a full vowel to deletion of the vowel, so too can pathways of **consonant weakening** be identified. The scale of **consonantal strength** in Figure 8.3 can be helpful in identifying cases of weakening.

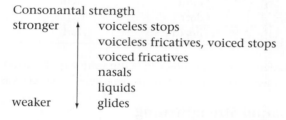

Consonantal strength
stronger   voiceless stops
  voiceless fricatives, voiced stops
  voiced fricatives
  nasals
  liquids
weaker   glides

(*Note:* Geminate consonants are stronger than their nongeminate counterparts.)

Figure 8.3 Scale of consonantal strength

Geminates weaken to nongeminates (**degemination**), stops weaken to fricatives (**frication**), and voiceless stops or voiceless fricatives weaken to voiced stops or voiced fricatives respectively (**voicing**). Weakening can ultimately result in the deletion of the consonant. Figure 8.4 is a typical pathway of weakening. (We use a double consonant here to represent gemination.)

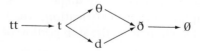

Figure 8.4 Typical pathway of consonant weakening

Consonants are particularly subject to weakening in an intervocalic environment. Parts of the pathway of consonantal weakening are exemplified in Table 8.10 with developments from the Romance languages.

Table 8.10 Consonantal weakening in Romance

Degemination (tt > t):	Latin	mi<u>tt</u>ere	>	Spanish	me<u>t</u>er	'to put'
Voicing (t > d):	Latin	mā<u>t</u>ūrus	>	Old Spanish	ma<u>d</u>uro	'ripe'
Frication (d > ð):	Old Spanish	ma<u>d</u>uro	>	Spanish	ma<u>d</u>uro [ð]	'ripe'
Deletion (ð > Ø):	Old French	[maðyr]	>	French	mûr	'ripe'

Rhotacism is a relatively common type of weakening that typically involves the change of [z] to [r]. Often rhotacism is preceded by a stage involving the voicing of [s] to [z]. Within the Germanic languages, for instance, [s] first became [z] in a particular intervocalic environment. This [z] remained in Gothic but became [r] in other Germanic languages such as English, German, and Swedish. The effects of the latter part of this change can be seen in the standard spellings of the words in Table 8.11.

Table 8.11 Rhotacism in English, German, and Swedish

Gothic	*English*	*German*	*Swedish*
maiza	more	mehr	mera
diuzam	deer	Tier	djur
huzd	hoard	Hort	—

In Modern English, rhotacism is the source of the alternation between [z] and [ɹ] in *was* and *were*. The [ɹ] resulted from earlier [z], which was originally intervocalic.

Consonantal Strengthening

Just as consonants weaken, they can also strengthen. **Glide strengthening** (the strengthening of a glide to an affricate) is particularly common, especially in word-initial position. For example the word-initial [j] sound in Latin words such as *jūdicium* 'justice' and *juvenis* 'young' became word-initial [ʤ] in the corresponding Italian words *giudizio* and *giovane*.

2.2 Segmental Change

Segments such as affricates are considered phonologically complex because they represent the fusing of a stop plus a fricative into a single segment: e.g., [dʒ] or [ts]. Such complex segments are commonly subject to simplification. A very common type of segmental simplification is **deaffrication**, which has the effect of turning affricates into fricatives by eliminating the stop portion of the affricate (see Table 8.12).

Table 8.12 Deaffrication in French

Old French	<u>c</u>ent	[ts]	French	<u>c</u>ent	[s]	'one hundred'
Old French	<u>g</u>ent	[dʒ]	French	<u>g</u>ent	[ʒ]	'people, tribe'

Since deaffrication of [tʃ] (as well as of [dʒ]) has not occurred in English, early borrowings from French maintain the affricate, while later borrowings have a fricative.

Thus, the words *chair* and *chain*, which were borrowed before deaffrication occurred, begin with [tʃ], while *chandelier* and *chauffeur*, borrowed after deaffrication, begin with [ʃ].

2.3 Auditorily Based Change

Although articulatory factors (particularly relating to ease of articulation) are of central importance in sound change as indicated in the discussion above, auditory factors also play a role. **Substitution** is a type of auditorily based change involving the replacement of one segment with another similar-sounding segment. A common type of substitution involves [f] replacing other voiceless nonstrident fricatives, such as velar [x] and interdental [θ]. Earlier in the history of English, [f] replaced [x] in some words, such as *laugh*, in standard varieties of English, while [f] replaced [θ] in all words in Cockney, a nonstandard dialect spoken in London.

So far we have treated sound changes without consideration of their effect on the sound pattern of the particular language as a whole. All the foregoing sound changes can lead both to new types of allophonic variation and to the addition or loss of phonemic contrasts. Examples of such cases are presented in the next section.

2.4 Phonetic versus Phonological Change

Sometimes sound change can lead to changes in a language's phonological system by adding, eliminating, or rearranging phonemes. Such **phonological change** can involve **splits**, **mergers**, or **shifts**.

Splits

In a phonological split, allophones of the same phoneme come to contrast with each other due to the loss of the conditioning environment, with the result that one or more new phonemes are created. The English phoneme /ŋ/ was the result of a phonological split (see Figure 8.5). Originally, [ŋ] was simply the allophone of /n/ that appeared before a velar consonant. During Middle English, consonant deletion resulted in the loss of [g] in word-final position after a nasal consonant, leaving [ŋ] as the final sound in words such as *sing*.

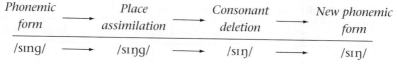

Phonemic form	→	Place assimilation	→	Consonant deletion	→	New phonemic form
/sing/	→	/sɪŋg/	→	/sɪŋ/	→	/sɪŋ/

Figure 8.5 Stages in the phonological split of [n] and [ŋ]

The loss of the word-final [g] created minimal pairs such as *sin* (/sɪn/) and *sing* (/sɪŋ/), in which there is a contrast between /n/ and /ŋ/. This example represents a typical phonological split. When the conditioning environment of an allophonic variant of a phoneme is lost through sound change, the allophone is no longer predictable and thus becomes contrastive (i.e., phonemic). The original phoneme (in Figure 8.6, /n/) splits into two phonemes (/n/ and /ŋ/).

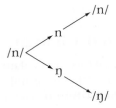

Figure 8.6   A phonological split

Mergers

In a phonological merger, two or more phonemes collapse into a single one, thereby reducing the number of phonemes in the language. The case of auditorily based substitution discussed above has this effect in Cockney English, where all instances of the interdental fricative /θ/ have become /f/ (see Figure 8.7). Consequently, the phonemes /θ/ and /f/ have merged into /f/, and words such as *thin* and *fin* have the same phonological form (/fɪn/). Similarly, /v/ and /ð/ have merged (e.g., /smuv/ for *smooth*).

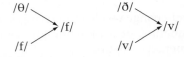

Figure 8.7   A phonological merger

Shifts

A phonological shift is a change in which a series of phonemes is systematically modified so that their organization with respect to each other is altered. A well-known example of such a change is called the **Great English Vowel Shift** shown in Table 8.13 and Figure 8.8. Beginning in the Middle English period and continuing into the eighteenth century, the language underwent a series of modifications to its long vowels, i.e., vowels that were pronounced with a longer duration.

Table 8.13   The Great English Vowel Shift

Middle English	Great Vowel Shift		Modern English	
/tiːd/	/iː/	>	/aj/	/tajd/	'tide'
/luːd/	/uː/	>	/aw/	/lawd/	'loud'
/geːs/	/eː/	>	/iː/	/gis/	'geese'
/sɛː/	/ɛː/	>	/iː/	/si/	'sea'
/goːs/	/oː/	>	/uː/	/gus/	'goose'
/brɔːkən/	/ɔː/	>	/oː/	/brokən/	'broken'
/naːmə/	/aː/	>	/eː/	/nem/	'name'

Figure 8.8 illustrates the changes that gradually affected the English long vowels.

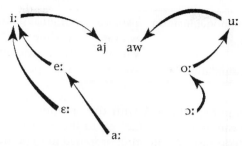

Figure 8.8   Changes brought about by the Great English Vowel Shift

2.5   Explaining Phonological Shift

The causes and even the details of the Great English Vowel Shift remain unclear. In fact, the causes of phonological shift in general are not well understood. A possible motivation in some cases may involve the notion of phonological space. Languages with seven or more vowels (e.g., English at the beginning of the Great English Vowel Shift) may have overcrowding of the phonological space. As a result, such languages often undergo **diphthongization** since the effect of the diphthongization of a pair of vowels is to reduce the seven-vowel system to a five-vowel system.

2.6   Sound Change and Rule Ordering

In describing language change, it is often crucial to identify the relative chronology, or order in which different changes have occurred. Three important changes in the history of English can be given as the (somewhat simplified) rules in Figure 8.9.

> 1) Voicing
> $\qquad$ C $\quad \rightarrow \quad$ [+voice] / [+voice] ___ [+voice]
>
> 2) Syncope
> $\qquad$ V $\quad \rightarrow \quad \varnothing$ / ___ C #
> $\qquad$ [–stress]
>
> 3) Suffix assimilation
> $\qquad$ C $\quad \rightarrow \quad$ [+voice] / C ___
> $\qquad\qquad\qquad\qquad$ [+voice]

Figure 8.9   Three rules in the history of English

These changes have played an important role in the evolution of English plural forms such as *hooves* (versus *hoof*) and *wolves* (versus *wolf*). Of the possible orderings of these three rules, only one will derive the contemporary pronunciation from the earlier (Old English) phonemic form. Two of the possible orderings are given in Table 8.14.

Table 8.14   Rule ordering in the history of English

Hypothesis A		Hypothesis B	
Original phonemic form	/wulfas/	Original phonemic form	/wulfas/
Voicing	wulvas	Voicing	wulvas
Syncope	wulvs	Suffix assimilation	(cannot apply)
Suffix assimilation	wulvz	Syncope	wulvs (incorrect)

If we assume hypothesis A with the ordering voicing, syncope, and suffix assimilation, we can account for the [vz] in the modern pronunciation of a word such as *wolves*. By contrast, the ordering proposed in hypothesis B would not account for the present pronunciation.

3   Morphological Change

In this section we discuss morphological changes resulting from analogy and reanalysis as well as changes involving the addition or loss of affixes.

3.1   Addition of Affixes

Borrowing has been a very important source of new affixes in English. During the Middle English period, many French words containing the suffix *-ment* (e.g., *accomplishment, commencement*) made their way into the language. Eventually, *-ment* established itself as a productive suffix in English and was used with bases that were not of French origin (e.g., *acknowledgment, merriment*). The ending *-able*, which converts a verb into an adjective (e.g., *readable, lovable*, etc.), followed a similar pattern. Although words with this ending (e.g., *favorable, conceivable*) were initially borrowed into English as whole units, eventually the suffix became productive and was used with new bases.

Not all new affixes are the result of borrowing. Lexical forms can become grammatical forms over time through a process called **grammaticalization**. Grammaticalized forms often undergo dramatic phonological reduction, as well as semantic change in which they can lose much of their original content; for example, the Latin word *habeō* '(I) have, hold, grasp' is the source of the Italian future suffix *-ò*. In the first stage of grammaticalization, *habeō* remained an independent word but underwent semantic reduction and functioned as an auxiliary verb indicating future tense: for example, *amāre habeō* 'I will love'. When two words are frequently adjacent, over time they can become fused together to form a single unit consisting of a base and an affix. This specific type of grammaticalization, where words develop into affixes (either prefixes or suffixes), is called **fusion** (see Table 8.15).

Table 8.15   Fusion resulting in a future tense suffix in Italian

Latin (two words)	→	base + affix	→	Italian (with suffix)	
amāre habeō		amār + ō		amerò	'I will love'
amāre habēmus		amār + ēmus		ameremo	'we will love'

A number of Modern English suffixes have been derived from earlier words by means of fusion (see Table 8.16).

Table 8.16   English suffixes resulting from fusion

Old English word		Modern English suffix
hād	'state, condition, rank'	-hood (childhood)
dōm	'condition, power'	-dom (freedom)
(ge-)līc	'similar, equal, like'	-ly (fatherly)

3.2   Loss of Affixes

Just as affixes can be added to the grammar, they can also be lost. Sometimes affixes simply fall into disuse for no apparent reason. For example, a number of Old English derivational affixes, including -oþ and -estre, are no longer used (see Table 8.17).

Table 8.17   Affixes no longer found in English

V + oþ	→	N (e.g., *hunt-oþ* 'hunting' from *hunt-ian* 'to hunt')
V + estre	→	N (e.g., *luf-estre* 'lover' from *luf-ian* 'to love')

It is also very common for affixes to be lost through sound change. For example, Old English had a complex system of affixes marking case and gender. Nouns were divided into three gender classes—masculine, neuter, and feminine. Assignment to a class was not based on sex (natural gender) but on grammatical gender; for example, the word for *stone* (Old English *stān*) and even a word for *woman* (*wīfmann*) were masculine, the word for *sun* (*sunne*) was feminine, and another word for *woman* (*wīf*) was neuter. Each gender class was associated with a different set of case endings (see Table 8.18).

Table 8.18   Old English case affixes

	Masculine	Neuter	Feminine
	hund 'dog'	dēor 'animal'	gief 'gift'
Singular			
NOMINATIVE	hund	dēor	gief-u
ACCUSATIVE	hund	dēor	gief-e
GENITIVE	hund-es	dēor-es	gief-e
DATIVE	hund-e	dēor-e	gief-e

Table 8.18   Continued

Plural			
NOMINATIVE	hund-as	dēor	gief-a
ACCUSATIVE	hund-as	dēor	gief-a
GENITIVE	hund-a	dēor-a	gief-a
DATIVE	hund-um	dēor-um	gief-um

The following Old English sentence contains all four case categories.

2) Se cniht   geaf gief-e   þæs hierd-es   sun-e.
    the youth-NOM gave gift-ACC the shepherd-GEN son-DAT
    'The youth gave a gift to the shepherd's son.'

By the fifteenth century, English case endings had changed radically as a result of consonant deletion and vowel reduction and deletion. Consequently, many of the earlier case and gender distinctions were obliterated. (The examples in Table 8.19 also include changes to the stem-internal vowels as the result of various processes, including the Great English Vowel Shift.)

Table 8.19   The loss of case affixes through sound change (in English *hound*)

	Old English	*Middle English (e = [ə])*	*Modern English*
Singular			
NOMINATIVE	hund	hund	hound
ACCUSATIVE	hund	hund	hound
GENITIVE	hund-es	hund-(e)s	hound's
DATIVE	hund-e	hund-(e)	hound
Plural			
NOMINATIVE	hund-as	hund-(e)s	hounds
ACCUSATIVE	hund-as	hund-(e)s	hounds
GENITIVE	hund-a	hund-(e)	hounds'
DATIVE	hund-um	hund-(e)	hounds

Whereas Old English had five distinct suffixes for cases, Middle English had only two suffixes, *-e* and *-es*, which, with the loss of schwa, were ultimately reduced to a single suffix *-s*, still used in Modern English for the plural and the possessive. This represents a typical example of how sound change can result in modification to the morphological component of the grammar.

3.3 Analogy

The drastic effects that sound change can have on the morphology of a language are often alleviated through analogy. For example, the plural of Old English *hand* 'hand' was *handa*. Vowel reduction and apocope applying to *handa* would have yielded a

Modern English plural form identical to the singular form, namely *hand*. The Modern English plural *hands* is obviously not the consequence of sound change. Rather, it is the result of earlier analogy with words such as Middle English *hund* 'hound' (see Table 8.19), which did form the plural with the suffix *-s*. This suffix, whose earlier form *-as* was predominant even in Old English, was extended by analogy to all English nouns with a few exceptions (*oxen, men, geese*, etc.). Other plural forms besides *hands* that were created on the basis of analogy include *eyes* (*eyen* in Middle English) and *shoes* (formerly *shooen*).

Continuing analogy along these lines is responsible for the development of the plural form *youse* (from *you*) in some English dialects. Each generation of English-speaking children temporarily extends the analogy still further by producing forms such as *sheeps, gooses*, and *mouses*. To date, however, these particular innovations have not been accepted by adult speakers of Standard English and are eventually abandoned by young language learners.

3.4 Reanalysis

As mentioned in Section 1.2, reanalysis can result in a new morphological structure for a word. It can affect both borrowed words and, particularly in cases where the morphological structure of the word is no longer transparent, native words. Reanalysis can result in new productive patterns (as in the case of *(-)burger*) or it can remain quite isolated, affecting perhaps only one word. Since the type of reanalysis exemplified by *hamburger* is not based on a correct analysis of a word (at least from a historical perspective) and does not usually involve a conscious or detailed study of the word on the part of the speaker, it is often called **folk etymology** (see Table 8.20).

Table 8.20 Folk etymology in English (native words and borrowings)

Modern word	Source
belfry	Middle English *berfrey* 'bell tower' (unrelated to *bell*)
bridegroom	Middle English *bridegome* (unrelated to *groom*) (compare Old English *brȳd* 'bride' and *guma* 'man')
muskrat	Algonquian *musquash* (unrelated to either *musk* or *rat*)
woodchuck	Algonquian *otchek* (unrelated to either *wood* or *chuck*)

Although reanalysis of individual words is common, affixes can also be affected, sometimes with new productive morphological rules developing as a result. This is the case of the Modern English adverbial suffix *-ly* (from Old English *-lic-e*). In Old English, adjectives could be derived from nouns by adding the suffix *-lic*. Adverbs, in turn, could be derived by adding the suffix *-e* to adjectives (including those derived with *-lic*) (see Table 8.21). At some point, the entire complex suffix *-lic+e* was reanalyzed as an adverbial suffix (rather than as an adjectival suffix *-lic* plus an adverbial suffix *-e*). It was then used by analogy to derive adverbs from adjectives in forms where it was not used before, resulting in Modern English *deeply* and other such words.

Table 8.21   The derivation of Old English adjectives and adverbs

Formation of an adjective from a noun	
[dæg]$_N$ + lic → [dæglic]$_A$	'daily' (e.g., as in "daily schedule")
Formation of an adverb from an adjective	
[dēop]$_A$ + e → [dēope]$_{Adv}$	'deeply'
Formation of an adverb from a derived adjective with -lic	
[dæg+lic]$_A$ + e → [dæglice]$_{Adv}$	'daily' (e.g., as in "she ran daily")

4   Syntactic Change

Like other components of the grammar, syntax is also subject to change over time. Syntactic changes can involve modifications to phrase structure (such as word order) and to transformations, as the following examples illustrate.

4.1   Word Order

All languages make a distinction between the subject and direct object. This contrast is typically represented through case marking or word order. Since Old English had an extensive system of case marking, it is not surprising that its word order was somewhat more variable than that of Modern English. In unembedded clauses, Old English placed the verb in second position (much like Modern German). Thus we find subject-verb-object order in simple transitive sentences such as the following.

3) S   V   O
   Hē   geseah   þone mann.
   'He   saw   the man.'

When the clause began with an element such as *þa* 'then' or *ne* 'not', the verb preceded the subject as in the following example.

4) V   S   O
   þa   sende   sēcyning   þone disc
   then   sent   the king   the dish
   'Then the king sent the dish.'

Although this word order is still found in Modern English, its use is very limited and subject to special restrictions, unlike the situation in Old English.

5)   V   S   O
   Rarely has he ever deceived me.

When the direct object was a pronoun, the subject-object-verb order was typical.

6) S   O   V
   Hēo   hine   lǣrde.
   She   him   advised
   'She advised him.'

The subject-object-verb order also prevailed in embedded clauses, even when the direct object was not a pronoun.

7)

	S	O		V	
þa	hē	þone cyning	sōhte,		hē bēotode.
when	he	the king	visited,		he boasted

'When he visited the king, he boasted.'

After case markings were lost during the Middle English period through sound change, fixed subject-verb-object order became the means of marking grammatical relations. As Table 8.22 shows, a major change in word order took place between 1300 and 1400, with the verb-object order becoming dominant.

Table 8.22 Word order patterns in Middle English

Year	1000	1200	1300	1400	1500
Direct object before the verb (%)	53	53	40	14	2
Direct object after the verb (%)	47	47	60	86	98

From SOV to SVO

Just as languages can be classified in terms of their morphology, languages can also be grouped on the basis of the relative order of subject (S), object (O), and verb (V) in basic sentences. Almost all languages of the world fall into one of three types: SOV, SVO, or VSO, with the majority of languages being one of the first two types. Just as languages change through time from one morphological type to another, they can also change from one syntactic type to another. A case in point is found in the history of English, which shows the development from SOV to SVO syntax.

Evidence indicates that the earliest form of Germanic from which English descended was an SOV language. One of the earliest recorded Germanic sentences, for example, has this word order. The sentence in *8* was inscribed on a golden horn (now called the Golden Horn of Gallehus) about 1,600 years ago.

8) Horn of Gallehus

S			O	V	
ek HlewagastiR	HoltijaR		horna	tawido
I Hlewagastir	of Holt		horn	made

'I, Hlewagastir of Holt, made the horn.'

Another type of evidence for an earlier SOV order is found in morphological fusion (see Section 3.1). Since fusion depends on frequently occurring syntactic patterns, it can sometimes serve as an indicator of earlier syntax. The OV compound, very common in Old English (as well as in Modern English), likely reflects an earlier stage of OV word order (see Table 8.23).

Table 8.23 Old English compounds with OV structure

manslæht	'man' + 'strike'	'manslaughter, murder'
æppelbǣre	'apple' + 'bear'	'apple-bearing'

If the earliest Germanic was SOV and Modern English is firmly SVO, then Old English represents a transitional syntactic type. In developing from SOV syntax to SVO syntax, languages seem to follow similar pathways. For example, Modern German, which developed from the same Germanic SOV source as English, shares two of Old English's distinguishing characteristics. Not only is the verb typically placed in the second position of the sentence in main clauses, preceded by the subject or some other element (such as an adverb), SOV order is employed for embedded clauses.

9) Modern German word order

    a. Verb in second position in unembedded clauses
      (Compare the Old English sentence in *4*.)

	V	S		O
Gestern	hatte	ich	keine	Zeit.
yesterday	had	I	no	time

      'I had no time yesterday.'

    b. SOV in embedded clauses
      (Compare the Old English sentence in *7*.)

	S	O	V
Als	er	den Mann	sah . . .
when	he	the man	saw

      When he saw the man . . .'

The change from SOV to SVO is not restricted to English and other Germanic languages. The same change is evident in completely unrelated languages such as those of the Bantu family of Africa. Since linguists are still not sure why languages change from one syntactic type to another, the causes of such change will undoubtedly remain an important area of investigation, especially since the relative order of verb and object (OV versus VO) has been closely linked with other word order patterns.

4.2   Inversion in the History of English

In Old and Middle English, Inversion (the operation that moves auxiliary verbs in front of the subject in yes-no questions) could apply to all verbs, not just auxiliaries, yielding forms that would be unacceptable in Modern English.

10) Speak they the truth?

During the sixteenth and seventeenth centuries, the Inversion rule was changed to apply solely to auxiliary verbs.

11) *Inversion (old form):* The V moves in front of the subject
They speak → Speak they?
They can speak → Can they speak?

    Inversion (new form): The Aux moves in front of the subject
They speak → *Speak they?
They can speak → Can they speak?

With this change, structures such as *Speak they the truth?* were no longer possible. The corresponding question came to be formed with the auxiliary *do* as in *Do they speak the truth?*

5 Lexical and Semantic Change

Another obvious type of language change involves modifications to the lexicon. The addition or loss of words often reflects cultural changes that introduce novel objects and notions and that eliminate outmoded ones.

5.1 Addition of Lexical Items

Addition is frequently the result of technological innovations or contact with other cultures. Such developments result in **lexical gaps** that can be filled by adding new words to the lexicon. New words are added either through the word formation processes available to the language or through borrowing.

Word Formation

The most important word formation processes are compounding and derivation, although other types, including conversion, blending, backformation, clipping, and acronyms can play a significant role.

Compounding and derivation have always been available to English speakers for the creation of new words. In fact, much of the compounding and derivation in Old English seems very familiar (see Table 8.24).

Table 8.24 Compounding and derivation in Old English

Noun compounds			
N + N	sunbēam		'sunbeam'
A + N	middelniht		'midnight'
Adjective compounds			
N + A	blōdrēad		'blood-red'
A + A	dēadboren		'stillborn'
Derived nouns			
[bæc]$_v$ + ere	→	bæcere	'baker'
[frēond]$_N$ + scipe	→	frēondscipe	'friendship'
Derived adjectives			
[wundor]$_N$ + full	→	wundorfull	'wonderful'
[cild]$_N$ + isc	→	cildisc	'childish'

Just as speakers of Modern English can use compounding and derivational rules to create new words (e.g., the N + N compound *airhead*), so could Old English speakers

---

LANGUAGE MATTERS   Dictionaries as Historical Records

There are some dictionaries, such as the *Oxford English Dictionary*, that provide us with a window on language change. A lexical entry includes not only definitions of the word, but also examples of how the word has been used in written documents over many years. Consider the citations for the word *linguist*:

1591. Shakespeare, *Two Gentlemen of Verona*. "Seeing you are beautiful, with goodly shape; and by your owne report A Linguist."
1695. Edwards, *Perfect Script*. "Here linguists and philologists may find that which is to be found no where else."

Information from: the *Oxford English Dictionary* 2e (1989): Definition of *linguist*. By Permission of Oxford University Press.

---

create new words such as the poetic N + N compound *hwælweg*, literally 'whale' + 'path', to mean 'sea'.

Even though many Old English compounding and derivational patterns have been maintained in Modern English, words that were acceptable in Old English are not necessarily still in use in Modern English, despite the fact that they are often quite understandable (see Table 8.25).

Table 8.25 Old English compound and derived forms that are no longer used

Noun compounds			
N + N	bōccræft ('book' + 'craft')		'literature' (compare *witchcraft*)
A + N	dimhūs ('dim' + 'house')		'prison'
Adjective compounds			
N + A	ælfscīene ('elf' + 'beautiful')		'beautiful as a fairy'
A + A	eallgōd ('all' + 'good')		'perfectly good'
Derived nouns			
[sēam]$_V$ + ere	→	sēamere	'tailor' (compare *seamster, seamstress*)
[man]$_N$ + scipe	→	manscipe	'humanity' (compare *friendship*)
Derived adjectives			
[word]$_N$ + full	→	wordfull	'wordy' (compare *wonderful*)
[heofon]$_N$ + isc	→	heofonisc	'heavenly' (compare *childish*)

Not all word formation processes available to Modern English speakers were found in Old English. For example, conversion (as in Modern English [summer]$_N$ → [summer]$_V$) was not possible in Old English. In fact, this process is typically not available to (synthetic) inflectional languages such as Old English, since change in a word's category in such languages is usually indicated morphologically; by definition, conversion does not involve the use of affixes.

Borrowing

As discussed in Section 1.2, language contact over time can result in an important source of new words: borrowing. Depending on the cultural relationship holding between languages, three types of influence of one language on the other are traditionally identified: **substratum**, **adstratum**, and **superstratum influence**.

Substratum influence is the effect of a politically or culturally nondominant language on a dominant language in the area. Both American English and Canadian French, for instance, have borrowed vocabulary items from Native American languages (see examples in Section 1.2). From a much earlier period in the history of English, the influence of a Celtic substratum is also evident, particularly in place names such as *Thames*, *London*, and *Dover*. Substratum influence does not usually have a major impact on the lexicon of the borrowing language. Borrowed words are usually restricted to place names and unfamiliar items or concepts. This situation reflects the fact that it is usually the speakers of the substratum language who inhabited the area first.

Superstratum influence is the effect of a politically or culturally dominant language on another language or languages in the area. For example, the Athabaskan language Gwich'in (Loucheux) (spoken in Alaska and Canada's Northwest Territories) has borrowed a number of governmental terms and expressions from English, including *bureaucratic, constituents, program, business, development,* and *political*.

LANGUAGE MATTERS   Getting Rid of French

The following whimsical piece, from the March 14, 2003, *Christian Science Monitor*, gives you an idea what English would be like without the influence of French.

The Franco-American ~~dispute~~ *falling out* over the best ~~approach~~ *way* to ~~disarming Iraq~~ *take away Iraq's weapons* has resulted in perhaps the highest ~~level of~~ anti-French feeling in the United ~~States~~ *Lands* since 1763.

A French-owned ~~hotel~~ *innkeeping* firm, Accor, has taken down the ~~tricolor~~ *three-hued* flag. In the House of ~~Representatives~~ *Burghers*, the ~~chairman~~ *leader* of the ~~Committee~~ *Body* on ~~Administration~~ *Running Things* has ~~renamed~~ *named anew* French fries "freedom fries" and French toast "freedom toast" in House ~~restaurants~~ *eating rooms*.

It is time for English-speaking ~~peoples~~ *folk* to throw off this cultural ~~imperialism~~ *lording-it-over-others* and ~~declare~~ *say* our linguistic freedom. It is time to ~~purify~~ *clean* the English ~~language~~ *tongue*. It will take some ~~sacrifices~~ *hardship* on everyone's part to get used to the new ~~parlance~~ *speech*. But think of the ~~satisfaction~~ *warm feeling inside* on the day we ~~are all able to~~ *can all* stare the *Académie Française* in the eye and say without fear of ~~reprisal~~ *injury*: "*Sumer is icumen in . . .*"

The Christian Science Monitor. "English Sans French." Reproduced with permission from the March 14, 2003 issue of *The Christian Science Monitor* (www.CSMonitor.com). © 2003 The Christian Science Monitor.

In the case of English, Norman French had a superstratum influence. The major impact of French on the vocabulary of English is related to a historical event—the conquest of England by French-speaking Normans in 1066. As the conquerors and their descendants gradually learned English over the next decades, they retained French terms for political, judicial, and cultural notions (see Table 8.26). These words were in turn borrowed by native English speakers who, in trying to gain a place in the upper middle class, were eager to imitate the speech of their social superiors. Not surprisingly, borrowing was especially heavy in the vocabulary areas pertaining to officialdom: government, the judiciary, and religion. Other areas of heavy borrowing include science, culture, and warfare.

Table 8.26 Some French loan words in English

Government	tax, revenue, government, royal, state, parliament, authority, prince, duke, slave, peasant
Religion	prayer, sermon, religion, chaplain, friar
Judiciary	judge, defendant, jury, evidence, jail, verdict, crime
Science	medicine, physician
Culture	art, sculpture, fashion, satin, fur, ruby
Warfare	army, navy, battle, soldier, enemy, captain

In some cases, French loan words were used in conjunction with native English words to convey distinctions of various sorts. For a minor crime, for example, the English word *theft* was employed, but for a more serious breach of the law, the French word *larceny* was used. The English also kept their own words for domestic animals, such as *cow, calf, sheep,* and *pig,* but adopted the French words for the meat from those creatures, namely *beef, veal, mutton,* and *pork.*

LANGUAGE MATTERS   Multiple Borrowings

Languages have been known to borrow back their own words. For example, the French word *biftek* comes from the English word *beefsteak.* However, earlier, English borrowed the French word *bœuf* as *beef.*

Adstratum influence refers to the situation where two languages are in contact and neither one is clearly politically or culturally dominant. In a city such as Montreal, with its large number of bilingual speakers, English and French inevitably influence each other, yielding words in Montreal English like *subvention* 'subsidy', *metro* 'subway', and *autoroute* 'highway'.

Earlier in the history of English, when the Scandinavians settled part of England beginning in 800 AD, there was substantial contact between the speakers of English and Scandinavian, resulting in an adstratum relationship. Adstratum contact usually results in the borrowing of common everyday words, such as these borrowed from Scandinavian languages: *anger, egg, gear, get, hit, root, seat, skill, skin, their, they,* and *window.* In fact, without consulting a dictionary, most English speakers could not distinguish between borrowings from Scandinavian languages and native English words.

Borrowed words from many other languages attest to various types of cultural contact and serve often to fill the lexical gaps such contact inevitably brings (see Table 8.27).

Table 8.27 Some lexical borrowings into English

Italian	motto, artichoke, balcony, casino, mafia, malaria
Spanish	comrade, tornado, mosquito, guitar, vigilante, marijuana
German	poodle, kindergarten, seminar, noodle, pretzel
Dutch	sloop, coleslaw, smuggle, gin, cookie, boom
Slavic languages	czar, tundra, polka, intelligentsia, robot
Native American languages	toboggan, opossum, wigwam, chipmunk, Mississippi, Omaha
Hindi	thug, punch (drink), shampoo, chintz

Although borrowing has been a very rich source of new words in English, it is noteworthy that loan words are least common among the most frequently used vocabulary items. This reflects a general tendency for highly frequent words to be relatively resistant to loss or substitution (see Table 8.28).

Table 8.28 Origin of the 5,000 most frequent words in English

Degree of frequency	*Source language (%)*			
	English	*French*	*Latin*	*Other*
First 1,000	83	11	2	4
Second 1,000	34	46	11	9
Third 1,000	29	46	14	11
Fourth 1,000	27	45	17	11
Fifth 1,000	27	47	17	9

5.2 Loss of Lexical Items

Just as words can be added to the lexicon, they can also be lost. Changes in society play an important role in the loss of words as lexical items often fall into disuse because the object or notion they refer to has become obsolete (see Table 8.29).

Table 8.29 Some Old English words lost through cultural change

dolgbōt	'compensation for wounding'
þeox	'hunting spear'
eafor	'tenant obligation to the king to convey goods'
flȳtme	'a blood-letting instrument'

LANGUAGE MATTERS   Borrowing Phrases

Sometimes languages borrow simple phrases or expressions and translate them word-for-word. The following are all examples of common English phrases that came from another language.

English phrase	*Source phrase*
brainwashing	Chinese *xǐnǎo*
flea market	French *marché aux puces*
antibody	German *Antikörper*
moment of truth	Spanish *el momento de la verdad*

5.3   Semantic Change

Although changes in word meaning take place continually in all languages, words rarely jump from one meaning to an unrelated one. Typically, the changes occur step by step and involve one of the following phenomena.

As Table 8.30 shows, **semantic broadening** is the process in which the meaning of a word becomes more general or more inclusive than its historically earlier form. In contrast, **semantic narrowing** is the process in which the meaning of a word becomes less general or less inclusive than its historically earlier meaning. In **amelioration**, the meaning of a word becomes more positive or favorable. The opposite change, **pejoration**, also occurs. Given the propensity of human beings to exaggerate, it is not surprising that the **weakening of meaning** frequently occurs. For example, our word *soon* used to mean 'immediately' but now simply means 'in the near future'.

Table 8.30   Semantic change

Change	Word	Old meaning	New meaning
Semantic broadening	bird	'small fowl'	'any winged creature'
	barn	'place to store barley'	'farm building for storage and shelter'
Semantic narrowing	hound	'any dog'	'a hunting breed'
	meat	'any type of food'	'animal flesh'
	disease	'any unfavorable state'	'illness'
Amelioration	pretty	'tricky, sly, cunning'	'attractive'
	knight	'boy'	'special title or position'
Pejoration	silly	'happy, prosperous'	'foolish'
	wench	'girl'	'wanton woman, prostitute'
Weakening of meaning	wreck	'avenge, punish'	'to cause, inflict'
	quell	'kill, murder'	'to put down, pacify'

Semantic shift is a process in which a word loses its former meaning and takes on a new, but often related, meaning (see Table 8.31). Sometimes a series of semantic shifts occurs over an extended period of time, resulting in a meaning that is completely unrelated to the original sense of a word. The word *hearse*, for example, originally referred to a triangular harrow (a farming implement). Later, it denoted a triangular frame for church candles and later still it was used to refer to the device that held candles over a coffin. In a subsequent shift, it came to refer to the framework on which curtains were hung over a coffin or tomb. Still later, *hearse* was used to refer to the coffin itself before finally taking on its current sense of the vehicle used to transport a coffin.

Table 8.31 Semantic shift

Word	Old meaning	New meaning
immoral	'not customary'	'unethical'
bead	'prayer'	'prayer bead, bead'

In the late twentieth century, the word *gay* underwent a dramatic and unusually rapid set of shifts. Just a few generations earlier, this word was typically used in the sense of 'lively, carefree, happy'. It then came to designate 'homosexual', and a phrase such as 'a gay film' would be interpreted in this sense.

LANGUAGE MATTERS   Dictionaries Help Track Meaning Changes

The word *girl* in Middle English was used to refer to a child of either sex. Note the following definition from the *Oxford English Dictionary*:

Girl. A child or young person of either sex; a youth or maiden.
1290. "And gret prece of gurles and men comen hire."
('And a great throng of children and men came here.')

Information from: the *Oxford English Dictionary* 2e (1989): Definition of *girl* By Permission of Oxford University Press.

One of the most striking types of semantic change is triggered by **metaphor**, a figure of speech based on a perceived similarity between distinct objects or actions. Metaphorical change usually involves a word with a concrete meaning taking on a more abstract sense, although the word's original meaning is not lost. The meanings of many English words have been extended through metaphor (see Table 8.32).

Table 8.32 Some examples of metaphor in English

Word	Metaphorical meaning
grasp	'understand'
yarn	'story'
high	'on drugs'

6   The Spread of Change

Up to this point, we have been concerned with the causes and description of linguistic change. Still to be dealt with is the question of how linguistic innovations spread. This section focuses on two types of spread, one involving the way in which an innovation is extended through the vocabulary of a language and the other involving the way in which it spreads through the population.

6.1   Diffusion through the Language

Some linguistic change first manifests itself in a few words and then gradually spreads through the vocabulary of the language. This type of change is called **lexical diffusion**. A well-attested example in English involves an ongoing change in the stress pattern of words such as *convert*, which can be used as either a noun or a verb. Although the stress originally fell on the second syllable regardless of lexical category, in the latter half of the sixteenth century three such words, *rebel*, *outlaw*, and *record*, came to be pronounced with the stress on the first syllable when used as nouns. As Figure 8.10 illustrates, this stress shift was extended to an increasing number of words over the next decades.

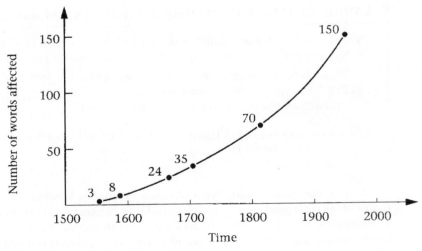

Figure 8.10   Diffusion of stress shift in English

This change still has not diffused through the entire vocabulary of English. There are about a thousand nouns of the relevant sort that still place the stress on the second syllable (e.g., *report*, *mistake*, and *support*). Table 8.33 illustrates the spread of this change to date.

Table 8.33   Stress shift in English (nouns)

Before the 16th century	During the 16th century	During the 18th century	Today
re'bel	'rebel	'rebel	'rebel
af'fix	af'fix	'affix	'affix
re'cess	re'cess	re'cess	'recess
mis'take	mis'take	mis'take	mis'take

This ongoing change can be observed in progress today. The noun *address*, for example, is pronounced by many people with stress on the first syllable as ['ædɹɛs], although the older pronunciation [ə'dɹɛs] is still heard. Some speakers alternate between the two pronunciations. This change may continue to work its way through the language until all nouns in the class we have been considering are stressed on the first syllable.

However, not all linguistic change involves gradual diffusion through the vocabulary of a language. Sound changes typically affect all instances of the segment(s) involved. For example, in some dialects of Spanish (such as Cuban) the consonantal weakening of [s] to [h] in syllable-final position affects all instances of *s* in those positions. The relevant rule can be stated as in Figure 8.11.

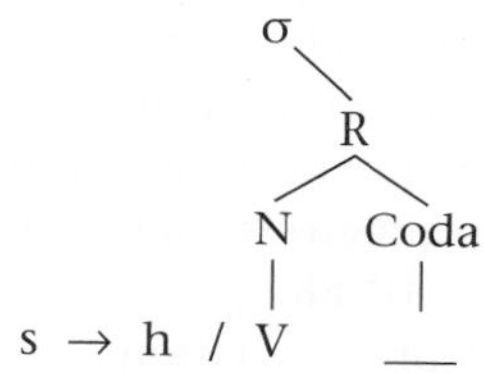

Figure 8.11   Consonant weakening of [s] to [h] in certain Spanish dialects

This rule has resulted in changes such as those exemplified in Table 8.34.

Table 8.34   The effects of the [s] to [h] change in Caribbean Spanish dialects

Standard pronunciation	New pronunciation	
[felismente]	[felihmente]	'happily'
[estilo]	[ehtilo]	'type'
[espaɲa]	[ehpaɲa]	'Spain'

This change is entirely regular, affecting all instances of syllable-final [s] in the speech of individuals who adopt it.

Two types of language change can thus be identified. One, exemplified by the stress shifts in bisyllabic English nouns of the type we have discussed, affects individual words one at a time and gradually spreads through the vocabulary of the language.

The other, exemplified by the consonant weakening of syllable-final [s] to [h] in some dialects of Spanish, involves an across-the-board change that applies without exception to all words.

6.2   Spread through the Population

For a language change to take place, the particular innovation must be accepted by the linguistic community as a whole. For example, although children acquiring English typically form the past tense of *go* as *goed* instead of *went*, *goed* has never received widespread acceptance. Doubtless the verb form in *he throve on fame* would be equally unacceptable to most speakers today. In earlier English, however, *throve* was the past tense form of *thrive* (compare *drive/drove*). At some point in the past then, the novel form *thrived* did receive general acceptance. It's no coincidence that the irregular form that survived is from a frequent verb, and the one that was lost is from a verb that is less commonly used. The frequency with which irregular forms are heard and used is a major determinant of their longevity.

Just as change sometimes begins with a small number of words, the effects of a change often appear first in the speech of only a small number of people. Social pressures often play an important role in whether a particular innovation will spread through the entire linguistic community. Since speakers can consciously or subconsciously alter the way they speak to approximate what they perceive to be a more prestigious or socially desirable variety of speech, once a change has taken hold in the speech of a particular group it may gradually spread to other speakers and ultimately affect the entire linguistic community.

There have been numerous examples of this in the history of English, notably the loss of postvocalic [ɹ] along the east coast of the United States. This change, which led to an 'r-less' pronunciation of words such as *far* as [faː], originated in parts of England in the seventeenth and eighteenth centuries. At that time, postvocalic [ɹ] was still pronounced throughout English-speaking settlements in North America. Two factors accounted for its loss in parts of this continent. First, the children of the New England gentry picked up the new pronunciation in British schools and subsequently brought it back to the colony. Second, the speech of newly arrived immigrants, including colonial administrators and church officials who enjoyed high social status in the colony, typically lacked the postvocalic [ɹ]. As a result, the innovation was widely imitated and ultimately spread along much of the east coast and into the south.

Social pressures were also involved in limiting the spread of this innovation. It did not penetrate Pennsylvania or the other midland states since the most prestigious group of settlers there were Quakers from northern England, an area that retained the postvocalic [ɹ]. Similarly, in Appalachia, the influence of Scottish and Irish settlers, whose dialects did not undergo the change in question, helped ensure the survival of postvocalic [ɹ]. More recently the 'r-less' pronunciation has become stigmatized in some areas, such as New York City, and we now see a trend to restoration of [ɹ] in environments where it had been deleted.

7 Language Reconstruction

When we compare the vocabulary items of various languages, we cannot help but notice the strong resemblance certain words bear to each other. By systematically comparing languages, we can establish whether two or more languages descended from a common parent and are therefore **genetically related**. The **comparative method** refers to the procedure of reconstructing earlier forms on the basis of a comparison of later forms. By means of such **comparative reconstruction** we can reconstruct properties of the parent language with a great degree of certainty.

7.1 Comparative Reconstruction

The most reliable sign of family relationships is the existence of **systematic phonetic correspondences** in the vocabulary items of different languages. Many such correspondences can be found in the sample of vocabulary items in Table 8.35 from English, Dutch, German, and Danish, all of which are members of the Germanic branch of the Indo-European family of languages.

Table 8.35   Some Germanic cognates, contrasted with unrelated Turkish

English	Dutch	German	Danish	Turkish
man	man	Mann	mand	adam
hand	hand	Hand	hånd	el
foot	voet	Fuß (ß = [s])	fod	ayak
bring	brengen	bringen	bringe	getir
summer	zomer	Sommer	sommer	yaz

Since the relationship between the phonological form of a word and its meaning is mostly arbitrary, the existence of systematic phonetic correspondences in the forms of two or more languages must point toward a common source. Conversely, where languages are not related, their vocabulary items fail to show systematic similarities. This can be seen by comparing words from Turkish, which is not related to the Germanic languages, with their counterparts in the languages in Table 8.35.

Words that have descended from a common source (as shown by systematic phonetic correspondences and, usually, semantic similarities) are called **cognates**. Cognates are not always as obvious as the Germanic examples in Table 8.35. Where languages from the same family are only distantly related, the systematic correspondences may be considerably less striking. This is exemplified in the data in Table 8.36 from English, Russian, and Hindi, all of which are distantly related to each other. Forms from the unrelated Turkish are included to emphasize the similarities among the first three languages.

Table 8.36 Some distantly related cognates compared to unrelated Turkish

English	*Russian*	*Hindi*	*Turkish (orthography)*
two	dva	dō	iki
three	tri	tīn	üç
brother	brat	bhāi	kardeş
nose	nos	nahī	burun
			*<ü> = [y]; <ç> = [tʃ]; <ş> = [ʃ]

Once the existence of a relationship between two or more languages has been established, an attempt can be made to reconstruct the common source. This reconstructed language, or **protolanguage**, is made up of **protoforms**, which are written with a preceding * (e.g., *hand*) to indicate their hypothetical character as reconstructions of earlier forms that have not been recorded or are not directly observable.

7.2   **Techniques of Reconstruction**

Reconstruction can be undertaken with some confidence because (as discussed in the previous sections) the processes underlying language change are systematic. Once the processes are uncovered by linguists, we can infer earlier forms of the language. Although it is possible to reconstruct all components of a protolanguage (its phonology, morphology, syntax, lexicon, and semantics), we will focus here on phonological reconstruction, the area in which linguists have made the most progress.

Reconstruction Strategies

Reconstruction of a protoform makes use of two general strategies. The most important one is the **phonetic plausibility strategy**, which requires that any changes posited to account for differences between the protoforms and later forms must be phonetically plausible. Secondarily, the **majority rules strategy** stipulates that if no phonetically plausible change can account for the observed differences, then the segment found in the majority of cognates should be assumed. It is important to note that the first strategy always takes precedence over the second; the second strategy is a last resort.

Consider the cognates in Table 8.37 (somewhat simplified) from members of the Romance family.

Table 8.37   Romance cognates

French	*Italian*	*Romanian*	*Spanish*	
[si]	[si]	[ʃi]	[si]	'yes'; 'and' (Rom.)

The data exemplify a correspondence between [s] and [ʃ] before the vowel [i]. To account for this, we could assume either that Romanian underwent a change that converted [s] to [ʃ] before [i] or that the other three languages underwent a change converting [ʃ] to [s] before [i], as shown in Figure 8.12.

Hypothesis A	
Protoform	*si
Sound change (Romanian only)	*s > ʃ / ___ i
Hypothesis B	
Protoform	*ʃi
Sound change (French, Italian, and Spanish)	*ʃ > s / ___ i

Figure 8.12 Hypotheses for reconstructing Proto-Romance 'yes'

Both reconstruction strategies favor hypothesis A. Most importantly, the phonetic change needed to account for the Romanian pronunciation involves palatalization before [i]. Since palatalization in this context is a very common phenomenon in human language, it is reasonable to assume that it occurred in Romanian. It would be much more difficult to argue that the protolanguage contained [ʃ] before [i] and that three languages underwent the change posited by hypothesis B, since depalatalization before [i] would be an unusual phonetic process. (The reconstructed *s posited in hypothesis A is also compatible with the majority rules strategy since three of the four languages in the data have [s] before [i].)

Reconstruction and the Catalog of Sound Changes

Although there are factors that can confound our attempt to determine the relative plausibility of various sound changes, the changes listed in the catalog in Table 8.2 can generally be considered highly plausible. Table 8.38 lists some plausible versus less plausible or even implausible changes based on that catalogue.

Table 8.38 Different rules in terms of their plausibility based on the catalog

Rule	Name of sound change in catalog
High probability	
t > tʃ / ___ i	palatalization/affrication
n > m / ___ b	assimilation (place of articulation)
t > d / V ___ V	voicing
k > Ø / V ___ C	consonant deletion (cluster simplification)
Low probability	
tʃ > t / ___ i	
m > n / ___ b	
d > t / V ___ V	
Ø > k / V ___ C	

Reconstructing Proto-Romance

Consider now the slightly more complex example in Table 8.39 involving data from several languages of the Romance family.

Table 8.39   Some Romance cognates

Spanish	Sardinian	French	Portuguese	Romanian	Original meaning
riba [riβa]	ripa	rive [ʁiv]	riba	rîpă [rɨpə]	'embankment'
amiga [amiɣa]	amica	amie [ami]	amiga	–	'female friend'
copa	cuppa	coupe [kup]	copa	cupă [kupə]	'cup, goblet'
gota	gutta	goutte [gut]	gota	gută [gutə]	'drop'

Note: Orthographic *c* represents [k] in all the above examples. [β] is a voiced bilabial fricative and [ɣ] a voiced velar fricative. [ɨ] is a high central unrounded vowel. Some details of vowel quality have been ignored.

Our goal here is to reconstruct the protoforms for these words in Proto-Romance, the parent language of the Modern Romance languages, which stands very close to Latin. Classical Latin was the literary language of ancient Rome, whereas Proto-Romance represents an attempt to reconstruct the spoken language spread throughout Europe that was the source of the various Romance languages.

Let us first consider the reconstruction of the Proto-Romance form for 'embankment'. Since the first two segments are the same in all the cognate languages, we can reconstruct Proto-Romance *r and *i on the basis of the majority rules strategy. In the case of the second consonant, however, there are differences between the cognates (see Table 8.40).

Table 8.40   Systematic correspondences in the cognates for 'embankment'

Spanish	Sardinian	French	Portuguese	Romanian
-β-	-p-	-v-	-b-	-p-

It is most important that we first think in terms of phonetic plausibility. In the absence of evidence to the contrary, we will assume that one of the segments found in the cognates ([p], [b], [v], or [β]) should be reconstructed for Proto-Romance. Logically possible changes ranked with respect to their phonetic plausibility are found in Table 8.41.

Table 8.41   Changes based on phonetic plausibility

Change in V__V	Name of change based on catalog	Phonetic plausibility
p > b	voicing	high
p > v	voicing (p > b) and frication (b > v)	high
p > β	voicing (p > b) and frication (b > β)	high
b > p		low
β > p		low
v > p		low

In terms of plausibility, the only possible reconstruction for Proto-Romance is *p. Proto-Romance *p underwent no change in Sardinian and Romanian, but in Portuguese it underwent intervocalic voicing and in Spanish it underwent both voicing and frication (that is, weakening) (see Table 8.42). (We assume that voicing preceded frication since Portuguese shows voicing but no frication.) If we assume that the final vowel of the protoform was still present in French when the consonant changes took place, we can conclude that voicing and frication occurred in this language as well. (In its written form, *rive* retains a sign of the earlier reduced vowel [ə].) These changes are phonetically plausible and thus expected.

Table 8.42 Summary of the changes affecting Proto-Romance *p

*p > p / V__V	no change in Sardinian or Romanian
*p > b / V__V	voicing in Portuguese
*p > b > β / V__V	voicing and frication in Spanish
*p > b > v / V__V	voicing and frication in French

Turning now to the final vowel, we note that three languages have full vowels, Romanian has [ə], and French has no vowel (see Table 8.43). Since vowel reduction and apocope are phonetically plausible changes, it is appropriate to posit a full vowel for the protolanguage. Furthermore, since the three languages with a full vowel all have [a], we can posit this vowel on the basis of the majority rules strategy. Accordingly, the reconstructed protoform is *ripa.

Table 8.43 Summary of the changes affecting Proto-Romance *a

Language	Change (word final)	Name of change(s)
Romanian	*a > ə	vowel reduction
French	*a > ə > Ø	vowel reduction and apocope

We can now outline the evolution of this word in French, which has the most complicated development of the six languages (see Table 8.44).

Table 8.44 Evolution of French *rive* from *ripa

Change	*ripa	Name of change
p > b / V __ V	riba	voicing
b > v / V __ V	riva	frication
a > ə / __ #	rivə	vowel reduction
ə > Ø / __ #	riv	apocope

In the case of the cognates for 'female friend' (the second row of Table 8.39), the first three segments are the same in all the languages in the data. According to the majority rules strategy we can reconstruct them as *ami-. In the reconstruction of the second consonant, however, we must appeal to our strategy of phonetic plausibility (see Table 8.45).

Table 8.45 Systematic correspondences in the second consonant of the cognates for 'female friend'

Spanish	Sardinian	French	Portuguese	Romanian
-ɣ-	-k-	-Ø	-g-	–

Once again, since intervocalic voicing, frication, and deletion are phonetically plausible changes, it is most appropriate to posit *k for the protoform (see Table 8.46).

Table 8.46 Summary of the changes affecting Proto-Romance *k

Language	Change (in V_V)	Name of change(s)
Portuguese	*k > g	voicing
Spanish	*k > g > ɣ	voicing and frication
French	*k > g > ɣ > Ø	voicing, frication, and deletion

In the case of the final vowel, we have the same situation we had in the previous form. The full vowel is found in Spanish, Sardinian, and Portuguese but there is no vowel in French. We can therefore assume the full vowel *a for the protoform, with subsequent vowel reduction and apocope in French. Consequently, we arrive at the protoform *amika.

Finally, applying the same procedure to the cognates in the final two rows of Table 8.39 yields the protoforms *kuppa 'cup' and *gutta 'drop'. All the languages in the data retain the initial consonant of both protoforms. The vowel *u is reconstructed on the basis of the majority rules strategy, since we have no phonetic grounds for choosing either [u] or [o] as the older vowel. The systematic correspondences involving the intervocalic consonants are given in Table 8.47.

Table 8.47 Systematic correspondences of the medial consonants of *kuppa and *gutta

Spanish	Sardinian	French	Portuguese	Romanian
-p-	-pp-	-p	-p-	-p-
-t-	-tt-	-t	-t-	-t-

Regardless of whether we are dealing with original *pp or *tt, the same pattern is evident in the case of both geminate types. There is a geminate stop consonant in Sardinian and a single consonant in Spanish, French, Portuguese, and Romanian. Since degemination is an expected sound change (see the catalog in Table 8.2), we assume that the protoforms contained geminate consonants that underwent degemination except in Sardinian. This is an example of a case where the phonetic plausibility strategy overrules the majority rules strategy (since four of the five languages have [p]/[t] whereas only one language has [pp]/[tt]). As far as the final vowels are concerned, the same pattern found in the previous examples is once again evident.

Proto-Romance *a was retained in Spanish, Sardinian, and Portuguese, reduced to [ə] in Romanian, and deleted in French (see Table 8.43).

Of the languages exemplified here, Sardinian is considered the most conservative since it has retained more of the earlier consonants and vowels. (In fact, the Sardinian words in the examples happen to be identical with the protoforms, but this degree of resemblance would not be maintained in a broader range of data.) In the case of the other Romance languages and changes we have discussed, the most to least conservative are Portuguese (degemination and voicing) and Romanian (degemination and vowel reduction); Spanish (degemination, voicing, and frication); and French (degemination, voicing, frication, consonant deletion, vowel reduction, and apocope).

Although Proto-Romance is not identical with Classical Latin, close similarity is expected. Accordingly, the fact that our reconstructions are so close to the Latin words gives us confidence in our methods of reconstruction (see Table 8.48).

Table 8.48 Comparison of Latin and Proto-Romance forms

Latin	Proto-Romance form
rīpa	*ripa
amīca (c = [k])	*amika
cuppa	*kuppa
gutta	*gutta

It is sometimes not possible to reconstruct all the characteristics of the protolanguage. For example, on the basis of our data we were not able to reconstruct vowel length (Latin had a distinction between long and short vowels) since there was no evidence of this characteristic in the cognate forms.

It is also worth noting that we are not always so fortunate as to have written records of a language we expect to be very close to our reconstructed language. In the case of the Germanic languages, for example, there is no ancient written language equivalent to Latin. We must rely completely on our reconstruction of Proto-Germanic to determine the properties of the language from which the modern-day Germanic languages descended. Furthermore, for many languages of the world we have no written historical records at all and for other languages, such as Native American languages, it is only very recently that we have written records.

In summary, when the forms of two or more languages appear to be related, we can, through a consideration of systematic phonetic correspondences among cognates, reconstruct the common form from which all the forms can be derived by means of phonetically plausible sound changes. The reconstructed forms are protoforms, and a reconstructed language, a protolanguage.

7.3 Internal Reconstruction

Sometimes it is possible to reconstruct the earlier form of a language even without reference to comparative data. This technique, known as **internal reconstruction**, relies on the analysis of morphophonemic variation within a single language. The key point is that the sound changes that create allomorphic and allophonic variation can be identified and then used to infer an earlier form of the morpheme. The data in Table 8.49 are from French; because of borrowing, English exhibits a parallel set of contrasts involving [k] and [ʃ].

Table 8.49   [k] / [s] correspondence in French

maʒik	'magic'	maʒis-jɛ̃	'magician'
loʒik	'logic'	loʒis-jɛ̃	'logician'
myzik	'music'	myzis-jɛ̃	'musician'

The root morpheme in each row exhibits two forms, one ending in [k], the other ending in [s]. The same methods and principles used in comparative reconstruction can be applied here to reconstruct the historically earlier form of the root morpheme. If a root ending in *s is posited, no phonetically plausible change can account for the [k] in the left-hand column. By contrast, if a root-final *k is posited, the [s] can be accounted for by assuming that the *k was fronted under the influence of the palatal glide [j] of the suffix (palatalization) and became an affricate [ts] (affrication), which was later simplified to a fricative [s] (deaffrication). All of these changes are phonetically plausible and listed in the catalog in Table 8.2. Accordingly, internal reconstruction indicates that at an earlier point in the development of French, the root morphemes in Table 8.49 contained the consonant *k.

8 Language Change and Naturalness

A striking fact about language change is that the same patterns of change occur repeatedly, not only within a particular language at different periods in its history but also across languages. Both the similarity of changes across languages as well as the directionality of language change suggest that some changes are more natural than others. This notion of **naturalness** is implicit in the phonetic plausibility strategy introduced in the section on comparative reconstruction.

If naturalness is a factor in language change, its manifestations should also be found in language acquisition and in language universals. This does seem to be the case. As a specific example, let us consider the frequently made claim that the CV syllable is the most natural of all syllable types. At least three different kinds of evidence can be brought forth in support of this claim. First, in terms of universals, virtually all languages of the world have CV syllables in their syllable type inventory, and some languages only have CV syllables. Second, a variety of sound changes have the effect of reducing less natural syllable types to the more natural CV type (see Table 8.50).

By contrast, such changes rarely, if ever, apply to a CV syllable to yield a different syllable type. Deletion of the C in a word-initial CV syllable is extremely rare, as is vowel epenthesis in a CV syllable or in a sequence of CV syllables.

Table 8.50 Sound changes yielding CV syllables

Deletion							
CCV	>	CV	Old English	cnēow	English	knee	/ni/
CVC	>	CV	Old Spanish	non	Spanish	no	
Vowel epenthesis							
CCVCV	>	CVCVCV	Italian	croce	Sicilian	kiruci	'cross'

Third, in terms of language acquisition, the CV syllable type is one of the first syllable types to be acquired and many phonetic processes found in child language have the effect of yielding CV syllables, just like the sound changes listed above (see Table 8.51).

Table 8.51 Phonetic processes in language acquisition yielding CV syllables

CCV → CV	tree → [ti]	(simplification of consonant clusters)
CVC → CV	dog → [dɑ]	(deletion of final consonants)

The precise effects of linguistic naturalness are not yet fully understood. For example, some sound changes actually do produce less natural syllables. Thus, syncope has the effect of reducing a sequence of CVCVCV syllables to the less natural CVCCV. Usually in such cases, a different motivation can be identified, such as the preference for shorter phonological forms over longer forms. But given the complexity of human language, not to mention human behavior in general, it should not be surprising that there are many different parameters of linguistic naturalness and that these can, in turn, lead to apparently conflicting changes in language over time. It remains an important task of the linguist to identify, rank, and ultimately explain relations of linguistic naturalness. The study of language change will continue to make an important contribution to this area.

Summing Up

Historical linguistics studies the nature and causes of language change. The causes of language change find their roots in the physiological and cognitive makeup of human beings. Sound changes usually involve articulatory simplification, as in the case of the most common type, **assimilation**. **Analogy** and **reanalysis** are particularly important factors in morphological change. **Language contact** resulting in **borrowing** is another important source of language change.

All components of the grammar, from phonology to semantics, are subject to change over time. A change can simultaneously affect all instances of a particular sound or form, or it can spread through the language word by word by means of **lexical diffusion**. Sociological factors can play an important role in determining whether or not a linguistic innovation is ultimately adopted by the linguistic community at large. Since language change is systematic, it is possible, by identifying the changes that a particular language or dialect has undergone, to reconstruct linguistic history and thereby posit the earlier forms from which later forms have evolved. Using sets of **cognates**, **comparative reconstruction** allows us to reconstruct the properties of the parent or **protolanguage** on the basis of **systematic phonetic correspondences**.

Studies in historical linguistics can provide valuable insights into relationships among languages and shed light on prehistoric developments. Furthermore, historical studies of language are of great importance to our understanding of human linguistic competence. In fact, it has often been stated that language change provides one of the most direct windows into the workings of the human mind. Furthermore, the study of language change contributes to our understanding of how social, cultural, and psychological factors interact to shape language. Finally, the integration of studies on language change, language acquisition, and language universals remains one of the most important challenges facing linguists today.

Key Terms

General terms and terms concerning the nature of change and its spread

analogy

articulatory simplification

borrowing

historical linguistics

hypercorrection

language contact

lexical diffusion

reanalysis

spelling pronunciation

General terms concerning sound change

assimilation

consonantal strength

deaffrication

dissimilation

epenthesis

geminate

glide strengthening

metathesis

phonetically conditioned change

segmental change

sequential change

substitution

weakening

Terms concerning sound change by assimilation

affrication

manner assimilation

nasalization

palatalization

partial assimilation

place assimilation

total assimilation

umlaut

voicing assimilation

Terms concerning sound change by weakening

apocope

consonant deletion

consonant weakening

degemination

deletion

frication

rhotacism	voicing
syncope	vowel reduction

Terms concerning phonological change

diphthongization	phonological (sound) change
Great English Vowel Shift	shifts
mergers	splits

Terms concerning morphological, syntactic, and lexical changes

adstratum influence	lexical gaps
folk etymology	substratum influence
fusion	superstratum influence
grammaticalization	

Terms concerning semantic change

amelioration	semantic narrowing
metaphor	semantic shift
pejoration	weakening of meaning
semantic broadening	

Terms concerning genetic relationships and reconstruction

cognates	naturalness
comparative method	phonetic plausibility strategy
comparative reconstruction	protoforms
genetically related (languages)	protolanguage
internal reconstruction	systematic phonetic correspondences
majority rules strategy	

Recommended Reading

Brinton, Laurel J., and Leslie K. Arnovick. 2011. *The English Language: A Linguistic History*. 2nd ed. Oxford: Oxford University Press.

Campbell, Lyle. 2013. *Historical Linguistics: An Introduction*. 3rd ed. Cambridge, MA: MIT Press.

Gelderen, Elly van. 2014. *A History of the English Language*. Rev. ed. Amsterdam: John Benjamins.

Hock, Hans Henrich, and Brian D. Joseph. 2009. *Language History, Language Change, and Language Relationship: An Introduction to Historical and Comparative Linguistics*. 2nd ed. New York: Mouton de Gruyter.

Hopper, Paul J., and Elizabeth Closs Traugott. 2003. *Grammaticalization*. 2nd ed. Cambridge, UK: Cambridge University Press.

Joseph, Brian D., and Richard Janda, eds. 2003. *The Handbook of Historical Linguistics*. Oxford: Blackwell.

Trask, R. L. 2015. *Historical Linguistics*. Ed. and rev. by Robert McColl Millar. 3rd ed. London: Routledge.

Exercises

1. Place names are often subject to spelling pronunciation. Transcribe your pronunciation of the following words and then compare your pronunciation with that recommended by a good dictionary. Do you think any of your pronunciations qualify as spelling pronunciations? (See Section 1.2.)
   a) Worcestershire
   b) Thames
   c) Edinburgh (Scotland; compare Edinburgh, Texas)
   d) Cannes (France)
   e) Newfoundland

2. Identify the following sound changes with reference to the catalog of sound changes provided in Table 8.2 and described in Section 2. In each pair of examples, focus on the segment(s) in bold only. The form on the left indicates the original segment(s) before the change and the form on the right indicates the segment(s) after the change. (The orthography is supplemented with IPA, in square brackets, where the intended pronunciation is not otherwise clear.)

a)	Sanskrit	**sn**eha	Pali	**sin**eha	'friendship'
b)	Old English	**hl**āf	English	loaf
c)	Latin	**i**uvenis [j]	Italian	**gi**ovane [dʒ]	'young'
d)	English	triath**l**on	dialect	triath[ə]lon
e)	Latin	vi**dua** [dw]	Spanish	viu**da** [wd]	'widow'
f)	Sanskrit	sa**pt**a	Pali	sa**tt**a	'seven'
g)	Latin	turtu**r**	English	turtle
h)	Pre-Spanish	*ven**r**é	Spanish	ven**dr**é	'I will come'
i)	Italian	mo**nd**o	Sicilian	mu**nn**u	'world'
j)	Old French	cire [**ts**]	French	cire [**s**]	'wax'
k)	Latin	pā**n**-	French	pai**n** [ɛ̃]	'bread'
l)	Latin	mu**lg**ēre	Italian	mu**ng**ere	'to milk'
m)	Latin	pa**c**are [k]	Italian	pa**g**are	'to pay'
n)	Old Spanish	ni**d**o	Spanish	ni**d**o [ð]	'nest'
o)	Latin	pe**cc**ātum [kk]	Spanish	pe**c**ado [k]	'sin'
p)	Pre-Latin	*hon**ō**sis	Latin	hon**ō**ris	'honor (GEN SG)'
q)	Old French	rai**g**e [dʒ]	French	ra**g**e [ʒ]	'rage'
r)	English	co**ff**ee	Chipewyan	[ka**θ**i]
s)	Latin	ma**re**	Portuguese	ma**r**	'sea'
t)	Latin	vī**c**īnitās	Spanish	ve**c**indad	'neighborhood'
u)	Gothic	**þl**iuan [θ]	English	**fl**ee
v)	Old English	(ic) si**ng**e	English	(I) si**ng**	
w)	Latin	su**mm**a	Spanish	su**m**a	'sum, gist'
x)	Latin	ōrnā**m**entum	Old French	orne**m**ent [ə]	'ornament'
y)	Pre–Old English	*l**ū**si	Old English	l**ȳ**s [y:]	'lice'

3. *i)* Describe the difference in obstruents between the two French dialects in the following data. Assume that the data are in phonetic transcription.
   ii) What sound change would you posit here? Why? (See Section 2.)
   iii) State the sound change in the form of a rule.

   (*Note:* [y] represents a high front rounded vowel; [ø] represents a mid front rounded vowel; [ʁ] represents a voiced uvular fricative.)

European French	Acadian French	
a) okyn	otʃyn	'none'
b) køʁ	tʃør	'heart'
c) ke	tʃe	'wharf'
d) kɛ̃:z	tʃɛ̃:z	'fifteen'
e) akyze	atʃyze	'accuse'
f) ki	tʃi	'who'
g) kav	kav	'cave'
h) kɔʁ	kɔr	'body'
i) kuʁiʁ	kurir	'run'
j) ɑ̃kɔ:ʁ	ɑ̃kɔ:r	'again'

4. *i)* What sound changes differentiate Guaraní from its parent language, Proto-Tupí-Guaraní, in the following data? (See Section 2.)
   ii) State these changes in rule form.

   (*Note:* [ɨ] represents a high central unrounded vowel.)

Proto-Tupí-Guaraní	Guaraní	
a) jukɨr	jukɨ	'salt'
b) moajan	moajã	'push'
c) puʔam	puʔã	'wet'
d) meʔeŋ	meʔẽ	'give'
e) tiŋ	tʃĩ	'white'
f) potiʔa	potʃiʔa	'chest'
g) tatatiŋ	tatatʃĩ	'smoke'
h) kɨb	kɨ	'louse'
i) men	mẽ	'husband'

5. *i)* Describe the three changes that took place between Proto-Slavic and Bulgarian in the following data. (The symbol ˘ over a vowel indicates that it is short.) (See Section 2.)
   ii) State these changes as rules and indicate, as far as possible, the order in which they must have applied. (See Section 2.6.)
   iii) Apply these rules to the Proto-Slavic word for 'adroit' to show how the Bulgarian form evolved.

Proto-Slavic	Bulgarian	
a) gladŭka	glatkə	'smooth'
b) kratŭka	kratkə	'short'
c) blizŭka	bliskə	'near'
d) ʒeʒĭka	ʒeʃkə	'scorching'

e) lovŭka   lofkə   'adroit'
f) gořika   gorkə   'bitter'

(Data for exercises 4 and 5 from: F. Columbus, *Introductory Workbook in Historical Phonology*. Cambridge, MA: Slavica, 1974.)

6. For each item, list all the sound changes required to derive the later form from the protoform. Where necessary, give the chronology of the sound changes. (See Section 2.)

   a) *feminam   Old French   femme (final e = [ə])   'woman'
   b) *lumine   Spanish   lumbre   'fire'
   c) *tremulare   Spanish   temblar   'tremble'
   d) *stuppam   Spanish   estopa   'tow'
   e) *populu   Romanian   plop   'poplar'

7. Taking into consideration the Great English Vowel Shift (Section 2.4), give all the changes necessary to derive the Modern English forms from the Old English forms. (*Note:* Assume, simplifying somewhat, that the Old English forms were pronounced as they are written.)

Old English	*Modern English*
a) brōde	brood [brud]
b) cnotta (c = [k])	knot [nɑt]
c) wīse	wise [wajz]
d) hlæfdige	lady [lejdi]

8. Compare the Old English singular and plural forms:

Singular	*Plural*	
bōc	bēc	'book(s)'
āc	æc	'oak(s)'

   Although the Old English words have a plural form that was brought about by umlaut (as in Old English gōs/gēs 'goose/geese'), the Modern English forms do not. Explain how the change in plural formation in Modern English could have come about. (See Sections 1.2, 3.3, and 3.4.)

9. Look up the following words in a good dictionary. Discuss any semantic changes that have affected the underlined portions since Old English. Do you think speakers of Modern English have reanalyzed any of these forms in terms of folk etymology? (See Sections 3.3 and 3.4.)

   a) wed<u>lock</u>
   b) witch<u>craft</u>
   c) stead<u>fast</u>
   d) after<u>ward</u>

10. As evident in the following sentence, Shona, a modern Bantu language, has SVO word order. (*Note*: The morpheme *ano-* marks present tense.)

    mwana   anotengesa   miriwo
    child   sells   vegetables
    'The child sells vegetables.'

By contrast, Shona's word structure reflects a different pattern, as evident in the following examples.

mwana   ano**mu**ona
child   **him**+*see*
'The child sees him.'

mukadzi   ano**va**batsira
woman   **them**+*help*
'The woman helps them.'

What do these examples indicate about earlier Shona or Proto-Bantu word order? (See Section 4.1.)

11. Consider the following lyrics from the Middle English song "Sumer is i-cumen in." Compare the Middle English lyrics with the Modern English translation and answer the questions that follow.

Original text
Sumer is i-cumen in;
Lhude sing, cuccu!
Grōweþ sēd, and blōweþ mēd,
And springþ þe wude nū.

Transcription
[sʊmər ɪs ɪkʊmən ɪn
luːdə sɪŋg kʊkku
grɔːwəθ seːd and blɔːwəθ meːd
and sprɪŋgθ ðə wʊdə nuː]

Translation
'Summer has come in;
Loudly sing, cuckoo!
Seed grows and meadow blooms
And the wood grows now.'

i) What affix converted the adjective *loud* into an adverb in Middle English? (See Section 3.4.)

ii) What accounts for the difference between the Middle English and Modern English pronunciation of the vowel in *loud*? (See Section 2.4.)

iii) What other words in this poem reflect this general shift? (See Section 2.4.)

iv) How has the relative ordering of the subject and verb changed since this was written? (See Section 4.1.)

v) How has the third-person singular present tense suffix changed since Middle English? (See Section 3.)

12. The following words found in various Cree dialects were borrowed from French as the result of contact between the two groups on the Canadian prairies. (Notice that the French determiner was not treated as a separate morpheme and was carried along with the borrowed word.) Why were these words borrowed? (See Section 5.1.)

	Cree	*French*	
a)	/labutoːn/	le bouton	'button'
b)	/lɪːbot/	les bottes	'boots'
c)	/lamilaːs/	la mélasse	'molasses'
d)	/lapwɪːl/	la poêle	'frying pan'
e)	/litɪː/	le thé	'tea'

13. All of the following English words at one time had meanings that are quite different from their current ones. Identify each of these semantic changes as an instance of narrowing, broadening, amelioration, pejoration, weakening, or shift. (See Section 5.3.)

Word	Earlier meaning
a) moody	'brave'
b) uncouth	'unknown'
c) aunt	'father's sister'
d) butcher	'one who slaughters goats'
e) witch	'male or female sorcerer'
f) sly	'skillful'
g) accident	'an event'
h) argue	'make clear'
i) carry	'transport by cart'
j) grumble	'murmur, make low sounds'
k) shrewd	'depraved, wicked'
l) praise	'set a value on'
m) ordeal	'trial by torture'
n) picture	'a painted likeness'
o) seduce	'persuade someone to desert his or her duty'
p) box	'a small container made of boxwood'
q) baggage	'a worthless person'
r) virtue	'qualities one expects of a man'
s) myth	'story'
t) undertaker	'one who undertakes'
u) hussy	'housewife'
v) astonish	'strike by thunder'
w) write	'scratch'
x) quell	'kill'

14. The following line is from *Troilus and Criseyde V* by Geoffrey Chaucer.

His lighte goost ful blisfully is went.
[hɪs liçtə gɔːst fʊl blɪsfʊlli ɪs wɛnt] ([ç] is a voiceless palatal fricative).
'His light spirit has gone very blissfully.'

a) How has the meaning of the word *ghost* changed since Chaucer's time? (See Section 5.3.)

b) Describe the changes that have taken place in the pronunciation of *light* and *ghost*. (See Section 2.)

15. Attempt to reconstruct the Proto-Germanic form for each pair of cognates. Focusing on the vowels, describe the changes that affected the Old English forms. (See Section 7.1.) (*Note*: y = [y], a high front rounded vowel; œ = [ø], a mid front rounded vowel; c = [k]; and j = [j].)

Gothic	Old English	
a) kuni	cyn	'kin'
b) badi	bed	'bed'

c) dōmjan	dœman	'to judge, to deem'
d) sōkjan	sœcan	'to seek'
e) bugjan	bycgan	'to buy'
f) nati	net	'net'

16. Reconstruct the Proto-Romance form for each set of cognates. Give all the changes necessary to derive each of the modern forms from the protoforms. If you are not sure how to proceed, return to Section 7. (*Note*: The Spanish and Romanian spelling <ie> represents the sequence /je/, and the Romanian spelling <ia> represents the sequence /ja/.)

Spanish	*Sardinian*	*Romanian*	
a) vida	bita	vită (ă = [ə])	'life'
b) sí	si	și (ș = [ʃ])	'yes'; 'and' (Rom.)
c) riso	rizu	rîs	'laugh'
d) miel	mele	miere	'honey'
e) hierro	ferru	fier	'iron'
f) piedra	pedra	piatră (ă = [ə])	'stone'
g) hierba	erva	iarbă (ă = [ə])	'grass'
h) oso	ursu	urs	'bear'
i) roto	ruttu	rupt	'broken'
j) lecho	lettu	–	'bed'

(Data from *Source Book for Linguistics* by W. Cowan and J. Rakusan. Philadelphia, PA: John Benjamins, 1987.)

 **LaunchPad Solo**
macmillan learning | For more helpful content and quizzes, go to the LaunchPad Solo for *Contemporary Linguistics* at **launchpadworks.com**.

First Language Acquisition

William O'Grady
Sook Whan Cho

*The only language that [people] learn perfectly is acquired [in]
childhood when no one can teach [them].*
–MARIA MONTESSORI, *The Absorbent Mind* (1949)

OBJECTIVES

In this chapter, you will learn:
• how first language acquisition is studied
• how children learn to understand and pronounce the sounds of their language
• how children develop a vocabulary
• how children's morphology develops
• what stages children go through in their production of sentences
• what factors influence first language acquisition

 **LaunchPad Solo** | For more helpful content and quizzes, go to the LaunchPad Solo
macmillan learning | for *Contemporary Linguistics* at **launchpadworks.com**.

A major landmark in human development is the acquisition of language. Most
children acquire language quickly and effortlessly, giving the impression that the
entire process is simple and straightforward. However, the true extent of children's
achievement becomes evident when we compare their success with the difficulties
encountered by adults who try to learn a second language. Understanding how children the world over are able to master the complexities of human language in the
space of a few short years has become one of the major goals of contemporary linguistic research.

This chapter provides a brief overview of the progress that has been made in this area. We will begin by considering the research strategies used by linguists and psychologists in the study of linguistic development. We will then describe some of the major findings concerning children's acquisition of the various parts of their language—phonology, vocabulary, morphology, syntax, and semantics. The chapter concludes with a brief examination of the contribution of the linguistic environment to language acquisition, the relationship between the emergence of language and cognitive development, and the possible existence of inborn linguistic knowledge.

1   The Study of Language Acquisition

Although we commonly refer to the emergence of language in children as "language acquisition," the end result of this process is actually a **grammar**—the mental system that allows people to speak and understand a language. There are at least two reasons for believing that the development of linguistic skills must involve the acquisition of a grammar.

First, mature language users are able to produce and understand an unlimited number of novel sentences. This can only happen if, as children, they have acquired the grammar for their language. Simple memorization of a fixed inventory of words and sentences would not equip learners to deal with previously unheard utterances— a basic requisite of normal language use.

A second indication that children acquire grammatical rules comes from their speech errors, which often provide valuable clues about how the acquisition process works. Even run-of-the-mill errors such as *doed, *runned, and *goed can be informative. Since adults don't talk that way, such errors tell us that children don't just imitate what they hear. Rather, they create rules of their own to capture the regularities that they observe in the speech of those around them.

LANGUAGE MATTERS   Darwin the Linguist

One of the first language diarists was Charles Darwin, who kept a detailed record of the development of his son. Among the observations in "A Biographical Sketch on an Infant" (1877) is the following anecdote: "At exactly the age of a year, he invented a word for food, namely *mum*. . . . And now instead of beginning to cry when he was hungry, he used the word in a demonstrative manner or as a verb, implying 'Give me food'."

In *The Descent of Man*, Darwin wrote that language "has justly been considered as one of the chief distinctions between man and the lower animals."

Information from: Charles Darwin, "A Biographical Sketch on an Infant," *Mind* 2 (1877): 285–294; Charles Darwin, *The Descent of Man, and Selection in Relation to Sex* (New York: D. Appleton, 1882), 84.

1.1 Methods

Two complementary methods of data collection are used in the study of child language—naturalistic observation and experimentation.

Two Approaches

In the **naturalistic approach**, investigators observe and record children's spontaneous utterances. One type of naturalistic investigation is the so-called **diary study**, in which a researcher (often a parent) keeps daily notes on a child's linguistic progress. Here's a short example, drawn from a diary tracking a child's early vocabulary development.

Date	Child's word	Adult word	Comment
June 9, 2003	krakuh	cracker	said several times to refer to Japanese crackers; used a few days later to refer to graham crackers
June 24, 2003	G	MG	said on several occasions while pointing at the MG symbol on her father's shirt; used on July 24 to refer to an actual MG roadster

Another way to collect naturalistic data involves regular taping sessions, often at biweekly intervals, to gather samples (usually an hour at a time) of the child interacting with his or her caregivers. Detailed transcripts are then made for subsequent analysis. A great deal of data of this type is available online through CHILDES (the Child Language Data Exchange System). Here is a small excerpt from a CHILDES transcript containing a fragment of a conversation between Adam (aged 2 years, 4 months) and his mother:

ADAM: read book.
MOT: papa bear.
MOT: yes.
ADAM: bunny rabbit.
MOT: did you see bunny rabbit?
ADAM: bunny rabbit rabbit running.
MOT: bunny rabbit running?

The CHILDES database includes thousands of hours of data from more than twenty languages.

Naturalistic studies tend to be **longitudinal** in that they examine language development over an extended period of time (sometimes as long as several years). As the name suggests, longitudinal studies take a long time to conduct, but they have the advantage of permitting researchers to observe development as an ongoing process in individual children.

Naturalistic data collection provides a great deal of information about how the language acquisition process unfolds, but it also has its shortcomings. The most serious of these is that particular structures and phenomena may occur rarely in children's everyday speech, making it difficult to gather enough information from natural speech samples to test hypotheses or draw firm conclusions. This problem is further compounded by the fact that speech samples from individual children capture only a small portion of their utterances at any given point in development. Because of the amount of time required to transcribe and analyze recordings, researchers typically have to be content with hour-long samples taken at weekly or biweekly intervals.

In **experimental studies**, researchers typically make use of specially designed tasks to elicit linguistic activity relevant to the phenomenon that they wish to study. The child's performance is then used to formulate hypotheses about the type of grammatical system acquired at that point in time.

Experimental research is typically **cross-sectional** in that it investigates and compares the linguistic knowledge of different children at a particular point in time. A typical cross-sectional study might involve conducting a single experiment with a group of two-year-olds, a group of four-year-olds, and a group of six-year-olds, taking each of these groups to be representative of a particular stage or cross-section of the developmental process.

Types of Experimental Studies

Experimental studies usually employ tasks that test children's comprehension, production, or imitation skills. One widely used method for testing comprehension calls for children to judge the truth of statements that are made about particular pictures or situations presented to them by the experimenter. Figure 9.1 offers an example of one such task. In this particular case, many preschool children respond by saying "no," justifying their answer by noting that one of the boxes doesn't have a ball on it!

A second method for testing comprehension involves supplying children with an appropriate set of props and then asking them to act out the meaning of a sentence—perhaps a passive structure such as *The truck was bumped by the car.* Children's responses can provide valuable clues about the type of grammatical rules being used to interpret sentences at various stages of development.

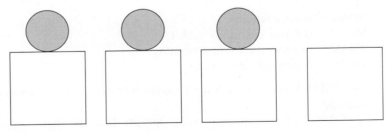

Figure 9.1 "Every ball is on a box."

In a typical production task, the experimenter presents the child with a situation that calls for a particular type of statement or question. In order to determine whether three-year-old children correctly order the auxiliary verb and the subject when asking *yes-no* questions, for instance, a researcher might design a game in which the child asks a puppet for his opinion about various pictures, as in the example in Figure 9.2.

Figure 9.2   "Ask the puppet if the dog is smiling."

If all goes well, the child will respond by asking a question, which allows us to look for signs of Inversion—the operation that places the auxiliary verb before the subject, as in *Is the dog smiling?*

Although production tasks can be useful for assessing certain types of linguistic knowledge, many structures are hard to elicit, even from adults, because they are used only in special contexts. (For example, passive sentences such as *The house was painted by students* are quite rare and are reserved for situations in which the speaker wants to highlight the undergoer of an action.) Moreover, because children's ability to comprehend language is often more advanced than their ability to produce sentences of their own, production tasks can provide an overly conservative view of linguistic development unless they are accompanied by other types of tests.

Experiments that have children imitate model sentences can also provide important clues about grammatical development. Although imitation might appear to be easy, it has been found that children's ability to repeat a particular structure provides a good indication of how well they have mastered it. For instance, a child who has not yet acquired auxiliary verbs will repeat the sentence *Mickey is laughing* as *Mickey laughing*.

The principal advantage of the experimental approach is that it allows researchers to collect data of a very specific sort about particular phenomena or structures. Experimentation is not without its pitfalls, however. In addition to the difficulty of designing a good experiment, there is always the possibility that a child's performance will be affected by extraneous factors, such as inattention, shyness, or a failure to understand what is expected. Nonetheless, by using experimental techniques together with naturalistic observation, linguists and psychologists have made significant progress toward understanding the language acquisition process. This chapter is devoted to a survey of this progress, beginning with the development of speech sounds.

2 Phonological Development

Children seem to be born with a perceptual system that is especially designed for listening to speech. Newborns respond differently to human voices than to other sounds, they show a preference for the language of their parents over other languages by the time they are two days old, and they can recognize their mother's voice within a matter of weeks.

From around one month of age, children exhibit the ability to distinguish among certain speech sounds. In one experiment, infants were presented with a series of identical [ba] syllables. These were followed by an occurrence of the syllable [pa]. A change in the children's sucking rate (measured by a specially designed pacifier) indicated that they perceived the difference between the two syllables and that they were therefore able to distinguish between [p] and [b].

2.1 Babbling

The ability to produce speech sounds begins to emerge around six months of age, with the onset of **babbling**. Babbling provides children with the opportunity to experiment with and begin to gain control over their vocal apparatus—an important prerequisite for later speech. Children who are unable to babble for medical reasons (because of the need for a breathing tube in their throat, for example) can subsequently acquire normal pronunciation, but their speech development is significantly delayed.

Despite obvious differences among the languages to which they are exposed, children from different linguistic communities exhibit significant similarities in their babbling. The tendencies in Table 9.1 are based on data from fifteen different languages,

---

LANGUAGE MATTERS   Hearing It All

Infants are even able to distinguish between sounds in unfamiliar languages. In one experiment, six- to eight-month-old infants who were being raised in English-speaking homes could hear contrasts among unfamiliar consonants in Hindi and Nlaka'pmx (a Native American language spoken on parts of Canada's west coast). By the time they were ten to twelve months old, though, this ability had begun to diminish.

Information from: P. Iverson, P. K. Kuhl, R. Akahane-Yamada, E. Diesch, Y. Tohkura, A. Kettermann, and C. Siebert, "A Perceptual Interference Account of Acquisition Difficulties for Non-native Phonemes," *Cognition* 87, 1 (2003): B47–57; P. K. Kuhl, K. A. Williams, F. Lacerda, K. N. Stevens, and B. Lindblom, "Language Experience Alters Phonetic Perception in Infants by Six Months of Age," *Science* 255 (1992): 606–608; Janet Werker, Valerie Lloyd, Judith Pegg, and Linda Polka, "Putting the Baby in the Bootstraps: Toward a More Complete Understanding of the Role of the Input in Infant Speech Processing," in *Signal to Syntax*, ed. J. Morgan and K. Demuth (Mahwah, NJ: Erlbaum, 1996), 427–447; Katherine Yoshida, Ferran Pons, Jessica Maye, and Janet Werker, "Distributional Phonetic Learning at Ten Months of Age," *Infancy* 15 (2010): 420–433.

including English, Thai, Japanese, Arabic, Hindi, and Mayan. (We focus here on consonant sounds, for which the data is somewhat more reliable than for vowels.)

Table 9.1   Cross-linguistic similarities in babbling

Frequently found consonants				Infrequently found consonants			
p	b	m		f	v	θ	ð
t	d	n		ʃ	ʒ	tʃ	dʒ
k	g			l	ɹ	ŋ	
s	h	w	j				

Such cross-linguistic similarities suggest that early babbling is at least partly independent of the particular language to which children are exposed. In fact, even deaf children babble, although their articulatory activity is somewhat less varied than that of hearing children.

2.2   Developmental Order

Babbling increases in frequency until the age of about twelve months, at which time it begins to give way to intelligible words. By the time children have acquired fifty words or so (usually by around eighteen months of age), they begin to adopt fairly regular patterns of pronunciation.

Although there is a good deal of variation from child to child in terms of the order in which speech sounds are mastered in production and perception, the following general tendencies seem to exist.

- As a group, vowels are generally acquired before consonants (by age three).

- Stops tend to be acquired before other consonants.

- In terms of place of articulation, labials are often acquired first, followed (with some variation) by alveolars, velars, and alveopalatals. Interdentals ([θ] and [ð]) are acquired last.

- New phonemic contrasts manifest themselves first in word-initial position. Thus, the /p/-/b/ contrast, for instance, is manifested in pairs such as *pat-bat* before *cap-cab*.

By age two, a typical English-speaking child has the inventory of consonant phonemes shown in Table 9.2.

Table 9.2   Typical consonant inventory at age two

Stops		Nasals	Fricatives	Other
p	b	m	f	w
t	d	n	s	
k	g			

By age four, this inventory is considerably larger and typically includes the sounds shown in Table 9.3.

Table 9.3   Typical consonant inventory at age four

Stops		Nasals	Fricatives		Affricates		Other	
p	b	m	f	v	tʃ	dʒ	w	j
t	d	n	s	z			1	ɹ
k	g	ŋ	ʃ					

Still to be acquired at this age are the interdental fricatives [θ] and [ð] and the voiced alveopalatal fricative [ʒ].

In general, the relative order in which sounds are acquired reflects their distribution in the world's languages. The sounds that are acquired early tend to be found in more languages whereas the sounds that are acquired late tend to be less common across languages.

2.3   Early Phonetic Processes

Children's ability to perceive the phonemic contrasts of their language develops well in advance of their ability to produce them. So even children who are unable to produce the difference between words like *mouse* and *mouth*, *cart* and *card*, or *jump* and *dump* may nonetheless be able to point to pictures of the correct objects in a comprehension task. Moreover, as the following experimenter's report vividly illustrates, children distinguish phonemes even when they cannot yet produce them.

> One of us spoke to a child who called his inflated plastic fish a *fis*. In imitation of the child's pronunciation, the observer said: "This is your *fis*?" "No," said the child, "my *fis*." He continued to reject the adult's imitation until he was told, "That is your *fish*." "Yes," he said, "my *fis*."

The child's reaction to the adult's initial pronunciation of *fish* shows that he could perceive the difference between /s/ and /ʃ/ and that he had correctly represented the word as /fɪʃ/ in his lexicon even though he could not yet produce it himself.

What precisely is responsible for the special character of the sound patterns in children's early speech? The key seems to lie in the operation of a limited number of universal phonetic processes.

Syllable Deletion

Because syllables bearing primary or secondary stress (marked below by ' and ˌ, respectively) are more noticeable than their unstressed counterparts, they tend to be more salient to children in the early stages of the language acquisition process. As a result, stressed syllables are more likely to be retained in children's pronunciation than are unstressed syllables (see Table 9.4).

Table 9.4 Differences in the retention of stressed and unstressed syllables

Word	Child's pronunciation
hip po 'po ta mus	[pɑs]
spa 'ghe tti	[gɛ]
'he li ˌcop ter	[ɛlkɑt]
kan ga 'roo	[wu]
'te le ˌphone	[fow]

Note: ' = primary stress; ˌ = secondary stress

However, unstressed syllables in final position tend to be retained, probably because the ends of words are easier to remember (see Table 9.5).

Table 9.5 Retention of unstressed syllables in final position

Word	Child's pronunciation
po 'ta to	[tejdo]
ba 'na na	[nænə]
to 'ma to	[mejdo]
'el e phant	[ɛlfən]

Syllable Simplification

Another frequent process in children's speech involves the systematic deletion of certain sounds in order to simplify syllable structure. In the data in Table 9.6, typical of the speech of two- and three-year-old children, consonant clusters are reduced by deleting one or more segments.

Table 9.6 Reduction of consonant clusters

Cluster	Strategy	Examples
[s] + stop	delete [s]	stop → [tɑp] small → [mɑ] desk → [dɛk]
stop + liquid	delete liquid	try → [taj] crumb → [gʌm] bring → [bɪŋ]
fricative + liquid	delete liquid	from → [fʌm] sleep → [sip]
nasal + voiceless stop	delete nasal	bump → [bʌp] tent → [dɛt]

Yet another common deletion process in early child language involves the elimination of final consonants, as in the following examples.

1) dog [dɑ]
  bus [bʌ]
  boot [bu]

Both the reduction of consonant clusters and the deletion of final consonants have the effect of simplifying syllable structure, bringing it closer to the consonant-vowel (CV) template that is universally favored by children and that is the most widely found pattern in human language in general.

Substitution

One of the most widespread phonetic processes in early language involves substitution—the systematic replacement of one sound by an alternative that the child finds easier to articulate (see Table 9.7). Common substitution processes include **stopping**, the replacement of a fricative by a corresponding stop; **fronting**, the moving forward of a sound's place of articulation; **gliding**, the replacement of a liquid by a glide; and **denasalization**, the replacement of a nasal stop by a nonnasal counterpart.

Table 9.7 Substitution in early speech

Process	Example	Change
Stopping (continuant → stop)	sing → [tɪŋ]	s → t
	sea → [ti]	s → t
	zebra → [dibɹə]	z → d
	thing → [tɪŋ]	θ → t
	this [dɪt]	ð → d, s → t
	shoes [tud]	ʃ → t, z → d
Fronting	ship → [sɪp]	ʃ → s
	jump → [dzʌmp]	dʒ → dz
	chalk → [tsɑːk]	tʃ → ts
	go → [dow]	g → d
Gliding	lion → [jajn̩]	l → j
	laughing → [jæfɪŋ]	l → j
	look → [wʊk]	l → w
	rock [wɑk]	ɹ → w
	story → [stowi]	ɹ → w
Denasalization	spoon → [bud]	n → d
	jam → [dæb]	m → b
	room → [wub]	m → b

Assimilation

Still another widespread phonetic process in child language is **assimilation**—the modification of one or more features of a segment under the influence of neighboring sounds. In the following examples, initial consonants have been voiced in anticipation of the following vowel.

2) tell   [dɛl]
   pig   [bɪg]
   push   [bʊs]
   soup   [zup]

Assimilation is also observed in children's tendency to maintain the same place of articulation for all of the consonants or vowels in a word. This can lead to the pronunciation of *doggy* as [gɑgi] (with identical consonants), and [bibi] for *baby* (with identical vowels in both syllables). Other examples include [fɛlf] for *self*, [kæklin] for *Cathleen*, and [næns] for *dance*.

3   Vocabulary Development

By age eighteen months or so, the average child has a vocabulary of fifty words or more. Common items include the words listed in Table 9.8.

Table 9.8 Common items in the first fifty words

Entities: Words referring to
    people: *daddy, mommy, baby*
    food/drink: *juice, milk, cookie, water, toast, apple, cake*
    animals: *dog, cat, duck, horse*
    clothes: *shoes, hat*
    toys: *ball, blocks*
    vehicles: *car, boat, truck*
    other: *bottle, key, book*

Properties: *hot, all-gone, more, dirty, cold, here, there*
Actions: *up, sit, see, eat, go, down*
Personal-social: *hi, bye, no, yes, please, thank-you*

Note: Hyphens are used here to indicate that these expressions are not yet segmented into their component words.

As Table 9.8 shows, noun-like words make up the single largest class in the child's early vocabulary, with verb- and adjective-like words being the next most frequent category types. Among the most frequent words are expressions for displeasure or rejection (such as *no*) and various types of social interaction (such as *please* and *bye*). Over the next months, this vocabulary grows rapidly, sometimes by as much as

LANGUAGE MATTERS   Moving Along

Every child develops at his or her own pace, of course, but to the extent that we can depict a "typical" profile for vocabulary development, it would look something like this. Note the relatively slow start (just fifty words in eighteen months), followed by a rapid acceleration that is sustained over a multiyear period.

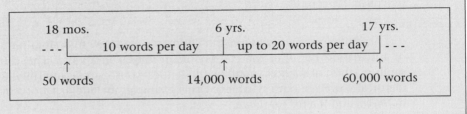

ten or twelve words a day. By age six, most children have mastered about 13,000 or 14,000 words.

Children seem to differ somewhat in the types of words that they focus on, especially in the early stages of language acquisition. One of these differences is reflected in the number of nouns in early vocabulary. Whereas some children have a relatively high proportion of such words (75 percent or more) by age two, other learners exhibit a much lower percentage of nouns (50 percent or less). Making up for the smaller number of nouns is a larger vocabulary of socially useful expressions such as *bye*, *go-away*, *stop-it*, *thank-you*, *I-want-it*, and so on.

3.1   Strategies for Acquiring Word Meaning

Children seem to draw on certain strategies when trying to determine the meaning of a new word. This is perhaps easiest to illustrate in the case of noun-type meanings, for which the following strategies appear to be employed.

3) Three strategies for learning the meanings of new words:

The Whole Object Assumption
A new word refers to a whole object.

The Type Assumption
A new word refers to a type of thing, not just to a particular thing.

The Basic Level Assumption
A new word refers to objects that are alike in basic ways (appearance, behavior, etc.).

To see how these strategies work, imagine that a father and his eighteen-month-old son are driving through the countryside and they encounter a sheep munching on the grass. The father points to the animal and says "sheep." What does the child think the word means? Does it mean 'white'? Or does it mean 'woolly'? Does it refer to the animal? Or to parts of the animal? Or does it refer to the fact that a particular animal is munching on grass?

The Whole Object Assumption allows the child to infer that the word *sheep* refers to the animal itself, not to its parts, not to its whiteness, and not to its woolliness. The Type Assumption allows him to infer that *sheep* refers to a type of animal, not to just one particular sheep. And the Basic Level Assumption leads him to guess that *sheep* is used to refer just to white, four-legged, woolly animals, and not to animals in general.

Contextual Clues

Another major factor in vocabulary development is the child's ability to make use of contextual clues to draw inferences about the category and meaning of new words. For instance, from early in the language acquisition process, children can use the presence or absence of determiners to distinguish between names and ordinary nouns. Two-year-old children who are told that a new doll is *a dax* will apply this label to similar-looking dolls as well. However, if they are told that the new doll is *Dax*, they assume that it refers just to the doll they have actually been shown. Like adults, these children treat *dax* as an ordinary noun when it is preceded by *a*, but as a name when there is no determiner.

In another experiment, three- and four-year-old children were asked to act out the meaning of sentences such as "Make it so there is *tiv* to drink in this glass (of water)." The only clues about the interpretation of *tiv* came from the meaning of the rest of the sentence and from the child's understanding of the types of changes that can be made to a glass of water. Not only did more than half the children respond by either adding or removing water, but some even remembered what *tiv* meant two weeks later!

For children to benefit from this sort of experience, they have to have some sense of what other speakers are talking about. The meaning of a new word can hardly be learned if the speaker is referring to one thing and the child is focused on another. Somehow, children have to be in sync with other humans—noticing what they notice and thinking what they are thinking.

This is no trivial matter. In fact, psychologists often note that being able to sense the intentions and thoughts of others in this way requires a theory of mind—an understanding of how other people think and see the world. This is part of what it takes to be a social creature—to fit in to a family and a society. Thus, using the Social Strategy stated in *4* helps children understand words in context.

4) *The Social Strategy*
   To figure out what new words mean, think like other people think.

A variety of experiments help illustrate how children use this strategy. In one experiment involving two-year-old children, an adult looked at and named a toy (saying, "Look! A modi!") just as the child's attention was drawn to another toy by lighting it up. When the children were then asked to retrieve the "modi," they consistently chose the object that the adult had been looking at. Somehow, the children knew that the adult was naming the toy that he was looking at when he spoke, regardless of what else was happening. That's how language is used in ordinary social situations, and part of learning a language involves realizing that simple fact.

3.2   Meaning Errors

The meanings that children associate with their early words sometimes correspond closely to the meanings employed by adults. In many cases, however, the match is less than perfect. The two most typical semantic errors involve **overextension** and **underextension**.

LANGUAGE MATTERS   Fast Mapping

How many times does a child have to hear a new word in order to learn it? In one study, eighteen-month-old children were able to learn pairs of new words after just three exposures. In a study of somewhat older children (two- to five-year-olds), a single encounter with a new word led to impressive success: 81 percent of the children could identify the word's referent the next time they heard it. The rapid learning of new words is called *fast mapping*.

Information from: C. Dollaghan, "Child Meets Word," *Journal of Speech and Hearing Research* 28 (1985): 449–454; C. Houston-Price, K. Plunkett, and P. Harris, "Word Learning Wizardry at 1:6," *Journal of Child Language* 32 (2005): 175–190.

Overextensions

In cases of overextension, the meaning of the child's word is more general or inclusive than that of the corresponding adult form. The word *dog*, for example, is frequently overextended to include horses, cows, and other four-legged animals. Similarly, *ball* is sometimes used for any round object, including a balloon, an Easter egg, a small stone, and so on. As many as one-third of children's words may be overextended at the fifty-word stage of vocabulary development (see Table 9.9).

Physical similarities seem to be a critical factor in children's first hypotheses about word meanings. As a result, children often overextend a word to include a set of perceptually similar objects that they know to have diverse functions. For example, one child used the word *moon* for the moon, grapefruit halves, and a crescent-shaped car light. Another child used the word *money* for a set of objects ranging from pennies to buttons and beads. If you reconsider the examples of overextension given in Table 9.9, you will see that they too can be explained in terms of visible similarities.

Table 9.9   Examples of overextension

Word	First referent	Subsequent extensions
tick tock	watch	clocks, gas meter, fire hose on a spool, scale with round dial
fly	fly	other small insects, specks of dirt, dust, child's toes, crumbs of bread
quack	duck	all birds and insects, flies, coins (with an eagle on the face)
candy	candy	cherries, anything sweet
apple	apples	balls, tomatoes, cherries, onions, biscuits
turtle	turtles	fish, seals
cookie	cookies	crackers, any dessert
kitty	cats	rabbits, any small furry animal
box	boxes	elevators
belt	belts	watch strap

Many overextensions may be deliberate attempts to compensate for vocabulary limitations. One indication of this is that particular overextensions often disappear as soon as children learn the right word for the objects that they have been mislabeling. For example, two-year-old Allen was using the word *dog* for dogs, cats, sheep, and other four-legged mammals, but he stopped doing so as soon as he learned the words *cat* and *sheep*. If he thought that *dog* meant 'animal', he could still have sometimes referred to cats and sheep as *dogs* (just as adults sometimes refer to them as animals). The fact that he didn't suggests that he never thought *dog* meant 'animal'; he had just been "borrowing" it until the right word came along.

A further indication that many overextensions are designed to compensate for vocabulary limitations comes from the fact that children seem to overextend more in their production than in their comprehension. Even children who sometimes use *dog* to refer to cows or horses typically point to the right animal when asked to show the dog to the experimenter (see Figure 9.3). This is not what one would expect if children thought that *dog* meant 'animal'.

Figure 9.3   A sample overextension test

Underextensions

Another possible type of word-meaning error in early language involves underextension, the use of lexical items in an overly restrictive fashion. Thus, *kitty* might be used to refer to the family pet but not to other cats. Or the word *dog* might be used for collies, spaniels, and beagles but not for chihuahuas.

Underextension errors often reflect children's propensity to focus on prototypical or core members of a category. The potential referents of many words differ in terms of how well they exemplify the properties associated with a particular concept. For example, among the potential referents of the word *dog*, golden retrievers and spaniels have more of the properties associated with the concept DOG (long hair, relative size, type of bark, and so on) than do chihuahuas. While the preference for a prototype can be overruled by factors such as the presence of a nontypical category member in the child's everyday experience (e.g., a chihuahua as a family pet), the internal structure of concepts can have an important influence on semantic development.

Verb Meanings

Meaning errors also occur with verbs. For example, some preschool children believe that *fill* means 'pour' rather than 'make full'. So, when asked to decide which of the two series of pictures in Figure 9.4 is an example of filling, they choose the second series—even though the glass remains empty!

Figure 9.4   Sample pictures used to test children's understanding of *fill*. From Gropen, Jess, Steven Pinker, Michelle Hollander, and Richard Goldberg, "Syntax and Semantics in the Acquisition of Locative Verbs," *Journal of Child Language*, 18 (1991): 115–51 (1 figure). Reprinted with the permission of Cambridge University Press.

Not surprisingly, children who make this sort of mistake tend to use *fill* in the wrong syntactic patterns as well.

5) And fill the little sugars up in the bowl . . . (Mark, at age 4 yrs., 7 mos.)
   Can I fill some salt into the [salt shaker]? (E, at age 5 yrs.)

These errors disappear as children come to realize that *fill* means 'make full' rather than 'pour into'.

Dimensional Terms

Terms describing size and dimensions are acquired in a relatively fixed order, depending on their generality (see Table 9.10). The first adjectives of this type to be acquired, *big* and *small*, are the most general in that they can be used for talking about any aspect of size (height, area, volume, and so on). In contrast, the second group of adjectives to emerge—*tall, long, short, high*, and *low*—can only be used for a single dimension (height or length). The remaining modifiers (*thick-thin, wide-narrow*, and *deep-shallow*) are still more restricted in their use since they describe the secondary or less extended dimension of an object. For instance, the dimension of a stick that we describe in terms of width or thickness is almost always less extended than the dimension that we describe in terms of height or length, which tends also to be perceptually more salient.

Table 9.10   Order of acquisition for dimensional adjectives

Step	Words	What they describe
1	*big-small*	any aspect of size
2	*tall-short, long-short, high-low*	a single dimension
3	*thick-thin, wide-narrow, deep-shallow*	a secondary dimension

The difficulty of dimensional adjectives for children is also evident in experimental tasks. In one experiment children aged three to five were shown pairs of objects—sometimes a big one and a tall one (pair [a] in Figure 9.5) and sometimes a big one and a long one (pair [b] in Figure 9.5). Younger children did well when asked to choose "the big one." However, when asked to choose "the tall one" or "the long one," they often picked the big one instead. This suggests that they are initially more sensitive to overall size than to a single dimension like height or length.

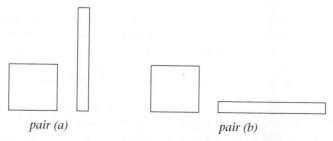

pair (a)   pair (b)

Figure 9.5   Dimensional adjective pairs: *big-tall* versus *big-long*

4   Morphological Development

As is the case with the sound pattern of language and with vocabulary, the details of morphological structure emerge over a period of several years. Initially, affixes are systematically absent and most words consist of a single root morpheme.

4.1   Overgeneralization

Because many common words have irregular inflection in English (*went* as the past tense form of *go*, *ran* as the past form of *run*, *men* as the plural form of *man*), children sometimes begin by simply memorizing inflected words on a case-by-case basis without regard for general patterns or rules. As a result, they may initially use irregular forms such as *men* and *ran* correctly. However, when they subsequently observe the generality of *-s* as a plural marker and *-ed* as a past tense marker (usually around age two and a half), they sometimes use these suffixes for the irregular forms—producing words such as *mans* and *runned*. (Errors that result from the overly broad application of a rule are called **overgeneralizations** or **overregularizations**.) Even occasional mixed forms such as *felled*, a blend of *fell* and *falled*, may occur during this period. (See Table 9.11.)

Table 9.11   The development of affixes

Stage	Affix acquisition	Examples
1	Case-by-case learning	PL *boys, men*; PAST *walked, ran*
2	Overuse of general rule	PL *mans*; PAST *runned*
3	Mastery of exceptions to the general rule	PL *men*; PAST *ran*

One of the best indications that children have mastered an inflectional rule comes from their ability to apply it to forms they have not heard before. In a classic experiment, children were shown a picture of a strange creature and told, "This is a wug." A second picture was then presented and the children were told, "Now, there's

---

LANGUAGE MATTERS   How Many Times Does It Take to Get It Right?

How many times does a child have to hear the adult form of an irregular verb before all overregularizations are eliminated? Several hundred times, according to one estimate. That's why children are often relatively quick at figuring out the right past tense form for frequently heard irregular verbs like *go* and *see*, but take much longer to master less common verbs such as *sink* or *win*.

Information from: Michael Maratsos, "More Overregularizations After All: New Data and Discussion on Marcus, Pinker, Ullman, Hollander, Rosen and Xu," *Journal of Child Language* 27 (2000): 183–212.

another wug. There are two of them. Now, there are two . . . ?" (see Figure 9.6). Even four- and five-year-old children did well with the plural forms of *wug* words, demonstrating that the general rules for inflection have been learned by that time, despite the occurrence of occasional errors.

This is a wug.

Now, there's another wug.
There are two of them.
Now, there are two . . . ?

Figure 9.6   The *wug* test. From Jean Berko Gleason, "The Child's Learning of English Morphology," *Word* 14: 150–77 (1958). Reprinted by permission of Jean Berko Gleason.

Although inflectional overgeneralization is very noticeable in young children's speech and can last into the school years, it doesn't affect all irregular verbs all the time. In fact, preschool children seem to overregularize verbs less than 25 percent of the time at any point in development. This suggests that the overgeneralization errors observed in early speech reflect lapses in accessing the appropriate irregular form from the lexicon rather than the failure to learn irregular forms per se.

4.2   A Developmental Sequence

An important result of early work on child language was the discovery that the development of bound morphemes and functional categories (such as determiners and auxiliaries) takes place in an orderly fashion that is quite similar across children. In a pioneering study of three children between the ages of twenty and thirty-six months, the **developmental sequence** in Table 9.12 was found to be typical.

Table 9.12   Typical developmental sequence for English nonlexical morphemes

1. *-ing*	5. past tense *-ed*
2. plural *-s*	6. third-person singular *-s*
3. possessive *-'s*	7. auxiliary *be*
4. *the, a*	

An interesting feature of this developmental sequence is that it seems to be at least partly independent of the frequency with which the various morphemes occur in adult speech (see Table 9.13). For example, the determiners *the* and *a* are the most frequent morphemes in the children's environment but are nonetheless acquired relatively late.

Table 9.13   Typical relative frequency of morphemes in parental speech

1. *the, a*	5. possessive *-'s*
2. *-ing*	6. third-person singular *-s*
3. plural *-s*	7. past tense *-ed*
4. auxiliary *be*	

This shows that frequency by itself cannot explain developmental order, although it may have some role to play in conjunction with other factors. (It's also clear that pronunciation by itself is not decisive either, since the three *-s* morphemes are acquired at different times.) What, then, determines the order of acquisition of non-lexical categories and bound morphemes?

Research on a variety of languages suggests that several factors are involved.

1. ***Frequent occurrence, especially in utterance-final position*** Children show a greater tendency to notice and remember elements that occur at the end of the utterance than those found in any other position.

2. ***Syllabicity*** Children seem to take greater notice of morphemes such as *-ing*, which can constitute syllables on their own, than the plural or possessive suffix *-'s*, whose principal allomorphs (/-s/ and /-z/) are single consonants.

3. ***Absence of homophony*** Whereas the word *the* functions only as a determiner in English, the suffix *-s* can be used to mark any one of three things: plural number in nouns, third-person singular in verbs, or possession. The resulting complication in the relationship between form and meaning may impede acquisition.

4. ***Few or no exceptions in the way it is used*** Whereas all singular nouns form the possessive with *-'s*, not all verbs use *-ed* to mark the past tense (*saw*, *read*, *drove*). Such exceptions hinder the language acquisition process.

5. ***Allomorphic invariance*** Whereas the affix *-ing* has the same form for all verbs, the past tense ending *-ed* has three allomorphs—/-t/ for verbs such as *chase*, /-d/ for forms such as *love*, and /-əd/ for verbs such as *decide*. This type of allomorphic variation, which also occurs with the plural, possessive, and third-person singular affixes in English, slows morphological development.

6. ***Clearly discernible semantic function*** Whereas morphemes such as plural *-s* express easily identifiable meanings, some morphemes (such as the third-person singular *-s*, as in *She works hard*) make no obvious contribution to the meaning of the sentence. Acquisition of this latter type of morpheme is relatively slow.

4.3   Word Formation Processes

The major word formation processes in English—derivation and compounding—both emerge early in the acquisition of English. The first derivational suffixes to show up in children's speech are the ones that are most common in the adult language (see Table 9.14).

Table 9.14   Suffixes in the speech of a child prior to age four

Ending	Meaning	Example
-er	'doer'	walk<u>er</u>
-ie	'diminutive'	dogg<u>ie</u>
-ing	'activity'	Runn<u>ing</u> is fun.
-ness	'state'	happi<u>ness</u>

Note: The suffix *-er* can also have an 'instrument' meaning, as in *cutter* 'something used for cutting', but this is less frequent in children's early speech.

Children as young as three demonstrate an ability to use derivation to make up names for agents when presented with questions such as the following.

> "I've got a picture here of someone who crushes things. What could we call someone who crushes things? Someone who crushes things is called a . . ."

Children exhibit a propensity for forming compounds, especially of the N-N type. When asked "What would you call a boy who rips paper?", they don't hesitate to respond "a paper ripper." However, some of the compounds found in the spontaneous speech of three- and four-year-olds do not follow the usual pattern for English compounds (e.g., the verb-noun pattern *open man* for 'someone who opens things' and *cutter grass* for 'grass cutter'), but these disappear by age five. Other early compounds have the right structure but are inappropriate because English already has words with the intended meaning (see Table 9.15).

Table 9.15   Some innovative compounds

Child's word	Intended meaning
car-smoke	'exhaust'
cup-egg	'boiled egg'
firetruck-man	'fire fighter'
plant-man	'gardener'
store-man	'clerk'
leg-pit	'area behind the knee'

Children's creativity with compounds points to a preference for building words from other words, perhaps because this places less demand on memory than does learning an entirely new word for each concept.

LANGUAGE MATTERS   It Takes a While

The full derivational system continues to develop well into the school years. Even ten-year-olds have some difficulty using suffixes to recognize the category of unfamiliar words, as when they are asked which of four words best fits in a sentence such as the following:

You can _____ the effect by turning off the lights.

intensify   intensification
intensity   intensive

They have even more trouble when the possible words are made up rather than real:

I wish Dr. Who would just _____ and get it over with.

transumpation   transumpative
transumpate   transumpatic

Information from: A. Tyler and W. Nagy, "The Acquisition of English Derivational Morphology," *Journal of Memory and Language* 28 (1989): 649–667.

Even the subtlest properties of word formation seem to be acquired in the preschool years. One such property involves the fact that an inflectional suffix such as the plural cannot occur inside compounds (compare **dogs catcher* with *dog catcher*). In one study, children as young as three years of age produced compounds that obeyed this constraint. Thus, when asked a question such as "What do you call someone who eats cookies?", they responded by saying *cookie eater* rather than **cookies eater*.

5   Syntactic Development

Like phonological and morphological development, the emergence of syntactic structure takes place in an orderly manner and reveals much about the nature of the language acquisition process. We will briefly survey some of the milestones in this developmental process here.

5.1   The One-Word Stage

As noted earlier, children begin to produce one-word utterances between the ages of twelve and eighteen months. A basic property of these one-word utterances is that they can be used to express the type of meaning that is associated with an entire sentence in adult speech. Thus, a child might use the word *dada* to assert 'I see Daddy', *more* to mean 'Give me more juice', and *up* to mean 'I want up'. Such utterances are called **holophrases** (literally 'whole sentences').

In forming holophrastic utterances, children seem to choose the most informative word that applies to the situation at hand. A child who wants juice, for example, would say *juice* rather than *want* since *juice* is more informative in this situation. Similarly, a child who notices a new doll would be more likely to say *doll* than *see*, referring to the most novel feature of the situation he or she is trying to describe.

Table 9.16 presents examples of the types of holophrastic meaning that children commonly express during the **one-word stage**.

Table 9.16 Semantic relations in children's one-word utterances

Semantic relation	Utterance	Situation
Agent of an action	*dada*	as father enters the room
Action or state	*down*	as child sits down
Undergoer (or theme)	*door*	as father closes the door
Location	*here*	as child points
Recipient	*mama*	as child gives mother something
Recurrence	*again*	as child watches lighting of a match

Comprehension appears to be considerably in advance of production in the one-word stage, and children are able to understand many multiword utterances during this period. One indication of this comes from an experiment in which children in the one-word stage listened to sentences such as *Big Bird is hugging Cookie Monster* as an experimenter tracked their gaze toward competing pictures: the children preferred to look at a depiction of Big Bird hugging Cookie Monster rather than the reverse situation.

5.2 The Two-Word Stage

Within a few months of their first one-word utterances, children begin to produce two-word mini-sentences. Table 9.17 provides a sampling of these utterances and the types of meaning they are commonly used to express. (Although these examples are from English, similar patterns are found in the early development of all languages.)

Table 9.17 Some patterns in children's two-word speech

Utterance	Intended meaning	Semantic relation
Baby chair	'The baby is sitting on the chair.'	agent-location
Doggy bark	'The dog is barking.'	agent-action
Ken water	'Ken is drinking water.'	agent-theme
Hit doggy	'I hit the doggy.'	action-theme
Daddy hat	'Daddy's hat'	possessor-possessed

Early multiword utterances tend to exemplify a relatively small number of "slot-and-frame" patterns: *It's-a__, more__, no__, see__,* and so on. It is unclear whether children have acquired syntactic categories such as noun, verb, and adjective at this point in their development. This is because the markers that help distinguish among syntactic categories in adult English (e.g., inflection such as the past tense suffix and functional categories such as determiners and auxiliary verbs) are absent during this period. To complicate matters still further, the relative shortness of the utterances produced during the **two-word stage** means that the positional differences associated with category distinctions in adult speech are often not manifested. Thus, words such as *busy* (an adjective in adult speech) and *push* (a verb) may appear in identical patterns.

6) Mommy busy.
   Mommy push.

While this does not show that children lack syntactic categories, it makes it difficult to demonstrate that they possess them. For this reason, researchers are split over whether to describe children's utterances in terms of the syntactic categories of adult speech.

A notable feature of children's two-word utterances is that they almost always exhibit the appropriate word order, and there is some reason to think that learners have a general word order rule by the time they are three years old. Not only do they use the right subject–verb–direct object order in their own speech, they are reluctant to abandon this pattern, even when experimenters present them with verbs used in novel orders. In one experiment, for instance, children aged two to four were taught made-up verbs (such as *tam*, *gop*, and *dack*) for novel actions involving puppet characters. The verbs were presented using the following orders:

7) *subject-verb-object order*: Elmo tammed the apple.
   subject-object-verb order: Elmo the apple gopped.
   verb-subject-object order: Dacked Elmo the apple.

Even very young children were far more likely to reproduce the experimenter's utterance when it contained the standard word order and rarely adopted an unusual word order for new verbs.

5.3   The Telegraphic Stage

After a period of several months during which their speech is largely limited to one- and two-word utterances, children begin to produce longer and more complex grammatical structures, drawing on an ever-growing store of words. As illustrated in the sentences in example *8*, a defining feature of these patterns is the frequent absence of bound morphemes and nonlexical categories.

8) Chair broken.
   Daddy like book.
   What her name?
   Man ride bus today.
   Car make noise.
   Me wanna show Mommy.
   I good boy.

Linguists often call such speech telegraphic, thanks to its resemblance to the clipped style of language found in the now-defunct telegram (a pretexting form of written communication that required paying by the word).

Although it is certainly true that many important morphemes are missing from children's early speech, these items do not go entirely unnoticed. As noted in Section 3.1, for instance, children as young as seventeen months can infer from the presence or absence of a determiner whether a novel word refers to a type of object (e.g., a doll) or to a particular object. Eighteen-month-olds pay more attention to sentences containing an *is + V-ing* pattern (e.g., *she is playing*) than to one containing the ungrammatical *she can playing*. And infants as young as eleven months of age are surprised when *a* or *the* is replaced by a nonsense syllable, or when it is used in the wrong place, as in *book the*.

The **telegraphic stage** is characterized by the emergence of quite elaborate types of phrase structure. As the examples in *8* show, children can form phrases consisting of a head and a complement (*like book, ride bus, show mommy*), phrases that include a modifier (such as *today* and *good*), and even full-fledged sentences. Table 9.18 summarizes the stages in the development of phrase structure.

Table 9.18   The development of phrase structure

Stage	Approx. age	Developments
Holophrastic	1–1.5 yrs.	single word utterances; no structure
Two-word	1.5–2 yrs.	early word combinations; presence of syntactic categories unclear
Telegraphic	2–2.5 yrs.	emergence of phrase structure

Language development from this point onward is rapid. As the examples in Table 9.19 illustrate, in a matter of just a few months children move from relatively primitive two- and three-word utterances at the beginning of the telegraphic stage to a broad range of morphologically and syntactically intricate sentence types.

Table 9.19   Sample utterances from a child's speech over an 11-month period

Age	Sample utterances
28 mos.	What doing? A bunny-rabbit walk Like some?
30 mos.	Take a button off. Dis a other one. Dat's a my pencil. Hand me a piece of paper.
32 mos.	This is heavy. You going faster? Where horses go? Go down right side.

Table 9.19   Continued

34 mos.	Let me have one.
	Some kind fishing rod.
	Want some milk in it.
	Heard you talking.
	Look at that train Ursula brought.
	Is this goes over here?
36 mos.	Do you want me eat with that fork?
	I want to sit on steps.
	I'm going give Robin that pencil.
	Why not he have ball?
	You going bring raisin tomorrow?
38 mos.	I want to see what's going on in there.
	Let's have something to read.
	Mommy cook something eat.
	I just went to sleep.
	I don't want to go to bed again.
	Mommy, I better go outside and hang yours outside . . .

Data adapted from: Steven Pinker, "Sample Utterances from a Child's Speech," *The Language Instinct* (New York: HarperCollins, 1994), 269–270. Copyright © 1994 by Steven Pinker. Reprinted by permission of HarperCollins Publishers.

5.4   Later Development

In the months following the telegraphic stage, children continue to acquire the complex grammar that underlies adult linguistic competence, including the operations that move various words and phrases to nonbasic positions in the sentence.

Yes-No Questions

In the very early stages of language acquisition, children signal *yes-no* questions by means of rising intonation alone. (Recall that auxiliary verbs are a relatively late development.)

9) See hole?
    I ride train?
    Ball go?
    Sit chair?

Even after individual auxiliary verbs make their appearance, there is often a delay of a few months before Inversion takes place in *yes-no* questions. In one study, for example, a young boy began using the auxiliary verb *can* at age two years, five months, but he did not use it in the presubject position until six months later.

An interesting—but infrequent—error in children's early use of Inversion in both *yes-no* and *wh* questions is exemplified in *10*.

10) *Can* he *can* look?
     What *shall* we *shall* have?
     Did you *did* came home?

In these sentences, the auxiliary verb occurs twice—once before the subject and once after it. It has been suggested that this pattern reflects an error in the use of Inversion that involves leaving a copy of the moved auxiliary behind in its original position.

Wh Questions

Wh questions emerge gradually between the ages of two and four. The first *wh* words to be acquired are typically *what* and *where*, followed by *who*, *how*, and *why*; *when*, *which*, and *whose* are relatively late acquisitions.

11) Where that?
     What me think?
     Why you smiling?
     Why not me drink it?

With the acquisition of auxiliary verbs, Inversion becomes possible. Interestingly, some children appear to find Inversion easier in *yes-no* questions, where it is the only movement operation, than in *wh* questions, where the *wh* word must also be moved. (For some reason, this is especially true in the case of *why* questions.) The following examples from children's speech all show the effects of moving the *wh* word but not the auxiliary verb.

12) What I did yesterday?
     Where I should sleep?
     Why that boy is looking at us?
     Why she doesn't like bananas?
     Why unicorns are pretend?

5.5   The Interpretation of Sentence Structure

The interpretation of sentences draws heavily on various features of syntactic structure. In this section, we will briefly consider some aspects of the acquisition of two interpretive phenomena that rely on information about syntactic structure.

Passives

Children learning English are able to use word order clues to interpret sentences at a very early point in the acquisition process. By the time their average utterance length is two words, they are able to respond correctly about 75 percent of the time to comprehension tests involving simple sentences such as *13*, in which *the truck* is the agent and *the car* is the undergoer (or theme).

13) The truck bumped the car.

However, children find it much harder to interpret certain other types of sentences correctly. This is especially true for passive sentences such as the one in *14*, in which more than just word order matters—the form of the verb and the presence of *by* jointly indicate that the first NP refers to the undergoer rather than the agent.

14) The car was bumped by the truck.

Although children produce passive sentences in their own speech from around age three, they have continuing difficulty responding appropriately to passive constructions in comprehension tests (see Table 9.20).

Table 9.20 Accurate interpretation of passive constructions

Group	Percentage correct
Nursery School	20
Kindergarten	35
Grade 1	48
Grade 2	63
Grade 3	88

Why should this be so? One possibility is that children expect the first NP in a sentence to refer to the agent. This is sometimes called the **Canonical Sentence Strategy**.

15) *The Canonical Sentence Strategy*
NP . . . V . . . NP is interpreted as
agent – action – undergoer

The Canonical Sentence Strategy works for active sentences such as *The truck bumped the car*, but not for passive sentences, where the first NP refers to the undergoer and the second NP to the agent.

16) Active sentence: The truck bumped the car.
                                              agent   *undergoer*
        Passive sentence: The car was bumped by the truck.
                                              undergoer   *agent*

Children employing the Canonical Sentence Strategy associate the first NP with the agent and the second NP with the undergoer, so when they hear the passive sentence in *16*, they think the car bumped the truck.

As the data in Table 9.20 show, this strategy is applied much less consistently by grade one children, who have evidently begun to realize that word order is not the only thing that determines a sentence's interpretation—the verbal construction (*was bumped*) and the presence of a preposition such as *by* also matter. A year or so later, children's scores start to rise dramatically, indicating that they have come to recognize the special properties of the passive construction.

Pronominals and Reflexives

Sometimes, even more abstract features of sentence structure are relevant for comprehension. For example, a defining feature of reflexive pronouns (*myself, himself, herself,* and so on) is that they look to a structurally higher NP for their interpretation. (This NP is called the **antecedent**; a structurally higher NP is said to **c-command** a structurally lower item.)

A sentence's structure can be represented in different ways, but everyone agrees that subjects are always higher than direct objects, no matter what else might be in the sentence.

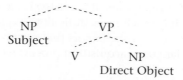

Figure 9.7 Subjects above direct objects in sentence structure

For that reason, it's possible for the antecedent to be the subject and for the reflexive pronoun to be the direct object, but not vice versa.

17) a. Direct object reflexive pronouns with subject antecedent:
    I hurt *myself* with the stapler.
   b. Subject reflexive pronoun with direct object antecedent:
    **Myself* hurt *me* with the stapler.

But even this is not enough—not only does the antecedent have to be higher, it has to be in the same clause.

18) **I* said [someone hurt *myself* with the stapler].

Things work the opposite way for pronominals such as *me, him,* and *her*: they can't have a higher antecedent in the same clause, but they can take an antecedent outside their clause.

19) a. A pronominal with a higher antecedent in the same clause:
    **I* hurt *me* with the stapler.
   b. A pronominal with an antecedent outside its clause:
    I said [someone hurt *me* with the stapler].

Despite the abstractness of these constraints, children appear not to have trouble using pronouns in their own speech. In one study of the use of *me* and *myself* in speech transcripts from three children aged two to five, researchers found a few errors of the following type.

20) Sample pronoun errors:
   Mistake involving *me*: I see *me*. (Adam, age 34 mos., looking through a telescope)
   Mistake involving *myself*: Don't you drop me . . . you hurt *myself*. (Abe, age 34 mos.)

Overall, though, the children misused *me* only about 5 percent of the time and made errors with *myself* less than 1 percent of the time. We will return to this point in Section 6.4.

6   What Makes Language Acquisition Possible?

In the preceding sections, we have seen that the language acquisition process extends over a period of several years. It is relatively easy to describe what takes place during these years, but it is much more difficult to explain *how* it happens. The sections that follow focus on some of the factors that may contribute to an eventual understanding of how the language acquisition process works.

6.1   The Role of Experience

First and foremost, children need to be exposed to language; they need to observe it being used by those around them as often as possible. One very clear indication of this comes from a two-and-a-half-year study of parental speech to forty-two children, who were seven to nine months old when the project began. The key finding revealed the consequences of limited exposure to speech in a very striking manner: children who hear a lot of language develop much faster than children who do not (see Table 9.21).

Table 9.21   Effects of exposure to language on development

High-level exposure to language				
Words/hour	*Words/day*	*Utterances/day*	*Utterances/year*	*After three years*
2,100	29,000	7,250	2.5 million+	7.5 million
Average vocabulary size at age thirty months: 766 words				
Average number of words learned in the next six months: 350				
Low-level exposure to language				
Words/hour	*Words/day*	*Utterances/day*	*Utterances/year*	*After three years*
620	8,680	2,170	800,000	2.5 million
Average vocabulary size at age thirty months: 357 words				
Average number of words learned in the next six months: 168				

Not only do children who are exposed to large amounts of speech know twice as many words at age thirty months than children who have fewer opportunities to hear language, they go on to do significantly better in school. One of the most important things that parents and other caregivers can do is speak to their children.

Do parents need to make special adjustments to their speech when talking to children? Probably not, although many subconsciously make some changes, producing what is sometimes called **motherese** or **caregiver speech**. Table 9.22 summarizes the principal features of the caregiver speech used by middle-class English-speaking caregivers.

Table 9.22   Some features of English caregiver speech

Phonetic	Slow, carefully articulated speech Higher pitch Exaggerated intonation and stress Longer pauses
Lexical and semantic	More restricted vocabulary Concrete reference to here and now
Syntactic	Few incomplete sentences Short sentences More imperatives and questions
Conversational	More repetitions Few utterances per conversational turn

Caregiver speech could be helpful to children in various ways. For example, exposure to slow, carefully articulated speech may make it easier for children to pick out words and to learn their pronunciation. (Remember that sentences consist of a continuous stream of speech sounds; there are generally no pauses between words.) Moreover, the acquisition of meaning may be facilitated by the fact that caregiver speech tends to concentrate on the here and now, especially the child's surroundings, activities, and needs. The examples in Table 9.23 help illustrate this. Exposure to language of this type may well make it easier to match morphemes, words, and phrases with meanings—a major part of the language acquisition process.

Table 9.23   Some examples of caregiver speech

Caregiver's utterance	Context
That's right, pick up the blocks.	the child is picking up a box of building blocks
That's a puppy.	the child is looking at a young dog
The puppy's in the basket.	the child is examining a puppy in a basket

Although potentially *helpful*, caregiver speech may not actually be *necessary* to the language acquisition process. In Western Samoa, for instance, speech to children is not simplified in the way it often is in North America, and caregivers do not try to reformulate children's unintelligible speech or make any special attempt to understand it. Yet Samoan children have no trouble learning Samoan. Evidently, the speech style typical of middle-class caregivers in North America is not essential for language acquisition.

LANGUAGE MATTERS   Do Children Learn by Imitating?

Popular opinion holds that children learn language simply by imitating the speech of those around them. This cannot be right, however. Not only do children tend not to repeat the speech of others, they are typically unable to imitate structures that they have not yet learned. For instance, children who have not yet started to invert the auxiliary verb and the subject in questions will avoid Inversion in their imitations.

> Model sentence: Why can't kitty stand up?
> Child's imitation: Why kitty can't stand up?

Children's own grammar, not the model provided by adult speech, determines what they will say at any given point of development.

Moreover, even in cultures where it is common, caregiver speech seems to have very selective effects on child language. For instance, the number of *yes-no* questions in caregiver speech seems to be correlated with the rate at which auxiliary verbs develop—apparently because auxiliaries occur in the salient sentence-initial position in *yes-no* questions (*Can Jennifer go?*). At the same time, though, many other features of caregiver speech seem *not* to affect child language. As we saw earlier (in Section 4.2), for example, the relative frequency of bound morphemes and nonlexical categories in caregiver speech apparently does not determine their order of acquisition.

In and of itself, then, caregiver speech cannot explain how language acquisition occurs. However, research into this subject may contribute to this goal in less direct ways by helping determine the types of linguistic experience that are most valuable to children. This in turn could help us identify the types of mechanisms and strategies involved in language acquisition.

6.2   The Role of Feedback

It is sometimes suggested that parents help their children learn language by correcting their "mistakes." However, studies of actual interactions between parents and children point in a quite different direction. In general, parents tend to be more concerned with the truth of children's utterances than with their grammaticality—one transcript of a parent-child conversation includes *That's right* as a response to the grammatical monstrosity *Mama isn't boy, he's a girl!*

Moreover, even when adults do attempt to correct children's grammatical errors, their efforts often have little effect. The following exchange between a child and his father is typical in this regard.

21) *Child*:   Want other one spoon, Daddy.
    Father: You mean, you want the other spoon.
    Child: Yes, I want other one spoon, please Daddy.
    Father: Can you say "the other spoon"?

Child: other . . . one . . . spoon.
Father: Say "other."
Child: other.
Father: "spoon."
Child: spoon.
Father: "other spoon."
Child: other . . . spoon. Now give me other one spoon?

Interestingly, however, some research suggests that subtler forms of feedback may have a role to play in the language acquisition process.

Recasts

Adults often respond to a child's utterance by repeating it, making adjustments to its form and/or content. (Responses of this sort are called **recasts**.)

22) *Child*:   Daddy here.
   Mother: Yes, Daddy is here.

   Child: Him go.
   Mother: Yes, he is going.

   Child: Boy chasing dog.
   Mother: Yes, the boy is chasing the dog.

   Child: The dog is barking.
   Mother: Yes, he is barking at the kitty.

Recasts provide children with potentially useful information—adding a missing verb (*is* in the first example), changing the form of a pronoun (*him* to *he* in the second example), and so on. However, parents usually don't correct errors, and sometimes they actually reformulate their children's *grammatical* utterances (as in the final example), so recasts also have the potential to be misleading.

It is not yet clear what role recasts play in language learning, and studies to date have yielded conflicting results. For instance, a study of the acquisition of *the* and *a* by three children revealed no link between the frequency of recasts and the rate at which their use of determiners increased—no matter how many recasts children heard, the rate of development stayed the same.

A quite different result emerged from an experiment in which four- and five-year-olds were taught made-up verbs with irregular past tense forms—for example, *pell* (with *pold* as its past tense). When the children first learned what the verbs meant (they were linked to various funny actions, such as hitting someone with a beanbag attached to a string), they heard only the *-ing* forms ('This is called *pelling*'). They therefore had no idea what the past tense forms should be. Just hearing an adult use *pold* to refer to a past pelling action had little or no effect, but being allowed to make "mistakes" such as *pelled* and then hearing an adult recast the sentence using *pold* had a major impact. In fact, a single recast was often enough to permit learning of the irregular form, which suggests that certain types of feedback have a role to play in the language acquisition process after all.

6.3   The Role of Cognitive Development

Because there are dramatic changes in both linguistic and nonlinguistic abilities during the first years of life, it is tempting to think that the two are somehow linked. Yet there is considerable evidence to suggest that language acquisition is to a large extent independent of other types of cognitive development. One such piece of evidence comes from the study of individuals whose general cognitive development is deficient but whose language is highly developed. For example, Rick performed so poorly at age fifteen on a variety of nonlinguistic tasks that his general cognitive level was estimated to be that of a preschool child. Yet, as the following examples illustrate, his speech manifests considerable syntactic and morphological sophistication—with appropriate use of affixes, nonlexical categories, and word order.

23) She must've got me up and thrown me out of bed.
     She keeps both of the ribbons on her hair.
     If they get in trouble, they'd have a pillow fight.
     She's the one that walks back and forth to school.
     I wanna hear one more just for a change.

LANGUAGE MATTERS   A Linguistic Savant

A particularly celebrated case of a dissociation between language and cognitive development involves Christopher. Now an adult, Christopher can read, write, and communicate in about twenty languages (including English, Danish, Dutch, Finnish, French, German, Modern Greek, Hindi, Italian, Norwegian, Polish, Portuguese, Russian, Spanish, Swedish, Turkish, and Welsh). He learned some of these languages as a child (based on minimal exposure) and taught himself others as an adolescent and adult, often with amazing speed, as the following account of his encounter with Dutch illustrates.

> Shortly before he was due to appear on Dutch television, it was suggested that he might spend a couple of days improving his rather rudimentary Dutch with the aid of a grammar and dictionary. He did so to such good effect that he was able to converse in Dutch—with facility if not total fluency—both before and during the programme. (p. 18)

Christopher has a nonverbal IQ (depending on the test) of between 56 and 76, and a mental age of 9 years, 2 months. He has trouble with addition (he can handle simple cases such as 12 + 13, but not carrying over as in 14 + 19); he is very bad at drawing; and he can't figure out how tic-tac-toe works. He is unable to care for himself and lives in a home for adults with special needs.

Information from: Neil Smith and Ianthi-Maria Tsimpli, *The Mind of a Savant* (Oxford: Blackwell, 1995). A short video (4:33) on Christopher is available on YouTube, and further information can be found in Neil Smith, Ianthi Tsimpli, Gary Morgan, and Bencie Woll, *The Signs of a Savant: Language against the Odds* (Cambridge, UK: Cambridge University Press, 2011).

At the same time, there are also documented cases of people whose IQ is within the normal range but who nonetheless have great difficulty with inflection for the past tense and plural, as illustrated by the examples in *24*. (There is reason to believe that this particular disorder is inherited.)

24) The boys eat four cookie.
    It's a flying finches, they are.
    The neighbors phone the ambulance because the man fall off the tree.

Case studies such as these suggest that certain aspects of language (in particular, morphology and syntax) are independent of nonlinguistic types of cognitive development. This in turn implies that the mental mechanisms responsible for the acquisition of those parts of the grammar are relatively autonomous and that their operation neither follows from nor guarantees general cognitive development.

6.4   The Role of Inborn Knowledge

There can be no doubt that some special quality of the human mind facilitates the acquisition of language. The only real question has to do with precisely what that special quality is.

A very influential view among linguists is that children are born with prior knowledge of the type of categories, operations, and principles that are found in the grammar of any human language. They therefore know, for example, that the words in the language they are acquiring will belong to a small set of syntactic categories (N, V, and so on) and that they can be combined in particular ways to create larger phrases (NP, VP, TP, etc.). The set of inborn categories, operations, and principles common to all human languages makes up what is often referred to as **Universal Grammar (UG)**.

The view that certain grammatical knowledge is inborn is known as **nativism**. Although nativism has roots in philosophy that date back thousands of years, its popularity in linguistics is due largely to the influence of Noam Chomsky, a linguist at the Massachusetts Institute of Technology. Chomsky's basic claim is that the grammars for human language are too complex and abstract to be learned on the basis of the type of experience to which children have access. Therefore, he argues, significant components of the grammar must be inborn. To illustrate this, we must consider a relatively complex example involving the notion of c-command alluded to earlier.

Principles A and B

As we have seen (Section 5.5), the interpretation of pronouns such as *himself* and *him* is regulated by two quite abstract principles.

25) *Principle A*
    A reflexive pronoun must have a c-commanding antecedent in the same clause.

    Principle B
    A pronominal must not have a c-commanding antecedent in the same clause.

These principles have played an important role in the study of language acquisition, and three arguments have been put forward in support of the claim that they are inborn.

First, the notion of c-command is quite abstract. It is not the type of concept that we would expect young children to discover simply by listening to sentences. Since we also know that no one teaches them about c-command, it makes sense to think that this notion is inborn and therefore does not have to be discovered or taught.

Second, the c-command relation seems to be universally relevant to the interpretation of pronouns. The universality of this restriction would be explained if Principles A and B were innate and hence part of the inborn linguistic knowledge of all human beings.

Third, as we saw earlier in this chapter, Principles A and B seem to be available to children from a very early stage in their development—even three-year-olds appear to have mastered the distinction between reflexives and pronominals in their own speech (although they do sometimes make mistakes in comprehension). Given the complexity of these principles, this provides additional evidence for the claim that they are inborn.

Parameters

Of course, not every feature of a language's grammar can be inborn. Its vocabulary and morphology must be learned, and so must at least part of its syntax. For example, UG stipulates that a phrase can include a head and its complements, but it does not specify the relative order of these elements. This differs from language to language, so that a child acquiring English must learn that heads precede their complements, whereas a child acquiring Korean must learn the reverse order.

26) Head-complement order in English and Korean:
    a. English (head–complement)
       read [that book]
    b. Korean (complement–head)
       [ku chayk] ilke
       that book read

UG includes a **parameter** for word order that offers a choice between head-initial and head-final order. (We ignore the positioning of specifiers for the purposes of the illustration in Table 9.24.)

Table 9.24   The word order parameter

Stipulated by UG	*Resulting options*
A phrase consists of a head and a complement	Head–Complement order [head-initial]
	Complement–Head order [head-final]

There are also phonological parameters: for example, languages can differ from each other in terms of whether they allow two or more consonants in the onset of a syllable—English does (e.g., *gleam*, *sprint*), whereas Japanese does not.

All of this suggests that part of the language acquisition process involves **parameter setting**—that is, determining which of the options permitted by a particular parameter is appropriate for the language being learned.

6.5   Is There a Critical Period?

One of the most intriguing issues in the study of language acquisition has to do with the possibility that normal linguistic development is possible only if children are exposed to language during a particular time frame or **critical period**. Evidence for the existence of such a period comes from the study of individuals who do not experience language during the early part of their lives.

One such individual is the much-discussed Genie, who was kept in a small room with virtually no opportunity to hear human speech from around age two to age thirteen. After many years of therapy and care, Genie's nonlinguistic cognitive functioning was described as "relatively normal" and her lexical and semantic abilities as "good." In terms of syntax and morphology, however, many problems remained, as evidenced in the sample utterances in Table 9.25.

Table 9.25   Some of Genie's utterances

Utterance	Meaning
Applesauce buy store.	'Buy applesauce at the store.'
Man motorcycle have.	'The man has a motorcycle.'
Want go ride Miss F. car.	'I want to go for a ride in Miss F.'s car.'
Genie have full stomach.	'I have a full stomach.'
Mama have baby grow up.	'Mama has a baby who grew up.'

As these examples show, Genie makes word order errors (the first two examples) and her speech does not contain nonlexical categories or affixes. (The 1997 Emmy Award–winning documentary about Genie, *Secret of the Wild Child*, is available for viewing online.)

Another revealing case study involved Chelsea, a deaf child who was misdiagnosed as mentally disabled and emotionally disturbed. Chelsea grew up without language and was not exposed to speech until the age of thirty-one, when she was finally fitted with hearing aids. After intensive therapy, she is able to hold a job and to live independently. However, her vocabulary consists of only 2,000 words and her sentences are badly formed, as the following examples help show.

27)   The woman is bus the going.
      Combing hair the boy.
      Orange Tim car in.
      The girl is gone the ice cream shopping buying the man.

Based on case studies such as these, it is now widely believed that the ability to acquire a first language in an effortless and ultimately successful way begins to decline from age six and becomes increasingly compromised with each passing year.

Summing Up

This chapter has been concerned with the problem of how children acquire the **grammar** of their first language. Research in this area deals with two major issues: the nature of the **developmental sequence** leading to the emergence of mature linguistic competence in the areas of phonology, vocabulary, morphology, and syntax, and the factors that make it possible for children to acquire a complex grammar. A number of factors may contribute to the child's acquisition of language, including the properties of **caregiver speech**, **recasts**, and inborn linguistic knowledge (**Universal Grammar**). We look to future research for deeper insights into the precise role of these and other factors.

Key Terms

General terms and terms concerned with research methods

cross-sectional   grammar
diary study   longitudinal
experimental studies   naturalistic approach

Terms concerning phonological development

babbling   gliding
denasalization   stopping
fronting

Terms concerning vocabulary, morphological, and syntactic development

antecedent   overextension
assimilation   overgeneralizations
c-command   overregularizations
Canonical Sentence Strategy telegraphic stage
developmental sequence   two-word stage
holophrases   underextension
one-word stage

Terms concerning factors contributing to language acquisition

caregiver speech   parameter
critical period   parameter setting
motherese   recasts
nativism   Universal Grammar (UG)

Recommended Reading

Ambridge, Ben, and Elena Lieven. 2001. *Child Language Acquisition: Contrasting Approaches.* Cambridge, UK: Cambridge University Press.

Berko Gleason, Jean, and Nan Bernstein Ratner. 2012. *The Development of Language.* 8th ed. Upper Saddle River, NJ: Pearson.

Blom, Elma, and Sharon Unsworth, eds. 2010. *Experimental Methods in Language Acquisition Research.* Amsterdam: John Benjamins.

Bloom, Paul. 2002. *How Children Learn the Meanings of Words.* Cambridge, MA: MIT Press.

Clark, Eve. 2009. *First Language Acquisition.* 2nd ed. Cambridge, UK: Cambridge University Press.

Hirsh-Pasek, Kathy, and Roberta Golinkoff. 2012. "How Babies Talk: Six Principles of Early Language Development." In *Re-visioning the Beginning: Developmental and Health Science Contributions to Infant/Toddler Programs for Children and Families Living in Poverty.* Edited by S. L. Odom, E. Pungello, and N. Gardner-Neblett, 77–101. New York: Guilford Press.

Lust, Barbara. 2006. *Child Language: Acquisition and Growth.* Cambridge, UK: Cambridge University Press.

O'Grady, William. 2005. *How Children Learn Language.* Cambridge, UK: Cambridge University Press.

Exercises

1. One piece of evidence that children acquire a grammar is their production of over-regularized past tense forms such as *doed*, *leaved*, and *goed*. Based on this model, what type of evidence should we look for in order to show that children have acquired the rule that creates comparative forms such as *bigger*, *richer*, and *taller*? (Hint: Think about adjectives that have irregular comparative forms in the adult language.)

2. In one naturalistic study, a search for passive structures in a sample of 18,000 utterances from sixty children yielded only nineteen examples produced by twelve of the children.
   i) Is this evidence that the other forty-eight children had not yet learned the passive structure? Why or why not?
   ii) How are the disadvantages of the naturalistic method exemplified here? (See Section 1.1.)

3. The following transcriptions represent the pronunciation of a two-year-old child. Indicate which phonetic processes have applied in each case. (See Section 2.3.)

a)	skin	[kɪd]	h)	thin	[tɪn]
b)	spoon	[bun]	i)	teddy	[dɛdi]
c)	zoo	[du]	j)	brush	[bʌt]
d)	John	[dɑn]	k)	lump	[wʌp]
e)	bath	[bæt]	l)	play	[pwej]
f)	other	[ʌdə]	m)	breakfast	[bɹɛkpəst]
g)	Smith	[mɪt]			

4. Drawing on the phonetic processes posited for the preceding exercise, predict one or more plausible immature pronunciations for each of the following words and specify which processes are at work. (See Section 2.3.)

a) show
b) please
c) spit
d) under
e) juice
f) thumb
g) zero
h) ring

5. Consider the following examples of overextensions, all of which have actually been observed in children's speech. What is the apparent basis for each of these overextensions? (See Section 3.2.)

Child's word	First referent	Overextensions
a) sch	sound of a train	music, noise of wheels, sound of rain
b) bow-wow	dog	sheep, rabbit fur, puppet
c) baby	baby	people in pictures
d) sizo	scissors	nail file, knife, screwdriver, spoon
e) policeman	policeman	mailman, sailor, doctor
f) strawberry	strawberry	grapes, raspberry
g) fireworks	fireworks	matches, light, cigarette
h) Batman	Batman logo on a T-shirt	any logo on a T-shirt

6. Since children have a tendency to focus on the prototypical members of categories in the acquisition of words, how might you expect children to underextend the following words? What members of the category might you expect children not to include? (See Section 3.)

a) bird
b) pet
c) toy

7. The allomorphic variation associated with the third-person singular verbal ending -s is identical to that found with plural -s.

i)   Make up a test parallel to the *wug* test discussed in Section 4.1.
ii) If possible, give your test to children between the ages of three and seven. Explain your results. To what extent are they similar to the ones discussed in the chapter?

8. Based on the discussion in Section 4.2 about the developmental sequence of morpheme acquisition, consider the acquisition in other languages of the morphemes corresponding to those listed in Table 9.12. Would you predict that these morphemes would be acquired in exactly the same order as their English equivalents? Why or why not?

9. Considering children's tendency to overgeneralize morphological rules, what might we expect a young child to use in the place of the following adult words? Justify your choice in each case. (See Section 4.1.)

a) fish (plural)
b) went
c) mice
d) ate

e) has

f) geese

g) brought

h) hit (past tense)

i) himself

j) women

10. Each of the following utterances is from the speech of a child in the two-word stage. Identify the semantic relation expressed by each of these utterances. (See Table 9.17.)

Intended meaning	*Child's utterance*
a) Jimmy is swimming.	Jimmy swim.
b) Ken's book	Ken book
c) Daddy is at his office.	Daddy office.
d) You push the baby.	Push baby.
e) Mommy is reading.	Mommy read.

11. Consider the following data from Jordie, a two-and-a-half-year-old child, in light of the list of morphemes in Table 9.12.

Intended meaning	*Jordie's utterance*
a) Where's my blanket?	Where my blanket?
b) Does it go right here, Mommy?	Go right here, Mommy?
c) It's running over.	Running over.
d) Here, it goes here.	Here, go here.
e) No, that's mine.	No, that mine.
f) Dinosaurs say gronk.	Dinosaur say gronk.
g) There's more.	There more.

i) Which of the morphemes in Table 9.12 are missing in Jordie's sentences but present in the intended meanings?

ii) List the morphemes that are present in both the intended meanings and in Jordie's speech.

12. Now consider the following utterances from a child named Krista. (See Section 4.)

Intended meaning	*Krista's utterance*
a) My name is Krista.	Mine name Krista.
b) My sister's name is Peggy.	Sister name Peggy.
c) The tape is right there.	Tape right there.
d) Daddy's book	Daddy book
e) I've got a book.	I'm got a book.
f) Read me a story.	Read me story.
g) I'll do it.	I'm do it.
h) He went outside.	He went outside.
i) Open the gate, please.	Open a gate, please.
j) Gramma's house	Gramma's house
k) Smell the flowers.	Smell flowers.
l) My shoes are on.	Shoes on.
m) The wee boy fell down.	Wee boy fell down.
n) That's my ball.	That's mines ball.

    i)   Which morphemes are missing in Krista's speech but present in the intended meanings?

    ii)   Krista uses the past tense twice in the above utterances. Do you think this is evidence that she has acquired the past tense morpheme? Why or why not?

    iii) Comment on Krista's difficulty with possessive pronouns.

    iv) Do you think she has acquired possessive -'s? Why or why not?

13. The following utterances were produced spontaneously by Holly, age three years. (See Sections 4 and 5.)

    a) I learned about loving moms.
    b) Put him in the bathtub.
    c) We eated gummy snakes.
    d) Thank you for giving these books us.
    e) I don't know.
    f) He bited my finger. (When corrected, she said: He bitted my finger.)
    g) I runned in the water.
    h) I rided on a elephant.

    i)   Has Holly acquired the past tense morpheme? How do you know?

    ii)   What is the evidence in Holly's speech that she has learned phrases that consist of a head, a complement, and/or a specifier?

    iii) What is the evidence that words such as *eat*, *know*, and *ride* are verbs for Holly and that words such as *bathtub*, *books*, and *water* are nouns for her?

14. It has been reported that hearing children growing up in homes with nonspeaking deaf parents cannot learn spoken language from radio or even television (see p. 278 of *The Language Instinct* by S. Pinker [New York: Morrow, 1994]).

    i)   What might be the reasons for this? (See Section 6.)

    ii)   What are the implications of these findings for our understanding of the type of experience that is required for language acquisition? (See Section 6.)

ten

Second Language Acquisition

John Archibald

> *When we talk about acquisition in SLA research, we are not talking about acquisition in the sense that one acquires polo ponies, Lladró figurines, or CBS, but rather in the sense that one acquires vicious habits, a taste for Brie, or a potbelly.*
>
> —KEVIN R. GREGG, *Linguistic Perspectives on Second Language Acquisition* (1989)

OBJECTIVES

In this chapter, you will learn:

- how the learner's first language and the language being learned interact to influence changes in the learner's grammar as he or she progresses
- what characterizes the phonology, syntax, and morphology of a second language learner's grammar
- how nonlinguistic factors may influence second language acquisition
- how second language classrooms help the learner by modifying language and focusing on form
- what alternatives exist for English language learners in U.S. schools

 **LaunchPad Solo** | For more helpful content and quizzes, go to the LaunchPad Solo
macmillan learning | for *Contemporary Linguistics* at **launchpadworks.com**.

The field of **second language acquisition** (SLA) research investigates how people attain proficiency in a language that is not their mother tongue. Whether we are talking about someone learning to read Greek in university, or someone becoming fluent in a third language in their forties, or a child acquiring a new language after moving to a new country, we refer to it as second language acquisition. The interesting phenomenon of children simultaneously acquiring two languages is generally investigated in the field known as **bilingualism** (which may be thought of as a subdiscipline of SLA research). In this chapter, we will primarily be concerned with second language acquisition in adults.

Over the years, the study of second language acquisition has been undertaken from a variety of different perspectives. In the 1950s and 1960s, the primary objective was pedagogic. Researchers were interested in trying to improve the way in which second languages were taught. Therefore, they were interested in discovering how those languages were learned. From the 1970s on, the focus moved from the teacher to the learner, and the field of second language (L2) instruction became somewhat separate.

This change in perspective was related to what was going on in linguistics, psychology, and first language acquisition research. All three of these areas shifted focus from the external to the internal in the 1960s. Linguistics became concerned with the mental grammar of the speaker, not just the description of the linguistic structures of a given language. Psychology shifted from behaviorism (which denied the importance of mental representations) to cognitive psychology, and research on first language acquisition focused on children's internal grammars rather than just their verbal production. These fields are also crucial to the study of SLA. Linguistics gives us a sophisticated and accurate description of what people are trying to learn (the second language) and what they already know (the first language). Psychology can provide us with a learning theory to account for how people acquire knowledge. Finally, the field of first language acquisition (which has been around longer than the field of second language acquisition) offers various findings that can be productively applied to SLA. For example, we know that children who are acquiring their first language (L1) have systematic grammars and that their utterances are not just bad imitations of the adult target. As we will see, second language learners, too, are developing a grammar that is systematic even if it is not nativelike.

1   The Study of Second Language Acquisition

In the case of first language acquisition, we may ascribe the difference between child and adult grammars to either cognitive or biological immaturity in the child. In the case of second language learning by adults, however, we cannot say that the learners are either cognitively or biologically immature. Rather, they are subject to an influence that is absent from the child's situation: the first language itself.

$$L1 \rightarrow \text{Interlanguage Grammar} \leftarrow L2$$

Figure 10.1   Linguistic influences on an interlanguage grammar

Figure 10.1 illustrates the fact that second language learners have a systematic **interlanguage (IL) grammar**—so called because it is a system of mental representations influenced by both the first and the second language and has features of each.

1.1   The Role of the First Language

One of the most easily recognizable traits of a second language learner's speech is that it bears a certain resemblance to the first language. Thus, someone whose first language is French is likely to sound different from someone whose first language is German when they both speak English. We see an example of this in the typical pronunciation of the English word *have* by speakers of French and German, as illustrated in Table 10.1. The form in Table 10.1, produced by French speakers, reflects the fact that French lacks the phoneme /h/, while the pronunciation associated with German speakers can be traced to the fact that German includes a rule of syllable-final obstruent devoicing (which changes the [v] to a [f]).

Table 10.1   Phonological transfer: French and German

English target	French speakers	German speakers
have [hæv]	[æv]	[hæf]

The term **transfer** is used to describe the process whereby a feature or rule from a learner's first language is carried over to the IL grammar. Other examples can be seen in Table 10.2.

Table 10.2   More phonological transfer: Spanish, English, and French

L1	L2	Example	Comment
Spanish	English	I espeak Espanish.	Spanish does not allow s + consonant sequences word-initially.
English	French	[ty] 'you' → [tu]	English does not have the front rounded vowel [y]. The English speaker substitutes the [u] sound.
Quebec French	English	Over dere.	The [ð] sound is replaced by [d].
European French	English	Over zere.	The [ð] sound is replaced by [z].
English	Spanish	[rio] 'river' → [ɹio]	Since English does not use [r] word-initially, an [ɹ] is substituted.

1.2   The Nature of an Interlanguage

The first language is not the only influence on the interlanguage grammar, since some properties of the IL can be traced to aspects of the L2. In the case of a German speaker who is learning English, for example, the IL grammar will contain some features of both German and English. Consider how a German learner of English might pronounce the words *back* and *bag*. Because of the German rule of Syllable Final Obstruent Devoicing, the German learner will pronounce both *back* and *bag* the same: [bæk]. However, in English, not only is the final consonant different in the words *back* and *bag*, but also the vowel before a voiced obstruent coda is lengthened, so native speakers of English will pronounce *back* as [bæk] and *bag* as [bæːg]. The German learner of English who has learned this rule may then produce [bæ:k] for *bag*, showing the influence of both the L2 rule of Vowel Lengthening and the L1 rule of Syllable Final Obstruent Devoicing, as illustrated in Table 10.3.

Table 10.3   Influence of L1 and L2 on the learner's interlanguage

Underlying form	*V Lengthening (L2 rule)*	*Syllable-Final Devoicing (L1 rule)*
/bæg/	[bæ:g]	[bæ:k]

This example serves to show us something about the nature of an interlanguage: it contains features of both the L1 and the L2. The speech of second language learners can exhibit nonnativelike characteristics in any linguistic domain, as shown in Table 10.4. When the interlanguage grammar stops changing, it is said to have **fossilized**.

Table 10.4   Types of errors found in the acquisition of English

L1	*Example*	*Error type*	*Comment*
Spanish	My wife is <u>embarrassed</u>. (meaning 'pregnant')	lexical	Spanish *embarazada* = 'pregnant'
Various	I live in a two-bedroom <u>department</u>.	lexical	The speaker chooses the wrong word.
Various	I <u>didn't took</u> the car.	morphological	English doesn't mark the past tense on both auxiliary and main verbs.
Various	She <u>get ups</u> late.	morphological	The speaker adds the agreement marker to the preposition, not the verb.
French	He <u>drinks frequently</u> beer.	syntactic	French places the main verb before the adverb.
Various	There's the man that I saw <u>him</u>.	syntactic	Some languages (e.g., Arabic, Turkish) allow pronouns in this position in a relative clause.

1.3   The Final State

So far we have been talking about the characteristics of the intermediate grammar. But a discussion of what an IL grammar looks like must consider the **target**: that is, what is to be acquired. The field of SLA, then, must address the issue of actual proficiency or **communicative competence**. Although knowledge of a language's grammar allows us to distinguish between grammatical and ungrammatical sentences, successful communication requires much more than this. The learner must also be able to use the language in a way that is appropriate to the situation or context. As Figure 10.2 helps illustrate, both grammatical accuracy and communicative ability are part of communicative competence.

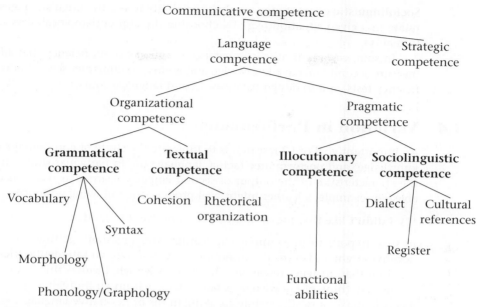

Figure 10.2 A model of communicative competence

LANGUAGE MATTERS   Even Though They Are Natural, L2 Mistakes Can Be Embarrassing

"It's those tiny details that do you in: a vowel here, a consonant there. Who would think it would make such a difference? Like the time I thought I was telling my roommate that the sink was plugged again. I said *kinor*. I meant *kiyor* . . . big deal. But Ruthie had no idea what I was trying to say. I ask you, how hard can it be to figure out that I meant *sink* and not *violin*? Oh, and there was the time her friends came calling, and asked if she was *yeshna* (there). I thought they were asking if she was *yeshena* (sleeping). I said yes and closed the door. They thought I was nuts. Fortunately, she woke up and explained that I was only Canadian."

–Janet McDonald on speaking Hebrew

What the model depicted in Figure 10.2 captures graphically is that the skills required to function in a second language go beyond **grammatical competence** in the core domains of linguistics: phonetics, phonology, morphology, syntax, and semantics. **Textual competence** recognizes the ability to organize and link sentences coherently in a spoken or written text. **Illocutionary competence** showcases the ability to understand and convey meaning via a variety of linguistic forms (e.g., by expressing a request via a direct command or via a question with *could*).

Sociolinguistic competence involves the ability to use the linguistic register appropriate to a given situation (e.g., by choosing the appropriate vocabulary or level of formality).

In sum, communicative competence is a model of proficiency that allows us to measure second language knowledge and ability, to construct second language proficiency tests, and to design balanced second language courses.

1.4   Variation in Performance

An important goal of L2 research is to integrate the study of **competence** (linguistic knowledge) and **performance** (actual language use in particular situations). One of the characteristics of the output of second language learners is that it is quite variable. For example, a learner might well produce the following sentence:

1) I **didn't** like **th**at movie so I told her I **no** want to go **d**ere.

In this (hypothetical) example, the learner is inconsistent, getting one of the two negatives right and correctly pronouncing one of the two interdental fricatives. The question that intrigues researchers has to do with what causes this sort of variation. We usually think of knowledge as fairly stable within an individual. For example, if a person makes a mistake while speaking in his or her native language, we tend not to question the speaker's competence in that language but rather to assume that some kind of performance error was made. So how do we account for learners who behave as if they know how to negate a verb or pronounce [ð] on some occasions but not others? Do they have the knowledge or don't they?

It is difficult to answer this question, in part because of considerations involving error frequency. If a second language learner gets something wrong 10 percent of the time, is it the same (in terms of competence) as getting it wrong 60 percent of the time? We would probably say that a nonnative speaker who gets the English past tense correct 10 percent of the time does not know it and that someone who gets it right 90 percent of the time does. But what of someone who gets it right somewhere between those two scores? This is a complex research question. The (admittedly simplistic) view adopted in this chapter is that variation falls into the realm of linguistic performance—it reflects the imperfect use of linguistic knowledge rather than deficits in the knowledge itself.

Linguistic performance clearly involves the interaction of a number of cognitive systems and has much in common with other skills. A crucial notion for the study of how skills develop involves the distinction between controlled and automatic processing. When acquiring a new skill (e.g., playing golf), we begin by having to devote a lot of conscious or controlled processing to the activity: feet apart, head down, elbow straight, white shoes, and so on. Once we become proficient, we just hit the ball; the activity has become automatic.

We need to shift processing from controlled to automatic because, as humans, we have a fixed processing capacity. We can't consciously process everything at once. Shifting some material into automatic processing frees up space for additional controlled processing. Consider an example from reading. When we first learn how to read, we devote much of our cognitive processing to determining what the written symbols stand for. When we are focusing on decoding the letters, we do not have the processing capacity to deal with things like reading for prejudice or bias. After a time, though, letter recognition happens automatically in our first language, and we can devote more of our cognitive capacity to higher-level skills.

That native speakers do this kind of thing automatically can be seen by the difficulty we have in proofreading. It is hard to suppress the information we're getting from the context since the mind tries to make sense of what it's reading. Conversely, when we are forced by exceptional circumstances to devote a lot of energy to decoding the print (e.g., a bad photocopy or fax), our higher-level processing slows down; we can't focus as much on the message when we are focusing on the form.

All of this is relevant to second language acquisition in that it can help explain the variable performance of L2 learners. When learners are focusing on the form of the L2 utterance, they may be able to produce it accurately. However, when there are extra demands, such as trying to communicate a complex thought or carry on a conversation in a noisy room, errors may occur. This suggests that the learner has a mental representation of the form in question (say, a negated verb or an interdental fricative) but can have difficulty implementing or accessing it under certain conditions.

2 Interlanguage Grammars

Let us turn now to a discussion of the specifics of what is acquired when learning the phonology, morphology, and syntax of a second language. The general question we are trying to answer here is: What is the structure of an interlanguage? Second language learners are acquiring grammars, and those grammars involve mental representations. Therefore, we can investigate the nature of those representations within the various subdomains of linguistic theory. We begin with phonology.

LANGUAGE MATTERS   The Subtleties in Learning New Lexical Items

"I suppose hearing a language is a different way of feeling the words. I don't suppose there are synonyms really. I wonder if *moon* means exactly the same thing as *luna*? I don't suppose it does; there's a slight difference. There should be—in every word. So that to learn any language is to find out different ways of viewing, of sensing the universe, the world, or ourselves."

–Jorge Luis Borges
The Royal Society of Arts. Copyright © 1983 by The Royal Society of Arts.

2.1   L2 Phonology

Let us consider what is to be acquired in the domain of phonology. Broadly speaking, we can distinguish between segmental and prosodic phonology. Segmental phonology has to do with the characteristics of phonological segments, like consonants and vowels. Prosodic phonology, however, has to do with phonological phenomena that affect more than a single segment (e.g., syllables and stress).

Segmental Phonology

Languages vary in their segmental inventory in that they choose a subset of the sounds found in human languages. There is thus a good chance that a second language learner will have to learn to produce and perceive some new sounds when acquiring a second language.

One of the most obvious characteristics of adult second language speech is that it is accented as the result of phonological and phonetic transfer from the native language. This is why native speakers of English can usually distinguish French-accented English from German-accented English. Consider the examples in Table 10.5.

Table 10.5   Examples of French- and German-accented English

English target	Quebec French speaker	German speaker
[ðə] 'the'	[də]	[zə]

Since both French and German lack the interdental fricative [ð], native speakers of those languages substitute a sound from their L1 that shares some features with the target sound. Speakers of Canadian French substitute a voiced alveolar stop, while German speakers substitute a voiced alveolar fricative. Particularly at a beginning level of proficiency, L2 learners pronounce words using their L1 phonological system.

A similar phenomenon can be seen in the phonology of loan words. When a word is borrowed from another language, its pronunciation is modified to suit the new phonological system. For example, when English borrowed the word *pterodactyl* from Greek, the initial consonant was dropped from the /pt/ onset, which is well formed in Greek but not in English. However, no such change was made in the word *helicopter* (with the same Greek root *pter* 'wing') since it already complied with the phonological pattern of English, thanks to the syllable break between /p/ and /t/.

Markedness

One question that has received a lot of attention in SLA research is why some sounds are harder to acquire in a second language than others. Perhaps some sounds are simpler than others. Or perhaps some sound systems are easier for speakers of a certain language to acquire. Would it be easier for a Japanese speaker to acquire English or Vietnamese? As might be expected, these are not simple issues. We cannot talk about the ease or difficulty of entire languages, but we may have something to say about individual sounds.

When linguists try to deal with the notions of ease or simplicity, they make use of the notion of **markedness**. Structures that are simple and/or especially common in human language are said to be **unmarked**, while structures that are complex or less common are said to be **marked**. So we might say that a sound that is found in relatively few of the world's languages (e.g., [θ]) is marked, while a sound that occurs in many of the world's languages (e.g., [t]) is unmarked.

Markedness is commonly approached from the perspective of language typology, which is concerned with the comparative study of similarities and differences among languages. Researchers have discovered certain **implicational universals** of the form "if a language has *x*, it will also have *y*." For example, if a language has nasal vowels (e.g., /ã/), then it will also have oral vowels (e.g., /a/). Crucial to the understanding of implicational universals is the fact that the implication is unidirectional. Thus a language that has oral vowels does not necessarily have nasal vowels. This allows us to identify /a/ as less marked than /ã/, in accordance with the following generalization.

2) *X* is more marked than *y* if the presence of *x* implies the presence of *y*, *but not vice versa.*

It is interesting to ask whether IL grammars obey such implicational universals and whether this can tell us something about the question of ease and difficulty of learning.

The **Markedness Differential Hypothesis** holds that structures that are typologically marked will be more difficult than their unmarked counterparts for second language learners. Remember the earlier example of Syllable Final Obstruent Devoicing in German, which explains why a word like *Hund* 'dog' is pronounced with a [t] at the end. German speakers learning English typically transfer this devoicing rule into their IL (producing [hæt] for [hæd] 'had') and must learn to make the contrast between [t] and [d] at the ends of words. We might be tempted to think that the principle underlying this phenomenon is something like "it's hard to learn to make contrasts that your L1 doesn't make." But when we look at another set of data, we see that this is not the case.

French makes a contrast between [ʃ] and [ʒ] in places where English does not, as Table 10.6 indicates. If it were invariably difficult for second language learners to make contrasts that are not found in their L1, we would expect English speakers to have difficulty learning to produce [ʒ] at the beginning of words. But they don't. English speakers seem able to learn to pronounce French words like *jaune* 'yellow' and *jeudi* 'Thursday' without trouble.

Table 10.6 The [ʃ]/[ʒ] contrast in English and French

	English [ʃ]/[ʒ]	*French* [ʃ]/[ʒ]
Initial	<u>s</u>ure [ʃ]/*[ʒ]	<u>ch</u>ant [ʃ]/<u>g</u>ens [ʒ] 'song' 'people'
Medial	a<u>ss</u>ure [ʃ]/a<u>z</u>ure [ʒ]	bou<u>ch</u>er [ʃ]/bou<u>g</u>er [ʒ] 'to fill up' 'to move'
Final	lea<u>sh</u> [ʃ]/lie<u>g</u>e [ʒ]	ha<u>ch</u>e [ʃ]/a<u>g</u>e [ʒ] 'h' 'age'

The notion of markedness can be used to explain why German speakers have difficulty making a new contrast in English, while English speakers don't have difficulty making a new contrast in French. The typological situation is as follows:

- There are languages that have a voicing contrast initially, medially, and finally (e.g., English).

- There are languages that have a voicing contrast initially and medially, but not finally (e.g., German).

- There are languages that have a voicing contrast initially, but not medially or finally (e.g., Sardinian).

These generalizations allow us to formulate the following implicational universal.

3) The presence of a voicing contrast in final position implies the presence of a voicing contrast in medial position, which in turn implies the presence of a voicing contrast in initial position.

We can represent this universal graphically as follows:

4) initial > medial > final
      C   B   A

The presence of A implies the presence of B and C (but not vice versa), and the presence of B implies the presence of C (but not vice versa). Therefore, A is the most marked and C is the least marked. This markedness differential explains the differing degrees of difficulty exhibited by the German and English L2 learners. The German speakers learning English are attempting to acquire a contrast in a universally more marked position (final) whereas the English speakers learning French are attempting to acquire a contrast in a universally unmarked position (initial).

Another way of looking at the acquisition of new sounds is not in terms of ease or difficulty of acquisition but rather in terms of *rate* of acquisition. The **Similarity Differential Rate Hypothesis** proposes that the rates of acquisition for dissimilar phenomena are faster than for similar phenomena. In other words, all other things being equal, learners will learn something that is unlike their first language structure *faster* than something that is similar to (and hence could be confused with) a first language structure. The data shown in Figure 10.3 describe the acquisition of English [ɹ] (in word-initial position) and English velarized [ɫ] (in word-final position) by a native speaker of Haitian Creole, which has a uvular [ʁ] and only an alveolar [l]. Note that there is virtually no acquisition of the velarized [ɫ] and little change in rate, whereas the rate of change for [ɹ] is much more dramatic. The dissimilar [ɹ] is acquired at a faster rate than the similar [ɫ].

Of course, the question of how to determine whether two features are similar or dissimilar is not always straightforward. To really test this hypothesis, we need to look at perceptual, phonetic, phonological, and even orthographic factors that could affect this judgment. Here we will just accept that the two *l*s are more similar than the two *r*s.

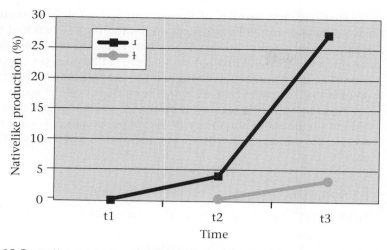

Figure 10.3 Differential rates of acquisition. Data adapted from: M. DeGaytan, "A Longitudinal Study of the Interlanguage Phonology of a Haitian Immigrant Learning English as a Second Language," Applied Project (Tempe: Arizona State University, 1997).

Acquiring New Features

One question that often comes up in the field of second language phonology is whether one can learn material that is not found in one's first language. Some have argued that if a phonological feature is lacking in the L1, then acquiring L2 contrasts based on that feature will be impossible. One study compared the relative success of Chinese learners of the English /l/ versus /ɹ/ contrast and the lack of success of Japanese learners attempting to acquire the same contrast. Both Japanese and some dialects of Mandarin Chinese lack the /l, ɹ/ contrast but, it was argued, Mandarin has the appropriate phonological *feature* in the L1, whereas Japanese lacks it. (The specific feature is not important for our discussion.) However, it appears that this is too strong a stance. In some cases, L2 learners *can* acquire contrasts based on features absent from their L1. We will give two brief examples.

LANGUAGE MATTERS Foreign Accent Syndrome

There have been several documented cases of what has become known as *foreign accent syndrome*, in which people have been known to suddenly acquire what sounds like a nonnative accent. A British English speaker, for example, may start to sound as if she has a Spanish accent. Or an American English speaker may acquire a British accent. The cases all result from underlying brain damage (from a stroke or some sort of cerebral trauma), but it appears that there is no one brain area that is related to this syndrome. In 2006, the *Journal of Neurolinguistics* (vol. 19, no. 5) devoted an entire issue to this subject.

First, Japanese learners of Russian can acquire Russian /r/ (even though they have difficulty with English /ɹ/). Second, it has been shown that English learners of Japanese can acquire the distinction between long (or geminate) and short consonants, even though English does not have that distinction. The details of why this is possible are complex (involving such things as phonetic salience), but the main point is that structures that are absent from the L1 can be acquired in the L2.

In addition to the segmental inventory, second language learners also have to acquire the prosodic phonology of the target language. For example, they have to acquire the principles of syllabification and stress assignment. We will now look at each in turn.

L2 Syllabification

Syllables have the hierarchical structure shown in Figure 10.4.

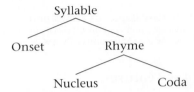

Figure 10.4   The internal structure of the syllable

The languages of the world vary in the type of syllable structures that they permit. For instance, some languages, such as Arabic, do not allow more than one consonant at the beginning or end of a syllable, so that the longest possible syllable is CVC. When speakers of some dialects of Arabic start learning English as a second language, they add the vowel /i/ after extra consonants.

5) *English target*   *Nonnative speaker's version*
   plant   [pi.lan.ti]
   Fred   [fi.rɛd]
   translate   [ti.ran.si.let]

Research on the acquisition of English by Mandarin Chinese speakers sheds light on the different types of repair strategies that are available to a learner whose L1 does not allow syllables of the same type and complexity as those found in the second language. (Mandarin Chinese allows only /n/ and /ŋ/ in coda position, but English allows many options, including consonant clusters.) There are two possible repair strategies: deletion and epenthesis.

6) *Target word*   *Deletion strategy*   *Epenthesis strategy*
   seed   [si]   [sidə]
   big   [bɪ]   [bɪgə]
   went   [wɛ]   [wɛntə]

As learners' proficiency increases, they make more epenthesis repairs than deletion repairs— a positive development because the epenthesized version is easier for listeners to understand.

Stress Assignment

L2 learners also have to acquire the stress patterns of the language they are trying to learn. Consider an example from Polish, a language in which word-level stress is always assigned to the penultimate (second-to-last) syllable. The transfer of this L1 principle results in one of the characteristics of a Polish accent in English: the tendency to place stress on the penultimate syllable of English words. The following examples illustrate a nonnative stress pattern in which the second-to-last syllable is always stressed.

7) *English target*   *Nonnative form*
   a'stonish   a'stonish
   main'tain   'maintain
   'cabinet   ca'binet

2.2 L2 Syntax

L2 learners also have to acquire the syntax of their new language. In this section, we will look at two facets of syntactic structure: the **Null Subject Parameter** and **Verb Raising**.

Null Subjects

According to the theory of Universal Grammar, the human language faculty includes both universal principles that account for what all natural languages have in common and parameters that account for cross-linguistic variation. Parameters are like linguistic switches (often binary) that can be set to a particular value as a result of the linguistic input. One of the first parameters to be proposed was the Null Subject (or Pronoun-Drop) Parameter. Essentially, this parameter is designed to account for the contrast between languages like French and English, which require overt subjects (e.g., *He speaks French/*Speaks French*), and languages like Spanish and Italian, which allow subjects to be omitted (e.g., Spanish *El habla español/Habla español* '[S/he] speaks Spanish').

8) *The Null Subject Parameter*
   The subject of a clause with a verb marked for tense [may/may not] be null.

Languages that allow null subjects tend to have other associated grammatical traits. For one, they tend to allow declarative sentences with the word order verb + subject as well as subject + verb, as in the following examples from Spanish.

9) a. Juan llegó.
       Juan arrived
   b. Llegó Juan.
       arrived Juan

Secondly, they tend to allow sentences like the following, in which a complementizer (here *que* 'that') is immediately followed by the trace (*t*) of a moved *wh* word.

10) Quién   dijo usted   que *t*   llegó?
    Who   said you   that   arrived
    'Who did you say arrived?'

As the following example shows, such sentences are unacceptable in Standard U.S. English.

11) *Who did you say [$_{CP}$ that [$_{TP}$ *t* arrived]]?
    (deep structure = *you did say that who arrived*)

In other words, languages like Standard U.S. English ([–null subject]) do not allow *that*-trace sequences, whereas languages like Spanish ([+null subject]) do.

Studies on L2 learners of English show that Spanish speakers are more likely to judge subjectless English sentences to be grammatical than are French speakers. This is consistent with the assumption that L1 parameter settings are transferred into the IL grammar, at least in the early stages. Learning a second language can be seen as involving the resetting of parameters that have different values in the L1 and the L2.

Moreover, when Spanish subjects are given a task that requires them to change a declarative sentence into a question, they are more likely to produce a sentence that contains a *that*-trace sequence than are French subjects. For example, if Spanish subjects are given a sentence like *Joshua believed that his father would be late* and asked to form a question asking about the underlined element, they are more likely than French subjects to produce a sentence like *Who did Joshua believe that* t *would be late?* This points toward the possibility that the admissibility of null subjects and the acceptability of *that*-trace sequences are somehow both related to the Null Subject Parameter (i.e., speakers of null subject languages are more likely to permit *that*-trace sequences).

However, there are complications. Remember that the Spanish and French subjects in the study we have been considering had to actually create their own sentences. Another study had both French and Spanish subjects simply judge the grammaticality of English sentences with a *that*-trace violation. Both groups were quite able to reject those sentences as ungrammatical. For some reason, there is a stronger L1 influence when learners have to form new sentences themselves.

Verb Raising

French and English differ in the setting of the Verb Raising Parameter (which is slightly simplified here).

12) *The Verb Raising Parameter*
   A main verb marked for tense [raises/does not raise] to T.

The transformation of Verb Raising takes a verb from within the VP and moves it to T (see Figure 10.5). English does not allow Verb Raising (as the operation is articulated here) but French does. Thus, in French the verb raises to T past a preverbal adverb, but in English it does not. This difference can be seen in the sentences in *13*, in which movement of the verb over the adverb separating it from the T position gives a bad result in English but a good result in French.

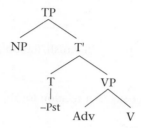

Figure 10.5   Verb Raising

13) a. *Marie watches often *t* television.
   b. Marie regarde souvent *t* la télévision.

Studies have shown that French speakers learning English initially assume that English allows Verb Raising. In order to learn English, they have to reset the value of the Verb Raising Parameter.

Markedness and the Subset Principle

Another interesting facet of a parameter-setting approach to SLA has to do with whether adult L2 learners can reset their parameters and whether the direction of difficulty posited by the Markedness Differential Hypothesis (see Section 2.1) can be captured in a parameter-setting model. The Null Subject Parameter can be used to address these questions. To understand how, we must first consider how a parameter-setting model instantiates the notion of markedness.

   If we consider the two settings of the Null Subject Parameter (+/–), we can see that the different values result in different grammars, as shown in the following sentences from English and Spanish.

14) [–null subject]:   I   speak   Spanish.
   [+null subject]:   Yo   hablo   español.
   Hablo   español.

As you can see, the [+null subject] setting generates more grammatical utterances than the [–null subject] setting does. Therefore the [–] setting is said to be a subset of the [+] setting. Graphically, this can be represented as in Figure 10.6.

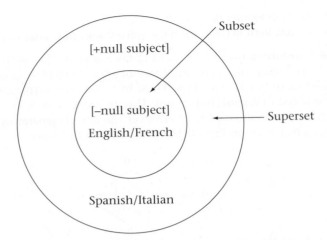

Figure 10.6   Subset/superset relation for the Null Subject Parameter

The **Subset Principle** stipulates that for first language learners, the initial or default setting will be the subset value (i.e., [–null subject] in the case of the Null Subject Parameter). When attempting to reset from subset to superset or from super-set to subset, second language learners need access to different types of evidence. Imagine a learner of English (who has the [–] setting) trying to learn Spanish. The learner's initial assumption will be the L1 parameter setting, which leads to the expectation that all sentences will have overt subjects. When faced with Spanish input, the learner will be exposed to grammatical utterances in the L2 that do not have overt subjects (e.g., *Hablo español* '[I] speak Spanish'), which indicates that the L1 setting is incorrect and needs to be reset. Data like this, which involves grammatical utterances to which one is actually exposed, is referred to as **positive evidence**.

Now imagine a learner whose L1 is Spanish ([+]) who is trying to learn English ([–]). The learner's initial assumption will be that English should be [+null subject], like the L1. The learner's IL grammar will allow both sentences with overt subjects and sentences without. Crucially, there will be no positive evidence in the English input directed at this learner to show that the L1 parameter setting is wrong. The learner will hear sentences with overt subjects, which are sanctioned by the current IL grammar, but there will be no direct indication that sentences with null subjects are not allowed. There is no pressure to reset the parameter. In this case, the learner will have to rely on **negative evidence** (i.e., observations about what is missing or ungrammatical in the data) to reset the parameter. In particular, the learner would either have to be explicitly told what is ungrammatical (**direct negative evidence**), or infer that it is ungrammatical on the basis of the fact that no one else ever says it (**indirect negative evidence**).

Given that direct positive evidence is available in one case (English → Spanish) and negative evidence is required in the other (Spanish → English), we might predict that it will be harder for Spanish speakers to learn the English value of the Null

Subject Parameter than vice versa. In fact, the prediction is borne out. Studies have shown that it is easier for English speakers to reset to the Spanish value of the Null Subject Parameter than it is for Spanish subjects to reset to the English setting.

Let us now consider how an approach based on typological universals would treat the same phenomenon. The presence of null subjects implies the presence of overt subjects, but not vice versa.

15) The presence of overt subjects is implied by the presence of null subjects.

According to this formulation, null subjects are more marked than overt subjects. The Markedness Differential Hypothesis predicts that structures that are more marked typologically will cause difficulty in second language acquisition. The Subset Principle, on the other hand, predicts that structures that are more marked will not cause difficulty because there will be clear evidence that the L1 setting is wrong. Although only the Subset Principle seems to make the correct prediction in the case of the null subjects, further research is necessary in order to see which approach is better able to handle a wider range of data.

2.3   L2 Morphology

The study of second language morphology has a slightly different flavor from the study of either L2 phonology or L2 syntax. L2 phonology has been studied for a long time, though the analyses have changed to reflect changes in linguistic theory. L2 syntax is a much younger field, and much of it has been informed by current linguistic theory. By contrast, L2 morphology has been studied more or less in a theoretical vacuum. In the 1970s, a number of studies collected data on the accuracy of second language learners on a variety of morphemes. This research drew on previous studies in the field of first language acquisition that had attempted to determine the order of acquisition of morphemes in L1 development. The **developmental sequence** in Table 10.7 was found.

Table 10.7   Developmental order for first language acquisition

Morpheme	Example
1. -*ing*	She is work*ing*.
2. plural -*s*	bottle*s*
3. irregular past	She *taught* French.
4. possessive -'*s*	a child'*s* toy
5. copula *be*	I *am* happy.
6. articles	*A* man read *the* book.
7. regular past	She walk*ed* quickly.
8. 3rd person singular -*s*	She walk*s* quickly.
9. auxiliary *be*	She *is* working.

Research on second language acquisition focused on whether the developmental sequence in L2 learning was the same as for L1 learning. The order in Table 10.8 was found.

Table 10.8 Developmental order for second language acquisition

1. *-ing*	4. auxiliary *be*	7. regular past
2. copula *be*	5. plural *-s*	8. 3rd person singular *-s*
3. articles	6. irregular past	9. possessive *-'s*

There are many similarities in the two orders, but also some differences. For example, note that auxiliary and copula *be* are acquired at a relatively earlier point in L2 than in L1 and that the possessive morpheme *-'s* is acquired later in L2 than in L1. To attempt to explain these patterns, we need to look a little more closely at the structures involved.

Children acquire *be* as a copula verb before they acquire *be* as an auxiliary verb. So they produce sentences that have only a copula verb (e.g., *He is hungry*) before they produce sentences that include an auxiliary plus a main verb (e.g., *He is working*) as shown in Figure 10.7.

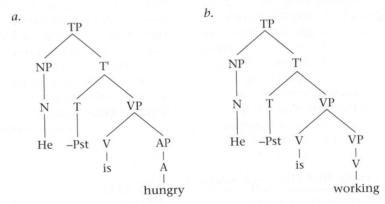

Figure 10.7 Sentence structure for copula versus auxiliary *be*

The structure in *b* has an extra level of complexity in that it has one VP within another. Differences in the L1 and L2 acquisition of *be* seem to arise from this complexity. In contrast to child L1 learners, adult L2 learners appear to be able to use both the simple copula and auxiliary verbs quite early on, presumably because they have both types of structure available to them from their L1.

Remember that English-speaking children acquire the three *-s* morphemes in the order plural, possessive, third-person singular in their first language. Phonetically, these morphemes have the same realization, so we can't say that the order reflects phonological complexity. The order might be explained by noting that noun plurality is a word-level phenomenon (e.g., *dogs*), possessive is a phrase-level phenomenon (e.g., [*the king of England*]'*s* horse, not **the [king]'s of England horse*), and third-person marking involves a relation between the verb and a phrase (the subject) elsewhere in the sentence (e.g., [*That man*] *usually watches TV*). Like the pattern noted for the development of copula and auxiliary *be*, children seem to be acquiring structures in order of complexity, as shown in Figure 10.8.

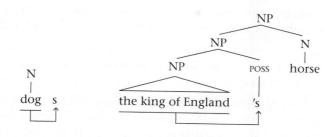

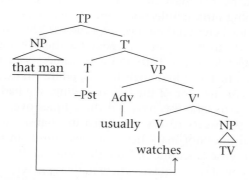

Figure 10.8 Structural implications for three types of /-s/ affix

In contrast, adult second language learners acquire the plural quite early but seem to get both the possessive and the third-person marking quite late—perhaps for reasons involving processing. (When concentrating on getting the words right, we do not always have the processing capacity to produce well-formed higher-level structures.) Interestingly, the adults do not seem to find interphrasal morphology (like third-person marking) more difficult than phrasal morphology (like possessives). This may be because the adults have already acquired the grammar for their first language, and that grammar most likely has both phrase-level and interphrasal morphological phenomena. In contrast, children could conceivably be building a sentence's structure from the bottom up (words → phrases → sentences).

In summary, we note that the order of acquisition data are intriguing in both first and second language acquisition, even though we await a conclusive explanation of the facts.

2.4 Morphology and Syntax

We conclude this section with a discussion of a recent theoretical approach that looks at the interaction of morphology and syntax in second language learners in an attempt to answer one of the questions we have already posed in this chapter: If someone leaves something out, does it really mean he or she doesn't have a representation for it? To answer this question, we will consider what second language learners know about tense. It is well known that nonnative speakers often make mistakes with the tense of a sentence, as exemplified in *16*.

16) You know, I *call* Bill this morning and nobody *answer*. And I *start* to worry . . . He either *stay* in Eliotville, because he said he *call* me last night, and he never did.

We might be tempted to say that this learner lacks knowledge of tense due to the lack of overt past-tense marking. Two theoretical positions have been put forward. The first is the **Impaired Representation Hypothesis**, which argues that the learners have some sort of underlying representation deficiency (i.e., problems with the representation of tense). The second is the **Missing Surface Inflection Hypothesis**, which argues that the learners have the correct underlying functional categories but have difficulty mapping surface inflection onto those categories.

How can we decide between these two hypotheses? We will use the data from a longitudinal case study to build our argument for the Missing Surface Inflection Hypothesis. The subject, known as Patty in the literature, is a native Mandarin (and Hokkien) speaker who first acquired English as an adult. An example of her English is given in *16* above. At the time of the first recording, she had been in the United States for about ten years. She was recorded three times over the next nine years. During that period, she was virtually immersed in English, and yet, as shown in Table 10.9, she often does not mark her past tense forms in **obligatory contexts** (contexts where past tense is required). Note that she supplies the past tense marking in about 34 percent of the contexts where native speakers do. Although Patty is clearly not placing the proper inflectional morphology on her verbs, we will argue that she does have targetlike knowledge of the tense feature.

Table 10.9   Patty's past-tense marking in obligatory contexts

Recording #	Patty's past tense marking/ obligatory contexts	%
1	24/69	34.78
2	191/548	34.85
3	46/136	33.82

In order to show that Patty does have knowledge of tense, we can look at the pronominal subjects of verbs with and without tense. The subject of a tense-bearing verb in English receives nominative case (e.g., *I*, *he*). In contrast, the subjects of verbs that lack tense marking do not receive nominative case (e.g., *me*, *him*), as can be seen by comparing the pronouns in the sentences in *17*.

17) a. I believe that [he   is a liar].

                    NOM   [tense marked]

    b. I believe [him   to be a liar].

                  ACC   [no tense]

In *17a* the second verb (*is*) is marked for tense and the pronoun has nominative case. In *17b*, in contrast, the second verb lacks tense (*to be*) and the preceding pronoun does not have nominative case. Note that *him* is not the object of the verb *believe*—you don't believe him; in fact, you think he's a liar. The point is that there is a connection between tense and nominative case marking.

Let us return to our two hypotheses about Patty. The Impaired Representation Hypothesis holds that because Patty does not use tense marking on her verbs, she should be unable to make the connection between tense and nominative case marking. In contrast, the Missing Surface Inflection Hypothesis suggests that Patty has the category of tense but has trouble with the overt morphological marking; it therefore predicts that she will demonstrate a connection between tense and case marking. So what does she do? The data in Table 10.10 clearly show that Patty correctly assigns nominative case to all pronominal subjects of a tense-bearing verb.

Table 10.10 Patty's use of nominative case on pronominal subjects

Recording #	Nominative subject pronouns/ Past tense contexts	%
1	49/49	100
2	378/378	100
3	76/76	100

Furthermore, Patty does not *incorrectly* mark pronouns in other contexts, as her sentences in *18* demonstrate.

18) It's best for *me* to stay in Shanghai.

    It is possibility for *me* to get out.

    That doesn't have anything to do with *me* leaving home.

These considerations suggest that Patty does have a mental representation of tense that governs case assignment, even though she has fossilized with respect to its morphological expression on verbs.

3 Factors Affecting SLA

So far, we've looked at some of the characteristics of an IL grammar. Now let's turn to a variety of factors that can influence second language acquisition. It is clear that there is much more variation in the grammars of people learning second languages than in the grammars of people learning first languages. This brings us to the question of what factors might help to account for that variation.

3.1 Age

One of the obvious ways in which language learners vary is in their age. People start learning second languages at different points in their lives. Could the age of onset of L2 learning cause different levels of final proficiency?

This is a question usually considered under what is known as the **Critical Period Hypothesis**. We know that biologically based critical periods exist in other species. For example, some birds can learn the song of their species only if exposed to it during a particular window of opportunity. If they hear the song too early or too late, then learning will not take place.

Is second language learning like this? Is there an optimal time (or critical period) to acquire a second language? The answer appears to be "yes and no." Proficiency in a language is a remarkably complex thing (see the discussion of communicative competence in Section 1.3). Usually, discussion of a possible critical period focuses on the area of phonological competence. Although people who begin SLA as adults tend to retain nonnativelike phonology in the target language, it is much more difficult to predict knowledge or ability in any of the other areas of communicative competence (syntax, cohesion, sociolinguistics, etc.) based upon age of acquisition.

In fact, even L2 phonology is not so straightforward as it might first appear to be. We can predict with a fair degree of certainty that people who start learning their L2 before the age of seven will have nativelike L2 speech and that people who start learning after fourteen or fifteen will probably have nonnativelike speech. But the results for people who start learning between the ages of seven and fourteen are much more varied. Some end up with accents, and some do not.

There is no current evidence of anything biological that prevents adults from acquiring proficiency in a second language. Factors that have been considered in the past (like brain lateralization) are now thought to have little predictive value in determining L2 ability. Recent research demonstrates that some people who start learning their second language as adults *are* able to reach a final state that is indistinguishable from native speakers. One study in the syntactic domain shows that near-native speakers perform like native speakers when it comes to speed and accuracy in grammaticality judgment tasks (involving sentences such as *Who did Mary meet the man after she saw* t?).

Similarly, studies have shown that some people (admittedly a minority, but they do exist) can start learning their second language as adults and perform within the range of native speakers when it comes to their pronunciation. When native speaker judges listen to recordings of both native and nonnative speakers (not knowing which is which) and give a global accent rating, there are always some native speakers who do not get a perfect rating and some nonnative speakers who can score more highly than these subjects. Currently, the critical period debate in SLA research is usually couched in terms of the question, "Do adults have access to Universal Grammar?" Rather than looking for changes in the brain that coincide with aging, researchers now look to see whether IL grammars are governed by the same constraints as human languages in general (e.g., English, Navajo, and Swahili).

If adults are engaged in the same kind of developmental process as children, then we would expect their IL grammars to be describable in terms of the same principles and parameters of UG that we use to describe all languages. Conversely, if adults are acquiring their second languages using qualitatively different learning mechanisms than are used to acquire an L1 (e.g., if they use general problem-solving abilities), then we might expect them to adopt hypotheses that are not sanctioned by Universal Grammar. Something like this may in fact happen in the acquisition of gender in French.

Children learning French as a first language seem to have very little trouble learning gender as they learn the words themselves (e.g., *le livre*, 'the book', is masculine; *la table*, 'the table', is feminine, and so on). However, adults whose first language does not have gender often have great difficulty learning French gender. They seem to set up complex (but incorrect) rules for predicting the gender of a given noun. For example, they may assume that words naming parts of the body (or some other semantic category) belong to one gender, or that words that end with a certain sound sequence belong to another. Rules like this sometimes allow nonnative speakers to guess the gender correctly, but they still perform significantly differently from native speakers. This is an example of how adults' greater capacity to formulate general rules can sometimes lead them down the wrong path.

3.2 Individual Differences

Learners vary in ways other than age. Broadly speaking, the researcher asks the question: If learners have a particular quality *x*, does this make them better at second language acquisition? For example, we might look at the effect of inhibition, left-handedness, or some other individual trait on L2 ability. As intuitively appealing as this avenue is, it is one that must be taken carefully. In particular, we must be explicit about three points:

- how we define and measure *x*
- what it means to be *better*
- what aspect of communicative competence we are referring to

Consider in this regard a trait like empathy. It has been argued that people who are empathetic are better language learners. This is an intuitively appealing notion. People who are empathetic can imagine what it feels like to be in someone else's shoes and they can look at things from another perspective. And second language learning certainly involves looking at things from a different perspective. But in SLA research, we need to find a more precise way to evaluate this hypothesis.

There are tests that claim to measure a person's empathy, but how well defined is the notion of empathy? Is one simply empathetic or not, or are there degrees of empathy? If there are degrees, do we see a correlation between degree of empathy and degree of L2 learning success? And what does it mean for empathetic learners to be better language learners than people who aren't empathetic? Do they make fewer errors? Less serious errors? Should we expect people with greater empathy to be better at everything in the L2? Or maybe just at phonology and sociolinguistic competence? On what basis could we make a prediction? These are not simple issues. We raise them not to argue that research in individual variation is misguided but to show some of the complex areas that need to be addressed before we can hope to establish a causal connection between a particular personality trait and success at second language learning.

Let us look at one set of factors that may influence second language learning.

Affective Factors

Affective factors have to do with the emotional side of learning a second language. Clearly there can be a great deal at stake emotionally when learning a second language, and it is possible that emotions affect how successful a second language learner is. Affective factors that have been studied include empathy, anxiety, inhibition, and risk-taking. In this section, we will look at one such factor: motivation.

Learners can vary with respect to the amount or type of motivation they have to learn a second language. If someone is highly motivated to learn, will that person do better at learning? In order to answer this question, we need to say a bit more about what it means to be motivated.

Traditionally, two types of motivation have been proposed: **instrumental motivation** and **integrative motivation**. Instrumental motivation involves wanting to learn the L2 for a specific goal or reason. For example, someone might need to pass a language requirement in order to get a graduate degree or a job with a government agency. Integrative motivation, in contrast, involves wanting to learn the L2 in order to learn more about a particular culture or fit into it better. For instance, someone might want to learn Japanese in order to learn more about a fascinating culture.

Studies have shown that the degree of integrative motivation correlates with the degree of success in language learning. That is, subjects who score highly on tests of integrative motivation do better on certain language tests than comparable subjects who score poorly on the same tests. However, under the right circumstances, studies have also shown that subjects with instrumental motivation rather than integrative motivation can also do well. In particular, integrative motivation may be less important for learners living outside the culture where the target language is spoken. Indeed, for learners of English as a foreign language, a desire to integrate into a native-speaking culture may be less important than the learner's desire to cultivate an **international posture**, symbolized in part by the ability to use English.

Attention in the twenty-first century has also been focused on the dynamic, individual, and contextual nature of motivation. The changeable nature of motivation has been studied on the microlevel within the course of single lessons and on the macrolevel as motivation waxes and wanes over weeks and months. Over both the short and long term, motivation may be linked to the individual's sense of **self-efficacy** (belief in his or her own capacity to succeed) and image of the ideal self as a competent user of the L2. Together, these may lead to self-regulated and motivated behavior that includes effort and persistence. The individual does not learn in a vacuum, however, and motivation also depends on the context of learning. For example, the behavior and attitudes of one's classmates and teacher as well as the value that L2 learning holds within the learner's community can all exert a powerful influence on the learner's motivation and subsequent success.

LANGUAGE MATTERS **Exceptional Language Learning Ability**

Although not all linguists are adept at acquiring communicative competence in second languages, the field of linguistics does attract some extraordinary language learners. One is Stephen Wurm, who grew up in a multilingual family, learning English from his father, Hungarian from his mother, Norwegian from his grandfather, and Finnish and Mongolian from his two grandmothers. In his career, he worked on endangered languages, including Aboriginal languages of Australia and Papua New Guinea. By his retirement, he had learned forty-eight languages.

Another extraordinary language learner among linguists was Ken Hale, who spoke over fifty languages. Professor Hale likened his ability in language learning to musical talent, saying that he needed to work one-on-one with a native speaker, first learning common nouns, then the sound system, and moving to complex sentences, which he claimed were more regular than simple sentences. Hale grew up in Arizona, and when he discovered he could speak Navajo as a young teenager, he would spend time sitting on a rock every day and talking to himself in Navajo. When he went to a boarding high school, he learned first Hopi, then Jemez from his roommates. As an adult, he continued to acquire Native American languages as well as European languages and a number of Aboriginal languages of Australia, including Warlpiri. At his memorial service in 2001, eulogies were offered in English, Hebrew, Hopi, Navajo, Warlpiri, and Wampanoag (a Native American language of Massachusetts that Hale had helped revitalize).

Information from: William Honan (1997), "To Masters of Language, a Long Overdue Toast," *New York Times* 31 Dec: B8; Samuel Jay Keyser, "Kenneth Locke Hale" (obituary), *Language* 79, 2 (2003): 411–422; and Wolfgang Saxon (2001), "Kenneth Hale, 67, Preserver of Nearly Extinct Languages" (obituary), *New York Times* 19 Oct., accessed through www.nytimes.com.

4 The L2 Classroom

It has been flippantly said that people have been successfully acquiring second languages for thousands of years, but when teachers get involved, the success rate plummets. This comment is probably more a reflection of people's unfortunate experience in certain types of language classrooms (which may have been dull or even physically threatening, depending on the century) than it is a statement about general pedagogic utility. However, the fact remains that language classrooms can be sheltered environments where students can benefit from being given the opportunity to learn and practice without being subject to the penalties for failure that can be imposed outside the classroom.

We should acknowledge at this point that there is really no such thing as *the* second language classroom. In reality, all classrooms are different because they have different people in them (both students and teachers).

4.1   Focus on Form

One of the most obvious characteristics of a second language class is the presence of a teacher who may provide explicit instruction about the actual form of the target language. Let us look at what we can learn from the research on what is known as **focus on form**. The term *focus on form* encompasses two distinct practices that tend to occur in most L2 classrooms: instruction about the language and explicit correction.

Most second language classes present the students with some sort of information about the language—noting, for example, that English requires an overt subject for a verb with tense or that French has nasal vowels. Instruction of this type is designed to improve the form (or **accuracy**) of the student's L2. In all likelihood, other activities that happen in the class will focus on giving the student a chance to improve **fluency** or particular sociolinguistic skills.

Error correction is also designed to improve the form of the student's L2. Regardless of the methodology used, in most classes today there is some focus on form and some error correction. The interesting research question is whether either of these practices can be shown to have a positive effect on the learner. Do students who get corrected do better than students who don't?

The question may not be as straightforward as it appears. Remember that it has frequently been argued in first language acquisition research that attempts at error correction are relatively infrequent and don't really affect children's grammars. Could it be different for adult second language learners? The learning environment is different in that adult learners (unlike children) are usually exposed to a fair amount of error correction. But does that make a difference? Not surprisingly, this question is difficult to answer. Some studies have argued that second language learners who receive correction develop at about the same pace as those who do not. Other studies have shown certain increases in accuracy as the result of correction.

LANGUAGE MATTERS   It Can Be Comforting to Hear Your Native Language

A seven-year-old Siberian tiger named Boris moved from a zoo near Montreal (in French-speaking Quebec) to a zoo in Edmonton (in English-speaking Alberta). At first, zookeepers found him shy and aloof. Then one zookeeper began to speak to him in French. Immediately, the tiger came over to her and seemed much friendlier. It's not just humans who get used to a particular language!

Information from: Katherine Harding, "Vive le Quebec Tigre" (news), *Globe and Mail*, 29 May 2007, accessed through www.theglobeandmail.com.

These results may not be as contradictory as they seem. The areas where correction seems to be most useful involve the use of lexical items. Feedback concerning certain structural phenomena may not be as effective. For example, the previously mentioned study of French speakers learning about the limited scope of Verb Raising in English (it applies only to copula and auxiliary verbs; see Section 2.2) found that while there were short-term improvements in the learners who were explicitly taught the relevant facts, there were no significant long-term effects. When the learners were tested a year later, they had reverted to their pre-instructional performance. Part of the reason for this poor performance may have been that the explicit instruction was not connected to a meaningful context.

But this doesn't mean that there is no place for explicit instruction in the classroom. Students benefit most when focus on form happens within a meaningful interaction. Research has shown that what is known as **spontaneous focus on form** can be beneficial to students' overall proficiency. There is a difference between **reactive focus on form** (when the teacher responds to an erroneous utterance with instruction) and **pre-emptive focus on form** (when a teacher or another student draws a learner's attention to a form that is anticipated to be problematic). An example of reactive focus on form would be the following exchange:

> *Student*: Sometimes they complain that.
> *Teacher*: They complain *about* that.

An example of pre-emptive focus on form can be seen in the following exchange:

> *Teacher*: Do you know what *ballet* is?
> *Student*: Ah, the classical music, the ladies . . .
> *Teacher*: Men and women, it's dance, it's a type of dance. Ballet.

This distinction can help explain some of the seemingly conflicting research results insofar as pre-emptive focus on form is more effective than reactive focus on form. Studies that didn't take this difference into account might have reached different conclusions.

In sum, adult students usually expect error correction, and teachers are accustomed to providing it. Assuming that the class is not devoted entirely to instruction that focuses on form (with no opportunity for meaningful practice), error correction doesn't seem to cause any harm. In a class with activities that focus on both form and fluency, the students tend to emerge with greater accuracy. Teachers who provide opportunities for interactions with both pre-emptive and reactive focus on form are serving the learners well.

4.2   Education in a Bilingual Environment

Students designated as **English learners (ELs)**—defined as students participating in language assistance programs—represent the fastest growing segment of the school population, accounting for over 9 percent of all pre-K through 12 pupils in the United States. While many ELs are recent immigrants, in fact over half of ELs in U.S. schools were born in the United States. ELs are more heavily distributed in states such as California, Texas, and New York, with the proportion of nonnative speakers of English accounting for more than 20 percent of the student population in some school districts. By far, the largest group of ELs speak Spanish as their first language (estimated at approximately 3.5 million in 2011–12), followed by speakers of Chinese (estimated at almost 90,000). A variety of programs exist to address the disparate needs of the EL population in U.S. schools. These programs are influenced not only by the linguistic needs of the ELs but also by the available resources and political beliefs of the community within which the ELs live.

Newcomer Programs

Newcomer programs are temporary transitional programs for new arrivals in the U.S., some of whom may be refugees escaping war in their own countries. Not only may the ELs have a low level of English, but they may also have educational gaps when they missed one or more years of school. Newcomer programs aim to help these students acquire English skills, strengthen their L1 literacy skills, provide some content instruction, and help acculturate students to the U.S. school environment so that they can move into mainstream classes as soon as possible. Successful programs also take account of the particular needs of their population, offering flexible scheduling and connecting with the family and social services.

English Immersion

English immersion may be the educational mode of choice either out of necessity or out of belief. On the one hand, English immersion for all ELs may be the only viable option if there are very few ELs in a school, if the ELs come from many different first language backgrounds, or if there is a lack of trained bilingual teachers. On the other hand, English immersion is mandated by law in California, Arizona, and Massachusetts, where voters decided that bilingual education should not be provided to ELs. In localities where bilingual education is not possible or not allowed, **structured English immersion (SEI)** may be the choice for ELs for their first year or two in the school district. In SEI, students are grouped according to their level of language proficiency and receive four hours or more per day of intensive English language instruction. During this time, academic content is very much subordinate to language instruction. Once they exit the program, ELs may still receive some language support.

Forms of ESL support may include **sheltered instruction**, in which ELs learn academic content that has been modified to take account of their language proficiency; teachers include language objectives in the lesson plan, modify input so that it is comprehensible to ELs, and provide manipulatives, activities, and opportunities for student interaction in order to make the content material accessible to ELs. In a **pull-out** or **push-in program**, ELs are mainstreamed but spend time with an ESL tutor or paraprofessional either outside or inside the classroom.

Bilingual Education

When a school has enough ELs sharing the same first language and the practice is allowed by law, it is possible to provide bilingual education in which students receive at least part of their daily instruction in the first language. Generally, bilingual education is offered at the elementary school level and introduces instruction in literacy in the first language to students whose primary language is not English. **Transitional bilingual education** does not aim for full biliteracy but is intended instead to provide instruction in the first language only so long as it takes the student to acquire enough English to take part in mainstream classes taught in English. Transitional bilingual education provides ELs with a foundation of literacy skills and content knowledge comparable to that of native English-speaking children, and research with Spanish speakers indicates that there is positive transfer of literacy skills from the first language to the second language. In contrast, **maintenance (or developmental) bilingual education** usually lasts for five or six years and has the goal of promoting bilingualism and literacy in both languages in addition to academic achievement for ELs.

Dual Language Programs/Two-Way Immersion (TWI)

Dual language programs (also known as **two-way immersion programs** or **TWI**) provide bilingual education for native speakers of English and ELs together. The vast majority of programs are Spanish/English, although other languages taught with English include Chinese, French, Korean, and Navajo.

Three criteria are used to classify a program as a TWI program. First, language minority and language majority students must be integrated academically and socially for at least half of the day. Second, content and literacy instruction must be given in both languages to all students; for example, in a Spanish TWI program, Spanish speakers and English speakers would be taught together in both English and Spanish. Third, the number of language minority and language majority students must be balanced, with neither group comprising more than two thirds of the class. Typically, these programs are used in elementary school, rather than in high school, and students join the program when they start school. In some programs, the minority language is used 80–90 percent of the time for the first year with gradual transitioning to a balanced use of both languages by the time students reach fourth grade. Other programs provide balanced instruction in both languages from the start.

One attraction of TWI programs is that, unlike one-way bilingual education, they offer bilingualism for all students, language-majority and language-minority alike. Furthermore, because the students are learning each other's native languages, language learning is enhanced by social interactions with native speakers, and academic excellence is promoted in both languages.

Effectiveness

The question of effectiveness of various programs for ELs is not trivial. If an EL does not understand what the teacher is saying or cannot read the textbook, he or she cannot make progress in the content subjects, with the result that the EL falls further and further behind academically. Nationwide, there is a large achievement gap between ELs and other students. For example, the national high school graduation rate (in 2011–12) was 80 percent for all students, but only 59 percent for ELs. As of

2013, measures of reading and math proficiency in eighth grade showed enormous gaps between ELs and other students, as Table 10.11 shows.

Table 10.11   Reading and math proficiency of eighth grade pupils

	Reading		Math	
Level	ELs	Non-ELs	ELs	Non-ELs
Below basic	70%	20%	69%	24%
Basic	27%	42%	26%	39%
Proficient	3%	33%	4%	28%
Advanced	0%	4%	1%	9%

Data from: "English Learners (ELs) and NAEP (National Assessment of Educational Programs)," January 2015. Accessed through the website of the Office of English Language Acquisition at www.ncela.ed.gov /files/fast_facts/OELA_FastFacts_ELsandNAEP.pdf.

In evaluating the effectiveness of programs for ELs it is important to note when the students' progress was measured. Typically, measures taken in early elementary school or when students first exit a bilingual program may show an advantage in English proficiency for pupils in English immersion. This is not surprising given the greater amount of class time spent on English in the early years. However, this advantage of English immersion over bilingual education does not last. By middle school, pupils who have had bilingual education or dual language immersion score higher than pupils in English-only immersion in tests of English proficiency and math. Various studies conducted over 30 years have in general shown long-term advantages for bilingual or dual-language programs over English immersion. One large-scale study examined student records of standardized test scores in reading, language arts, and math from over 200,000 students who had participated in various forms of bilingual education, English-only ESL, or English-language mainstream education with no special language support. Students who had participated in bilingual or dual language programs were the only ones to reach the 50th percentile in both the first and second languages and to maintain their achievement over time. This group also had the fewest dropouts. The group with the lowest scores were those students who had entered the English language mainstream with no language support programs; this group also accounted for the largest percentage of dropouts.

Heritage Language Programs

Heritage language programs are designed to maintain, preserve, or revive heritage languages of indigenous people, immigrants, or refugees. They can be community-based or associated with an educational institution. Heritage language programs for Native Americans have taken a number of different forms, some more successful than others in encouraging heritage language use among children. At one extreme are programs that include a few minutes of language instruction per day in a heritage language that children no longer speak; such programs, although well-intentioned, have generally provided students with some possible sense of pride in the heritage language but little in the way of language skills other than a handful of vocabulary words. A more effective model for preschoolers is a **language nest**, a term coined originally in New Zealand for preschool language immersion programs for Maori children, and now being tried in a variety of settings in the United States. However, if the heritage language is not used in the home, in the community, or at school, then it can be quickly forgotten once children leave the nest.

Among groups with a larger base of native speakers of the heritage language within the surrounding community, bilingual or immersion programs have been developed in schools. In Hawaii, for example, as of 2015–16, 21 public schools were designated as Hawaiian language immersion schools. Typically, in these schools, Hawaiian is used exclusively in the first years and English gradually introduced in fifth grade and onwards. Evaluation of ninth grade students in this program revealed that they scored as highly on English language standardized tests as their peers in nonimmersion programs and were attaining mastery of the Hawaiian language as well. Similarly in the scattered Yupik-speaking villages of Alaska, various forms of bilingual education have been developed to encourage Yupik language maintenance among English-dominant students or to encourage acquisition of English along with initial content instruction in Yupik for Yupik-speaking students. In Montana, an immersion program for grades K–8 was created with Blackfoot as the language of instruction, and a handful of schools in North and South Dakota are experimenting with immersion in the Lakota language.

Benefits of Bilingualism

One of the reasons for the interest in bilingual programs is the evidence that second language learning is correlated with other benefits. All of the following have been found in certain second language learners:

- increased syntactic complexity in the L1

- increased sensitivity to the needs of the listener

- higher scores on the Scholastic Aptitude Test

- higher scores on tests of analogical reasoning

- higher scores on tests of mathematical ability

- delay in the onset of symptoms in cases of dementia

Summing Up

This chapter has dealt with a number of issues in the field of second language acquisition. We investigated the notion of an **interlanguage** grammar and the influence of both the source and target languages on this grammar in terms of **transfer** and developmental errors. Proficiency in a second language requires both knowledge and ability, something captured in a model of **communicative competence**. A learner must acquire knowledge in all linguistic domains (phonetics, phonology, morphology, syntax, and semantics) as well as the ability to use that knowledge in a variety of social contexts.

What is easy or difficult to acquire in a second language has been investigated from a variety of perspectives. We focused on Universal Grammar (the **Subset Principle**) and typological universals (the **Markedness Differential Hypothesis**). However, it is not just universals that influence second language learning; the specific characteristics of an individual can also affect the process. **Affective factors** influence second language learning. So too do factors such as **focus on form** and bilingual education.

The field of second language acquisition is remarkably diverse, in part because of what is involved in L2 learning. Someone who is attempting to learn an additional language must develop new mental representations and develop facility at accessing those representations in a variety of circumstances. The field of SLA research must therefore draw on philosophy (theories of mind), psychology (theories of learning, theories of performance), linguistics (theories of linguistic structure), and pedagogy (theories of instruction). This is probably the main reason why we have not established anything like a comprehensive theory of how second languages are learned. But bit by bit, piece by piece, we're starting to put together some pieces of the puzzle.

Key Terms

General terms concerning the study of second language acquisition

bilingualism
fossilized
interlanguage (IL)

second language acquisition
transfer

Terms concerning second language proficiency

communicative competence
competence
grammatical competence
illocutionary competence

performance
sociolinguistic competence
target
textual competence

Terms concerning interlanguage grammars

developmental sequence
direct negative evidence
Impaired Representation
 Hypothesis
implicational universals
indirect negative evidence
marked
markedness
Markedness Differential
 Hypothesis

Missing Surface Inflection
 Hypothesis
negative evidence
Null Subject Parameter
obligatory contexts
positive evidence
Similarity Differential Rate
 Hypothesis
unmarked
Verb Raising

Terms concerning other factors affecting second language acquisition

affective factors
Critical Period Hypothesis
instrumental motivation

integrative motivation
international posture
self-efficacy

Terms related to the second language classroom

accuracy	pre-emptive focus on form
fluency	reactive focus on form
focus on form	spontaneous focus on form

Terms related to education in a bilingual environment

dual language (two-way immersion [TWI]) programs	newcomer programs
English immersion	pull-out program
English learners (ELs)	push-in program
heritage language programs	sheltered instruction
language nest	structured English immersion (SEI)
maintenance (developmental) bilingual education	transitional bilingual education

Recommended Reading

Archibald, John, ed. 2000. *Second Language Acquisition and Linguistic Theory*. Oxford: Blackwell.

Grosjean, François. 2010. *Bilingual: Life and Reality*. Cambridge, MA: Harvard University Press.

Hawkins, Roger. 2001. *Second Language Syntax: A Generative Introduction*. Oxford: Blackwell.

Herschensohn, Julia, and Martha Young-Scholten, eds. 2013. *The Cambridge Handbook of Second Language Acquisition*. Cambridge, UK: Cambridge University Press.

Meisel, Jürgen M. 2011. *First and Second Language Acquisition: Parallels and Differences*. Cambridge, UK: Cambridge University Press.

Ritchie, William C., and Tej K. Bhatia. 2009. *The New Handbook of Second Language Acquisition*. Bingley, UK: Emerald Group.

White, Lydia. 2003. *Second Language Acquisition and Universal Grammar*. Cambridge, UK: Cambridge University Press.

Exercises

1. Consider the changes that would result if a particular L1 transfered aspects of its phonology to the L2.

    i) Write the following sentence in phonetic transcription. *The bad guys tried to climb out and thought they had made it until they saw the dog.*

    ii) Now transcribe the sentence again and apply these changes:

    a) Devoice word-final obstruents.
    b) Turn interdental fricatives into alveolar fricatives.
    c) Delete the second consonant of a word-final consonant cluster.
    d) Delete glottal fricatives.

2. Indicate the type of error (phonological, morphological, syntactic, or lexical) found in the following sentences. (See Section 2.)
   a) She play tennis almost every day.
   b) I no get on the train on time.
   c) There are many nationalities live in my city.
   d) I'm not a very good cooker.
   e) You should get your hairs cut.
   f) Look at that goose with antlers!
   g) I miss the bus, yesterday.
   h) Tank you very much.

3. Some dialects of Arabic break up clusters by inserting an epenthetic vowel before a problematic consonant (unlike the dialect illustrated in example 5 of Section 2.1). How would a speaker of this dialect pronounce the words *plant*, *transport*, and *translate*? Write each word with the epenthetic [i] in the correct place and periods separating syllables.

4. In your second language learning experience, what is an example of an L2 property that seemed very different from your L1 and that you found easy to learn? What is an example of something different that you found hard to learn? What do you think might have led to the difference in ease of learning? Relate your experience to factors discussed in Section 2.1.

5. In second language learners whose first language does not allow coda consonants, we sometimes see variation in the production of English codas. Examine the following phrases and propose an explanation as to why some stops in coda position are deleted and others are produced. Segments in **boldface** are produced while ~~struckthrough~~ segments are deleted. Focus only on either boldface or struck-through segments for this question. (See Section 2.1.)
   a) cu**p** of coffee
   b) ba~~ck~~ to work
   c) me**t** on the train
   d) ba~~d~~ with numbers

6. In the following sentences produced by the same speaker, why might we find variation in the accuracy of the production of the interdental fricative? (Hint: consider aspects of the complexity of the two sentences.) (See Section 1.4.)
   a) Put [ð]at box over [ð]ere.
   b) Not having been swamped by [d]e waves, [d]eir yacht crossed [d]e line first.

7. Consider a Spanish learner of English and an English learner of Spanish. Do you think it would be more difficult for an English speaker to learn to drop pronominal subjects and produce grammatical Spanish sentences like "No speak French" or for a Spanish speaker to learn that pronominal subjects cannot be dropped and hence to avoid producing ungrammatical English sentences like "No speak German"? What factors led you to your answer? (See Section 2.2.)

8. What explanation would you give for a native speaker of French who produced the English sentence *I drink frequently coffee*? How could you explain the fact that when the same speaker produces the sentence *He is frequently late*, it is grammatical? Do any other English verbs have the same properties as *be*? For assistance, see Section 2.2 in this chapter and Chapter 5, Section 4.1.

9. Consider the possible responses of a teacher when a student produces the following ungrammatical sentence: *Why he should bring a sweater?*

    Teacher A: *That should be "why should he bring a sweater?"*
    Teacher B: *He should?*
    Teacher C: *Think about what you know about WH questions with modals in them.*
    Teacher D: *Because it might be cold in the theater.*

    What do you see as the pros and cons of each of the responses? What might influence your response? (See Section 4.1.)

10. Imagine that you are teaching English to a group of L2 learners. How might you respond to the following nontargetlike utterances? What do you think the intended utterance was? If you tried to explain the nature of the errors, what would you say? (See Section 4.1.)
    a) I very appreciate your help.
    b) My country develops very fast, but between people disappear emotion, friendship, and conscience.
    c) I was disgusted for the film.
    d) I will give some information about who I am, where did I come from, and what has made me who I am today.
    e) Me, I'll not go ever to that place!
    f) Is raining.
    g) I bought in Japan.

11. Based on what you have learned about the pros and cons of various language programs (see Section 4.2), respond to the following statement:

    It's the school system's job to make sure that nonnative speakers of English learn English. They need English in order to be able to succeed in this country. We want them to succeed. If we encourage them to speak their own language, then ghettoes will form and they'll never learn English. And if we want them to learn English, then obviously they need to be exposed to more English. What good is it knowing how to speak another language in North America? What they need is English, English, and more English.

eleven

Psycholinguistics: The Study of Language Processing

Gary Libben

> *Words! Mere words! How terrible they were! How clear, and vivid, and cruel! One could not escape from them. And yet what subtle magic there was in them!*
>
> —OSCAR WILDE, *The Picture of Dorian Gray* (1891)

OBJECTIVES

In this chapter, you will learn:

- what methods psycholinguists use to study language processing
- how linguistic concepts and principles contribute to understanding language comprehension and production
- how psycholinguistic models are used to explain language processing

 **LaunchPad Solo** | For more helpful content and quizzes, go to the LaunchPad Solo
macmillan learning | for *Contemporary Linguistics* at **launchpadworks.com**.

We engage in language processing every day of our lives. This processing takes place when we watch television, listen to the radio, read a passing billboard while driving, or discuss the weather. Usually these language activities are carried out with great ease and in a completely subconscious manner. We might sometimes be aware that we are searching for a word, composing a sentence, or straining to understand someone else, but we are never aware of the actual mechanisms and operations involved in producing and understanding language.

Psycholinguistics is the study of these language-processing mechanisms. Psycholinguists study how word meaning, sentence meaning, and discourse meaning are computed and represented in the mind. They study how complex words and sentences are composed in speech and how they are broken down into their constituents in the acts of listening and reading. In short, psycholinguists seek to understand how language is "done."

We begin this introduction to the field of psycholinguistics by discussing some methods used by psycholinguists to probe language representation and processing in the mind. This is followed by a summary of recent research on language processing in the domains of phonetics, phonology, morphology, and syntax. Finally, we discuss how these various aspects of linguistic processing work together to make the everyday acts of speaking, listening, and reading appear so simple and effortless. Although psycholinguists study both production and comprehension, this chapter focuses primarily on language processing during comprehension and therefore draws mostly on data from listening and reading.

1   Methods of Psycholinguistic Research

The key fact that guides psycholinguistic methodology is that language users are unaware of the details of language processing. Simply paying attention to what you are doing will not provide reliable insights into how you access words or build sentences. Perhaps the reason for this is that in normal use, language processing must occur very quickly. By shielding mental linguistic operations from the conscious mind, the language-processing system may be maximizing its ability to operate with speed and efficiency.

In order to get a sense of just how subconscious language processing is, you might try the following exercise: give a friend a page of text to read silently and sit opposite him or her. Carefully observe your friend's eyes as they move across the text. You will notice that the eyes do not move smoothly from left to right but rather proceed in a series of jerks called **saccades**. Like most of us, your friend probably has the subjective impression that his or her eyes are moving very evenly across the page. But that subjective impression is incorrect. We are simply not constructed to be able to monitor many of our automatic activities, including language processing.

A substantial additional challenge for the psycholinguistic researcher comes from the fact that most of language processing involves not observable physical events such as eye movement but rather mental events that cannot be observed directly. Research in this field therefore requires that mental language-processing events be inferred from observable behavior. Consequently, a large part of psycholinguistic research is concerned with the development of new (and often very clever) techniques to uncover how language processing is accomplished. Some of these techniques are presented in the following sections.

1.1   Field Methods: Slips of the Tongue

Some of the earliest and most influential studies of language processing examined the spontaneous slips of the tongue produced during speech. One kind of slip of the tongue is known as a **Spoonerism**—after Reverend William A. Spooner, who was head of New College, Oxford between 1903 and 1925. Reverend Spooner was famous for producing a great many, often humorous, speech errors. Here are some of his more well-known mistakes.

1) What he intended: You have missed all my history lectures.
   What he said: You have hissed all my mystery lectures.

2) What he intended: noble sons of toil
   What he said: noble tons of soil

3) What he intended: You have wasted the whole term.
   What he said: You have tasted the whole worm.

4) What he intended: the dear old Queen
   What he said: the queer old dean

Beginning in the 1960s, Victoria Fromkin began to study these and other naturally occurring slips of the tongue and noted that they can be very revealing of the manner in which sentences are created in speech. For instance, as can be seen in the examples above, the characteristic pattern in Reverend Spooner's errors is a tendency to exchange the initial consonants of words in the utterance. When these segment exchanges create new words (as opposed to nonwords as in *fire and brimstone → bire and frimstone*), the result is often humorous. But here's the important psycholinguistic point: in order for these exchanges to occur, the sentence would have to be planned out before the person begins to say it. Otherwise, how would it be possible in example *1* for the first segment of the sixth word *history* to be transported backwards so that it becomes the first segment of the third word (*missed → hissed*)?

Another important observation that Fromkin made was that speech errors also often involve "mixing and matching" morphemes within words. Consider the following slips of the tongue.

5) Intended: rules of word formation
   Produced: words of rule formation

6) Intended: I'd forgotten about that.
   Produced: I'd forgot aboutten that.

7) Intended: easily enough
   Produced: easy enoughly

All these errors involve morphemes being exchanged within a sentence. As is the case for sound exchange errors, these slips of the tongue provide evidence that a sentence must be planned out to some degree before speech begins. They also provide evidence that the morpheme, rather than the word, is the fundamental building block of English sentence production. Note how in example *5* the inflectional suffix *-s* remains in its original place, while the nouns *rule* and *word* reverse positions. In examples *6* and *7*, it is the suffixes that move while the stems remain in their original positions. These examples all suggest that morphological components of words can function independently during sentence planning (and also in sentence misplanning).

As can be seen from these examples, slips of the tongue can offer a fascinating window to the mechanisms involved in language production and to the role that linguistic units such as phonemes and morphemes play in that production. But because slips of the tongue are naturally occurring events, the researcher has no control over when and where they will occur and must simply wait for them to happen. In this way, the analysis of slips of the tongue is a **field technique** and differs from the **experimental paradigms** discussed in the following sections. In these experimental paradigms, the researcher takes an active role in controlling the circumstances under which language is processed, the stimuli to which the experimental participants are exposed, and the ways in which participants may respond to these stimuli.

1.2 Experimental Methods: Words in the Mind

One of the most intense areas of psycholinguistic research has been the investigation of how words are organized in the mind. We are all in possession of a vocabulary that forms the backbone of our ability to communicate in a language. In many ways, this vocabulary must be used the way a normal dictionary is used. It is consulted to determine what words mean, how they are spelled, and what they sound like. But the dictionary in our minds, our mental lexicon, must also be substantially different from a desktop dictionary. It must be much more flexible, accommodating the new words that we learn with ease. It must be organized so that words can be looked up extremely quickly—word recognition takes less than one-third of a second and the average adult reads at a rate of about 250 words per minute. It must allow us to access entries in terms of a wide variety of characteristics. **Tip-of-the-tongue phenomena**, in which we are temporarily unable to access a word, are particularly revealing with respect to how flexible access to the mental lexicon can be—we have all experienced episodes in which we eventually retrieve words on the basis of their meaning, sound, spelling, first letter, or even what they rhyme with.

LANGUAGE MATTERS   Early Research and Experimentation

Sigmund Freud (1856–1939) allowed his patients to speak as freely as possible, recorded their utterances, and sought to find meaning in unintentional speech errors, which he called *Fehlleistungen* ('faulty actions'). In his 1901 book *The Psychopathology of Everyday Life*, Freud discusses numerous speech errors, which he analyzed as revealing unconscious desires, memories, or conflicts—the infamous "Freudian slips."

Early Experimentation

Although primarily interested in memory, Hermann Ebbinghaus (1850–1909) may be considered the first to have conducted psycholinguistic experiments. In 1885, he reported his use of nonsense syllables (e.g., *bim*, *lup*) as the basis of investigations into human learning, retention, and recall.

Many psycholinguists conceive of the mental lexicon as a collection of individual units as in Figure 11.1. In this figure, the lexicon is shown as a space in which entries of different types are stored and linked together. The main questions that are asked about the mental lexicon are these: (1) How are entries linked? (2) How are entries accessed? (3) What information is contained in an entry?

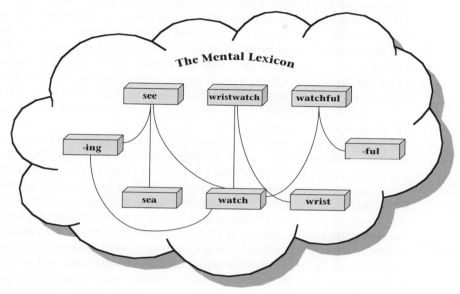

Figure 11.1   Units in the mental lexicon

Although these questions are simple and straightforward, there is no way to answer them directly because the human mental lexicon cannot be observed. So the psycholinguist must use special experimental methods to understand how words are organized, accessed, and represented in the mind. We will briefly discuss the two most common of these methods—**lexical decision** and **priming**.

Lexical Decision

In the lexical decision paradigm, the experimental participant (in this example, a native speaker of English) is seated in front of a computer screen. A word appears in the middle of the screen and the participant must judge as quickly as possible whether the word is a real English word and press a button labeled "yes" or a button labeled "no."

This task is very easy for participants to carry out. They typically see and judge hundreds of words in a single fifteen-minute session. In most lexical decision experiments, there are two **dependent variables**—that is, things that are being measured: the time that it takes for a participant to respond (**response latency**) and the accuracy of the participant's judgment (**response accuracy**). A response is judged as correct if a participant responds "yes" to a real word such as *glove* or *sadness* and "no" to a nonword such as *blove* or *sadding*.

Lexical decision experiments usually involve comparing participants' performance on one set of stimuli (e.g., nouns) to their performance on another set of stimuli (e.g., verbs). The key to the importance of the experimental paradigm is that in order for a participant to respond "no" to a stimulus such as *blove* or "yes" to a real word such as *glove*, the participant's mental lexicon must be accessed. The lexical decision task can therefore be used to measure the speed and accuracy with which words in the mental lexicon are accessed. It has been found in many experiments that participants take about half a second (500 milliseconds) to press the "yes" button for frequently used words such as *free* but almost three-quarters of a second to press the "yes" button for less common words such as *fret*. This finding has been called the **frequency effect**. Assuming that longer response times reflect processing that is more difficult or complex, this finding suggests that our mental dictionaries are organized so that words that we typically need more often (the frequent words) are more easily and quickly available to us.

Another way in which the lexical decision task can be used to explore language representation and processing is to investigate the speed and accuracy with which participants press the "no" button for different types of stimuli. It has been found, for example, that pronounceable nonwords such as *plib* show slower "no" response times than unpronounceable nonwords such as *nlib*. Thus, participants' lexical decisions seem to take into account the phonotactic constraints of the language. It has also been found that nonwords that sound like real words (e.g., *blud*, *phocks*) take longer to reject than stimuli that are nonwords both visually and phonologically. Again this tells us that aspects of phonology are automatically activated during word reading. (Note that in the lexical decision task, the participant never has to pronounce the word aloud.)

The Priming Paradigm

The priming paradigm very often involves the lexical decision task and can be considered an extension of it. Recall that in lexical decision tasks, different categories of stimuli (e.g., concrete versus abstract words) are compared in terms of participants' response latency and accuracy. Priming experiments typically involve the same procedure as the lexical decision task except that the word to be judged (now called the **target**) is preceded by another stimulus (called the **prime**). What is measured is the extent to which the prime influences the participant's lexical decision performance on the target stimulus.

The priming paradigm is an excellent technique for probing how words are related in the mind. One of the first experiments using this paradigm showed that response time is faster when a target is preceded by a semantically related prime (e.g., *cat-dog*) as compared to when it is preceded by an unrelated prime (e.g., *bat-dog*). Results of this sort lead us to the view that words are related in the mind in terms of networks. On the basis of evidence from these priming experiments, psycholinguists reason that when a word such as *cat* is seen, its representation is activated in the mind, and that activation spreads to other words in the lexical network that are semantically related (e.g., *dog*). Because the mental representation for *dog* has already been activated through the prime, it is in a sense "warmed up" so that when the participant later sees it on the screen as the target, response time is faster than it other-wise would have been. This is called the **priming effect** (as shown in Figure 11.2).

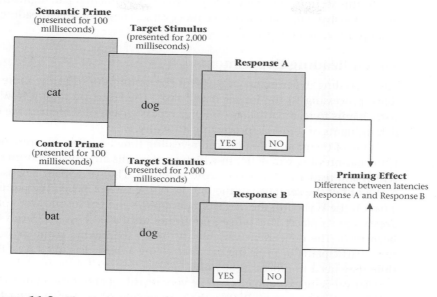

Figure 11.2   The structure of a lexical decision experiment with semantic priming

In recent years, the priming paradigm has been used to explore many aspects of the representation of words in the mind, and researchers have explored many types of priming in addition to the semantic priming described above. For example, prim-ing effects have been found for orthographically similar words (e.g., *couch-touch*), for phonologically similar words (e.g., *light-bite*), and for word roots and complex forms (e.g., *legal-illegality*). This last finding, which suggests that words are represented in the mind in terms of their constituent morphemes, will be discussed further in Sec-tion 2.2.

1.3   Experimental Methods: Sentence Processing

The lexical decision and priming paradigms offer interesting insights into how words are processed but are of limited use in exploring the processing of sentences. The main reason for this is that the types of questions asked about sentence processing tend to be different from those asked about the mental lexicon. Because every sen-tence is different, sentence processing must rely on a particular type of computation (as opposed to a particular type of storage, in the case of words). It is presumed that in sentence processing (i.e., in reading or listening), a sentence is understood through the analysis of the meanings of its words and through the analysis of its syntactic structure. Psycholinguists refer to this type of unconscious automatic analysis as **pars-ing**. Much of the research on sentence processing is concerned with the principles and steps in parsing, its speed, and the manner and conditions under which it can break down.

In this section, we review two groups of experimental paradigms that have been used extensively to study sentence processing. These are timed-reading experiments and eye-movement experiments.

Timed-Reading Experiments

Timed-reading experiments begin with the assumption that the more difficult sentence processing is, the longer it will take. Therefore, by timing how long it takes participants to read particular sentence types or parts of sentences, we can study the determinants of sentence-processing difficulty.

One of the more common and revealing timed-reading experimental paradigms is the bar-pressing paradigm, in which participants are seated in front of a computer screen and read a sentence one word at a time. The participant begins by seeing the first word of the sentence in the middle of the screen. When the participant presses a bar on the keyboard, the first word disappears and the second word of the sentence appears in its place. This process continues until all the words in the sentence have been read. The dependent variable in these experiments is the amount of time it takes participants to press the bar after seeing a particular word (i.e., the amount of time they need to process that word).

Bar-pressing experiments can be very revealing about the manner in which sentence processing occurs. Rather than producing equal bar-pressing times across a sentence, participants show a pattern that reflects the syntactic structure of the sentence. An example of such a pattern is shown in Figure 11.3, which displays bar-pressing times for the sentence *The Chinese, who used to produce kites, used them in order to carry ropes across the rivers.*

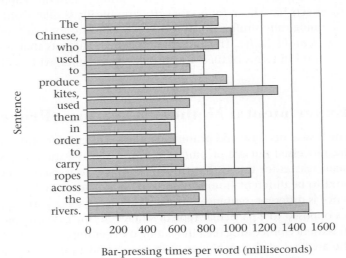

Figure 11.3   Bar-pressing times in sentence reading. From "On-Line Processing of Written Text by Younger and Older Children" by E. A. Stine in *Psychology and Aging* 5 (1): 68–78. March 1990. Published by American Psychological Association. © 1990.

As can be seen in Figure 11.3, participants show longer bar-pressing times for processing content words such as nouns and verbs and relatively less time for words such as determiners, conjunctions, and prepositions. Of particular interest is the length of the pause at the clause boundaries—especially at the end of the relative clause (*kites*) and the end of the full sentence (*rivers*). This increased processing time is interpreted as reflecting the extra amount of time required to integrate preceding information into a complete clause structure.

Eye Movements

We have already noted that sentence reading involves a series of jerky eye movements called saccades. A number of events occur during these jerky movements. When the eyes are at rest they take a "snapshot" of two or three words. These snapshots usually last from 200 to 250 milliseconds. While the snapshot is being taken, the language-processing system calculates where to jump to next. During a jump to the next fixation location (usually about eight letters to the right), the reader is essentially blind.

The details of eye movements in sentence reading are studied with sophisticated laboratory procedures in which a participant is often seated in front of a computer screen on which text is displayed. Eye movements are tracked by a device that illuminates the participant's eyes with low-intensity infrared light and records the reflection. The eye-position data are linked to the position of text on the screen so that it is possible to determine how the eyes move from one text position to another.

This technique has revealed that fixation times are typically longer for less frequent words and that the points of fixation are typically centered on words such as nouns and verbs, rather than on function words such as determiners and conjunctions. Difficult sentence structures create longer fixation times as well as many more regressive saccades. **Regressive saccades** are backward jumps in a sentence and are usually associated with misparsing or miscomprehension. On average, backward saccades make up 10 to 15 percent of the saccades in sentence reading. But syntactically complex sentences and semantically anomalous sentences (e.g., *The pizza was too hot to drink*) create many more regressive saccades. It has also been found that poor readers jump back and forth through sentences much more often than good readers do.

1.4   Brain Activity: Event-Related Potentials

Perhaps one of the most exciting techniques to be used in psycholinguistic research is the study of **event-related potentials (ERPs)** produced by the brain during language processing. As a research technique, the ERP paradigm has the same basic advantage as eye-movement studies. The participant simply sits in front of a computer screen and reads. This is a relatively natural language-processing activity that, unlike lexical decision or bar pressing, is similar to what participants do in normal language-processing situations.

ERP experiments measure electrical activity in the brain. Electrodes are placed on a participant's scalp and recordings are made of voltage fluctuations resulting from the brain's electrical activity. There is a significant difference between ERP recordings and the more familiar EEG (electroencephalogram) recordings. In the EEG, all the electrical activity of the brain is recorded. This electrical activity results from a very large number of background brain activities that are always going on. The advantage of the ERP approach is that it uses a computer to calculate what part of the brain's electrical activity is related to a stimulus event (in our case, words or sentences on a screen). This is done by a process of averaging. The computer records the instant at which a stimulus is presented and compares the voltage fluctuation immediately following the stimulus presentation to the random background "noise" of the ongoing EEG. By repeating this process many times with stimuli of a particular type, random voltage fluctuations are averaged out and the electrical potentials related to that stimulus type can be extracted. The resulting wave forms are the event-related potentials.

The ERP pattern is typically presented as a line graph in which time is shown from left to right; voltage is shown on the vertical axis, with negative values on top and positive values on the bottom. An example of an ERP graph is provided in Figure 11.4.

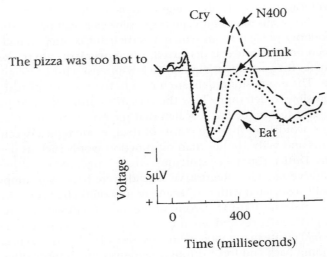

Figure 11.4 ERPs elicited by sentence-final words that are congruent, incongruent, and very incongruent with the sentence context. From *Language, Communication, and the Brain* by Fred Plum. Copyright © 1988, Lippincott, Williams & Wilkins. Used by permission of Lippincott, Williams & Wilkins.

Figure 11.4 also displays one of the most interesting psycholinguistic findings using ERPs. It turns out that in the processing of implausible sentences, the brain displays a characteristic ERP sign of surprise. Consider the following sentences:

8) a. The pizza was too hot to eat.
    b. The pizza was too hot to drink.
    c. The pizza was too hot to cry.

The sentences in *8* are arranged in order of semantic plausibility. In the first case, the last word fits in perfectly well with the sentence and would typically be expected by the reader. As can be seen in Figure 11.4, the ERP for this sentence shows a positive voltage associated with the last word. In the case of *8b*, however, in which the last word does not make sense (people do not drink pizza), the ERP is much more negative. As is shown in the horizontal axis, this negative wave occurs 400 milliseconds after the onset of the word. For this reason, this signal of semantic anomaly is called the N400 (negative wave at 400 milliseconds after stimulus presentation). The N400 is even stronger in the case of sentence *8c*, which is even less congruent with the sentence context (*drink* is at least associated with food).

The N400 effect can be obtained not only at the ends of sentences but in any sentence position. This fact suggests that sentence processing is immediate and online. When reading a sentence, we do not wait until the entire string is complete; rather, we are constantly building interpretations of the sentence as it unfolds. Whenever what we see or hear contradicts our expectations based on our ongoing interpretive processes, an N400 ERP component is observed.

LANGUAGE MATTERS   Simple Experiments Can Be Very Revealing

One of the most revealing psycholinguistic experiments requires no laboratory and no special equipment. In fact, you can try it with a friend: simply tell your friend that in this experiment, you will say a word out loud and his or her task (as a participant in the experiment) is to try as hard as possible to not understand the word. You can give fair warning by counting down "3, 2, 1," and then saying the word (e.g., *water*). Of course, as long as the participant can actually hear the word, it is impossible to not understand it. This is probably the fundamental truth of language processing: it is automatic and obligatory.

The N400 was the first stable language-related ERP wave to be extensively documented. More recently, a number of other ERP signature waves have been isolated. The P600 wave and the ELAN (early left anterior negativity) have been claimed to be markers of syntactic anomaly (e.g., **The men is here*), in contrast to the semantic anomaly marked by the N400 wave. We should expect that as research in this domain becomes more fine-grained, new ERP patterns associated with language processing will be revealed.

1.5   Language Corpora and Databases

Recent technological advances have enabled the creation of databases of many millions of words. These new databases and language corpora make it possible for psycholinguists to incorporate many more variables concerning language use into their experimental analyses. Thus, in addition to the word frequency variable, for example, researchers are able to analyze factors such as how early in life a particular word is typically acquired (age of acquisition), the number of different syntactic contexts in which it can occur, the number of complex words that have that word as a morphological constituent (morphological family size), and the semantic properties of the words that it has as neighbors in both speech and writing. This capability has greatly increased the sophistication of both the design and statistical analysis of recent psycholinguistic investigations. Finally, projects such as the English Lexicon Project have created databases of words that can be used as stimuli in psycholinguistic experiments as well as databases of lexical decision response times that have been obtained over multiple experiments using those words (see the website of the English Lexicon Project).

Google Ngram is an interesting and very easy-to-use tool that demonstrates the power of large corpora built from the millions of books that Google has digitized. With the Google Ngram Viewer tool, anybody can examine the relative frequency of words or phrases in written English, over years or centuries. The tool also allows users to analyze differences in lexical category and analyze words with different inflections. Figure 11.5 provides an example of how Google Ngram can be used.

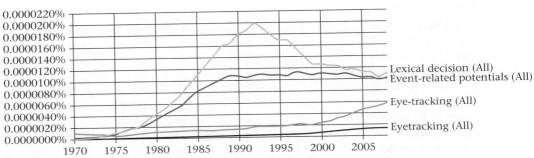

Figure 11.5   Google Ngram analysis of the relative frequencies of the words *lexical decision*, *event-related potentials*, and *eye-tracking* from 1970 to 2008 (which is the most recent date currently offered by Google).

Values on the vertical axis in Figure 11.5 represent frequency—the percentage of words in any given time period that consists of the search words. The data show the peaking of *lexical decision* in the early 1990s, the rise of *event-related potentials*, and the more recent ascendency of *eye-tracking*. Currently, hyphenated and nonhyphenated versions of words (e.g., *eye-tracking* vs. *eyetracking*) must be entered separately.

2   Language Processing and Linguistics

In the preceding sections, we discussed some of the methods that psycholinguists use to investigate how language is processed. One of the most important results of such psycholinguistic investigations is that many of the concepts and principles used by linguists to describe and understand the structure of language in terms of phonetics, phonology, morphology, and syntax have been found to also play an important role in the understanding of how language is produced and comprehended during activities such as speaking, listening, reading, and writing. In this section, we will focus on these points of contact between theoretical linguistics and psycholinguistics. In doing this, we will highlight the correspondence between the study of language processing and concepts that are central to the study of phonetics, phonology, morphology, and syntax.

2.1   Phonetics and Phonology

The study of phonetics and phonology reveals that the sound system of language is richly structured and contains different levels of representation. Thus, as discussed in Chapters 2 and 3, individual segments can be characterized in terms of place and manner of articulation or with respect to a matrix of phonological features. Sequences of sounds can be grouped into syllabic structures, and allophonic variation can be described in terms of underlying phonemes and surface allophones. How much of this structure plays a role in language processing? The simple answer to this question is all of it! The more complex answer, and of course also the more accurate answer, is that language processing shows evidence that features, phonemes, and syllable structure all capture some aspects of the way in which we process language but that speech production and perception is a complex activity that involves much more than these phonetic and phonological representations.

To see why this is the case, consider what might occur when you hear the sentence *The dog bit the cat*. Because the utterance unfolds in time, you will first hear the segment /ð/ and then the segment /ə/. (In fact, you do not hear these segments separately; rather, you create them out of a continuous sound stream.) As soon as these segments are identified, you have already accessed the representation for the word *the* in your mental lexicon. When the next segment comes up in the sound stream, you already know that it is the beginning of a new word and you also know that this word will probably be a noun. The phonetic analysis that follows identifies the segments [d], [ɔ], and [g] and the corresponding lexical entry *dog*. Now come the first segments of the word *bit*. In principle, the first two phonemes /bɪ/ could be the first two segments of the word *believe*, but you are not likely to consider this possibility because your developing interpretation of the sentence is biasing you toward the word *bit*, which is associated in your mind with *dog*.

As can be appreciated from this example, language processing involves the interplay of information that develops simultaneously at many different levels of analysis. The person hearing the sentence *The dog bit the cat* is performing a phonetic analysis to isolate phonemes and word boundaries and to relate these to items in the mental lexicon. This inductive analysis is referred to as **bottom-up processing**. But we do not wait until we have analyzed all the phonemes in a sentence before we begin to try to understand it. Rather, we begin interpretation of a sentence spontaneously and automatically on the basis of whatever information is available to us. For this reason, by the time we get to the word *bit*, we are not only recognizing it using bottom-up processing but are also employing a set of expectations to guide phonetic processing and word recognition. This is called **top-down processing**. In normal language use, we are always engaged in both bottom-up and top-down activities. We never just process features, or phonemes, or syllables. We process language for the purposes of understanding each other.

In Section 3 of this chapter, we will discuss how phonetic and phonological analysis fit into other processes involved in speaking and listening. For now, however, we will concentrate on three levels of linguistic structure that seem fundamental to phonetic and phonological representation: features, phonemes, and syllables.

Features

In both linguistics and psycholinguistics, the term *feature* is used to refer to the most basic level of representation. It is therefore always associated with bottom-up processing in language. In the processing of sound, it refers to characteristics of individual phonemes (e.g., [± voice], [± continuant], etc.). The most straightforward evidence concerning the role of such features comes from the analysis of slips of the tongue. Some examples are presented in Table 11.1.

Table 11.1   The role of features in speech errors

Intended	Actually produced
a. big and fat	pig and vat
b. Is Pat a girl?	Is bat a curl?
c. Cedars of Lebanon	Cedars of Lemanon

The errors in Table 11.1 follow a pattern, but that pattern can only be understood with reference to a system of phonological features. In all three examples, the errors involve a phonological feature. In example *a*, the feature [voice] has been exchanged between the words *big* and *fat* to create the new words *pig* and *vat* (remember that /b-p/ and /f-v/ only differ in the feature [voice]).

This same pattern of voice feature exchange can be seen in example *b*, where *Pat* becomes *bat* and *girl* becomes *curl*. Finally, the error in *c* is particularly intriguing because it involves just a single feature change: the voiced labial stop /b/ becomes [+nasal] under the influence of the /n/ in the next syllable, yielding an /m/ and the pronunciation *Lemanon*. Such examples offer evidence that language production makes use of the individual feature components of phonemes and that the phonemes that we produce in speech may actually be put together "on the fly" out of bundles of such features.

Phonemes

We have seen in Section 1.1 that Spoonerisms show evidence of entire phonemes being misplaced during sentence planning. The phonemic unit of representation also plays a central role in psycholinguistic models of speech processing, such as the **cohort model** proposed by William Marslen-Wilson in the 1980s. This model states that in word comprehension, words are analyzed by hearers from beginning to end. So, for example, when we hear the word *glass*, we initially consider all the words that begin with the sound [g]. When the next sound [l] is recognized, the number of possible words (the **cohort**) is reduced to those words that begin with [gl]. This process continues until the cohort of possible words is reduced to one—the word that is being recognized. In a number of experiments, Marslen-Wilson investigated whether this beginning-to-end analysis of spoken words proceeds one phoneme at a time, one cluster at a time, or one syllable at a time. He and his colleagues found that the phoneme seems to be the fundamental unit of auditory word recognition.

Syllables

Although in the cohort model, the phoneme rather than the syllable seems to be the fundamental unit of auditory word recognition, other evidence points to the syllable playing an important role in speech perception. In one study, participants were presented with disyllabic words (e.g., *bullet*) and disyllabic nonwords (e.g., *sullet*) and were asked to press a button if a particular target unit was in the stimulus. The target units were either syllables (e.g., *let*) or segments (e.g., *t*). It was found for both words and nonwords that participants were significantly faster at identifying syllable targets than at identifying single segment targets. The researchers concluded that syllable identification was faster because in normal auditory analysis, participants first break down stimuli into syllables and then into individual segments as the situation demands.

Another source of evidence concerning the role of the syllable in language processing comes from observing participants' performance on word-blending tasks. In such tasks, participants are given two monosyllabic words such as *bug* and *cat* and are required to blend the words together to make a new word. Now, what sounds better: (*bug* + *cat* = *bat*) or (*bug* + *cat* = *but*)? Notice that the first option makes use of internal syllable structure, combining the onset of the first word/syllable with the rhyme (nucleus plus coda) of the second word/syllable. The second option, in contrast, combines the first two sounds of the first word with the last sound of the second word, making no reference to syllable structure. Typically, participants prefer the first option: that is, they are much better at creating word blends that make use of syllable structure than those that don't. The fact that English speakers find such divisions easier and more natural suggests that words are represented in speakers' minds in terms of their syllables and syllable constituents.

2.2   Morphological Processing

Morphology is the study of words, including their structure and their interpretation. The psycholinguistic study of morphology seeks to understand how word structure plays a role in language processing. In the following sections, we will summarize some psycholinguistic research that reveals how morphological structures and principles play a substantial role in the representation of words in the mind and in word recognition.

Morpheme Activation

Words such as *blackboard*, *happiness*, and *watching* are made up of two morphemes. In the case of the compound *blackboard*, both morphemes are roots. In the case of *happiness*, one morpheme is a root and the other is a derivational suffix. Finally, in the case of *watching*, one morpheme is a root and the other is an inflectional affix. The first question we will address is whether the individual morphological components of words play a role in processing.

The answer to this question seems to be a straightforward yes. For most multimorphemic words, individual morphemes are automatically activated during word recognition. One source of evidence for this conclusion comes from priming experiments in which it is found that multimorphemic words will prime semantic associates of their constituents in a lexical decision experiment. Thus, when a participant is exposed to a multimorphemic word such as *suntan*, the activation of that word in the mind will facilitate the recognition of *moon*, which is highly associated with the initial morpheme of *sun* but not with the whole word *suntan*. The facilitation, therefore, must arise from independent activation of the morphemes within a word.

LANGUAGE MATTERS   SPAM: A Morphological Blend

In 1937, the luncheon meat SPAM was introduced. The previous name for the product was Hormel Spiced Ham and it was produced by the Hormel Foods Corporation. In 1936, the company had a contest offering one hundred dollars for the best new name for the product. The prize was won by Kenneth Daigneau, the brother of the company's vice-president. Like the participants in the psycholinguistic experiments discussed above, Mr. Daigneau chose to combine the onset of the first word *spiced* and the rhyme of the second word *ham*.

There are two proposals about how this activation of morphemes might occur. The first is that it derives from structured morphological representations in the mind. According to this view, multimorphemic words such as *happiness* and *blackboard* are represented in the mind as [happy + ness] and [black + board], and when we access such words, first their whole word forms and then their constituent morphemes are automatically activated. This view is termed **postlexical decomposition**, because the constituents of a multimorphemic word are activated only after the representation of the whole lexical item is activated. In other words, whole word access occurs first, morphological decomposition second.

An alternative view is that the activation of constituent morphemes results from a computational mechanism that scans a word and isolates individual morphemes in much the same way as individual words are isolated when we see or hear sentences. This view is termed **prelexical decomposition**, because the constituent morphemes are activated through a computational process (called **morphological parsing**) rather than through the morphological representation of the word in the mind. In this case, morphological decomposition occurs first, and whole-word access occurs second. These alternative views are represented in Figure 11.6.

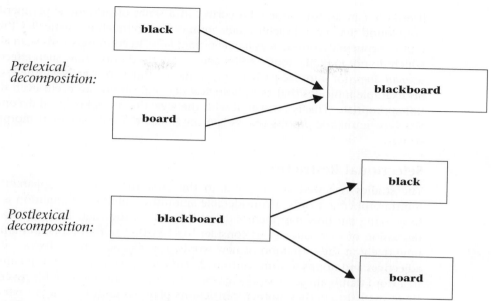

Figure 11.6 Prelexical and postlexical decomposition

Recent research has shown that, interestingly, both these views are correct. In a semantic priming experiment, multimorphemic words such as *barking* were presented to participants as primes in order to measure their effect on monomorphemic target words. Words like *barking* have ambiguous roots: *bark* can be a noun that means 'the outside of a tree' or a verb that means 'the sound that a dog makes'. In the multimorphemic word *barking*, however, the root can only have the verb meaning. The researchers asked the question: Will *barking* affect the processing of both *dog* (an associate of the verb) and *tree* (an associate of the noun)? If the processing of *tree* (as well as *dog*) is affected, this would be evidence for prelexical morphological decomposition, because there would be no reason for the meaning of *tree* to be activated by the entire word *barking*.

Indeed, both *dog* and *tree* were affected by the prime word *barking*. The word *dog* was recognized more quickly following the presentation of the word *barking*—a priming effect. Recognition of the incorrect associate (*tree*) was also affected, but in the opposite direction: the processing of the word *tree* was slowed down. In other words, a negative priming effect was observed. This led to the conclusion that during prelexical decomposition, *bark* and -*ing* were accessed separately, allowing both meanings of *bark* to be activated before one was suppressed.

Perhaps even more dramatic evidence of automatic and obligatory morphological decomposition comes from a set of experiments that have investigated priming effects among words that look multimorphemic but are not. An example of such a word is *corner*. It looks like it contains the root *corn* and the suffix -*er*. But of course it does not mean 'someone who corns'. In a series of priming experiments, it has been found that a word such as *corner* primes *corn* in much the same way that a truly multimorphemic word such as *hunter* primes *hunt*. In contrast, words such as *scandal*, which do not look like root + suffix combinations, do not show such effects. Seeing *scandal* does not improve participants' response times to *scan*. Nevertheless, the *corner* example indicates that morphological decomposition can occur even when it is not appropriate. This is consistent with the view that morphological decomposition is a very automatic process that is "on the lookout" for all apparent morphological strings.

Selectional Restrictions

The studies reviewed above point to the view that even for apparently simple multimorphemic words, a considerable amount of mental computation is involved in working out how morphemes do and do not fit together. To complete our brief discussion of this issue, let us consider the fact that not all roots and affixes combine freely in the formation of new words. For instance, the suffix *-ize* attaches to adjectives and nouns to form verbs (e.g., *nationalize, hospitalize*), but it cannot apply to a word that is already a verb (e.g., **understandize*). The question for psycholinguistic research is: Do these formal restrictions play a role in the way in which native speakers of English process new words?

In an experiment in morphological processing, participants were presented with nonsense roots (e.g., *birm*) that had prefixes and suffixes attached to them. Because they contained nonsense roots, none of these words made much sense (e.g., *rebirmable, rebirmize, rebirmity*). But notice that, as is shown in Figure 11.7, *rebirmable* and *rebirmize* are morphologically legal, whereas *rebirmity* violates a morphological constraint—the prefix *re-* attaches to a verb to create another verb (as in *redo*), and the suffix *-ity* attaches to an adjective to create a noun (as in *insane–insanity*). The form *rebirmity* is illegal because *re-birm* has to be a verb and therefore can't take the suffix *-ity*, whereas *birm-ity* has to be a noun and therefore can't occur with the prefix *re-*. In experiments with these sorts of stimuli, it was found that processing times were significantly longer for the illegal nonsense words than for the morphologically legal words. These results suggest that knowledge of the selectional restrictions of affixes does indeed form part of the word-processing system and that violation of these restrictions creates difficulty for automatic lexical processing, which would of course go unnoticed by the language user but is discernible through psycholinguistic techniques.

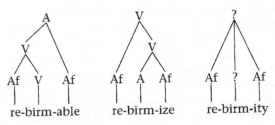

Figure 11.7 Morphologically legal and illegal affixed nonsense roots

2.3 Syntax

Syntax is the system of rules and categories that underlies sentence formation in human language. One of the fundamental insights in the study of syntax is that sentences are unique events. That means that virtually all the sentences that you read in this chapter are sentences that you have never encountered before. They are typically made up of familiar words, but the particular combination of words and the manner in which they are arranged are unique to each sentence. The question that we will consider in this section is: How are these syntactic structures created during sentence processing?

The Syntax Module

One very simple possibility for how sentences are processed is that production and comprehension employ the system of rules that are used by syntacticians to describe sentence structure. This possibility suggests that speakers use the Merge operation to create deep structure representations and employ Move operations to derive the surface structure characteristics of a sentence. Many psycholinguistic experiments examined this possibility by testing, for example, whether sentences that have undergone many Move operations take longer to process than sentences with fewer such operations. It turned out that the number of Move operations that a sentence had undergone did not predict processing time. Researchers concluded that there is at least some difference between the rules that native speakers use to generate and comprehend sentences and the rules that linguists use to characterize the linguistic knowledge of native speakers. It was therefore necessary to postulate a special module for sentence processing, called the **syntactic parser**, and another for grammatical knowledge.

It should be noted that in discussing how processing takes place, the term *module* has a special meaning. It refers to a mechanism of processing that is relatively autonomous from other processing mechanisms. The idea of **processing modules** has been very important and controversial in many domains of human information processing. To get a sense of how processing may involve the coordination of separate modules, consider what occurs when you watch a movie. The movie director, in order to obtain a variety of effects, relies on processing modularity. The director knows that in watching an adventure film, your stomach will take a dip when the airplane on the screen goes into a dive or when the canoe goes over the falls. He or she knows that you cannot stop this from happening even though you are aware that you are sitting in a chair that is not moving. Similarly, you will be frightened by the sudden appearance of a monster, even though you know that you are really in no danger. All these effects result from processing modularity. The bottom-up information that comes from processing modules cannot be turned off by the top-down information that you are seated in a stationary and safe environment.

A variety of psycholinguistic studies have investigated whether this same sort of modularity is present in syntactic processing. In other words, they look at whether syntactic parsing operates in an automatic and obligatory manner that is relatively independent of the activity of other processing systems. The syntactic parser is understood to be a system that makes use of grammatical knowledge but that also contains special procedures and principles that guide the order in which elements of a sentence are processed and the manner in which syntactic structure is built up. Because our parsing ability is based on our grammatical knowledge of our language, it is usually the case that there is a close correspondence between sentence parsing and grammatical structure. However, because the parsing module has its own set of principles, sentences that are grammatically complex are not necessarily difficult to parse, while some sentences with relatively simple syntactic structure can create substantial parsing problems. Two sources of evidence have been very important in the exploration of modularity in sentence processing. These are **garden path sentences** and **sentence ambiguity**.

Garden Path Sentences

Some sentences are extraordinarily difficult to understand even though they are not very complex syntactically. These sentences are called garden path sentences because they lead the syntactic parser down the garden path to the wrong analysis. Perhaps the most famous garden path sentence is the one given in 9.

9) The horse raced past the barn fell.

This sentence is perfectly grammatical but almost impossible to understand. The reason for this is that as we read the sentence, we build up a syntactic structure in which *the horse* is the subject of the sentence and *raced past the barn* is the VP. When we get to the word *fell*, we are surprised because the sentence we have built up has no room for an extra VP (see Figure 11.8a). The correct interpretation for the sentence requires that *fell* be the head of the main VP and that *raced past the barn* be a clause (a reduced version of *which was raced past the barn*) that attaches to the NP *the horse* (see Figure 11.8b). The sentence thus has an interpretation parallel to that of the unambiguous sentence *The statue taken from the gallery shattered*.

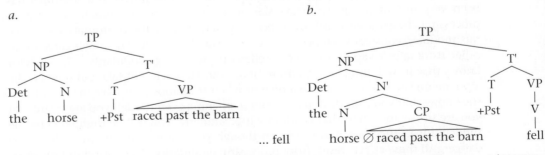

Figure 11.8 A garden path sentence. The garden path effect is shown in *a*. The correct interpretation is represented in *b*.

The ways in which native speakers misunderstand garden path sentences reveal how the parser might work. It seems that we construct syntactic representations from the beginning of the sentences to the end and that our sentence parsers are organized so that we make a number of assumptions about how a sentence will proceed. This can be seen by considering the garden path sentence in *10*.

10) Since Jay always walks a mile seems like a short distance to him.

This sentence is not as difficult to process as the sentence in *9*, but you probably noticed yourself having to backtrack after an initial misanalysis. Your parser is inclined to build a single VP out of the string *walks a mile*, when in fact *walks* and *a mile* belong to different clauses. This tendency has been extensively studied by psycholinguists. The backtracking that you might have noticed in your own reading shows up in eye-movement studies in which participants have been found to show more regressive saccades and longer fixation times for these sentences than for sentences that do not require backtracking.

It has been claimed that the garden path effect results from two principles of parsing: **minimal attachment** and **late closure**. The principle of minimal attachment states that, all other things being equal, we do not build more syntactic structure (like the extra embedded phrase in Figure 11.8b) than is absolutely necessary. The principle of late closure states that we prefer to attach new words to the clause currently being processed as we proceed through a sentence from beginning to end. The result of late closure can be discerned in sentence *10*, where we are inclined to add the NP *a mile* to the VP headed by *walks* rather than beginning a new clause.

Now, there is one last point to be made concerning what garden path sentences can tell us about how people process sentences. Try reading the sentence in *10* again. You might find that although you now know the correct analysis for the sentence, you misread it the second time just as you did the first time. This suggests that the parsing system is in fact a module that operates automatically and independently.

Sentence Ambiguity

Another important clue to how syntactic processing is accomplished comes from the study of ambiguity. Consider the sentence in *11*.

11) They all rose.

The last word in *11* is ambiguous. The word *rose* can be related to either *stand* or *flower*. However, the sentence context leads us clearly to favor the *stand* version of the word. Does the sentence context therefore inhibit activation of the other meaning of *rose*? This question was investigated in a lexical decision experiment in which the sentence in *11* served as the prime. After seeing the sentence, participants were presented with either the word *flower* or *stand*. The researchers found that the sentence facilitated lexical decision response times to both words. That is, both meanings for the word *rose* were activated, even though the sentence clearly presented a bias in favor of one reading over the other.

Even more revealing was a follow-up priming experiment that was identical to the one just described except that there was a pause of several hundred milliseconds between the prime and the target. When the pause was present, the priming effect disappeared for the meaning that was unrelated to the sentence context (i.e., *flower*).

This suggests that in fact sentence processing proceeds in two stages. In the first stage, all possible representations and structures are computed. In the second stage, one of these structures is selected and all others are abandoned.

Of course, all this happens very quickly and subconsciously, so that we as native speakers of a language are never aware that for a sentence such as *12*, we compute two possible interpretations.

12) The tuna can hit the boat.

In reading this sentence, you ended up imagining either

> *a.* tuna meat that is packed in a small round can, *or*
> *b.* a large fish swimming toward a boat

The point of the psycholinguistic experiments just described is this: no matter which interpretation you arrived at (*a* or *b*), you probably considered both of them, chose one, discarded the other, and forgot about the whole thing in less than a second.

3   Putting It All Together: Psycholinguistic Modeling

Up to this point, our discussion of psycholinguistic research has been restricted to examining characteristics of phonetic, phonological, morphological, and syntactic processing and the relation between the concepts used in theoretical linguistics and in psycholinguistics. It is important to note, however, that psycholinguistic research seeks to discover not only which types of representations play a role in language processing but also how these representations and processes fit together to make activities such as speaking, listening, reading, and writing possible.

Psycholinguistic researchers present their ideas about how language is "done" in terms of models. A **psycholinguistic model** incorporates the results of experiments into a proposal about how processing takes place. In other words, it is a statement of what happens when. Suppose, for example, we wished to present the finding discussed in Section 2.3 that a sentence such as *They all rose* will prime both the words *flower* and *stand*. The model might look like Figure 11.9.

For our present purposes, it is not important whether this model is actually correct. The purpose of the model is simply to illustrate how psycholinguistic hypotheses can be represented. This model, which looks very much like a computer flow chart, says that when processing a sentence such as *They all rose*, we first perform phonological analysis. This is followed by lexical access, in which all words with matching phonological representations are accessed (including the two words *rose*). Information from lexical access feeds the syntactic parsing module, and information from both the lexical access module and the parsing module are fed to the representation pruning module (the module that discards multiple representations). Finally, the model states that an interpretation becomes conscious only in the final stage of analysis and that there is only one-way information flow to conscious interpretation (in other words, the conscious mind cannot "peek" at how things are going).

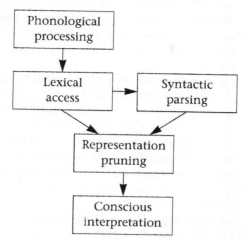

Figure 11.9   A serial psycholinguistic model of sentence processing

You will note that in creating this model, we have taken two kinds of shortcuts. First, we have created a novel name (i.e., *pruning*) to describe an operation that has been deduced from the results of psycholinguistic experimentation. Second, our model uses the box notation as a shorthand for a constellation of processes. Thus, it is understood that as the model becomes more elaborate, each one of the boxes in Figure 11.9 would be expanded into a flow chart of its own.

As you inspect the model in Figure 11.9, you should find that it is really very inadequate. It is missing much important detail, it seems to characterize only one aspect of sentence processing, and it avoids any mention of how meaning is accessed or how sentence interpretation actually takes place. In other words, to be a model of any real value, it would have to be much more elaborate.

Indeed, the types of psycholinguistic models that have been proposed in recent years are very elaborate. This is a good thing. We want models to be as detailed and comprehensive as possible, to take a great deal of experimentation into account and, perhaps most importantly, to show how linguistic and nonlinguistic operations work together in the processing of language.

3.1   The Use of Metaphors in Psycholinguistic Modeling

Perhaps the most important characteristic of the model presented in Figure 11.9 is the fact that it obviously could not reflect what really happens in the mind of a language user. It is exceedingly unlikely that our minds possess boxes and arrows (or their equivalents). This model, like all psycholinguistic models, employs metaphors for language representations and language processing. The value of these metaphors is that they allow researchers to make specific claims about how language processing works, which can then be tested. For example, through its architecture, the model in Figure 11.9 claims that phonological processing precedes lexical access, which in turn precedes syntactic processing. This claim can then be tested in an experiment that investigates whether all phonological processing is complete before syntactic processing begins.

We see, then, that psycholinguistic models have dual functions. They summarize specific research findings and generate specific hypotheses. They also have the very important function of embodying general perspectives on how language processing works. This is again accomplished through the use of metaphors. These metaphors have the effect of shaping how we conceive of language in the mind and what kinds of questions are asked by psycholinguistic researchers. Finally, these metaphors provide the means by which major families of models can be contrasted in order to test which ones most accurately describe language processing. In the following sections, we review three of the most important current issues in psycholinguistic modeling: serial versus parallel processing models, single-route versus multiple-route models, and finally, symbolic versus connectionist models.

Serial versus Parallel Processing Models

Let us return to Figure 11.9. By employing the metaphor of a computer program that operates sequentially, the **serial processing model** in Figure 11.9 not only makes a claim about sentence processing but also claims that language processing proceeds in a step-by-step manner. In contrast, a **parallel processing model** claims that phonological, lexical, and syntactic processes are carried out simultaneously. Figure 11.10 represents an example of a parallel processing model. Here information does not flow in a sequential manner. Rather, all modules operate simultaneously and share information. The model in Figure 11.10 claims, therefore, that when we hear a sentence, we begin phonological, lexical, and syntactic processes at the same time. As each type of processing proceeds, it informs the other.

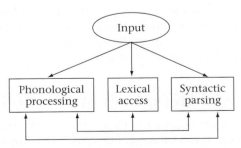

Figure 11.10   A parallel psycholinguistic model of sentence processing

In recent research, serial and parallel processing models have been very important for understanding the extent to which bottom-up and top-down processing
interact. Serial models correctly characterize those aspects of language processing that
are modular and are driven by strict bottom-up procedures, such as phonetic perception. Parallel processing models, in contrast, are more effective than serial models at
characterizing complex processes such as sentence comprehension.

Single-Route versus Multiple-Route Models

Put most directly, **single-route models** claim that a particular type of language processing is accomplished in one manner only. **Multiple-route models** claim that a
language-processing task is accomplished through (usually two) competing mechanisms. Consider, for example, the task of reading English words. Here there are three
possibilities: (1) we read a word by looking it up in our mental lexicon based on its
visual characteristics; (2) we convert a visual input into a phonological representation first, and this phonological representation becomes the basis for comprehension; or (3) we do both at the same time. Options (1) and (2) represent single-route
models in the sense that they claim that reading is accomplished in one way. Option
(3), which is represented in Figure 11.11, represents a multiple-route model in that
it claims that both mechanisms are employed. Usually such multiple-route models
employ the additional metaphor of a horse race by claiming that for some words
(e.g., very frequent short words) the direct route is faster but for others (e.g., rare
words) the phonological conversion route is faster and wins the race.

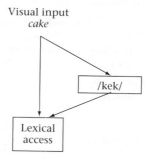

Figure 11.11   A multiple-route model of word reading

In recent psycholinguistic investigations, the multiple-route approach has been
very influential in modeling whether multimorphemic words are decomposed into
their constituent morphemes during word recognition or are accessed as whole
words. It has been found that although both procedures are active all the time, the
whole-word recognition route wins the race for frequent bimorphemic words such as
blackboard. However, in the case of less frequent words such as *breadboard* or novel
multimorphemic forms such as *blueboard*, the morphological decomposition route is
the one that provides the basis for comprehension.

Symbolic versus Connectionist Models

The final modeling contrast that we review in this section is the contrast between symbolic and connectionist models. These types of models represent fundamentally different views about the nature of mental representations. **Symbolic models** (which include all the ones we have discussed so far) claim that linguistic knowledge must make reference to rules and representations consisting of symbols corresponding to phonemes, words, syntactic category labels, and so forth. **Connectionist models** claim that the mind can be best understood by reference to large associations of very simple units (often called **nodes**) that more closely approximate the kinds of processing units (i.e., neurons) that we know the brain to be composed of. Connectionist models typically do not contain direct representations for language units such as words but rather represent these units as an association of nodes. This difference is exemplified in Figure 11.12.

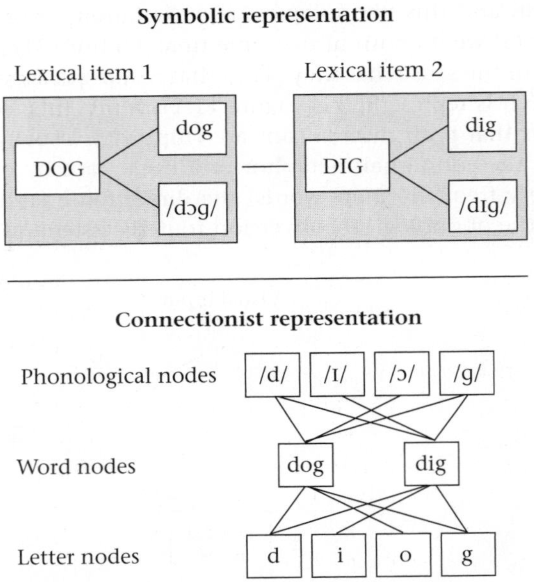

Figure 11.12 Symbolic versus connectionist representations for the words *dog* and *dig* in the mind

In one sense, the two kinds of representations in Figure 11.12 represent exactly the same information—namely, the graphemic and phonological makeup of the words *dog* and *dig*. In another sense, however, they are very different. The connectionist representation shows words as having reality only in the sense that they are bundles of associations between phonological and graphemic nodes. (In some connectionist approaches, the word *nodes* is not used at all.) In the symbolic representation, words do indeed have discrete representations in the mind, and each representation contains information regarding the word's sound and spelling.

3.2   Which Model Is Right?

Almost certainly, none of the models that we have discussed is correct. All models represent a researcher's claim about the most current version of the truth. Because psycholinguistics is a very young field, we can expect that any current version of the truth will be very far from the real truth (if there is one). Perhaps this is why psycholinguistic models are so important. They give us the vocabulary with which to ask major questions about mental processing.

Implementing and Testing Models Computationally

Currently, the best way to evaluate the value of a psycholinguistic model is to implement it as a computer program and to evaluate whether the patterns of performance of the computer program accord with the performance of humans carrying out language tasks. Thus the merit of a proposed psycholinguistic model increases if it makes the same kinds of mistakes that humans do, if it performs more poorly on language structures that humans also find difficult, and if its performance changes over time in accordance with the way in which human performance changes across the lifespan. In this way, psycholinguistic models that incorporate human learning theory are particularly valuable to our ability to capture the dynamic nature of human language processing.

Big Questions, Emerging Perspectives, and the Next Steps

The alternative approaches to psycholinguistic modeling that we have discussed above capture important questions: Is it reasonable to postulate mental representations that correspond to phonemes, words, and phrases, or are mental representations distributed over a large number of nodes? Does the mind settle into a best way to perform a task, or are all processes horse races between alternative ways to solve a problem? Do mental operations proceed in a step-by-step manner?

These are all big questions and big issues. The more we investigate the details, the more we realize that language processing offers our best clues to the secrets of human cognition and the more we appreciate how well guarded those secrets are. In the past quarter-century of psycholinguistic research, we have learned a great deal about language representation and processing. In the first part of this chapter, we concentrated on the research techniques that have made these advances possible. In this final section of the chapter, we have focused on the still unresolved major issues.

Although we do not yet know which models are right or which hybrids will be most effective in our evolving understanding of human cognition, the research we have reviewed in this chapter points to a view of language processing that is characterized by massive storage of language forms and by extensive connections among these forms. Language processing also seems to involve automatic and obligatory computational procedures that break down complex language structures into their phonological, morphological, and syntactic constituents during language comprehension and build them up again during production. We are thus able to conclude that the language system is, paradoxically, fast and automatic but not necessarily efficient. The reason for this is probably that the language-processing system is designed to exploit all the linguistic resources of the human brain—its massive storage ability, its apparently unlimited capacity for associations among representations, and finally, its ability to carry out complex computation within modular subsystems. So whereas theoretical characterizations of language structure strive, quite appropriately, for elegance and simplicity, the language-processing system might strive for exactly the opposite—namely, extensive redundancy. The exact manner in which different and perhaps redundant methods of "doing language" might coexist in a single human brain has been the subject of a great deal of recent research and debate among psycholinguists and constitutes the next big research challenge in the field.

Summing Up

Psycholinguistics is the study of language processing. The field is defined both by a subject matter and a particular methodology. Psycholinguists study how people perform the functions of language comprehension and production. They seek to discover the nature of the mental representations that serve these functions and the nature of the cognitive operations and computations that are employed when we understand and produce language.

Because language processing involves computations and representations that cannot be observed and measured directly, psycholinguists have devised special experimental techniques to investigate language processing. Some of these techniques, such as **lexical decision** and **priming**, measure a participant's response time and **response accuracy** to linguistic stimuli. Other techniques measure eye movement while participants are reading silently, and yet others measure electrical activity in the brain during language processing.

Language processing involves many **processing modules** that are specialized for a particular language-processing task and that interact with other modules in restricted ways. Thus, language processing involves a constant interplay between **bottom-up** and **top-down processing**. We process phonetic features, phonemes, and words all at the same time. We construct syllable representations, morphological representations, and syntactic representations in a spontaneous and obligatory manner. As conscious beings, we are aware of the results of our processing but not of the processing itself.

In general, psycholinguistic studies have revealed that many of the concepts employed in the analysis of sound structure, word structure, and sentence structure also play a role in language processing. However, an account of language processing also requires that we understand how these linguistic concepts interact with other aspects of human processing to enable language production and comprehension.

Psycholinguists typically present their views of how language production and comprehension are achieved in terms of processing models. These models are at the heart of research in psycholinguistics and allow researchers to express the significance of particular research findings, to predict the outcomes of future experiments, and to debate the fundamental characteristics of human cognition.

Key Terms

General terms and terms concerning psycholinguistic methods

dependent variables	priming effect
event-related potentials (ERPs)	psycholinguistics
experimental paradigms	regressive saccades
field technique	response accuracy
frequency effect	response latency
lexical decision	saccades
parsing	Spoonerism
prime	target
priming	tip-of-the-tongue phenomena

Terms concerning language processing

bottom-up processing	postlexical decomposition
cohort	prelexical decomposition
cohort model	processing modules
garden path sentences	sentence ambiguity
late closure	syntactic parser
minimal attachment	top-down processing
morphological parsing	

Terms related to psycholinguistic models

connectionist models	psycholinguistic model
multiple-route models	serial processing model
nodes	single-route models
parallel processing model	symbolic models

Recommended Reading

Carroll, David. 2007. *Psychology of Language*. Belmont, CA: Wadsworth.

Field, John. 2004. *Psycholinguistics: The Key Concepts*. London: Routledge.

Gaskell, Gareth M., ed. 2007. *Oxford Handbook of Psycholinguistics*. Oxford: Oxford University Press.

Menn, Lise. 2010. *Psycholinguistics: Introduction and Applications*. San Diego, CA: Plural.

Exercises

1. How do psycholinguistic investigations of language differ from theoretical linguistic investigations? (Review information presented in Sections 1–2.)

2. Consider the following slips of the tongue. What does each reveal about the process of language production? (See Section 1.1.)
   a) They *laked* across the *row*.
   b) The spy was *gound* and *bagged*.
   c) I will *zee* you in the *pank*.

3. Imagine that you read that a psycholinguist has reported an experiment in which a priming effect was found for morphological roots on suffixed past tense forms in a lexical decision task. (See Section 1.2.)
   - *i)* State the dependent variable in the experiment (i.e., the thing that is observed and measured).
   - *ii)* Give an example of a prime stimulus.
   - *iii)* Give an example of a target stimulus.

4. Complete the following sentences by filling in the blanks. In each case, what type of top-down processing and bottom-up processing guided your decision? (See Section 2.)
   - a) The children _____ running in the park.
   - b) All _____ movies I like have happy endings.
   - c) He tends to see everything as _____ and white.

5. Recall that according to the cohort model, a word is recognized from beginning to end, one phoneme at a time. According to the cohort model, how many phonemes of each of the following words would have to be processed before a hearer would be sure which word had been spoken? (See Section 2.1.)
   - a) giraffe
   - b) splat
   - c) computerize

6. Write the sentences in examples *9* and *10* from Section 2.3 on separate index cards. Take a few other cards and write a normal sentence on each of them. Now, have some friends try to read aloud the sentences on the cards. What kind of evidence shows that the sentences are more difficult to process?

7. What is a processing model? Try to describe the process of reading single words in terms of a processing model that contains specific modules. (See Section 2.)

8. Imagine yourself as a psycholinguist trying to devise experiments to investigate how people do language. What experiments would you make up to address the following questions? Be as specific as possible about how you would interpret the question and about what you would do to try to find an answer through psycholinguistic experimentation.
   - a) Are semantically abstract words easier to process than semantically concrete ones?
   - b) Are simple clauses more difficult to understand than conjoined clauses?
   - c) Do people read words from beginning to end?
   - d) Do people with different levels of education process language in fundamentally different ways?
   - e) Does the way you parse a sentence depend on what language you speak?

twelve

Brain and Language

Gary Libben

The problem of neurology is to understand man himself.
—WILDER PENFIELD, "Foreword," *The Anatomy of the Brain and Nerves* (1965)

OBJECTIVES

In this chapter, you will learn:

• how the human brain is structured as it relates to language
• how neurolinguists have investigated the brain and language
• what studies of brain damage tell us about the brain and language

 **LaunchPad Solo**
macmillan learning | For more helpful content and quizzes, go to the LaunchPad Solo
for *Contemporary Linguistics* at **launchpadworks.com**.

In this chapter we will be concerned with the branch of neuroscience that has as its goal the understanding of how language is represented and processed in the brain. This field of study is called **neurolinguistics**. Although the study of the relationship between brain and language is still in its infancy, much has already been learned about which parts of the brain are involved in various aspects of language production and comprehension. The field of neurolinguistics has also done much to deepen the way we think about the nature of linguistic competence.

The chapter provides a brief survey of brain structure and the methods that are currently available to study the brain. This is followed by a discussion of the different types of language disturbance that result from brain damage and a discussion of how phonology, morphology, syntax, and semantics may be represented in the brain. The chapter concludes by reviewing the current answers to the important neurolinguistic question: Where is language?

455

1 The Human Brain

Contained within your skull is about 1,400 grams of pinkish-white matter. It may be the most complex 1,400 grams in the galaxy. For most of human history, however, the role of the brain as the center of mental life remained completely unknown. Even the Greek philosopher Aristotle believed that its primary function was to cool the blood.

We now know much more about the structure and functioning of the brain. But in many ways we are still quite like Aristotle, finding it hard to believe that this wrinkled mass of nerve cells could be the stuff that dreams, fears, and knowledge are made of. Nevertheless, it is, and the task of brain science (**neuroscience**) is to understand how the breadth and depth of human experience is coded in brain matter.

The brain is composed of nerve cells, or **neurons**, that are the basic information-processing units of the nervous system. The human brain contains about 10 billion neurons that are organized into networks of almost unimaginable complexity. This complexity results from the fact that each neuron can be directly linked with up to ten thousand other neurons. But the brain is not simply a mass of interconnected neurons. It is composed of structures that seem to play specific roles in the integrated functioning of the brain. The following sections provide a brief overview of these structures.

1.1 The Cerebral Cortex

The brain encompasses all the neurological structures above the spinal cord and appears to have evolved from the bottom up. The lower brain structures are shared by almost all animals. These structures are responsible for the maintenance of functions such as respiration, heart rate, and muscle coordination that are essential to the survival of all animals. As we move farther away from the spinal cord, however, we begin to find structures that have developed differently in different species. At the highest level of the brain, the **cerebral cortex**, the differences are most pronounced. Reptiles and amphibians have no cortex at all, and the progression from lower to higher mammals is marked by dramatic increases in the proportion of cortex to total amount of brain tissue. The human brain has the greatest proportion of cortex to brain mass of all animals.

In humans, the cortex (from Latin 'bark of a tree') is the gray outer covering of the wrinkled mass, the **cerebrum**, that sits like a cap over the rest of the brain. The wrinkled appearance results from the cortex being folded in upon itself. This folding allows a great amount of cortical matter to be compressed into the limited space provided by the human skull (in much the same way as the folding of a handkerchief allows it to fit into a jacket pocket). It has been estimated that up to 65 percent of the cortex is hidden within its folds.

It is the human cortex that accounts for our distinctness in the animal world, and it is within the human cortex that the secrets of language representation and processing are to be found. The remainder of our discussion of brain structure, therefore, will focus on the features of the cerebral cortex.

1.2   The Cerebral Hemispheres

The most important orientation points in mapping the cortex are the folds on its surface. These folds have two parts: **sulci** (pronounced /sʌlsaj/; singular: **sulcus**), which are areas where the cortex is folded in, and **gyri** (pronounced /dʒajraj/; singular: **gyrus**), which are areas where the cortex is folded out toward the surface.

Figure 12.1 shows a human brain as seen from above, illustrating the many sulci and gyri of the cortex. A very prominent feature is the deep sulcus (in this case called a **fissure** because of its size) that extends from the front of the brain to the back. This fissure, which is known as the **longitudinal fissure**, separates the left and right **cerebral hemispheres**. In many ways, the cerebral hemispheres can be considered to be separate brains; they are in fact often referred to as the left brain and the right brain. There are two main reasons for this.

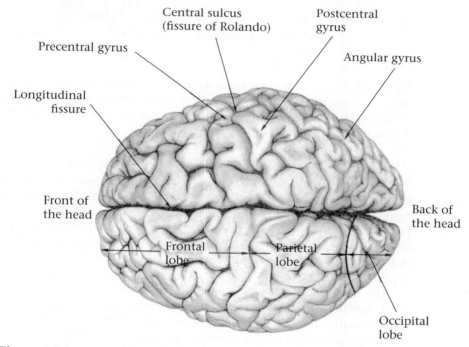

Figure 12.1   The cerebral hemispheres seen from above. Note the many sulci and gyri of the cortex and the prominence of the longitudinal fissure that separates the left and right hemispheres.

First, as shown in Figure 12.2, the hemispheres are almost completely anatomically separate. The main connection between them is a bundle of nerve fibers known as the **corpus callosum**, whose primary function is to allow the two hemispheres to communicate with one another.

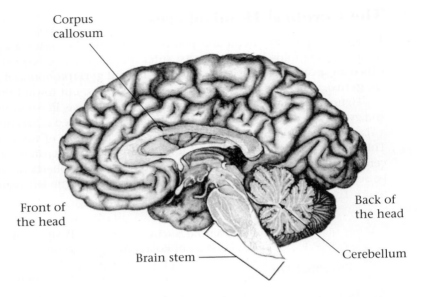

Corpus
callosum

Front of
the head

Back of
the head

Brain stem

Cerebellum

Figure 12.2   The right hemisphere seen from the inside. In this picture the corpus callosum has been cut so that one hemisphere may be separated from the other. Note how
the cerebral cortex caps the lower structures (the brain stem and cerebellum), which are
whitish in color.

Second, the cerebral hemispheres show considerable functional distinctness. In
terms of muscle movement and sensation, each hemisphere is responsible for half
the body—oddly enough, the opposite half. Thus the left hemisphere controls the
right side of the body and the right hemisphere controls the left side of the body.
These **contralateral** (contra = opposite; lateral = side) responsibilities of the cerebral
hemispheres account for the fact that people who suffer damage to one hemisphere
of the brain (e.g., as a result of a stroke or accident) will exhibit paralysis on the
opposite side of the body.

The hemispheres also show functional distinctness with respect to higher cognitive functions. In general, the left hemisphere seems to excel in analytic tasks
such as arithmetic, whereas the right hemisphere excels in tasks that require an
overall appreciation of complex patterns such as the recognition of familiar faces and
melodies.

Despite the fact that the hemispheres show such specialization, we should be
cautious about making sweeping generalizations about left brain versus right brain
abilities or strategies. In all probability, complex mental activities involve the coordinated functioning of both hemispheres. The representation of language in the brain
provides a useful example of this.

Most right-handed individuals have language represented in the left cerebral
hemisphere and are therefore said to be left **lateralized** for language. But not every

aspect of language is represented in the left hemisphere of right-handers. Adults who have had their left cerebral hemispheres surgically removed (a procedure sometimes required to treat seizures) lose most, but not all, of their linguistic competence. They typically lose the ability to speak and process complex syntactic patterns but retain some language comprehension ability. Clearly, it must be the right hemisphere that is responsible for whatever language-processing ability remains.

It has also been reported that right-handed patients who suffer damage to the right cerebral hemisphere exhibit difficulty in understanding jokes and metaphors in everyday conversation. These patients are able to provide only a literal or concrete interpretation of figurative sentences such as *He was wearing a loud tie*. They frequently misunderstand people because they cannot use loudness and intonation as cues to whether a speaker is angry, excited, or merely joking. Thus, the right hemisphere has a distinct role to play in normal language use.

Finally, consideration of language representation in the brains of left-handers makes matters even more complex. Contrary to what might be expected, few left-handers have a mirror image representation for language (that is, language localization in the right hemisphere). Rather, they tend to show significant language representation in both hemispheres. Thus, left-handers are generally less lateralized for language.

To sum up, although the left and right hemispheres have different abilities and different responsibilities, complex skills such as language do not always fall neatly into one hemisphere or the other. Research into why this is the case constitutes an important part of neuroscience. This research promises to reveal much about the cerebral hemispheres and about the individual representations and processes that constitute language.

1.3   The Lobes of the Cortex

We have seen that the cerebral hemispheres make distinct contributions to the overall functioning of the brain. In addition, each hemisphere contains substructures that appear to have distinct responsibilities. The substructures of the cortex in each hemisphere are called **lobes**. The lobes of the cerebrum can be located with reference to prominent sulci, fissures (deep sulci), and gyri, which are useful as orientation points in much the same way that rivers and mountain ranges are useful in finding particular locations on a map. As can be seen in Figure 12.3, the **central sulcus** (also called the fissure of Rolando) extends from the top of the cortex to another groove known as the **lateral fissure** (also called the Sylvian fissure). These two features are important in the delineation of the cerebral lobes. The **frontal lobe** lies in front of the central sulcus and the **parietal lobe** lies behind it. The **temporal lobe** is the area beneath the lateral fissure. The fourth lobe, the **occipital lobe**, is not clearly marked by an infolding of the cortex, but can be identified as the area to the rear of the **angular gyrus** (which has been found to play an important role in reading).

Figure 12.3 shows the left hemisphere of the brain. It indicates the location of each lobe and its specialized functions. (Some of the functions listed, such as those related to movement and the senses, are located in both hemispheres.) Assuming that this is the brain of a right-hander, it is also possible to identify those areas of the cortex that have a particular role to play in language processing, as we will see.

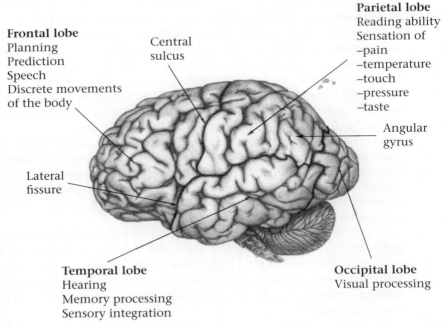

Frontal lobe
Planning
Prediction
Speech
Discrete movements
of the body

Central
sulcus

Lateral
fissure

Parietal lobe
Reading ability
Sensation of
–pain
–temperature
–touch
–pressure
–taste

Angular
gyrus

Temporal lobe
Hearing
Memory processing
Sensory integration

Occipital lobe
Visual processing

Figure 12.3   The left hemisphere seen from the outside

2   Investigating the Brain

Imagine that you could open the top of a living human being's skull and observe the brain while the individual is engaged in activities such as reading, writing, watching a football game, or having a heated argument. What would you see? The answer is—nothing! To the outside observer, the working brain shows no evidence of its activity. This is clearly a problem for the field of neurolinguistics, which requires the use of special investigative techniques to uncover the secrets of where and how language is processed in the brain. In addition, these special techniques must meet the ethical requirements of research on human subjects. While other neuroscientists are able to do much of their research using animal subjects, this option is not available to neurolinguists.

Imposing as they may be, the problems of investigating the processing of language in the brain are not insurmountable. Recent decades have seen a number of technological advances that have greatly facilitated the investigation of the question: What is going on in the brain when people are engaged in language behavior?

In the following sections, we discuss some of the techniques of neurolinguistic investigation.

2.1   Autopsy Studies

Until recently, the only way to study the brain was through **autopsy studies**. This technique was most often carried out with patients who were admitted to hospitals displaying a neurological disorder. Careful observations were made of a patient's behavior, and subsequent to his or her death, the brain was examined to determine which areas were damaged. By comparing the area of brain damage and the type of disorder the patient displayed while alive, neurologists could develop theories about the role of the damaged brain part(s) in normal brain functioning.

LANGUAGE MATTERS   Paul Broca

When Paul Broca conducted his first studies of aphasia, he was thirty-seven years old. He was already known for being a bold thinker and a strong supporter of Charles Darwin's new and controversial theory of evolution. Darwin had published his landmark book two years earlier. In that same year, 1859, Broca had founded the Anthropological Society of Paris. Broca's work on aphasia lasted less than ten years. By the 1870s, his interests had turned to other things. He founded the scientific journal *Revue d'anthropologie* in 1872 and was elected to the French Senate in 1879. He also advanced the treatment of brain aneurysms. And it was in fact a brain aneurysm that caused his death in 1880 at the age of fifty-six. His scientific contributions, however, continue to have an impact almost 150 years later.

A famous example of this type of analysis comes from the work of Paul Broca, a nineteenth-century French neurologist. In 1860, Broca observed a patient who had been hospitalized for more than twenty years in Paris. For most of his hospitalization, the patient was almost completely unable to speak but appeared to understand everything that was said to him. Toward the end of his life (he died at age fifty-seven), he also developed a paralysis of the right arm and leg. Immediately after the patient's death (as a result of an unrelated infection), Broca examined the brain. It showed severe damage (called a **lesion**) in the lower rear area of the left frontal lobe. Broca concluded that because the patient was unable to speak, this part of the frontal lobe must normally be responsible for speech production. Since that time, many other autopsy studies have supported Broca's conclusions. This portion of the left frontal lobe is now called **Broca's area** (see Figure 12.4, which shows this and other language-processing areas of the left hemisphere). As will be discussed in Section 3.1, the impairment of the ability to speak as a result of brain damage is called **Broca's aphasia**.

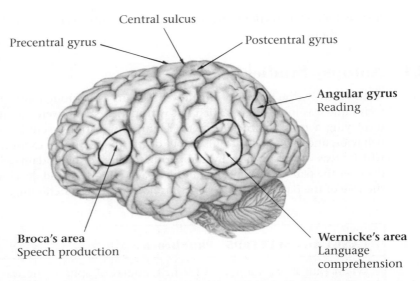

Central sulcus

Precentral gyrus

Postcentral gyrus

Angular gyrus
Reading

Broca's area
Speech production

Wernicke's area
Language
comprehension

Figure 12.4 Language processes in the left hemisphere. Damage to Broca's area is usually associated with nonfluent speech and difficulty processing complex syntactic patterns. Damage to Wernicke's area (see Section 3.2) is usually associated with comprehension disturbances. Damage to the area around the angular gyrus results in reading impairment.

LANGUAGE MATTERS   Phrenology: A Discredited Theory

Franz Joseph Gall was born in 1758 in southwestern Germany. After moving to Vienna, he founded the field of phrenology, which can be considered to have three basic claims:

1. The mind can be divided into discrete mental "organs."
2. Particular development in any area results in expanded brain size in that location.
3. This expansion presses on the skull, and produces bumps, which can then be identified and interpreted by the trained phrenologist.

Although it is extremely unlikely that Gall's original mental organs (e.g., combativeness, hope) are correct, the more general idea of mental organs remains a key part of current neuropsychological debate.

We now consider claims *2* and *3* to be largely unsubstantiated. But, interestingly, Gall was reported to be extraordinarily good at assessing the abilities and traits of complete strangers (allegedly using his method of feeling the skull). In his time, Gall gained both fame and notoriety. Forced to leave Vienna, he eventually settled in France, where his work was also discredited within scientific circles.

2.2   Images of the Living Brain

Autopsy analysis has been and continues to be an important tool in the understanding of the brain. But an autopsy can be carried out only after the patient's death. Therefore, whatever information it reveals about the nature and extent of the patient's brain damage can no longer be of any use in his or her treatment. One of the earliest techniques used to understand how the living brain processes language was pioneered in Canada by the Montreal-based neurosurgeon Wilder Penfield. This technique was developed to map the brain of a person who was about to undergo neurosurgery. Prior to the surgical procedure, a portion of the skull was removed and the surface of the brain was stimulated with electrodes carrying small electrical charges in order to map which areas of the individual's brain were involved in particular functions. This would allow the physicians to better assess how surgery might affect the post-operative abilities of the patient and assist the patient and family in weighing the risk-benefit ratio of the planned intervention. Such preoperative procedures greatly assisted early attempts to produce a functional map of the human cerebral cortex. Interestingly, it was also found that direct electrical stimulation of the brain resulted in temporary loss, rather than enhancement, of function.

Since Penfield's pioneering work in the 1950s, the sophistication of preoperative techniques has increased greatly. It is now possible to insert electrodes deep into the living brain and isolate the function of a very small number of neurons (i.e., fewer than a thousand at a time). But this, of course, remains a very invasive technique that would only be carried out on patients whose neurological impairment may require brain surgery. Other techniques that are, comparatively speaking, much less invasive have been devised and refined since Penfield's work.

Computerized axial tomography (also called **CT scanning**) is a technique that uses a narrow beam of X-rays to create brain images that take the form of a series of brain slices. CT scans offered neuroscientists their first opportunity to look inside a living brain. However, like autopsy studies, CT scanning provides a static image of the brain; it is most useful in identifying brain lesions and tumors. In order to study the brain in action, other techniques are required that are sensitive to dynamic activity.

One such dynamic technique is **positron emission tomography** (also called **PET** scanning). This technique capitalizes on one of the brain's many interesting properties—it is extremely hungry for glucose and oxygen. Although the brain accounts for only about 2 percent of total body weight, it consumes about 20 percent of the oxygen the body uses while at rest. This oxygen is, of course, carried to the brain by the blood.

In the PET technique, positron-emitting isotopes, which function as radioactive tracers, are injected into the arteries in combination with glucose. The rate at which the radioactive glucose is used by specific regions of the brain is recorded while the subject is engaged in various sorts of cognitive activities. These recordings are used to produce maps of areas of high brain activity associated with particular cognitive functions. Examples of such PET maps are represented in Figure 12.5.

Although PET is much less invasive than electrical stimulation of the brain, which requires prior removal of portions of the skull, it is hardly a technique that

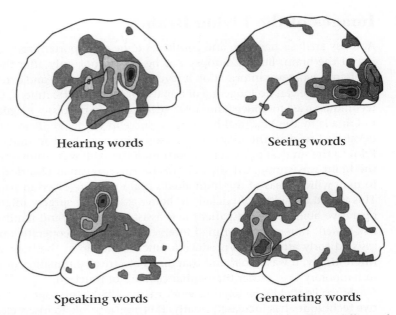

Figure 12.5   PET scans show how blood flow to the brain shifts to different locations, depending on which task is being performed. Data adapted from: Gerald D. Fischbach, "Mind and Brain," by Gerald D. Fischbach. Copyright © 1992 by Professor Marcus E. Raichle. Used by permission of Professor Marcus E. Raichle.

most people would volunteer for because of the perceived risks associated with the injection of the radioactive tracer. The two techniques that we will review next also make use of changes in blood flow within the brain in order to associate cognitive function with specific brain regions, but they do so without injection.

At present, **functional magnetic resonance imaging (fMRI)** is the preferred means of gaining information about the functional anatomy of the brain. The technique also monitors increases in blood flow to specific areas of the brain. It does so by making use of the fact that blood is rich in iron. Although iron constitutes only 0.004 percent of the human body, 65 percent of it is found within the hemoglobin of red blood cells. The fMRI technique uses powerful magnetic fields to track this iron, and hence the blood flow within the brain. fMRI installations are currently very expensive and therefore not available at all research centers. Nevertheless, the technique has already yielded dramatic evidence of activity in particular parts of the brain during language-processing tasks.

A final extremely promising technique for the study of how language is processed in the brain is **magnetoencephalography**, or **MEG**. The MEG technique records very subtle changes in the magnetic fields generated within the brain. Although MEG also requires a very expensive apparatus, it has advantages over all the other techniques discussed so far. In contrast to PET, it is noninvasive, and like fMRI, it provides detailed information on which parts of the brain are involved in particular types of language processing (speaking, hearing, reading, or writing). Its key advantage

---

LANGUAGE MATTERS   **Language Learning Strengthens the Brain**

Using MRI scans of the brain, researchers in Sweden compared the brains of military interpreters undergoing intensive language training with the brains of medical students, also intensively involved in learning. The researchers discovered that, after three months, the intensive language learners had increased thickness of the brain cortex (the gray matter associated with memory formation) in three specific areas related to acoustic-phonetic processing and the articulatory network. Furthermore, the language learners experienced growth in the volume of the hippocampus (which has a role in learning and storing information in long-term memory). Similar results were not observed in the brains of the medical students.

Information from: J. Mårtensson, et al., "Growth of Language-Related Brain Areas after Foreign Language Learning," *NeuroImage* 63 (2012): 240–244.

---

is that it also provides time resolution that is greatly superior to that of fMRI. Using the MEG technique, researchers are able to gain a millisecond-by-millisecond record of how the brain responds to a stimulus event, such as the presentation of a single word. In this way, MEG provides detailed information on both the timing and location of activity in the brain.

Modern brain-imaging techniques such as fMRI and MEG have greatly increased our knowledge of where language processing takes place in the brain. It has been found, for example, that when subjects speak, much blood flows to the left hemisphere of the cortex and to Broca's area in particular. When subjects read, much blood flows to the occipital lobe (because it is responsible for visual processing), to the angular gyrus (which has a special role to play in reading), and to other areas of the left hemisphere. These observations support the view that the left hemisphere is primarily responsible for language in most people and that there are specific language areas within the left hemisphere.

Finally, functional brain imaging studies are playing an important role in increasing our understanding of the differences that might exist between the use of one's first language and that of a second language. Second-language processing has been shown to involve a wider variety of cortical sites. This supports the view that the less automatic nature of language use in a second language requires the involvement of diverse mental processes in addition to those specifically dedicated to language.

2.3   Learning from Hemispheric Connections and Disconnections

In the techniques that have been described, information about language representation in the brain is gained through an investigation of the brain itself. In this section, we review an alternative approach—one that examines behavior that can be associated with a particular brain hemisphere.

Dichotic Listening Studies

Dichotic listening studies have been extremely important in accumulating knowledge about the specialization of the cerebral hemispheres. The technique capitalizes on the property of the brain that we discussed in Section 1.2—namely, that each hemisphere is primarily wired to the opposite side of the body (including the head). So most of the input to your right ear goes to the left hemisphere of your brain. Now, if the left cerebral hemisphere is indeed specialized for language processing in right-handers, these individuals should process language better through the right ear.

If you are right-handed, you will probably be able to verify this by observing the difference between holding a telephone to your right ear and holding it to your left ear during a conversation. When the phone is held to the right ear, the speech will seem louder and clearer. This phenomenon is known as the **right ear advantage (REA)**. In the laboratory technique, stereo earphones are used and different types of stimuli are presented to each ear. In general, the right ear shows an advantage for words, numbers, and Morse code, whereas the left ear shows an advantage for the perception of melodies and environmental sounds such as bird songs.

Split Brain Studies

If the left hemisphere is wired to the right ear, why is it possible to understand speech presented to the left ear? There are two reasons for this. The first is that the auditory pathways to the brain are not completely crossed—there are also secondary links between each hemisphere and the ear on the same side of the body. The second is that after the right hemisphere receives information from the left ear, that information can be transferred to the left hemisphere via the corpus callosum—the bundle of fibers that connects the two hemispheres.

Evidence concerning the crucial role that the corpus callosum plays in normal brain functioning comes from the study of patients who have had this pathway surgically severed (a rare procedure used to treat severe forms of epilepsy by preventing seizures from spreading to both hemispheres). Studies that have investigated the effects of this surgery on cognition—so-called **split brain experiments**—have provided dramatic illustrations of what happens when the hemispheres cannot communicate with one another.

It appears from the behavior of split brain patients that although the right hemisphere does show some language understanding, it is mute. In one of the many split brain experiments, a patient is blindfolded and an object, such as a key, is placed in one hand. When the key is held in the right hand, the patient can easily name it, because the right hand is connected to the left hemisphere, which can compute speech output. However, when the key is placed in the left hand, the patient cannot say what it is. The right hemisphere, which receives information from the left hand, knows what is there (as is shown by the person's ability to draw the object with the left hand), but it can neither put this into words nor transfer the information across the severed corpus callosum to the left brain.

Split brain experiments have presented new and important knowledge about the functioning of the brain. In terms of overall investigative methodology, however, they are not quite as exotic as they seem. In fact, the logic of split brain experiments is identical to the logic employed by Broca in 1860. In both cases, the researcher endeavors to learn how the normal brain works by examining which functions are lost as a result of the brain damage. In the case of split brain studies, the damage is surgically induced. In the case of Broca's aphasia, disease caused an "experiment in nature." In Section 3, we return to these experiments in nature and examine what they reveal about language representation in the brain.

3   Aphasia

The term **aphasia** refers to the loss of language ability as a result of damage to the brain. The most common cause of aphasia is **stroke** (also called a cerebrovascular accident). A stroke occurs when the normal flow of blood to the brain is disrupted, preventing neurons from receiving oxygen and nutrients. Aphasia can also be caused by blows to the head, brain infection, brain tumors, and brain hemorrhage. Currently, aphasia affects more than 1 million people in North America. The syndrome is equally common in men and women, and is most likely to occur in persons over the age of fifty.

In general, the amount and type of aphasic disturbance that a patient will exhibit depends on the extent and location of the brain damage. Most individuals who suffer aphasic impairment experience a mixture of deficits in speaking, listening, reading, and writing. However, some other forms of aphasia are much more specific. In these more specific forms, particular skills are lost and others remain intact. The study of these specific aphasias can tell us much about the building blocks of language in the brain. In the next two sections, we discuss the two most widely studied specific aphasias.

3.1   Nonfluent Aphasia

Nonfluent aphasia (also called **motor aphasia**) results from damage to parts of the brain in front of the central sulcus. Recall that part of the frontal lobe is concerned with motor activity and that the bottom rear portion of the frontal lobe (Broca's area) is responsible for the articulation of speech (see Figure 12.4). Not surprisingly, therefore, nonfluent patients show slow, effortful speech production (hence the term *nonfluent*). The most severe form of nonfluent aphasia is **global aphasia**. In this type of aphasia, the patient is completely mute. Of the less severe forms, Broca's aphasia is the most informative with respect to language in the brain.

The speech of Broca's aphasics is very halting. Patients have great difficulty in accurately producing the needed phonemes to say a word. For example, a patient who wishes to produce the sentence in *1a* would be likely to produce an utterance like the one in *1b*.

1) a. It's hard to eat with a spoon.
   b. . . . har eat . . . wit . . . pun

LANGUAGE MATTERS   Brain Size Is Not the Whole Story

Although humans have relatively large brains (only those of elephants are bigger), an even more important factor than size may be the amount of cortex (related to the amount of folding into gyri and sulci) and the proportion of uncommitted cortex—areas not assigned a specific sensory function, such as vision or smell. The amount of uncommitted cortex is related to the degree of flexibility for learning. As shown in the diagram below, humans have a great deal of uncommitted cerebral cortex. Human intelligence is made possible by the richness of associations within that cortex.

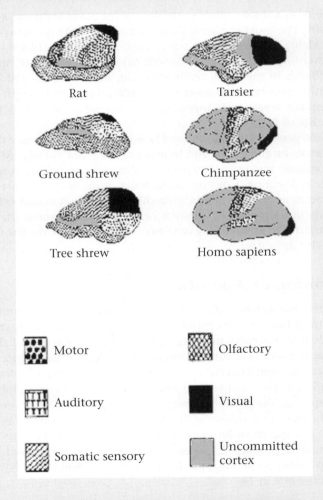

Rat

Tarsier

Ground shrew

Chimpanzee

Tree shrew

Homo sapiens

Motor   Olfactory

Auditory   Visual

Somatic sensory   Uncommitted cortex

Adapted from: Wilder Penfield, *The Mystery of the Mind* © 1975 Princeton University Press, 2003 renewed PUP. Reprinted by permission of Princeton University Press.

The ellipsis dots (. . .) between the words in *1b* indicate periods of silence in the production of the utterance. Sentences produced at this slow rate also tend to lack normal sentence intonation. This common characteristic of the speech of Broca's aphasics is called **dysprosody**. Note how the patient simplifies the consonant clusters in the words *hard* and *spoon* and changes the /θ/ to /t/ in the word *with*. The speech errors that result from these sorts of phonemic errors are called **phonemic paraphasias**.

It is tempting to think that the impairment of speech production in Broca's aphasia is caused by the fact that Broca's area is adjacent to the motor strip that controls movement of the facial muscles. The problem with this hypothesis is that damage to Broca's area usually produces only mild weakness of the muscles on the opposite side of the face and no permanent damage. Yet for some reason, even people who can still control the muscles used in speech cannot use language properly after damage to Broca's area. This suggests that Broca's area has a language-specific responsibility.

Broca's Aphasia as a Syntactic Disorder

Returning to the utterance in *1b*, note that the patient also omits a number of words that would normally be used in this utterance. The words that are omitted are *it*, *is*, *to*, and *a*. Often dubbed **function words**, items of this sort belong to categories and subcategories (pronoun, copula verb, preposition, determiner, and so on) that have a very limited membership. They typically do not carry stress and cannot be inflected. Their omission by Broca's aphasics creates a telegraphic style of speech that consists mostly of nouns, verbs, and adjectives.

One possible account of the speech of Broca's aphasics is that it results from an economy of effort. Speech production is very effortful for these patients, so they use as few words as possible because they are "paying" by the word. (Interestingly, the words that are dropped are the very items that we tend to omit from short text messages: "I will meet you in the baggage claim" becomes "Meet you baggage claim.") But other characteristics of their linguistic abilities point to a deeper cause—the disturbance of syntactic competence.

In addition to omitting function words, Broca's aphasics tend to omit inflectional affixes such as *-ing*, *-ed*, and *-en* in words such as *running*, *chased*, and *broken*. They also show difficulty judging the grammaticality of sentences. For example, given sentences such as the ones in *2*, Broca's aphasics will not always be able to determine which ones are grammatical and which ones are not.

2) a. The boy ate it up.
   b. *The boy ate up it.
   c. *Boy ate it up.
   d. The boy ate up the cake.

Finally, a close examination of the comprehension of Broca's aphasics offers further support for the view that there is a syntactic component to the disorder.

3) a. The mouse was chased by the cat.
   b. The dog was chased by the cat.
   c. The cat was chased by the mouse.

Broca's aphasics tend to interpret sentences such as *3a* correctly because knowledge about the behavior of cats and mice helps them infer the meaning. However, they are unsure about sentences such as *3b*, in which knowledge of the world is not a reliable guide to comprehension, and they tend to interpret a sentence such as *3c* as though it means 'The cat chased the mouse'. When we read a sentence like *3c*, we recognize it as describing an unlikely event, but our interpretation is driven by the syntax of the sentence (including the presence of the auxiliary verb *be* and the preposition *by*), not by our knowledge of the world. Many Broca's aphasics appear not to have this ability.

These sorts of observations have led many neurolinguists to reconsider the traditional view that Broca's aphasia is simply a production deficit. The possibility that Broca's aphasia also involves some central disturbance of syntactic competence is intriguing and may lead to a deeper understanding of how syntactic knowledge is represented in the brain. We will return to this question in Section 4.

A final point about Broca's aphasia is of a less technical nature but is of great importance to the understanding of the syndrome as a whole. Most Broca's aphasics are acutely aware of their language deficit and are typically very frustrated by it. It is as though they have complete understanding of what they should say, but to their constant dismay, they find themselves unable to say it. This plight of Broca's aphasics is consistent with our understanding of the role of the frontal lobe, which is usually the site of lesions in the syndrome. Broca's area plays an extremely important role in language; however, it does not seem to be involved in the semantic relationships between words and the relationship between units of language and units of thought. The neurological basis of these meaning relationships remains almost entirely unknown. From the analysis of nonfluent aphasia in general and Broca's aphasia in particular, however, we suspect that these semantic relationships are the responsibility of areas of the brain that lie behind the central sulcus—in the temporal and parietal lobes of the brain (see Figure 12.3). This suspicion is supported by the type of language deficits associated with damage to the temporal and parietal lobes.

3.2 Fluent Aphasia

The type of aphasia that results from damage to parts of the left cortex behind the central sulcus is referred to as **fluent aphasia** (or **sensory aphasia**). This type of aphasia stands in sharp contrast to nonfluent aphasia. Fluent aphasics have no difficulty producing language but have a great deal of difficulty selecting, organizing, and monitoring their language production.

The most widely studied type of fluent aphasia is called **Wernicke's aphasia**. The syndrome is named after the German physiologist Carl Wernicke, who, in 1874, published a now famous report of a kind of aphasia that was almost the complete opposite of Broca's aphasia. It was determined from autopsy data that this type of aphasia was associated with a lesion in the temporal lobe just below the most posterior (rear) portion of the lateral fissure. In severe cases, the lesion could also extend upward into the lower portion of the parietal lobe. This area of the brain is now known as **Wernicke's area** (see Figure 12.4).

LANGUAGE MATTERS   Carl Wernicke

Carl Wernicke was born in Prussia and was only twenty-six years old when he published his landmark study of aphasia. At the time, he was a medical intern and had the opportunity to observe a number of persons with aphasia. Those patients who showed difficulty in language comprehension were of particular interest to him. Wernicke's ideas were very much influenced by his teacher and mentor, the neuroanatomist Theodor Meynert, who also taught Sigmund Freud in Vienna. Meynert's influence motivated Wernicke to link his theory of brain function to networks of specific brain locations. Wernicke went on to become an international authority in neuroanatomy and brain disorders. He completed his *Textbook of Brain Disorders* in 1883 and, together with three other authors, *Atlas of the Brain* in 1903. Wernicke only lived to be one year older than Paul Broca, and like Broca, his death may have been caused by damage to the brain. Wernicke died in 1905 at age fifty-seven as a result of injuries sustained in an accident while riding his bicycle through the forest.

In contrast to Broca's aphasics, Wernicke's aphasics are generally unaware of their deficit. Their speech typically sounds very good: there are no long pauses; sentence intonation is normal; function words are used appropriately; word order is usually correct. The problem is that the patient rarely makes any sense. The following is a conversation between an examiner (E) and a Wernicke's patient (P).

4) *E:* How are you today, Mrs. A?
   P: Yes.
   E: Have I ever tested you before?
   P: No. I mean I haven't.
   E: Can you tell me what your name is?
   P: No, I don't I . . . right I'm right now here.
   E: What is your address?
   P: I cud /kʌd/ if I can help these this like you know . . . to make it.
   We are seeing for him. That is my father.

The patient in this conversation produces a number of errors, but most of them are different from the kinds of errors made by Broca's aphasics. While the patient is able to produce some well-formed structures (e.g., *no, I don't*), these structures appear intermittently amidst various unrelated fragments. Not only are these constructions unrelated to each other, they are also unrelated to the examiner's questions. It appears that the patient has no understanding of the questions being asked.

This patient displays a significant but not severe form of Wernicke's aphasia. Her speech appears to result from a semirandom selection of words and short phrases. In very severe cases of this syndrome, phonemes are also randomly selected and the result is speech that has the intonational characteristics of English but actually contains very few real words of the language. This is termed **jargon aphasia**.

The type of deficit found in Wernicke's aphasia leads us to a greater understanding and a deeper consideration of the nature of language comprehension. Wernicke's aphasia is primarily a comprehension deficit. But as we have seen, when comprehension breaks down, most of what we call language ability breaks down with it. Patients cannot express themselves because they cannot understand what they have just said and then use that understanding in the planning of what to say next. In a very real sense, these patients have lost contact with themselves (and therefore with the rest of the world). Wernicke's patients cannot have coherent trains of thought—the brain damage does not allow the parts of the train to be connected. It is interesting to note that Wernicke's patients have difficulty planning and executing many types of sequenced behavior, such as purchasing groceries, getting home by bus, or washing laundry.

In summary, our discussion of fluent and nonfluent aphasia has demonstrated how normal language use is a marriage of content and form. In the case of nonfluent aphasia, form is compromised but the content of language remains relatively intact. In contrast, fluent aphasia is characterized by a rapid flow of form with little content.

4   Acquired Dyslexia and Dysgraphia

Reading and writing involve a complex array of perceptual and motor skills. In this section, we will consider impairments of reading and writing that are caused by damage to the brain. The impairment of reading ability is called **acquired dyslexia** (or **acquired alexia**). The impairment of writing ability is called **acquired dysgraphia** (or **acquired agraphia**). In both cases, the term *acquired* indicates that the patient possessed normal reading and/or writing ability prior to brain damage and distinguishes the syndromes from developmental dyslexia and developmental dysgraphia, which deal with disturbances of reading and writing development in children.

4.1   Reading and Writing Disturbances in Aphasia

Acquired dyslexia and dysgraphia typically accompany the aphasic syndromes that we considered in Section 3. Most Broca's aphasics show writing disturbances that are comparable to their speaking deficits. In other words, a patient who cannot pronounce the word *spoon* will also not be able to write it correctly. The resulting error in writing (e.g., *poon*) is called a **paragraphia**. In spontaneous writing, Broca's aphasics also tend to omit function words and inflectional affixes. Finally, while the silent reading of Broca's aphasics is very good, their reading aloud shows the same telegraphic style as their spontaneous speech. These observations reinforce the view that the deficit in Broca's aphasia is much more than a speech articulation deficit. It is a production deficit at a very deep level of language planning.

Wernicke's aphasics also show reading and writing deficits that match their deficits in speaking and listening. The writing of Wernicke's aphasics is formally very good. They typically retain good spelling and handwriting. However, like their speaking, what they write makes little sense. Reading comprehension is also severely impaired in Wernicke's aphasia. Patients can see the letters and words but cannot make any sense of them. Again, the conclusion to be drawn is that Wernicke's aphasia, like Broca's aphasia, involves a central disturbance of language competence—the knowledge that underlies language functioning. In such cases of central language disturbance, whatever impairment the patient has in listening and speaking will be matched in reading and writing.

4.2 Acquired Dyslexia as the Dominant Language Deficit

In addition to the reading and writing deficits that accompany aphasia, there are many cases in which the disruption of reading and writing ability is the dominant symptom. This typically follows damage in and around the angular gyrus of the parietal lobe. An analysis of these types of disabilities has led to some very interesting theories about the nature of reading (at least in English).

Before we proceed to discuss two contrasting types of acquired dyslexia, it might be worthwhile to reflect on the abilities involved in the reading of words. Up to this point in the chapter, you have read over five thousand words. Some of these words (such as the function words) are very familiar to you, and you probably recognized them as wholes. But others, such as *angular gyrus*, are words that you probably read for the first time. How then could you know how to pronounce them? Many theorists believe that readers maintain a set of spelling-to-sound rules that enable them to read new words aloud. These rules are important in the development of reading ability and in the addition of new words to our reading vocabulary.

Phonological dyslexia is a type of acquired dyslexia in which the patient seems to have lost the ability to use spelling-to-sound rules. Phonological dyslexics can only read words that they have seen before. Asked to read a word such as *blug* aloud, they either say nothing or produce a known word that is visually similar to the target (e.g., *blue* or *bug*).

Surface dyslexia is the opposite of phonological dyslexia. Surface dyslexics seem unable to recognize words as wholes. Instead, they must process all words through a set of spelling-to-sound rules. This is shown by the kinds of errors they make. Surface dyslexics do not have difficulty reading words such as *bat* that are regularly spelled. However, they read irregularly spelled words such as *yacht* by applying regular rules and thus producing /jɑtʃt/. The most interesting aspect of surface dyslexics' reading ability is that they understand what they produce, not what they see. For example, a surface dyslexic would be likely to read the word *worm* as /wɔɹm/ (and not /wɚm/). When asked what the word means, the patient would answer, "The opposite of *cold*."

Data from acquired dyslexia allow researchers to build models that specify the components of normal reading ability and their relationship to each other. Clearly, this type of analysis plays a very important role in the development of our understanding of language, the mind, and the brain.

5   Linguistic Theory and Aphasia

Looking at aphasia in terms of linguistic theory gives us a new perspective on language in the brain. Linguistic theory has been traditionally concerned with the structure of language, not with how it is used in listening, speech production, reading, and writing. In contrast, the traditional way of looking at aphasia has been in terms of what the patient can and cannot do. The involvement of theoretical linguists in the study of aphasia has caused a minor revolution in the field. Aphasia researchers have begun to think about the deficit in terms of the loss of semantic features, phonological rules, and perhaps syntactic tree structures. Theoretical linguists have also found that the study of aphasia offers an important area for testing theoretical distinctions such as the one between derivational and inflectional affixes. In this section, we will look at some of the areas in which the marriage of theoretical linguistics and neurolinguistics has been most fruitful. This fruitfulness has usually meant an increase in the sophistication of the questions that are asked about aphasia. It has also meant the discovery of new and often bizarre aphasic phenomena.

5.1   Features, Morphemes, and Meaning

In the area of phonology, we have found that the phonemic paraphasias of Broca's aphasics usually differ from the target phoneme by only one distinctive feature (recall example *1* in Section 3.1: *with* → /wɪt/) and can therefore be easily described by phonological rules. Observations such as these lead us to believe that phonological features and rules might be good tools to characterize how language is represented and produced.

In the area of morphology, the study of aphasia has offered empirical support for the theoretical distinction between inflection and derivation. As we have discussed, Broca's aphasics show a sensitivity to this distinction in their omission of affixes in speech. Inflectional affixes are commonly dropped, but derivational affixes are usually retained. Perhaps most interesting is the tendency of some aphasics to produce the basic forms of morphemes in reading and repetition. Asked to repeat the word *illegal*, for example, some aphasics will produce *inlegal*, using the most unrestricted form of the negative prefix rather than the allomorph that should occur before a base beginning with /l/. Again, errors such as these point to the possibility that phonological processes such as nasal assimilation and the notion of underlying form are not only an elegant way to represent linguistic competence but are also relevant to the processing of language in the brain.

The study of aphasia also has the potential to shed light on the nature of semantic representations. Most of the work in this area has concentrated on the many subvarieties of acquired dyslexia. In a syndrome known as **deep dyslexia**, patients produce reading errors that are systematically related to the word that they are asked to read (in the sense that they share some semantic features but not others). Given the word *mother*, for example, a deep dyslexic may read *father*.

The detailed study of semantic deficits associated with brain damage has also led to some very surprising discoveries. Most aphasics and dyslexics find abstract words much more difficult to process than concrete words. But there have been reports of concrete word dyslexia in which the patient shows exactly the opposite problem (having difficulty with concrete words such as *table*). There has even been a report of a patient who shows a selective inability to read words that refer to fruits and vegetables.

5.2 Agrammatism

In Section 3.1, we observed that many theorists now believe that Broca's aphasia involves a central syntactic deficit. The syndrome that is characterized by telegraphic speech has been given the name **agrammatism**—to indicate that grammatical ability has been lost. Agrammatism is the aphasic disturbance that has been most studied by linguists. It is characterized by the omission of function words such as *it*, *is*, *to*, and *a*; by the omission of inflectional affixes; and by comprehension deficits in cases where the correct interpretation of a sentence is dependent on syntax alone.

In recent years, many linguists have become involved in the problems of characterizing the agrammatic deficit. These problems have raised both specific questions, such as exactly what a function word is, and general questions, such as whether it is possible to lose syntax. The involvement of linguists has also generated cross-linguistic studies of agrammatism that provide interesting insights into the interaction between characteristics of the syndrome and characteristics of particular languages.

5.3 The Loss of Syntactic Competence

Another, much more general, challenge is to define what it means to possess syntactic competence such that we can speak of its loss. This challenge has forced researchers to address the question: What is the essence of syntactic knowledge? Is it the hierarchical arrangement of elements? Is it the representation of abstract entities such as the +Q feature and traces?

Some researchers have suggested that agrammatism involves the loss of the ability to deal with the details of syntactic structure, especially when there has been movement. They claim that agrammatics rely on word order rather than structure to interpret sentences and that they employ a default strategy that treats the first NP as the agent. This strategy works reasonably well for simple sentences in which the first NP can be assigned the thematic role of agent and the second NP can be assigned the role of undergoer (theme), as in sentence *5a*. It results in miscomprehension, however, for sentences such as *5b* and *5c*, where the first NP does not have the role of agent.

5) a. The girl kissed the boy.
   b. The girl was kissed.
   c. It was the girl that the boy kissed.

Other researchers have argued that agrammatism does not involve the loss of syntactic competence, but rather an alteration of that competence. They have claimed that agrammatics have full-fledged syntactic structure but can no longer represent the traces that indicate an NP's position in deep structure. As a result, they are unable to recognize that the subject NP in *5b* is the undergoer since they do not realize that it is the complement of the verb in deep structure.

5.4   Agrammatism in Other Languages

Data from other languages has suggested that the original characterization of agrammatism as a syndrome in which function words and inflectional affixes are lost may not reflect the true nature of this phenomenon.

In English, affixes are typically attached to a base that is itself a free form. The past form of the verb *visit*, for example, is created by the addition of *-ed*; the third person singular is created by the addition of *-s*. However, not all languages work this way. In Semitic languages, such as Hebrew, the base is typically a string of three consonants, which is unpronounceable in its uninflected form. Inflected words are produced by inserting vowels into this triconsonantal skeleton. For example, the Hebrew root for the verb *to write* is /ktv/. The masculine third person present form of the verb is /kɔtɛv/ and the masculine third person past form is /katav/. If Hebrew agrammatics simply lose inflectional affixes the way they do in English, they should not be able to produce any verbs. As it turns out, Hebrew agrammatics do produce verbs, but instead of dropping inflectional forms, they choose randomly among them. This sort of evidence has provided a convincing argument against the view that agrammatic language results from a simple economy of effort. Rather, it seems that it is a linguistic deficit that involves the misselection of linguistic forms. It is only in languages such as English, where the base is also a legal free form, that the agrammatism is characterized by affix omission.

6   Language in the Brain: What's Where?

We have seen that, in an important sense, normal language use involves the integrated functioning of the entire cortex. Even right-handers who are strongly left lateralized for language show some language deficit in cases of damage to the right hemisphere. Finally, virtually all forms of aphasia are accompanied by word-finding difficulties. This observation suggests that the storage and retrieval of word forms may be diffusely represented in the brain.

Recent evidence has suggested that lexical knowledge is centered in the temporal lobes. Yet, as was originally discussed by Sigmund Freud in his 1891 book *On Aphasia* (Freud studied aphasia before turning to his better-known work on psychoanalysis), knowledge of a word can be characterized as a rich set of associations. Some of these are actually part of the word—for example, what it looks like, what it sounds like, how it is pronounced, and how it is written. But other aspects are not necessarily linguistic—for example, what the referent of the word feels, or sounds, or smells, or looks like. Given these considerations, it is hardly surprising that the representation of a word in the brain may best be considered to be a network rather than a single entity.

LANGUAGE MATTERS Where Is Universal Grammar?

In two experiments, native speakers of German were given rules for Italian and for Japanese, neither of which the subjects knew. For each language, the subjects were given six rules and were then asked to judge whether sentences in the language were grammatical or not, according to the rules they had been given. Three rules were real rules of the language and complied with principles of Universal Grammar (UG) but differed from the language-specific parameters of German (e.g., put the object before the verb in Japanese). The other three rules were fake and did not comply with principles of UG (e.g., to negate a sentence, put the negative after the third word of the sentence).

When the subjects made their grammaticality judgments, the experimenters looked at reaction time and fMRI images of brain activity. Subjects took longer to make grammaticality judgments when fake rules instead of real rules were involved. In addition, the fMRI showed no pattern of brain activation when fake rules were involved. However, when real rules were involved, there was consistent brain activation in a specific part of Broca's area.

Information from: M. Musso et al., "Broca's Area and the Language Instinct," *Nature Neuroscience* 6, 7 (2003): 774–781.

In recent years, an interesting view of how words are represented in the brain has been put forward using the concept of a **cell assembly**. This concept, first developed by Donald Hebb at McGill University in the 1940s, claims that neurons that are repeatedly activated together come to be associated with each other, creating a cell assembly. Individual words in the brain could each be represented as cell assemblies of this sort and could differ in their brain location in accordance with the nature of the associations that form a particular word's assembly (or network). Figure 12.6 shows a suggestion for how action-related words (e.g., *run, jump*) could differ from object-related words (e.g., *barn, tree*). As shown in this figure, action words are represented more anteriorly and object words are represented more posteriorly. Of course, many, but not all, action words are verbs and many, but not all, object-related words are nouns. Thus, this difference may coincide with a general verb-versus-noun difference in how words are represented in the brain.

There seems to be good evidence that the verb-noun distinction does correspond to differences in brain location. There is less consensus, however, for the reason why. It could be that because verbs are typically associated with actions, they are represented more anteriorly (near the motor strip). Or it could be purely related to their grammatical category. Recently, some scholars have made this latter claim and supported it with evidence from case studies which suggest that patients with anterior lesions are more likely to have difficulty with verbs, whereas patients with posterior lesions are more likely to have difficulty with nouns.

Object-related words   Action-related words

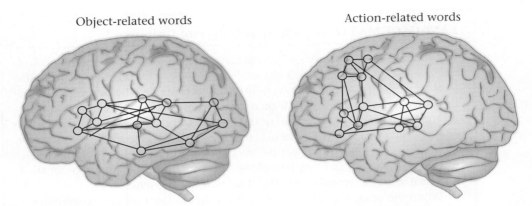

Figure 12.6   A view of how words could be represented in the brain. Data adapted from: Figure 2a in F. Pulvermüller, "Brain Reflections of Words and Their Meaning," in *Trends in Cognitive Sciences*, 5(12): 517–524, 2001, with permission from Elsevier.

The issue of *why* certain areas of the brain are associated with certain aspects of language is not restricted to the representation of words. We have seen, for example, that Broca's area is particularly involved in syntactic processing. Is this because there is a special place for syntax in the brain? Is it perhaps that syntactic processing represents very complex sequencing, and Broca's area is related to the planning of complex motor sequences? These are questions that are currently under intense debate among neurolinguists.

The nature of the debate can serve to remind us that ultimately, the goal of neurolinguistics is to understand, in neurological terms, what language is. Knowing *where* certain functions are performed in the brain is only the first step. What we really want to understand is how those functions are performed by the brain and why, in the development of our species, particular locations (perhaps because of their cell organization or patterns of neuronal connections) have advantages over others for particular language representations and tasks.

Summing Up

This chapter is concerned with how language is represented and processed in the human brain. **Dichotic listening** studies and **split brain experiments** have shown that the left hemisphere of the brain carries most of the responsibility for language processing in right-handed individuals. Neuroscientists have also used **autopsy studies, computerized axial tomography, positron emission tomography, functional magnetic resonance imaging**, and **magnetoencephalography** to determine the relationship between particular areas of the left hemisphere and specific language functions. It has been found that **Broca's area** is primarily responsible for speech production, **Wernicke's area** is primarily responsible for language comprehension, and the area surrounding the **angular gyrus** plays an important role in reading. Most of our knowledge concerning language representation in the brain comes from the study of **aphasia**—language disturbance resulting from damage to the brain. Neuro-linguists, trained in both linguistics and **neuroscience**, carefully examine the manner in which linguistic competence is affected by brain damage. Their goal is to increase our understanding of how linguistic knowledge is coded in brain matter and how this knowledge is used in the processes of language comprehension and production.

Key Terms

General terms

neurolinguistics

neuroscience

Terms concerning the structure of the brain

angular gyrus
Broca's area
central sulcus
cerebral cortex
cerebral hemispheres
cerebrum
contralateral
corpus callosum
fissure
frontal lobe
gyrus/gyri

lateral fissure
lateralized
lobes
longitudinal fissure
neurons
occipital lobe
parietal lobe
sulcus/sulci
temporal lobe
Wernicke's area

Terms concerning how language in the brain is studied

autopsy studies
Broca's aphasia
computerized axial tomography
  (CT scanning)
dichotic listening studies
functional magnetic resonance
  imaging (fMRI)

lesion
magnetoencephalography (MEG)
positron emission tomography (PET)
right ear advantage (REA)
split brain experiments

Terms concerning language deficit and brain damage

acquired dysgraphia (*or* agraphia)
acquired dyslexia (*or* alexia)
agrammatism
aphasia
cell assembly
deep dyslexia
dysprosody
fluent aphasia
function words
global aphasia

jargon aphasia
motor aphasia
nonfluent aphasia
paragraphia
phonemic paraphasias
phonological dyslexia
sensory aphasia
stroke
surface dyslexia
Wernicke's aphasia

Recommended Reading

Caplan, D. 1993. *Language: Structure, Processing, and Disorders*. Cambridge, MA: MIT Press.
Ingram, J. 2007. *Neurolinguistics: An Introduction to Spoken Language Processing and Its Disorders*. New York: Cambridge University Press.
Stemmer, B., and H. A. Whitaker. 2008. *Handbook of the Neuroscience of Language*. New York: Elsevier.

Exercises

1. What distinguishes the human brain from a nonhuman brain? (See Section 1.)

2. In what ways can the cerebral hemispheres be considered to be two separate brains? (See Section 1.2.)

3. Below is an unlabeled diagram of the left hemisphere. Choose four contrasting colors and color each lobe of the cortex. Use arrows to point to the central sulcus, the lateral fissure, and the angular gyrus. Finally, use a pencil to indicate areas of lesion that would result in Broca's aphasia, Wernicke's aphasia, and acquired dyslexia. Label these areas. (See Figures 12.3 and 12.4; Sections 3–4.)

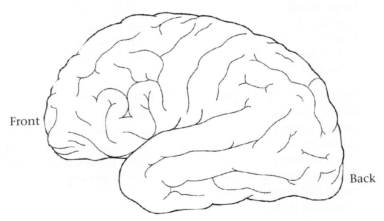

Front

Back

4. What are the relative advantages and disadvantages of the various techniques used to investigate the brain? Consider ethics, cost, intrusiveness, and type of information yielded. (See Section 2.)

5. What do dichotic listening tests tell us about the specialization of the cerebral hemispheres? What types of stimuli would be interesting to present dichotically? (See Section 2.3.)

6. To what extent is it possible to learn how the normal brain functions by studying brain-damaged patients? What can the study of aphasia tell us about normal language competence? (See Section 3.)

7. Contrast the differences in behavior between fluent and nonfluent aphasics. What could explain these differences? (See Sections 3.1 and 3.2.)

8. Describe the differences between phonological and surface dyslexia. (See Section 4.2.)

9. Many researchers have claimed that agrammatism (see Section 5.2) involves a loss of syntactic knowledge. Imagine a type of aphasia that involves a loss of *phonological* knowledge. How would patients with this type of aphasia behave?

 **LaunchPad Solo** | For more helpful content and quizzes, go to the LaunchPad Solo
macmillan learning | for *Contemporary Linguistics* at **launchpadworks.com**.

t h i r t e e n

Language in Social Contexts

Gerard Van Herk
Janie Rees-Miller

> *Us Yoopers don't need no grammar 'cause we speak goodly.*
> —Popular Saying in an Elementary School
> in Michigan's Upper Peninsula

OBJECTIVES

In this chapter, you will learn:

- how place, class, ethnicity, and gender can influence variation in language
- how dialectal variation develops over time
- how various forms of isolation can lead to dialectal variation
- how language contact affects language use and development
- how language use is influenced by social interaction
- how societies deal with language

 **LaunchPad Solo**
macmillan learning | For more helpful content and quizzes, go to the LaunchPad Solo
for *Contemporary Linguistics* at **launchpadworks.com**.

Sociolinguistics is the study of the relationship between society and language. Language is central to how we deal with other people, and the way we use language says a lot about us. Details of word choice, syntax, and pronunciation reveal us to be members of a particular **speech community**, a group of people who share social conventions, or **sociolinguistic norms**, about language use. When the first author speaks English, most people can tell he's North American (he pronounces *schedule* with a [sk] sound), Canadian (he rhymes *shone* with *gone*, not *bone*), and probably from Quebec (he drinks *soft drinks* and keeps his socks in a *bureau*). And language also tells people with shared norms something about their place in the speech

483

> **LANGUAGE MATTERS   One Commercial for Two Languages**
>
> The Indic languages Urdu and Hindi are considered separate languages because they're spoken in different countries—Urdu in Pakistan, Hindi in India. But they're mutually intelligible, so speakers of both languages can understand Bollywood films (in Hindi) on Sunday afternoon television in Canada. One barrier to communication is that the languages have different writing systems (Arabic for Urdu, Devangari for Hindi). Clever advertisers get around that problem by using neither system. Instead, words in commercials are often phonetically spelled using the Latin alphabet, which viewers are familiar with from English.

community: he's probably under eighty (he pronounces *whale* and *wail* the same), but he's definitely not young (he almost never ends sentences with a questionlike rising intonation). When he speaks French, most people can tell he's probably from Quebec (he pronounces *tu* with a [ts] sound) and definitely English (he has English [ɪ] and he says *so* a lot). Of course, members of his speech community don't have to wait for a sentence about whales, schedules, and beverages to place him. Dozens of features mark his speech. Some are **salient features** (noticeable) and recognized within the community as having a particular social meaning; they're also called **sociolinguistic markers**. Other features, such as vowel height or the choice between *used to* and *would*, are "below the radar" but can be shown by large-scale study to be associated with particular social characteristics; these features are called **sociolinguistic indicators**. A speech community's norms affect both markers and indicators. Because these norms are shared by all members of a speech community, sociolinguists study the language of the community, not the speech (or perceptions of the speech) of a single speaker.

These broad definitions allow us to speak of speech communities of very different sizes. Boston is a speech community—its members share norms about what to call soft drinks (*tonics*) and whether *marry* and *merry* are pronounced the same (they're not). But in a sense, all speakers of English form a (very big) speech community—we share norms about putting adjectives before nouns, for example, and we can usually more or less understand each other. This criterion—**mutual intelligibility**—is what linguists usually use to determine whether people are speaking the same language or not. If people from two different places—say, Birmingham, Alabama, and Birmingham, England—can understand each other, then they're speaking the same language, and the systematic differences in their speech reflect different **dialects**, or subsets, of the same language.

In practice, as Chapter 7 notes, mutual intelligibility is not always used to decide whether two different ways of speaking should be considered different languages or dialects of the same language. Speakers of Swedish and Norwegian, for example, can understand each other, but Swedish and Norwegian are considered two different languages because they're found in two different countries. The Chinese situation is the opposite—Cantonese and Mandarin are *not* mutually intelligible, but their speakers consider them dialects because they are spoken in the same country and words of similar meaning in each language are written using the same characters.

Another aspect of the naming issue is that many nonlinguists reserve the term *language* for what linguists might call the **standard** variety—the language taught in school, used in formal writing, and often heard from newscasters and other media figures who wish to project authority (or at least competence). All other varieties of the language—those we call **nonstandard**—get called dialects. There are almost always value judgments attached to this practice: the standard is seen as good, pure, clear, and rule-governed—a "real language"—whereas "dialects" are perceived as broken, chaotic, limited, or impermanent. Many sociolinguists avoid the naming problem by using the value-neutral term **variety** for any subset of a language: the standard variety, as well as regional, class, or ethnic varieties. Others reclaim the term *dialect* and speak of the standard dialect, as well as regional dialects, **sociolects**, or **ethnolects**. They'll often say, "Everybody has a dialect."

Two other naming problems related to dialects need to be cleared up. Nonlinguists often call nonstandard varieties **slang**. To linguists, *slang* refers only to words—either words new to the language or old words or phrases with new meanings. Slang is usually associated with younger speakers—in fact, a good indicator that a slang term is finished is when middle-aged university professors start using it. Most slang is faddish or short-lived—you don't hear many people saying *groovy* or *the bee's knees* anymore, and *crib* and *dope* and *wack* sound dated now. Some slang terms hang on, however, and become part of the standard language—*mob*, *freshman*, and *glib* all started out as slang. Unlike slang, a dialect is usually distinct in multiple linguistic domains—lexicon, morphology, syntax, and phonology/phonetics.

A second term sometimes used for dialects is **accent**, which linguists use to refer only to pronunciation. Although dialects usually include accent differences, dialect and accent boundaries don't have to match. For example, many people speak Standard English (in terms of grammar and lexicon), but with an accent reflecting their ethnicity, class, and/or region—think of Martin Luther King Jr., or former President Bill Clinton. The reverse situation (standard accent, nonstandard grammatical features) is much less common. Try imitating Prince Charles saying, "Ain't no woman like the one I got."

To really study how language and society affect each other, we need to consider the social characteristics of the person speaking—such things as region, gender, age, or class—as well as the social relationships between participants in a conversation and the treatment of language by societies. Each of these objects of study requires its own methods and approaches.

1 Language Variation and Social Distinctions

It's sometimes said that in any society, social distinctions will develop, and where there are social distinctions, we can expect to find them reflected in linguistic distinctions. The branch of linguistics that tries to measure and explain that connection is known as variation theory, or **variationist sociolinguistics**.

Central to the practice of variationist sociolinguistics is the concept of **structured variation**. In any language variety, there are many linguistic features that can be produced in more than one way. For example, many varieties of English have more than one way to pronounce the sounds represented by the letter combination *th* in *thin*, *that*, *brother*, or *path*. In this case, *th* is what we call the **variable**—the thing with several possible realizations. Do people say *brother*, or *brudder*, or *bruvver*, or *bro'er*? Each possible realization (interdental fricative, alveolar stop, labiodental fricative, glottal stop, etc.) is called a **variant**. Across all the words of the language, the variant that is likely to surface depends on **linguistic factors** like position in the word, voicing, and the like. A variable is something like a phoneme, or underlying representation; the variants are like allophones, or surface realizations; and the linguistic factors include what phonologists would call phonetic environments.

But then sociolinguists complicate the analysis, in an attempt to model the complicated situation of language in everyday use. In phonology, rules are usually assumed to apply *every time* a particular environment is found. In other words, the rules are **categorical**. In sociolinguistic analyses, the "rules," or **constraints**, are usually **probabilistic**—more or less likely to apply. So interdentals might be more *likely* to be pronounced as stops at the beginning of the word, or when they're voiced, or even with particular lexical items like *this* or *that*, but each linguistic factor explains only part of the variation. At its most complex, sociolinguistic research considers all these factors together, and with the help of computer programs, calculates how much each factor contributes to the likely outcome (see Figure 13.1).

In our *th* example—and in much variationist work—the focus is on linguistic factors affecting variation. In fact, variationist sociolinguistics is sometimes described as "too much linguistics and not enough socio." But the "socio" component does show up in two different ways. First, variationist research is usually conducted among speakers of nonstandard varieties; this research has made important contributions to our understanding that nonstandard varieties are, like the standard, governed by subtle and complex linguistic rules. In fact, a well-known early paper by William Labov, a pioneer of sociolinguistics, is entitled "The Logic of Nonstandard English." Second, variationist work also concerns itself with **social factors** that influence variation in a structured way. In the case of *th*, the choice of variant might be affected by the speaker's age, sex, or degree of education. We assume some variation within the speech of an individual (**intraspeaker variation**), especially in terms of style shifting, but most of this work looks at how speech varies according to speakers' social characteristics. In other words, researchers are looking at **interspeaker variation**. In theory, any speaker characteristic could have linguistic consequences; in practice, research has shown that several social factors are particularly important. In the following sections, we look at those factors one by one.

The linguistic variables a researcher wants to investigate will give rise to one or more specific hypotheses or research questions that are normally tied to a particular speech community. The speech community plus the research questions or hypotheses will then suggest how **informants** (also called **consultants**) should be selected. In what is called a judgment sample, the researcher may decide that she wants, for example, ten informants over the age of sixty and ten under the age of thirty, and that each group should have an equal number of men and women. Armed with these criteria, the researcher then works her contacts within the community to fill those categories. Another possibility is to use a snowball sample in which an already participating informant is asked to introduce other potential informants; this can be a useful way to penetrate **social networks**. A third possibility is a random sample, in which a researcher would choose every fifth house in a residential neighborhood, for example, or every tenth name in the phone book and seek to interview that person.

The most well-known modern means of obtaining linguistic data is through the use of a **sociolinguistic interview**, which is based on the assumption that when people pay attention to their speech, they will speak most carefully and aim to speak as closely to the standard as they can. The interview is designed to elicit a range of speaking styles from most careful in reading a list of words and reading a passage to less formal in an informal interview, and then to most casual when the informant is telling a personal narrative that involves some strong emotion. The most well-known question to elicit such a story is asking the informant to tell about a near-death experience, but other, less intrusive possibilities are asking about a local natural disaster or a childhood memory of being unfairly punished. During the interview the researcher is recording the interview for analysis later.

Once the interviews have been conducted, the researcher faces the task of analyzing the data. In the recordings or transcripts of recordings, she must first identify the variants of the linguistic variables under investigation and find ways of coding these variants. Some, such as vowel height, may be **gradient variables** with a full range of possible values that can be plotted through acoustic analysis. Others, however, may be **discrete variables** with easily distinguishable variants, such as use of [ɪn] versus [ɪŋ] for -*ing*. These steps in doing variationist research are summarized in Figure 13.1.

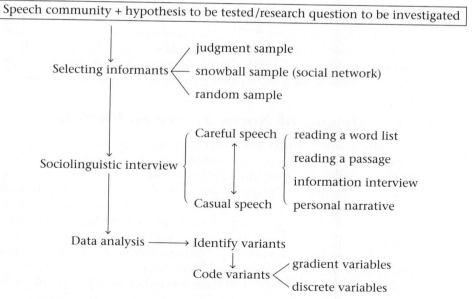

Figure 13.1 Steps in variationist research

2   Place

Geographical location is probably the most-studied social factor affecting variation. If it's true that we talk *like* who we talk *with*, it makes good sense that we will share linguistic features with our neighbors. **Dialectology**, the study of regional differences in language, is the oldest major branch of sociolinguistics. Early linguistics had a major historical focus, and linguists turned to the study of traditional rural dialects because those varieties preserved older speech features and thus held many clues to earlier stages of the language. In order to collect data, the field-worker would find informants with little contact outside their region, typically **NORMs** (nonmobile old rural males). The informant would respond to literally hundreds of questions eliciting data on pronunciation, grammar, and lexicon. In the 1930s work on the linguistic atlases of the United States, a large number of questions focused on agricultural themes, such as what the terms were for various farm implements and their parts, or how one called different types of livestock in from the pasture. After fieldwork was completed, results could be tabulated.

Although the questions we ask today may differ (and be rather less time-consuming), the method of dealing with the results remains more or less the same. A line called an **isogloss** can be drawn on a map to separate geographical areas where one linguistic feature is preferred over another. Where there is a group of isoglosses, called an **isogloss bundle**, a dialect boundary may be established. One such isogloss bundle in the 1930s fieldwork separated the North—where the terms *pail*, *darning needle* (for 'dragonfly'), and *whiffletree or whippletree* ('pivot bar on a horse-drawn wagon') were preferred—from the Midland south of the isogloss bundle, where the terms *bucket*, *snake feeder*, and *swingletree*, respectively, were more common (see Figure 13.2).

Even in the 1960s, when extensive fieldwork was conducted for the *Dictionary of American Regional English* (*DARE*), the preference was still for older, more rural informants: almost 70 percent lived in rural areas or small towns, and almost two-thirds were aged sixty or older. More contemporary work in dialectology seeks to survey a broader range of speakers, including young people and city dwellers.

2.1   The Origins of North American English

In Europe, where much early dialect study was done, countries long settled by speakers of the same language have had the time to develop distinct regional varieties. These varieties reflect settlement patterns that are often more than a thousand years old. For example, the major dialect areas of England still largely match the areas settled by different groups—Angles, Saxons, and Jutes—about fifteen hundred years ago. Natural barriers, such as mountain ranges, have helped limit interdialect contact, thus allowing dialects to develop along their own distinct paths.

The same basic combination of factors—origins of the early settlers and limits on intervariety contact—also explain dialect differences in North American English. The New England area of the United States was settled largely by people from East Anglia.

darning needle (= dragonfly)

whiffletree, whippletree (= swingletree)

pail

Figure 13.2   An isogloss bundle across Pennsylvania separating North and Midland

Most of the people who settled along the coast farther south came from the south of England, while the later arrivals, who moved into the inland Appalachian area, were Scots Irish, originating in Scotland and northern Ireland. Each group brought the speech patterns of its home area with it. By the time of the American Revolution (1776–83), three major dialect areas had developed in the eastern United States: a Northern variety in New England and the Hudson Valley, the Midland dialect of Pennsylvania, and the Southern dialect (see Figure 13.3). These varieties were already becoming distinct from British English and from each other.

In fact, many of the existing dialect patterns in North America today can be traced to routes of migration, settlement, and trade, as shown in Figure 13.3. The dialect area of the North follows the migration route along the Erie Canal and the Great Lakes. The migration route west on the old National Road (along the approximate route of present-day I-70) allowed the settlement of the North Midland with the dividing line between North and South Midland roughly along the Ohio River. The South Midland region spreads out into the mountains of West Virginia, Kentucky, and Tennessee. The dialect area of the South reflects migration and settlement sweeping southward through North Carolina and north Georgia with another route heading westward parallel with the Gulf coast.

THE NORTH

1. Northeastern New England
2. Southeastern New England
3. Southwestern New England
4. Inland North
5. The Hudson Valley
6. Metropolitan New York

THE MIDLAND

North Midland

7. Delaware Valley (Philadelphia)
8. Susquehanna Valley
10. Upper Ohio Valley (Pittsburgh)
11. Northern West Virginia

South Midland

9. Upper Potomac & Shenandoah
12. Southern West Virginia &
    Eastern Kentucky
13. Western Carolina & Eastern
    Tennessee

THE SOUTH

14. Delmarva (Eastern Shore)
15. The Virginia Piedmont
16. Northeastern North Carolina
17. Cape Fear & Peedee Valleys
18. The South Carolina Low Country

Figure 13.3   Regional dialects of American English. Eastern dialects are numbered; other (more tentative) dialect boundaries are indicated by dotted lines. Arrows indicate direction of major migrations.

As waves of English-speaking settlers moved westward, they took their dialects with them. The three major American dialects spread west, blurring and merging as they went—dialect maps of North America show a fanning out from the east and a general mixed dialect in the westernmost areas of the United States (see Figure 13.3). We can assume that the western pioneers encountered a rich mixture of regional accents and vocabulary. As their children and grandchildren grew up together, there was considerable **dialect leveling** in which extreme regional features from the east were worn down over time, and a new dialect evolved. Even after much migration across the continent and great social change, the dialect distinctions laid down more than three hundred years ago remain strong.

LANGUAGE MATTERS   New England and Postvocalic *r*

At the time of the first settlements in America in 1607 and 1620, speakers in most parts of Britain pronounced the **postvocalic *r***, in other words the *r* after a vowel at the end of a syllable. One area in which the postvocalic *r* had already weakened was East Anglia, the area from which many of the Pilgrims and Puritans originated. New England town records from the seventeenth century provide evidence that dropping of postvocalic *r* had become a New England characteristic—as it still is today. Misspellings such as *Mos* (for *Morse*), *fouth* (for *fourth*), *Geoge* (for *George*), and *Chals* (for *Charles*) show clearly that postvocalic *r* was not pronounced. It was not until about the time of the Revolutionary War that dropping of postvocalic *r* became widespread in London and southeast England generally.

2.2   Regional Variation in Lexical Items

Despite the ubiquity of various forms of media connecting us to the wider world, regional differences in lexical items still exist. For example, a carbonated soft drink is called *soda* in the Northeast, *pop* in the Inland North and much of the North Midland, *tonic* in eastern New England, and *coke* in the South. Similarly, depending on the region of the country, a sandwich on a large roll with a variety of meats and cheeses may be called a *grinder* (New England), a *hero* (New York City and Long Island), a *hoagie* (Philadelphia), a *poorboy* (New Orleans), or a *sub* (generally). There are regional differences in the names of various creepy-crawlies; for example, the miniature freshwater lobsterlike creature is a *crayfish* in the North, a *crawdad* in the South Midland, and a *crawfish* in the South. The insect that lights up on summer evenings is a *firefly* in the West, a *lightning bug* in the Midland, and either name for most of the rest of the country.

Regional lexical items may also reflect the language patterns of original settlers. For example, a number of expressions that have become associated with Pittsburgh (although they are used more generally in the North Midland) are *jag* 'tease', *nebby* 'nosy', *slippy* 'slippery', and *redd up* 'clean up, tidy up'. These expressions can all be traced to the Scots Irish who immigrated to America and settled in the Midland area in the eighteenth century. In Michigan's upper peninsula, on the other hand, local vocabulary items such as *pasty* 'a handheld meat pie with vegetables' and *sisu* 'fortitude in the face of adversity' reflect settlement by Cornish miners and Finns, respectively.

2.3   Regional Variation in Phonology

There is a great deal of regional diversity in the pronunciation of vowels immediately preceding liquids and nasals. For instance, there is considerable dialectal variation in how orthographic <e> and <a> are pronounced when followed by [ɪ] in words such as *Mary*, *merry*, and *marry*. Some speakers have a two-way distinction, others have a three-way distinction, while in much of the Midwest, the distinction is neutralized to [ɛ] when the vowel is followed by [ɹ]. Thus, *Mary*, *merry*, and *marry* all sound the same, as do *Harry* and *hairy*, *Barry* and *berry*, *fairy* and *ferry*.

Another dialectal difference is the effect that a nasal has on preceding vowels. Throughout the rural South and into southern Ohio, central Indiana, Illinois, Missouri, and Kansas, the vowels [ɪ] and [ɛ] have merged as [ɪ] before a nasal. Thus, both *him* and *hem* are pronounced as [hɪm], and one must specify whether a [pɪn] is for sticking (*pin*) or for writing (*pen*).

A dialectal change in progress is the **low back merger** of [ɔ] and [ɑ] in words such as *caught* and *cot*, *hawk* and *hock*, and *dawn* and *Don*. Although the two sounds remain distinct in much of the Midwest, the South, and the mid-Atlantic states, they have merged in northeastern New England, in western Pennsylvania and central Ohio, in northern Minnesota, and throughout the West (with the possible exception of the large cities of San Francisco, Los Angeles, and Denver). One sign that this merger is in the process of expanding is that it is more strongly represented by younger speakers than older speakers. We will take up in more detail some systematic changes in the regional pronunciation of vowels in Section 3.

When dialectal differences based on lexicon are superimposed on dialectal differences based on phonology, the results are actually remarkable similar, as is shown in Figure 13.4.

Figure 13.4 Dialect boundaries based on lexical items and a phonological survey. (The solid line represents dialect boundaries found in the Phonological Atlas survey; the dashed line represents dialect boundaries based on lexical items.)

2.4   Regional Differences in Morphology and Syntax

Regional differences in morphology and syntax are relatively few but nonetheless noticeable for newcomers in an area. One difference involves the problem of standard English *you*, which must serve as both singular and plural. In New York City, a socially stigmatized solution is the plural *youse*; in Pittsburgh and parts of Appalachia, it is *y'ins* (or *you'uns*). Throughout the South and in the South Midland, the problem is solved by the regionally standard forms *y'all* and *you-all*.

In addition to *y'all*, a distinctive grammatical feature of the South is the use of double modals such as *might could* or *might should*, in which the *might* serves to lessen the force of *could* or *should*. Although the urban South has been swamped with migrants from other dialect regions and many distinctively southern features are disappearing, *y'all* and double modals persist as robust markers of regional identity. Another such marker is the quasi-modal *fixin' to*, which is used for the immediate future. Except for weather prediction (*It's fixin' to rain*), *fixin' to* is restricted to the immediate future in which some intentionality is involved; thus in *1* the first sentence is acceptable, while the second is not:

1) Sorry, I can't talk to you now. I'm fixin' to leave.
   *That house is fixin' to fall down.

Appalachian English has a number of distinctive grammatical features, including counterfactual *liketa*, as in *I laughed so hard I liketa died*, and the use of *right* as a degree word, as in *It's right nice weather today*. A couple of interesting syntactic differences exist between standard American English and Appalachian English in relative clauses. In most dialects of American English, the complementizer *that* and the trace of a *wh-* element moved from subject position are not acceptable in sentences such as *2*.

2) *Who did you say that *t* called?

However, this type of structure is perfectly acceptable in Appalachian English. Interestingly, in some areas of Appalachia and in other southern-based dialects, it is possible to delete the relative pronoun even when it is the subject of a relative clause:

3) That man lives down the road is crazier than a loon.

Recent work on grammatical features of the Midland dialect has listed a number of items that are particular to the Midland and may be traced to the influence of Scots Irish settlers in the eighteenth century. One feature of Midland English that is so widespread that it is standard within the region is the verb *needs* plus a past participle, as in the sentences in *4a* and *4b*. This form can also be found with the verbs *want* and *like*, as in *4c* and *4d*, although these forms are not as universally acceptable as those after *need*.

4) a. The car needs washed.
   b. The document needs checked.
   c. The dog wants fed.
   d. Babies like cuddled.

A possible extension is also the use of a prepositional adverb after the verbs *want* and *need* as well:

5) a. The cat wants out.
   b. Excuse me, can you move? I need by.

Finally, positive *anymore* can be used in a sentence without a negative, in which case it means 'recently, these days' in contrast with past times. The expression is perhaps more acceptable at the beginning of the sentence, as in *6a*, but it can also be used in other positions, as in *6b*.

6) a. Anymore, I'd just as soon read a book as watch TV.
   b. There are a lot of male nurses anymore.

New Conceptions of Place and Space

Contemporary sociolinguists are developing different ways to think of space. We borrow ideas from cultural geographers to distinguish between physical distance and social perceptions of distance. Some places seem closer because we can easily travel there thanks to highways or the routes followed by airlines, buses, or ferries. For example, a sound change affecting cities around the Great Lakes seems to be creeping down Interstate 55 to St. Louis. And some linguistic innovations seem to spread first from big city to big city, jumping over intervening small towns and only later diffusing into the surrounding regions. Even when a change does diffuse into rural areas, it may be realized differently than it is in the city. This is because some of those living in the more rural areas identify proudly as "country" and use their speech as a marker to distinguish themselves from city dwellers. Studies of "country talk" in places like Texas and California have suggested that varieties identified as country have become **enregistered**. That is, particular linguistic features have become symbolic markers that are linked with the specific idealized cultural values associated with "country" as opposed to "city." In this way, space reinforces other social distinctions—you speak like who you speak to, and you tend to speak to people like you!

3   Time

All spoken languages change. Elsewhere in this book, you've explored the linguistic processes involved in that change. Sociolinguists are interested in the relationship between change over time and the variation found in a community at a single point in time. Think of big changes, like the Great Vowel Shift of earlier English. Presumably, people in England didn't all go to bed one night pronouncing their words one way and wake up the next morning with a completely different vowel system. At some point, either everybody used both the old and the new pronunciation, or some people always used the old way and some always used the new, or some combination of those two happened. In other words, change over time results in variation in each time period. Add to that the reasonable assumption that people's basic grammar doesn't change that much during their lifetime, and you get a powerful insight: you can see change happening by looking at the differences between old and young speakers. This idea, called the **apparent time hypothesis**, has opened up whole new areas of research—as one major sociolinguistic article puts it, we can use the present (variation) to explain the past (change). This is particularly true if we use the tools of variation—sound recordings and measurement tools—and probabilities.

Consider *whale* and *wail*. Over a *very* long period of time, English speakers have moved toward pronouncing them the same. What were once two separate phonemes—/w/ and /ʍ/—have merged for many speakers, especially those born after 1950. We can see this change happening by looking at some findings of research by Canadian sociolinguist Jack Chambers. As the graph in Figure 13.5 shows, older speakers have lower rates of **phoneme merger**, while younger speakers almost always merge the two sounds. This research done in Canada reflects the situation in much of the United States today. However, in the U.S. South, the distinction is still maintained.

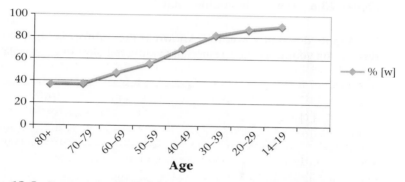

Figure 13.5 Percentage of speakers with [w], not [ʍ], in words like *which* and *whine* in central Canada, by age. Data from: J. K. Chambers,"Patterns of Variation Including Change," in *The Handbook of Language Variation and Change*, edited by J. K. Chambers, Peter Trudgill, and Natalie Schilling-Estes (Oxford: Blackwell, 2002), fig. 14.5, 360. © Blackwell Publishers 2002. Reprinted by permission of Blackwell Publishing.

Changes like this are easy to see when they involve an entire segment—two formerly separate sounds merge, or an alternative pronunciation dies out, or is born. A lot of sound change is subtler than that, though, especially when we look at vowels. Vowels may shift in the vowel space, sometimes so slightly that the change is only evident through acoustic analysis. Modern technology has let us track some big changes that are happening in North American vowel pronunciations. One dramatic shift, affecting about 40 million speakers in the U.S. Midwest, is known as the **Northern Cities Shift**. A **vowel shift** occurs when a series of vowel phonemes undergo reorganization. The Northern Cities Shift began in the metropolitan areas of Chicago, Detroit, Cleveland, and Buffalo, and has now spread to smaller cities around the Great Lakes. In order to understand the changes taking place in the Northern Cities Shift, see Figure 13.6.

The earliest changes in the Northern Cities Shift began over 100 years ago and involved the low vowels [æ] and [ɑ]. First, the [æ] in words like *bag* or *cad* was raised and diphthongized to [ɪə], so *Ann* sounded like *Ian*. Then the sound [ɑ] in words like *cod*, *pop*, *hot*, and *Chicago* was fronted. To someone not participating in the Northern Cities Shift, the word *block* would sound more like *black*. As the sound [ɛ] as in *desk* was backed, that pushed the [ʌ] sound in *cud*, *bug*, or *dull* farther back, so the word *bus* could sound like *boss* to someone unfamiliar with the shift.

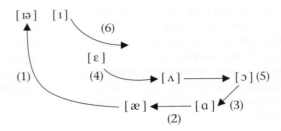

Figure 13.6   The Northern Cities Shift

A quite different vowel shift known as the **California Shift** seems to be in progress among young speakers (especially young females) in California (see Figure 13.7).

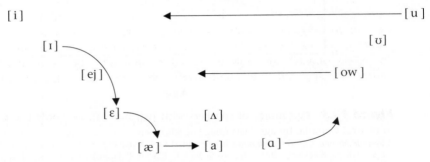

Figure 13.7   The California Shift

The nonlow tense back vowels are fronted, giving the stereotypical valley girl and surfer dude pronunciation of words like *dude* and *eeeuuw*. The vowels [ɑ] and [ɔ] are merged to a backed [ɑ]; this then leaves room for [æ] to move back. The result is that *sax* sounds more like *socks*. With the [æ] space free, [ɛ] is lowered, so that *sex* sounds more like *sax*. The [ɪ] moves down toward the [ɛ] space, with the result that *six* sounds more like *sex*.

The findings of apparent-time studies can sometimes be confirmed by **real-time studies**. In Montreal, speakers first interviewed by sociolinguists in the 1970s have been revisited and reinterviewed several times now. For some of their variant linguistic features, apparent-time findings are confirmed; for others, researchers have found some change even in individual speakers. We can also work farther into the past.

Recordings made in the 1960s for the *Dictionary of American Regional English* (*DARE*) can provide evidence of the pronunciation of speakers born in the nineteenth century, which can be compared with speakers today, giving an estimated 50-year difference in real time and an approximately 100-year difference in apparent time. For example, a recent study compared recordings of speakers born in the 1880s from the Midland and Northern dialect areas of northeastern Ohio with speakers from the same areas born in the 1980s. Among the findings were that the low back vowel merger of /ɑ/ and /ɔ/ is relatively recent in the Midland area, but in the North, the fronted /ɑ/ and raised /æ/ of the Northern Cities Shift probably date back to the nineteenth century. Written corpora, especially letters and other personal writings, can also provide a window into the lexicon and grammar of earlier times. For example, a large corpus of letters to and from soldiers in the Civil War shows that the use of *you all* to designate plural *you* was well-established in the English of the South but not of the North during the 1860s.

4   Isolation

As mentioned in the discussion of dialectology, speech communities that are isolated in some way seem to preserve older ways of speaking, just as they might also preserve traditional music or farming methods. The isolation involved can be **physical isolation**, isolated from *everybody*; **linguistic isolation**, isolated from speakers of the same or a similar language; or **social isolation**, isolated by conventions or attitudes. These three types of isolated speech communities can act as a sort of linguistic time machine for us—as long as we're cautious enough to remember that even isolated speech communities change over time, perhaps in ways very different from mainstream speech.

4.1   Physical Isolation: The Case of Smith Island

With modern transportation and communication, few speech communities are physically isolated any longer. Some small island communities, though, still remain relatively isolated in the twenty-first century. One of these is Smith Island, Maryland, actually a small group of islands in the Chesapeake Bay and accessible only by boat. The original inhabitants from Cornwall in southwest England settled the island in the late seventeenth century. Since then, a localized variety of English has developed on the island, owing its features to the dialect of the original inhabitants, the lifestyle that developed on the island, and the natural course of language change over time.

In terms of phonology, the islanders retain a **relic form** that preserves the pronunciation of the early settlers; word-initial [s] is voiced, so *sink* is pronounced as *zink*, which was characteristic of southwestern British English of the seventeenth century. There have also been innovations in the island phonology that do not reflect the pronunciation of the original settlers. For example, [aj] is raised to [ʌj] in words like *night* and *mine*, and [aw] is fronted so that *house* sounds almost like *hace*.

Morphologically, Smith Islanders preserve the relic form of **a-prefixing**, which can add an *a-* to verbs ending in *-ing*, such as *The men went a-huntin'*. Another distinct feature, which appears to be increasing in use, is the **regularization** of the past tense verb *be* to *weren't* when it is used in the negative. (*It weren't me. She weren't home.*) The island dialect also includes many specialized lexical items related to the way the islanders make their living, such as many expressions having to do with catching crabs and with the various life stages of crabs.

When communities are isolated geographically such as Smith Island has been, it is often the case that increased contact with other speech communities leads to the loss of the local dialect. On Smith Island, however, the dialect not only seems to be holding its own but actually increasing its distinctiveness among younger speakers. Possible reasons for this include the fact that high school students no longer have to go to boarding school but can return to the island each night. Smith Island has not become a tourist destination, so contact with mainlanders is on the mainland, not on the island. Finally, the small population has always prided itself on its independence, and language is a marker of that independence.

4.2   Linguistic Isolation: The Case of Quebec French

Quebec French is so distinct and so filled with interesting variation that it is actually one of the language varieties most studied by sociolinguists. In fact, several major theoretical concepts in sociolinguistics (beyond the scope of an introductory text) have been developed through work on this variety.

Like Smith Island English, Quebec French is a good example of how isolated language varieties retain older features of a language while undergoing their own internally motivated processes of language change. New France was settled early by French colonists. However, in 1763, with the British victory in the French and Indian War, the French lost their claim in Canada, and French immigration ceased. For more than two centuries, French in North America has been isolated, but the isolation has been linguistic rather than physical. The metaphor of an island of French surrounded by a sea of English is often heard, and English influence is sometimes invoked to explain why the French spoken in Quebec (and elsewhere in Canada) is different from the European standard variety. Certainly, some English words have been borrowed into Quebec French: a restaurant might give you a *bill* (rather than a *facture*) for your order of *bines* ('beans') and *toast* (rather than *fèves* or *haricots* and *rôties*). On the other hand, Quebecers park in a *terrain de stationnement*, whereas in France they use the English loan word *le parking*. And people in both Quebec and France look forward to *le weekend*. Other distinct Quebec French forms reflect retention of older relic forms, such as *flambe* for 'flame' (rather than the European *flamme*) or *doutance* (rather than *doute*) for 'suspicion'. In some cases, words have developed distinct meanings in Quebec French: *traversier* means 'ferry' in Quebec and 'crossing' in France, *ma blonde* means 'my girlfriend' in Quebec and 'my blonde' in France, and *dépanneur* means 'repairman' in France but 'convenience store' in Quebec (in both French and English).

Some syntactic differences observed in Canadian French, although sometimes attributed to contact with English, seem to represent either processes that started centuries ago or internally motivated changes. For example, recently unearthed early recordings by folklorists show that the loss of *ne* in casual speech, as when people say *Je sais pas* instead of *Je ne sais pas* for 'I don't know', was widespread even in speakers born as early as 1846. And research on the use of the subjunctive mood in one area of Quebec seems to show the form strengthening its association with a few verbs and linguistic contexts rather than undergoing across-the-board English-induced decline. Other features of Quebec French morphosyntax include the use of *Je vas* (instead of *vais*) for 'I go' and the replacement of the standard form *nous* ('we') with *on* (originally 'one', as in 'one never knows'), as shown in Table 13.1. Quebecers are also more likely to refer to just one person as *tu* ('you', originally informal) rather than the more formal *vous*. These last few changes all work together to produce a regularization of the verb-marking system, as is shown in Table 13.1.

Table 13.1 Present tense verb forms for *go* in standard and spoken Quebec French

Meaning	Standard (European) French	Spoken Quebec French
'I go'	*je vais*	*je **vas*** (pronounced *va*)
'you (SG) go'	usually *vous allez*	***tu vas***
's/he goes'	*elle/il va*	*elle/il va*
'we go'	*nous allons*	***on va***
'you (PL) go'	*vous allez*	*vous allez*
'they go'	*elles/ils vont*	*elles/ils vont*

As a Quebecer visiting Paris for the first time, one of us quickly realized how many phonetic features of his French were distinctive. He diphthongized (and lowered) his /ɛ/, so that he said [pajr] where they said [pɛːʁ] (*père*, 'father'). He also diphthongized many nasalized vowels, so that he said [prẽjs] where they said [pʁɛ̃s] (*prince*, 'prince'). His short high vowels, [i] and [u], were lax in word-final closed syllables (syllables ending with a consonant). So he said [vɪt] where they said [vit] (*vite*, 'quickly'). Most noticeable of all, he palatalized his /t/ and /d/ before high front vowels and glides, so that he said [tˢydᶻi] where they said [tydi] (*tu dis*, 'you say'). Well, actually, most of them said *vous dites*, and considered his use of *tu* a bit presumptuous. They also wondered how *ma blonde* could have dark hair.

Linguistic isolation is more common than you might think. Around the world, languages and language varieties, cut off from their sources, have kept some older features and developed their own unique innovations. In the Dominican Republic, the African American community of Samaná has spoken English since 1824, surrounded by Spanish speakers. Cajuns in Louisiana have maintained their own variety of French, although now only the elderly generation uses French. Pennsylvania German, which includes some relic forms, is still spoken in communities of Old Order Amish. And in Turkey, the descendants of Jews who fled the Spanish Inquisition five centuries ago still speak a form of Spanish that preserves some features of medieval Spanish. We also see a less severe and shorter-lived version of linguistic isolation in immigrant neighborhoods, whose members often find when revisiting their original homelands that language has moved on without them.

4.3   Social Isolation: The Case of Urban African American English

Social isolation refers to a situation in which a smaller speech community is in some way restricted in social interaction with the larger surrounding speech community that shares the same language. Urban African American English (AAE) exemplifies a unique dialect that developed as a result of social isolation. (A description of the linguistic features of AAE is to be found in Section 6.2.)

Prior to World War I, few African Americans lived in cities, particularly in the North; after World War I and continuing through the 1920s and 1930s in particular, African Americans from small rural communities in the South migrated in great numbers to urban areas, such as New York, Chicago, Detroit, Philadelphia, Washington, D.C., Los Angeles, and Baltimore in what is known as the Great Migration. The migration continued throughout the twentieth century. In northern cities, African American migrants faced segregated housing and a climate in the white community that discouraged racial mixing. Although discriminatory practices in housing are now outlawed, racial isolation and de facto segregation still exist in many American inner cities.

At its beginning, the Great Migration of the 1920s and 1930s brought together speakers of various southern rural dialects. Through a process of dialect leveling, some features unique to particular southern localities were lost, and some southern relic forms fell into disuse in urban AAE. At the same time, independent innovations began to develop within the urban African American speech community. Because of social isolation, though, AAE speakers have not participated in linguistic changes—such as the Northern Cities Shift—which have affected the speech of white speech communities in the same regions. The process of innovation within urban AAE continues today with African American youth in cities leading the way. Urban AAE has become a powerful cultural symbol, and innovations spread from city to city and outwards from the cities to less urban areas and even to small isolated rural communities.

Less extreme cases of social isolation are often found, and many speech communities prove resistant to change. The sociolinguist Lesley Milroy has proposed the notion of social networks to explain why this happens. **Dense** and **multiplex social networks**—where a small group of people interact with each other often and in multiple ways—are much less likely to change. If your neighbors are also your friends, and your coworkers, and your coworshippers, and your in-laws, and your children and theirs go to school together and play together, the intensity and frequency of your contacts with them will reinforce your traditional way of speaking. In this model, change is brought into the community by people with looser ties, those who work or go to school or hang out elsewhere. For example, work on the island of Ocracoke on North Carolina's Outer Banks has shown that select distinctive features of the endangered local dialect are most strongly maintained by a group of middle-aged men with dense multiplex networks. They play poker together several times a week, generally work in fishing or other marine activities, and share strong local loyalty and pride. In the face of loss of the island dialect through contact with tourists and with the mainland, the poker players assert their island identity through their speech.

5 Contact

The other side of isolation, of course, is **language contact**—with speakers of other varieties or of other languages. We've already considered the possibility of dialect leveling, where similar dialects that come into contact with each other tend to keep their shared features and get rid of the things that are different (usually by adopting the variant found in the socially or numerically dominant language). A whole range of other phenomena can happen when speakers of different *languages* meet and move toward bilingualism.

5.1 Code-Switching and Borrowing

In bilingual or multilingual speech communities, such as the New York Puerto Rican community, who use English and Spanish daily, or the middle class in Lebanon, for whom trilingualism in Lebanese Arabic, French, and English is the norm, members commonly engage in **code-switching**; that is, they use two or more languages in conversation. In what is known as **situational code-switching**, the different languages may be used in different domains. For example, in east Africa, Swahili is typically used for official business, but the local tribal language is used within the family and with close friends from the same tribe. When people from one speech community join in conversation with those from another, they may code-switch to a language that all understand. Alternatively, participants in a conversation may choose to code-switch to a language that excludes others; for example, international male students in the cafeteria on a U.S. campus may code-switch to their own language to talk about the pretty girls at the next table.

In other cases, code-switching can happen in the same sentence, as in *Sometimes I'll start a sentence in English y termino en español* ('. . . and finish in Spanish'). This is not random grasping at words, but skilled linguistic behavior. For example, the Dutch sentence *Ik kocht het laatste exemplaar* 'I bought the last copy' could not be code-switched with English on alternate words: **Ik bought het last exemplaar*. Instead, switching can only happen at certain points. In this sentence, the subject and verb could be in one language with the NP that is the verb complement in the other: *I bought het laatse exemplaar* or *Ik kocht the last copy*.

Code-switching on this local level can serve a number of functions within the conversation. It may be used as a sort of tag or discourse marker that is external to the structure of the sentence. For example, a Japanese-English bilingual says, *He is in Japan yo* 'He is in Japan, I'm telling you,' switching to Japanese for the tag 'I'm telling you'. If a quotation is involved, code-switching to another language for the quotation serves as a way to set it off linguistically. In addition, code-switching can lend emphasis or call attention to the content of the message. It can be used to end an argument or to separate personal opinion from fact.

Sometimes, though, use of another language for a word or expression just seems to be a **nonce borrowing**—a one-off—to fill a **lexical gap**. In this case, typically, the borrowed expression is adapted to fit the morphology of the matrix language. For example, speakers of Acadian French in Canada's Maritime provinces borrow English verbs and inflect them as if they were French verbs: *J'ai parké* 'I parked', or *J'ai hangé around* 'I hung around'. The same situation is observed in Spanish of the U.S. Southwest. English words are borrowed and integrated into Spanish sentences, such as *Las brecas de la troca no trabajan* 'The brakes of the truck don't work'. In this sentence, the choice of the verb is also influenced by English; in standard Spanish, *funcionar* would be used for machines, with *trabajar* reserved for people. Southwest Spanish also makes use of **loan translation**, which means an expression in one language (English here) is translated word-for-word into another language (Spanish in this case). For example, 'run for mayor' would be *hacerse candidato para alcalde* in standard Spanish, but Southwest Spanish translates each English word directly, creating the loan translation *correr por mayor*.

Borrowings may also result from language contact situations in which few speakers are bilingual. In these cases, words are borrowed, typically nouns, especially related to new activities, cultural items, or natural phenomena. For example, English settlers in America borrowed the words *moccasin, wigwam, squash* (the vegetable), *moose,* and *skunk* from Native American languages. Verbs may also be borrowed to a lesser extent, with the occasional adjective or adverb. Function words such as prepositions or determiners are almost never borrowed. Once a word is truly borrowed, it loses its association with the original language and is adapted to the pronunciation and morphosyntax of the borrowers. So the Spanish *el legarto* 'the lizard' became *alligator*, and when we say *alligator*, we do not associate it with 'the lizard'.

5.2 Contact Languages: Mixed Languages, Lingua Francas, Pidgins, and Creoles

Occasionally, in heavy switching communities, you will hear sentences where virtually all the content words (nouns, verbs) are borrowed and adapted, while all the function words are from the matrix language. One of us heard a coworker say, "Tu peux pas parker ton truck dans le spot du station wagon du boss" ('You can't park your truck in the spot reserved for the boss's station wagon'). If that sort of process became the norm in a language-contact situation, you might eventually end up with a **mixed language**.

Mixed Languages

Mixed languages are not common, and researchers who work on language contact argue (often fiercely) over whether they really exist and what they tell us about language. One strong candidate for mixed language status is Michif, still spoken in North Dakota and the plains provinces of Canada among the Métis, people of mixed Cree and French descent. In Michif, most nouns and the words associated with them are derived from French, while most verbs and the words associated with them are derived from Cree (see Table 13.2).

Table 13.2 French-origin noun morphology and Cree-origin verb morphology in Michif

PAR LA QUEUE	apoci-pit-ew	kihtwam	LE LOUP	ase-kiwe-pahta-w
by the tail	*inside out-pull-he/him*	*again*	*the wolf*	*back go.home-run-he*
'He pulled him inside out by the tail, and the wolf ran home again.'				

Information from: Peter Bakker and Maarten Mous, eds., *Mixed Languages: 15 Case Studies of Language Intertwining* (Amsterdam: IFOTT, 1994). © Professor Peter Bakker and Professor Maarten Mous.

Lingua Francas

In areas of great linguistic diversity, such as Africa, people who do not share the same first language must interact daily and thus require a **lingua franca**, a term meaning a common language chosen for communication. Among the languages used as lingua francas, West African Pidgin English, which is no one's native language, is used widely for trade in sub-Saharan countries on the western coast. In east Africa, Swahili, a native language on the coast, serves a far wider area as a lingua franca for business and religion. In postcolonial nations, such as the Democratic Republic of Congo, the former colonial language—French in this instance—may be used as the lingua franca among educated Africans who speak different tribal languages. Throughout the world in the twenty-first century, English serves as the international lingua franca, giving rise to the endearing acronym **ELF (English as Lingua Franca)**. Norms for use of ELF by nonnative speakers in communication with other nonnative speakers are developing in ways that differ from native speaker norms.

Pidgins

Contact situations where speakers have restricted access to each other's language can sometimes lead to the formation of a **pidgin**—a rudimentary language with minimal grammatical rules and a small lexicon. By definition, a pidgin has no native speakers, and many pidgins are predominantly used as a lingua franca. Example *7* shows three examples of English-based pidgins.

7) a. *Chinese Pidgin English*
   Before my sell-um   for ten dollar.
   PAST   1 SG sell-TRANSITIVE for ten dollar
   'I sold it for ten dollars.'

   b. *Neo-Melanesian Pidgin*
   mi stap lɔŋŋ bɪglajn, mi kətɪm   kopra.
   'I was in the work-group, cutting copra.'

   c. *Nauru Pidgin English (spoken on the Pacific island of Nauru)*
   Mi hasɪbən flɛn   no waɪfu.
   my husband friend no wife
   'My husband's friend has no wife.'

The examples in *7* illustrate some linguistic features of pidgins. Pidgins are distinguished from other languages in that they have only a small number of grammatical categories and very little grammatical complexity. For example, pidgins do not generally have complement clauses nor do they have bound morphemes to mark agreement, tense, or number. As *7a* illustrates, past tense meaning is conveyed with the use of an adverb of time, *before*, and the word *dollar* is not marked for plurality. All three examples in *7* show use of invariable pronouns; in other words, instead of different pronouns *I, me, my* for subject, object, and possessive, there is just one form. Another feature of English-based pidgins, shown in *7a* and *7b*, is the use of *-um* or *-im* to mark a transitive verb (a verb that takes an object). Typically, too, the lexicon of a pidgin will be relatively limited. As a result, one word may have multiple meanings. In Chinese Pidgin English, for example, *pay* had the meaning of both 'pay' and 'give'. In Chinook Jargon, a Native American pidgin of the Northwest coast, *muckamuck* meant 'eat' as well as 'drink' and even 'bite'. Substrate words may also be used, such as the West African *nyam* 'eat food', which is commonly found in Atlantic pidgins and creoles. Pidgin phonology also tends to be simplified. For example, in English-based pidgins and creoles the interdental fricatives [θ] and [ð] are typically replaced by stops [t] and [d], which are more common in world languages. Pidgins do not generally use tone phonemically, even when the speakers of a particular pidgin have tones in their native languages. And as *7c* shows in the words for *husband* and *wife*, epenthesis may be used to create CV syllables and avoid obstruent codas.

Socially, pidgins tend to develop in two different contact situations. Each situation involves one or more groups having limited access to the **lexifier language**, the language that supplies the basic wordstock for the pidgin. Trade is one such situation. Australian Pidgin English and Chinese Pidgin Portuguese are trade pidgins that

---

LANGUAGE MATTERS   Russenorsk, a Nautical Pidgin

Russenorsk arose in the early 1800s as the result of contact between Russian and Norwegian fishermen working on the Arctic coast of Norway. Russenorsk has dual variants for many words, some lexified from Russian and some from Norwegian, as well as a few words of Dutch or English origin, as the following shows:

Kak	ju	wil	skaffom	ja	drikke	te . . .
what	2SG	want	eat	and	drink	tea

'If you want to eat and drink tea . . .'

Kak is Russian, *ju* is English, *wil* is Norwegian, and *skaffom* is international nautical jargon possibly derived from Dutch.

Information from: Peter Bakker, "Pidgins," in *Pidgins and Creoles: An Introduction*, edited by Jacques Arends, Pieter Muysken, and Norval Smith (Amsterdam: John Benjamins, 1995), 25–40.

developed from European lexifier languages. In the Pacific Northwest, North American natives developed the trade pidgin Chinook Jargon. The other common pidgin formation situation is when people from many language backgrounds are brought together to work on large plantations as slaves or indentured workers. Tok Pisin, a language of the South Pacific that is now a full **creole**, originally developed this way.

If a pidgin operates as a lingua franca, as in trade situations, it may persist in its simplified form for a long time. In plantation situations, though, the children of the original pidgin speakers may learn the pidgin as a first language, and it may become the native language of the new community. When this happens, the pidgin becomes a full-fledged language known as a creole.

Creoles

When a pidgin becomes a creole, its inventory of lexical items and grammatical rules expands dramatically, usually in only one or two generations. One word-formation process used extensively in creoles is conversion (also known as zero derivation; see Chapter 4). For example, in Berbice Dutch—an extinct creole of the coast of Guyana—*kapu* can mean 'to cut', 'a cut', and 'operation'; *kurkuru* means 'black, become black, blacken'; and *sara* can be used to mean both 'to fall' and 'to drop'. Creoles also frequently use compounding to create new words, as illustrated in *8* by Tok Pisin—the creole that is the official language of Papua New Guinea.

8) mausgras   (mouth + grass)   'moustache'
    gras nogut   (grass + no good)   'weed'
    daiman   (die + man)   'corpse'

Reduplication is also very common in creoles and can be used to indicate a variety of meanings, as shown in *9* by Sranan—an English-based creole of Surinam—and by Fa d'Ambu—a west African Portuguese-based creole spoken on an island off the coast of Equatorial Guinea.

9) a. *Sranan*
       fatu   'fat'   fat(u)fatu   'a bit fat'
       ferfi   'paint'   ferfiferfi   'to paint a lot'

    b. *Fa d'Ambu*
       kitsyi 'small'   kitsyikitsyi 'very small'
       gavu   'good'   gagavu   'very good'

Creoles worldwide also share remarkably similar grammatical characteristics. For example, creoles commonly have invariable pronouns, limited bound morphology, and an SVO word order. Also, creoles have a number of preverbal elements used to mark tense and aspect (e.g., duration of the action of the verb). The examples in *10* serve to illustrate some of the common features of creoles.

10) a. *Australian Roper River Creole*
       de bin alde   luk   dat big tri
       3PL PAST always look that big tree
       'They always looked for a big tree.'

b. *Sranan*
a   ben e   sidon fow en anu   na ondro en kakumbe
3SG PAST PROG sit   fold 3SG hand LOC under 3SG chin
'He was sitting as usual with his chin on his hands.'

c. *Saramaccan*
A   tei goni suti   di pingo
He take gun shoot the pig
'He shot the pig with a gun.'

Examples *10a* and *10b* both mark the past tense with the preverbal particle *bin* or *ben*. In *10b*, the progressive aspect is also marked with a preverbal particle *e*. The example in *10c* contains a **serial verb construction**, which occurs when two or more verbs are strung together without any conjunction to express ideas such as instrumentality or direction. Example *10c* also illustrates simplified phonology that is typical of both pidgins and creoles. Optimal CV syllables have been created through deletion or epenthesis, and the less common fricative [ʃ] has been replaced with the most common [s]. Some typical characteristics of pidgin and creole languages are summarized in Table 13.3.

Table 13.3   Some linguistic characteristics of pidgins and creoles

Phonology	CV syllables
	substitution of unmarked sounds for marked sounds
	phonemic tone rare
Morphology	limited bound morphology
	limited inflection (tense, aspect, agreement, number)
	invariable pronouns
Syntax	SVO order
	separate words to mark time, duration, or action
	serial verbs
	complement clauses rare (pidgins)
Lexicon	multiple meanings for one word
	conversion (zero derivation)
	frequent use of compounding
	reduplication
	some borrowings from substratum language(s)

Several theories have developed to account for the similarities among creoles. One argument is that creoles the world over have developed from a single template language, which acted as a sort of structural frame into which the actual words of different lexifier languages were slotted. This frame might have been a **protopidgin**, perhaps spread by sailors and slavers, or a stripped-down version of one or another West African language. This scenario is called the **relexification hypothesis**.

Another idea, known as the **language bioprogram hypothesis**, attributes similarities in creoles to the way in which children go about learning language. The key idea is that children restructure the basic input of pidgins, supplementing and extending what they hear in similar ways. The result is a set of creoles that are remarkably alike.

Because pidgins and creoles have tended to develop without documentation, it is unlikely that either hypothesis will garner conclusive proof. However, observations of the development of Tok Pisin into a full-fledged creole (and the official language of Papua New Guinea) in recent years confirm that major changes occur when a pidgin becomes a community's native language, which is consistent with some version of the bioprogram.

Often, creoles coexist with a local version of their original lexifier languages. This leads to a range of language varieties between the most creole-like, called the **basilect**, and the least creole-like, the **acrolect**. Intermediate stages are called **mesolects**. This range is known as the **creole continuum**. We often assume that the basilect represents something close to the original creole variety, with mesolects reflecting a wearing away of those deep creole features under the influence of the acrolect—a sort of bottom-up explanation. This scenario is supported by evidence that basilectal features drop out as we move up the continuum, sometimes being replaced by a form that looks like the standard but continues to behave like the original basilectal feature. For example, mesolectal past tense markers *did* and *had* may be affected by the same linguistic factors as the basilectal marker *bin*. In other cases, however, there seems to be a break in the middle, as when bare forms like *she see him* represent a single event at the basilectal end, but a recurring or habitual one in the high mesolect. In those situations, a combination of top-down and bottom-up explanations may be needed. Barbadian (creole) English, or Bajan, provides an example. Bajan is often assumed to show little variation. However, as Table 13.4 shows, a range of creole features exists.

Table 13.4 Some features of Barbadian (Creole) English

Linguistic feature	Example
1. Completive *done*	It **done** set there since last year.
2. Present tense *–s* absence	He **send** somebody.
3. Unmarked past tense	Two day before she **pass** away, I **tell** her to start crying now.
4. Copula (*be* verb) absence	**She lucky** that I ain't throw it on her.
5. *Ain't*	It **ain't** concern you.
6. Unmarked possessives	You know some **people** cake, you cut it here, you find a lump.
7. Object forms as subjects	**Them** ain't want to hear you.
8. Subject forms as objects	I ain't mind **she**.

Information from: Gerald Van Herk, "Barbadian Lects: Beyond Meso," in *Contact Englishes of the Eastern Caribbean*, edited by Michael Aceto and Jeffrey B. Williams (Amsterdam: John Benjamins, 2003), 241–264. With kind permission by John Benjamins Publishing Company, Amsterdam/Philadelphia.

6 Distinctions within a Community: Class, Ethnicity, and Gender

So far, we've looked at social factors that apply to almost everyone in a community. The kinds of change, isolation, and contact we've been discussing affect entire regional groups. Here, we'll look at what language variation tells us about distinctions within regional communities. These distinctions include class, ethnicity, and gender, among others, as well as the interactions between them.

6.1 Class

Class, or **socioeconomic status (SES)**, is a classic social distinction in studies of industrialized societies and has played a role in sociolinguistic studies from the beginning of the discipline. We sociolinguists haven't always had an easy time determining just which social class level to assign to the people we interview. Sometimes, we resort to complex weighting scales involving income, amount of education, type of housing, and prestige associated with one's occupation. Over time, we seem to have settled on occupational prestige as the major indicator of class.

A finding across many speech communities has been that certain linguistic variants are more closely associated with the upper classes and that these variants carry the most prestige. For example, in most varieties of English, *these things* is a more

---

LANGUAGE MATTERS   Going Up

The famous **department store study** by William Labov in New York demonstrated that prestige is not an automatic function of a person's income but relates to context and expectations. The researcher asked employees in three different department stores for directions to a department located on the store's fourth floor and tabulated how many of their answers involved pronunciation of the [ɹ] in each word (*r*-fulness being the prestige form). Labov found that even though all the employees earned similar (low) wages, those who worked in the higher-prestige stores used more of the higher-prestige variant. Labov hypothesized that store employees borrowed prestige from their customers and that this was reflected in their unconscious language choices.

An interesting and creative follow-up to Labov's classic survey studied language on the TV reality show *Say Yes to the Dress*, which films bridal consultants as they try to sell a wedding dress to a prospective bride. The study investigated use of postvocalic *r* by five salespeople in a New York City bridal salon. Researchers found a significant correlation between the bride's stated budget for the dress and the consultant's use of postvocalic *r*: The less the bride could spend on the dress, the more the salesperson dropped postvocalic *r*; the higher the bride's budget, the more postvocalic *r* was pronounced.

prestigious utterance than *dem tings*. It involves two higher-prestige forms, one pho-nological (interdental fricatives rather than dental or alveolar stops), the other syn-tactic or lexical (demonstrative *these* instead of *them*).

Classic sociolinguistic studies, such as William Labov's study of New York's Lower East Side, analyzed people's language in situations that encouraged different degrees of attention to speech, from naturalistic interviews to formal word-list read-ing (see Figure 13.8). They found a strong relationship between class and careful speech styles (those involving a lot of attention to speech). No matter what the task, higher-class speakers used more prestige variants. And no matter what the class, care-ful style correlated with prestige variants. In other words, as Labov put it, a careful pipefitter spoke like a casual salesman, at least in the use of linguistic variables that had social meaning in his speech community. Generally, people of all classes showed the same rate of increase in the use of prestige forms in careful speech. The exception was members of the second-highest class, who sharply increased their use of prestige forms when paying a great deal of attention to speech—in other words, they over-compensated, or in Labov's terminology, they showed (social) **hypercorrection**. This tendency among the second-highest class has shown up in studies in many different communities; it is generally attributed to **linguistic insecurity** among a social group attempting to move up the class ladder.

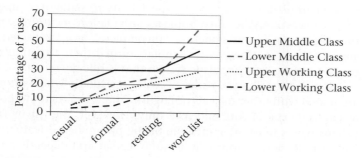

Figure 13.8 Rates of standard pronunciation of /ɹ/ (as in *car*) across social classes and formality of tasks in New York City. Note how the *second*-highest class becomes extremely standard in the most formal task. Information from: William Labov, *Sociolinguistic Patterns* (Philadelphia: University of Pennsylvania Press, 1972), 73. © University of Pennsylvania Press 1972. Reprinted with permis-sion of the University of Pennsylvania Press.

The concepts of prestige or status seem to transfer across cultures better than the narrower term *class*. In societies where movement between status groups is very difficult, such as in the caste system of traditional India, rigid rules have developed (see Table 13.5). Members of different castes will often have categorical rules govern-ing word choice. This may sound extreme, but North American English is not that different in this respect. How many of us can say *You shall do as I say*, or *whilst*, or describe something as *rather thrilling*, without sounding like we're desperately striv-ing for the social heights?

We'll return to issues of class and prestige when we talk about standard languages and prescriptivism in Section 8.

Table 13.5   Caste differences in Bangalore Kannada

	Brahmin	*Non-Brahmin*
'it is'	ide	ayti
'inside'	-alli	-aga
'sit'	kut-	kunt-

Information from: Peter Trudgill, *Sociolinguistics: An Introduction to Language and Society* (New York: Penguin, 1974).

6.2   Ethnicity: The Case of African American English

If linguistic distinctions reflect a society's social distinctions, it's no surprise that we find racial or ethnic differences in language. In North America, the ethnic variety (or ethnolect) that has received the most attention by far from sociolinguists is **African American English (AAE)**. This is at least partly to make up for an earlier deficit—AAE was often ignored or marginalized in discussions of North American English until the civil rights movement picked up steam in the 1960s. This shortage of serious study allowed an unearned veneer of respectability to settle over suggestions that the distinct features of AAE resulted from lazy articulation or cultural deprivation, or showed that the language was somehow "incomplete" or a "restricted code" not suited to abstract thought. However, as scholars turned their attention to AAE, they discovered a supraregional linguistic system that is rule-governed.

Some of the characteristics of AAE, particularly where phonology is concerned, are shared with other dialects of English, and it is difficult to point to single features as characteristic of AAE and AAE only. However, the list in Table 13.6, while not exhaustive, is illustrative of some of the phonological features of AAE. Consonant cluster reduction word-finally is quite regular and depends on voicing of the final

Table 13.6   Some phonological features of AAE

Phonological feature	*Example*
Consonant cluster reduction word-finally	test → tes, desk → des
Deletion of postvocalic liquids	help → [hɛp], ball → [bɔ], car → [kɑ]
Stopping of [ð] word-initially	the man → [də] man
Change of [θ] to [f], and [ð] to [v] word-medially and word-finally	mouth → [mawf] the brother → [də bɹʌvə] smooth → [smuv]

two consonants. The second element in a cluster is deleted word-finally if it shares the same [± voice] feature with the preceding consonant. Thus, *test* becomes *tes, desk* becomes *des, hand* becomes *han,* but *pant* does not become **pan.* The deletion rule operates before the addition of the plural suffix, since the plural of *tes* is *tesses* and the plural of *des* is *desses.* Although other varieties of English simplify consonant clusters word-finally, AAE is more likely than other varieties to delete the second consonant even when a vowel follows, as in *lif up* (for *lift up*).

The morphosyntactic features of AAE illustrate the rule-governed and systematic nature of AAE. Some of these features are listed in Table 13.7.

Table 13.7 Some morphosyntactic features of AAE

Morphosyntactic feature	Example
absence of possessive *-s*	John hat, Byron car
absence of 3SG present *-s*	she talk, he sing
absence of PL *-s* when quantifier given	three dog, some cat
multiple negation	He don' know nothin'.
inversion with indefinite negative subject	Don' nobody talk like that.
stressed *bín* for state begun in remote past and still continuing	She bín married. I bín known him.
habitual *be*	The coffee be cold (= always). He be tired out (= habitually).
copula deletion	She nice. He in the kitchen. He tired out (= temporarily).
come to express indignation	She come goin' in my room.

The *-s* morph marking the possessive, the third-person singular present, and the plural may be absent. AAE shares with some other varieties of English (including the English written by Chaucer) the possibility for multiple negation, but it also allows inversion when the subject of the sentence is an indefinite negative:

11) Don't nobody talk like that.
     'Absolutely no one talks like that.'
     *Don't John talk like that.
     *Don't everybody talk like that.

As the starred examples in *11* show, when the subject of the sentence names a specific person, the inversion is unacceptable; likewise, it is unacceptable when the subject is not a negative.

AAE has a much richer aspectual system (the forms that indicate duration or type of activity of the verb) than standard English, and the examples listed in Table 13.7 are not exhaustive. In AAE, the stressed *bín* denotes a state, condition, or activity begun in the remote past and continued to the present. It is not simply a deletion of the standard English auxiliary verb *have* with the same meaning as in standard English *have/has been*. For an AAE speaker, *She bín married* means that she got married a long time ago and is still married, whereas most non-AAE speakers would interpret it as meaning that she is no longer married.

The use of **habitual (invariant)** *be* to mark a habitual or repeated state, condition, or action is illustrated in *12*.

12) a. This room be cold.
       *This room be cold today.
    b. He be tired out.
       *He be tired out right now.

As the starred examples show, the use of habitual *be* means that the state is constant or habitual, not one that is a temporary condition or onetime occurrence. Conversely, copula deletion may be used for a temporary or onetime state of affairs. Thus, *He tired out* can mean that he is tired out today or right now, but not necessarily as a habitual state.

Another aspectual marker in AAE is *come* used to express indignation. Although other varieties of English have similar structures with *come*, it is obviously not a verb of motion in this AAE structure when it is used as in *13*.

13) She come goin' into my room without knockin'.

As this sentence illustrates, *come* and *go* cannot both be verbs of motion. Instead, *come* expresses the speaker's annoyance.

The lists given here of AAE features are not meant to be exhaustive, nor are they meant to suggest that all speakers of AAE use exactly these forms. Just as speakers of Appalachian English, for example, will differ according to their specific geographical origin, level of education, and socioeconomic status, so too will speakers of AAE. Similarly, it must be remembered that speakers of any variety of English may be bidialectal or multidialectal and will accommodate to a greater or lesser extent to the setting in which they find themselves and the interlocutors with whom they are speaking.

In the discussion of features of AAE, we noted that some of the features were shared with other dialects of English. In Table 13.8, you can see that varieties of English align with each other in complex ways. AAE and Newfoundland English both express habitual actions with *be*; AAE and Caribbean creoles both use zero copula forms, and *done* in perfect constructions; and almost everybody uses unmarked forms for some past tense verbs (especially *come*, *run*, and *give*). Even varieties that share forms may have different frequencies of use, or different rules for when to use them. It's this complexity that keeps sociolinguists busy sorting out the origins and internal systems of different varieties.

Table 13.8 Comparing varieties of English

Function	Standard	Nonstandard	Newfoundland English	AAE	Caribbean creoles
Recent perfect	I've just eaten.	I **done** ate.	I'm **after** eating.	I **done** ate.	I **done** eat.
Auxiliary/ Copula	He's coming. He's a fool.	**He's** coming. He's a fool.	He's coming. He's a fool.	He coming. He a fool.	He coming. He a fool.
Habitual	She always, sometimes, often, usually sings.	She always, sometimes, often, usually sings.	She **bees singing.** She **does be** singing.	She **be singing.** She **steady** singing.	She **does/da** sing. She **does be** singing.
Past	She came. She saw it.	She **come.** She **seen** it.	She **come.** She **seen** it.	She **come.** She **seen** it.	She **come.** She **see** it.

Note: Speakers of a nonstandard variety may also use the standard form, to varying degrees. This table represents their least standard uses.

Notice, too, that Newfoundland English, AAE, and creoles can all use verb forms to express distinctions that standard English can't (standard speakers need to use adverbs like *usually* or *just*). In other words, in these respects, these nonstandard varieties are *more* complex and precise than the standard language, contrary to common linguistic prejudice.

The 1980s saw a growth of interest in tracing the origins of the distinctive features of AAE. As with pidgins and creoles, the lack of historical documentation of the variety limited the data available to researchers, and perhaps encouraged speculation. Over the past two decades, however, a remarkable number of sources of information on earlier AAE have been discovered. These include isolated African American communities in Nova Scotia and Samará in the Dominican Republic, writings by travelers of past centuries, the dialogue of old plays, old letters by semiliterate authors, and recordings made in the 1930s and 1940s of elderly ex-slaves. Researchers disagree, often strongly, about what the data from these sources tell us about where AAE came from. Some argue that contemporary AAE features like copula deletion (e.g., *he bad*) show that AAE was once a creole, or something like it; others argue that the AAE of isolated communities shows features (and linguistic factors affecting them) that more closely resemble the earlier English dialects preserved in places like Newfoundland (e.g., *people goes*). Information from both positions converges, though, in showing that AAE has always been a complete, highly structured language variety; the features of AAE today have not appeared overnight.

Contemporary AAE continues to provide avenues of research for sociolinguists. For one thing, new grammatical features seem to be developing, including the use of past perfects with simple past meaning (e.g., *had went* for *went*). And research is moving past the previous focus on the grammatical consistency of the variety to look at regional diversity in AAE's sound system. Sociolinguists are also beginning to pay back a variety that has supplied the data for so much study, by developing teaching materials that help AAE speakers to bridge the dialect gap in the school system.

6.3 Gender

Sociolinguists generally find differences in language use that reflect socially assigned sex roles, or **gender roles**. One frequent finding is that when language variation in a community is stable (no change is occurring), women use more of the standard forms associated with official (overt) prestige and switch to prestige forms when paying more attention to their speech. British sociolinguist Peter Trudgill found that men not only use more nonstandard forms than women but also claim to use even more of them than they actually do. Trudgill explained this by proposing the idea of **covert prestige**—a sort of linguistic street credibility that men aim for to prove their masculinity. The second gender difference that often surfaces is that when change *does* occur, women use more of the incoming forms than men. This is especially true with **change from above**, changes that are noticeable in the community and work from the upper classes down. Some sociolinguists suggest that women use overt prestige forms and adopt changes from above because of linguistic insecurity. But these differences may also reflect gender expectations that limit women's ability to demonstrate toughness or the fact that women more often do the jobs that require standard speech, such as teacher or receptionist. And women may lead change simply because of their role as child caregivers. If women adopt a new form, it *becomes* a change because children grow up hearing it from women.

Researchers have also noted gender differences in **discourse**, the way conversations are structured. Early studies found that in public mixed-sex settings, men talked more, interrupted more, and controlled the topic more than women. In private mixed-sex settings, various case studies noted that women seemed to put in more work than men to keep conversations going. In what has been labeled the **dominance approach**, researchers interpreted these findings as a reflection of men's dominant position in society. Other researchers, using a **differences approach**, observed single-sex conversations among children and noted the tendency of girls to express affiliation and of boys to engage in one-upmanship. They believe that these childhood tendencies become characteristics of adult gendered speech in which women's speech is classified as cooperative, while men's is dubbed competitive. Researchers who follow the differences approach explain this as evidence of a cultural difference in the upbringing of men and women and their consequent expectations about appropriate linguistic behavior.

However, we should be careful not to make stereotypical generalizations without attention to context. Close analysis of individual conversations reveals that the same linguistic behavior can have different meanings depending on context. For example, overlapping speech may signal an interruption as another speaker competes for the floor, but it may also be a sign of a cooperative conversation in which participants are involved in jointly co-constructing meaning together. In fact, analysis of conversations of single-sex groups has shown that men and women alike engage in competitive and cooperative conversational moves, depending on context such as the topic or stage of topic development.

More recent work on language and gender has made use of the notion of **performativity**. Individuals enact or perform their culturally shaped gendered identity through various symbolic behaviors, of which language is one. Men use male-associated language to "be a man" and assert a stereotypical heterosexual masculinity. For example, in a study of language use among fraternity men, even individuals with monogamous relationships with women participated in weekly ritualized story-telling sessions about sexual exploits as a way of asserting their masculinity with their other fraternity members. Women also perform and reinforce their gender. In the second author's corpus of compliments on a U.S. college campus, women in unstructured settings used compliments to each other on clothing or hairstyles as a way of reinforcing cultural norms of femininity that demand daily effortful attention to appearance.

Performativity may also be manifest in grammar. In Japanese, the choice of first-person pronoun is constrained not only by the level of formality but also by gender of the speaker. Professional women in positions of authority (such as school principals) walk a tightrope between choosing a pronoun that carries authority (typically one of the male choices) and one that is considered socially appropriate for female use (typically lacking in authority). Japanese schoolgirls also wrestle with pronoun choice that will reflect their identity as members of their social network. And among Japanese lesbians, pronoun choice reveals their specific sexual orientation and identity. Performing one's gender even extends to voice quality. Men have deeper voices than women because male vocal folds are longer. That, however, is not the whole story. Research in Britain has shown that men's voices are even deeper than longer vocal folds would predict and suggests that the rest of the difference is social. In other words, men who buy into their gender role overdo it. Not only that, one way of further deepening the voice is through **creaky voice** (also called **vocal fry**), which involves compression of the vocal folds and very slow vibration of one end of the vocal cords. Creaky voice has been reported among British men and interpreted as a sign of authority and extreme masculinity. A similar finding of exaggerated voice quality comes from Japan. Japanese women's voices have a higher average pitch than American women's voices. There being no physiological explanation for this, the difference can be ascribed to Japanese and American cultural expectations of how a woman should sound.

Just as some individuals may choose to perform their gender in stereotypical ways, others may choose to opt out. The creaky voice phenomenon noted as a sign of masculinity in Britain has been noted particularly among young women in the United States. It seems to have originated in California, spread to the Pacific Northwest, and is now becoming widespread enough to have attracted media attention. In a matched guise study, hearers judged its use to be nonaggressive and informal and characteristic of an educated, upwardly mobile young woman. Some recent Canadian research suggests that people who describe themselves as avoiding traditional sex roles also avoid the poles of traditional male or female pronunciations. Work on the speech of men perceived by listeners as gay finds that listeners base their judgments on the use of phonetic features that are also associated with female speech. This also suggests that it is more practical to think of gendered language as a continuum rather than either/or.

6.4   Situation-Specific Factors

Study after study has shown that factors like gender and region affect language use. But ticking off these factors on a sociolinguistic checklist doesn't mean that we've explained a community's language use.

In many situations, completely different aspects of social reality may be reflected in language use. In rural Guyana, language use varies according to whether people work in plantation fields or not. Some speakers use particular variants to show their identification with local values. In fact, in Ocracoke Island and also among speakers of Cajun Vernacular English, researchers have observed a **performance register** in which speakers exaggerate distinctive features of their local dialect to reinforce their local identity and perhaps to impress the tourists. Recently, some scholars have adopted the term **community of practice** to explain some language variation—people who come together to engage in some shared activity are likely to develop shared language practices. Penelope Eckert investigated language use in a Detroit-area high school and found that it reflected membership in one of two groups—*jocks* (who identify with the official system of the institution) and *burnouts* (who don't). The first author's work on online youth subcultures shows that people can adapt their language to reflect participation in groups like hip-hop fans, tweens, and nerds.

A second issue to keep in mind is that all of these social categories *intersect*. It's the combination of social forces that is played out in language use. Eckert's jocks and burnouts were not identical to middle- and working-class groups, but membership in these groups reinforced students' streaming toward those classes. And being a jock or burnout meant different things for men and women. A gender effect was also clear with online subcultures. For example, male and female hip-hop fans showed strong differences in language use, whereas nerds rejected the most gender-specific terms.

7   Social Interaction and Language

We humans aren't sociolinguistic robots, programed to speak a certain way because of our region, gender, ethnicity, age, and the like. Instead, we reveal (or perform) our social roles in extended language interaction, or discourse. And society also has rules, or conventions, about how discourse should proceed. Linguists use **discourse analysis** to look at the structure of a conversation and what it reveals about the roles of the participants. Some aspects of discourse, such as conversational maxims, are covered at the end of Chapter 6. Here, we look at two methods of analyzing discourse. We also examine the effects of power differences on communication.

7.1   Ethnography of Communication

Ethnography of communication is a way to analyze discourse by using the same sort of methods that anthropologists might use to study other aspects of a culture, such as religious practices. Within **speech situations** (circumstances involving the use of speech), cultures have developed conventions governing interactions, or **speech events**. Ethnography of communication analysis pulls apart speech events into their component parts. The components of speech events include the setting, the participants, their purposes as well as the end results, the sequence of exchanges, and the norms that govern how one acts in that particular type of event.

If we have **communicative competence**, we understand the implicit rules so that we can use language in a way that is appropriate for the participants, the situation, and the context. For most of us, communicative competence includes control of **style**, or how formal our speech is. We use formal style when we are looking for (overt) prestige and when we pay attention to our speech; we use informal style in more relaxed situations and/or when overt prestige is not our goal. The related term **register** also describes a type of speech, but it is more closely associated with a specific speech situation, so we can speak of a *legal register* or *ritual language register*. Sometimes the boundary between register and genre is fuzzy; sociolinguists speak of a *recipe register*, although we can also think of *recipe* as a genre—it's a widely recognized category of event with its own name. Both style and register are associated with particular phonological, lexical, or syntactic properties. The same sentiment is expressed by the formal *I shall never surrender* and the informal *I ain't never quittin'!* And recipe register is full of imperatives (*Place chicken legs in bag containing spiced flour*) and zero object constructions (*Shake vigorously*, where the shaking refers to the chicken).

A register associated with a particular occupation or activity often develops its own special vocabulary items, known as **jargon**. Jargon can involve special terms, as when linguists refer to *fricatives* or *complementizers*, or specialized meanings for existing words, as when we give particular linguistic meanings to the words *register* or *style*. Jargon makes communication more effective for in-group members—rather than constantly saying, "those sounds where our phonation is all hissy," we can use the term *fricatives*. But jargon also excludes nonmembers and creates barriers to participation, as you may have noticed through the course of this book.

7.2   Ethnomethodology

Act sequences and norms tell us something about the conventions of conversation. One way to investigate these conventions is through **ethnomethodology**. This method allows us to search large collections of recorded natural speech to discover patterns in the distribution of utterances. One very common structure is the **adjacency pair**, a sort of minimal act sequence in which a specific type of utterance by one speaker is followed by a specific type by someone else. An obvious example is *question-answer*, but other recurring examples include *compliment-acceptance* and *offer-refusal*. Sometimes the first part permits more than one response: in a store, an offer (*Can I help* *you?*) can trigger either acceptance (*Yes, I'm looking for an Arcade Fire T-shirt*) or refusal (*No thanks, just browsing*). Sometimes one utterance type can be interpreted as another. For example, in cultures where direct requests are discouraged, an overt compliment (*What a nice hat!*) will be interpreted as a request (*May I have it?*). In other cultures, the same compliment may be interpreted as an attribution of wealth (*You must be rich to afford such a hat*) leading up to a request for money, thus requiring a denial (*This old thing? I've had it forever*).

A form of ethnomethodology, **conversation analysis** deals with who speaks when. It includes identification of **conversational openings** (*How are you?*) and **closings** (*Well, gotta get back to work*). As well, it studies **turn-taking**. At the end of a conversational turn, the speaker may try to determine who should speak next (for example, by asking a question of a particular person) or may open the floor to any participant who has something to contribute. If nobody takes over, the original speaker may continue. Sometimes, the turn-boundary cues are subtler, including the use of intonation or discourse markers (*so . . .* or *but . . .*). Cross-culturally, differences in turn-taking cues may cause confusion. Linguists have identified communities with a **high involvement style**, such as Eastern European Jews in New York or radio talk show callers in Jamaica. Here, turns will often overlap (one speaker will start before another finishes). In other communities, including among the Western Apache, a longer pause is required to signal the end of a turn. A speaker who hasn't developed communicative competence in these communities might be seen by Jamaicans as unwilling to participate and by the Western Apache as monopolizing the conversation.

7.3   Solidarity and Power

Even when participants in a conversation share norms, the conversation may be somewhat unbalanced, depending on the status of the speakers. Participants may express closeness or intimacy, and thus shared status (**solidarity**), or they may maintain a difference in power and signal the relative social standing of each participant (the **power** relationship). One clear example of this is found in **address terms**—what the participants call each other. Participants can express solidarity and shared status through reciprocal naming, as when friends call each other by their first names. When there is a perceived power difference, as with age differences or work relationships, we often see nonreciprocal naming. A teacher or boss, for example, may call students or employees by their first names, while students or employees may use title and last name: *Professor Rivero, Mr. Kadonoff*. If you've worked in factories, you've probably observed a gradient form of address: a fellow worker named Vijay Kumar is *Vijay*, a foreman of the same name is *Mr. Vijay*, while the "big boss" would be *Mr. Kumar*.

Many languages can express power relationships through a different form of address—the choice of pronoun meaning *you*. Generally, the **T form** is used reciprocally among family and close friends, while the **V form** is used reciprocally among

---

LANGUAGE MATTERS "I Thou Thee, Thou Traitor!"

English used to have a T/V system in which the familiar second-person singular forms were *thou* and *thee*, and the plural forms were *ye* and *you*. In Shakespeare's time, *thou* was used not only for intimates but also from a superior to an inferior, and the shift to *thou* where social convention would demand *you* expressed the speaker's extreme contempt for the addressee. During Sir Walter Raleigh's trial on charges of treason in 1603, Sir Edward Coke, the attorney general prosecuting the case, fiercely attacked the accused, declaring, "All that he did was at thy instigation, thou viper; for I thou thee, thou traitor."

---

people who have roughly equal status but are not close. (The T and V terminology comes from the French pronouns *tu* and *vous*.) When participants are of unequal status, the powerful employ the T forms to address the less powerful, while the less powerful use V forms to address the powerful. Societies can differ on where to draw the line between people who need T-ing or V-ing; Quebec French speakers will use *tu* more readily than European French speakers. This distinction carries so much significance that languages sometimes have a verb meaning 'using the T form': in German, it's *duzen*; in French, it's *tutoyer*. People will sometimes formally admit somebody into their friendship circle by saying, "You may *tutoyer* me."

In some societies, we find **diglossia**—distinctly different varieties acting as social registers. The high (H) variety is used in formal situations, official proclamations, and the like; the low (L) variety is used among friends: in effect, diglossia involves entire languages or language varieties acting like V and T forms. Examples include Paraguay (Spanish and Guaraní), Morocco (Standard Arabic and Moroccan Arabic, or Darija), Switzerland (Standard German and Schwyzerdütsch), and Javanese, as Table 13.9 shows.

Table 13.9 Dialect of the Prijajis (Javanese)

Level	are	you	going	to eat	rice	and	cassava	now
High	menapa	pandjenengan	badé	dahar	sekul	kalijan	kaspé	semanika
Low	apa	sampéjan	arep	neda	sega	lan	kaspé	saiki

Another way in which power imbalances reveal themselves in interaction is through linguistic **accommodation**: speakers modifying their language patterns to make them more like those of the people they're talking to. In a classic study, a Welsh travel agent was wired for sound and recorded through her business day. She adapted her speech to include more local, working-class features when speaking to working-class customers.

8 How Societies Deal with Language

So far, we've been taking language as our object of study and looking at how social forces can shape it. But society and language also interact at a strictly social level. In other words, society can treat language in the same way it treats clothing, the arts, or business—as a thing to be debated and regulated. In this section, we look briefly at how societies approach language as a social object.

Most speech communities feature more than one language variety. As we've seen in our discussions of English, sometimes one variety is called the standard and is claimed to be more "correct" than others. Some countries (notably France and Italy) have formal academies responsible for maintaining the purity of language. English has never had a formal academy, but for centuries, our linguistic insecurity has been fed by newspaper columnists, authors of dictionaries and grammars, and other self-proclaimed defenders of the language. The standard language industry probably had its heyday between about 1750 and 1900, when a growing middle class trying to move up the linguistic ladder provided a ready market for ever-stricter rules about correct language use. This is the time period that gives us such inappropriate analogies with mathematics as *Two negatives make a positive*. (As the linguist Steven Pinker has pointed out, that should mean it's all right to use *three* negatives, as in *I can't never get no satisfaction*.) The demand for **prescriptive grammars** (the ones that tell us how to use language) remains strong today, judging by the success of books like *Eats, Shoots, and Leaves*.

The standard is difficult, if not impossible, to define objectively. We can agree that some forms, like *ain't*, are probably not part of the standard—at least not anymore. Others, like *There's dozens of ways*, are on the boundary. The standard is slightly easier to pin down on social grounds. It's the language of the upper socioeconomic classes and of educated people, the language of literature or printed documents (including this textbook), the variety taught in schools and used by broadcasters; in American English, it's the accent of the Midwest. In effect, the standard is the language of powerful people. By this definition, however, any idea of "correctness" disappears. We're left with a sociolect. What's interesting to sociolinguists is the *idea* of a standard: the widely held belief that some ways of speaking are not just different but inherently correct. (Presumably, this is less of an issue for researchers in other disciplines—astronomers don't worry about whether Neptune is "better" than Mercury.) Because of this belief in the correctness of the standard, language sometimes serves as a barrier to education and employment for speakers of other varieties.

Attitudes toward language have been implicitly involved in much of our discussion so far. The idea of a standard language legitimizes the marginalization of other varieties. People often describe nonstandard varieties as lazy, illogical, or sloppy, although they may not feel comfortable saying the same things about the people who speak them. On the whole, though, it's not always easy to determine attitudes toward languages. Working in the field of **perceptual dialectology**, researchers in Michigan have encouraged speakers to use maps to rate regional varieties in categories such as "pleasantness" or "correctness." As you might expect, respondents considered Michigan speech to be the most correct. The speech of the U.S. South was seen as extremely incorrect, but pleasant. Language attitudes can also be revealed by deconstructing media images. What accents do you hear from characters who are supposed to be stupid? Criminal? Wise? Pretentious?

Attempts to find objective evidence supporting popular linguistic attitudes and prejudices sometimes result in odd **language myths**. It's easy to be puzzled by the once-popular idea that African American English resulted from its speakers having large lips, or by Korean parents having their children undergo tongue surgery (called a frenulotomy) in the belief that more flexible tongues will lead to accentless English. Other language myths are more widespread, especially the idea that some language varieties have tiny vocabularies or are not capable of expressing complex or abstract

---

LANGUAGE MATTERS   The Matched Guise Test

The **matched guise test**, first developed in Canada, tries to get past people's professed viewpoints to gauge their deeply held language attitudes. In the test, subjects listen to a range of recordings of people speaking and are asked to rate the speakers according to traits like social class, intelligence, and friendliness. What the subjects don't know is that they're actually listening to the same speaker or speakers several times, using different accents or speaking different languages. Because the only thing that differs between recordings is the accent or language, any differences in ratings are taken to reflect differences in attitudes toward the language varieties involved. Early experiments showed that both English and French speakers rated French recordings lower in intelligence. In the years since, matched guise studies have fairly consistently shown a solidarity/prestige split. Standard speakers are seen as more competent, smarter, even taller! Nonstandard speakers are seen as warmer and friendlier. Matched guise studies in the United States have shown that human resources personnel are likely to assign lower-status jobs to speakers of African American English, as well as to speakers with Hispanic or Asian accents.

A real-world application of the matched guise test is found in California, where the linguist John Baugh and his associates have spent years collecting information for housing-discrimination cases. They phone landlords and ask about advertised apartments, using identical sentences but adopting African American, Hispanic, or standard American accents. If apartments are available to standard speakers but are either unavailable or more expensive when nonstandard speakers call, discrimination is assumed.

Information from: Thomas Purnell, William Idsardi, and John Baugh, "Perceptual and Phonetic Experiments on American English Dialect Identification," *Journal of Language and Social Psychology* 18,1 (1999): 10–30.

ideas. Although these notions may reassure people who wish to dismiss those language varieties, they have no basis in fact. The opposite notion is also popular—that certain languages have massive vocabularies for particular items. This is sometimes known as The Great Eskimo Vocabulary Hoax (also the title of a book on the subject), after its most commonly expressed example. In reality, Inuit and Yupik languages (both spoken in the far North) have roughly the same number of words for snow as English does.

Of course, languages do sometimes find themselves at a loss for words. This is particularly true when a language moves into new domains, typically when a community language becomes a language of power. Different language groups have dealt with this in different ways. Some languages borrow words. When English became the language of British government and the law hundreds of years ago, it borrowed many of the terms needed from French (*attorney, governor general*). When the creole language Tok Pisin became the official language of Papua New Guinea, it borrowed legal terms from English (the Tok Pisin term for *public solicitor* is *pablik salisita*). In other situations, governments establish bodies to oversee **language planning**, which often includes coming up with homegrown solutions to lexical gaps. In Quebec, the *Office québécois de la langue française* works to develop French-based terms for new or imported concepts (e.g., for lesser-known foodstuffs imported from other countries) and to implement government legislation on language.

Government involvement in language planning often includes the declaration of an **official language** for a particular region or country as a result of legislation. When a language is made an official language, it often privileges the political and economic power of the ethnic group that speaks that language. In some cases, official language designations are a response by a majority group to a perceived increase in status or power of a minority group. A good example of this situation is the attempt by "English-only" groups to have English declared the official language of the United States. Currently, over half of the states have some sort of law giving English official status. In Canada, French and English are the official languages (at the federal level); most provinces conduct official business in either English or French. The Northwest Territories has *eleven* official languages: Chipewyan, Cree, English, French, Gwich'in, Inuinnaqtun, Inuktitut, Inuvialuktun, North Slavey, South Slavey, and Tlicho, although services in all eleven are not available everywhere.

Language planning policies often have their greatest impact in regulating the language of schooling, which in turn places differential barriers on access to education. Proponents of minority-language education or bilingual education argue that teaching subject matter such as science or geography in students' first language levels the playing field by removing the linguistic barrier to learning. However, these minority-language education programs are sometimes interpreted by majority-language groups as resistance to assimilation, leading to backlash. In California, the Oakland school district's attempt to recognize the legitimacy of AAE in the learning process was harshly criticized. Currently, three states forbid bilingual education, while other jurisdictions restrict funding. In the past, home languages have been banned in schools, with harsh punishments for their use. Welsh was banned in

---

LANGUAGE MATTERS Language Planning in Tanzania

The objectives of Tanzania's Institute of Kiswahili Research illustrate the activities of language planning groups that work to expand the role and usefulness of official languages in postcolonial situations:

- To undertake research in various aspects of Kiswahili morphology, syntax, phonology, sociolinguistics, and dialectology.

- To undertake research in Kiswahili lexicography and compile general and subject dictionaries.

- To compile terminologies and coin new terms for different academic and/or specialized fields.

- To coordinate and provide translation services to government offices, parastatal organizations, industries, institutions, and individuals in and outside the country.

- To carry out research in oral and written literature, theater arts, folklore, and the cultures of the Tanzanian and East African societies.

- To cooperate with other institutions in the development of Kiswahili language and provide consultancy services in different aspects of Kiswahili language and literature.

- To publish teaching material on/in Kiswahili for schools, colleges, and universities.

- To see to it that Kiswahili acquires a strong foundation for becoming a medium of instruction for primary, secondary, and tertiary levels of education.

Information from: Institute of Kiswahili Research.

Welsh schools, and Native American languages such as Lakota and Apache were banned at residential schools in the United States.

In many cases, minority languages are in danger of dying out. Immigrant languages continue to be spoken elsewhere, so their decline here leads to decreased diversity but not to **language death**. The situation is different for Native American languages, many of which now have fewer than one hundred speakers, and for minority languages around the world. Major efforts are being made to support endangered languages through the development of dictionaries, reading materials, and school systems, but the past history of endangered languages is not encouraging. Languages usually come "back from the brink" only when major political and social will is involved. One such example is Hebrew, which has been built up to become the official language of Israel.

Summing Up

Sociolinguistics is the study of language in its social contexts. Linguistic variation between **speech communities** reflects social factors such as region, change over time, isolation, and language contact. These social factors can influence the development of distinctive lexical items, phonology, morphology, and syntax. Contact situations lead to bilingualism, **code-switching**, and **borrowing**, as well as to such contact-driven language types as **mixed languages**, **lingua francas**, **pidgins**, and **creoles**. Within speech communities, language reflects important social distinctions, including class, ethnicity, and gender, as well as the interactions between these factors and locally relevant norms.

Discourse analysis looks at language in interactions, using such methods as **ethnography of communication** and **ethnomethodology**. Individual speakers adapt their use of **style**, **register**, and **jargon** to fit each interaction, as well as to reflect **solidarity** and **power** relationships between speakers. Often, the language of a high-status group will become known as the **standard** language; this variety will be described as more "correct" than other varieties, based largely on attitudes toward the variety. Attitudes can restrict the social mobility of nonstandard speakers. **Language planning** involves attempts by a society to regulate language use through the choice of an **official language** and the language of education and sometimes even by banning languages.

Through analysis of language variation, fifty years of sociolinguistic research confirms that variation is highly patterned and is affected by a range of linguistic and social factors. This patterning helps reveal the social meaning of language and sociolinguistic competence of speakers, who use language to situate themselves with respect to other speakers and the norms of their society.

Key Terms

General terms

accent
dialects
mutual intelligibility
nonstandard
salient features
slang
sociolinguistic indicators

sociolinguistic markers
sociolinguistic norms
sociolinguistics
speech community
(speech) variety
standard

Terms concerning language variation

categorical (rules)
constraints
interspeaker variation
intraspeaker variation
linguistic factors
probabilistic

social factors
(sociolinguistic) variable
structured variation
variant
variationist sociolinguistics

Terms concerning gathering and analyzing data

consultants
dialectology
discrete variables
gradient variables
informants

isogloss
isogloss bundle
NORMs
sociolinguistic interviews

Terms concerning regional variation and change over time

apparent-time hypothesis
California Shift
dialect leveling
enregistered
low back merger

Northern Cities Shift
phoneme merger
postvocalic *r*
real-time studies
vowel shift

Terms concerning dialect development through isolation

a-prefixing
dense social networks
linguistic isolation
multiplex social networks
physical isolation

regularization
relic form
social isolation
social networks

Terms related to languages in contact

acrolect
basilect
borrowings
code-switching
creole
creole continuum
ELF (English as Lingua Franca)
language bioprogram hypothesis
language contact
lexical gap
lexifier language

lingua franca
loan translation
mesolect
mixed language
nonce borrowing
pidgin
protopidgin
relexification hypothesis
serial verb construction
situational code-switching

Terms concerning social class, gender, and ethnic variation

African American English (AAE)
change from above
community of practice
covert prestige
creaky voice (vocal fry)
department store study
differences approach
discourse
dominance approach

ethnolects
gender roles
habitual (invariant) *be*
hypercorrection
linguistic insecurity
performance register
performativity
socioeconomic status (SES)
sociolects

Terms concerning social interaction and language

adjacency pair	high involvement style
communicative competence	jargon
conversation analysis	register
conversational closings	speech events
conversational openings	speech situations
discourse analysis	style
ethnography of communication	turn-taking
ethnomethodology	

Terms concerning solidarity and power

accommodation	solidarity
address terms	T form
diglossia	V form
power	

Terms concerning how societies deal with language

language death	official language
language myths	perceptual dialectology
language planning	prescriptive grammars
matched guise test	

Recommended Reading

Chambers, J. K. 2009. *Sociolinguistic Theory: Linguistic Variation and Its Social Significance*. Rev. ed. Oxford: Blackwell.

Chambers, J. K., Peter Trudgill, and Natalie Schilling-Estes. 2002. *The Handbook of Language Variation and Change*. Oxford: Blackwell.

Lippi-Green, Rosina. 2012. *English with an Accent: Language, Ideology, and Discrimination in the United States*. 2nd ed. London: Routledge.

Meyerhoff, Miriam. 2011. *Introducing Sociolinguistics*. 2nd ed. London: Routledge.

Milroy, Leslie, and Matthew Gordon. 2003. *Sociolinguistics: Method and Interpretation*. Oxford: Blackwell.

Schneider, Edgar W., ed. 2008. *Varieties of English*. Vols. 1–4. Berlin: Mouton de Gruyter.

Wolfram, Walt, and Natalie Schilling. 2016. *American English: Dialects and Variation*. 3rd ed. Oxford: Wiley Blackwell.

Wolfram, Walt, and Ben Ward, eds. 2006. *American Voices: How Dialects Differ from Coast to Coast*. Malden, MA: Blackwell.

Exercises

1. In each of the following sentences, you can probably make an educated guess about one or two of the following categories: the speaker's region, age, level of education or socioeconomic status, gender, or ethnicity. For each sentence, write

what you would assume about the speaker, cite two specific linguistic examples in the sentence, and explain how these examples provide evidence for your judgments about the speaker. (You may find useful information in Sections 1, 2, and 6.)

a) Anymore, the oil needs changed every month.
b) From whom might one obtain that information?
c) I see y'all have dinner on the table; you must be fixin' to eat.
d) An' I'm all, "Dude, like that totally sucks, man!"
e) Oy vey! Who wants to schlep that stuff all over town!
f) Oh, I just love that new sweater on you. Teal is your color.
g) Me an' him wasn't doin' nothin'.
h) Mommy, I have a tummy ache.
i) She be studyin' at her des' all the time.

2. In one dialect of American English (Tidewater Virginia), [aj] is monophthongized to [a] according to a rule. Examine the data below, and write what the rule is.

	Word	Phonetic transcription		Word	Phonetic transcription
a)	snipe	[snajp]	i)	my	[ma]
b)	ride	[rad]	j)	bike	[bajk]
c)	prize	[pɹaz]	k)	five	[fav]
d)	nice	[najs]	l)	write	[ɹajt]
e)	mile	[mal]	m)	scribe	[skɹab]
f)	white	[ʍajt]	n)	life	[lajf]
g)	nine	[nan]	o)	time	[tam]
h)	tithe	[tað]	p)	type	[tajp]

3. Copy the following question, and ask at least five people from different regions about the words. What results do you obtain, and how do you explain those results? (You can refer to Section 2.3.)

Do the words in each pair sound the same or different to you?
a) cot, caught
b) fail, fell
c) gem, Jim
d) marry, merry
e) pool, pull

4. i) Explain the regional differences in pronunciation you might expect to hear in the following words: *box, Ann, dude, back, fourth floor.* (You can refer to Sections 2.3, 3, and 6.1.)

ii) Now make a copy of sentences *a–e* in *iii*, and ask five people from different regions to read each aloud. As they are distracted by filling in the blank, you will be paying attention to how they pronounce the words from the list in *i*.

iii) Transcribe how each person said the target word in the sentence. Did you hear what you expected to hear? Why or why not?

a) The box is sitting over there on the _____.

b) I invited Ann and _____.

c) Look at that dude on the _____.

d) A strange noise is coming from the back of the _____.

e) On the fourth floor you'll find _____.

5. List the slang terms your generation would use for each of the following terms. (Slang and language change are discussed in Sections 1 and 3.)

a) an attractive girl or guy

b) an ugly girl or guy

c) a best friend

d) a super-easy class

e) drunk

f) vomit

i) Talk to someone in your parents' and in your grandparents' generation, and write the slang terms they used when they were young for the same things.

ii) How do your slang terms sound to the older generations? How do their terms sound to you? Are any of their terms still used? What does this problem tell you about how language changes over time?

6. Review the uses of code-switching in Section 5.1. For each of the examples below, explain what function the code-switching is serving.

a) In an English class taught to students who are Tamil-speaking, the teacher speaks in English and then switches to Tamil (underlined).

What is the past tense of swim*?* [silence] *Come on . . .* [silence] *enna piLLayal, itu teriyaataa? Poona vakuppilai connaniinkal.* ('What, children, you don't know this? You told me in the last class.')

b) A Japanese-English bilingual is speaking (Japanese is underlined).

Dakedo I don't like New York. ('But I don't like New York.')

c) A Papua New Guinea child is narrating the story of a cartoon (that had no dialogue) in Tok Pisin and English (English is underlined).

Lapun man ia kam na tok, "Oh you poor pussycat," na em go insait.
('The old man came and said, "Oh you poor pussycat," and then he went inside.')

d) A Puerto Rican mother in New York is calling her child in Spanish and switches to English (English is underlined).

Ven acá, ven acá. Come here, you. ('Come here, come here.' Come here, you.)

e) A Puerto Rican boss and his secretary in New York are discussing Mr. Bolger, to whom the boss has just sent a letter. Their conversation is in English and then switches to Spanish (Spanish is underlined).

Boss: *Ah, this man William Bolger got his organization to contribute a lot of money to the Puerto Rican parade. He's very much for it. ¿Tú fuiste a la parada?* ('Were you at the parade?')

Secretary: *Sí, yo fui.* ('Yes, I was').

Boss: *¿Y cómo te estuvo?* ('How did you like it?') [The conversation continues in Spanish.]

f) The following conversation was conducted in Slovenian concerning the origin of a certain type of wheat, but the speaker switched to German in the last line (German is <u>underlined</u>).

A: *Vigələ ma yə sa ameircə.*   ('Wigele got them from America.')
B: *Kanada pridə.*   ('It comes from Canada.')
A: <u>*Kanada mus i sogn nit.*</u>   ('<u>I would not say Canada.</u>')

7. Review the linguistic characteristics of pidgins and creoles in Section 5.2, and look for examples in the following data from Jamaican creole. Use the examples from Jamaican creole to answer the questions that follow. (Note: Although the data are not written in IPA, the orthography is intended to capture the pronunciation.)

a) good-belly   'good natured'   hard-ears   'stubborn'
    nyami-nyami   'voracious eater, greedy '   nyam   'eat, food'
    tiif (from *thief*) 'steal, thief'   smaal smaal 'very small'
b) Jan tiif di mango yesidee.   'John stole the mango yesterday.'
c) Dem a waak go a maakit.   'They're walking (thither) to the market.'
d) Mi tek naif kot di bred.   'I cut the bread with a knife.'
e) Im a nyam im dina.   'He is eating his dinner.'

i)   What are two characteristics of pidgin/creole phonology? Cite an example of each and explain it.

ii)   What are two characteristics of verbs and how they are marked in creoles? Cite an example of each and explain it.

iii) What is a characteristic of pronouns in pidgin/creole? Cite an example each from two different sentences and explain each one.

iv) What are three characteristics of the lexicon in pidgins and creoles? Cite an example of each and explain it.

8. Examine a text written in African American English and identify ten different linguistic features that differ from standard American English. Write each example and explain how it illustrates one characteristic feature. You may use an excerpt from a literary text (such as *Their Eyes Were Watching God* by Zora Neale Hurston or *The Color Purple* by Alice Walker), or you may choose the lyrics of a contemporary rap song. (Refer to Section 6.2.)

9. Imagine a conversation in a cafeteria line in which a young chemistry prof is trying to talk her timid cousin into going to a rock concert with her. Now change two of the components of the speech event and consider how the conversation would be different. (See Section 7.1.)

10. Each of these sentences contains at least one odd feature—something disliked by prescriptive grammarians (now or in the past) or something that sounds wrong to us but used to be required by prescriptivists. Find the feature. How wrong does it sound to you? (See Section 8.)
a) A new mall is building next to the highway.
b) Send an e-mail to Clarisse and myself.
c) Send an e-mail to Clarisse and I.

d) You should have went home earlier.

e) I'm arrived at the airport.

f) There's hundreds of peasants with torches outside the castle.

g) Ask your father when he was at the store did he buy the coffee.

h) I seen five or six moose last summer.

i) I'm loving the *Glass Boys* album.

j) This class needs more workers and less complainers.

11. Spend a week actively aware of language variation that you hear or read by continually thinking, "Is this something I haven't heard before? Is this something that not everyone would say? How might this be said by somebody of a different age, ethnicity, gender, or social class?" Make a list of your observations.

 **LaunchPad Solo** macmillan learning | For more helpful content and quizzes, go to the LaunchPad Solo for *Contemporary Linguistics* at **launchpadworks.com**.

Writing and Language

William O'Grady
Michael Dobrovolsky

Letters
continue to fall
like precise rain
along my way.

—PABLO NERUDA, "Ode to Typography" (1964)

OBJECTIVES

In this chapter, you will learn:

- how different types of writing systems have developed from earliest times
- how different types of alphabetic systems emerged
- how various types of non-European writing systems developed
- how historical factors have led to the modern English spelling system
- how writing and reading are related

 **LaunchPad Solo**
macmillan learning | For more helpful content and quizzes, go to the LaunchPad Solo
for *Contemporary Linguistics* at **launchpadworks.com**.

Speaking and writing are different in both origin and practice. Our ability to use language is as old as humankind and reflects the biological and cognitive modifications that have occurred during the evolution of our species. Writing, the symbolic representation of language by graphic signs or symbols, is a comparatively recent cultural development, having occurred within the past five thousand years and only in certain parts of the world. Most of the world's languages have no tradition of writing, and many lack a writing system even today.

2 The Early History of Writing

It is surprising that we cannot say with certainty how a comparatively recent cultural phenomenon like writing originated. We do know that writing developed in stages, the earliest of which involved direct representation of objects. This is sometimes called **prewriting**.

2.1 Prewriting

Figures and scenes depicted on cave walls and rock faces in the Americas, Africa, and Europe as much as fifteen thousand years ago, and perhaps even earlier, may have been forerunners of writing. Some of these drawings may represent a type of preliterate stage that did not evolve into a full-fledged writing system.

These drawings depict a wide range of human and animal activity and may even have been intended for purposes of linguistic communication. Some illustrations were doubtless a form of religious symbolism to request a successful hunt or other benefits. Perhaps some were for purely aesthetic purposes. Still others, such as those depicting the phases of the moon, may have been part of some form of record keeping. For example, the cave paintings of Lascaux, France, dating back to 15,000 B.C., have been interpreted as religious magic. Among the realistic paintings of animals are hundreds of abstract signs. As Figure 14.3a shows, some are feather or branchlike signs, others are parallel marks suggesting animal tracks, and others are box-shaped signs, possibly representing traps or enclosures. Figure 14.3b shows an incised eagle bone from Le Placard, France, that dates back some thirteen to fifteen thousand years. The incisions, which vary subtly, have been analyzed as a record of lunar phases. Pictorial records thus link the origins of writing with the history of representational art.

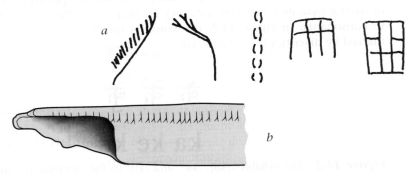

Figure 14.3 *a.* Abstract signs, Lascaux cave; *b.* Le Placard eagle bone

An even more direct connection links the origin of writing with record keeping. It has been suggested that the idea of writing had its origin in small clay tokens and counters that were used in record keeping and business transactions in the ancient Middle East. These small, fire-baked pieces of clay were apparently used for thousands of years before writing emerged (see Figure 14.4). Counters representing cattle and other goods were stored on shelves or in baskets. Eventually, people began to make an impression of the tokens on soft clay tablets rather than storing and shipping the tokens themselves. This may have led to the idea that other objects and events in the world could be represented symbolically in graphic form.

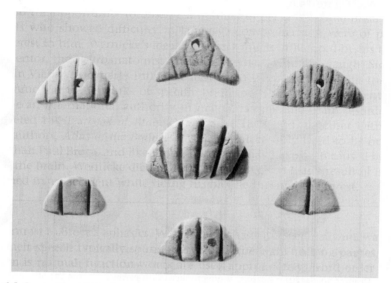

Figure 14.4   Ancient Mesopotamian tokens. RMN-Grand Palais/Art Resource, NY.

2.2   Pictograms

Whatever their purpose, there is no doubt that pictures were among the precursors of the written word. Early writing systems all evolved from pictorial representations called **pictograms** or picture writing. Each pictogram was an image of the object or concept that it represented and, as far as we know, offered no clues to pronunciation. Pictorial representations of this sort have been found among people throughout the ancient and modern world. Figure 14.5 illustrates several examples of Native American picture writing made by a Dakota named Lonedog; they depict the following unrelated events: death as the result of smallpox, the building of a log cabin, the killing of someone with a spear, and the eclipse of the sun.

Figure 14.5   Native American pictography: some Dakota records of significant events.
Information from: Hans Jensen, *Sign, Symbol, and Script: An Account of Man's Efforts to Write*, 3rd ed., trans. George Unwin (London: George Allen and Unwin, 1970), 43.

Pictograms are still used today, often reflecting the function of this form of pre-writing as a memory aid. Many signs indicating roadside services or information in parks are pictographic in nature, as are the standardized set of symbols for Canada's Workplace Hazardous Materials Information System to identify classes of hazards (see Figure 14.6).

Figure 14.6   Contemporary pictograms: Workplace Hazardous Materials Information System symbols. © All Rights Reserved. *Do You Know These Vital Signs? The Hazard Symbols of WHMIS.* Health Canada, 2011. Adapted and reproduced with permission from the Minister of Health, 2016.

As we consider developments that emerge from pictographic representation, it is important to remember that ancient pictograms are not writing in any sense of the word. They do not represent linguistic elements such as segments, syllables, morphemes, or words. They are not written in a sequence that matches the language's word order, and they often provide only limited clues about their intended meaning.

3   The Evolution of Writing

The earliest known logographic writing came from Sumeria, from where it spread to surrounding areas about five thousand years ago. Over time, inherently ambiguous pictograms came to be used to represent abstract notions, as their use was extended to include related concepts. For example, as shown in Figure 14.7, the pictogram for 'fire' was also used for 'inflammation', the pictogram for 'hand' was employed to signify 'fist' as well as a particular unit of measurement, and the symbol for 'foot' came to stand for 'go', 'move', and 'go away'.

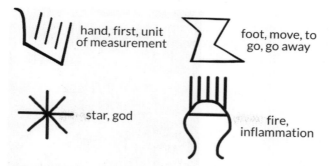

Figure 14.7 Sumerian pictograms. Information from: Hans Jensen, *Sign, Symbol, and Script: An Account of Man's Efforts to Write*, 3rd ed., trans. George Unwin (London: George Allen and Unwin, 1970), and René Labat, *Manuel d'épigraphie akkadienne: Signes, syllabaire, idéogrammes*, 5th ed. (Paris: P. Geuthner, 1976).

Sumerian writing also combined signs to express abstract meanings. For example, a head with fire coming out of the crown indicated 'anger', as shown in Figure 14.8.

Figure 14.8 The Sumerian sign for 'anger'. Information from: René Labat, *Manuel d'épigraphie akkadienne: Signes, syllabaire, idéogrammes*, 5th ed. (Paris: P. Geuthner, 1976).

Although its evolution was gradual, we can state with some certainty that Sumerian writing represented words (it was logographic rather than just pictographic) because from a fairly early stage, it was written in a consistent linear order that appears to reflect the order of words in speech. We cannot say with certainty at what date pictures began to be read as words, but once this practice took hold, the stage was set for the evolution to phonographic writing.

3.1   Rebuses and the Emergence of Writing

Phonographic writing made its appearance around 3000 B.C. with the first use of Sumerian symbols to represent sound rather than just meaning. This major development in the history of writing was made possible by the use of the **rebus principle**, which allows a sign to be used for any word with the same pronunciation as the word for which it was originally intended. In the inscription of an economic transaction in Figure 14.9, for example, the symbol in the upper left-hand corner, which was originally used to represent the word *gi* 'reed', represents a homophonous word with the meaning 'reimburse'.

Figure 14.9   Early Sumerian cuneiform tablet. © The Metropolitan Museum of Art. Image source: Art Resource, NY.

Thanks to the rebus principle, concepts that could not be directly depicted by a pictogram/logogram could be represented in writing. Thus, the sign for the word *ti* 'arrow', ➤➤, was also used for the word *ti* 'life'.

3.2   Toward Syllabic Writing

Once the breakthrough toward phonographic writing had been made, it did not take long (in historical terms) before syllabic writing began to emerge. Within about five hundred to six hundred years, signs that clearly represent not just homophonous words but parts of words—specifically, syllables—had become well established in Sumerian writing. For example, the syllable *kir* was represented by the syllabic signs for *ki* and *ir*, written in sequence. (By allowing the function of the symbols to overlap in this way, they avoided the need for a special sign for *r*.) Figure 14.10 illustrates this with the help of Sumerian cuneiform signs that are discussed in more detail in the following section.

ki   +   ir   =   kir

Figure 14.10   Overlapped Sumerian syllabic signs. Data from: Hans Jensen, *Sign, Symbol and Script: An Account of Man's Efforts to Write*, 3rd ed., trans. George Unwin (London: George Allen and Unwin, 1970), 95.

Sumerian writing never developed into a pure syllabary, however. Logographic elements were interspersed with syllabic ones, and many syllabic signs were used to represent syllables with other pronunciations as well.

Cuneiform

Over the centuries, Sumerian writing was simplified and eventually came to be produced with the use of a wedge-shaped stylus that was pressed into soft clay tablets.

This form of writing, initiated in the fourth millennium B.C., has come to be known as **cuneiform** (from Latin *cuneus* 'wedge'). In time, a change in writing practices led the cuneiform signs to be modified so that they ended up bearing even less resemblance to their pictographic origins than before. Figure 14.11 illustrates this development for two words.

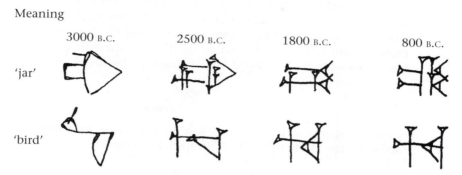

Figure 14.11   Changes in cuneiform writing. Adapted from *The Origins of Writing* by Wayne M. Senner, by permission of the University of Nebraska Press. Copyright 1989 by the University of Nebraska Press.

The cuneiform system was borrowed by the Elamites and Akkadians in the third millennium B.C., a little later by the Persians, and in the second millennium B.C. by the Hittites far to the north in the ancient region of Anatolia (modern Asian Turkey). Cuneiform writing persisted until about the first few centuries of the Christian era in some areas and then disappeared from use, not to be rediscovered until the nineteenth century. It was first deciphered from Old Persian texts, a breakthrough that led to the deciphering of Akkadian, Sumerian, and Hittite, among other languages that employed it. This script was used for thousands of years but was generally replaced by systems of writing employed by the Semitic peoples of the Eastern Mediterranean.

3.3   Another Middle Eastern Writing System: Hieroglyphs

At about the time Sumerian pictography was flourishing, a similar system of pictorial communication was in use in Egypt. The Egyptian signs have become known as **hieroglyphs** (meaning 'sacred inscriptions' in Greek). The earliest texts display about five hundred such symbols. Like Sumerian pictograms, the hieroglyphic signs at first represented objects, but later they became logographic as they began to be associated with words.

Egyptian hieroglyphs developed into a mixed system of logographic writing and phonographic writing. Although hierogryphs derived from pictures, they could be used as pictograms, as phonograms, or as **determinatives**—signs that indicated the meaning of a word. For example, the sign for the heart and trachea was ⚷; this represented the word itself: *nfr*. (Only the consonants of words represented by hieroglyphs are known with certainty. The Egyptians did not represent vowels—these can only be partially reconstructed from transcriptions in Greek and other languages that were made much later.) Eventually, this sign came to be disassociated from the word it represented and was used to transcribe other words that consisted of or included the same sounds, such as the word for 'good', which also contained the consonants *nfr*.

Hieroglyphic symbols eventually came to be used to represent individual consonant phonemes by application of what is called the **acrophonic principle** (from Greek *acros* 'extreme'): a consonant was represented by a picture of an object whose pronunciation began with that sound. In this way, the first consonant of a word-sign came to be what the sign stood for. For example, the hieroglyph for 'horned viper'

is read logographically as *f-t*. Thanks to the acrophonic principle, this sign was also used to represent the phoneme /f/ in spellings such as *fen* 'pleasant'.

As we will see in the next section, the acrophonic principle was crucial to the development of true alphabets. In Egyptian writing, however, it was only part of a system that mixed logographic and phonographic elements.

Figure 14.12 provides some additional examples of hieroglyphs. Hieroglyphs were used with decreasing frequency until Christian times. By the second century A.D., Egyptian began to be written with Greek letters, and by the third century A.D., hieroglyphs had been replaced by the Greek alphabet.

zaa-j   ndtjj-j
son-my   savior-my

Figure 14.12   Egyptian hieroglyphs (c. 1500 B.C.).

3.4   The Emergence of Alphabets

Alphabetic writing emerged slowly from mixed writing systems over a long period in the Middle East. Building on this tradition of mixed writing, the Semitic peoples of ancient Phoenicia (modern Lebanon) devised an abjad writing system consisting of twenty-two symbols for consonants (but none for vowels) as early as 1000 B.C. This system was written horizontally, right to left, as had been common in earlier scripts. It ultimately led to the development of many alphabetic writing systems, including both the Greek and Latin alphabets.

The pictorial (and eventually logographic) origins of the Phoenician alphabet are evident in some of its symbols. Figure 14.13 illustrates the creation of alphabetic symbols from the logograms corresponding to an ox's head, a throwing stick (some say a camel's hump), and a wavy flow of water.

Figure 14.13 Pictorial and logographic origins of some signs in the Phoenician alphabet.

These symbols eventually came to be used to represent the consonant phonemes of words by application of the acrophonic principle (see Section 3.3). In this way, *'ālep* was used to represent a glottal stop; *gīml*, the consonant /g/; and *mēm*, the consonant /m/. The Phoenicians were a trading people, and their alphabetic writing spread to adjacent countries and beyond. Eventually, the Greeks acquired and adapted the Phoenician alphabet.

The Greek Alphabet

The Greeks developed the Phoenician writing system into the world's first full alphabet, with separate symbols for each consonant and vowel. (Phoenician symbols for consonant sounds not found in Greek were adapted to represent Greek vowels.) Figure 14.14 illustrates the evolution of the Classical Greek and ultimately the Latin (Roman) alphabet from the original Phoenician consonantal signs.

Phoenician *'ālep* represented a glottal stop. Since Greek had no such phoneme, the *'ālep* was employed to represent the vowel /a/ in Greek. Phoenician *hē* ⟨symbol⟩ (/h/) was used to represent the Greek vowel /e/, and other signs were added to the system by the Greeks, including Φ for /f/, X for /kʰ/ and then /ks/, ψ for /ps/, and Ω for /oː/.

The Phoenician names for the letters (*'ālep, bēt, gīml, dālet*, and so on) were maintained by the Greeks (as *alpha, beta, gamma, delta*, and so on), but the possible pictorial origins were lost, and the names carried no other meaning. The writing system itself gained its name from the first two letters of the series: *alphabet*.

Unlike Phoenician, which was written right to left, the earliest inscriptions in ancient Greek reversed the direction of writing at the end of each line. If the first line of a text was written right to left, the next line continued left to right, then right to left, and so on. This practice was typical of many old writing systems and is known as **boustrophedon** (Greek for 'as the ox turns'), since it was said to resemble the pattern made by plowing a field. Eventually, this practice was abandoned, and Greek was written left to right.

Phoenician			Greek			Latin	
Name	IPA	Symbol	Name	Early Symbol	Classical Symbol	Early Symbol	Classical Symbol
'alep	?	𐤀	alpha	A	A	A	A
bēt	b	𐤁	beta	8	B		B
gīml	g	𐤂	gamma	𐌂	Γ		C
dālet	d	𐤃	delta	Δ	Δ	D	D
hē	h	𐤄	epsilon	E	E	E	E
wāw	w	Y	digamma	ꟻ		ꟻ	F
							G
zayin	z	I	zeta	I	Z		
hēt	ħ	日	eta	日	H	日	H
tēt	tˤ	⊗	theta	⊗	θ		
yōd	j	𐤉	iota	⟨	I	I	I
							(J)
kāp	k	𐤊	kappa	⋊	K	⋊	K
lāmed	l	𐤋	lambda	Γ	Λ		L
mēm	m	𐤌	mu	⋔	M	⋔	M
nūn	n	𐤍	nu	ꓤ	N	ꓤ	N
sāmek	s	𐤎					
ʕayin	ʕ	o	ŏmicron	O	O	O	O
pē	p	𐤐	pi	⊓	Π		P
çādē	sˤ	𐤑	san	M			
qōp	q	Φ	qoppa	ϙ			Q
reš	r	𐤓	rho	𐌓	P		R
šin	ʃ	W	sigma	⟩	Σ	⟩	S
tāw	t	X	tau	X			T
			upsilon		Y	V	V
			chi		X		X
							Y
			omega		Ω		Z

Figure 14.14 Evolution of the Greek and Latin alphabets from Phoenician signs. David Diringer, "Alphabet," *The Encyclopedia Americana*, 1968 edition. All rights reserved. Reprinted by permission of Scholastic Library Publishing, Inc.

The Roman Alphabet

When Greek colonists occupied southern Italy in the eighth and seventh centuries B.C., they brought their alphabet with them. It was in turn taken up and modified by the Etruscan inhabitants of central Italy, a non-Latin-speaking people who were a political and cultural power before the rise of Rome. It is believed that the Romans acquired their alphabet through the Etruscans. As the Romans grew in power and influence during the following centuries, first as masters of Italy and later of Europe, the Roman alphabet spread throughout their empire.

Under the Romans, the Greek/Etruscan alphabet was again modified, this time with some symbols influenced by the Etruscans. Innovations included *C* for the phoneme /k/ and *G* for /g/. The oldest inscriptions also retained *K* for /k/ in some words, but it was generally replaced by *C*. Similarly, *Q*- was retained before /u/. Roman script (which at the time consisted only of upper-case letters) also employed Greek *U* (= *V*), *X*, *Y*, and *Z*, and moved *Z* to the end of the alphabet. The symbols Φ, Θ, ψ, and Ω were among those discarded, and *H* was converted back to a consonant symbol.

Some subsequent changes were made in the alphabet as it was adapted by various peoples of the Roman Empire. In English, for example, *W* was created from two juxtaposed *V*s. Spanish employs a tilde (˜) over *n* (ñ) to signify a palatal nasal, as in *año* /aɲo/ 'year', and French uses a cedilla under *c* (ç) to indicate the dental fricative /s/, as in the spelling of *français* [fʁãsɛ] 'French'.

4   Some Non-European Writing Systems

This section focuses on the nature and development of writing systems that originated outside the Middle East. While some of these systems emerged in response to external influences, others seem to have been entirely independent innovations. We will briefly examine the writing systems of China, Japan, and Korea, as well as a script developed for use with Cherokee in the United States.

4.1   Chinese Writing

The Chinese system of writing developed out of pictograms that eventually came to represent morphemes (most of which are also words). The oldest inscriptions are the oracle texts, written on animal bones and tortoise shells and dating back to about 1200 B.C. These include many recognizable images, such as ☉ 'sun' and ☽ 'moon'.

A change toward more symbolic signs began at an early date as more abstract notions were symbolized, such as ‿ 'above' and ⌒ 'below'. Symbols were also combined to extend meanings metaphorically. For example, the sign for 'to tend (animals)' 牧 is composed of 牛 'cow' and 攴 'hand and whip'. 'To follow' 从 is two men in sequence, and so on. In time, the characters became more abstract. Figure 14.15 shows the historical development of the symbol for 'dog'.

Figure 14.15   Historical development of the Chinese symbol for 'dog'. Data from: Jerry Norman, *Chinese* (Cambridge, UK: Cambridge University Press, 1988), 59. Reprinted with the permission of Cambridge University Press.

Calligraphy is an ancient and respected art in China, and Chinese writing exists in a number of styles. The script is usually written from left to right along a horizontal axis, although newspapers and older texts are written in vertical columns that are read downwards, beginning on the right side of the page. The units of contemporary Chinese writing are called **characters**. Many monosyllabic words are presented in true logographic fashion by a character consisting of a single symbol. For example, the Mandarin words [ʃǒu] 'hand' and [mǎ] 'horse' are written 手 and 馬, respectively. However, the overwhelming majority of characters (one estimate is 99 percent) consist of two parts.

The main component of a two-part character, called the **phonetic determinative**, provides information about the pronunciation of the corresponding morpheme. Although about four thousand different phonetic determinatives are used in Chinese writing, they represent pronunciation very imperfectly. Tone, which is contrastive in the Chinese family of languages, is not represented at all, and many phonetic determinatives indicate only part of the morpheme's pronunciation. For instance, the determinative in column C of Table 14.1 is used for a wide variety of words ending in *ao* without regard for tone or for whether the initial consonant is *j*, *n*, *r*, or some other element. Furthermore, because of sound changes over the last centuries, about one-third of all phonetic determinatives provide little or no useful information about current pronunciation. Finally, because Chinese languages have many homophones, even the most informative phonetic determinatives can be used for many different words.

Chinese characters also include a semantic component, called the **radical** or key, which provides clues about the morpheme's meaning. There are about two hundred different radicals in contemporary Chinese writing. Table 14.1 provides examples of some of the characters that can be formed by combining phonetic determinatives with radicals. Notice that only the phonetic determinative in column A indicates the precise pronunciation (ignoring tone) of the four characters in which it appears. The other determinatives supply helpful, but incomplete, phonetic information.

Table 14.1 Some Chinese characters

	Semantic radical	*Phonetic determinatives as pronounced in Mandarin*			
		A 敖 (*áo*)	*B* 參 (*cān*)	*C* 堯 (*yāo*)	*D* 甫 (*fǔ*)
1	亻 'person'	傲 (*ào*: 'proud')	傪 (*cān*: 'good')	僥 (*jiǎo*: 'lucky')	俌 (*fǔ*: 'help')
2	扌 'hand'	擨 (*ào*: 'shake')	摻 (*shán*: 'seize')	撓 (*náo*: 'scratch')	捕 (*bǔ*: 'catch')
3	木 'wood'	檄 (*āo*: 'barge')	椮 (*shēn*: 'beam')	橈 (*náo*: 'oar')	楠 (*fú*: 'trellis')
4	氵 'water'	漱 (*ào*: 'stream')	渗 (*shèn*: 'leak')	澆 (*jiāo*: 'sprinkle')	浦 (*pǔ*: 'creek')

Data from: John DeFrancis, *Visible Speech: The Diverse Oneness of Writing Systems* (Honolulu: University of Hawaii Press, 1989), 107. © 1989 John DeFrancis. Reprinted with permission of the University of Hawaii Press.

The usefulness of the information supplied by the radicals also varies. The characters in row 1 represent morphemes whose meaning is at best indirectly associated with that of the radical ('person'), but the radicals in rows 2, 3, and 4 are much more informative: the characters in row 2 all denote actions involving the hand, while those in row 3 refer to things made of wood and those in row 4 all have something to do with liquids.

Although neither phonetic determinatives alone nor semantic radicals alone suffice to identify the morphemes that they are used to represent, they are more than adequate when used in conjunction with each other. Despite these complexities—one authority has described the system as "outsized, haphazard, inefficient, and only partially reliable"—Chinese writing provides its users with an effective way to represent the words and morphemes of their language. Moreover, the lack of efficiency is offset by the fact that the same literary script can be understood by speakers of different Chinese languages. Although a speaker of Mandarin and a speaker of Cantonese may pronounce the word for 'fire' differently—/xwǒ/ and /fɔ́/, respectively—both can read it from the same character (火), since Chinese writing does not represent a word's phonemic segments individually.

In the mid-twentieth century, the government of the People's Republic of China introduced simplified characters (some newly invented) in an attempt to promote literacy. At the same time, a system of writing Mandarin with a modified Latin alphabet, called **pinyin**, was also introduced. Pinyin is used as a subsidiary system for writing such things as street signs, addresses, and brand names as well as for teaching children how to pronounce characters. It is also sometimes used to input Chinese into an electronic device (computer, cell phone, etc.), which then automatically converts it into characters.

4.2   Japanese Writing

The writing system of modern Japanese is arguably the most complicated in the world. Its use requires knowledge of three distinct scripts, including a pair of syllabaries—**hiragana** and **katakana**—which were created by modifying Chinese characters. Although Japanese can be written exclusively with either syllabary, normal writing involves the use of Chinese characters (called **kanji** in Japanese) in addition to hiragana and katakana. Kanji symbols are typically used to represent all or part of a word's root while affixes are represented by hiragana symbols. The phrase *in the man's car*, for example, can be written as in Figure 14.16, with the roots 'man' and 'car' represented by kanji and affixes such as *no* (marking possession) and *de* (marking location) written in hiragana.

Figure 14.16   The Japanese phrase meaning 'in the man's car' written in a mixture of kanji and hiragana

The katakana syllabary, whose symbols are less rounded than their hiragana counterparts (see Figure 14.17), is used to write onomatopoeic words as well as words borrowed into Japanese from other languages.

Hiragana chart

COLUMN / LINE	A	I	U	E	O
SINGLE VOWEL	あ A	い I	う U	え E	お O
K	か KA	き KI	く KU	け KE	こ KO
S	さ SA	し SHI	す SU	せ SE	そ SO
T	た TA	ち CHI	つ TSU	て TE	と TO
N	な NA	に NI	ぬ NU	ね NE	の NO
H	は HA	ひ HI	ふ FU	へ HE	ほ HO
M	ま MA	み MI	む MU	め ME	も MO
Y	や YA		ゆ YU		よ YO
R	ら RA	り RI	る RU	れ RE	ろ RO
W	わ WA				を O
N (in a coda)	ん N				

Katakana chart

COLUMN / LINE	A	I	U	E	O
SINGLE VOWEL	ア A	イ I	ウ U	エ E	オ O
K	カ KA	キ KI	ク KU	ケ KE	コ KO
S	サ SA	シ SHI	ス SU	セ SE	ソ SO
T	タ TA	チ CHI	ツ TSU	テ TE	ト TO
N	ナ NA	ニ NI	ヌ NU	ネ NE	ノ NO
H	ハ HA	ヒ HI	フ FU	ヘ HE	ホ HO
M	マ MA	ミ MI	ム MU	メ ME	モ MO
Y	ヤ YA		ユ YU		ヨ YO
R	ラ RA	リ RI	ル RU	レ RE	ロ RO
W	ワ WA				ヲ O
N (in a coda)	ン N				

Figure 14.17 Hiragana and katakana syllabaries and their phonetic values. (The conventions for representing voicing, vowel length, and gemination are not indicated here.) Adapted from Len Walsh, *Read Japanese Today* (North Clarendon, VT: Tuttle, 2009). Reprinted with permission from Tuttle Publishing, www.tuttlepublishing.com.

Finally, it should be noted that the Roman alphabet, which the Japanese call *romaji*, is also making inroads. It is not unusual to see all four writing systems used together, especially in advertising.

Learning to read Japanese is a formidable task, in part because of the way the various scripts are intermingled and in part because of complexities in the use of kanji symbols, which can have more than one pronunciation depending on whether they are used to represent a word of Chinese or Japanese origin. For example, Japanese has two morphemes with the meaning 'mountain'—/san/, which is of Chinese origin, and the native Japanese /jama/. Both are written with the kanji character 山.

4.3 Korean Writing

Korean was once written with Chinese characters, which had been introduced in the first centuries A.D. However, Korean suffixes could not be easily represented by Chinese writing. Various devices were used to alleviate this problem, but inadequacies persisted. Finally, King Sejong (1419–52) created an alphabetic script called **hangul**. After some modifications over the centuries, it became the standard Korean writing system. An especially interesting feature of hangul is that symbols are grouped together into syllable-sized clusters (see Figure 14.18).

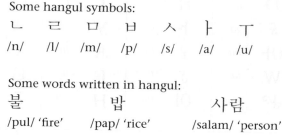

Figure 14.18 Some hangul symbols

Another intriguing feature of hangul is that it typically provides a single spelling for each morpheme, regardless of contextually induced variations in its pronunciation. For instance, the word for 'rice' has the same spelling (see above), regardless of whether it is pronounced /pap/ (the basic pronunciation) or /pam/, as happens in front of a nasal consonant (e.g., /pam man/ 'rice only').

Like Japanese, Korean also makes use of Chinese characters (called **hanja**), although in a more restricted way. Approximately half the vocabulary of contemporary Korean is of Chinese origin, and many words of this type are written with the help of Chinese characters in newspapers and in scientific articles. However, this practice has been reduced somewhat in recent years in South Korea, and it has been eliminated entirely in North Korea.

The relationship between symbol and phoneme in English orthography was significantly disturbed in the Middle English period as the phonological pattern of the language began to change. To see an example of this, we need only consider the Great Vowel Shift, which dramatically altered the pronunciation of long vowels—converting /i:/ into /aj/, /e:/ into /i/, /a:/ into /e/, and so on. Because Old English orthography used the same symbol for long and short vowels, complications arose when the pronunciation of the long vowels changed. Thus, the letter *i*, which had formerly been used only to represent the phonetically similar /i:/ and /i/, ended up representing the very dissimilar /aj/ (the descendant of /i:/) and /ɪ/ (the descendant of /i/). The end result can be seen in the spelling of *hide* and *hid*, *write* and *written*, *ride* and *ridden*, *wide* and *width*, and many other words.

Additional complications arose following the invasion of England by French-speaking Normans in the eleventh century. The use of English in official documents declined and regional orthographies developed in the absence of a national standard. To make matters worse, scribes who were trained primarily to write French and Latin made a number of questionable changes to English spelling. Among those that have survived are the use of *ch* rather than *c* for /tʃ/ (*cheese*, *chin*, etc.), *th* rather than þ (thorn) and ð (eth) for /θ/ and /ð/ (*thin*, *this*), and *c* rather than *s* for /s/ (*grace*, *ice*, *mice*).

Toward the end of the fifteenth century, yet another trend developed—the practice of spelling words in a manner that reflected their etymological origin. Enduring examples of this influence are found in the spelling of the words *debt*, *doubt*, *receipt*, and *salmon* (formerly spelled *dette*, *doute*, *receite*, and *samon*), all of which were given a silent consonant to make them look more like the Latin words from which they descended.

LANGUAGE MATTERS   How Do You Spell 'Shakespeare'?

During William Shakespeare's time (1564–1616), English spelling was still in a state of flux, which may explain why there were so many spellings for his name—Shakespeare, Shakespere, Shakespear, Shakspear, among others. Shakespeare himself wrote his name in different ways and wavered on the spelling of many words in his plays—he used three different spellings for *more*, three for *-ness*, and five for *sheriff*, to mention a few examples.

By the 1500s, English orthography had become increasingly irregular and idiosyncratic, with many different spellings in use for the same word. The word *pity*, for example, could be spelled *pity*, *pyty*, *pitie*, *pytie*, *pittie*, and *pyttye*. As printing presses came into greater use and books became more widely available, the need to reform and regularize English orthography became apparent. In the late 1500s and early 1600s, a number of individuals (most notably Richard Mulcaster and Edmond Coote) formulated and published spelling rules, which were gradually adopted by printers and other literate speakers of English. While these rules were far from perfect, they at least had the effect of stabilizing English spelling. By the 1700s, English orthography was more or less fixed.

The vast majority of the spelling conventions introduced during this period are still in use today. One of the most famous, proposed by Mulcaster in 1582, involves the use of 'silent' *e* at the end of words to indicate a preceding long (tense) vowel, as in *late* and *bone*. Even here, though, there are complications and exceptions, as can be seen in the modern spelling of *have*, *done*, and *come*, which contain lax vowels. In these cases, the *e* represents a word-final /ə/ that has since been lost.

5.2   Obstacles to Reform

Over the years, there have been numerous proposals for the reform of English orthography, including ones put forward by Benjamin Franklin, George Bernard Shaw, and Noah Webster. However, far-reaching reforms are unlikely for a variety of reasons. For one thing, they would require a long and difficult period of transition. As the following tongue-in-cheek suggestion (variously attributed to Mark Twain, M. J. Shields, and W. K. Lessing) shows, reform would not be painless even if it took place over a period of many years.

> For example, in Year 1 that useless letter 'c' would be dropped to be replased either by 'k' or 's', and likewise 'x' would no longer be part of the alphabet. The only kase in which 'c' would be retained would be the 'ch' formation, which will be dealt with later. Year 2 might reform 'w' spelling, so that 'which' and 'one' would take the same konsonant, wile Year 3 might well abolish 'y' replasing it with 'i' and Iear 4 might fiks the 'g–j' anomali wonse and for all.
>
> Jenerally, then, the improvement would kontinue iear bai iear with Iear 5 doing awai with useless double konsonants, and Iears 6–12 or so modifaiing vowlz and the rimeining voist and unvoist konsonants. Bai Iear 15 or sou, it wud fainali be posibl tu meik ius ov thi ridandant leterz 'c', 'y' and 'x'—bai now jast a memori in the maindz of ould doderers—tu replais 'ch', 'sh' and 'th' rispektivli.
>
> Fainali, xen, after sam 20 iers ov orxogrephkl riform, we wud hev a lojikl, kohirnt speling in ius xrewawt xe Ingliy spiking werld . . .

People who knew only the reformed spelling system would have difficulty reading books written in traditional orthography. Those who wished to read any of the millions of books or articles currently in print would therefore have to either learn the traditional spelling system or have the documents that interested them converted into the new orthography.

A second factor militating against serious orthographic reform has to do with the dialectal variation found within English. Because English is spoken in more parts of the world than any other language, it has many different dialects. Any attempt to establish an orthography based on a principle of one phoneme, one symbol would result in serious regional differences in spelling. For instance, speakers of Boston English would write *far* as *fa* since they do not pronounce syllable-final /ɪ/. Speakers of some dialects of Newfoundland English would write both *tin* and *thin* as *tin* and both *den* and *then* as *den* since they have no /t/-/θ/ or /d/-/ð/ distinction. Moreover, while Americans in western states would have identical spellings for *cot* and *caught* (since these words are homophones in their speech), speakers of English in many other parts of the United States and the world pronounce them differently and would therefore spell them differently as well.

Other Considerations

Even if considerations relating to practicality and dialectal variation did not rule out major reforms to our orthography, there might still be reasons for retaining at least some of the current spelling conventions.

One advantage of the contemporary system is that it often indicates derivational relationships among words. For instance, if the words *music* and *musician* or *sign* and *signature* were spelled phonetically, it would be difficult to perceive the relationship between them since the root is pronounced differently in each case.

1) music   [mjuzɪk]   musician   [mjuzɪʃ-n̩]
   sign   [sajn]   signature   [sɪgn-ɪtʃɨ]

As illustrated in Table 14.5, there are many other such cases where English orthography ignores differences in pronunciation so that a morpheme can have the same or nearly the same spelling in different words.

Table 14.5   Examples of a single English spelling for roots with different
                   pronunciations

electric – electri<u>c</u>ity	[k] and [s] represented as *c*
inser<u>t</u> – inser<u>t</u>ion	[t] and [ʃ] as *t*
righ<u>t</u> – righ<u>t</u>eous	[t] and [tʃ] as *t*
bom<u>b</u> – bom<u>b</u>ard	Ø and [b] as *b*
dam<u>n</u> – dam<u>n</u>ation	Ø and [n] as *n*
impre<u>ss</u> – impre<u>ss</u>ion	[s] and [ʃ] as *ss*
analo<u>g</u>y – analo<u>g</u>ous	[dʒ] and [g] as *g*
res<u>ig</u>n – res<u>ig</u>nation	[aj] and [ɪ] as *i*; Ø and [g] as *g*
ch<u>a</u>ste – ch<u>a</u>stity	[ej] and [æ] as *a*
pl<u>ea</u>se – pl<u>ea</u>sant	[i] and [ɛ] as *ea*

Examples such as these show that English orthography often seeks to provide a single spelling for the variants of a morpheme, even if this means ignoring alternations among phonemes. This is sometimes called a *deep orthography* or a *morphophonemic orthography*. Once this aim is taken into account, it is possible to see the usefulness of orthographic conventions that allow *c* to stand for both /k/ (*electric*) and /s/ (*electricity*), *t* to represent both /t/ (*insert*) or /ʃ/ (*insertion*), and so on.

Morphological considerations are reflected in English orthography in other ways as well. Consider in this regard the spelling of the following words.

2) mess   lapse
   crass   dense
   kiss   house
   floss   mouse

Although these words all end in the phoneme /s/, this segment is not represented as a simple *s*. Instead, the *s* is either doubled to *ss* (when preceded by a lax vowel, as in the first column) or followed by an *e* (in all other cases, as exemplified in the second column). This reflects a general rule of English orthography, which reserves word-final *s* mostly for inflectional suffixes (particularly, the plural and the third-person singular). Thus, a single word-final *s* is permitted in the word *laps* (the plural of *lap*) but not in *lapse*.

Another example of morphological influence is found in the rule that prohibits a final *ll* in polysyllabic words—*plentiful, excel, repel*, and so on. As the following examples show, this rule is systematically suspended in two morphological patterns: compounds (the first column) and derivations consisting of a prefix and its base (the second column).

3) baseball   unwell
   spoonbill   resell
   landfill   recall

Yet another morphologically constrained rule of English orthography usually converts postconsonantal *y* in a polysyllabic root to *i* in front of a suffix.

4) carry   carri-ed
   merry   merri-ly
   marry   marri-age
   candy   candi-es
   beauty   beauti-ful

The existence of conventions and practices such as these demonstrates that English orthography is much more than a system for phonemic transcription. Its intricacies can be understood only through the careful study of the history and structure of the linguistic system that it is used to represent.

6 Writing and Reading

The three types of writing described earlier in this chapter each represent different types of linguistic units—morphemes and words in the case of logographic systems, syllables in the case of syllabaries, and consonants and vowels in the case of alphabets. Because of these differences, each orthography places different demands on readers. We know that different parts of the brain are used for reading logographic writing systems compared to phonographic orthographies such as syllabaries and alphabets. Because phonological structure is largely irrelevant to logographic writing, people suffering from phonological deficits caused by damage to the brain typically do not lose the ability to write and read logograms. In contrast, the use of syllabaries and alphabets can be severely disrupted by this type of disorder. Indeed, there are reports of Japanese stroke patients who are unable to use hiragana or katakana (the Japanese syllabaries) but retain mastery of kanji (the logographic writing system).

LANGUAGE MATTERS   Do Spelling Irregularities Hurt Young Readers?

Perhaps. One study reports that children whose language has highly regular symbol-phoneme correspondences (e.g., Greek, Finnish, German, Spanish, and Italian) can read both words and nonwords at almost 100 percent accuracy by the middle of first grade. In contrast, children learning to read English have success rates around 34 percent, on average. Children whose language falls somewhere in the middle in terms of orthographic regularity (Danish, Portuguese, and French) show mean success rates of around 75 percent.

Information from: J. C. Ziegler and U. Goswami, "Becoming Literate in Different Languages: Similar Problems, Different Solutions," *Developmental Science* 9, 5 (2006): 429–453.

Further information about the relationship between language and writing systems comes from the study of the congenitally deaf. Because their hearing impairment undermines their access to the phonological units that alphabets represent, they often have significant difficulty learning to read orthographies of this type.

The type of linguistic unit represented by an orthography also has an effect on how children with normal hearing learn to read. Each system has its own advantages and disadvantages. Children learning Chinese characters have little difficulty understanding what each symbol represents, but it takes them many years to learn enough symbols to be able to write and read all the items in their vocabulary. (Knowledge of several thousand separate symbols is required just to read a newspaper.) Even educated people typically know only a few thousand characters and must use dictionaries for new or unfamiliar words.

This problem does not arise in syllabic and alphabetic orthographies. Because languages have far fewer syllable types and phonemes than morphemes or words, the entire inventory of symbols can be learned in a year or two and then used productively to write and read new words. This is the major advantage of sound-based orthographies over word-based writing systems.

There is reason to think that children find syllabaries easier to master than alphabets. Children learning syllabaries (such as Japanese hiragana) are reported to have fewer reading problems than children learning alphabetic orthographies. Of course, the difficulties associated with learning an alphabetic orthography can be compounded by irregularities in the system itself. This is at least part of the reason that children learning to read English are more likely to have problems than are children learning to read a language with a more regular system of spelling.

The advantage of syllabaries over alphabets for young readers apparently stems from the fact that children have less difficulty identifying syllables than phonemes. One study revealed that 46 percent of four-year-olds and 90 percent of six-year-olds can segment words into syllables. In contrast, virtually no four-year-olds and only about two-thirds of all six-year-olds can segment words into phoneme-sized units.

LANGUAGE MATTERS   Processing the Words

A common source of problems in reading, writing, and spelling is developmental dyslexia, a learning disability of neurological origin that may affect 10 to 15 percent of the population to some degree. Research suggests that dyslexics process certain types of information in different parts of the brain than do nondyslexics and that they have particular trouble discriminating among the sounds within words. Even a small processing problem can disrupt the relationship between symbols on the page and the corresponding words, creating an unrecognizable jumble of letters.

Hav ingdys lexiac anmake it hardtodo wellins chool.
Eaxly trexxmxnt xs impxrtant.

You can find out more about dyslexia from the International Dyslexia Association website.

Since learning to read involves an understanding of the type of unit represented by written symbols, it is not surprising that syllabaries are generally easier for young children to learn.

Of course, it must be remembered that syllabaries may have disadvantages of other sorts. While syllabic writing is feasible for languages such as Japanese that have a relatively small number of syllable types, it would be quite impractical in English, where there are dozens of different syllable structures. Ultimately, an orthography must be judged in terms of its success in representing language for the purpose of reading and writing. There is no doubt that an alphabetic orthography is superior to a syllabary for representing the phonological structure of English.

Summing Up

The development of writing has been one of humanity's greatest intellectual achievements, built on the relationship between graphic symbols and spoken language. The graphic representation of language has included **pictograms**, **logograms**, **syllabic writing**, and **alphabetic writing**.

Many of the large number of writing systems in use today owe their origin directly or indirectly to the Semitic writing systems of the eastern Mediterranean, where writing first emerged in Mesopotamia and Egypt. As the idea of writing spread, new forms of the signs were independently invented, and sound-symbol correspondences were altered to accommodate individual languages. Some two thousand years after the first ancient Near Eastern writing systems appeared, the Phoenician alphabet was invented, later to be adopted and adapted by the Greeks. The Greek alphabet in turn was adapted by the Romans.

In Asia, Chinese **characters**, which are logograms, are used in the writing systems of Japan and Korea. The Japanese system also uses a **syllabary**, while the Korean writing system is based on an alphabet.

Syllabaries are particularly suited to the phonological structure of languages such as Japanese and Cherokee, and are actually easier to learn to read than alphabetic writing. English **orthography** has a number of irregularities, some of which can be traced to historical developments. However, there are a number of reasons making reform undesirable.

Key Terms

Terms concerning types of writing

alphabetic writing
logograms
logographic (writing)
orthography

phonographic (writing)
syllabary
syllabic writing

Terms related to the history of writing

abjads
abugidas
acrophonic principle
boustrophedon
cuneiform

determinatives
hieroglyphs
pictograms
prewriting
rebus principle

Terms related to non-European writing systems

characters
hangul
hanja
hiragana
kanji

katakana
phonetic determinative
pinyin
radical

Recommended Reading

Collier, Mark, and Bill Manley. 2003. *How to Read Egyptian Hieroglyphs*. Rev ed. Berkeley: University of California Press.

Daniels, Peter T., and William Bright. 1996. *The World's Writing Systems*. Oxford, UK: Oxford University Press.

DeFrancis, John. 1989. *Visible Speech: The Diverse Oneness of Writing Systems*. Honolulu: University of Hawaii Press.

Gelb, I. 1952. *A Study of Writing*. Chicago: University of Chicago Press.

Jensen, Hans. 1970. *Sign, Symbol and Script: An Account of Man's Efforts to Write*. 3rd ed. Translated by George Unwin. London: George Allen and Unwin.

Rogers, Henry. 2005. *Writing Systems: A Linguistic Approach.* Malden, MA: Blackwell.

Sampson, Geoffrey. 2015. *Writing Systems.* 2nd ed. Sheffield: Equinox.

Senner, Wayne M., ed. 1989. *The Origins of Writing.* Lincoln: University of Nebraska Press.

Treiman, Rebecca, and Brett Kessler. 2014. *How Children Learn to Write Words.* New York: Oxford University Press.

Upward, Christopher, and George Davidson. 2011. *The History of English Spelling.* Malden, MA: Blackwell.

Exercises

1. Suppose you are the user of a pictographic writing system that can already represent concrete objects in a satisfactory way. Using the pictographic symbols of your system, propose ideographic extensions of these symbols to represent the following meanings.

   a) hunt   f) cook
   b) cold   g) tired
   c) fast   h) wet
   d) white   i) angry
   e) strength   j) weakness

2. Construct a syllabary for English that can be used to spell the following words. What problems do you encounter?

foe	law	shoe
slaw	slow	slowly
lee	day	daily
sue	pull	shop
ship	loop	food
lock	shock	unlock
locked	shocked	pulled
shops	locker	shod
float	splint	schlock

3. How does English orthography capture the morphophonemic alternations in the following words? Begin your analysis with a phonemic transcription of the forms. (See Section 5.2.)

a) hymn	hymnal	
b) part	partial	
c) recite	recitation	
d) reduce	reduction	
e) design	designation	
f) critical	criticize	criticism
g) analog	analogous	analogy

4. After discussing the forms in exercise 3, consider the following forms. Does the spelling system treat all cases of allomorphic variation the same way?
   a) invade   invasion
   b) concede   concession
   c) assume   assumption
   d) profound   profundity

5. Briefly outline the advantages and disadvantages of the three major types of writing that have evolved throughout history.

 **LaunchPad Solo** | For more helpful content and quizzes, go to the LaunchPad Solo
macmillan learning | for *Contemporary Linguistics* at **launchpadworks.com**.

Cerebrovascular accident   *See* **Stroke**.

Cerebrum   The wrinkled gray outer part of the human brain where higher intellectual functions take place.

Change from above   A change that begins in the speech of the members of the upper classes and spreads to the lower social classes.

Characters   The units of the contemporary Chinese writing system, many of which consist of two parts—a **phonetic determinative** and a **radical**.

Class 1 affixes   A group of affixes that (in English) often trigger changes in the consonant or vowel segments of the base and may affect the assignment of stress.

Class 2 affixes   A group of affixes that tend to be phonologically neutral in English, having no effect on the segmental makeup of the base or on stress assignment.

Class (sound)   A group of sounds that shares certain phonetic properties (e.g., all voiced sounds).

Classificatory verbs   In Athabaskan languages of North America, verb stems that are matched with noun classes on the basis of the type of movement or handling involved in the verb meaning.

Classifier constructions   In sign languages, the combination of hand shapes for different types of nouns with different manners of movement and location in space. Similar to **classificatory verbs** in Athabaskan languages.

Clear *l*   An *l* sound made with the tongue tip touching the alveolar ridge and no secondary places of articulation.

Clipping   A word-formation process that shortens a polysyllabic word by deleting one or more syllables (e.g., *prof* from *professor*).

Clitic   A word that is unable to stand alone as an independent form for phonological reasons.

Cliticization   The process by which a **clitic** is attached to a word.

Closed syllable   A syllable with a coda (e.g., both syllables in *camping*).

Closing   A discourse unit conventionally used to end a conversation.

Coarticulation   An articulation in which phonemes overlap to a certain extent.

Coda (Co)   The elements that follow the nucleus in the same syllable (e.g., [ɹf] in *surf*).

Code-switching   The systematic alternation between language systems in discourse.

Cognates   Words of different languages that have descended from a common source, as shown by systematic phonetic correspondences (e.g., English *father* and German *Vater*).

Cognitive development   The emergence of the various mental abilities (such as language) that make up the human intellect.

Cohort   In a psycholinguistic model of spoken-word recognition, a set of possible words. (*See also* **Cohort model**.)

Cohort model   A model of spoken-word recognition according to which word recognition proceeds by isolating a target word from a set of words that share initial segments.

Coinage   *See* **Word manufacture**.

Communicative competence   A speaker's underlying knowledge of the linguistic and social rules or principles for language production and comprehension in particular speech situations.

Community of practice   A group of individuals who come together for a shared purpose and hence develop shared language practices.

Comparative method   In historical linguistics, the reconstruction of properties of a parent language through systematic comparison of its descendant languages.

Comparative reconstruction   The reconstruction of properties of a parent language through comparison of its descendant languages.

Competence   The mental system that underlies a person's ability to speak and understand a given language; distinguished from **performance**.

Complement   A syntactic constituent that provides information about entities and locations implied by the meaning of the **head**.

Complementary distribution   The distribution of allophones in their respective phonetic environments such that one never appears in the same phonetic context as the other (e.g., the distribution of long and short vowels in English).

Complement clause   A sentence-like construction that is embedded within a larger structure (e.g., *that his car had been totaled* in *Jerry told Mary that his car had been totaled*).

Complementizer (C)   A **functional category** that takes a TP complement, forming a CP (complementizer phrase) (e.g., *whether* in *I wonder whether Lorna has left*).

Complex word   A word that contains two or more morphemes (e.g., *theorize, unemployment*).

Componential analysis   The representation of a word's **intension** in terms of smaller semantic components called features.

Compound word   A word made up of two or more words (e.g., *greenhouse, pickpocket*).

Compounding   Creating a new word by combining two or more existing words (e.g., *fire + engine*).

Computational linguistics   The area of common interest between linguistics and computer science.

Computerized Axial Tomography   A technique for observing the living brain that uses a narrow beam of X-rays to create brain images that take the form of a series of brain slices (also called **CT scanning**).

Concatenative (morphology)   A term used for the morphological process that builds word structure by assembling morphemes in an additive, linear fashion.

Concord   A kind of agreement in which determiners and adjectives agree with their noun (e.g., in number or case).

Concordance   An index of words showing every occurrence of each word in its context.

Conflation pattern   A class of meanings created by combining semantic elements such as manner and motion or direction and motion.

Conjugation   The set of inflected forms associated with a verb (also called a verbal paradigm).

Conjunction (Con)   A **functional category** that joins two or more categories of the same type, forming a coordinate structure (e.g., *and* in *a man and his dog*).

Connectionist model   A psycholinguistic theory built around the claim that the mind can be best modeled by reference to complex associations of simple units that approximate neurons.

Connotation   The set of associations that a word's use can evoke (e.g., in Wisconsin, *winter* evokes ice, snow, bare trees, etc.). (*See also* **Denotation**.)

Consonant deletion   A phonetic process that deletes a consonant (e.g., the deletion of [θ] in *fifths*).

Consonant weakening   A lessening in the time or degree of a consonant's closure.

Consonantal   A major class feature that characterizes sounds produced with a major obstruction in the vocal tract.

Consonantal strength   Increasing time or degree of a consonant's closure.

Consonants   Sounds that are produced with a narrow or complete closure in the vocal tract.

Constituent   One or more words that make up a syntactic unit (e.g., *the apple* in *the apple fell onto the floor*). (*See also* **Coordination test, Substitution test**, and **Movement test**.)

Constraints   Conditions that govern the form of a linguistic element (e.g., [ɹ] is deleted after a vowel).

Constricted glottis (CG)   A laryngeal feature that characterizes sounds made with the glottis closed (in English, only [ʔ]).

Consultants   Native speakers of a language or language variety who provide data to a linguist (also called **informants**).

Continuant   A manner feature that characterizes sounds made with free or nearly free airflow through the oral cavity: vowels, fricatives, glides, and liquids.

Continuants   Sounds that are produced with a continuous airflow through the mouth.

Contour tones   Tones that change pitch on a single syllable.

Contradiction   A relationship between sentences wherein the truth of one sentence requires the falsity of another sentence (e.g., *Raymond is married* contradicts *Raymond is a bachelor*).

Contralateral   The control of the right side of the body by the left side of the brain and vice versa.

Contrast   Segments are said to contrast when their presence alone may distinguish forms with different meanings from each other (e.g., [s] and [z] in the words *sip* and *zip*).

Conversation analysis   *See* **Ethnomethodology**.

Conversational closing   *See* **Closing**.

Conversational implicature   Information that is understood through inference but is not actually said.

Conversational maxims   *See* **Maxims**.

Conversational opening   *See* **Opening**.

Conversion   A word-formation process that assigns an already existing word to a new syntactic category (also called **zero derivation**) (e.g., *nurse* [V] from *nurse* [N]).

Cooperative Principle   The general overarching guideline thought to underlie conversational interactions: Make your contribution appropriate to the conversation.

Coordinate structure   A phrase that is formed by joining two (or more) categories of the same type with a conjunction such as *and* or *or* (e.g., *those men and that woman*).

Coordination   The process of grouping together two or more categories of the same type with the help of a conjunction (e.g., *Mary and the white horse*).

Coordination schema   A blueprint for conjoining two categories of the same type with a **conjunction** (e.g., [extremely poor]$_{AP}$ but [very honest]$_{AP}$).

Coordination test   A test used to determine if a group of words is a **constituent** by joining it to another group of words with a conjunction such as *and* or *or*.

CORONAL   A place feature that characterizes sounds made with the tongue tip or blade raised (e.g., [t, d, s, θ]).

Corpus   A collection of texts that provides a database (e.g., for a computer grammar).

Corpus analysis   A technique for building lexicons by means of automated analysis of a body of texts.

Corpus callosum   The bundle of nerve fibers that serves as the main connection between the cerebral hemispheres, allowing the two hemispheres to communicate with one another.

Covert prestige   Prestige that is attached to nonstandard linguistic forms (e.g., because they are associated with physical labor and masculinity).

Creaky voice   A type of phonation in which vocal folds are compressed and vibrate slowly at one end during speech (also called **Vocal fry**).

Creativity   The characteristic of human language that allows novelty and innovation in response to new thoughts, experiences, and situations.

Creole   A language that originated as a **pidgin** and has become established as a first language in a speech community.

Creole continuum   The range of creole forms, extending from the variety that shows the least influence from the standard language from which the creole arose to the variety that shows the most influence.

Cricoid cartilage   The ring-shaped cartilage in the larynx on which the thyroid cartilage rests.

Critical period   A particular time frame during which children have to be exposed to language if the acquisition process is to be successful.

Critical Period Hypothesis   The hypothesis that achievement of nativelike proficiency in a second language depends on age of acquisition and is rarely attainable unless the learner begins second language acquisition during the **critical period**.

Cross-sectional (research)   Research that investigates and compares subjects selected from different developmental stages.

CT scanning   *See* **Computerized Axial Tomography**.

Cuneiform   Writing invented in the fourth millennium B.C. in Mesopotamia and produced by pressing a wedge-shaped stylus into soft clay tablets.

Dark *l* *See* **Velarized *l*.**

Dative The **case** form characteristically used to mark a recipient.

Deaffrication A type of segmental simplification that turns affricates into fricatives by eliminating the stop portion of the affricate (e.g., [dʒ] becoming [ʒ]).

Declension *See* **Nominal paradigm**.

Deep dyslexia A type of **acquired dyslexia** in which the patient produces a word that is semantically related to the word he or she is asked to read (e.g., producing *father* when asked to read *mother*).

Deep structure The structure generated by the phrase structure rules in accordance with the subcategorization properties of the heads.

Degemination The weakening of a **geminate** consonant (double consonant) to a nongeminate consonant (e.g., [tt] becoming [t]).

Degree word (Deg) A **functional category** that serves as the specifier of a preposition or an adjective (e.g., *quite* in *quite tired*, *very* in *very near the house*).

Deictics Forms whose use and interpretation depend on the location of the speaker and/or addressee within a particular setting (e.g., *this/that, here/there*).

Delayed release (DR) A manner feature that refers to the release of the stop in affricate consonants.

Deletion A process that removes a segment from certain phonetic contexts (e.g., the pronunciation of *fifths* as [fɪfs]).

Denasalization A common substitution process in child language acquisition that involves the replacement of a nasal stop by a nonnasal counterpart (e.g., *come* is pronounced [kʌb]).

Denotation Entities that a word or expression refers to (also called its **referents** or **extension**).

Dense social networks **Social networks** in which almost everyone in the network knows everyone else in the network.

Dentals Sounds made with the tongue placed against or near the teeth.

Department store study A study by William Labov investigating the correlation between pronunciation of *r* after a vowel and social class in New York City: workers in higher-class department stores in New York pronounced the *r* in the words *fourth floor* more often than workers in lower-class department stores.

Dependent variable In an experiment, the behavior or event that is measured.

Derivation (1) In morphology, a word-formation process by which a new word is built from a stem—usually through the addition of an affix—that changes the word class and/or basic meaning of the word. (2) The set of steps or rule applications that results in the formation of a sentence in syntax or of a phonetic representation from an underlying form in phonology.

Derived (phonology) Resulting from the application of phonological rules to underlying representations.

Descriptive (grammar) A grammar that seeks to describe human linguistic ability and knowledge, not to prescribe one system in preference to another. (*See also* **Prescriptive [grammar]**.)

Determinative A symbol used in non-alphabetic writing systems to assist the reader in knowing the intended meaning or pronunciation of a word.

Determiner (Det) A **functional category** that serves as the specifier of a noun (e.g., *a, the, these*).

Deterministic parsers Sentence processors that pursue no more than one analysis at a time.

Devanagari script Writing system that developed in India and was used for Sanskrit.

Developmental bilingual education An educational program for language minority students usually lasting throughout elementary school in which language proficiency and literacy in both the minority language and the majority language are promoted (also called **maintenance bilingual education**).

Developmental sequences The stages of linguistic development that are relatively invariant across language learners.

Devoicing   Voicing assimilation in which a sound becomes voiceless because of a nearby voiceless sound (e.g., the *l* in *place* is devoiced because of the voiceless stop preceding it).

Diacritics   Marks added to a phonetic symbol to alter its value in some way (e.g., a circle under a symbol to indicate voicelessness).

Dialect   A regional or social variety of a language characterized by its own phonological, syntactic, or lexical properties.

Dialect leveling   In a region with many dialects, the process by which certain dialectal features are lost and a more homogeneous dialect emerges.

Dialectology   A branch of linguistics concerned with the analysis and description of regional varieties of a language.

Diaphragm   The large sheet of muscle that separates the chest cavity from the abdomen and helps maintain the air pressure necessary for speech production.

Diary study   A type of naturalistic investigation in which a researcher (often a parent) keeps daily notes on a child's linguistic progress.

Dichotic listening studies   Research based on an experimental technique in which the subject listens to different sounds in each ear.

Differences approach   The view that male-female communication patterns reflect cultural differences in the ways men and women have been socialized and their expectations and norms of communication.

Diglossia   The relationship between multiple varieties spoken by one speech community but with sharply distinct domains of use.

Diphthongization   A process in which a monophthong becomes a diphthong (e.g., [i:] became [aj] during the Great English Vowel Shift).

Diphthongs   Vowels that show a noticeable change in quality within a single syllable (e.g., the vowel sounds in *house* and *ride*).

Direct negative evidence   Language instruction involving correction or focus on form.

Direct object   The NP **complement** of a verb (e.g., *a fish* in *Caleb caught a fish*).

Discourse   A set of utterances that constitute a speech event.

Discourse analysis   The field that deals with the organization of texts, including ways in which parts of texts are connected and the devices used for achieving textual structure.

Discourse markers   Expressions such as *on the other hand* and *therefore* that show the relationship of ideas within a text.

Discrete variable   A variable (such as *going to* versus *will* for the future) that can be realized as either one form or the other with no possible in-between form.

Dissimilation   A process whereby one segment becomes less like another segment in its environment (e.g., *anma* 'soul' in a form of Latin became *alma* in Spanish).

Distinctive feature   A feature that serves to distinguish contrastive forms (e.g., the feature [voice] is distinctive in English because it underlies the contrast between /p/ and /b/, /t/ and /d/, etc.).

Distribution   The set of elements with which an item can co-occur.

***Do* insertion**   The syntactic rule that places *do* into an empty T position, making **inversion** possible in English questions.

Dominance approach   The view that male-female communication patterns reflect male dominance in the society at large.

DORSAL   A place feature that represents sounds produced when the body of the tongue is involved (e.g., vowels and [k, g]).

Dorsum (of the tongue)   The body and back of the tongue.

Double-blind test   A test in which a subject's responses are interpreted independently by someone other than the administrator of the test.

Downdrift   The maintenance of a distinction among the pitch registers of an utterance even as the overall pitch of the utterance falls.

D-structure   *See* **Deep structure**.

Dual   The pronominal form in some languages that designates two and only two.

Dual-language programs   *See* **Two-way immersion (TWI) programs**.

Dysprosody   The lack of sentence intonation, a common characteristic of the speech of Broca's aphasics.

Ejectives   Stops or affricates that are made with simultaneous closure of the glottis and constriction of the throat, producing a distinctive "popping" sound.

Enclitic   A **clitic** that attaches to the end of a word.

Endangered language   Language that is falling out of use and is likely to become extinct.

Endocentric compound   A compound word in which one member identifies the general class to which the meaning of the entire word belongs (e.g., *dog food* is a type of food in English). (*See also* **Exocentric compound**.)

English as lingua franca (ELF)   English used as an international language of communication among people who are not native speakers of English.

English immersion   Teaching academic courses to nonnative speakers of English in the United States through the medium of English-only.

English learners (ELs)   Nonnative speakers of English, particularly used for those in U.S. schools (previously known as Limited English Proficient [LEP] students).

Enregistered   A dialect is said to be enregistered when particular linguistic features have become symbolic of idealized cultural values associated with the speakers of the dialect.

Entailment   A relation between sentences in which the truth of one sentence necessarily implies the truth of another (e.g., *Gary is Bernice's husband* entails the sentence *Bernice is married*).

Environment   The phonetic context in which a sound occurs.

Epenthesis   A process that inserts a segment into a particular environment (e.g., the insertion of a schwa in the pronunciation of *athlete* as [æθəlɪt]).

Eponyms   Words created from names (e.g., *quixotic* from *Don Quixote*).

Ergative   The case associated with the subject of a **transitive verb** (but not that of an **intransitive verb**).

Ergative-absolutive pattern   Sentence pattern in which **ergative** case is assigned to the **agent** of a **transitive verb**, but **absolutive** case is assigned to the subject of an **intransitive verb** or the object of a transitive verb.

Ethnic slurs   Socially stigmatized names for ethnic groups.

Ethnography of communication   A type of discourse analysis that concentrates on how language is used to achieve communicative goals in particular social situations.

Ethnolect   A dialect spoken by a particular ethnic group.

Ethnomethodology   A type of discourse analysis that focuses on the structural relationship between utterances in conversations.

Ethnonyms   Socially preferred names for ethnic groups.

Event-related potentials (ERPs)   A measurement of electrical activity in the brain that is correlated with the presentation of particular stimulus events.

Evidentiality   A system of morphological contrasts indicating the type of evidence for the truth of a statement.

Evidentials   Morphological or syntactic elements (frequently **enclitic** morphemes) that indicate the speaker's source of information for the statement he or she is making.

Exclusive (pronoun)   A type of first-person plural pronoun whose referents do not include the addressee. (*See also* **Inclusive [pronoun]**.)

Exocentric compound   A compound whose meaning does not follow from the meaning of its parts (e.g., *redneck*, since its referent is not a type of neck).

Experimental paradigm   A method of investigation that involves a particular way of presenting stimuli and a particular way of measuring responses.

Experimental studies   Studies in child language in which researchers make use of specially designed tasks to elicit linguistic activity relevant to a particular phenomenon.

Extension   The set of entities to which a word or expression refers (also called its **denotation** or **referents**).

Feature (phonological)   The smallest unit of analysis of phonological structure, combinations of which make up segments (e.g., [nasal], [continuant]).

Feature hierarchy   A hierarchical representation of how features are related to each other.

Features (semantic)   The semantic components that make up a word's **intension**.

Field technique   A method of study that does not involve manipulation and control of factors in a laboratory, but rather involves observing phenomena as they occur.

Fissure   A relatively deep **sulcus** of the cerebral cortex.

Fixed stress   Stress whose position in a word is predictable.

Fixed stress languages   Languages in which the position of stress in words is predictable. (*See also* **Fixed stress**.)

Flap   A sound commonly identified with *r* and produced when the tongue tip strikes the alveolar ridge as it passes across it (e.g., in North American English, the medial consonant in *bitter* and *bidder*).

Flapping   A phonetic process in which an alveolar stop is pronounced as a voiced flap between vowels, the first of which is generally stressed (e.g., ['bʌtɹ̩] → ['bʌɾɹ̩]).

Fluency   Second language speech that is produced automatically and without noticeable hesitation.

Fluent aphasia   The **aphasia** that occurs due to damage to parts of the left cortex behind the central sulcus, resulting in fluent speech but great difficulty selecting, organizing, and monitoring language production (also called **sensory aphasia**).

Focus on form   In second language teaching, the practice of giving explicit instruction about the second language and overtly correcting errors.

Folk etymology   Reanalysis of a word that is based on an incorrect historical analysis

(e.g., *hamburger* being reanalyzed into two morphemes, *ham* and *burger*).

Formants   The main frequencies of a speech wave.

Fossilized   Characteristic of an **interlanguage** grammar that has reached a plateau (i.e., ceased to improve).

Free form   An element that can occur in isolation and/or whose position with respect to neighboring elements is not entirely fixed.

Free morpheme   A **morpheme** that can be a word by itself (e.g., *fear*).

Free stress   Stress whose position in a word is not predictable and must be learned on a case-by-case basis.

Free stress languages   Languages in which the position of stress in words is not predictable. (*See also* **Free stress**.)

Free variation   The free alternation of allophones and/or phonemes in a given environment (e.g., *sto*[pʔ], *sto*[p]; /ɛ/*conomics*, /i/*conomics*).

Frequency effect   The common experimental finding that words that occur more frequently in a language are processed more quickly and more accurately.

Frication   The weakening of a stop to a fricative (e.g., [d] becoming [ð]).

Fricatives   Consonants produced with a continuous airflow through the mouth, accompanied by a continuous audible noise (e.g., [f], [ʃ]).

Front   *See* **Front vowel**.

Front vowel   A vowel that is made with the tongue positioned in the front of the oral cavity (e.g., the vowel sounds in *seal* and *bat*).

Frontal lobe   The lobe of the brain that lies in front of the central sulcus and in which Broca's area is located.

Fronting   A common substitution process in child language acquisition that involves the moving forward of a sound's place of articulation (e.g., *cheese* pronounced as [tsiz]).

Full reduplication   A morphological process that duplicates the entire word (e.g., in Turkish, tʃabuk 'quickly'/tʃabuk tʃabuk 'very quickly').

Function words Words such as determiners and conjunctions that specify grammatical relations rather than carry semantic content.

Functional analysis An approach to syntactic analysis that attempts to understand syntactic phenomena in terms of their communicative function.

Functional category A word-level syntactic category whose members specify grammatical relations rather than carry semantic content (e.g., auxiliary verbs, conjunctions, determiners, and degree words) (also called **nonlexical category**).

Functional magnetic resonance imaging (fMRI) A brain imaging technique that yields information on areas of high brain activity during the performance of cognitive tasks.

Fusion A morphological change in which a word becomes an affix over time (e.g., English affixes such as *-hood*, *-dom*, and *-ly* used to be words).

Fusional languages Languages in which words typically consist of several morphemes, and the morphemes that are affixes often mark several grammatical categories simultaneously (e.g., Russian).

Fuzzy concepts Concepts that do not have clear-cut boundaries that distinguish them from other concepts (e.g., the concept POOR).

Garden path sentence A sentence that is difficult to process and interpret because its structure biases sentence parsing toward an incorrect analysis.

Geminates Double consonants (e.g., [tt]) that are articulated for a longer period of time than the corresponding single consonant (e.g., [t]).

Gender *See* **Noun class**.

Gender roles Roles or occupations that are traditionally associated with only one sex.

Genetic classification The categorization of languages according to the ancestor languages from which they developed.

Genetic relationships Relationships among languages that have descended from a common ancestor language. (*See also*

Genetic classification and **Genetically related languages**.)

Genetically related languages Languages that have descended from a common parent (e.g., German and Italian have both descended from Indo-European).

Genitive The **case** form characteristically used to mark a possessor.

Given information Knowledge that the speaker assumes is available to the addressee at the time of the utterance, either because it is shared by both or because it has already been introduced into the discourse (also called **old information**).

Glide strengthening The strengthening of a glide to an affricate (e.g., [j] becoming [dʒ]).

Glides Sounds that are produced with an articulation like that of a vowel, but move quickly to another articulation (e.g., [j], [w]).

Gliding A common substitution process in child language acquisition that involves the replacement of a liquid by a glide (e.g., *play* is pronounced [pwej]).

Global aphasia The most severe form of **nonfluent aphasia**, in which the patient is completely mute.

Glottalization A consonant that is made with simultaneous closure of the glottis and constriction of the throat. Glottalized stops and affricates (**ejectives**) are the most common glottalized consonants.

Glottals Sounds produced by using the vocal folds as the primary articulators (e.g., [h], [ʔ]).

Glottis The space between the **vocal folds**.

Goal A **thematic role** that describes the end point for a movement (e.g., *Mary* in *Terry gave the skis to Mary*).

Graded (membership) A concept whose members display varying degrees of the characteristics that are considered typical of the concept.

Gradient variable A variable that can be realized with a range of subtle options (e.g., the vowel [ɑ] is pronounced further to the front in the **Northern Cities Shift**, and some speakers will front it more than other speakers).

Grammar   The mental system of rules and categories that allows humans to form and interpret the words and sentences of their language.

Grammatical (sentence)   A sentence that speakers judge to be a possible sentence in their language.

Grammatical competence   Competence in the structural aspects at or below the sentence level.

Grammatical hierarchies   In the classification of languages, the degrees of **markedness** of particular structures in the world's languages, going from least marked (i.e., most common) to most marked (i.e., least common).

Grammaticalization   The change of a lexical form into a grammatical form (e.g., an **affix** or member of a **functional category**).

Grammaticalized concepts   Concepts that are expressed as affixes or nonlexical categories (e.g., the concept of OBLIGATION as expressed by the auxiliary verb *must*).

Great English Vowel Shift   A series of nonphonetically conditioned modifications to long vowels that occurred from the Middle English period to the eighteenth century.

Grimm's Law   A set of consonant shifts that took place between Proto-Indo-European and Proto-Germanic.

Gyri   Plural of **gyrus**.

Gyrus   An area where the cerebral cortex is folded outward.

Habitual (invariant) *be*   Uninflected *be* used to indicate a habitual state or action in **African American English** (e.g., *The coffee be cold* means 'the coffee is usually cold').

Hangul   The alphabetic script used to represent Korean, the symbols of which are grouped to represent the syllables of individual morphemes.

Hanja   The Korean word for the Chinese characters used in Korean writing.

Head (of a phrase)   The category around which a phrase is built (e.g., V is head of VP, N is head of NP, A of AP, P of PP).

Head (of a word)   The morpheme that determines the category of the entire word in a compound (e.g., *bird* in *blackbird*).

Head complement parameter   A parameter that offers two versions of the **X' Schema**—one in which the head precedes its complement and one in which the head follows its complement.

Head-final (language)   Language in which the **head** of a phrase follows its **complement** (e.g., the verb comes after the direct object in the VP).

Head-initial (language)   Language in which the **head** comes before its **complement** (e.g., the verb comes before the direct object in the VP).

Headless compound   A compound word whose category cannot be traced to either component (e.g., *dropout* is a noun, although *drop* is a verb and *out* is a preposition).

Heavy syllable   Syllable that has either a **coda** or two elements in the **nucleus** (e.g., a diphthong or a long vowel).

Heritage language programs   Educational programs designed to preserve, maintain, or revive the ancestral languages of indigenous peoples, immigrants, or refugees in the United States.

Hieroglyphs   An ancient Egyptian writing system that used stylized pictures as pictograms, logograms, and consonant phonemes.

High   A DORSAL feature that characterizes sounds produced with the tongue body raised.

High involvement style   A style of turn-taking in a conversation in which speaker turns overlap.

High vowel   A vowel that is made with the tongue raised (e.g., the vowel sounds in *beat* and *lose*).

Hiragana   The Japanese syllabary that is used in conjunction with **katakana** and **kanji** to write Japanese.

Historical linguistics   The linguistic discipline that is concerned with the description and the explanation of language change over time.

Holophrases   Utterances produced by children in which one word expresses the type of meaning that would be associated with an entire sentence in adult speech (e.g., *up* used to mean 'Pick me up').

Homographs   Different words with the same spelling (e.g., *bow* [bow] for shooting arrows, and *bow* [baw] meaning 'bend at the waist').

Homonyms   Different words with the same pronunciation and the same spelling—that is, they are both homophones and **homographs** (e.g., *light* 'not heavy' and *light* 'illumination').

Homophony   The situation in which a single form has two or more entirely distinct meanings (e.g., *club* 'a social organization', *club* 'a blunt weapon').

Host   The element to which a **clitic** is attached.

Hypercorrection   Overgeneralization of particular rules in a language in an attempt to speak (or write) "correctly."

Illocutionary competence   The ability to understand a speaker's intent and to produce a variety of forms to convey intent.

Illocutionary force   The intended meaning of an utterance.

Immersion   A method of teaching a second language to children in which students are given most of their content courses and school activities in the target language.

Impaired Representation Hypothesis   The hypothesis that states that second language learners who produce errors lack an underlying representation of the structure in which they have produced errors.

Implementation   A practical application of a formal system.

Implicational universals   A universal of language that specifies that the presence of one trait implies the presence of another (but not vice versa).

Inalienably possessed nouns   Nouns that must always have a pronominal possessor indicated; usually parts of the body or kinship terms.

Inanimate   A noun class category in some languages generally assigned to nonliving referents. (*See also* **Animate**.)

Inclusive (pronoun)   A type of first-person plural pronoun whose referents include the addressee. (*See also* **Exclusive [pronoun]**.)

Incorporation   The combination of a word (usually a noun) with a verb to form a compound verb.

Indirect negative evidence   The assumption that nonoccurring structures in the linguistic environment are ungrammatical.

Indo-European family   The **language family** that includes most of the languages in a broad curve from northern India through western Asia (Iran and Armenia) to Europe.

Infix   An **affix** that occurs within a base.

Inflection   The modification of a word's form to indicate the grammatical subclass to which it belongs (e.g., the *-s* in *books* marks the plural subclass).

Inflectional language   *See* **Fusional languages**.

Informants   *See* **Consultants**.

Initialisms   Abbreviations that are pronounced as a series of letters rather than as words (e.g., *LA* for Los Angeles).

Insertion rule   An operation that adds an element to a tree structure.

Instrumental motivation   The desire to achieve proficiency in a new language for utilitarian reasons, such as a job promotion.

Integrative motivation   The desire to achieve proficiency in a new language in order to participate in the social life of the community that speaks the language.

Intension   An expression's inherent sense; the concepts that it evokes.

Intercostals   The muscles between the ribs that help to maintain the air pressure necessary for speech production.

Interdentals   Sounds made with the tongue placed between the teeth (e.g., [θ], [ð]).

Interlanguage (IL)   The changing grammatical system that an L2 learner is using at a particular period in his or her acquisition of a second language as he or she moves toward proficiency in the target language.

Internal change   A process that substitutes one nonmorphemic segment for another to mark a grammatical contrast (e.g., *sing, sang, sung*).

Internal reconstruction   The reconstruction of a **protolanguage** that relies on the analysis of morphophonemic variation within a single language.

International Phonetic Alphabet (IPA) A system for transcribing the sounds of speech that attempts to represent each sound of human speech with a single symbol.

International posture   Desire of a language learner to be associated with a global perspective, symbolized in part by use of English.

Interspeaker variation   Variation that occurs across individuals (e.g., some speakers distinguish between [ɔ] in *caught* and [ɑ] in *cot*, while other speakers do not).

Intonation   Pitch movement in spoken utterances that is not related to differences in word meaning.

Intransitive   *See* **Intransitive verb**.

Intransitive verb   A verb that does not take a direct object (e.g., *sleep*).

Intraspeaker variation   Variation that occurs within the speech of a single individual (e.g., an individual may sometimes pronounce the *wh* in a word such as *what* with the voiceless labiovelar glide [ʍ] and sometimes with the voiced [w]).

Inversion   A **transformation** that moves the element in the T position to a position in front of the subject, formulated as: Move T to C.

Isogloss bundle   Convergence of several lines drawn on a dialect map to represent boundaries between dialects.

Isoglosses   Lines drawn on a dialect map to represent boundaries between dialects.

Isolate   A language that is not known to be related to any other living language (e.g., Basque, Kutenai).

Isolating languages   Languages whose words typically consist of only one morpheme (e.g., Mandarin) (also called **analytic languages**).

Jargon   (1) Vocabulary peculiar to a particular field; (2) a simple pidgin used in very limited circumstances.

Jargonaphasia   A symptom of severe cases of **Wernicke's aphasia** in which speech contains very few real words of the language.

Kanji   The Japanese word for the Chinese characters used to write Japanese.

Katakana   The Japanese syllabary that is used in conjunction with **hiragana** and **kanji** to write Japanese.

LABIAL   A place feature that characterizes sounds articulated with one or both lips.

Labials   Sounds made with closure or near closure of the lips (e.g., the initial sounds of *win* and *forget*).

Labiodentals   Sounds involving the lower lip and upper teeth (e.g., the initial sounds of *freedom* and *vintage*).

Labiovelars   Sounds made with the tongue raised near the velum and the lips rounded at the same time (e.g., the initial sound of *wound*).

Language bioprogram hypothesis   The hypothesis that similarities among creoles reflect linguistic universals both in terms of first language acquisition and with respect to processes and structures that are innate.

Language contact   Interaction between speakers of one language and speakers of another language or dialect.

Language death   The situation in which there are no more native speakers of a language.

Language family   In language classification, a group of languages with a historical origin in the same **protolanguage**.

Language myths   Unsubstantiated beliefs about a language or language variety (e.g., that Eskimo languages have hundreds of words for 'snow').

Language nest   An educational program for preschoolers in which a (usually endangered) minority language is used exclusively.

Language planning   Official policy with the goal of increasing or limiting the domain of use of a particular language or languages.

Laryngeal features Phonological features that represent laryngeal states (e.g., [voice], [spread glottis], and [constricted glottis]).

Larynx The boxlike structure located in the throat through which air passes during speech production; commonly known as the voice box.

Late closure A parsing principle that claims that in sentence comprehension, humans prefer to attach new words to the clause currently being processed.

Lateral (feature) A manner feature that characterizes a sound made with the sides of the tongue lowered (e.g., varieties of *l*).

Lateral (sound) A sound made with the sides of the tongue lowered (e.g., varieties of [l]).

Lateral fissure The fissure that separates the temporal lobe from the frontal and parietal lobes in the brain.

Lateral fricative A **lateral sound** made with a narrow enough closure to be classified as a fricative.

Lateralization The unilateral control of cognitive functions by either the left or the right side of the brain (e.g., language is lateralized to the left hemisphere in most people).

Lateralized *See* **Lateralization**.

Laterals Sounds made with the sides of the tongue lowered (e.g., varieties of *l*).

Lax vowels Vowels that are made with a placement of the tongue that results in relatively less vocal tract constriction (e.g., the vowel sounds in *hit* and *but*).

Length The subjective impression of time occupied by the duration of a **phone**.

Lesion Severe damage to the brain.

Lexical ambiguity A situation in which a single form has two or more meanings (e.g., a *trunk* is a 'piece of luggage' or an 'elephant nose').

Lexical category The word-level syntactic categories noun (N), verb (V), adjective (A), and preposition (P).

Lexical decision An experimental paradigm in which a person sees or hears a stimulus and must judge as quickly as possible whether or not that stimulus is a word of his or her language.

Lexical diffusion Linguistic change that first manifests itself in a few words and then gradually spreads through the vocabulary of the language.

Lexical gaps Gaps in the lexicon that result from technological innovation or contact with another culture.

Lexicalization The process whereby concepts are encoded in the words of a language (e.g., the concepts of MOTION and MANNER are both encoded by the word *roll*).

Lexicon A speaker's mental dictionary, which contains information about the syntactic properties, meaning, and phonological representation of a language's words.

Lexifier language The language that provides most of the lexical items to a contact variety.

Light syllable A syllable with just a vowel or a syllabic liquid or nasal in the syllable **rhyme** (e.g., the syllable *see*).

Lingua franca A language that is used when speakers of two or more different languages come into contact and do not know each other's languages.

Linguistic competence Speakers' knowledge of their language, which allows them to produce and understand an unlimited number of utterances, including many that are novel.

Linguistic factors Factors such as position in a word, voicing, and so forth that can influence how a **variant** is realized.

Linguistic insecurity The degree to which speakers believe that their own variety is not standard.

Linguistic isolation The situation in which the members of a **speech community** are not in contact with other speakers of the same language (e.g., Quebec French is surrounded by English in North America).

Linguistics The discipline that studies the nature and use of language.

Linguistic typology An approach to language classification that classifies languages according to their common structural characteristics without regard for **genetic relationships**.

Linguistic universals   Structural characteristics that occur across the languages of the world.

Liquids   A class of consonants containing *l* and *r* sounds and their variants.

Loan translation   An expression in one language translated word-for-word into another language.

Lobes   Substructures of the hemispheres of the brain that appear to have distinct responsibilities (e.g., **frontal lobe**, **temporal lobe**).

Location   A **thematic role** that specifies the place where an action occurs (e.g., *the SkyDome* in *The athletes practiced in the SkyDome*).

Locative   The **case** form characteristically used for the noun that is *in*, *to*, or *at* a location.

Logogram   A written symbol representing a morpheme or word.

Logographic writing   A type of writing in which symbols represent morphemes or even entire words.

Longitudinal fissure   The fissure that extends from the front of the brain to the back and separates the left and right cerebral hemispheres.

Longitudinal studies   Studies that examine language development over an extended period of time.

Long vowels   Vowels that are articulated for a longer period of time than corresponding **short vowels**.

Loudness   The subjective impression of a speech sound's volume relative to the sounds around it.

Low back merger   The merger of the phonemes /ɑ/ as in *cot* and /ɔ/ as in *caught*.

Low (feature)   A DORSAL feature that characterizes sounds made with the tongue body lowered.

Low (sound)   A sound made with the tongue lowered (e.g., [a], [ɑ], [æ]).

Low vowel   A vowel that is made with the tongue lowered (e.g., the vowel sounds made in the words *c<u>a</u>t* and *t<u>o</u>p*).

Macrofamilies   *See* **Phyla**.

Magnetoencephalography (MEG)   A technique that provides detailed information on which parts of the brain are involved in language-processing activity by recording changes in magnetic fields generated within the brain.

Major class features   Phonological features that represent the classes consonant, obstruent, nasal, liquid, glide, and vowel.

Major diphthongs   Diphthongs in which there is extreme tongue movement from the initial vowel to the glide (e.g., [aj], [ɔj], and [aw]).

Majority rules strategy   A secondary strategy used to reconstruct protoforms, which stipulates that the segment found in the majority of cognates should be assumed to be part of the **protoform**. (*See also* **Phonetic plausibility strategy**.)

Maintenance bilingual education   *See* **Developmental bilingual education**.

Manner assimilation   Becoming more like a neighboring sound in manner of articulation.

Manner features   Phonological features that represent **manner of articulation**.

Manners of articulation   The various configurations produced by positioning the lips, tongue, velum, and glottis in different ways (e.g., nasal, fricative, liquid).

Marked   Occurring less commonly in world languages. (*See also* **Marked traits** and **Markedness theory**.)

Markedness   The quality of being relatively complex or rare in world languages. (*See also* **Marked traits** and **Markedness theory**.)

Markedness Differential Hypothesis   The hypothesis that L2 elements that are different and more **marked** than the L1 elements will cause difficulty in learning L2.

Markedness theory   A theory that classifies traits or patterns of languages as marked (those that are considered to be more complex and/or universally rarer) and unmarked (those that are considered to be less complex and/or universally more common).

Marked traits   Complex or less common features or characteristics of languages.

Matched guise test   A test of language attitudes that asks subjects to evaluate recordings of the same person speaking different language varieties.

Matrix   A representation of sounds in which all the relevant distinctive features and their values are placed in an array.

Matrix clause   The larger TP in which a **complement clause** occurs.

Matrix language   The dominant language in a **code-switching** exchange.

Maxim of Manner   A principle that is thought to underlie the efficient use of language and is formulated as: Avoid ambiguity and obscurity; be brief and orderly.

Maxim of Quality   A principle that is thought to underlie the efficient use of language and is formulated as: Try to make your contribution one that is true. (Do not say things that are false or for which you lack adequate evidence.)

Maxim of Quantity   A principle that is thought to underlie the efficient use of language and is formulated as: Do not make your contribution more or less informative than required.

Maxim of Relevance   A principle that is thought to underlie the efficient use of language and is formulated as: Be relevant.

Maxims   The specific principles that ensure that conversational interactions satisfy the **Cooperative Principle**.

Meaning   The message or content that a sign or utterance conveys.

Mental lexicon   *See* **Lexicon**.

Merge   A syntactic operation that combines elements to create phrases and sentences.

Merger   A change in a phonological system in which two or more phonemes collapse into one, thereby reducing the number of phonemes in that language.

Mesolect   A **creole** variety that falls between an **acrolect** and a **basilect** in terms of the amount of influence from the standard language.

Metaphor   The understanding of one concept in terms of another, sometimes responsible for language change (e.g., 'argument' understood in terms of 'war': *She annihilated him in the debate*).

Metathesis   A process that reorders a sequence of segments (e.g., in child language, pronouncing *spaghetti* as [pəskɛri]).

Mid vowels   Vowels that are made with the tongue neither raised nor lowered (e.g., the vowel sounds in *set* and *Coke*).

Minimal attachment   A proposed parsing principle that claims that in sentence comprehension, humans tend to attach incoming material into phrase structure using the fewest nodes possible.

Minimal pair   Two forms with distinct meanings that differ by only one segment found in the same position in each form (e.g., [ʃɪp] and [ʃip]).

Minor diphthongs   **Diphthongs** in which there is not a great change in articulator position from the initial vowel to the glide (e.g., [ej] and [ow]).

Missing Surface Inflection Hypothesis   The hypothesis that states that second language learners who produce errors may actually have correct underlying representations for the structure in which they have made errors but have difficulty mapping these underlying representations to their surface forms.

Mixed languages   Languages that intertwine features from two different source languages (e.g., Michif, which derives from French and Cree).

Modal auxiliaries   English **auxiliary verbs** in the T position that are not inflected for agreement with the subject (e.g., *may, can, will, must, could*) but may show tense (e.g., *could, would* may be past).

Modifier   An optional element that describes a property of a **head** (e.g., *blue* in *that blue car*, or *that Gloria likes* in *the car that Gloria likes*).

Morpheme   The smallest unit of language that carries information about meaning or function (e.g., *books* consists of the two morphemes *book + s*).

Morphological parsing   The computational process in the brain that analyzes constituent morphemes of a word.

Morphology   The system of categories and rules involved in word formation and interpretation.

Morphophonemics Rules that account for alternations among **allomorphs**.

Morphophonology *See* **Morphophonemics**.

Motherese The type of speech that is typically addressed to young children (also called **caregiver speech**).

Motion verbs Words that can describe motion through space (e.g., *come, go,* and *move* in English).

Motor aphasia *See* **Nonfluent aphasia**.

Move A syntactic operation that transports an element to a new position within a particular sentence.

Movement test A test used to determine if a group of words is a **constituent** by moving it as a single unit to a different position within the sentence.

Multiple-route model A psycholinguistic theory built around the claim that a particular type of language processing can be accomplished in more than one manner.

Multiplex social networks **Social networks** in which the connections are based on several kinds of relationships.

Murmur *See* **Breathy voice**.

Mutual intelligibility The criterion that is sometimes used to distinguish between a language and a dialect: Mutually intelligible varieties of a language can be understood by speakers of each variety and are therefore dialects of the same language.

Narrow transcription Phonetic transcription that uses a fairly elaborate set of symbols and **diacritics** to show phonetic detail.

Nasal A manner feature that characterizes any sound made with the **velum** lowered.

Nasal phones Sounds produced by lowering the **velum**, allowing air to pass through the nasal passages.

Nasal vowels Vowels produced with a lowered **velum** so that air passes through the oral and nasal cavities at the same time.

Nasalization A kind of **assimilation** in which the **velum** is lowered and air passes through the nose for sounds adjacent to a nasal sound (e.g., the nasal quality of the *a* in *bank*).

Native speakers Those who have acquired a language as a child in a natural setting.

Nativism The view that certain grammatical knowledge is inborn.

Natural class A class of sounds that shares a **feature** or features (e.g., voiced stops).

Naturalistic approach An approach to investigating child language in which researchers observe and record children's spontaneous verbal behavior.

Naturalness A criterion that guides language reconstruction by determining whether or not changes are natural.

Near-minimal pair Two forms with distinct meanings that contrast segments in nearly identical environments.

Negative evidence Information as to the ungrammatical nature of utterances.

Network density The degree to which speakers in a **social network** all know each other.

Neurolinguistics The study of how language is represented and processed in the brain.

Neurons The basic information-processing units of the nervous system (also called nerve cells).

Neuroscience The scientific study of the brain.

Newcomer programs Programs designed to provide intensive language instruction, literacy development, and cultural orientation for English language learners who arrive in U.S. schools with very low-level skills in English and/or little previous experience in school.

New information Knowledge that is introduced into the discourse for the first time.

Nominal paradigm The set of related forms associated with a noun (also called a **declension**).

Nominative The **case** form characteristically used to mark a subject.

Nominative-accusative pattern Sentence pattern in which the subject of the sentence is identified by nominative **case**, and the direct object is marked by accusative **case**.

Nonce borrowings   Words from one language that are used spontaneously in another language by bilinguals but are not part of the vocabulary of the other language.

Nonconcatenative mophology   Morphology in which words are not built up in a linear fashion (e.g., in the Arabic words *kitaab* 'book' and *maktuub* 'letter', the root morpheme is *k-t-b*). (*See* also **Concatenative morphology**.)

Nonfluent aphasia   Aphasia that results from damage to parts of the brain in front of the central sulcus and that is characterized by slow, effortful speech production (also called **motor aphasia**).

Nonlexical category   *See* **Functional category**.

Nonmodal auxiliaries   Auxiliary verbs that show agreement with the subject, originate in VP, and raise to T when there is no **modal auxiliary**; in English, the auxiliary verbs *be* and *have* when they occur with a main verb (e.g., *was* writing; *have* seen).

Nonstandard (dialect)   A variety of language that differs from the standard dialect in systematic ways.

Nonstridents   Coronal fricatives and affricates that have less acoustic noise than **stridents** ([θ, ð] are nonstridents).

Nonsyllabic (sounds)   Sounds that do not act as syllable peaks, as distinguished from **syllabic** sounds.

Nonterminal (intonation) contour   Rising or level intonation at the end of an utterance, often signaling that the utterance is incomplete.

Nonterminals   Parts of a structure that are not lexical items, for example VP, NP, Det, N'. (*Compare with* **terminals**.)

NORMs   An **acronym** for *nonmobile older rural males*, who were the informants sought by earlier linguists studying traditional rural dialects.

Northern Cities Shift   The systematic change in vowel sounds taking place in cities around the Great Lakes. (*See also* **Shift**.)

Noun (N)   A **lexical category** that typically names entities, can usually be inflected for number and possession (in English), and

functions as the **head** of a noun phrase (e.g., *key, Bob, perception*).

Noun class   A grammatical category dividing nouns into classes often based on shared semantic properties (also called **gender**).

Noun incorporation   *See* **Incorporation**.

NP Movement   A transformation that moves a noun phrase into the subject position.

Nucleus (N)   A vocalic element that forms the core of a syllable (e.g., the vowel [æ] is the nucleus of the first syllable of *Patrick*).

Null Subject Parameter   A cross-linguistic variation that allows some languages to drop subject pronouns, while other languages require an overt grammatical subject.

Number   The morphological category that expresses contrasts involving countable quantities (e.g., in English, the two-way distinction between singular and plural).

Obligatory contexts   Contexts in which a certain form is required and would be supplied by a native speaker (e.g., In *He walks to school every day*, the *-s* on the end of *walk* is obligatory).

Oblique NP   A noun phrase that combines with a preposition.

Obstruent   Any nonsonorant consonant: fricatives, affricates, oral stops.

Occipital lobe   The area of the brain to the rear of the angular gyrus in which the visual cortex is located.

Official language   A language that has been designated by political or other official authorities as the working language of a region, nation, or other group.

Old information   *See* **Given information**.

One-word stage   A stage of first language acquisition at which children characteristically produce one-word utterances.

Onomatopoeic words   Words that sound like the thing that they name (e.g., *plop, hiss*).

Onset   The portion of a syllable that precedes the **nucleus** (e.g., /spl/ in *spleen*).

Opening   A discourse unit conventionally used to begin a conversation.

Open syllable   A syllable that has no **coda**.

Oral phones   Sounds produced with the velum raised and the airflow through the nasal passage cut off.

Ordered rule application   In a phonological **derivation**, an application of rules in which the rules must be applied in a certain order to derive the surface form from the **underlying representation**.

Ordered rules   Rules that must be applied in a particular order. *See* **ordered rule application**.

Orthography   A set of conventions for representing language in written form; spelling.

Overextension   A developmental phenomenon in which the meaning of a child's word overlaps with that of the equivalent adult word but also extends beyond it (e.g., *dog* is used to refer to other animals as well as dogs).

Overgeneralization   A developmental phenomenon that results from the overly broad application of a rule (e.g., *falled* instead of *fell*).

Overregularization   *See* **Overgeneralization**.

Palatalization   The effect that front vowels and the palatal guide [j] typically have on velar, alveolar, and dental stops, making their place of articulation more palatal (e.g., the first sound of *keep* is palatalized).

Palatals   Sounds produced with the tongue on or near the palate (e.g., [j]).

Palate   The highest part of the roof of the mouth.

Palatoalveolar   *See* **Alveopalatal (area)**.

Paragraphia   Writing errors made by Broca's aphasics that have characteristics corresponding to their speech.

Parallel processing model   A psycholinguistic theory built around the claim that phonological, lexical, and syntactic processes are carried out simultaneously.

Parameter   The set of alternatives for a particular phenomenon made available by **Universal Grammar** to individual languages.

Parameter setting   The determination of which option permitted by a particular **parameter** is appropriate for the language being learned.

Paraphrases   Two sentences that have the same basic meaning (e.g., *A Canadian wrote that book* is a paraphrase of *That book was written by a Canadian*).

Parietal lobe   The lobe of the brain that lies behind the central sulcus and above the temporal lobe.

Parser   A program or mental process for doing grammatical analysis.

Parsing   The procedure through which speech or text is analyzed by assigning categories to words and assigning structure to strings of words.

Partial assimilation   The assimilation of only some features of a neighboring segment (such as when a vowel becomes nasalized in the neighborhood of a nasal consonant).

Partial reduplication   A morphological process in which part of a stem is repeated to form a new word (e.g., in Tagalog, *takbuh* 'run' and *tatakbuh* 'will run').

Partial suppletion   A morphological process that marks a grammatical contrast by replacing part of a morpheme (e.g., *think/thought*).

Parts of speech   *See* **Syntactic categories**.

Passive (sentence)   A sentence whose grammatical subject is the **theme** (the entity affected by the action of the verb) (e.g., *The report was prepared by the committee members*).

Patient   The recipient of an action (e.g., *dolphin* in *Marilyn fed the dolphin*).

Perceptual dialectology   The study of the attitudes of nonlinguists toward regional or other types of language variation.

Pejoration   A semantic change in which the meaning of a word becomes more negative or unfavorable (e.g., the meaning of *wench* used to be 'girl').

Performance   Actual language use in particular situations.

Performance register   When speakers exaggerate distinctive features of their dialect to reinforce their identification as members of their speech community.

Performativity   The idea that men and women act out their concept of their own gender identity through speech, gesture, and other observable behaviors.

Person   A morphological category that typically distinguishes among the first person (the speaker), the second person (the addressee), and the third person (anyone else) (e.g., in English, the difference between *I*, *you*, and *she/he/it*).

Person hierarchy   In some languages, such as those in the Algonquian family, the system that governs the order in which pronominal affixes appear on a stem.

Pharyngeals   Sounds made through the modification of airflow in the **pharynx** by retracting the tongue or constricting the pharynx.

Pharynx   The area of the throat between the **uvula** and the **larynx**.

Phoenician script   An early writing system that had twenty-two consonantal signs, devised by the Semitic peoples of ancient Phoenicia as early as 1000 B.C.

Phoneme merger   When two phonemes lose their distinctiveness and become one phoneme (e.g., for many speakers of North American English, the vowels in *caught* and *cot* are no longer distinct phonemes).

Phonemes   Distinctive sounds in a language that contrast with other sounds in that language (e.g., the sounds [ɪ] and [i] as in *rich* and *reach* contrast with each other as separate phonemes in English but not in Spanish).

Phonemic level   *See* **Phonemic representation**.

Phonemic paraphasias   Speech errors that result from phonemic substitutions and omissions (e.g., *spoon* may be pronounced as *poon*).

Phonemic representation   The representation that consists of the phonemes to which allophones belong; predictable phonetic information is not represented.

Phonemic transcription   A type of transcription of sounds where phonetic details are ignored and only phonemic contrast is recorded.

Phones   Any sounds used in human language (also called **speech sounds**).

Phonetically conditioned change   Sound change that begins as subtle alterations in the sound pattern of a language in particular phonetic environments.

Phonetic determinative   The part of a Chinese character that provides information about the pronunciation of the corresponding morpheme.

Phonetic level   *See* **Phonetic representation**.

Phonetic plausibility strategy   The primary strategy used to reconstruct protoforms that requires any sound changes posited to be phonetically plausible. (*See also* **Majority rules strategy**.)

Phonetic representation   What is actually produced in speech after rules have been applied to the **underlying representation** (i.e., predictable variants, or **allophones**).

Phonetics   The study of the inventory and structure of the sounds of language.

Phonetic sound change   A sound change that results in a new allophone of an already existing phoneme.

Phonetic transcription   A type of transcription of sounds in which not only phonemic differences but also phonetic details are recorded.

Phonographic writing   A type of writing in which symbols represent syllables or segments.

Phonological (sound) change   A sound change that results in the addition, elimination, or rearrangement of phonemes (e.g., splits, mergers).

Phonological dyslexia   A type of acquired dyslexia in which the patient seems to have lost the ability to use spelling-to-sound rules and can only read words that they have seen before.

Phonological processes   *See* **Processes**.

Phonological representation   *See* **Phonemic representation**.

Phonological rules   Rules that relate the underlying forms of words to their phonetic forms.

Phonology   The component of a grammar made up of the elements and principles that determine how sounds pattern in a language.

Phonotactics   The set of constraints on how sequences of segments pattern.

Phrase   A unit of syntactic structure that is built by combining words together so that the phrase consists of a **head** and an optional **specifier** and/or **complement** (e.g., *the apple, Bob, hurried to class*).

Phrase structure rule   A rule that specifies how a syntactic **constituent** is formed out of other smaller syntactic constituents (e.g., NP → Det N').

Phrase structure schema   The blueprint for the internal structure of phrases. (*See also* **X' Schema**.)

Phyla   The groups into which purportedly related language **stocks** are placed (also called superstocks).

Physical isolation   A situation in which a speech community is geographically isolated from other speech communities (e.g., island communities).

Pictograms   Pictorial representations of objects or events.

Pidgin   A **lingua franca** with a highly simplified grammatical structure that has emerged as a mixture of two or more languages and has no native speakers.

Pinyin   The system of writing Mandarin Chinese with a modified Latin alphabet, used for such things as street signs and brand names.

Pitch   The auditory property of a sound that enables us to place it on a scale that ranges from low to high.

Place features   Phonological features that represent place of articulation.

Place node   A node in the feature geometry in autosegmental phonology, which dominates major place features.

Place or manner assimilation   The process by which one segment becomes more like another in either the place at which it is articulated or the manner by which it is articulated.

Places of articulation   The points at which the airstream is modified in the vocal tract to produce **phones** (also called points of articulation).

Plural   An inflectional category associated with nouns with more than one referent.

Points of articulation   *See* **Places of articulation**.

Polysemy   The situation in which a word has two or more related meanings (e.g., *bright* 'intelligent', *bright* 'shining').

Polysynthetic languages   Languages in which single words can consist of long strings of lexical categories and affixes, often expressing the meaning of an entire sentence in English (e.g., Inuktitut).

Positive evidence   Grammatical utterances in the learner's linguistic environment.

Positron Emission Tomography (PET)   A brain imaging technique that uses radioactive isotopes to measure changes in brain metabolism associated with particular cognitive and behavioral tasks.

Postlexical decomposition   The process by which the constituents of a multimorphemic word are activated in the brain through the representation of the whole lexical item.

Postposition   A P that occurs after its complement. (*See also* **Preposition**.)

Postvocalic *r*   An *r* that occurs after a vowel in the same syllable (e.g., the *r* in *core* or *darling*).

Power   The degree of control that one group or individual may hold over another.

Pragmatics   Speakers' and addressees' background attitudes and beliefs, their understanding of the context of an utterance, and their knowledge of how language can be used for a variety of purposes.

Predicate   A traditional term for the verb phrase in a sentence.

Preemptive focus on form   In second language classrooms, giving explicit language instruction in preparation for a task or activity.

Prefix   An **affix** that is attached to the front of its base (e.g., *re-* in *replay*).

Prelexical decomposition   The computational process by which the individual morphemes of a multimorphemic word are scanned and isolated in the brain.

Preposition (P)   A minor **lexical category** whose members typically designate relations in space or time (e.g., *in*, *before*); they come before the NP complement with which they combine to form a PP.

Prescriptive (grammar)   A grammar that aims to state the linguistic facts in terms of how they *should* be. (*See also* **Descriptive [grammar]**.)

Presupposition   The assumption or belief implied by the use of a particular word or structure.

Prewriting   Possible forerunners of writing, such as incised bone or clay counters used to keep records.

Primary place of articulation   The most important place where the airflow is modified (e.g., in [w], which is made with the tongue raised near the velum and the lips rounded, the velum is the primary place of articulation).

Primary stress   The most prominent stress of a word.

Prime   In a priming experiment, this is the stimulus that is expected to affect a subject's **response accuracy** and **response latency** to the following stimulus.

Priming   A situation in which the presentation of a stimulus makes it easier to process the following stimulus.

Priming effect   In a priming experiment, this is the extent to which a priming stimulus facilitates the processing of the next stimulus.

Principle A   The syntactic principle that constrains the interpretation of reflexive pronouns and is formulated as: A **reflexive pronoun** must have an antecedent (within the same clause) that c-commands it.

Principle B   The syntactic principle that constrains the interpretation of pronominals and is formulated as: A **pronominal** must not have an antecedent (within the same clause) that c-commands it.

Principle of Compositionality   A principle underlying sentence interpretation that is formulated as: The meaning of a sentence is determined by the meaning of its component parts and the manner in which they are arranged in syntactic structure.

Probabilistic (rules)   Rules that are not absolute but are more or less likely to apply.

Processes   *See* **Articulatory processes**.

Processing module   A unit of processing that is relatively autonomous from other processing units.

Proclitic   A **clitic** that attaches to the beginning of a word.

Productivity   In morphology, the relative freedom with which affixes can combine with bases of the appropriate category.

Progressive assimilation   Assimilation in which a sound influences a following segment.

Pronominal   A pronoun whose interpretation may, but does not have to, be determined by an antecedent in the same sentence (e.g., *he*, *her*).

Pronoun (Pro)   A minor **lexical category** whose members can replace a noun phrase and look to another element for their interpretation (e.g., *he*, *herself*, *it*).

Prosodic properties   *See* **Suprasegmental properties**.

Prosody   Rhythm, prominence, or intonation, often used to separate parts of a sentence, emphasize selected elements, or communicate other important information.

Protoform   The form that is reconstructed as the source of cognate words in related languages.

Proto-Indo-European (PIE)   The proto-language from which evolved most of the languages of Europe, Persia (Iran), and the northern part of India.

Protolanguage   The reconstructed language that is presumed to be the common source for two or more related languages (e.g., Proto-Indo-European).

Protopidgin   The reconstructed ancestor language that is hypothesized to be the ancestor for all **pidgins**.

Prototypical   Characteristic of the best exemplars of a concept (e.g., robins or sparrows are prototypes of the concept BIRD).

Psycholinguistic model A schematic representation based on experimental results of how language is processed mentally.

Psycholinguistics The study of the mental processes and representations involved in language comprehension and production.

Pull-out program An ESL program for nonnative speakers of English in U.S. schools in which they are taken outside their mainstream classrooms for some portion of the day.

Push-in program An ESL program for nonnative speakers of English in U.S. schools in which an ESL tutor joins them in their mainstream classrooms for some portion of the day.

Q feature In syntax, a feature in the **complementizer** position that marks a sentence as a question and that may attract elements (such as an **auxiliary verb**) to the complementizer position.

Radical The part of a Chinese character that provides clues about the morpheme's meaning (also called a key).

Reactive focus on form In second language classrooms, giving explicit language instruction in response to an error.

Reading The interpretation for a particular utterance.

Real-time studies Studies that investigate language change by collecting data over a period of time.

Reanalysis A source of language change that involves an attempt to attribute an internal structure to a word that formerly was not broken down into component morphemes (e.g., *ham* + *burger*).

Rebus principle In writing, the use of a sign for any word that is pronounced like the word whose meaning the sign represented initially.

Recast A repetition of a child's or second language learner's utterance that includes adjustments to its form and/or content.

Recursion Repeated application of the same rule to create a more and more complex sentence, such as a series of embedded clauses (e.g., *This is the cat that killed the rat*

that ate the malt that lay in the house that Jack built).

Reduced A phonological characteristic of schwa [ə], indicating a weakly articulated, unstressed variant of stressed vowels.

Reduced vowel *See* **Schwa**.

Redundancy The use of different modalities to convey the same information.

Reduplication A morphological process that repeats all or part of the base to which it is attached. (*See also* **Partial reduplication** and **Full reduplication**.)

Referents The set of entities to which a word or expression refers (also called its **denotation** or **extension**).

Referring expression generation In **computational linguistics**, the task of producing an NP that identifies a particular **referent**.

Referring expressions Words or expressions (typically nouns or pronouns) that name entities (e.g., *Johanna, the class, they*).

Reflexive pronoun A pronoun that must have a c-commanding antecedent, usually in the same clause (e.g., *himself, herself*).

Regional dialect A speech variety spoken in a particular geographical area (e.g., Appalachian English).

Register A speech variety appropriate to a particular speech situation (e.g., formal versus casual).

Register tones Tones that have a stable pitch over a single syllable.

Regressive assimilation Assimilation in which a sound influences a preceding segment.

Regressive saccades Eye movements in which the eyes dart backward to a section of text that has been previously read.

Regularization The process by which forms in a language are made more regular (e.g., the past tense of *thrive* used to be *throve* but has changed over time to the regular past tense form *thrived*).

Relational analysis A syntactic analysis in which phenomena are described in terms of grammatical relations such as **subject** and **direct object** rather than morphological patterns or the order of words.

Relative clause   A sentence-like construction that follows a noun (in English) and gives information about the noun it follows (e.g., the linguistics class *that my favorite professor teaches*).

Relative pronouns   *Wh* words (e.g., *who* or *which*) that come at the beginning of a **relative clause**.

Relexification hypothesis   The hypothesis that **creoles** are formed by using words from one language and the grammatical system of another.

Relic forms   Forms that used to be widespread in a language but have survived only in a particular dialect (e.g., **a-prefixing** is a relic form in Appalachian English).

Representations   Models of one aspect of language (e.g., phonological representation, syntactic representation).

Response accuracy   The correctness of a subject's responses to particular stimuli in an experiment.

Response latency   The amount of time taken by a subject in an experiment to respond to a stimulus.

Retroflex   Sounds produced by curling the tongue tip back into the mouth (e.g., American English [ɹ]).

Rhotacism   A type of weakening that typically involves the change of /z/ to /r/.

Rhyme (R)   The **nucleus** and the **coda** of a syllable (e.g., [uts] in the word *boots*).

Right ear advantage (REA)   A phenomenon where speech is louder and clearer when it is heard in the right ear than in the left ear for right-handed people.

Root (of a word)   In a complex word, the morpheme that remains after all affixes are removed (e.g., *mind* in *unmindfulness*).

Root (of the tongue)   The part of the tongue that is contained in the upper part of the throat.

Round   A place feature that characterizes sounds made by protruding the lips (e.g., [ɔ], [w]).

Rounded (sounds)   Sounds made with the lips protruding (e.g., [ow], [ɔ]).

Rounding   The act of protruding the lips to make **rounded sounds**.

Saccades   The quick and uneven movements of the eyes during reading.

Salient features   Linguistic variables that are easily perceived by a speech community.

Sandhi   Change in pronunciation of a segment when it is adjacent to another sound at word or morpheme boundaries.

Schwa   The mid lax unrounded vowel that is characterized by briefer duration than any of the other vowels (also called a **reduced vowel**) (e.g., the underlined vowels in C*a*n*a*da, s*u*ppose).

Secondary place of articulation   A second and less important place where the airflow is modified (e.g., in [w], which is made with the tongue raised near the velum and the lips rounded, the lips are the secondary place of articulation).

Secondary stress   The second most prominent stress in a word.

Second language acquisition (SLA)   The acquisition of a language that is not one's native language.

Segmental change   A sound change that affects a segment.

Segments   Individual speech sounds.

Self-efficacy   A language learner's belief in his or her own capacity to succeed.

Semantic broadening   The process in which the meaning of a word becomes more general or more inclusive than its historically earlier form (e.g., the word *aunt* used to mean only 'father's sister').

Semantic decomposition   *See* **Componential analysis**.

Semantic features   The components of meaning that make up a word's **intension** (e.g., *man* has the feature [+human]; *dog* has the feature [–human]).

Semantic narrowing   The process in which the meaning of a word becomes less general or less inclusive than its historically earlier meaning (e.g., the word *meat* used to mean any type of food).

Semantic role labeling   The task of identifying the **thematic roles** of phrases in a sentence.

Semantics   The study of meaning in human language.

Semantic shift   The process in which a word loses its former meaning, taking on a new, often related meaning (e.g., *immoral* used to mean 'not customary').

Sensory aphasia   *See* **Fluent aphasia**.

Sentence (IP)   A syntactic unit consisting of a noun phrase and a verb phrase.

Sentence ambiguity   The possibility that a sentence can be interpreted in more than one way.

Sequential change   Sound change that involves sequences of segments (e.g., **assimilation**).

Serial processing model   A psycholinguistic theory built around the claim that language processing proceeds in a step-by-step manner.

Serial verb construction   A construction in which two or more verb phrases are strung together without a conjunction, often to express instrumentality or direction.

Setting   Contextual information having to do with the physical environment in which a sentence is uttered.

Sheltered instruction   A type of English as a second language (ESL) program that combines English language instruction with instruction in academic content for English language learners in U.S. schools.

Shift   A change in a phonological system in which a series of phonemes is systematically modified so that their organization with respect to each other is altered (e.g., the **Great English Vowel Shift**).

Short vowels   Vowels in which there is no lengthening of the duration of the vowel.

Sibilants   *See* **Stridents**.

Similarity Differential Rate Hypothesis   The hypothesis that claims that the rates of acquisition for dissimilar phenomena in two languages are faster than for similar phenomena.

Simple vowels   Vowels that do not show a noticeable change in quality during their production (also called monophthongs) (e.g., the vowel sounds of *cab* and *get*).

Simple word   A word that consists of a single **morpheme** (e.g., *horse*).

Single-route model   A psycholinguistic theory built around the claim that a particular type of language processing is accomplished in one manner only.

Singular   An inflectional category associated with nouns with a single referent.

Situational code-switching   Switching between languages for clearly identifiable reasons, such as when reporting the speech of another or when the topic of conversation switches from personal to business affairs.

Slang   An informal nonstandard speech variety characterized by newly coined and rapidly changing vocabulary.

Social factors   Nonlinguistic factors that correlate with variation in speech (e.g., in New York City, dropping the *r* in words such as *fourth floor* is more common among speakers of lower socioeconomic status).

Social isolation   A situation in which members of a speech community are isolated because of social conventions or attitudes (e.g., the speakers of urban African American English in the 1920s and 1930s).

Social networks   The connections between members of a social group, including whether all members of the group know each other and the number of contexts in which they interact.

Socioeconomic status (SES)   The social rank a person has based on factors such as level of education, income, occupation, etc.

Sociolects   Language varieties based on social factors, such as **socioeconomic status** of the speakers.

Sociolinguistic competence   The ability to understand and produce a variety of social dialects in appropriate circumstances.

Sociolinguistic indicators   Linguistic variables that are not noticed by listeners.

Sociolinguistic interviews   Interviews designed to elicit a range of natural speech styles from informants, including formal to casual conversation.

Sociolinguistic markers   Linguistic variables that are noticeable to the listener.

Sociolinguistic norms   Conventions for use of language structures in particular social situations.

Sociolinguistics The study of the social aspects of language.

Sociolinguistic variables Alternative ways of saying the same thing.

Solidarity The degree of intimacy or similarity that one group or individual may feel for another.

Sonorant (feature) A major class feature that characterizes all and only the "singables": vowels, glides, liquids, and nasals.

Sonorant (sound) A sound that is "singable," in contrast with an **obstruent**.

Sonority The degree of resonance of a sound.

Sonority Requirement A phonological constraint that requires **sonority** to increase before the nucleus of a syllable and decrease after the nucleus.

Sonority scale A scale that classifies sounds according to their relative degrees of resonance.

Sonorous Characterized by a relatively open vocal tract with relatively little obstruction of airflow as a sound is made (e.g., vowels are sonorous sounds).

Sound change A systematic change of sounds that took place over a long period.

Sound class *See* **Class (sound)**.

Sound shift The systematic modification of a series of phonemes (e.g., Grimm's Law).

Source A **thematic role** that describes the starting point for a movement (e.g., *Maine* in *The senator sent the lobster from Maine to Nebraska*).

Spatial metaphor Use of a word that is primarily associated with spatial orientation to talk about physical and psychological states.

Specifier A word that helps to make more precise the meaning of the **head** of the phrase and that occurs immediately beneath XP (e.g., *the* in *the book*).

Spectrogram An acoustic recording that graphically shows the frequency, intensity, and time of sounds.

Speech community A group whose members share both a particular language or variety of language and the norms for its appropriate use in social context.

Speech event An identifiable type of discourse associated with a particular speech situation.

Speech situation The social situation in which language is used.

Speech sounds *See* **Phones**.

Speech variety The language or form of language used by any group of speakers.

Spelling pronunciation One factor in sound change, where a new pronunciation reflects the spelling of the word (e.g., *often*).

Split brain experiments Studies that investigate the effects of surgically severing the **corpus callosum**.

Splits Phonological changes in which two allophones become separate phonemes due to the loss of the conditioning environment.

Spontaneous focus on form In second language classrooms, giving explicit but unplanned language instruction as the need arises in the course of a lesson.

Spoonerisms A type of speech error, named after Reverend William A. Spooner, in which words or sounds are rearranged with often humorous results.

Spread glottis (SG) A laryngeal feature that refers to the position of the **vocal folds** and that distinguishes unaspirated from aspirated sounds.

S-structure *See* **Surface structure**.

Standard (language) The prestige variety of a language that is employed by the government and media, is used and taught in educational institutions, and is the main or only written variety.

Stem The base to which an inflectional **affix** is added (e.g., *modification* is the stem for *-s* in the word *modifications*).

Stocks In language classification, groups of related language families.

Stopping In child language acquisition, the replacement of a fricative by a corresponding stop (e.g., *zebra* is pronounced [dibrə]).

Stops Sounds made with a complete and momentary closure of airflow through the vocal tract (e.g., [p], [t], [k]).

Stress *See* **Stressed vowels**.

Stressed vowels   Vowels that are perceived as relatively more prominent due to the combined effects of pitch, loudness, and length.

Strident   A place feature of fricatives and affricates characterized by greater acoustic noise (in English, [s, z, ʃ, ʒ, tʃ, dʒ]).

Stridents   The noisier coronal fricatives and affricates (in English, [s, z, ʃ, ʒ, tʃ, dʒ]) (also called **sibilants**).

Stroke   A hemorrhage in the brain or the blockage or rupture of an artery, causing brain damage (also called a **cerebrovascular accident**).

Structurally ambiguous   A property of phrases or sentences whose component words can be combined in more than one way (e.g., *fast cars and motorcycles*).

Structured English immersion (SEI)   Education for nonnative speakers of English in U.S. schools in which they are given intensive language instruction for a large part of the school day with much less time devoted to academic content.

Structured variation   Variation in language that is correlated with factors such as age, sex, or **socioeconomic status**.

Style   The level of formality associated with a linguistic structure or set of structures classified along a continuum from most informal to most formal.

Subcategorization   The classification of words in terms of their complement options (e.g., the verb *devour* is subcategorized for a complement NP).

Subject   The NP occurring immediately under IP (e.g., *Irene* in *Irene is a tailor*).

Subject-object agreement   Agreement of verbs in person and number with their subjects and objects.

Subordinate clauses   Sentence-like constructions that are embedded inside other sentences (e.g., the string of words beginning with *that* in *Jamie told me that Johanna is graduating soon*).

Subset Principle   The initial or default setting of a parameter will correspond to the option that permits fewer patterns.

Substitution (of sounds)   Replacement of one segment with another similar-sounding segment.

Substitution test   A test used to determine if a group of words is a syntactic **constituent** by replacing it with a single word.

Substratum influence   The influence of a politically or culturally nondominant language on a dominant language in the area (e.g., the borrowing of words into English from Native American languages).

Suffix   An **affix** that is attached to the end of its base (e.g., *-ly* in *quickly*).

Sulci   Plural of **sulcus**.

Sulcus   An area in the brain where the **cerebral cortex** is folded in.

Superstratum influence   The influence of a politically or culturally dominant language on a less dominant language in the area (e.g., the effects of Norman French on English during the Middle English period).

Suppletion   A morphological process that marks a grammatical contrast by replacing a morpheme with an entirely different morpheme (e.g., *be/was*).

Suprasegmental   Above the individual speech sound. (Syllables are suprasegmental.)

Suprasegmental properties   Those properties of sounds that form part of their makeup no matter what their place or manner of articulation: pitch, loudness, and length (also called **prosodic properties**).

Surface dyslexia   A type of acquired dyslexia in which the patient seems unable to recognize words as wholes, but must process all words through a set of spelling-to-sound rules (e.g., *yacht* would be pronounced /jætʃt/).

Surface representation   In phonology, the form that is actually produced by a speaker (also called **phonetic representation**).

Surface structure   The structure that results from the application of whatever transformations are appropriate for the sentence in question (also called **S-structure**).

Syllabary   A set of signs used for writing the syllables of a language.

Syllabic   A major phonological class feature assigned to segments that function as the nuclei of syllables (vowels and liquids).

Syllabic (sounds)   Sounds that could be peaks of syllables (e.g., vowels in English).

Syllabic liquids   Liquids that function as syllabic nuclei (e.g., the *l* in *bottle*).

Syllabic nasals   Nasals that function as syllabic nuclei (e.g., the *n* in *button*).

Syllabic writing   A type of writing in which each symbol represents a syllable.

Syllable   A unit of linguistic structure that consists of a syllabic element and any segments that are associated with it. (*See also* **Onset**, **Nucleus**, **Coda**.)

Syllable weight   The composition of a syllable **rhyme**; a **heavy syllable** has a coda, while a **light syllable** does not.

Symbolic model   A psycholinguistic theory built around the claim that models of linguistic knowledge make reference to rules and representations consisting of symbols such as phonemes, words, syntactic category labels, and so forth.

Syncope   The deletion of a word-internal vowel (e.g., the deletion of the schwa in *police*).

Synonyms   Words or expressions that have the same meanings in some or all contexts (e.g., *buy* and *purchase*).

Syntactic category   The category into which an element is placed depending on the type of meaning that it expresses, the type of affixes it takes, and the type of structure in which it occurs (includes both lexical and functional categories).

Syntactic parser   The theoretical construct that accounts for the human ability to assign grammatical categories and hierarchical structure to elements in a stream of language input.

Syntax   The system of rules and categories that underlies sentence formation in human language.

Synthetic language   A language that makes extensive use of polymorphemic words (e.g., words containing a root and one or more affixes) (also called an **inflectional language**) (e.g., Spanish).

Systematic gaps   Nonoccurring forms that would violate the phonotactic constraints of a language (e.g., in English *mtlow).

Systematic phonetic correspondences   Sound correspondences between two or more related languages that are consistent throughout the vocabularies of those languages.

Target   (1) In second language acquisition, the language the learner is learning. (2) In a priming experiment, the stimulus to which a subject must respond and for which **response accuracy** and **response latency** are measured.

Telegraphic speech   Speech lacking functional categories and bound morphemes.

Telegraphic stage   The stage in child language acquisition in which children's utterances are generally longer than two words but lack bound morphemes and most functional categories.

Temporal lobe   The lobe of the brain that lies beneath the lateral fissure and in which Wernicke's area is located.

Tense (feature)   A DORSAL feature that expresses the distinction between a **tense** and a **lax vowel**.

Tense (verb)   In syntax and morphology, an inflectional category indicating the time of an event or action relative to the moment of speaking.

Tense vowels   Vowels that are made with a relatively tense tongue and greater vocal tract constriction than a **lax vowel** (e.g., the vowel sounds in *heat* and *boat*).

Terminal (intonation) contour   Falling intonation at the end of an utterance, signaling that the utterance is complete.

Terminals   The lexical items or prefixes, suffixes, stems, or words of a language.

Textual competence   Competence in the organization of language beyond the sentence.

T form   In languages with more than one form of *you*, the informal or intimate form of *you*. (*Compare with* **V form**.)

Thematic grid   The part of a word's lexical entry that carries information about the thematic roles that it assigns.

Thematic role   The part played by a particular entity in an event (e.g., agent, theme, source, goal, location).

Theme   The **thematic role** of the entity directly affected by the action of the verb (e.g., *the ball* in *Tom caught the ball*).

Thyroid cartilage   The cartilage that forms the main portion of the larynx, spreading outward like the head of a plow.

Tiers   Different levels of structure in which only certain elements are represented (e.g., in phonology, a syllabic tier and a tonal tier; in morphology, an affix tier and a root tier).

Tip (of the tongue)   The narrow area at the front of the tongue.

Tip-of-the-tongue phenomena   Instances of temporary inability to access a word in the mental lexicon.

Tone   Pitch differences that signal differences in meaning.

Tone language   A language in which differences in word meaning are signaled by differences in pitch.

Tone placement   In a tone language, **inflection** by changing the tone (e.g., in Mono-Bili, past is marked by a high tone on the verb, while future is marked by a low tone).

(Tongue) back   *See* **Back**.

(Tongue) blade   *See* **Blade**.

(Tongue) body   *See* **Body**.

(Tongue) dorsum   *See* **Dorsum**.

(Tongue) root   *See* **Root**.

(Tongue) tip   *See* **Tip**.

Top-down parsing   A method of sentence analysis in which the entire sentence is considered first, before its component parts.

Top-down processing   A type of mental processing using a set of expectations to guide phonetic processing and word recognition.

Topic   What a sentence or group of sentences is about.

Topicalization   The process by which the topic of a sentence is moved to the front of the sentence (e.g., *Vanilla pudding I like*).

Total assimilation   The **assimilation** of all the features of neighboring segments.

Trace   The empty element, marked by the symbol *t*, that is left in syntactic structure after an element has been moved.

Trachea   The tube below the larynx through which air travels when it leaves the lungs, commonly known as the windpipe.

Transfer   The process by which the first language (L1) influences the **interlanguage** grammar of the learner of a second language.

Transformation   A type of syntactic rule that can move an element from one position to another.

Transformational generative grammar   A widely accepted approach to syntactic analysis in which syntactic phenomena are described in terms of building phrase structures and moving elements (transformations) as a result of **Merge** and **Move** operations.

Transitional bilingual education   An educational program for language minority students in which initial instruction is provided in the minority language along with the majority language, but full literacy in the minority language is not a goal. (*Compare with* **developmental bilingual education**.)

Transitive   *See* **Transitive verb**.

Transitive verb   A verb that takes a **direct object** (e.g., *hit*).

Tree   A diagram that represents the internal organization of a word, phrase, or sentence.

Trill   An *r*-like sound that is made by passing air over the raised tongue tip, allowing it to vibrate.

Truth conditions   The circumstances under which a sentence is true.

Turn-taking   The changeover between speakers' turns in a conversation.

Two-way immersion (TWI) programs   Educational programs that provide instruction in two languages for language minority students and language majority students together (also known as **dual-language programs**).

Two-word stage   A stage of first language acquisition in which children normally utter two succeeding words to make a sentence.

Typological plausibility   A criterion that guides language reconstruction by referring to universals or existing properties of language.

Umlaut   The effect that a vowel (or sometimes a glide) in one syllable can have on the vowel of another (usually preceding) syllable.

Underextension   A developmental phenomenon in which a child uses a lexical item to denote only a subset of the items that it denotes in adult speech (e.g., *car* used to refer to only moving cars).

Underlying   Unpredictable and basic (e.g., features of a phonemic segment before **derivation**).

Underlying form   *See* **Underlying representation**.

Underlying representation   In phonology, a form from which phonetic forms are derived by rule.

Universal Grammar (UG)   The system of categories, operations, and principles shared by all human languages and considered to be innate.

Universal tendencies   Patterns or traits that occur in all or most languages.

Unmarked   Tending to be relatively common in world languages and/or less complex. (*See also* **Unmarked traits**.)

Unmarked traits   Those characteristics of language that are considered to be less complex and/or universally more common in languages.

Unordered rule application   In a phonological **derivation**, an application of rules in which the outcome will be the same regardless of the order in which rules are applied.

Unreleased stop   At the end of a **stop**, the articulator remains at the place of articulation (e.g., the tongue stays at the alveolar ridge at the end of [t]).

Uvula   The small fleshy flap of tissue that hangs down from the velum.

Uvulars   Sounds made with the tongue near or touching the **uvula**.

Variable   *See* **Sociolinguistic variables**.

Variant   One of a set of several possible forms that can be used to express the same function or meaning.

Variationist sociolinguistics   The branch of linguistics that studies the connection between social distinctions and variation in language.

Velarized *l*   An *l* sound in which the tongue tip touches the alveolar ridge and also has an additional constriction at the velum (also called **dark *l***).

Velars   Sounds made with the tongue touching or near the **velum** (e.g., [ŋ], [k]).

Velum   The soft area toward the rear of the roof of the mouth.

Verb (V)   A **lexical category** that typically designates actions, sensations, and states; can usually be inflected for **tense**; and functions as the **head** of a verb phrase (e.g., *see, feel, remain*).

Verbal paradigm   The set of inflected forms associated with a verb (also called a **conjugation**).

Verb Raising   A cross-linguistic variation involving whether the verb does or does not raise to I.

Verb Raising transformation   A syntactic rule that moves the verb to the I position in **S-structure** in languages such as French.

(Verb) tense   *See* **Tense (verb)**.

V form   In languages with more than one form of *you*, the formal form of *you*. (*Compare with* **T form**.)

Vocal cords   *See* **Vocal folds**.

Vocal folds   A set of muscles inside the larynx that may be positioned in various ways to produce different glottal states (also called **vocal cords**).

Vocal fry   *See* **Creaky voice**.

Vocal tract   The oral cavity, nasal cavity, and pharynx.

Voice   A laryngeal feature that distinguishes between **voiced** and **voiceless** sounds.

Voiced   The glottal state in which the **vocal folds** are brought close together but not tightly closed, causing air passing through them to vibrate (e.g., [æ], [z], [m] are voiced).

Voiceless   The glottal state in which the **vocal folds** are pulled apart, allowing air to pass directly through the glottis (e.g., [t], [s], [f] are voiceless).

Voicing   (1) A kind of assimilation in which a sound becomes **voiced** because of a nearby voiced sound. (2) A historical process of **consonant weakening** in which voiceless stops or fricatives become voiced.

Voicing assimilation   The process in which one sound becomes more like another sound in terms of whether it is **voiced** or **voiceless**.

Vowel harmony   Phonological phenomenon in which all vowels of a word share one or more features (e.g., all [+back, +round]).

Vowel qualities   Vowel sounds.

Vowel reduction   A process that converts a full vowel, typically unstressed, to the short, lax **schwa**.

Vowels   Resonant, syllabic sounds produced with less obstruction in the vocal tract than that required for glides.

Vowel shift   *See* **Shift**.

Weakening (phonetic)   A type of **assimilation** in which a lessening in the time or degree of a consonant's closure occurs (also called lenition).

Weakening of meaning   The process in which the meaning of a word has less force (e.g., *soon* used to mean 'immediately' but now means 'in the near future').

Wernicke's aphasia   The **aphasia** that results in fluent but nonsensical speech, sometimes characterized by **jargonaphasia**.

Wernicke's area   The area of the brain involved in the interpretation and the selection of lexical items.

***Wh* Movement**   A **transformation** that moves a *wh* phrase to the beginning of the sentence, formulated as: Move a *wh* phrase to the specifier position under CP.

***Wh* Movement Parameter**   The parameter that determines whether a *wh* element must move to the specifier position of CP or not.

***Wh* question**   A sentence that begins with a *wh*- word such as *who, what, where, when* (e.g., *Who did you see?*).

Whisper   The glottal state in which the **vocal folds** are adjusted so that the front portions are pulled close together while the back portions are apart.

Word   The smallest free form found in language.

Word-based morphology   Morphology that can form a new word from a base that is itself a word (e.g., *re-do* and *treat-ment* in English).

Word manufacture   The creation of a word from scratch, sometimes with the help of a computer (also called **coinage**) (e.g., *Kodak*).

Writing   The representation of language by graphic signs or symbols.

XP rule   A phrase structure rule that deals with maximal categories, which states that a maximal category XP consists of an optional specifier and an X'.

X' rule   A phrase structure rule that deals with intermediate categories, which states that an intermediate category X' consists of a head, X, and any optional complements.

X' Schema   The template for phrase structure, indicating that a phrase is hierarchically organized with a head, complement, and specifier.

***Yes-no* questions**   Questions that require an answer of either *yes* or *no* (e.g., *Is linguistics interesting? Do you speak a second language?*).

Zero derivation   *See* **Conversion**.

SOURCES

Chapter 1   Language: A Preview

The information on the density of nerves controlling the vocal cords at the end of Section 1 is from John Colapinto's article "Giving Voice" in the *New Yorker*, March 4, 2014, 48–57. The discussion of word creation in Section 2 is based on an article by Eve Clark and Herb Clark, "When Nouns Surface as Verbs" in *Language* 55 (1979): 767–811. The Walbiri data are based on K. Hale's article "Person Marking in Walbiri" in *A Festschrift for Morris Halle*, edited by S. Anderson and P. Kiparsky (New York: Holt, Rinehart and Winston, 1973). The quote at the end of Section 3.2 is from the book by Steven Pinker titled *The Language Instinct: How the Human Mind Creates Language* (New York: Morrow, 1994), 370. The data on word order preferences are from *Typology and Universals* by William Croft (New York: Cambridge University Press, 1990), 46. Derek Bickerton's *Language and Species* (Chicago: University of Chicago Press, 1990) and Steven Pinker's *The Language Instinct: How the Human Mind Creates Language* (New York: Morrow, 1994) provide different views of the emergence of language in the human species.

The exercises for this chapter were prepared by Joyce Hildebrand.

Chapter 2   Phonetics

Information on the International Phonetic Alphabet can be obtained from the International Phonetic Association, University College, Gower Street, London, WC1E 6BT, UK (http://www.langsci.ucl.ac.uk/ipa/). The estimate of 600 consonants and 200 vowels comes from Peter Ladefoged in a talk given at the University of Hawaii, April 27, 1999. Sarcee data are taken from E.-D. Cook, "Vowels and Tones in Sarcee" in *Language* 47 (1971): 164–179; Gaelic data are courtesy of James Galbraith. Bini data are adapted from *A Course in Phonetics*, 4th ed., by P. Ladefoged (Toronto: Harcourt, 2001). For a discussion of glottal states, see Jimmy G. Harris, "The State of the Glottis for Voiceless Plosives" in *Proceedings of the 14th International Congress of Phonetic Sciences*, 3 (1999): 2041–44.

Chapter 3   Phonology

The view of the phoneme outlined in this chapter draws on classic work by pioneers in phonology from the later nineteenth and early half of the twentieth century. A still valuable presentation of classic phonemic analysis is found in H. A. Gleason, Jr.'s *An Introduction to Descriptive Linguistics* (Toronto: Holt, Rinehart and Winston, 1961). The discussion of syllable structure draws on the ideas put forward by G. N. Clements in "The Role of the Sonority Cycle in Core Syllabification" in *Papers in Laboratory Phonology I: Between the Grammar and the Physics of Speech*, edited by J. Kingston and M. Beckman (London: Cambridge University Press, 1990), 283–333. The data for Cree in the appendix are from Y. Carifelle and M. Pepper (personal communication).

Data sources for problems are as follows: for Inuktitut, B. Harnum (personal communication); for Mokilese, S. Harrison's *Mokilese Reference Grammar* (Honolulu: University of Hawaii Press, 1976); for Gascon, R. C. Kelly's *A Descriptive Analysis of Gascon* (Amsterdam: Mouton, 1978); for Passamaquoddy, *Kolusuwakonol, Philip S. LeSourd's English and Passamaquoddy-Moliseet Dictionary*, edited by Robert Leavitt and David Francis (Perry, ME: Passamaquoddy-Maliseet Bilingual Program, 1986); for Canadian French, D. C. Walker's *The Pronunciation of Canadian French* (Ottawa: University of Ottawa Press, 1984) and A. Teasdale (personal communication); for English fast speech, G. Zhang, *Phonological Representation and Analyses of Fast Speech Phenomena in English*, M.A. thesis, Memorial University of Newfoundland, 1994; for Tamil, R. Radhakrishnan (personal communication).

Chapter 4   Morphology

The estimate that the average high school student knows 60,000 "basic" words comes from *The Language Instinct* by S. Pinker (New York: Morrow, 1994), 150. The introduction to words and morphemes draws on the classic treatments found in L. Bloomfield's *Language* (New York: Holt, Rinehart and Winston, 1933), H. A. Gleason's *An Introduction to Descriptive Linguistics* (New York: Holt, Rinehart and Winston, 1961), and C. F. Hockett's *A Course in Modern Linguistics* (New York: Macmillan, 1958). The discussion of word formation seeks to portray those aspects of recent and current work that represent widely accepted views and are appropriate for presentation in an introductory textbook. Much of this work is summarized in the following books: *Morphology: Word Structure in Generative Grammar* by John Jensen (Amsterdam: John Benjamins, 1990), *Morphology* by Francis Katamba (London: Macmillan, 1993), and *Morphological Theory* by Andrew Spencer (Cambridge, MA: Blackwell, 1991), and the many references cited therein. For a detailed discussion on nonconcatenative morphology, see *A-Morphous Morphology* by S. Anderson (New York: Cambridge University Press, 1992).

The Arabic examples in Section 1.2 are from p. 17 of the book by Spencer cited above. The tier-based analysis of Arabic word structure is based on work by John McCarthy, including his article "A Prosodic Theory of Nonconcatenative Morphology," *Linguistic Inquiry* 12 (1981): 373–418. The facts concerning the requirement that *-ant* combine with a base of Latin origin (Section 2.1) are noted on p. 71 of the book by Katamba cited above.

The examples of conversion given in Section 5.2 come largely from the discussion in the books by Jensen (cited above, pp. 92–93) and pp. 229–231 of *English Word-Formation* by Laurie Bauer (New York: Cambridge University Press, 1983). The examples of Malay blends come from "Malay Blends—CV or Syllable Templates" by M. Dobrovolsky, unpublished manuscript, University of Calgary. The data on Slavey onomatopoeia are from "Slavey Expressive Terms" by M. Pepper, *Kansas Working Papers in Linguistics* 10 (1985): 85–100. The definition of *stem* introduced in Section 4 is from the article by S. Anderson, "Morphological Theory," in *Linguistics: The Cambridge Survey*, Vol. 1, edited by F. Newmeyer (New York: Cambridge University Press, 1988), 163. The discussion of the difference between regular and irregular inflection draws on information from "Rules of Language" by S. Pinker in *Science* 253 (August 1991): 530–535. The data in the section on tense come principally from "Tense, Aspect and Mood" by S. Chung and A. Timberlake in *Language Typology and Syntactic Description,* Vol. 3, edited by T. Shopen (London: Cambridge University Press, 1985), 202–258.

The examples used in the section on morphophonemics were taken from the discussion of this subject written by Michael Dobrovolsky for the third edition of this book.

Exercises whose authorship is not otherwise noted were prepared by Joyce Hildebrand. The data in problem 17 are from *Writing Transformational Grammars* by A. Koutsoudas (New York: McGraw-Hill, 1966). The Zapotec data and romanization are from *Grammática de la lengua zapoteca* by an anonymous author, published in 1897 in Mexico by the Oficina Tip. de la Secretaría de Formento. The Kwakum data are from Malcolm Guthrie's book *The Bantu Languages of Western Equatorial Africa* (Oxford: Oxford University Press, 1953).

Chapter 5   Syntax

Transformational grammar is the most popular of the half-dozen major contemporary syntactic theories. Traditionally, it is the theory taught in introductory linguistics courses, both because it is so widely used and because many of the other approaches that exist today have developed in response to it. The particular system outlined here involves a variety of simplifications to make it appropriate for presentation in an introductory course.

The system of subcategorization employed here is loosely based on the one outlined in *Generalized Phrase Structure Grammar* by G. Gazdar, E. Klein, G. Pullum, and I. Sag (Cambridge, MA: Harvard University Press, 1979), which describes a nontransformational approach to syntax.

The information on inversion in Appalachian English comes from *Appalachian Speech* by Walt Wolfram and Donna Christian (Arlington, VA: Center for Applied Linguistics, 1976).

The Welsh data in Section 5.4 is from "Welsh Syntax and VSO Structure" by Richard Sproat in *Natural Language and Linguistic Theory* 3 (1985): 173–216.

The exercises for this chapter were prepared by Joyce Hildebrand.

Chapter 6   Semantics

Surveys of the nature of word meaning and semantic relations can be found in many introductory books on semantics, including those recommended below and at the end of the chapter. A prominent advocate of componential analysis is Ray Jackendoff, whose book *Semantic Structures* (Cambridge, MA: MIT Press, 1991) reviews earlier ideas and offers new proposals. The discussion of a semantic constraint on double object patterns draws on the proposal put forward by Steven Pinker in *Learnability and Cognition* (Cambridge, MA: MIT Press, 1989). The discussion of fuzzy categories and graded membership in Section 2 draws from Part 1 of *Women, Fire, and Dangerous*

Things by G. Lakoff (Chicago: University of Chicago Press, 1987) and the references cited there. The discussion of metaphor takes as its starting point the book *Metaphors We Live By* by G. Lakoff and Mark Johnson (Chicago: University of Chicago Press, 1982). The four Inuktitut words for *snow* in Table 6.7 are from *The Handbook of American Indian Languages* by F. Boas (Washington: Smithsonian Institution, 1911); for a longer list of words for *snow*, see *Dictionnaire français-eskimau du parler de l'Ungava* (Québec: Presses de l'Université Laval, 1970); see also "The Great Eskimo Vocabulary Hoax" by G. Pullum in *Natural Language and Linguistic Theory* 7 (1989): 275–281. The discussion of verbs of motion is based on the paper "Lexicalization Patterns: Semantic Structure in Lexical Form" by L. Talmy in *Language Typology and Syntactic Description*, Vol. 3, edited by T. Shopen (New York: Cambridge University Press, 1985), 57–149. Data on Hidatsa assertion morphemes in the same section are from *Hidatsa Syntax* by G. H. Matthews (The Hague: Mouton, 1965).

The treatment of structural ambiguity, thematic role assignment, and pronoun interpretation in this chapter presents slightly simplified versions of classic views widely held within generative grammar. For a summary of the last two issues, see *Introduction to Government and Binding Theory*, 2nd ed., by L. Haegeman (Cambridge, MA: Blackwell, 1994). The discussion of constructional meaning is based on *Constructions: A Construction Grammar Approach to Argument Structure* by A. Goldberg (Chicago: University of Chicago Press, 1995).

The data used in the discussion of deixis come from "Deixis" by S. Anderson and E. Keenan in *Language Typology and Syntactic Description*, Vol. 3, edited by T. Shopen (New York: Cambridge University Press, 1985), 259–308. The discussion of topicalization draws on "Major Functions of the Noun Phrase" by A. Andrews in *Language Typology and Syntactic Description*, Vol. 1, edited by T. Shopen (New York: Cambridge University Press, 1985), 62–154. The discussion of the Cooperative Principle and the maxims of conversation is based primarily on "Logic and Conversation" by Paul Grice in *Syntax and Semantics*, Vol. 3, edited by P. Cole and J. Morgan (New York: Academic Press, 1975), 41–58 and the paper "Pragmatic Theory" by L. Horn, in *Linguistics: The Cambridge Survey*, Vol. 1, edited by F. Newmeyer (New York: Cambridge University Press, 1988), 113–145.

The exercises for this chapter were prepared by Joyce Hildebrand.

Chapter 7   Classification of Languages

The section on the threat to linguistic diversity was written by William O'Grady. It draws heavily on information in *Vanishing Voices: The Extinction of the World's Languages* by Daniel Nettle and Suzanne Romaine, as well as from the following sources: "New Knowledge: Findings from the Catalog of Endangered Languages ('ELCAT')," a paper by Lyle Campbell, Raina Heaton, Eve Okura, and John Van Way, presented at the 2013 meeting of the Linguistic Society of America; "The Case for Linguistic Diversity," by Luisa Maffi in *Terralingua Langscape* 2, 8 (Autumn 2011), **http://www .terralingua.org/**; and UNESCO's policy statement "Language Vitality and Endangerment" at **http://unesdoc.unesco.org/images/0018/001836/183699E.pdf**. Additional information can be found at the Ethnologue website (**www.ethnologue.com**) and at the website of the Summer Institute of Linguistics (**www.sil.org/sociolx/ndg-lg -home.html**).

The section on linguistic typology draws on data from the book by B. Comrie, *The Languages of the Soviet Union* (London: Cambridge University Press, 1981) and from the book by J. Greenberg, *The Languages of Africa* (Bloomington: Indiana University Press, 1966). Other material for this section comes from *Tone: A Linguistic Survey*, edited by V. Fromkin (New York: Academic Press, 1978); J. Hawkins's article "On Implicational and Distributional Universals of Word Order" in *Journal of Linguistics* 16 (1980): 193–235; M. Dryer's article "The Greenbergian Word Order Correlations" in *Language* 68 (1992): 81–132; *Patterns of Sounds* by I. Maddieson (Cambridge: Cambridge University Press, 1984); M. Ruhlen's book *A Guide to the Languages of the World* (Language Universals Project: Stanford University, 1976); *The World's Major Languages*, edited by B. Comrie (Oxford: Oxford University Press, 1990); and the four-volume series *Universals of Human Language*, edited by J. Greenberg (Stanford, CA: Stanford University Press, 1978).

The discussion of morphological typology draws on information presented in B. Comrie's book, mentioned above. The estimate of the relative frequency of languages in which the subject precedes the direct object is based on information in W. Croft, *Typology and Universals* (New York: Cambridge University Press, 1990). The data on OVS and OSV languages (and their romanization) are from "Object-Initial Languages" by D. Derbyshire and G. Pullum, *International Journal of American Linguistics* 47 (1981): 192–214. The discussion of consonant systems in Section 2.4 is based on "Phonetic Universals in Consonant Systems" by B. Lindblom and I. Maddieson in *Language, Speech and Mind: Studies in Honor of Victoria Fromkin*, edited by L. Hyman and C. Li (New York: Routledge & Kegan Paul, 1988), 62–78.

The section on language families is based on the books by B. Comrie and J. Greenberg mentioned above, the book by M. Ruhlen cited above and another book by Ruhlen titled *A Guide to the World's Languages, Vol. 1: Classification* (Stanford, CA: Stanford University Press, 1987), and C. F. and F. M. Voegelin's *Classification and Index of the World's Languages* (New York: Elsevier, 1978). Additional data derive from C. D. Buck's book *A Dictionary of Selected Synonyms in the Principal Indo-European Languages* (Chicago: University of Chicago Press, 1949); *The American Heritage Dictionary of Indo-European Roots*, revised and edited by C. Watkins (Boston: Houghton Mifflin, 1985); the three-volume *Russisches Etymologisches Wörterbuch*, compiled by M. Vasmer (Heidelberg: Carl Winter Universitätsverlag, 1950–58); "Syntactic Reconstruction and Finno-Ugric," an article by L. Campbell in *Historical Linguistics 1987*, edited by H. Andersen and K. Koerner (Amsterdam: John Benjamins, 1990); and the Proto-Baltic Dictionary database developed by the first author of this chapter.

Chapter 8   Historical Linguistics

The textbooks by Campbell, Hock, Labov, and Trask listed in the Recommended Reading provide much more detailed discussions of most of the major topics in this chapter. They are also excellent sources for references relating to particular topics.

Hock is particularly important for providing detailed discussions of syntactic change and the role of typology in reconstruction.

Overviews of historical linguistics as it applies to the development of English are presented in *A History of the English Language* by N. F. Blake (Houndmills, UK: Macmillan, 1996), in *A Biography of the English Language*, 2nd ed., by C. M. Millward (New York: Holt, Rinehart and Winston, 1996), and in *An Historical Study of English: Function, Form and Change* by Jeremy Smith (New York: Routledge, 1996).

The catalog of sound changes is adapted from catalogs proposed by Theo Vennemann in the article "Linguistic Typologies in Historical Linguistics" in *Società di linguistica italiana* 23 (1985): 87–91 and a book entitled *Preference Laws for Syllable Structure and the Explanation of Sound Change* (Amsterdam: Mouton de Gruyter, 1988). Section 2 has also benefited from unpublished material (particularly the manuscript "Linguistic Change") kindly made available by Theo Vennemann (University of Munich) to the author during his stay in Munich from 1980–85.

The data on word order in Old and Middle English come from the book by Joseph Williams, *Origins of the English Language: A Social and Linguistic History* (New York: Free Press, 1975). The examples of English loan words in Gwich'in (Loucheux) are given in *Dene* 1, 1 (1985), published by the Dene Language Terminology Committee, Yellowknife, Northwest Territories. The discussion of borrowing and semantic change in English draws on materials in the book by Williams.

The table depicting lexical diffusion of the stress change in English nouns derived from verbs is taken from the book by Jean Aitchison, *Language Change: Progress or Decay?* (New York: Universe Books, 1985). Aitchison's remarks are based on the article by M. Chen and W. Wang, "Sound Change: Actuation and Implementation" *Language* 51 (1975): 255–281. The data on the realization of [s] as [h] in Spanish were provided by the late Herbert Izzo of the University of Calgary.

The Germanic cognates used to illustrate family relationships are based on Leonard Bloomfield's classic work, *Language* (New York: Holt, Rinehart and Winston, 1933). Some of the Romance cognates in this section come from *Proto-Romance Phonology* by Robert A. Hall, Jr. (New York: Elsevier, 1976).

Exercise 2 on European and Acadian French is based on data provided by George Patterson, whose generosity we hereby acknowledge. The data for exercises 4 (Guaraní) and 5 (Bulgarian) are from F. Columbus's *Introductory Workbook in Historical Phonology* (Cambridge, MA: Slavica, 1974). Exercise 10 on Shona is based on data provided by David Bellusci. The data for exercise 16 in Proto-Romance are drawn from *Source Book for Linguistics* by W. Cowan and J. Rakušan (Philadelphia: John Benjamins, 1987).

Chapter 9   First Language Acquisition

The estimate of the proportion of language use captured in speech samples is from "Input and First Language Acquisition" by Elena Lieven in *Lingua* 120 (2010): 2546–2556. For more information on the misinterpretation of *every*, see "Quantifying Kids" by Bart Geurts in *Language Acquisition* 11 (2003): 197–218.

Pioneering work on infant perception is reported in "Developmental Studies of Speech Perception" by P. Eimas in *Infant Perception: From Sensation to Cognition*,

Vol. 2, edited by L. Cohen and P. Salapatek (New York: Academic Press, 1975), 193–231. More recent work is reported by J. Mehler, E. Dupoux, T. Nazzi, and G. Dehaene-Lambertz in "Coping with Linguistic Diversity: The Infant's Viewpoint" and by J. Werker, V. Lloyd, J. Pegg, and L. Polka in "Putting the Baby in the Bootstraps: Toward a More Complete Understanding of the Role of the Input in Infant Speech Processing," both in *Signal to Syntax*, edited by J. Morgan and K. Demuth (Mahwah, NJ: Erlbaum, 1996). The ability to use phonetic contrasts to distinguish between words is examined in "Perception and Production in Child Phonology: The Testing of Four Hypotheses" by M. Edwards in *Journal of Child Language* 1 (1974): 205–219. The cross-linguistic data on babbling are summarized and discussed on pp. 9–11 of *Phonological Acquisition and Change* by J. Locke (San Diego: Academic Press, 1983); see also "Adaptation to Language: Evidence from Babbling and First Words in Four Languages" by B. de Boysson-Bardies and M. Vihman in *Language* 67 (1991): 297–319. For a recent discussion of the relevance of babbling to the development of control over the vocal tract, see S. Pinker's *The Language Instinct* (New York: Morrow, 1994), 266. Differences between children's production and perception of speech sounds are found in *The Acquisition of Phonology: A Case Study* by N. Smith (New York: Cambridge University Press, 1973); the *"fis* phenomenon" is reported in "Psycholinguistic Research Methods" by J. Berko and R. Brown in *Handbook of Research Methods in Child Development*, edited by P. Mussen (New York: John Wiley and Sons, 1960). David Ingram's *Phonological Disability in Children* (London: Edward Arnold, 1976) contains many useful examples of early phonetic processes. The discussion of syllable deletion draws on information in "A Role for Stress in Early Speech Segmentation" by C. Echols, in *Signal to Syntax*, edited by J. Morgan and K. Demuth (Mahwah, NJ: Erlbaum, 1996), and in "The Acquisition of Prosodic Structure: An Investigation of Current Accounts of Children's Prosodic Development" by M. Kehoe and C. Stoel-Gammon in *Language* 73 (1997): 13–44. The data on developmental order for speech sounds come from Chapter 8 of *First Language Acquisition: Method, Description and Explanation* by D. Ingram (New York: Cambridge University Press, 1989).

The sample vocabulary in Table 9.8 is from p. 149 of the book by Ingram cited above. For a brief survey of work on rate of vocabulary development, see *How Children Learn Language* by William O'Grady (Cambridge, UK: Cambridge University Press, 2005), 7–8. Differences among children in terms of the types of words in their early vocabulary were first noted by K. Nelson in "Structure and Strategy in Learning to Talk" in *Monographs of the Society for Research in Child Development* 38, 149 (1973): 1–135. The *"dax* experiment" on proper and common nouns is reported by N. Katz, E. Baker, and J. Macnamara in their article, "What's in a Name? A Study of How Children Learn Common and Proper Nouns" in *Child Development* 45 (1974): 469–473; the *"tiv* experiment" is from "The Child as Word Learner" by S. Carey in *Linguistic Theory and Psychological Reality*, edited by M. Halle, J. Bresnan, and G. Miller (Cambridge, MA: MIT Press, 1978). The discussion of strategies for learning word meaning is based on the proposals outlined in *Categorization and Naming in Children: Problems of Induction* by E. Markman (Cambridge, MA: MIT Press, 1989). The Social Strategy is discussed by Michael Tomasello in his article "The Social-Pragmatic Theory of Word Learning," in *Pragmatics* 10 (2000): 401–413. The contrast between overextension in production and comprehension is described on pp. 152–153 of the book by Ingram cited above. The report of overextension in the speech of Allen is based on the discussion on p. 92 of *The Lexicon in Acquisition* by Eve Clark (New York: Cambridge University Press, 1993). The experimental study on overextension was carried out by J. Thomson and R. Chapman and reported in "Who Is 'Daddy' Revisited: The Status of Two-Year-Olds' Over-extended Words in Use and Comprehension" in *Journal of Child Language* 4 (1977): 359–375. The experiment on *pour* and *fill* can be found in "Syntax and Semantics in the Acquisition of Locative Verbs" by J. Gropen, S. Pinker, M. Hollander, and R. Goldberg in *Journal of Child Language* 18 (1991): 115–151. The experiment on dimensional terms was carried out by P. Harris and J. Morris and is reported in "The Early Acquisition of Spatial Adjectives: A Cross-linguistic Study" in *Journal of Child Language* 13 (1986): 335–352.

The remarks on inflectional overgeneralization are based in part on *Overregularization in Language Acquisition* by G. Marcus, S. Pinker, M. Ullman, M. Hollander, T. Rosen, and F. Xu, *Monographs of the Society for Research in Child Development*, Serial No. 228, Vol. 57, No. 4 (1992). The pioneering work on developmental order for English bound morphemes and lexical categories was done by R. Brown and reported in his book *A First Language: The Early Stages* (Cambridge, MA: Harvard University Press, 1973); see also "Universal and Particular in the Acquisition of Language" by D. Slobin in *Language Acquisition: The State of the Art*, edited by E. Wanner and L. Gleitman (New York: Cambridge University Press, 1982). The original *"wug test"* was done by J. Berko and is reported in her article "The Child's Learning of English Morphology" in *Word* 14 (1958): 150–177. The work on the development of derivational affixes and compounding in English is based on information reported in the book by Eve Clark recommended below and in the article by E. Clark and B. Hecht, "Learning to Coin Agent and Instrument Nouns" in *Cognition* 12 (1982): 1–24. The data on the acquisition of the prohibition against inflection within compounds are from "Level-Ordering in Lexical Development" by P. Gordon in *Cognition* 21 (1985): 73–93. Word order errors within compounds are reported in "Coining Complex Compounds in English: Affixes and Word Order in Acquisition" by E. Clark, B. Hecht, and R. Mulford in *Linguistics* 24 (1986): 7–29.

The data on four-year-olds' preference for SVO word order with nonsense verbs are from "Characterizing English-Speaking Children's Understanding of SVO Word Order" by Nameera Akhtar in *Journal of Child Language* 26 (1999): 339–356 and from "Early Word Order Representations: New Arguments against Old Contradictions," by Julie Franck, Servine Millotte, and Romy Lassotta in *Language Acquisition* 18 (2011): 121–135. The early sensitivity to the difference between *is V-ing* and *can V-ing* is documented in "Sensitivity to Discontinuous Dependencies in Language Learners" by Lynn Santelmann and Peter Jusczyk in *Cognition* 69 (1998): 105–134. The data on the development of question structures are based on the classic article by E. Klima and U. Bellugi, "Syntactic Regularities in the Speech of Children" in *Psycholinguistic Papers*, edited by J. Lyons and R. Wales (Edinburgh: Edinburgh University Press, 1966). The auxiliary copying error in question structures is the subject of an experiment reported by M. Nakayama, "Performance Factors in Subject-Auxiliary Inversion," *Journal of Child Language* 14 (1987): 113–126. The developmental order for *wh* words is documented by L. Bloom, S. Merkin, and J. Wootten, "*Wh* Questions: Linguistic Factors That Contribute to the Sequence of Acquisition," *Child Development* 53 (1982): 1084–1092. For a discussion of the absence of inversion in *why* questions, see "Language Acquisition Is Language Change" by Stephen Crain, Takuya Goro, and Rosalind Thornton in *Journal of Psycholinguistic Research* 35 (2006): 31–49. Other descriptions confirming the main points of this account can be found in Chapter 9 of the book by Ingram cited above. The data on the acquisition of passive structures come from a study by E. Turner and R. Rommetveit, reported in their article "The Acquisition of Sentence Voice and Reversibility" in *Child Development* 38 (1967): 650–660. The data on children's use of *me* and *myself* come from "Children's Knowledge of Binding and Coreference: Evidence from Spontaneous Speech" by P. Bloom, A. Barss, J. Nicol, and L. Conway in *Language* 70 (1994): 53–71.

The data on the effects of exposure to language in Section 6 are from *Meaningful Differences in the Everyday Experience of Young American Children*, by Betty Hart and Todd Risley (Baltimore: Paul H. Brookes, 1995). The role of correction in language development is examined in "Derivational Complexity and the Order of Acquisition in Child Speech" by R. Brown and C. Hanlon in *Cognition and the Development of Language*, edited by J. Hayes (New York: John Wiley and Sons, 1970). The data on mothers' reactions to children's ungrammatical and grammatical utterances come from "Brown and Hanlon Revisited: Mothers' Sensitivity to Ungrammatical Forms" by K. Hirsh-Pasek, R. Treiman, and M. Schneiderman in *Journal of Child Language* 11 (1984): 81–88. The relationship between *yes-no* questions in maternal speech and the development of auxiliaries is discussed by E. Newport, H. Gleitman, and L. Gleitman in their article, "Mother, I'd Rather Do It Myself: Some Effects and Noneffects of Maternal Speech Style" in *Talking to Children*, edited by C. Snow and C. Ferguson (New York: Cambridge University Press, 1977); see also the discussion in the book by C. Gallaway and B. Richards, *Input and Interaction in Language Acquisition* (Cambridge, UK: Cambridge University Press, 1994). The "other one spoon" example is reported on p. 161 of an article by M. Braine, "The Acquisition of Language in Infant and Child" in *The Learning of Language*, edited by C. E. Reed (New York: Appleton-Century-Crofts, 1971). The recast experiment involving nonsense verbs is from "The Contrast Theory of Negative Evidence" by M. Saxton in *Journal of Child Language* 24 (1997): 139–161.

The description of Genie and of Rick is based on "Abnormal Language Acquisition and the Modularity of Language" by S. Curtiss in *Linguistics: The Cambridge Survey*, Vol. 2, edited by F. Newmeyer (New York: Cambridge University Press, 1988), 96–116. Chelsea's case is discussed by S. Curtiss in "The Independence and Task-Specificity of Language" in *Interaction in Human Development*, edited by A. Bornstein and J. Bruner (Hillsdale, NJ: Erlbaum, 1989). Christopher is the subject of a book by N. Smith and I. Tsimpli, *The Mind of a Savant: Language Learning and Modularity* (Cambridge, MA: Blackwell, 1995). The examples of sentences produced by speakers who have problems with inflection are from p. 49 of *The Language Instinct* by S. Pinker, cited above.

Exercises for this chapter were prepared by Joyce Hildebrand.

Chapter 10   Second Language Acquisition

The model of communicative competence is an adaptation of L. Bachman's *Fundamental Considerations in Language Testing* (Oxford: Oxford University Press, 1990). The Markedness Differential Hypothesis was developed by F. Eckman in "Markedness and the Contrastive Analysis Hypothesis" in *Language Learning* 27 (1977): 315–330. The discussion of the Similarity Differential Rate Hypothesis comes from R. Major, "Further Evidence for the Similarity Differential Rate Hypothesis" in *New Sounds 97*, edited by J. Leather and A. James (Klagenfurt, Austria: University of Klagenfurt, 1997).

The data from Arabic syllabification come from E. Broselow, "Prosodic Phonology and the Acquisition of a Second Language" in *Linguistic Theory in Second Language Acquisition*, edited by S. Flynn and W. O'Neil (Dordrecht: Kluwer, 1988). The stress data were reported in J. Archibald, *Language Learnability and L2 Phonology* (Dordrecht: Kluwer, 1993). The Null Subject analysis is drawn from L. White, *Universal Grammar and Second Language Acquisition* (Amsterdam: John Benjamins, 1989). The Verb Movement study can be found in L. White, "Adverb Placement in Second Language Acquisition: Some Effects of Positive and Negative Evidence in the Classroom" in *Second Language Research* 7 (1991): 133–161. The data on epenthesis versus deletion strategies come from Chilin Wang's 1995 dissertation "The Acquisition of English Word-Final Obstruents by Chinese Speakers" (State University of New York at Stony Brook).

The L2 morphology data can be found in H. Zobl and J. Liceras, "Functional Categories Acquisition Order" in *Language Learning* 44, 1 (1994): 159–180. The discussion of Patty is taken from D. Lardiere, "Mapping Features to Forms in Second Language Acquisition," in *Second Language Acquisition and Linguistic Theory*, edited by J. Archibald (Oxford: Blackwell, 2000). This issue is also discussed in P. Prévost and L. White, "Missing Surface Inflection or Impairment in Second Language Acquisition? Evidence from Tense and Agreement," in *Second Language Research* 16, 2 (2000): 103–133. The French gender information is discussed in S. Carroll, "Second-Language Acquisition and the Computational Paradigm," in *Language Learning* 39, 4 (1989): 535–594. The ultimate attainment results for syntax come from Lydia White and Fred Genesee, "How Native Is Near-Native? The Issue of Ultimate Attainment in Adult Second Language Acquisition," *Second Language Research* 12 (1996): 238–265. The discussion of ultimate attainment in phonology comes from T. Bongaerts, S. Mennen, and F. Slik, "Authenticity of Pronunciation in Naturalistic Second Language Acquisition: The Case of Very Advanced Late Learners of Dutch as a Second Language," *Studia Linguistica* 54, 2 (2000): 298–308. The instrumental/integrative distinction comes from R. Gardner, J. B. Day, and P. D. MacIntyre, "Integrative Motivation, Induced Anxiety and Language Learning in a Controlled Environment," in *Studies in Second Language Acquisition* 14, 2 (2000): 197–214. The term *international posture* has been in use in the motivation literature since its introduction by Tomoko Yashima in "Willingness to Communicate in a Second Language: The Japanese EFL Context," which appeared in *Modern Language Journal* 86, 1 (2002): 54–66. The work of Zoltán Dőrnyei, along with his students and associates, has had great influence on the investigation of motivation in recent years, and the article by Freerkien Waninge,

Zoltán Dőrnyei, and Kees DeBot, "Motivational Dynamics in Language Learning: Change, Stability, and Context," which appeared in *Modern Language Journal* 98, 3 (2014): 704–723, summarizes some of the most recent work that is in turn summarized in this chapter.

The L2 classroom discussion owes much to R. Allwright and K. Bailey, *Focus on the Language Classroom: An Introduction to Classroom Research for Language Teachers* (Cambridge, UK: Cambridge University Press, 1991). The evidence from focus-on-form was presented by P. Lightbown and N. Spada, "Focus-on-Form and Corrective Feedback in Communicative Language Teaching: Effects on Second Language Learning," in *Studies in Second Language Acquisition* 12, 4 (1990): 429–448. The discussion of focus-on-form draws on C. Doughty, "Cognitive Underpinnings of Focus on Form," in *Cognition and Second Language Instruction*, edited by Peter Robinson in the Cambridge Applied Linguistics Series (Cambridge, UK: Cambridge University Press, 2001).

Section 4.2 was written by Janie Rees-Miller. Figures on the numbers of ELs are found in a webpage on English language learners posted in May 2015 by the National Center for Educational Statistics, accessed at **http://nces.ed.gov/programs/coe /indicator_cgf.asp** and on a variety of pages hosted by the Office of English Language Acquisition and posted in January 2015, accessed through **www.ncela.us /files/fast_facts/OELA**. The OELA website is also the source for ELs' performance on reading and math proficiency tests and graduation rates from high school.

Newcomer programs are described in the executive summary of *Helping Newcomer Students Succeed in Secondary Schools and Beyond* by Deborah Short and Beverly Boyson (Washington, DC: Center for Applied Linguistics, 2012), accessed online through the website of the Center for Applied Linguistics (**www.cal.org**). The *English Learner Toolkit for State and Local Education Agencies*, published in 2015 by the National Center for English Language Acquisition, describes not only the responsibilities of schools in the United States but also the types of programs for ELs. It was accessed online via **www2.ed.gov/about/offices/list/oela/english-learner-toolkit/index .html**. Various types of programs for ELs are described and evaluated for effectiveness in Ilana Urmansky and Sean Rearson, "Reclassification Patterns among Latino English Learner Students in Bilingual, Dual Immersion, and English Immersion Classrooms" in *American Educational Research Journal* 20, 10 (2014): 1–34, and in an article by Rachel Valentino and Sean Reardon titled "Effectiveness of Four Instructional Programs Designed to Serve English Learners: Variation by Ethnicity and Initial English Proficiency" in *Educational Evaluation and Policy Analysis* 37, 4 (2015): 612–637. Two-way immersion programs are also described in Elizabeth Howard and Julie Sugarman, "Two-Way Immersion Programs: Features and Statistics," Digest EDO-FL-01-01 (2001), accessed at **www.cal.org/resources/digest/0101twi.htm**. Virginia Collier and Wayne Thomas conducted the large-scale study of 200,000 students in various types of programs and reported the results in "The Astounding Effectiveness of Dual Language Education for All" in *NABE Journal of Research and Practice*, 2, 1 (Winter 2004): 1–20.

Among the sources used for the description of various types of heritage language programs is the webpage of the Resource Network for Linguistic Diversity devoted to language maintenance, accessed at **http://www.rnld.org/language_maintenance**

and the links provided there. The film *Rising Voices, Hótȟaŋiŋpi* documents revitalization efforts for Lakota; the film was shown at the 2016 Linguistic Society of America Annual Meeting in Washington, D.C., and is described at **http://risingvoicesfilm .com/**.

Chapter 11   Psycholinguistics

Some of the "slip of the tongue" material in Section 1.1 is drawn from Victoria Fromkin's chapter on speech production (pp. 272–300) in *Psycholinguistics*, edited by Jean Berko-Gleason and Nan Bernstein Ratner (Philadelphia: Harcourt Brace, 1998).

The discussion of eye-movement data in psycholinguistics was based on the article by K. Rayner and S. Sereno, "Eye Movements in Reading" in the *Handbook of Psycholinguistics*, edited by M. A. Gernsbacher (New York: Academic Press, 1994), 57–81, as well as in the book by K. Rayner and A. Pollatsek, *The Psychology of Reading* (Englewood Cliffs, NJ: Prentice-Hall, 1989).

The material on event-related potentials is discussed in an excellent review article by Marta Kutas and Cyma Van Petten in Gernsbacher's *Handbook of Psycholinguistics* cited above (pp. 83–133). The syllable-processing experiment cited in the syllable section was reported in "Phoneme Monitoring, Syllable Monitoring, and Lexical Access" by J. Segui, U. Frauenfelder, and J. Mehler in the *British Journal of Psychology* 72 (1981): 471–477, and is discussed by R. E. Remes in "On the Perception of Speech" in the Gernsbacher *Handbook*.

The word-blending studies are reported in a series of studies conducted by Rebecca Treiman; see "The Structure of Spoken Syllables: Evidence from Novel Word Games" in *Cognition* 15 (1983): 49–74. A cross-linguistic study using a forced-choice version of these word games is reported in G. E. Wiebe and B. L. Derwing's paper, "A Forced-Choice Blending Task for Testing Intra-syllabic Break Points in English, Korean, and Taiwanese," in *The Twenty-First LACUS Forum* (Chapel Hill, NC: LACUS, 1994).

The morphological priming experiments are summarized in an article by William Marslen-Wilson, Lorraine Komisarjevsky Tyler, Rachelle Waksler, and Lianne Older, "Morphology and Meaning in the English Mental Lexicon" in *Psychological Review* 101 (1994): 3–33. The experiments on selectional restrictions are reported in Gary Libben's article, "Are Morphological Structures Computed During Word Recognition?" in *Journal of Psycholinguistic Research* 22 (1993): 535–544, and in his article, "Computing Hierarchical Morphological Structure: A Case Study," in *Journal of Neurolinguistics* 8 (1994): 49–55. The priming experiment employing suffixed ambiguous roots (e.g., *barking*) is reported in Roberto G. de Almeida and Gary Libben's article, "Is There a Morphological Parser?" in *Morphology 2000,* edited by W. Dressler and S. Bendjaballah (Philadelphia: John Benjamins, 2001).

The section on the processing of garden path sentences is taken from Lynn Frazier's article, "Sentence Processing: A Tutorial Review," in *Attention and Performance (XII): The Psychology of Reading,* edited by M. Coltheart (London: Lawrence Erlbaum, 1987), 559–596. These sentence types are also discussed in David Caplan's book, *Language: Structure Processing and Disorders* (Cambridge, MA: MIT Press, 1994).

The study of sentence ambiguity was conducted by M. K. Tannenhaus, G. N. Carlson, and M. S. Seidenberg and reported in "Do Listeners Compute Linguistic Representations?" in *Natural Language Parsing*, edited by D. R. Dowty, L. Karttunen, and A. M. Zwicky (New York: Cambridge University Press, 1985).

Chapter 12　Brain and Language

David Caplan's 1996 book *Language: Structure, Processing and Disorders* (Cambridge, MA: MIT Press) offers a comprehensive overview of the breakdown of language in aphasia and its relation to normal processing. His 1987 book *Neurolinguistics and Linguistic Aphasiology: An Introduction* (Cambridge, UK: Cambridge University Press) is an excellent introduction to the field and provides important historical background. A more practical approach to aphasia and its treatment is to be found in J. C. Rosenbek, L. L. Lapointe, and R. T. Wertz's book *Aphasia: A Clinical Approach* (Austin, TX: PRO-ED, 1995). The discussion of the MEG technique was based on the overview chapter by A. C. Papanicolaou, P. G. Simos, and L. F. H. Basile in B. Stemmer and H. Whitaker's *Handbook of Neurolinguistics* (referenced below). The discussion of agrammatism was drawn from the rich literature that includes M.-L. Kean's edited volume *Agrammatism* (New York: Academic Press, 1985) and Yosef Grodzinsky's challenging proposals in *Theoretical Perspectives on Language Deficits* (Cambridge, MA: MIT Press, 1990). An alternative approach to Grodzinsky's can be found in David Caplan and Nancy Hildebrandt's book, *Disorders of Syntactic Comprehension* (Cambridge, MA: MIT Press, 1988). A very readable and insightful book that offers an experiential perspective on aphasic disturbance is Howard Gardner's *The Shattered Mind* (New York: Knopf, 1975).

The material on acquired dyslexia is drawn from *Deep Dyslexia*, edited by M. Coltheart, J. Patterson, and J. C. Marshall (London: Routledge & Kegan Paul, 1980), and *Surface Dyslexia*, edited by K. E. Patterson, J. C. Marshall, and M. Coltheart (Hillsdale, NJ: Lawrence Erlbaum, 1986), as well as Y. Zotterman's book *Dyslexia: Neuronal, Cognitive, and Linguistic Aspects* (Oxford: Pergamon Press, 1982).

Finally, an early overview of developments in the field of neurolinguistics as a whole is available in the *Handbook of Neurolinguistics*, edited by B. Stemmer and H. Whitaker (New York: Academic Press, 1998).

Chapter 13　Language in Social Contexts

The discussion of American dialects makes use of a number of sources: Wolfram and Schilling, *American English*, 3rd ed. (listed in the Recommended Reading); Craig M. Carver, *American Regional Dialects: A Word Geography* (Ann Arbor: University of Michigan, 1989); various chapters in Edgar Schneider, ed., *Varieties of English, Vol. 2: The Americas and the Caribbean* (New York & Berlin: Mouton de Gruyter, 2008); the edited volume *American Voices: How Dialects Differ Coast to Coast* (listed in the Recommended Reading); the extremely detailed *Atlas of North American English* by William Labov, Sharon Ash, and Charles Boberg (New York: Mouton de Gruyter,

2006), and its website, which can be accessed at **http://www.atlas.mouton-content .com/**.

Steps in conducting sociolinguistic research were informed by Crawford Feagin's chapter "Entering the Community: Fieldwork" in the edited volume by Chambers, Trudgill, and Schilling-Estes listed in the Recommended Reading. Description of dialectological work done in the 1930s and 1940s derives from the description by Carver in the work previously cited. Information on post-vocalic *r* in New England comes from Richard W. Bailey, *Speaking American: A History of English in the United States* (New York: Oxford University Press, 2012). Regional lexical items were gleaned from Carver, chapters in *American Voices*, and the online Harvard Survey conducted by Bert Vaux, whose dialect maps and results were accessed at **http://www4.uwm.edu/FLL /linguistics/dialect/maps.html**. The Yale Grammatical Diversity Project, accessed at **http://microsyntax.sites.yale.edu/**, has information and examples on a number of regional variants. Further grammatical features of Midland English are discussed in an article by Erica Benson titled "*Need* + Prepositional Adverb in the Midland: Another Feature *Needs* In," which appeared in the *Journal of English Linguistics* 40 (2012): 224–255. The notion of enregisterment is discussed in a number of recent articles, including "Mobility, Indexicality, and the Enregisterment of 'Pittsburghese'" by Barbara Johnston, Jennifer Andrus, and Andrew Danielson in the *Journal of English Linguistics* 34 (2006): 77–104, and in "Everyone Up Here: Enregisterment and Identity in Michigan's Keweenaw Peninsula" by Kathryn Remlinger in *American Speech* 84, 2 (2009): 118–137. This article is also the source of the quotation at the beginning of the chapter. The enregisterment of country talk in Texas is proposed in an article titled "Country Talk" by Lauren Hall-Lew and Nola Stephens in the *Journal of English Linguistics* 40, 3 (2012): 256–280. Differences between urban and country are also treated in "Country Ideology and the California Vowel Shift" by Robert Podesva, Annette D'Onofrio, Janneke Van Hofwegen, and Seung Kyung Kim in *Language Variation and Change* 27, 2 (2015): 157–186.

Information on the pronunciation of *wh* words—and on most central issues in variation theory—is found in J. K. Chambers, Peter Trudgill, and Natalie Schilling-Estes, eds., *The Handbook of Language Variation and Change* (previously cited). Sources for the vowel shift in California include a paper titled "You *So* Don't Talk Like Me: An Exploration of Southern California Sound Changes across the Generations," presented by Allyn Partin-Hernandez at the 2005 Linguistic Society of America annual meeting in Oakland, CA, and Penelope Eckert's "California Vowels" accessed at **www.stanford.edu/~eckert/vowels.html**. The shift is also treated in relevant chapters in *Varieties of English* and *American Voices* (both cited above).

The discussion of real-time studies in U.S. English using early recordings or written documentation are based in part on an article by Erik Thomas, "A Longitudinal Analysis of the Durability of the Northern-Midland Dialect Boundary in Ohio," which was published in *American Speech* 85 (2010): 375–430, and an article by Michael Ellis and Michael Montgomery, "About *ALL*: Studies in Nineteenth Century American English 1," which appeared in *American Speech* 86 (2011): 340–354.

The information on Smith Island is taken from Natalie Schilling-Estes's chapter in *American Voices* (cited above), and the development of urban African American

English draws on Walt Wolfram's chapter in *Varieties of English* (cited above). Detailed social networks information is found in Lesley Milroy, *Language and Social Networks* (Oxford: Blackwell, 1987). Information on the Ocracoke dialect is found in W. Wolfram and N. Schilling-Estes, "Moribund Dialects and the Endangerment Canon: The Case of the Ocracoke Brogue," *Language* 71 (1995): 696–721.

The discussion of code-switching is informed by Suzanne Romaine's book *Bilingualism*, 2nd ed. (Cambridge, MA: Blackwell, 1995) and the book *Language Contact and Bilingualism* by René Appel and Pieter Muysken (London: Edward Arnold, 1987). The Dutch example of code-switching comes from an article titled "Code-Switching Is Much More Than Careless Mixing: Multilinguals Know the Rules" by Jacomine Nortier in 2011 for the online magazine *Multilingual Living* (accessed through the magazine website at **www.multilingualliving.com**). Examples of borrowing in Southwest Spanish come from the chapter by Mary Ellen Garcia in *Languages and Dialects in the U.S.*, edited by Marianna DiPaolo and Arthur Spears (New York: Routledge, 2014).

The section on lingua franca, pidgins, and creoles has drawn heavily on information and examples presented in *Pidgins and Creoles: An Introduction*, edited by Jacques Arends, Pieter Muysken, and Norval Smith (Amsterdam: John Benjamins, 1995). Other sources include René Appel and Pieter Muysken, *Language Contact and Bilingualism* (cited above); Janet Holmes, *An Introduction to Sociolinguistics* (New York: Longman, 1992); and D. Bickerton, "The Language Bioprogram Hypothesis," *The Behavioral and Brain Sciences* 7, 2 (1984): 173–221. The Barbadian English data is from Gerard Van Herk, "Barbadian Lects: Beyond Meso," in Michael Aceto and Jeffrey P. Williams, *Contact Englishes of the Eastern Caribbean* (Amsterdam: John Benjamins, 2003). A great deal of work on class—including the *r*-lessness studies reported here—can be found in William Labov, *Sociolinguistic Patterns* (Philadelphia: University of Pennsylvania Press, 1972).

The study of post-vocalic *r* in the TV show *Say Yes to the Dress* is reported in "(r) You Saying Yes to the Dress?: Rhoticity on the Bridal Reality Television Show" by Maeve Eberhardt and Corinne Downs, which appeared in the *Journal of English Linguistics* 43, 2 (2015): 118–142.

An accessible description of covert prestige is found in Peter Trudgill, *Sociolinguistics: An Introduction to Language and Society* (Toronto: Penguin, 2000), which was also the source of the caste differences material. The section on African American English is based on W. Wolfram and N. Schilling (previously cited); papers on John Rickford's website devoted to ebonics at **http://www.stanford.edu/~rickford /ebonics/**; an untitled column by Jack Sidnell in *Anthropology Newsletter* 38, 3 (1997): 8; and Lisa Greene's *African American English* (Cambridge: Cambridge University Press, 2002).

The discussion of gender owes much to the collected articles as well as editorial commentary in *Language and Gender: A Reader*, 2nd ed., edited by Jennifer Coates and Pia Pichler (Malden, MA: Wiley-Blackwell, 2011). Information on gendered language use in Japan was also informed by chapters written by Ikuko Patricia Yuasa, Yoshiko Matsumoto, and Ayumi Miyazaki in the book *Gendered Practices in Language*, edited by Sarah Benor, Mary Rose, Devyani Sharma, Julie Sweetland, and Qing Zhan (Stanford, CA: CSLI, 2002). Ikuko Patricia Yuasa has also done work on creaky voice, as reported in "Creaky Voice: A New Feminine Voice Quality for Young Urban-Oriented Upwardly-Mobile American Women" in *American Speech* 85 (2010): 315–337. The work on contemporary compliments is in the article "Compliments Revisited: Contemporary Compliments and Gender" by Janie Rees-Miler and published in the *Journal of Pragmatics* 43, 11 (2011): 2673–2688.

The ethnography of communication is treated in John Gumperz and Dell Hymes, *Directions for Sociolinguistics: The Ethnography of Communication* (New York: Holt, Rinehart and Winston, 1972). The ideas behind T and V pronouns are first detailed in Roger Brown and Albert Gilman, "The Pronouns of Power and Solidarity," in *Style in Language*, edited by T. Sebeok (Cambridge, MA: MIT Press, 1960). This is also the source for the information in the Language Matters box "I thou thee, thou traitor!" in Section 7.3.

The classic work on diglossia is Charles A. Ferguson, "Diglossia," *Word* 15 (1959): 325–340. The accommodating Welsh travel agent is described in Nik Coupland, "Accommodation at Work: Some Phonological Data and Their Implications," *International Journal of the Sociology of Language* 46 (1984): 49–70. For language myths and more, read Geoffrey K. Pullum, *The Great Eskimo Vocabulary Hoax and Other Irreverent Essays on the Study of Language* (Chicago: University of Chicago Press, 1991).

Most of the exercises were written by Janie Rees-Miller. Exercise 2 is based on a phenomenon shared by Terrell Morgan (personal communication), himself a native of the Tidewater Virginia area. Exercise 6 on code-switching uses examples from the books cited earlier by Romaine and by Appel and Muksyen. The example of the teacher code-switching to Tamil was published in a chapter titled "Constructing Hybrid Postcolonial Subjects: Codeswitching in Jaffna Classrooms" by Suresh Canagarajah in the book *Voices of Authority: Education and Linguistic Difference*, edited by Monica Heller and Marilyn Martin Jones (Westport, CT: Ablex, 2001). The example of the boss and secretary code-switching from English to Puerto Rican Spanish was originally used by Joshua Fishman in *Sociolinguistics: A Brief Introduction* (Rowley, MA: Newbury House, 1971). Exercise 7 on Jamaican creole utilizes data from Donald Winford's book *An Introduction to Contact Linguistics* (Malden, MA: Blackwell, 2003) and from the online *Rasta/Patois Dictionary*, accessed at **www.niceup.com/patois.html**.

Chapter 14   Writing and Language

Comprehensive surveys of the development of writing and of the world's writing systems are found in the following books: H. Jensen, *Sign, Symbol and Script*, trans. G. Unwin (London: George Allen and Unwin, 1970); I. Gelb, *A Study of Writing* (Chicago: University of Chicago Press, 1952); John DeFrancis, *Visible Speech: The Diverse Oneness of Writing Systems* (Honolulu: University of Hawaii Press, 1989); and P. Daniels and W. Bright, *The World's Writing Systems* (Oxford: Oxford University Press, 1996). The possibility that pure syllabaries may not exist was called to the authors' attention by W. Poser of the University of Pennsylvania (personal communication). The idea that writing may have originated in record keeping with clay tokens is taken from Denise Schmandt-Besserat, "Two Precursors of Writing: Plain and Complex Tokens," in *The Origins of Writing*, edited by W. M. Senner (Lincoln: University of

Nebraska Press, 1989), 27–42. The section on the prehistoric precursors of writing and the emergence of writing systems in Mesopotamia and Egypt was revised by Janie Rees-Miller, drawing on archaeological interpretations of the material remains for these time periods. Sources include André Leroi-Gourhan's article "Les animaux et les signes" in *Lascaux inconnu*, XIIᵉ supplément à Gallia Préhistoire, edited by Arlette Leroi-Gourhan and J. Allain (Paris: Centre National de la Recherche Scientifique, 1979); *A History of the Ancient Near East circa 3000–323 B.C.* by Marc Van de Mieroop (Malden, MA: Blackwell, 2004); and *Middle Egyptian: An Introduction to the Language and Culture of Hieroglyphs* by James P. Allen (Cambridge: Cambridge University Press, 2000).

The discussion of Arabic writing is based on "The Arabic Alphabet" by James A. Bellamy in the book edited by Senner noted above. John DeFrancis (University of Hawaii), Robert Fisher (York University), and Brian King (University of British Columbia) all provided insightful and helpful comments (especially regarding Chinese writing)—so many, in fact, that we were not able to make use of all of them here. Their views are not necessarily those reflected in the chapter, however. The discussion of Chinese writing is derived from DeFrancis (in the book cited above); the presentation of Japanese writing is also indebted to DeFrancis, as well as to M. Shibatani, *The Languages of Japan* (Cambridge, UK: Cambridge University Press, 1990). The discussion of Sequoyah and the Cherokee syllabary draws in part on an article in the online *Cherokee Phoenix* about a new exhibit at the local museum, titled "CHC Exhibit Showcases Cherokee Syllabary" by Roger Graham (January 25, 2016, accessed at **www .cherokeephoenix.org**). Other online information about Sequoyah and the syllabary came from the website of the Sequoyah Birthplace Museum **www.sequoyahmuseum .org**) and the webpage devoted to the Cherokee language and writing system accessed at **www.omniglot.com**).

The discussion of the history of English spelling is based on *A History of English Spelling* by D. G. Scragg (New York: Barnes & Noble, 1974). The examples of spelling rules sensitive to morphological structure come from the book by D. W. Cummings, *American English Spelling* (Baltimore: Johns Hopkins University Press, 1988). Data on children's ability to segment words into syllables and phonemes come from I. Y. Liberman, reported in the book by E. Gibson and H. Levin, *The Psychology of Reading* (Cambridge, MA: MIT Press, 1975). For more information on reading problems in English and their relationship to phonemic awareness, see "Speech Development Patterns and Phonological Awareness in Preschool Children" by V. Mann and J. Foy in *Annals of Dyslexia* 5 (2007): 51–74; for a comparison of reading problems across languages, see "Becoming Literate in Different Languages: Similar Problems, Different Solutions" by J. Ziegler and Y. Gosami in *Developmental Science* 9 (2006): 429–453. John Sören Pettersson of Uppsala University commented extensively and helpfully on an earlier version of this chapter.

LANGUAGE INDEX

INDEX